W9-BUI-862

Random House Webster's Pocket French Dictionary

Second Edition

French • English
English • French
Français • Anglais
Anglais • Français

Edited by
Francesca L.V. Langbaum
UNIVERSITY OF VIRGINIA

Revised by
Susan Husserl-Kapit, Ph.D.

RANDOM HOUSE
NEW YORK

Random House Webster's Pocket French Dictionary,
Second Edition

This book was originally published as the *Random House French Dictionary, Second Edition* in 1996. The first edition of this work was published by Random House, Inc., in 1983.

This book is available for special purchases in bulk by organizations and institutions, not for resale, at special discounts. Please direct your inquiries to the Random House Special Sales Department, toll-free 888-591-1200 or fax 212-572-4961.

Please address inquiries about electronic licensing of reference products, for use on a network or in software or on CD-ROM, to the Subsidiary Rights Department, Random House Reference, fax 212-940-7370.

Visit the Random House Reference Web site at
www.randomwords.com

Typeset and printed in the United States of America

1998 Random House Edition
0 9 8 7 6 5 4 3
ISBN: 0-375-70156-7
December 2000

New York   Toronto   London   Sydney   Auckland

Concise Pronunciation Guide

The following concise guide describes the approximate pronunciation of the letters and frequent combinations of letters occurring in the French language. A study of it will enable the reader to pronounce French adequately most of the time. While the guide cannot list all the exceptions to the established pronunciations, or cover the manner in which adjacent words affect each other in speech, such exceptions and variations will readily be learned as one develops facility in the language.

French Letter	Description of Pronunciation
a, à	Between *a* in *calm* and *a* in *hat*.
â	Like *a* in *calm*.
ai	Like *e* in *bed*.
au	Like *oa* in *coat*.
b	As in English. At end of words, usually silent.
c	Before *e, i, y*, like *s*. Elsewhere, like *k*. When *c* occurs at the end of a word and is preceded by a consonant, it is usually silent.
ç	Like *s*.
cc	Before *e, i*, like *x*. Elsewhere, like *k*.
ch	Usually like *sh* in *short*. *ch* is pronounced like *k* in words of Greek origin before *a, o*, and *u* and before consonants.
d	At beginning and in middle of words, as in English. At end of words, usually silent.
e	At end of words, normally silent; indicates that preceding consonant letter is pronounced. Between two single consonant sounds, usually silent. Elsewhere, like English *a* in *sofa*.
é	Approximately like *a* in *hate*.
è, ê, ei	Like *e* in *bed*.
eau	Like *au*.
ent	Silent when it is the third person plural ending.
er (end of words)	At end of words of more than one syllable, usually like *a* in *hate*, the *r* being silent; otherwise like *air* in *chair*.
es	Silent at end of words.
eu	A vowel sound not found in English; like French *e*, but pronounced with the lips rounded as for *o*.

French Letter	Description of Pronunciation
ez	At end of words, almost always like English *a* in *hate*, the *z* being silent.
f	As in English; silent at the end of a few words.
g	Before *e, i, y*, like *z* in *azure*. Elsewhere, like *g* in *get*. At end of words, usually silent.
gn	Like *ni* in *onion*.
gu	Before *e, i, y*, like *g* in *get*. Elsewhere, like *g* in *get* plus French *u* (see below).
h	In some words, represents a slight tightening of the throat muscles (in French, called "aspiration"). In most words, silent.
i, î	Like *i* in *machine*.
ill	(-il at end of words) like *y* in *yes*, in many but not all words.
j	Like *z* in *azure*.
k	As in English.
l	As in English, but always pronounced "bright," with tongue in front of mouth.
m, n	When double, and when single between two vowel letters or at beginning of word, like English *m* and *n* respectively. When single at end of syllable (at end of word or before another consonant), indicates nasalization of preceding vowel.
o	Usually like *u* in English *mud*, but rounder. When final sound in word, and often before *s* and *z*, like *ô*.
ô	Approximately like *oa* in *coat*.
oe, oeu	Like *eu*.
oi	Approximately like a combination of the consonant *w* and the *a* of *calm*.
ou, oû, où	Like *ou* in *tour*.
p	At end of words, usually silent. Between *m* and *t*, *m* and *s*, *r* and *s*, usually silent. Elsewhere, as in English.
pn, ps	Unlike English, when *pn* and *ps* occur at the beginning of words the *p* is usually sounded.
ph	Like *f*.
qu	Usually like *k*.

French Letter	Description of Pronunciation
r	A vibration either of the uvula, or of the tip of the tongue against the upper front teeth. See above under *er*.
s	Generally, like *s* in *sea*. Single *s* between vowels, like *z* in *zone*. At end of words, normally silent.
sc	Before *e* or *i*, like *s*. Elsewhere, like *sk*.
t	Approximately like English *t*, but pronounced with tongue tip against teeth. At end of words, normally silent. When followed by *ie, ion, ium, ius*, and other diphthongs beginning with a vowel, *t* generally is like English *s* in *sea* (unless the *t* itself is preceded by an *s* or an *x*).
th	Like *t*.
u, û	A vowel sound not found in English; like the *i* in *machine* but with lips rounded as for *ou*.
ue	After *e* or *g* and before *il*, like *eu*.
v	As in English.
w	Usually like *v;* in some people's pronunciation, like English *w*.
x	Generally sounds like *ks;* but when the syllable *ex* begins a word and is followed by a vowel, *x* sounds like *gz*. At end of words, usually silent.
y	Generally like *i* in *machine;* but when between two vowels, like *y* in *yes*.
z	Like *z* in *zone*. At end of words, often silent (see above under *ez*).

Note on Pronunciation

A few minutes' study of the *Concise Pronunciation Guide* on pages v–vii will enable you to pronounce most French words without having to look each word up in the dictionary. For the relatively few cases in which the pronunciation does not follow the usual pattern, this dictionary provides a transcription in simple and familiar symbols.

ă	bat	ô	order
ā	cape	œ	[a vowel made with the lips rounded in position for *o* as in *over*, while trying to say *a* as in *able*]
â	dare		
ä	calm		
à	[a vowel intermediate in quality between the *a* of *cat* and the *a* of *calm*, but closer to the former]	oi	oil
		ŏŏ	book
		ōō	ooze
ĕ	set	ou	loud
ē	bee	ŭ	up
ĭ	big	ū	cute
ī	bite	û	burn
N	[a symbol used to indicate nasalized vowels. There are four such vowels in French, found in *un bon vin blanc* (œn bŏN văN blăN)]	Y	[a vowel made with the lips rounded in position for *oo* as in *ooze*, while trying to say *e* as in *easy*]
		ə	[indicates the sound of *a* in *alone*, *e* in *system*, *i* in *easily*, *o* in *gallop*, *u* in *circus*]
ŏ	hot		
ō	no		

Irregular Verbs

Infinitive	Pres. Part.	Past Part.	Pres. Indic.	Future
aller	allant	allé	vais	irai
asseoir	asseyant	assis	assieds	assiérai
atteindre	atteignant	atteint	atteins	atteindrai
avoir	ayant	eu	ai	aurai
battre	battant	battu	bats	battrai
boire	buvant	bu	bois	boirai
conduire	conduisant	conduit	conduis	conduirai
connaître	connaissant	connu	connais	connaîtrai
courir	courant	couru	cours	courrai
craindre	craignant	craint	crains	craindrai
croire	croyant	cru	crois	croirai
devoir	devant	dû	dois	devrai
dire	disant	dit	dis	dirai
dormir	dormant	dormi	dors	dormirai
écrire	écrivant	écrit	écris	écrirai
envoyer	envoyant	envoyé	envoie	enverrai
être	étant	été	suis	serai
faire	faisant	fait	fais	ferai
falloir	———	fallu	(il) faut	(il) faudra
joindre	joignant	joint	joins	joindrai
lire	lisant	lu	lis	lirai
mettre	mettant	mis	mets	mettrai
mourir	mourant	mort	meurs	mourrai
naître	naissant	né	nais	naîtrai
ouvrir	ouvrant	ouvert	ouvre	ouvrirai
plaire	plaisant	plu	plais	plairai
pleuvoir	pleuvant	plu	(il) pleut	(il) pleuvra
pouvoir	pouvant	pu	peux	pourrai
prendre	prenant	pris	prends	prendrai
recevoir	recevant	reçu	reçois	recevrai
rire	riant	ri	ris	rirai
savoir	sachant	su	sais	saurai
suffire	suffisant	suffi	suffis	suffirai
suivre	suivant	suivi	suis	suivrai
tenir	tenant	tenu	tiens	tiendrai
valoir	valant	valu	vaux	vaudrai
venir	venant	venu	viens	viendrai
vivre	vivant	vécu	vis	vivrai
voir	voyant	vu	vois	verrai
vouloir	voulant	voulu	veux	voudrai

Abbreviations

abbr.	abbreviation	*lit.*	literal, literally
adj.	adjective	*m.*	masculine
adv.	adverb	*med.*	medical
arch.	architecture	*mil.*	military
arith.	arithmetic	*n.*	noun
art.	article	*naut.*	nautical
comm.	commercial	*pl.*	plural
conj.	conjunction	*pred.*	predicate
eccles.	ecclesiastical	*prep.*	preposition
f.	feminine	*pron.*	pronoun
fig.	figurative	*sg.*	singular
geog.	geography	*tr.*	transitive (used only
geom.	geometry		with verbs which also
gramm.	grammar,		have reflexive use to
	grammatical		indicate intransitive
interj.	interjection		meaning)
interr.	interrogative	*vb.*	verb
intr.	intransitive		

à, *prep.* at, in, to.

abaisser, *vb.* depress, lower.

abandon, *n.m.* desertion, abandonment.

abandonné, *adj.* forlorn.

abandonner, *vb.* forsake, leave (desert). **s'a.,** give up, resign oneself.

abasourdir, *vb.* astound.

abat-jour, *n.m.* lampshade.

abattage, *n.m.* slaughter.

abattement, *n.m.* depression, dejection.

abattoir, *n.m.* slaughterhouse.

abattre, *vb.* depress, reduce; slaughter. **s'a.,** alight.

abbaye, *n.f.* abbey.

abbé, *n.m.* abbot.

abbesse, *n.f.* abbess.

abcès, *n.m.* abscess.

abdiquer, *vb.* abdicate.

abdomen, *n.m.* abdomen.

abeille, *n.f.* bee.

aberrant, *adj.* absurd.

aberration, *n.f.* aberration.

abîme, *n.m.* abyss.

abîmer, *vb.* injure, spoil.

abject, *adj.* abject, low.

aboiement, *n.m.* barking.

abolir, *vb.* abolish.

abolition, *n.f.* abolition.

abominable, *adj.* vile, objectionable.

abondamment, *adv.* fully.

abondance, *n.f.* plenty.

abondant, *adj.* plentiful. **peu a.,** scanty.

abonder de, *vb.* abound in.

abonné, *n.m.* subscriber.

abonnement, *n.m.* subscription.

abonner, *vb.* **s'a.,** subscribe.

abord, 1. *n.m.* approach. **2.** *adv.* **d'a.,** at first.

abordable, *adj.* approachable, affordable.

aborder, *vb.* accost.

aboutir, *vb.* end (in).

aboyer, *vb.* bark.

abrégé, *n.m.* summary.

abréger, *vb.* abridge, shorten, abbreviate.

abreuver, *vb.* water (animals).

abréviation, *n.f.* abbreviation.

abri, *n.m.* shelter. **à l'a. de,** safe from.

abricot, *n.m.* apricot.

abriter, *vb.* shelter.

abroger, *vb.* repeal.

abrupt (-pt) *adj.* steep.

abrutir, *vb.* exhaust. **s'a.,** become dazed.

absence, *n.f.* absence.

absent, *adj.* absent. **rester a.,** stay away.

absenter, *vb.* **s'a.,** go away.

abside, *n.f.* apse.

absinthe, *n.f.* absinthe.

absolu, *adj.* utter, absolute.

absolument, *adv.* absolutely.

absolution, *n.f.* absolution.

absorbant, *adj. and n.m.* absorbent.

absorbé dans, *adj.* intent on.

absorber, *vb.* engross, absorb. **s'a. dans,** pore over.

absorption, *n.f.* absorption.

absoudre, *vb.* absolve.

abstenir, *vb.* forbear. **s'a. de,** abstain from.

abstinence, *n.f.* abstinence.

abstraction, *n.f.* abstraction.

abstrait, *adj.* abstract.

absurde, *adj.* absurd, preposterous.

absurdité, *n.f.* nonsense, absurdity.

abus, *n.m.* abuse.

abuser de, *vb.* abuse.

académie, *n.f.* academy.

académique, *adj.* academic.

acajou, *n.m.* mahogany.

accablant, *adj.* oppressive.

accabler, *vb.* overwhelm, burden.

accalmie, *n.f.* lull.

accaparer, *vb.* get a corner on.

accéder, *vb.* reach.

accélérateur, *n.m.* accelerator.

accélération, *n.f.* acceleration.

accélérer, *vb.* quicken, hurry.

accent, *n.m.* stress, emphasis, accent.

accentuer, *vb.* accentuate, accent, emphasize.

acceptable, *adj.* acceptable.

acceptation, *n.f.* acceptance.

accepter, *vb.* accept, admit.

accepteur, *n.m.* accepter.

accès, *n.m.* access, approach; fit (of anger); bout (of fever).

accessible, *adj.* accessible.

accessoire, *n.m. and adj.* accessory, adjunct.

accident, *n.m.* crash, accident.

accidenté, *adj.* damaged; (terrain) hilly.

accidentel, *adj.* accidental.

acclamation, *n.f.* acclamation.

acclamer, *vb.* acclaim, cheer.

accommodant, *adj.* accommodating.

accommoder, *vb.* accommodate.

accompagnateur, *n.m.* accompanist, (travel) guide.

accompagnement, *n.m.* accompaniment.

accompagner, *vb.* accompany, go with.

accompli, *adj.* accomplished, complete, perfect.

accomplir, *vb.* accomplish, achieve, fulfill, carry out, perform.

accomplissement, *n.m.* performance, accomplishment, fulfillment, achievement.

accord, *n.m.* agreement, harmony; settlement; chord, tune. **être d'a.,** agree, concur.

accorder, *vb.* grant, bestow; allow; tune. **s'a.,** agree.

accouchement, *n.m.* delivery (baby).

accoucher, *vb.* deliver (baby).

accoucheur, *n.m.* **médecin-a.,** obstetrician.

accouder, *vb.* **s'a.,** lean.

accourir, *vb.* flock, run up.

accoutumer, *vb.* accustom, habituate.

accréditer, *vb.* accredit.

accro, *n.m.* (drug) addict.

accroc, *n.m.* tear, snag; hitch (fig.).

accrocher, *vb.* hook, hitch, hang (up).

accroissement, *n.m.* growth, addition.

accroître, *vb.* increase.

accroupir, *vb.* **s'a.,** squat, crouch.

accru, *adj.* greater, increased.

accueil, *n.m.* reception, greeting.

accueillir, *vb.* receive, greet.

acculer, *vb.* corner.

accumuler, *vb.* heap up.

accusateur, *n.m.* accuser.

accusatif, *n.m.* accusative.

accusation, *n.f.* accusation.

accusatrice, *n.f.* accuser.

accusé, *n.m.* defendant.

accuser, *vb.* arraign, accuse.

acerbe, *adj.* bitter.

acharné, *adj.* eager, relentless.

acharner, *vb.* **s'a.,** go at intensely.

achat, *n.m.* purchase.

acheminer, *vb.* start (toward).

acheter, *vb.* buy.

acheteur, *n.m.* buyer.

achèvement, *n.m.* completion.

achever, *vb.* complete, finish, achieve.

acide, *adj. and n.m.* acid.

acidité, *n.f.* acidity.

acier, *n.m.* steel.

acné, *n.f.* acne.

acolyte, *n.m.* associate.

acompte, *n.m.* deposit, installment.

à-côté, *n.m.* side-issue.

à-c.s., extras.

à-coup, *n.m.* jolt. **par à-c.s.,** by fits and starts.

acoustique, *n.f.* acoustics.

acquérir, *vb.* acquire, get, obtain.

acquiescement, *n.m.* acquiescence, compliance.

acquiescer à, *vb.* acquiesce, consent.

acquisition, *n.f.* acquisition, purchase.

acquittement, *n.m.* acquittal.

acquitter, *vb.* acquit.

âcre, *adj.* sharp.

acrobate, *n.m.f.* acrobat.

acrobatie, *n.f.* acrobatics.

acte, *n.m.* act. **a. notarié,** deed. **a. de naissance,** birth certificate.

acteur, *n.m.* actor.

actif, 1. *n.m.* assets *(comm.).* 2. *adj.* active.

action, *n.f.* action, deed, act; *(comm.)* share.

action de contrôle en retour, *n.f.* feedback.

actionnaire, *n.m.* shareholder.

actionner, *vb.* operate.

activement, *adv.* busily.
activer, *vb.* activate, fan, hurry.
activité, *n.f.* activity.
actrice, *n.f.* actress.
actualiser, *vb.* update.
actualité, *n.f.* topicality.
actualités, *n.f.pl.* current events, TV news.
actuel, *adj.* present.
actuellement, *adv.* now, at present.
acuité, *n.f.* acuteness.
acuponcture, *n.f.* acupuncture.
adaptateur, *n.m.* adapter.
adaptation, *n.f.* adaptation.
adapter, *vb.* adapt, fit, adjust, suit.
additif, *n.m.* additive.
addition, *n.f.* addition, bill.
additionnel, *adj.* additional.
additionner, *vb.* add.
adepte, *n.m.f.* follower.
adéquat, *adj.* appropriate.
adhérent, *n.m.* member.
adhérer, *vb.* adhere, join.
adhésif, *adj.* adhesive.
adieu, *n.m. and interj.* good-bye, farewell. **faire ses adieux**, take one's leave.
adjacent, *adj.* adjacent.
adjectif, *n.m.* adjective.
adjoindre, *vb.* add, attach.
adjoint, *n.m.* fellow-worker, associate.
adjuger, *vb.* grant, award.
admettre, *vb.* allow, admit, grant.
administrateur, *n.m.* administrator, director, manager.
administratif, *adj.* administrative.
administration, *n.f.* administration, direction.
administrer, *vb.* administer, manage.
admirable, *adj.* admirable.
admirateur, *n.m.* admirer.
admiration, *n.f.* admiration.
admirer, *vb.* admire.
admissible, *adj.* eligible.
admission, *n.f.* confession, admission.
adolescence, *n.f.* adolescence.
adolescent, *adj. and n.m.* adolescent.
adonner, *vb.* **s'a. à**, indulge in, become addicted to.
adopter, *vb.* adopt.

adoptif, *adj.* adoptive.
adoption, *n.f.* adoption.
adoration, *n.f.* adoration.
adorer, *vb.* worship, adore.
adosser, *vb.* **s'a. à**, lean on.
adoucir, *vb.* soothe, soften, sweeten.
adresse, *n.f.* address; skill, ability.
adresser, *vb.* address (a letter); direct. **s'a. à**, apply to.
adroit, *adj.* skillful, clever, handy.
aduler, *vb.* adulate.
adulte, *adj. and n.m.f.* adult.
adultère, *n.m.* adultery.
adultérer, *vb.* adulterate.
advenir, *vb.* happen, occur.
adverbe, *n.m.* adverb.
adversaire, *n.m.f.* opponent.
adverse, *adj.* adverse.
adversité, *n.f.* adversity.
aéré, *adj.* airy.
aérer, *vb.* air (a room).
aérien, *adj.* aerial, overhead.
aérobic, *n.m.* aerobics.
aérodynamique, *adj.* streamlined, aerodynamic.
aérogare, *n.f.* airline (city) terminal.
aéroglisseur, *n.m.* hovercraft.
aérogramme, *n.m.* airmail letter, aerogram.
aéronautique, 1. *n.m.* aeronautics. 2. *adj.* aeronautical.
aéroport, *n.m.* airport.
aérospatial, *adj.* aerospace.
affable, *adj.* affable.
affaiblir, *vb.* weaken.
affaire, *n.f.* affair, matter; deal; *(pl.)* business. **se tirer d'a.**, manage (somehow). **homme d'a.s**, businessman.
affairé, *adj.* busy.
affairer, *vb.* **s'a.**, be busy.
affaissement, *n.m.* collapse.
affaisser, *vb.* **s'a.**, collapse.
affaler, *vb.* **s'a.**, collapse.
affamé, *adj.* hungry, famished.
affamer, *vb.* starve.
affectation, *n.f.* affectation.
affecter, *vb.* affect; assign.
affectif, *adj.* emotional.
affection, *n.f.* affection.
affectueux, *adj.* affectionate.
affermir, *vb.* strengthen.
affiche, *n.f.* poster.

afficher, *vb.* post, announce.
affilée (d'), *adv.* in a row.
affilier, *vb.* affiliate.
affiner, *vb.* refine.
affinité, *n.f.* affinity.
affirmatif, *adj.* affirmative.
affirmation, *n.f.* statement.
affirmer, *vb.* assert, state, maintain, testify, affirm.
affliction, *n.f.* affliction.
affligé, *adj.* sorrowful.
affliger, *vb.* distress, afflict, grieve.
affluence, *n.f.* crowd. **heures d'a.,** rush hour.
affluent, *n.m.* tributary.
affluer, *vb.* flow into.
affolement, *n.* panic.
affoler, *vb.* drive mad.
affranchir, *vb.* free.
affranchissement, *n.m.* postage.
affréter, *vb.* charter (boat).
affreusement, *adv.* terribly.
affreux, *adj.* dreadful, terrible, horrid, dire.
affront, *n.m.* affront, insult.
affronter, *vb.* confront, face.
afin, 1. a. de, *prep.* in order to. **2.** *conj.* **a. que,** so that.
Africain, *n.m.* African.
africain, *adj.* African.
Afrique, *n.f.* Africa.
agacer, *vb.* vex, irritate.
âge, *n.m.* age. **d'un certain â.,** elderly. **le moyen â.,** the Middle Ages.
âgé, *adj.* aged.
agence, *n.f.* (*comm.*) agency.
agencer, *vb.* organize, arrange.
agenda, *n.m.* datebook.
agenouiller, *vb.* **s'a.,** kneel.
agent, *n.m.* agent. **a. de police,** policeman. **a. de change,** stockbroker.
agglomération, *n.f.* built-up area, town.
aggloméré, *n.m.* chipboard.
agglomérer, *vb.* **s'a.,** pile up.
agglutiner, *vb.* stick together.
aggraver, *vb.* aggravate.
agile, *adj.* nimble.
agir, *vb.* act. **s'a. de,** be a question of.
agitateur, *n.m.* agitator.
agitation, *n.f.* excitement, disturbance, commotion, flutter.

agité, *adj.* upset, excited.
agiter, *vb.* agitate, wave, wag, shake, stir. **s'a.,** toss; flutter.
agneau, *n.m.* lamb.
agonie, *n.f.* agony.
agoniser, *vb.* be dying.
agrafe, *n.f.* clasp, staple.
agrafer, *vb.* clasp, staple.
agrafeuse, *n.f.* stapler.
agrandir, *vb.* enlarge.
agréable, *adj.* likable, pleasant, enjoyable, agreeable.
agréer, *vb.* accept, consent.
agrégation, *n.f.* aggregation; fellowship.
agrément, *n.m.* pleasure, approval.
agresser, *vb.* attack.
agresseur, *n.m.* aggressor, attacker.
agressif, *adj.* aggressive, hostile.
agression, *n.f.* aggression.
agricole, *adj.* agricultural.
agriculture, *n.f.* agriculture.
agripper, *vb.* **s'a. à,** grab.
agroalimentaire, *n.m.* food industry.
agrumes, *n.m.pl.* citrus fruit(s).
aguerrir, *vb.* harden.
aguets, *n.m.pl.* **être aux a.,** be on the look-out.
aguicher, *vb.* entice.
ahurir, *vb.* bewilder, fluster.
aide, *n.f.* help, aid.
aider, *vb.* help, aid.
aïe, *interj.* ouch!
aïeul (ä yœl), *n.m.* grandfather.
aïeule (ä yœl), *n.f.* grandmother.
aïeux, *n.m.pl.* ancestors.
aigle, *n.m.f.* eagle.
aiglefin, *n.m.* haddock.
aigre, *adj.* sour.
aigu, *m.* **aiguë** *f. adj.* shrill, sharp, pointed.
aiguille, *n.f.* needle.
aiguisé, *adj.* keen.
aiguiser, *vb.* sharpen.
ail (ä ē) *n.m.* garlic.
aile, *n.f.* wing.
aileron, *n.m.* fin.
ailleurs, *adv.* elsewhere. **d'a.,** in addition, anyhow.
aimable, *adj.* kind, pleasant, amiable.
aimant, *n.m.* magnet.

aimer, vb. love, like.
aine, n.f. groin.
aîné (ĕ´ nā), **1.** adj. and n.m. elder. **2.** adj. eldest, senior.
ainsi, adv. thus, so, like this.
air, n.m. air, looks. **en plein a.,** in the open air.
aire, n.f. area.
aisance, n.f. ease, affluence.
aise, n.f. ease, comfort. **à l'a.,** comfortable.
aisé, adj. substantial, well-to-do; easy.
aisselle, n.f. armpit.
ajourner, vb. put off. **s'a.,** adjourn.
ajouter, vb. add.
ajustage, n.m. fitting.
ajuster, vb. fit, fix, adjust.
alarme, n.f. alarm.
alarmer, vb. alarm.
albâtre, n.m. alabaster.
albatros, n.m. albatross.
album, n.m. album.
albumine, n.f. albumin.
alcool (-kōl), n.m. alcohol.
alcoolique (-kōl-), adj. and n.m.f. alcoholic.
alcoolisé, adj. alcoholic (drink).
alcootest, n.m. Breathalyzer test.
alcôve, n.f. alcove.
aléas, n.m.pl. hazards.
aléatoire, adj. uncertain, random.
alentour, adv. around.
alentours, n.m.pl. neighborhood, surroundings.
alerte, n.f. spry, active, alert.
algarade, n.f. altercation.
algèbre, n.f. algebra.
Alger, n.f. Algiers.
Algérie, n.f. Algeria.
Algérien, n.m. Algerian.
algérian, adj. Algerian.
algue, n.f. seaweed.
alias, adv. alias.
alibi, n.m. alibi.
aliéné, n.m. lunatic.
aliéner, vb. alienate.
aligner, vb. line up.
aliment, n.m. food.
alimentation, n.f. feeding.
alimenter, vb. feed.
alinéa, n.m. paragraph.
aliter, vb. **s'a.,** take to one's bed.
allaiter, vb. nurse, feed.
allécher, vb. tempt.

allée, n.f. path, avenue, aisle.
allégation, n.f. allegation.
alléger, vb. lighten, soothe.
allégresse, n.f. glee, delight, mirth.
alléguer, vb. plead, allege.
Allemagne, n.f. Germany.
Allemand, n.m. German (person).
allemand, 1. n.m. German (language). **2.** adj. German.
aller, vb. go. **s'en a.,** go away. **a.,** fit. **se laisser a.,** drift. **a. bien,** be well. **a. mal,** be not well. **a. et retour,** round trip.
allergique, adj. allergic.
alliage, n.m. alloy.
alliance, n.f. alliance, union.
allié, 1. n.m. ally, relation. **2.** adj. allied.
allier, vb. ally. **s'a. à,** join with.
allô, interj. hello.
allocation, n.f. allowance. **a.s familiales,** family allowance.
allocution, n.f. short speech.
allonger, vb. lengthen, prolong.
allons, interj. well, come now.
allouer, vb. grant.
allume-cigare, n.m. cigar lighter.
allumer, vb. light.
allumette, n.f. match.
allure, n.f. pace, gait.
allusion, n.f. hint, allusion. **faire a. à,** allude to.
almanach (-nä), n.m. almanac.
aloi, n.m. **de bon a.,** of genuine quality.
alors, 1. adv. then. **2.** conj. **a. que,** when.
alouette, n.f. lark.
alourdir, vb. weigh down.
Alpes, n.f.pl. Alps.
alphabet, n.m. alphabet.
alphabétiser, vb. teach to read and write.
alpinisme, n.m. mountaineering.
Alsace, n.f. Alsace.
altérer, vb. change.
alternatif, adj. alternate.
alternative, n.f. alternative.
alterner, vb. alternate.
Altesse, n.f. Highness (title).
altitude, n.f. altitude.
alto, n.m. viola.
altruisme, n.m. altruism.
aluminium, n.m. aluminum.
amabilité, n.f. kindness.

amadouer, vb. soothe, coax.

amaigrir, vb. to make thin(ner).

amalgame, n.m. combination.

amalgamer, vb. amalgamate.

amande, n.f. kernel; almond.

amant, n.m. lover.

amarrer, vb. moor.

amas, n.m. hoard, mass.

amasser, vb. hoard, gather, amass.

amateur, n.m. amateur. **a. de,** lover of.

ambassade, n.f. embassy.

ambassadeur, n.m. ambassador.

ambassadrice, n.f. ambassadress.

ambiance, n.f. atmosphere.

ambiant, adj. surrounding.

ambigu m., **ambiguë** f. adj. ambiguous.

ambiguïté, n.f. ambiguity.

ambitieux, adj. ambitious.

ambition, n.f. ambition.

ambre, n.m. amber.

ambulance, n.f. ambulance.

ambulant, adj. traveling.

âme, n.f. soul.

amélioration, n.f. improvement.

améliorer, vb. improve.

aménagement, n.m. development.

aménager, vb. fit up.

amende, n.f. fine. **mettre à l'a.,** fine.

amendement, n.m. amendment.

amender, vb. amend.

amener, vb. bring, lead.

amenuiser, vb. **s'a.,** dwindle, lessen.

amer (-r), adj. bitter.

Américain, n.m. American.

américain, adj. American.

Amérique, n.f. America.

A. du Nord, North America.

A. du Sud, South America.

amertume, n.f. bitterness.

ameublement, n.m. furniture.

ami m., **amie** f. n. friend.

amiable, adj. conciliatory. **à l'a.,** out of court.

amiante, n.m. asbestos.

amical, adj. friendly, amicable.

amidon, n.m. starch.

amiral, n.m. admiral.

amitié, n.f. friendship.

ammoniaque, n.f. ammonia.

amniocentèse, n.f. amniocentesis.

amoindrir, vb. lessen, reduce.

amollir, vb. soften.

amonceler, vb. pile up. **s'a.,** pile up, (fig.) accumulate.

amont, adv. **en a.,** upstream, uphill.

amorce, n.f. bait, beginning.

amorcer, vb. bait, begin.

amorphe, adj. listless.

amortir, vb. deaden, soften.

amortisseur, n.m. shock absorber.

amour, n.m. love.

amoureux, 1. n.m. lover. 2. adj. in love, amorous.

amour-propre, n.m. vanity, pride, conceit.

ampère, n.m. amp(ere).

ample, adj. ample, spacious.

ampleur, n.f. plenty; compass.

amplificateur, n.m. amplifier.

amplifier, vb. increase, enlarge, develop.

ampoule, n.f. blister; (electric) bulb.

amputer, vb. amputate.

amusant, adj. funny, enjoyable.

amusement, n.m. fun, pastime, entertainment.

amuser, vb. entertain. **s'a.,** have a good time.

amygdale, n.f. tonsil.

an, n.m. year.

analogie, n.f. analogy.

analogique, adj. analogue.

analogue, adj. similar, analogous.

analphabète, n.m.f. illiterate.

analyse, n.f. analysis.

analyser, vb. analyze.

ananas, n.m. pineapple.

anarchie, n.f. anarchy.

anathème, n.m. anathema.

anatomie, n.f. anatomy.

ancêtre, n.m. forefather, ancestor.

anche, n.f. reed.

anchois, n.m. anchovy.

ancien m., **ancienne** f. adj. ancient, old; former.

ancre, n.f. anchor.

ancrer, vb. anchor.

Andorre, n.f. Andorra.

andouille, n.f. sausage made of chitterlings; (colloquial) idiot.

âne m., **ânesse** f. n. ass, donkey.

anéantir, vb. annihilate, destroy.

anecdote, n.f. anecdote.

anémie, n.f. anemia.

ânerie, n.f. stupidity.

anesthésie, *n.f.* anesthesia.

anesthésique, *adj. and n.m.* anesthetic.

ange, *n.m.* angel.

angine, *n.f.* throat infection.

Anglais, *n.m.* Englishman.

anglais, *adj. and n.m.* English.

Anglaise, *n.f.* Englishwoman.

angle, *n.m.* angle, corner.

Angleterre, *n.f.* England.

angoissant, *adj.* in anguish.

angoisse, *n.f.* agony, pang, anguish.

anguille, *n.f.* eel.

anguleux, *adj.* angular.

anicroche, *n.f.* hitch.

animal, *adj. and n.m.* animal.

animateur, *n.m.* leader, organizer.

animation, *n.f.* animation.

animer, *vb.* enliven, animate.

anis, *n.m.* aniseed.

ankyloser, *vb.* **s'a.**, become stiff.

animosité, *n.f.* animosity.

anneau, *n.m.* ring, circle.

année, *n.f.* year; vintage.

annexe, *n.f.* annex.

annexer, *vb.* annex.

annexion, *n.f.* annexation.

anniversaire, *n.m.* anniversary; birthday.

annonce, *n.f.* advertisement; announcement.

annoncer, *vb.* advertise; announce.

annotation, *n.f.* annotation.

annoter, *vb.* annotate.

annuaire, *n.m.* directory.

annuel, *adj.* yearly, annual.

annuité, *n.f.* annual payment.

annulaire, *n.m.* ring finger.

annulation, *n.f.* cancellation.

annuler, *vb.* cancel, void, annul.

anodin, *adj.* harmless, minor.

ânonner, *vb.* stammer.

anonyme, *adj.* anonymous.

anorak, *n.m.* anorak.

anorexie, *n.f.* anorexia.

anormal, *adj.* irregular, abnormal.

anse, *n.f.* handle; bay (water).

antagonisme, *n.m.* antagonism.

antarctique, *adj.* antarctic.

antécédent, *adj. and n.m.* antecedent.

antécédents, *n.m.pl.* record.

antenne, *n.f.* antenna.

antérieur, *adj.* previous; fore, front.

anthracite, *n.m.* anthracite.

antichambre, *n.f.* entrance hall.

anticipation, *n.f.* anticipation.

anticiper, *vb.* anticipate.

anticorps, *n.m.* antibody.

antidote, *n.m.* antidote.

antihistaminique, *n.m.* antihistamine.

Antilles, *n.f.pl.* West Indies.

antilope, *n.f.* antelope.

antinucléaire, *adj.* antinuclear.

antipathie, *n.f.* antipathy.

antiquaire, *n.m.* antique dealer.

antique, *adj.* ancient, antiquated, antique.

antiquité, *n.f.* antiquity.

antisémite, **1.** *n.m.* anti-Semite. **2.** *adj.* anti-Semitic.

antiseptique, *adj. and n.m.* antiseptic.

antre, *n.m.* den.

anxiété, *n.f.* anxiety, worry.

anxieux, *adj.* anxious.

août (ōō), *n.m.* August.

apaiser, *vb.* allay, quiet, appease.

apanage, *n.m.* **l'a. de**, privilege of.

aparté, *n.m.* aside.

apathie, *n.f.* apathy.

apatride, *n.m.* stateless person.

apercevoir, *vb.* perceive. **s'a. de**, realize.

aperçu, *n.m.* outline.

apéritif, *n.m.* appetizer.

à-peu-près, *n.m.* approximation.

apeuré, *adj.* scared.

aphone, *adj.* voiceless.

apitoyer, *vb.* move (emotionally).

aplanir, *vb.* even off.

aplatir, *vb.* flatten.

aplomb, *n.m.* poise, boldness.

apogée, *n.m.* peak.

apologie, *n.f.* vindication.

apoplexie, *n.f.* apoplexy.

apostolique, *adj.* apostolic.

apostrophe, *n.f.* apostrophe.

apothéose, *n.f.* crowning glory.

apôtre, *n.m.* apostle.

apparaître, *vb.* appear.

appareil, *n.m.* gear, appliance, device. **a. photographique**, camera.

apparence, *n.f.* appearance, looks.

apparent, *adj.* noticeable, apparent.

apparenté, *adj.* related.
apparition, *n.f.* appearance, ghost.
appartement, *n.m.* apartment.
appartenir, *vb.* belong; pertain.
appât, *n.m.* bait.
appauvrir, *vb.* impoverish.
appel, *n.m.* call, appeal.
appeler, *vb.* call, summon, appeal. **s'a.,** be named.
appendice, *n.m.* appendix.
appesantir, *vb.* **s'a.,** grow heavier.
appétissant, *adj.* appetizing.
appétit, *n.m.* appetite.
applaudir, *vb.* applaud.
applaudissements, *n.m.pl.* applause.
applicable, *adj.* applicable.
application, *n.f.* application, industry.
appliqué, *adj.* industrious.
appliquer, *vb.* apply (put on), stick. **s'a.,** work hard.
appoint, *n.m.* contribution.
appointements, *n.m.pl.* salary.
apport, *n.m.* contribution.
apporter, *vb.* bring, fetch.
apposer, *vb.* affix.
appréciable, *adj.* appreciable.
appréciation, *n.f.* appreciation.
apprécier, *vb.* appreciate, value.
appréhension, *n.f.* apprehension.
apprendre, *vb.* learn. **a. à,** teach (to). **a. par cœur,** memorize.
apprenti, *n.m.* apprentice.
apprentissage, *n.m.* apprenticeship.
apprêt, *n.m.* preparation.
apprêter, *vb.* **s'a.,** prepare, get ready.
apprivoiser, *vb.* tame.
approbation, *n.f.* endorsement, approval, approbation.
approche, *n.f.* approach.
approcher, *vb.* **s'a. de,** approach, go toward.
approfondir, *vb.* deepen.
appropriation, *n.f.* appropriation.
approprier, *vb.* **s'a.,** take over, appropriate.
approuver, *vb.* approve.
approvisionnement, *n.m.* supply.
approvisionner, *vb.* supply.
approximatif, *adj.* approximate.
appui (-pwē), *n.m.* support.
appuyer (-pwē-), *vb.* support, endorse, advocate. **a. sur,** emphasize.

âpre, *adj.* bitter.
après, 1. *adv., prep.* after. **2.** *conj.* **a. que,** after. **d'a.,** according to.
après-demain, *n.m.* day after tomorrow.
après-midi, *n.m.f.* afternoon.
âpreté, *n.f.* harshness, bitterness.
à-propos, *n.m.* fitness.
apte à, *adj.* apt, suitable for.
aptitude, *n.f.* fitness, ability, aptitude.
aqualit, *n.m.* waterbed.
aquarelle (-kwa-), *n.f.* watercolor.
aquarium (-kwa-), *n.m.* aquarium.
aquatique (-kwa-), *adj.* aquatic.
aqueux, *adj.* watery.
Arabe, *n.m.f.* Arab, Arabian.
arabe, 1. *n.m.* Arabic. **2.** *adj.* Arab, Arabian, Arabic.
arachide, *n.f.* peanut.
araignée, *n.f.* spider. **toile d'a.,** cobweb.
arbitrage, *n.m.* arbitration.
arbitraire, *adj.* arbitrary.
arbitre, *n.m.f.* umpire, arbitrator.
arbitrer, *vb.* arbitrate.
arbre, *n.m.* tree.
arbrisseau, *n.m.* shrub.
arc (-k), *n.m.* arc, arch, bow.
arc-boutant, *n.m.* flying buttress.
arc-en-ciel, *n.m.* rainbow.
archaïque (ärk-), *adj.* archaic.
arche, *n.f.* arch (of bridge); ark. **a. de Noé,** Noah's Ark.
archéologie, *n.f.* archeology.
archet, *n.m.* bow.
archevêque, *n.m.* archbishop.
archi-, *prefix.* very.
archipel, *n.m.* archipelago.
architecte, *n.m.* architect.
architectural, *adj.* architectural.
architecture, *n.f.* architecture.
archives, *n.f.pl.* files, archives.
arctique, *adj.* arctic.
ardemment, *adv.* eagerly.
ardent, *adj.* eager, fiery, ardent.
ardeur, *n.f.* ardor.
ardoise, *n.f.* slate.
arène, *n.f.* arena, ring.
arête, *n.f.* fish bone.
argent, *n.m.* silver, money.
argenté, *adj.* silver(y).

argenterie, *n.f.* silverware.

Argentin, *n.m.* Argentine.

argentin, *adj.* Argentine.

argile, *n.f.* clay.

argot, *n.m.* slang.

argument, *n.m.* argument (reasoning).

argumenter, *vb.* argue (reason).

aride, *adj.* arid.

aristocrate, *n.m.f.* aristocrat.

aristocratie, *n.f.* aristocracy.

aristocratique, *adj.* aristocratic.

arithmétique, *n.f.* arithmetic.

arme, *n.f.* weapon; arm.

armée, *n.f.* army.

armement, *n.m.* armament.

arme nucléaire, *n.f.* nuclear weapon.

armer, *vb.* arm.

armistice, *n.m.* armistice.

armoire, *n.f.* cupboard, closet, wardrobe.

armure, *n.f.* armor.

arnaque, *n.f.* swindle.

aromatique, *adj.* aromatic.

arome, *n.m.* flavor, aroma.

arpenter, *vb.* pace.

arrache-pied, *adv.* **d'a.,** relentlessly.

arracher, *vb.* snatch.

arrangement, *n.m.* arrangement, settlement.

arranger, *vb.* settle, trim, fix, arrange.

arrestation, *n.f.* arrest, apprehension. **en état d'a.,** under arrest.

arrêt, *n.m.* stop.

arrêté, *n.m.* decree.

arrêter, *vb.* stop, check, halt, arrest.

arrhes, *n.f.pl.* deposit.

arrière, *adv.* behind, back. **en a.,** backward. **marche a.,** reverse (gear).

arriéré, 1. *n.m.* arrear. **2.** *adj.* backward.

arrière-garde, *n.f.* rear guard.

arrivée, *n.f.* arrival.

arriver, *vb.* happen, reach, arrive.

arrogance, *n.f.* arrogance.

arrogant, *adj.* arrogant.

arroger, *vb.* arrogate, assume.

arrondir, *vb.* round off.

arrondissement, *n.m.* district.

arroser, *vb.* water, sprinkle; baste (meat).

arsenal, *n.m.* arsenal.

arsenic, *n.m.* arsenic.

art, *n.m.* art. **beaux-a.s,** fine arts.

artère, *n.f.* artery.

artériel, *adj.* arterial.

arthrite, *n.f.* arthritis.

arthrose, *n.f.* osteoarthritis.

artichaut, *n.m.* artichoke.

article, *n.m.* article, item; entry. **a. de fond,** editorial.

articulation, *n.f.* joint, articulation.

articuler, *vb.* articulate.

artifice, *n.m.* artifice.

artificiel, *adj.* artificial.

artificieux, *adj.* artful.

artillerie, *n.f.* artillery.

artisan, *n.m.* craftsman, artisan.

artiste, *n.m.f.* artist.

artistique, *adj.* artistic.

as (äs), *n.m.* ace.

ascenseur, *n.m.* elevator.

ascension, *n.f.* ascent (of a mountain).

ascète, *n.m.f.* ascetic.

aseptique, *adj.* aseptic.

aseptiser, *vb.* disinfect.

Asiatique, *n.m.f.* Asian.

asiatique, *adj.* Asian.

Asie, *n.f.* Asia.

asile, *n.m.* haven, refuge, asylum.

aspect (-pě), *n.m.* looks, appearance, aspect.

asperger, *vb.* sprinkle.

asperges, *n.f.pl.* asparagus.

aspérité, *n.f.* bump.

asphalte, *n.m.* asphalt.

asphyxier, *vb.* suffocate.

aspirateur, *n.m.* vacuum cleaner.

aspiration, *n.f.* aspiration, longing.

aspirer, *vb.* aspire, breathe.

aspirine, *n.f.* aspirin.

assaillant, *n.m.* assailant.

assaillir, *vb.* assail, attack.

assaisonner, *vb.* season.

assassin, *n.m.* assassin, murderer.

assassinat, *n.m.* assassination, murder.

assassiner, *vb.* assassinate, murder.

assaut, *n.m.* assault, attack.

assemblage, *n.m.* collection.

assemblée, *n.f.* congregation, assembly.

assembler, *vb.* convene, gather. **s'a.,** assemble.

assener, *vb.* deal (a blow).

assentiment, *n.m.* assent.

asseoir, *vb.* seat. **s'a.,** sit down.

assermenté, *adj.* sworn.

assertion, *n.f.* assertion.

asservir, *vb.* enslave.

assez (de), *adv.* enough (of); pretty much.

assidu, *adj.* assiduous, industrious.

assiduité, *n.f.* industry.

assiéger, *vb.* besiege.

assiette, *n.f.* plate.

assigner, *vb.* assign.

assimiler, *vb.* assimilate.

assis, *adj.* seated.

assistance, *n.f.* those present.

assister à, *vb.* attend, be present at.

association, *n.f.* soccer; association, company; connection.

associé, 1. *n.m.* partner, associate. **2.** *adj.* associated.

associer, *vb.* associate.

assoiffé, *adj.* thirsty.

assombrir, *vb.* **s'a.,** grow dark.

assommer, *vb.* murder, slaughter.

Assomption, *n.f.* (*eccles.*) Assumption.

assorti, *adj.* matching.

assortiment, *n.m.* assortment.

assortir, *vb.* match; tune.

assoupir, *vb.* **s'a.,** get drowsy.

assouplir, *vb.* make supple.

assourdir, *vb.* deafen.

assouvir, *vb.* satisfy, appease.

assujetti, *adj.* subject.

assujettir, *vb.* subject.

assumer, *vb.* assume.

assurance, *n.f.* assurance, insurance.

assuré, *adj.* sure.

assurer, *vb.* insure; assure. **s'a. de,** make certain.

assureur, *n.m.* insurer.

astérisque, *n.m.* asterisk.

asthme, *n.m.* asthma.

astiquer, *vb.* polish.

astre, *n.m.* star.

astronaute, *n.m.* astronaut.

astronome, *n.m.* astronomer.

astronomie, *n.f.* astronomy.

astuce, *n.f.* shrewdness; trick.

astucieux, *adj.* tricky.

atelier, *n.m.* studio, (work)shop.

athée, *n.m.f.* atheist.

Athènes, *n.f.* Athens.

athlète, *n.m.f.* athlete.

athlétique, *adj.* athletic.

atlantique, *adj.* Atlantic.

atlas (-s), *n.m.* atlas.

atmosphère, *n.f.* atmosphere.

atmosphérique, *adj.* atmospheric.

atome, *n.m.* atom.

atomique, *adj.* atomic.

atout, *n.m.* trump.

atroce, *adj.* atrocious, outrageous.

atrocité, *n.f.* atrocity.

attachement, *n.m.* attachment, affection.

attacher, *vb.* tie, fasten, join, attach.

attaque, *n.f.* attack.

attaquer, *vb.* attack.

attardé, *adj.* belated.

attarder, *vb.* **s'a.,** linger; delay.

atteindre, *vb.* reach, attain; strike.

atteint, *adj.* stricken.

atteinte, *n.f.* reach. **hors d'a.,** out of reach.

attelage, *n.m.* team.

atteler, *vb.* hitch up, harness.

attenant, *adj.* adjoining.

attendre, *vb.* wait (for), await. **s'a. à,** expect.

attendrir, *vb.* soften, move. **se laisser a.,** relent.

attendrissement, *n.m.* feeling, emotion.

attentat, *n.m.* criminal attack, outrage.

attente, *n.f.* expectation, wait.

attenter à, *vb.* make an attempt on.

attentif, *adj.* thoughtful, attentive.

attention, *n.f.* notice, heed, attention. **faire a.,** heed, pay attention.

atténuer, *vb.* extenuate.

atterrir, *vb.* land.

attester, *vb.* attest.

attirant, *adj.* attractive.

attirer, *vb.* attract, entice, lure.

attitude, *n.f.* attitude.

attouchement, *n.m.* touch.

attraction, *n.f.* attraction.

attrait, *n.m.* charm.

attraper, *vb.* catch.

attrayant, *adj.* attractive.

attribuer, *vb.* ascribe, attribute.

attribut, *n.m.* attribute, characteristic.

attrister, *vb.* grieve.

au, *m.,* **à la,** *f.,* **aux,** *pl. prep.* to the, in the.

aubaine, *n.f.* godsend.

aube, *n.f.* dawn.

auberge, *n.f.* inn.

aubergine, *n.f.* eggplant.

aubergiste, *n.m.* innkeeper.

aucun, *pron.* none.

aucunement, *adv.* not at all.

audace, *n.f.* audacity.

audacieux, *adj.* daring, bold.

au-delà, *adv.* beyond.

au-dessous, 1. *adv.* below. **2.** *prep.* **au-d. de,** beneath, under.

au-dessus, 1. *adv.* above. **2.** *prep.* **au-d. de,** over, above.

audience, *n.f.* audience.

Audimat, *n.m.* (trademark) TV ratings.

audiovisuel, *adj.* audiovisual.

auditeur, *n.m.* listener.

auditoire, *n.m.* audience, assembly.

auge, *n.f.* trough.

augmentation, *n.f.* increase, raise, rise.

augmenter, *vb.* increase.

augure, *n.m.* omen, augury. **de bon a.,** auspicious. **de mauvais a.,** ominous.

augurer, *vb.* augur.

aujourd'hui, *adv.* today.

aumône, *n.f.* alms.

aumônier, *n.m.* chaplain.

auparavant, *adv.* before (time).

auprès de, *prep.* next, near, beside.

auréole, *n.f.* halo.

aurore, *n.f.* dawn.

ausculter, *vb.* examine with a stethoscope.

auspice, *n.m.* auspice.

aussi, *adv.* too, also; so, as; therefore.

aussitôt, *adv.* immediately.

austère, *adj.* austere, severe.

austérité, *n.f.* austerity.

Australie, *n.f.* Australia.

Australien, *n.m.* Australian.

australien, *adj.* Australian.

autant, *adv.* so much, as much. **a.**

que, as (so) much as. **d'a. que,** since. **a. plus,** so much the more.

autel, *n.m.* altar.

auteur, *n.m.* author, originator.

authentique, *adj.* true, genuine, authentic.

auto, *n.f.* auto.

auto-, *prefix.* self-, auto-.

autobus (-s), *n.m.* bus.

automatique, *adj.* automatic.

automne (-tôn), *n.m.* fall.

automobile, *n.f.* automobile.

autonomie, *n.f.* autonomy.

autopsie, *n.f.* autopsy.

autorail, *n.m.* train car.

autorisation, *n.f.* license, authorization.

autoriser, *vb.* authorize.

autoritaire, *adj.* authoritative.

autorité, *n.f.* authority.

autoroute, *n.f.* highway.

auto-stop, *n.m.* hitchhiking.

autour, 1. *adv.* around. **2.** *prep.* **a. de,** around.

autre, 1. *adj.* other. **2.** *pron.* other, else. **l'un l'a.,** one another. **quelqu'un d'a.,** someone else.

autrefois, *adv.* formerly.

autrement, *adv.* otherwise.

Autriche, *n.f.* Austria.

Autrichien, *n.m.* Austrian.

autrichien, *adj.* Austrian.

autruche, *n.f.* ostrich.

autrui, *pron.* someone else, others.

auxiliaire, *adj.* auxiliary.

avalanche, *n.f.* avalanche.

avaler, *vb.* swallow.

avance, *n.f.* advance. **d'a.,** beforehand. **en a.,** fast (clock).

avancé, *adj.* forward, advanced.

avancement, *n.m.* advance; advancement; promotion.

avancer, *vb.* proceed; come *or* go forward *or* onward.

avances, *n.f.pl.* advance. **faire des a. à,** make approaches to.

avant, 1. *n.m.* fore, bow. **2.** *adv.,* *prep.* before. **3.** *conj.* **a. que,** before. **en a.,** forward, onward. **en a. de,** ahead of.

avantage, *n.m.* advantage.

avantageux, *adj.* advantageous; favorable; profitable.

avant-bras, *n.m.* forearm.

avant-garde, *n.f.* vanguard.

avant-hier (-yâr), *n.m.* day before yesterday.
avant-toit, *n.m.* eaves.
avare, 1. *n.m.f.* miser. **2.** *adj.* miserly, stingy.
avarice, *n.f.* avarice.
avec, *prep.* with.
avenant, *adj.* comely. **à l'a.,** accordingly.
avenir, *n.m.* future.
Avent, *n.m. (eccles.)* Advent.
aventure, *n.f.* adventure.
aventurer, *vb.* **s'a.,** take a chance.
aventureux, *adj.* adventurous.
aventurier, *n.m.* adventurer.
avenue, *n.f.* avenue.
avérer, *vb.* **s'a.,** prove (to be).
averse, *n.f.* shower (rain).
aversion, *n.f.* aversion, dislike.
avertir, *vb.* notify, warn.
avertissement, *n.m.* warning.
avertisseur d'incendie, *n.m.* fire alarm.
aveu, *n.m.* admission, confession.
aveugle, *adj.* blind.
aveuglement, *n.m.* blindness.
aveuglément, *adv.* blindly.

aveugler, *vb.* blind.
aviateur, *n.m.* flier, aviator.
aviation, *n.f.* air force, aviation.
avide, *adj.* eager, greedy, avid.
avidité, *n.f.* greediness.
avilir, *vb.* debase, disgrace.
avion, *n.m.* airplane. **a. de bombardement**, bomber. **par a.,** via air mail.
avis, *n.m.* notice, opinion, advice (comm.).
aviser, *vb.* inform, notify. **s'a. (de)**, decide.
avocat, *n.m.* lawyer; advocate.
avoine, *n.f.* oat.
avoir, *vb.* have. **il y a,** ago.
avortement, *n.m.* abortion.
avoué, *n.m.* attorney, lawyer.
avouer, *vb.* confess, admit, avow.
avril (-l), *n.m.* April.
axe, *n.m.* axis.
axer, *vb.* center.
axiome, *n.m.* axiom.
ayatollah, *n.m.* ayatollah.
azote, *n.m.* nitrogen.
azur, *n.m.* azure, blue.
azuré, *adj.* azure.

B

babeurre, *n.m.* buttermilk.
babil, *n.m.* babble.
babiller, *vb.* babble.
bâbord, *n.m. (naut.)* port.
babouin, *n.m.* baboon.
baby-foot, *n.m.* table football.
bac, *n.m.* ferryboat. **passage en b.,** ferry, high school diploma.
baccalauréat, *n.m.* high school diploma.
bachelier, *n.m.* graduate.
bachot, *n.m.* (colloquial) high school diploma.
bacille (-l), *n.m.* bacillus.
bactérie, *n.f.* bacterium.
bactériologie, *n.f.* bacteriology.
badaud, *adj.* silly.
baffe, *n.f.* (colloquial) slap.
bagages, *n.m.pl.* luggage.
bagatelle, *n.f.* trifle.
bagnole, *n.f.* (colloquial) car.
bague, *n.f.* ring.
baguette, *n.f.* wand, stick; long, thin loaf of bread.

baie, *n.f.* bay; creek; berry.
baigner, *vb.* bathe.
baigneur, *n.m.* bather.
baignoire (bĕn wär), *n.f.* bathtub.
bail, *n.m.* lease.
bâillement, *n.m.* yawn.
bâiller, *vb.* yawn.
bâillon, *n.m.* gag.
bain, *n.m.* bath.
baïonnette, *n.f.* bayonet.
baiser, *n.m. and vb.* kiss (hand, forehead, etc.).
baissé, *adj.* downcast.
baisser, *vb.* lower, sink.
bal, *n.m.* ball (dance).
balade, *n.f.* stroll.
baladeur, *n.m.* portable cassette player or radio; (trademark) Walkman.
balai, *n.m.* broom. **b. à laver,** mop.
balance, *n.f.* scales, balance.
balancement, *n.m.* rocking, swinging.

balancer, *vb.* rock, swing, sway. **se b.**, roll, hover.

balayer, *vb.* sweep.

balbutier, *vb.* stammer.

balcon, *n.m.* balcony.

baldaquin, *n.m.* canopy.

baleine, *n.f.* whale.

ballade, *n.f.* ballad.

balle, *n.f.* bullet, ball; bale.

ballet, *n.m.* ballet.

ballon, *n.m.* balloon.

ballot, *n.m.* bundle.

ballotter, *vb.* shake.

balnéaire, *adj.* seaside.

balsamique, *adj.* balmy.

bambin, *n.m.* small child.

bambou, *n.m.* bamboo.

ban, *n.m.* ban. **mettre au b.**, ban.

banal, *adj.* trite.

banane, *n.f.* banana.

banc, *n.m.* bench.

bancaire, *adj.* banking.

bandage, *n.m.* bandage.

bande, *n.f.* strip, stripe; pack, gang, band.

bande magnétique, *n.f.* tape.

bande vidéo, *n.f.* videotape.

bandit, *n.m.* bandit, robber, knave.

banlieue, *n.f.* suburbs.

bannière, *n.f.* banner.

bannir, *vb.* banish.

bannissement, *n.m.* banishment.

banque, *n.f.* bank. **billet de b.**, banknote.

banqueroute, *n.f.* bankruptcy.

banquet, *n.m.* banquet, feast.

banquier, *n.m.* banker.

baptême (bä têm), *n.m.* christening, baptism.

baptiser (bä tē-), *vb.* christen, baptize.

Baptiste (bä tēst), *n.m.* Baptist.

baptistère (bä tēs-), *n.m.* baptistery.

bar, *n.m.* bar; bass (fish).

baraque, *n.f.* booth, stall; (colloquial) house.

baratin, *n.m.* smooth talk.

barbare, **1.** *n.m.f.* barbarian **2.** *adj.* barbarian, barbarous, wild.

barbarie, *n.f.* cruelty.

barbe, *n.f.* beard.

barbouiller, *vb.* daub, blur.

barbu, *adj.* bearded.

baril, *n.m.* barrel, keg.

baromètre, *n.m.* barometer.

baron, *n.m.* baron.

baroque, *adj.* baroque, weird.

barque, *n.f.* boat.

barrage, *n.m.* dam.

barre, *n.f.* bar, rail(ing). **b. du gouvernail**, helm.

barreau, *n.m.* bar.

barrer, *vb.* shut out.

barricade, *n.f.* barricade.

barrière, *n.f.* gate; bar, barrier; fence.

barrique, *n.f.* barrel, cask.

bas, *n.m.* stocking.

bas *m.*, **basse** *f. adj.* base, low, soft. **en b.**, down(ward), downstairs. **b. côté**, aisle.

bascule, *n.f.* seesaw. **chaise à b.**, rocking-chair.

basculer, *vb.* fall over.

base, *n.f.* base, basis.

basilic, *n.m.* basil.

basket, *n.m.* basketball; sneaker.

Basque, *n.m.* Basque (person).

basque, **1.** *n.m.* Basque (language). **2.** *adj.* Basque.

basse, *n.f.* bass (voice).

basse-cour, *n.f.* barnyard.

bassesse, *n.f.* baseness.

bassin, *n.m.* basin, dock.

bataille, *n.f.* battle.

bataillon, *n.m.* battalion.

bâtard, *adj. and n.m.* bastard.

bateau, *n.m.* boat.

bâtiment, *n.m.* building.

bâtir, *vb.* build.

bâton, *n.m.* stick, staff.

battant, *n.m.* flap, door.

batte, *n.f.* bat.

battement, *n.m.* beat.

batterie, *n.f.* battery; drums.

battre, *vb.* beat, strike; flap, pulsate. **se b.**, fight.

baume, *n.m.* balm.

bavard, *adj.* talkative, gossipy.

bavardage, *n.m.* gossip, chatter.

bavarder, *vb.* gossip, chat(ter).

bavette, *n.f.* bib.

bavure, *n.f.* smudge, mistake.

bazar, *n.m.* bazaar.

BCBG, *adj.* preppy. (bon chic bon genre).

BD, *n.f.* comic strip. (bande dessinée).

béatitude, *n.f.* bliss.

beau, bel *m.,* **belle** *f. adj.* beautiful, handsome, fair, lovely, fine. **avoir b.,** (to do something) in vain. **faire b.,** be fine (weather).

beaucoup (de), *adj.* a lot, a great deal; much, many. **de b.,** by far.

beau-frère, *n.m.* brother-in-law.

beau-père, *n.m.* father-in-law; stepfather.

beauté, *n.f.* beauty. **grain de b.,** mole.

bébé, *n.m.* baby.

bec, *n.m.* beak, bill; spot; burner. **b. sucré,** sweet tooth.

bécane, *n.f.* (colloquial) bike.

bêche, *n.f.* spade.

bêcher, *vb.* dig.

becqueter, *vb.* peck.

bée, *adj.* **rester bouche b.,** stand gaping.

bégayer, *vb.* stammer.

beignet, *n.m.* fritter.

bêler, *vb.* bleat.

Belge, *n.m.f.* Belgian.

belge, *adj.* Belgian.

Belgique, *n.f.* Belgium.

bélier, *n.m.* ram.

belle-fille, *n.f.* daughter-in-law.

belle-mère, *n.f.* mother-in-law; stepmother.

belligérant, *adj. and n.m.* belligerent.

bémol, *n.m.* flat (music).

bénédiction, *n.f.* blessing, benediction.

bénéfice, *n.m.* benefit, advantage, profit.

bénéficier, *vb.* benefit, profit.

bénin *m.,* **bénigne** *f. adj.* benign.

bénir, *vb.* bless.

béquille, *n.f.* crutch.

berceau, *n.m.* cradle, bower.

bercer, *vb.* rock.

berge, *n.f.* bank (river, etc.).

berger, *n.m.* shepherd.

besogne, *n.f.* (piece of) work.

besoin, *n.m.* need, want. **avoir b.,** need.

bestiaux, *n.m.pl.* cattle.

bétail, *n.m.* cattle, animals.

bête, 1. *n.f.* beast, animal. **2.** *adj.* stupid, dumb.

bêtise, *n.f.* nonsense.

béton, *n.m.* concrete.

betterave, *n.f.* beet.

Beur, *n.m.f.* North African in France of immigrant parents.

beurre, *n.m.* butter.

bévue, *n.f.* blunder, boner.

biais, *n.m.* slant; bias. **en b.,** at an angle.

bibelot, *n.m.* trinket.

biberon, *n.m.* baby's bottle.

Bible, *n.f.* Bible.

bibliothèque, *n.f.* library; bookcase.

biblique, *adj.* biblical.

bicyclette, *n.f.* bicycle. **faire de la b.,** cycle.

bidet, *n.m.* bidet.

bidon, *n.m.* can.

bidonville, *n.m.* shanty town.

bien, *n.m.* good; *(pl.)* goods, property, estate. **faire du b. à,** benefit.

bien, *adv.* well. **b. entendu,** of course. **aller b.,** be well. **vouloir b.,** be willing. **b. que,** although.

bien-aimé, *n.m. and adj.* darling.

bien-être, *n.m.* welfare.

bienfaisant, *adj.* beneficent, kind, humane.

bienfait, *n.m.* benefit.

bienfaiteur, *n.m.* benefactor.

bienheureux, *adj.* blessed.

biséant, *adj.* proper.

bientôt, *adv.* soon.

bienveillance, *n.f.* benevolence, kindness.

bienveillant, *adj.* benevolent, kindly.

bienvenu, *adj.* welcome.

bière, *n.f.* beer, ale.

biffer, *vb.* cancel, erase.

bifteck, *n.m.* beefsteak.

bifurquer, *vb.* branch off, fork.

bigamie, *n.f.* bigamy.

bigot, *n.m.* bigot.

bigoterie, *n.f.* bigotry.

bijou, *n.m.* jewel.

bijouterie, *n.f.* jewelry.

bilan, *n.m.* balance sheet; outcome.

bile, *n.f.* bile. **se faire de la b.,** worry.

bilingue, *adj.* bilingual.

billard, *n.m.* billiards.

bille, *n.f.* marble (toy).

billet, *n.m.* ticket, note. **b. de banque,** banknote.

billetterie, *n.f.* ticket dispenser.

billion (-l-), *n.m.* billion.

biochimie, *n.f.* biochemistry.

biographie, *n.f.* biography.

biologie, *n.f.* biology.

bis, 1. *n.m.* encore. **2.** *adv.* A or a (in addresses).

biscuit, *n.m.* biscuit.

bise, *n.f.* (colloquial) kiss.

bisou, *n.m.* (colloquial) kiss.

bit, *n.m.* bit.

bizarre, *adj.* queer, odd, strange.

blâme, *n.m.* blame.

blâmer, *vb.* blame.

blanc *m.,* **blanche** *f. adj.* white, blank. **en b.,** blank.

blancheur, *n.f.* whiteness.

blanchir, *vb.* whiten.

blanchisserie, *n.f.* laundry.

blasé, *adj.* sophisticated.

blasphème, *n.m.* blasphemy.

blasphémer, *vb.* curse, blaspheme.

blatte, *n.f.* cockroach.

blé, *n.m.* wheat.

bled, *n.m.* inland country.

blême, *adj.* pale.

blesser, *vb.* wound, hurt, injure.

blessure, *n.f.* wound, hurt, injury.

bleu, *adj.* blue; extremely rare (meat).

bloc, *n.m.* pad, block.

blocus (-s), *n.m.* blockade.

blond, *adj.* fair, blond(e).

bloquer, *vb.* block.

blottir, *vb.* **se b.,** cower.

blouse, *n.f.* blouse.

blouson, *n.m.* windbreaker.

blue jeans, *n.m.pl.* blue jeans.

bluff, *n.m.* bluff.

bluffeur, *n.m.* bluffer.

bobine, *n.f.* spool, reel.

bœuf (bœf), *n.m.* ox, beef. **jeune b.,** steer.

bogue, *n.m.* bug (computers).

Bohême, *n.f.* Bohemia.

bohème, 1. *n.m.f.* bohemian, happy-go-lucky person. **2.** *n.f.* artistic underworld. **3.** *adj.* bohemian.

Bohémien, *n.m.* Bohemian; gypsy.

bohémien, *adj.* Bohemian.

boire, *vb.* drink. **b. à petits coups,** sip.

bois, *n.m.* wood, forest, lumber.

boiserie, *n.f.* woodwork.

boisseau, *n.m.* bushel.

boisson, *n.f.* beverage, drink.

boîte, *n.f.* box; can (food). **b. aux lettres,** mail-box.

boiter, *vb.* limp.

boiteux, *adj.* lame.

bol, *n.m.* bowl.

bombardement, *n.m.* bombardment.

bombarder, *vb.* bomb, bombard.

bombe, *n.f.* bomb, shell.

bombe à neutrons, *n.f.* neutron bomb.

bon *m.,* **bonne** *f. adj.* good, kind. **de b. heure,** early. **b. marché,** cheap.

bon, *n.m.* bond.

bonbon, *n.m.* candy, bonbon.

bond, *n.m.* bound, leap.

bonder, *vb.* overcrowd, jam.

bondir, *vb.* bound, leap, spring.

bonheur, *n.m.* happiness.

bonhomme, *n.m.* fellow.

bonjour, *interj. and n.m.* good morning.

bonne, *n.f.* maid.

bonnement, *adv.* simply.

bonnet, *n.m.* cap, hood.

bonsoir, *interj. and n.m.* good evening.

bonté, *n.f.* kindness, goodness.

bord, *n.m.* edge, rim, brim. **b. du toit,** eaves.

bordeaux, *n.m.* Bordeaux (wine).

border, *vb.* bound, edge, border, hem.

borne, *n.f.* bound, limit.

borner, *vb.* bound, limit.

Bosnie-Herzégovine, *n.f.* Bosnia (and) Herzegovina.

bosquet, *n.m.* clump (trees).

bosse, *n.f.* bump.

bosselure, *n.f.* dent.

bosser, *vb.* (colloquial) work.

bossu, *adj.* hunchbacked.

botanique, *n.f.* botany.

botte, *n.f.* boot; bunch.

Bottin, *n.m.* (trademark) phone book.

bottine, *n.f.* ankle boot.

bouche, *n.f.* mouth.

boucher, *vb.* stop up.

boucher, *n.m.* butcher.

boucherie, *n.f.* butcher shop.

bouchon, *n.m.* cork.

boucle, *n.f.* curl, loop, buckle. **b. d'oreille,** earring.

boucler, *vb.* curl.

bouclier, n.m. shield.
bouder, vb. sulk.
boudin, n.m. black pudding.
boue, n.f. mud.
bouée, n.f. buoy.
boueur, n.m. scavenger.
boueux, adj. muddy.
bouffe, n.f. (colloquial) food, grub.
bouffée, n.f. puff.
bouffon, n.m. clown, fool.
bouffonerie, n.f. antic(s).
bouger, vb. stir, move, budge.
bougie, n.f. candle; spark plug.
bouillabaisse, n.f. bouillabaisse.
bouillir, vb. boil.
bouilloire, n.f. kettle.
bouillon, n.m. broth.
bouillonner, vb. bubble.
bouillotte, n.f. kettle.
boulanger, n.m. baker.
boulangerie, n.f. bakery.
boule, n.f. ball.
bouleau, n.m. birch.
bouledogue, n.m. bulldog.
boulevard, n.m. boulevard.
bouleversement, n.m. upset.
bouleverser, vb. upset, overturn.
boulot, n.m. (colloquial) work.
boum, 1. n.m. bang. **2.** n.f. party.
bouquet, n.m. cluster, bunch, bouquet.
bouquiniste, n.m. (secondhand) bookseller.
bourbeux, adj. sloppy.
bourdon, n.m. bumblebee.
bourdonnement, n.m. buzz.
bourdonner, vb. hum, buzz.
bourg, n.m. borough, village.
bourgeois, adj. middle-class, bourgeois.
bourgeoisie, n.f. middle class.
bourgeon, n.m. bud.
bourgeonner, vb. bud.
bourgogne, 1. n.m. Burgundy (wine). **2.** n.f. **la B.,** Burgundy.
bourre, n.f. stuffing.
bourreau, n.m. executioner, hangman; brute.
bourrelet, n.m. pad.
bourrer, vb. stuff, pad.
bourru, adj. gruff.
bourse, n.f. purse, bag; stock exchange; scholarship, fellowship.
boursoufler, vb. bloat.

bousculer, vb. jostle.
bousiller, vb. bungle.
boussole, n.f. compass.
bout, n.m. end, tip, butt, stub.
bouteille, n.f. bottle.
boutique, n.f. shop.
bouton, n.m. button, bud; pimple.
boutonnière, n.f. buttonhole.
boxe, n.f. boxing.
boxeur, n.m. boxer.
boycotter, vb. boycott.
bracelet, n.m. bracelet.
braconnier, n.m. poacher.
brailler, vb. bawl.
braise, n.f. coals, embers.
brancard, n.m. stretcher.
branche, n.f. branch, bough, limb.
branché, adj. trendy.
brandir, vb. brandish.
branler, vb. waver.
braquer, vb. aim, point.
bras, n.m. arm.
brasse, n.f. fathom; breaststroke.
brasser, vb. brew.
brasserie, n.f. brewery; beer-joint.
bravade, n.f. bravado.
brave, adj. fine, good, brave.
braver, vb. brave, face, defy.
bravoure, n.f. courage.
break, n.m. station wagon.
brebis, n.f. lamb.
brèche, n.f. breach, gap.
bref, 1. adj. m., **brève** f. brief, short. **2.** adv. in short.
Brésil, n.m. Brazil.
Bretagne, n.f. Brittany.
brevet, n.m. commission. **b. d'invention,** patent.
bribe, n.f. scrap, bit.
bricoler, vb. do odd jobs.
bride, n.f. bridle.
brider, vb. curb.
bridge, n.m. bridge (game).
brièveté, n.f. brevity.
brigade, n.f. brigade.
brigadier, n.m. corporal.
brigant, n.m. robber, knave.
brillant, adj. brilliant, bright, glowing.
briller, vb. shine, glisten, glare.
brin, n.m. blade (grass).
brindille, n.f. twig.
brioche, n.f. bun.
brique, n.f. brick.

briquet, *n.m.* lighter. **pierre à b.,** flint.

brise, *n.f.* breeze.

briser, *vb.* break, shatter, smash.

britannique, *adj.* British.

brocart, *n.m.* brocade.

broche, *n.f.* spit, spindle; brooch.

brochette, *n.f.* skewer.

brochure, *n.f.* pamphlet.

broder, *vb.* embroider.

broderie, *n.f.* embroidery.

bronchite, *n.f.* bronchitis.

bronze, *n.m.* bronze.

broquette, *n.f.* tack.

brosse, *n.f.* brush.

brouhaha, *n.m.* uproar.

brouillard, *n.m.* fog, mist.

brouiller, *vb.* jumble, embroil; scramble (eggs). **se b.,** quarrel.

brouillon, *n.m.* (rough) draft.

broussailles, *n.f.pl.* brushwood.

brousse, *n.f.* **la b.,** the bush.

brouter, *vb.* browse.

broyer, *vb.* crush.

bruine, *n.f.* drizzle.

bruiner, *vb.* drizzle.

bruissement, *n.m.* rustle.

bruit, *n.m.* noise, clatter; report, rumor.

brûler, *vb.* burn.

brume, *n.f.* mist. **b. légère,** haze.

brumeux, *adj.* foggy, misty.

brun, *adj.* brown.

brune, *adj. and n.f.* brunette.

brusque, *adj.* abrupt, curt, blunt, gruff, brusque.

brut, *adj.* crude, gross.

Bruxelles, *n.f.* Brussels.

brutal, *adj.* brutal, savage.

brutalité, *n.f.* brutality.

brute, *n.f.* brute.

bruyant, *adj.* noisy, loud.

bruyère, *n.f.* heath, heather.

bûche, *n.f.* log.

bûcheron, *n.m.* wood-cutter.

budget, *n.m.* budget.

buffet, *n.m.* buffet.

buffle, *n.m.* buffalo.

buis, *n.m.* box (tree).

buisson, *n.m.* bush, shrub, thicket.

buissonneux, *adj.* bushy.

bulbe, *n.m.* bulb.

Bulgarie, *n.f.* Bulgaria.

bulle, *n.f.* bubble; (papal) bull.

bulletin, *n.m.* bulletin, ticket.

bureau, *n.m.* office, bureau; desk. **b. de location,** box office.

burin, *n.m.* chisel.

burlesque, *adj.* ludicrous.

bus, *n.m.* bus.

buste, *n.m.* bust.

but, *n.m.* aim, goal, purpose.

butin, *n.m.* spoils, booty.

butte, *n.f.* hill, knoll.

buvard, *n.m.* blotter.

buvette, *n.f.* bar.

C

ça, *pron.* that.

cabane, *n.f.* cabin, hut.

cabaret, *n.m.* cabaret; tavern.

cabine, *n.f.* cabin, booth.

cabinet, *n.m.* closet; office. **c. de toilette,** lavatory. **c. de travail,** study.

câble, *n.m.* cable, rope.

câbler, *vb.* cable.

câblogramme, *n.m.* cablegram.

cacahuète, *n.f.* peanut.

cacao, *n.m.* cocoa.

cacher, *vb.* hide, conceal. **se c.,** lurk.

cacher, *m.,* **cachère** *f. adj.* kosher.

cachet, *n.m.* seal.

cadavre, *n.m.* corpse.

cadeau, *n.m.* gift, present.

cadence, *n.f.* cadence.

cadet, 1. *n.m.* cadet. **2.** *adj.* junior.

cadran, *n.m.* dial.

cadre, *n.m.* frame.

café, *n.m.* coffee; café.

cage, *n.f.* cage.

cahier, *n.m.* notebook.

caille, *n.f.* quail.

caillot, *n.m.* clot.

caillou, *n.m.* pebble.

caisse, *n.f.* crate, case, box.

caissier, *n.m.* cashier, teller.

cajoler, *vb.* coax.

calamité, *n.f.* calamity.

calcium, *n.m.* calcium.

calcul, *n.m.* calculation.

calculateur, *n.m.* calculator.

calculatrice, *n.f.* calculator.

calculer, vb. figure, reckon, calculate.

cale, n.f. hold (ship).

calembour, n.m. pun.

calendrier, n.m. calendar.

calibre, n.m. caliber.

calicot, n.m. calico.

callosité, n.f. callus.

calmant, n.m. sedative.

calme, adj. and n.m. quiet, calm.

calmer, vb. soothe, quiet, calm.

calomnie, n.f. slander.

calomnier, vb. slander.

calorie, n.f. calorie.

calotte, n.f. crown (of hat).

Calvaire, n.m. Calvary.

camarade, n.m.f. comrade; companion, mate.

camaraderie, n.f. companionship, fellowship.

cambrioleur, n.m. burglar.

camembert, n.m. Camembert cheese.

camera, n.f. camera.

caméscope, n.m. camcorder.

camion, n.m. truck.

camoufler, vb. camouflage.

camp, n.m. camp.

campagnard, 1. n.m. countryman, peasant. **2.** adj. peasant.

campagne, n.f. country; campaign.

camper, vb. camp.

camphre, n.m. camphor.

Canada, n.m. Canada.

Canadien, n.m. Canadian.

canadien, adj. Canadian.

canaille, n.f. rabble; scoundrel.

canal, n.m. channel, canal.

canapé, n.m. sofa, couch; canapé.

canard, n.m. duck.

canari, n.m. canary.

cancer (-r), n.m. cancer.

cancérogène, adj. carcinogenic.

candeur, n.f. purity; candor.

candidat, n.m. candidate, applicant.

candidature, n.f. candidacy.

candide, adj. frank, open, candid.

canevas, n.m. canvas. **gros c.,** burlap.

canicule, n.f. heat wave.

canin, adj. canine.

canne, n.f. cane, stick.

canneberge, n.f. cranberry.

cannelle, n.f. cinnamon.

cannibale, adj. and n.m.f. cannibal.

canoë (-ō ā), n.m. canoe.

canon, n.m. cannon.

canot, n.m. boat, canoe. **c. automobile,** motorboat.

cantaloup, n.m. cantaloupe.

cantine, n.f. canteen, dining hall.

cantique, n.m. hymn.

canton, n.m. district, canton.

caoutchouc (-chōō), n.m. rubber.

cap (-p), n.m. cape (headland).

capable, adj. efficient, fit, capable, competent.

capacité, n.f. capability; capacity.

cape, n.f. cape (clothing).

capitaine, n.m. captain.

capital, adj. and n.m. capital.

capitale, n.f. capital (city).

capitaliser, vb. capitalize.

capitalisme, n.m. capitalism.

capitaliste, n.m.f. capitalist.

caporal, n.m. corporal.

capot, n.m. hood.

capote, n.f. hood.

câpre, n.f. caper.

caprice, n.m. whim, fancy.

capricieux, adj. fickle, capricious.

capsule, n.f. capsule.

captif, adj. and n.m. captive.

captiver, vb. captivate, charm.

captivité, n.f. captivity.

capture, n.f. capture.

capturer, vb. capture.

capuchon, n.m. hood.

car, conj. for.

caractère, n.m. character, nature, disposition; type.

caractériser, vb. characterize; distinguish; mark.

caractéristique, adj. characteristic.

carafe, n.f. decanter, water-bottle.

caraïbe, adj. Caribbean.

Caraïbes, n.f.pl. **les C.,** the Caribbean.

caramel, n.m. caramel.

carat, n.m. carat.

caravane, n.f. caravan.

carbone, n.m. carbon.

carboniser, vb. char.

carburant, n.m. fuel.

carburateur, n.m. carburetor.

carcasse, n.f. shell; carcass.

cardinal, n.m. cardinal.

Carême, *n.m.* Lent.
caresse, *n.f.* caress.
caresser, *vb.* fondle, stroke, caress.
cargaison, *n.f.* cargo.
caricature, *n.f.* caricature.
carie, *n.f.* decay.
carillon, *n.m.* chime.
carillonner, *vb.* chime.
carnaval, *n.m.* carnival.
carnet, *n.m.* notebook.
carnivore, *adj.* carnivorous.
carotte, *n.f.* carrot.
carré, *n.m. and adj.* square.
carreau, *n.m.* diamond (cards); pane; tile.
carrefour, *n.m.* crossroads.
carrément, *adv.* bluntly, altogether.
carrière, *n.f.* career; scope; quarry.
carriole, *n.f.* (light) cart.
carrosse, *n.m.* coach.
cartable, *n.m.* school bag.
carte, *n.f.* chart, map, card. **c. de crédit,** credit card. **c. du jour,** bill of fare.
carton, *n.m.* cardboard; box, carton.
cartouche, *n.f.* cartridge.
cas, *n.m.* case; event.
cascade, *n.f.* waterfall.
cascadeur, *n.m.* stuntman.
case, *n.f.* pigeonhole; hut, shed.
caserne, *n.f.* barracks.
casier, *n.m.* filing cabinet, compartment.
casque, *n.m.* helmet.
casque a écouteurs, *n.m.pl.* headphones.
casquette, *n.f.* cap.
cassable, *adj.* breakable.
casse-croûte, *n.m.* snack.
casser, *vb.* break, crack.
casserole, *n.f.* pan.
cassette, *n.f.* 1. casket. 2. cassette.
cassis, *n.m.* black currant.
cassure, *n.f.* break.
caste, *n.f.* caste.
castor, *n.m.* beaver.
casuel, *adj.* casual.
catalogue, *n.m.* catalogue.
cataracte, *n.f.* cataract.
catarrhe, *n.m.* catarrh.
catastrophe, *n.f.* disaster, catastrophe.
catéchisme, *n.m.* catechism.

catégorie, *n.f.* category.
cathédrale, *n.f.* cathedral.
catholicisme, *n.m.* Catholicism.
catholique, *adj.* Catholic.
cauchemar, *n.m.* nightmare.
cause, *n.f.* case; cause.
causer, *vb.* chat; cause.
causerie, *n.f.* chat, talk.
causette, *n.f.* chat.
caution, *n.f.* bail, security.
cavalerie, *n.f.* cavalry.
cavalier, *n.m.* rider, horseman; escort.
cave, *n.f.* cellar, cavern.
cavité, *n.f.* cavity.
CD, *n.m.* compact disc.
ce (sa), cet (sèt) m., cette (sèt) f., ces (sā) *pl. adj.* that, this.
ceci, *pron.* this.
cécité, *n.f.* blindness.
céder, *vb.* yield, give in, cede.
cédille, *n.f.* cedilla.
cèdre, *n.m.* cedar.
ceindre, *vb.* gird.
ceinture, *n.f.* belt, sash.
cela, *pron.* that.
célébration, *n.f.* celebration.
célèbre, *adj.* famous, noted.
célébrer, *vb.* celebrate.
célébrité, *n.f.* celebrity.
céleri, *n.m.* celery.
céleste, *adj.* heavenly, celestial.
célibataire, 1. *n.m.* bachelor. **2.** *adj.* single.
celle, *pron. f.* See **celui.**
cellule, *n.f.* cell.
celluloïd (-lô ēd), *n.m.* celluloid.
celtique, *adj.* Celtic.
celui *m.,* **celle** *f.,* **ceux** *m.pl.,* **celles** *f.pl. pron.* the one. **celui-ci,** this one; the latter. **celui-là,** that one; the former.
cendre, *n.f.* ashes, cinders.
cendrier, *n.m.* ashtray.
censé, *adj.* **être c. faire,** be supposed to do.
censeur, *n.m.* censor, vice-principal.
censure, *n.f.* censure.
censurer, *vb.* censor.
cent, *adj. and n.m.* hundred. **pour c.,** percent.
centaine, *n.f.* about a hundred.
centenaire, *adj. and n.m.* centenary, centennial.

centième, *adj.* hundredth.
centigrade, *adj.* centigrade.
centimètre, *n.m.* centimeter.
central, *adj.* central.
centraliser, *vb.* centralize.
centre, *n.m.* center.
cep, *n.m.* vine stock.
cependant, *adv.* however, still, yet.
cercle, *n.m.* circle, ring, hoop; club.
cercueil, *n.m.* coffin.
céréale, *adj. and n.f.* cereal.
cérémonial, *adj. and n.m.* ceremonial.
cérémonie, *n.f.* ceremony. **sans c.,** informal.
cérémonieux *adj.* formal, ceremonious.
cerf (sér), *n.m.* deer.
cerf-volant, *n.m.* kite.
cerise, *n.f.* cherry.
certain, *adj.* certain, sure; *(pl.)* some.
certes, *adv.* indeed.
certificat, *n.m.* credentials; certificate.
certifier, *vb.* certify.
certitude, *n.f.* certainty, assurance.
cerveau, *n.m.* brain.
cervelle, *n.f.* brains.
cessation, *n.f.* stopping, cessation.
cesser, *vb.* stop, desist, cease.
cession, *n.f.* assignment (law).
cet, cette, *pron.* See **ce.**
chacun, *pron.* everybody, everyone; each.
chagrin, 1. *n.m.* grief, vexation. **2.** *adj.* fretful.
chagriner, *vb.* grieve.
chaîne, *n.f.* chain; range.
chaîne stéréo, *n.f.* stereo system.
chaînon, *n.m.* link.
chair, *n.f.* flesh.
chaire, *n.f.* pulpit, rostrum.
chaise, *n.f.* chair.
chaland, *n.m.* barge.
châle, *n.m.* shawl.
chaleur, *n.f.* warmth, heat, glow.
chaloupe, *n.f.* launch.
chambre, *n.f.* room, chamber; House (parliament). **c. à coucher,** bedroom.
chameau, *n.m.* camel.
chamois, *n.m.* chamois.

champ, *n.m.* field.
champagne, *n.m.* champagne.
champêtre, *adj.* rural.
champignon, *n.m.* mushroom.
champion, *n.m.* champion.
championnat, *n.m.* championship.
chance, *n.f.* luck; risk, chance.
chanceler, *vb.* stagger, reel.
chancelier, *n.m.* chancellor.
chandail, *n.m.* sweater.
chandelier, *n.m.* candlestick.
chandelle, *n.f.* candle.
change, *n.m.* exchange.
changeant, *adj.* changeable.
changement, *n.m.* change, shift.
changer, *vb.* alter, shift, change.
chanson, *n.f.* song.
chant, *n.m.* song, chant. **c. du coq,** cock-crow.
chantage, *n.m.* blackmail.
chanter, *vb.* sing, chant.
chanteur, *n.m.* singer.
chantier, *n.m.* (work)yard.
chaos (k-), *n.m.* chaos.
chaotique (k-), *adj.* chaotic.
chapeau, *n.m.* hat, bonnet.
chapelle, *n.f.* chapel.
chaperon, *n.m.* chaperon.
chapiteau, *n.m.* capital.
chapitre, *n.m.* chapter.
chapon, *n.m.* capon.
chaque, *adj.* every, each.
char, *n.m.* chariot. **c. d'assaut,** (military) tank.
charbon, *n.m.* coal. **c. de bois,** charcoal.
charcuterie, *n.f.* delicatessen.
charge, *n.f.* load, charge.
charger, *vb.* load, burden, charge.
chariot, *n.m.* wagon; baggage cart.
charisme, *n.m.* charisma.
charitable, *adj.* charitable.
charité, *n.f.* charity.
charlatan, *n.m.* charlatan.
charmant, *adj.* delightful, lovely, charming.
charme, *n.m.* spell, charm.
charmer, *vb.* charm.
charnel, *adj.* carnal.
charnu, *adj.* fleshy.
charpente, *n.f.* framework.
charpentier, *n.m.* carpenter.
charretier, *n.m.* carter.
charrette, *n.f.* cart.
charrue, *n.f.* plow.

charte, *n.f.* charter.

chasse, *n.f.* hunt(ing), chase.

châsse, *n.f.* shrine.

chasse-neige, *n.m.* snowplow.

chasser, *vb.* hunt; chase; drive away.

chasseur, *n.m.* hunter; bellboy.

châssis, *n.m.* (window) sash; chassis.

chaste, *adj.* chaste.

chasteté, *n.f.* chastity.

chat *m.,* **chatte** *f. n.* cat.

châtaigne, *n.f.* chestnut.

château, *n.m.* mansion, castle.

châtier, *vb.* punish, chastise.

chaton, *n.m.* kitten.

chatouiller, *vb.* tickle.

chatouilleux, *adj.* ticklish.

chaud, *adj.* hot, warm.

chaudière, *n.f.* boiler.

chauffage, *n.m.* heating.

chauffer, *vb.* heat, warm.

chauffeur, *n.m.* driver, chauffeur.

chaumière, *n.f.* cottage.

chaussée, *n.f.* road.

chausser, *vb.* wear shoes. **se c.,** put on shoes.

chaussette, *n.f.* sock.

chaussure, *n.f.* footgear.

chauve, *adj.* bald.

chauve-souris, *n.f.* bat.

chaux, *n.f.* lime.

chavirer, *vb.* capsize.

chef, *n.m.* leader, chief.

chef-d'œuvre (shĕ-), *n.m.* masterpiece.

chemin, *n.m.* road. **c. de fer,** railway. **à mi-c.,** halfway. **c. de table,** table runner.

chemineau, *n.m.* tramp.

cheminée, *n.f.* fireplace, chimney; funnel.

chemise, *n.f.* shirt. **c. de nuit,** nightgown.

chemisier, *n.m.* blouse.

chêne, *n.m.* oak.

chenille, *n.f.* caterpillar.

chèque, *n.m.* check.

chèque de voyage, *n.m.* traveler's check.

cher (-r), *adj.* dear, expensive.

chercher, *vb.* seek, look for, search. **aller c.,** fetch.

chère, *n.f.* fare, food. **aimer la**

bonne c., be fond of good living.

faire bonne c., have a good meal.

chéri, *adj. and n.m.* beloved, darling.

chérir, *vb.* cherish.

chétif, *adj.* puny.

cheval, *n.m.* horse. **à c.,** on horseback. **monter à c.,** ride (horseback). **fer à c.,** horseshoe.

chevaleresque, *adj.* chivalrous.

chevalerie, *n.f.* chivalry.

chevalet, *n.m.* easel; knight.

chevalier, *n.m.* knight.

cheveu, *n.m., pl.* **cheveux,** hair.

cheville, *n.f.* ankle; peg.

chèvre, *n.f.* goat.

chevreau, *n.m.* kid.

chevreuil, *n.m.* roe.

chevron, *n.m.* rafter.

chevroter, *vb.* quaver.

chevrotine, *n.f.* buckshot.

chez, *prep.* at . . .'s (house, office, shop, etc.).

chic, *adj.* stylish.

chien, *n.m.* dog.

chienne, *n.f.* bitch.

chiffon, *n.m.* rag.

chiffonner, *vb.* crumple.

chiffre, *n.m.* figure.

chiffrer, *vb.* figure.

Chili, *n.m.* Chile.

Chilien, *n.m.* Chilean.

chilien, *adj.* Chilean.

chimie, *n.f.* chemistry.

chimiothérapie, *n.f.* chemotherapy.

chimique, *adj.* chemical.

chimiste, *n.m.f.* chemist.

Chine, *n.f.* China.

Chinois, **1.** *n.m.* Chinese (person).

chinois, **1.** *n.m.* Chinese (language). **2.** *adj.* Chinese.

chiper, *vb.* (colloquial) swipe.

chiquenaude, *n.f.* flip.

chirurgie, *n.f.* surgery.

chirurgien, *n.m.* surgeon.

chlore (k-), *n.m.* chlorine.

chloroforme (k-), *n.m.* chloroform.

choc, *n.m.* shock, clash, brunt.

chocolat, *n.m.* chocolate.

chœur (k-), *n.m.* choir, chorus.

choisir, *vb.* choose, select, pick.

choix, *n.m.* choice.

chômage, *n.m.* stoppage (of work).

chômer, *vb.* be unemployed.

choquer, *vb.* shock, clash.

choral (k-), *adj.* choral.

chose, *n.f.* thing, matter. **quelque c.,** anything.

chou, *n.m.* cabbage.

choucroute, *n.f.* sauerkraut.

chouette, 1. *n.f.* owl. **2.** *adj.* great, neat.

chou-fleur, *n.m.* cauliflower.

choyer, *vb.* pamper.

chrétien (k-), *adj. and n.m.* Christian.

chrétienté (k-), *n.f.* Christendom.

christianisme (k-), *n.m.* Christianity.

chronique (k-), **1.** *n.f.* chronicle. **2.** *adj.* chronic.

chronologique (k-), *adj.* chronological.

chronomètre (k-), stopwatch.

chronométrer (k-), *vb.* time.

chrysanthème (k-), *n.m.* chrysanthemum.

chuchoter, *vb.* whisper.

chut (shŸt), *interj.* sh!

chute, *n.f.* fall, drop, downfall.

Chypre, *n.f.* Cyprus.

cible, *n.f.* target.

cicatrice, *n.f.* scar.

cidre, *n.m.* cider.

ciel, *n.m.,* sky. *(pl.)* **cieux,** heaven.

cierge, *n.m.* (church) candle.

cigale, *n.f.* locust.

cigare, *n.m.* cigar.

cigarette, *n.f.* cigarette.

ci-gît, *adv. and vb.* here lies.

cigogne, *n.f.* stork.

ci-joint, *adj.* enclosed.

cil (-l), *n.m.* eyelash.

cime, *n.f.* top, summit.

ciment, *n.m.* cement.

cimenter, *vb.* cement.

cimetière, *n.m.* churchyard, cemetery.

cinéaste, *n.m.f.* film-maker.

cinéma, *n.m.* cinema.

cinémathèque, *n.f.* film library.

cinglant, *adj.* scathing.

cinq (-k), *adj. and n.m.* five.

cinquante, *adj. and n.m.* fifty.

cinquième, *adj. and n.m.f.* fifth.

cintre, *n.m.* semicircle; arch.

circonférence, *n.f.* circumference.

circonflexe, *adj.* circumflex.

circonscription, *n.f.* **c. électorale,** borough.

circonscrire, *vb.* circumscribe.

circonstance, *n.f.* event, circumstance. **c. critique,** emergency.

circonvenir, *vb.* circumvent.

circuit, *n.m.* circuit. **hors c.,** disconnected.

circulaire, *adj.* circular.

circulation, *n.f.* traffic; circulation.

circuler, *vb.* circulate, turn, revolve.

cire, *n.f.* wax.

cirer, *vb.* polish, shine.

cireur, *n.m.* bootblack.

cirque, *n.m.* circus.

cirrhose, *n.f.* cirrhosis.

cisailles, *n.f.pl.* shears.

ciseau, *n.m.* chisel; *(pl.)* scissors.

ciseler, *vb.* chisel.

citadelle, *n.f.* citadel.

citation, *n.f.* quotation, citation.

cité, *n.f.* city. **droit de c.,** citizenship.

citer, *vb.* quote, cite.

citoyen, *n.m.* citizen.

citron, *n.m.* lemon. **c. pressé,** lemonade.

citrouille, *n.f.* pumpkin.

civil (-l), **1.** *n.m.* civilian. **2.** *adj.* civil.

civilisation, *n.f.* civilization.

civilisé, *adj.* civilized.

civiliser, *vb.* civilize.

civique, *adj.* civic.

clair, *adj.* clear, bright. **c. de lune,** moonlight.

clairière, *n.f.* glade, clearing.

clairon, *n.m.* bugle.

clameur, *n.f.* clamor, outcry.

clandestin, *adj.* clandestine.

clapoteux, *adj.* choppy (sea).

claque, *n.f.* slap.

claquement, *n.m.* smack.

claquer, *vb.* slap, smack; chatter (teeth); bang.

clarifier, *vb.* clarify.

clarinette, *n.f.* clarinet.

clarté, *n.f.* clarity; light.

classe, *n.f.* class.

classement, *n.m.* classification.

classer, *vb.* classify, order, file, grade.

classeur, n.m. file, filing cabinet.
classification, n.f. classification.
classifier, vb. classify.
classique, adj. classic, classical.
clause, n.f. clause.
clavecin, n.m. harpsichord.
clavicule, n.f. collarbone.
clavier, n.m. keyboard.
clef (klā), **clé**, n.f. key.
clémence, n.f. clemency.
clément, adj. merciful.
clerc, n.m. clerk.
clergé, n.m. clergy.
clérical, adj. clerical.
cliché, n.m. cliché; snapshot; negative.
client, n.m. customer, patron, client.
clientèle, n.f. customers; practice.
cligner (de l'œil), vb. wink.
clignoter, vb. blink, wink.
clignotant, n.m. turn signal.
climat, n.m. climate.
climatisation, n.f. air conditioning.
climatiser, vb. air-condition.
clin, n.m. **c. d'œil**, wink.
clinique, 1. n.f. clinic. **2.** adj. clinical.
cloche, n.f. bell.
clocher, n.m. belfry. **de c.**, parochial.
cloison, n.f. partition.
cloître, n.m. cloister, convent.
clôture, n.f. fence.
clou, n.m. nail.
clouer, vb. nail, tack.
club (-b), n.m. club.
coaguler, vb. coagulate.
coalition, n.f. coalition.
coasser, vb. croak (frogs).
cobaye, n.m. guinea pig.
coca, n.m. Coke (trademarked name of soft drink).
cocaïne, n.f. cocaine.
cochon, n.m. pig.
coco, n.m. **noix de c.**, coconut.
cocon, n.m. cocoon.
cocotte, n.f. casserole.
cocu, n.m. cuckold.
code, n.m. code; laws.
code postal, n.m. zip code.
cœur, n.m. heart.
coffre, n.m. bin; coffer.
cognac, n.m. brandy, cognac.

cogner, vb. bump, strike, run into, knock (down).
cohérent, adj. coherent.
cohésion, n.f. cohesion.
coiffer, vb. dress (hair).
coiffeur, n.m. hairdresser, barber.
coiffure, n.f. hairdo.
coin, n.m. corner, wedge.
coincé, adj. stuck; inhibited.
coincer, vb. get stuck, jam.
coïncidence (kō ăn-), n.f. coincidence.
coïncider (kō ăn-), vb. coincide.
col, n.m. collar; pass.
colère, n.f. anger, temper. **en c.**, angry.
colimaçon, n.m. snail.
colique, n.f. diarrhea.
colis, n.m. parcel.
collaborateur, n.m. fellow-worker.
collaboration, n.f. assistance, collaboration.
collaborer, vb. work together, collaborate.
collant, n.m. pantyhose.
collatéral, adj. collateral.
colle, n.f. glue, paste.
collecte, n.f. collection.
collectif, adj. collective.
collection, n.f. collection.
collectionneur, n.m. collector.
collège, n.m. secondary school.
collègue, n.m.f. colleague.
coller, vb. glue, paste, stick.
collier, n.m. necklace; collar (dog).
colline, n.f. hill.
collision, n.f. collision.
colombe, n.f. dove.
Colombie, n.f. Colombia.
colon, n.m. settler, colonist.
colonel, n.m. colonel.
colonial, adj. colonial.
colonie, n.f. settlement, colony.
coloniser, vb. colonize.
colonne, n.f. column.
coloré, adj. colorful.
colorer, vb. color.
colossal, adj. huge, colossal.
colosse, n.m. giant, colossus.
colporter, vb. peddle.
colporteur, n.m. peddler.
combat, n.m. fight, battle. **hors de c.**, disabled.
combattant, adj. and n.m. combatant.

combattre, *vb.* fight.
combien (de), *adv.* how much, how many.
combinaison, *n.f.* combination; slip, B.V.D.'s.
combine, *n.f.* trick, scheme.
combine, *n.m.* (phone) receiver.
combiner, *vb.* devise, combine.
comble, *n.m.* climax, top.
combler, *vb.* heap up, fill.
combustible, 1. *n.m.* fuel. **2.** *adj.* combustible.
combustion, *n.f.* combustion.
comédie, *n.f.* comedy.
comédien, *n.m.* actor, comedian.
comestible, *adj.* edible.
comète, *n.f.* comet.
comique, *adj.* funny, comic(al).
comité, *n.m.* committee.
commandant, *n.m.* major, commander.
commande, *n.f.* order; commission.
commandement, *n.m.* command, commandment.
commander, *vb.* order, command.
commanditer, *vb.* finance.
comme, 1. *adv.* as, how. **2.** *prep.* as, like. **c. il faut,** proper, decent.
commémoratif, *adj.* memorial.
commémorer, *vb.* commemorate.
commencement, *n.m.* beginning, start.
commencer, *vb.* begin, start.
comment, *adv.* how.
commentaire, *n.m.* comment, commentary.
commentateur, *n.m.* commentator.
commenter, *vb.* comment on.
commerçant, *n.m.* trader.
commerce, *n.m.* trade, commerce.
commercer, *vb.* trade.
commercial, *adj.* commercial.
commettre, *vb.* commit.
commis, *n.m.* clerk.
commissaire, *n.m.* commissary, commissioner.
commissariat, *n.m.* police station.
commission, *n.f.* errand; commission.
commode, 1. *n.f.* dresser, bureau. **2.** *adj.* handy, convenient; comfortable.
commodité, *n.f.* convenience.

commun, *adj.* joint, common.
communauté, *n.f.* community.
commune, *n.f.* commune, town(ship).
communicatif, *adj.* communicative.
communication, *n.f.* communication.
communion, *n.f.* communion.
communiquer, *vb.* communicate.
communisme, *n.m.* communism.
communiste, *adj. and n.m.f.* communist.
commutateur, *n.m.* switch.
compacité, *n.f.* compactness.
compact (-kt), *adj.* compact.
compact disc, *n.m.* compact disc.
compagne, *n.f.* mate, companion.
compagnie, *n.f.* company.
compagnon, *n.m.* mate, fellow, companion.
comparable, *adj.* comparable.
comparaison, *n.f.* comparison.
comparaître, *vb.* appear.
comparatif, *adj. and n.m.* comparative.
comparer, *vb.* compare.
compartiment, *n.m.* compartment.
compas, *n.m.* compass.
compassion, *n.f.* sympathy, compassion.
compatible, *adj.* compatible.
compatissant, *adj.* sympathetic, compassionate.
compatriote, *n.m.f.* compatriot.
compensation, *n.f.* amends; compensation.
compenser, *vb.* compensate.
compétence, *n.f.* qualification, efficiency, competence.
compétition, *n.f.* competition.
compiler, *vb.* compile.
complaire, *vb.* please.
complaisance, *n.f.* kindness, compliance.
complaisant, *adj.* obliging, kind.
complément, *n.m.* object; complement.
complet, 1. *n.m.* suit. **2.** *adj.* full, thorough, complete.
compléter, *vb.* complete.
complexe, *adj. and n.m.* complex.
complexité, *n.f.* complexity.

complication, *n.f.* complication.

complice, *n.m.f.* party to, accomplice.

compliment, *n.m.* compliment.

compliqué, *adj.* intricate, involved, complicated.

compliquer, *vb.* complicate.

complot, *n.m.* plot.

comporter, *vb.* se c., act, behave.

composant, *adj. and n.m.* component.

composé, *adj. and n.m.* compound.

composer, *vb.* compound, compose.

compositeur, *n.m.* composer.

composition, *n.f.* essay, theme, composition.

composter, *vb.* date-stamp, punch.

compote, *n.f.* stewed fruit.

compréhensible, *adj.* understandable.

compréhensif, *adj.* comprehensive.

compréhension, *n.f.* comprehension.

comprendre, *vb.* understand, realize; comprise, include. **c. mal,** misunderstand.

compresse, *n.f.* compress.

compression, *n.f.* compression.

comprimé, *n.m.* tablet (med.).

comprimer, *vb.* compress.

compromettre, *vb.* compromise.

compromis, *n.m.* compromise.

comptabilité, *n.f.* accounting, bookkeeping.

comptable, *n.m.* accountant.

comptant, *adv.* payer c., pay cash.

compte, *n.m.* account, count. **rendre c. de,** account for. **tenir c. de,** allow for.

compte-gouttes, *n.m.* dropper.

compter, *vb.* count, reckon. c. sur, rely on.

compteur, *n.m.* meter.

comptoir, *n.m.* counter.

comte, *n.m.* count.

comté, *n.m.* county.

comtesse, *n.f.* countess.

concave, *adj.* concave.

concéder, *vb.* grant, concede.

concentration, *n.f.* concentration.

concentrer, *vb.* condense; concentrate.

concept (-pt), *n.m.* concept.

conception, *n.f.* conception.

concernant, *prep.* concerning.

concerner, *vb.* concern.

concert, *n.m.* concert.

concerter, *vb.* organize, prepare.

concession, *n.f.* grant, license, admission, concession.

concessionnaire, *n.m.* dealer.

concevable, *adj.* conceivable.

concevoir, *vb.* conceive, imagine.

concierge, *n.m.f.* janitor, doorkeeper, porter.

concile, *n.m.* council.

conciliation, *n.f.* conciliation.

concilier, *vb.* reconcile, conciliate.

concis, *adj.* concise.

concision, *n.f.* conciseness.

concitoyen, *n.m.* fellow citizen.

concluant, *adj.* conclusive.

conclure, *vb.* complete, conclude, infer.

conclusion, *n.f.* conclusion.

concombre, *n.m.* cucumber.

concourir, *vb.* concur, contribute, compete.

concours, *n.m.* contest.

concret, *adj.* concrete.

concrétiser, *vb.* put in concrete form.

concurrence, *n.f.* competition.

concurrent, *n.m.* rival, competitor.

condamnation (-dá nä-), *n.f.* conviction, condemnation, sentence.

condamner (-dä nä), *vb.* convict, doom, condemn, sentence.

condensation, *n.f.* condensation.

condenser, *vb.* condense.

condescendance, *n.f.* condescension.

condescendre, *vb.* condescend.

condiment, *n.m.* condiment.

condisciplé, *n.m.* classmates.

condition, *n.f.* condition.

conditionnel, *adj. and n.m.* conditional.

conditionnement, *n.m.* conditioning.

conditionner, *vb.* condition.

condoléance, *n.f.* condolence. **faire ses c.s à,** condole with.

condominium, *n.m.* condominium.

conducteur, *n.m.* conductor.

conduire, *vb.* lead, take, drive, conduct. **se c.,** behave, act.

conduite, *n.f.* behavior, conduct.

cône, *n.m.* cone.

cône de charge, *n.m.* warhead.

confection, *n.f.* making (e.g. clothes); ready-made garment.

confédération, *n.f.* confederacy, confederation.

confédéré, *adj. and n.m.* confederate.

conférence, *n.f.* lecture, talk, conference.

conférer, *vb.* confer, grant.

confesser, *vb.* confess, admit.

confesseur, *n.m.* confessor.

confession, *n.f.* denomination; confession.

confiance, *n.f.* trust, belief, confidence. **digne de c.,** dependable.

confiant, *adj.* confident.

confidence, *n.f.* confidence.

confident, *n.m.* confidant.

confidentiel, *adj.* confidential.

confier, *vb.* confide, entrust. **se c. à,** trust.

configuration, *n.f.* configuration.

confiner, *vb.* confine, limit.

confirmation, *n.f.* confirmation.

confirmer, *vb.* confirm.

confiserie, *n.f.* confectionery.

confisquer, *vb.* confiscate.

confit, *adj.* candied.

confiture, *n.f.* jam, jelly.

conflit, *n.m.* conflict.

confondre, *vb.* confuse, confound.

confondu, *adj.* overwhelmed.

conforme à, *adv.* in accordance with.

conformément, *adv.* in accordance.

conformer, *vb.* conform. **se c. à,** comply with.

conformité, *n.f.* accordance.

confort, *n.m.* comfort.

confortable, *adj.* cozy, snug, comfortable.

confrère, *n.m.* colleague.

confronter, *vb.* confront.

confus, *adj.* confused.

confusion, *n.f.* confusion.

congé, *n.m.* discharge; leave of absence.

congédier, *vb.* discharge, dismiss.

congélateur, *n.m.* freezer.

congeler, *vb.* congeal.

congénère, *n.m./f.* fellow human.

congénital, *adj.* congenital.

congestion, *n.f.* congestion.

conglomération, *n.f.* conglomeration.

congrès, *n.m.* congress, assembly, conference.

conjecture, *n.f.* guess, conjecture.

conjoint, 1. *n.m.* spouse, **2.** *adj.* joint.

conjonction, *n.f.* conjunction.

conjugaison, *n.f.* conjugation.

conjugal, *adj.* conjugal.

conjuguer, *vb.* conjugate.

conjuration, *n.f.* conspiracy.

conjurer, *vb.* conspire, plot.

connaissance, *n.f.* knowledge, acquaintance. **sans c.,** unconscious. **faire la c. de,** meet.

connaisseur, *n.m.* connoisseur.

connaître, *vb.* be acquainted with, know.

connecté, *adj.* on line.

connecter, *vb.* connect.

connexion, *n.f.* connection.

conquérir, *vb.* conquer.

conquête, *n.f.* conquest.

consacrer, *vb.* consecrate, devote, dedicate, hallow.

conscience, *n.f.* conscience, consciousness.

consciencieux, *adj.* conscientious.

conscient, *adj.* conscious.

conscription, *n.f.* draft.

conscrit, *adj. and n.m.* conscript.

consécration, *n.f.* consecration.

consécutif, *adj.* consecutive.

conseil, *n.m.* advice, counsel; council, board; staff.

conseiller, 1. *vb.* advise, counsel, **2.** *n.m.* advisor.

consentement, *n.m.* consent.

consentir, *vb.* consent, assent, accede.

conséquence, *n.f.* outgrowth, result, consequence.

conséquent, *adj.* consequent; consistent. **par c.,** consequently.

conservateur, *adj. and n.m.* conservative.

conservation, n.f. conservation.

conservatoire, n.m. academy; conservation area.

conserve, n.f. canned food, pickle.

conserver, vb. keep; preserve, can.

considérable, adj. considerable.

considération, n.f. consideration.

considérer, vb. consider.

consigne, n.f. checkroom; (mil.) orders.

consigne automatique, n.f. (luggage) locker.

consigner, vb. consign.

consistance, n.f. consistency.

consistant, adj. consistent.

consister, vb. consist.

consœur, n.f.(female) colleague.

consolateur, n.m. comforter.

consolation, n.f. comfort, solace.

console, n.f. bracket.

consoler, vb. comfort, console.

consolider, vb. consolidate, strengthen.

consommateur, n.m. consumer.

consommation, n.f. consumption; end, consummation.

consommé, adj. consummate.

consommer, vb. consummate, complete; consume.

consomption, n.f. consumption.

consonne, n.f. consonant.

conspirateur, n.m. conspirator.

conspiration, n.f. conspiration.

conspirer, vb. conspire.

conspuer, vb. boo.

constamment, adv. continually, constantly.

constance, n.f. constancy, firmness.

constant, adj. constant, firm.

constat, n.m. certified report, statement.

constater, vb. observe, state as a fact.

constellation, n.f. constellation.

consterné, adj. aghast.

consterner, vb. dismay.

constipation, n.f. constipation.

constipé, adj. constipated; tense.

constituant, adj. constituent.

constituer, vb. constitute.

constitution, n.f. constitution.

constitutionnel, adj. constitutional.

constructeur, n.m. builder.

constructif, adj. constructive.

construction, n.f. construction.

construire, vb. construct, build.

consul, n.m. consul.

consulat, n.m. consulate.

consultation, n.f. consultation.

consulter, vb. consult.

consumer, vb. consume.

contact (-ct), n.m. touch, contact.

contagieux, adj. contagious.

contagion, n.f. contagion.

contaminer, vb. contaminate.

conte, n.m. tale, story.

contemplation, n.f. contemplation.

contempler, vb. survey, observe, contemplate.

contemporain, adj. contemporary.

contenance, n.f. compass, capacity.

contenir, vb. hold, restrain, contain.

content de, adj. glad of, contented with. **c. de soi-même**, complacent.

contentement, n.m. content(ment), satisfaction. **c. de soi-même**, complacency.

contenter, vb. please, satisfy.

contentieux, n.m. litigation.

contenu, n.m. contents.

conter, vb. tell.

contestable, adj. questionable.

contestataire, n.m. protester.

contester, vb. challenge (dispute), object to, contest.

conteur, n.m. story-teller.

contexte, n.m. context.

contigu, m., **contiguë** f. adj. adjoining.

continent, n.m. continent.

continental, adj. continental.

contigences, n.f.pl. contingencies.

contingent, n.m. quota.

continu, adj. continuous.

continuation, n.f. continuation, continuance.

continuel, adj. continual.

continuer, vb. carry on, keep on, go on, continue.

continuité, n.f. continuity.

contorsion, n.f. contortion.

contour, n.m. outline.

contourner, vb. go round.

contraceptif, n.m. contraceptive.

contracter, *vb.* contract.
contraction, *n.f.* contraction.
contractuel, *n.m.* traffic warden.
contradiction, *n.f.* discrepancy, contradiction.
contradictoire, *adj.* contradictory.
contraindre, *vb.* coerce, force.
contrainte, *n.f.* compulsion.
contraire, 1. *n.m.* reverse. **2.** *adj.* contrary. **au c.,** on the contrary.
contrarier, *vb.* thwart, vex, annoy, oppose, keep (from).
contrariété, *n.f.* annoyance.
contraste, *n.m.* contrast.
contraster, *vb.* contrast.
contrat, *n.m.* contract.
contravention, *n.f.* traffic ticket.
contre, *prep.* against.
contre-balancer, *vb.* counterbalance.
contrebande, *n.f.* smuggling; contraband.
contrecarrer, *vb.* thwart.
contre-cœur, *adv.* **à c.,** unwillingly.
contrecoup, *n.m.* consequence.
contredire, *vb.* contradict.
contrée, *n.f.* district, province.
contrefaire, *vb.* forge, counterfeit.
contrefort, *n.m.* buttress.
contremaître, *n.m.* foreman.
contre-partie, *n.f.* counterpart.
contrepoids (-pwä), *n.m.* counterbalance.
contresens, *n.m.* misinterpretation.
contretemps, *n.m.* mishap.
contribuer, *vb.* contribute.
contribution, *n.f.* share, contribution; tax.
contrôle, *n.m.* check.
contrôle des naissances, *n.m.* birth control, contraception.
contrôler, *vb.* control, check.
contrôleur, *n.m.* checker, collector.
controverse, *n.f.* controversy.
contusion, *n.f.* bruise, contusion.
convaincre, *vb.* convince.
convaincu, *adj.* positive.
convalescence, *n.f.* convalescence.
convalescent, *n.m.* convalescent.
convenable, *adj.* becoming, appropriate, suitable, congenial.
convenance, *n.f.* convenience.
convenir à, *vb.* suit, fit, befit, agree.

convention, *n.f.* convention; contract.
conventionnel, *adj.* conventional.
convenu, *adj.* agreed.
converger, *vb.* converge.
conversation, *n.f.* talk, conversation.
converser, *vb.* talk, converse.
conversion, *n.f.* conversion, change.
convertir, *vb.* convert, transform.
convexe, *adj.* convex.
conviction, *n.f.* conviction.
convive, *n.m.* guest, companion.
convivial, *adj.* convivial, userfriendly.
convocation, *n.f.* summons.
convoi, *n.m.* convoy, funeral procession.
convoiter, *vb.* covet.
convoitise, *n.f.* covetousness.
convoquer, *vb.* summon, call.
convulsion, *n.f.* convulsion.
coopératif (kŏ ŏ-), *adj.* cooperative.
coopération (kŏ ŏ-), *n.f.* cooperation.
coopérative (kŏ ŏ-), *n.f.* cooperative.
coopérer (kŏ ŏ-), *vb.* cooperate.
coordonner (kŏ ŏr-), *vb.* coordinate.
copain, *n.m.* pal, chum.
copie, *n.f.* copy; exercise.
copier, *vb.* copy.
copieux, *adj.* copious.
copine, *n.f.* (female) pal, chum.
coq (-k), *n.m.* rooster.
coque, *n.f.* **œuf à la c.,** boiled egg.
coquet, *adj.* flirtatious, pretty.
coquille, *n.f.* shell.
coquin, *adj. and n.m.* rogue, rascal.
cor, *n.m.* horn; corn.
corail, *n.m., pl.* **coraux,** coral.
corbeau, *n.m.* raven, crow.
corbeille, *n.f.* basket.
corde, *n.f.* rope, string, cord.
cordial, *adj.* hearty, cordial.
cordon, *n.m.* rope.
cordonnier, *n.m.* shoemaker.
Corée, *n.f.* Korea.
coreligionnaire, *n.m.* member of the same religion.
corne, *n.f.* horn.
corneille, *n.f.* crow.

cornemuse, *n.f.* bagpipe.
cornet, *n.m.* cone.
cornichon, *n.m.* gherkin.
corporation, *n.f.* corporation.
corporel, *adj.* bodily.
corps, *n.m.* body.
corpulent, *adj.* burly.
corpuscule (-sk-), *n.m.* corpuscle.
correct (-kt), *adj.* right, correct.
correcteur, *n.m.* proofreader, examiner.
correction, *n.f.* correction, correctness; beating.
corrélation, *n.f.* correlation.
correspondance, *n.f.* (train) connection: similarity; correspondence.
correspondant, 1. *n.m.* correspondent. **2.** *adj.* similar, corresponding.
correspondre, *vb.* correspond.
corriger, *vb.* mend, reclaim, correct.
corroborer, *vb.* corroborate.
corroder, *vb.* corrode.
corrompre, *vb.* bribe, corrupt.
corrompu, *adj.* corrupt.
corruption, *n.f.* bribery, graft, corruption.
corsage, *n.m.* bodice, blouse.
Corse, *n.f.* Corsica. *n.m.f.* Corsican.
corse, *adj.* Corsican.
corset, *n.m.* corset.
cortège, *n.m.* procession.
corvée, *n.f.* chore.
cosmétique, *adj. and n.m.* cosmetic.
cosmonaute, *n.m.* cosmonaut.
cosmopolite, *adj. and n.m.f.* cosmopolite.
costaud, *adj.* strong, sturdy.
costume, *n.m.* attire, dress.
cote, *n.f.* quotation, rating.
côte, *n.f.* rib; coast.
côté, *n.f.* side, way. **mettre de c.,** put to one side (save; discard). **à c. de,** beside.
coteau, *n.m.* hill.
côtelette, *n.f.* chop, cutlet.
coton, *n.m.* cotton.
cou, *n.m.* neck.
couche, *n.f.* layer; bed; stratum; diaper.

coucher, *vb.* put to bed. **se c.,** lie down; set.
couchette, *n.f.* bunk, berth.
coucou, *n.m.* cuckoo.
coude, *n.m.* elbow.
coudoyer, *vb.* jostle.
coudre, *vb.* sew, stitch.
couette, *n.f.* duvet.
couler, *vb.* flow, sink, run; cast (metal).
couleur, *n.f.* hue, color; suit (cards).
couloir, *n.m.* corridor.
coup, *n.m.* blow, stroke, hit, bump, knock, cast. **c. de feu,** discharge (gun). **c. d'œil,** glance, look. **c. de pied,** kick. **c. de poing,** punch.
coupable, *adj.* guilty, to blame.
coupe, *n.f.* cut; goblet. **c. de cheveux,** haircut.
couper, *vb.* cut.
couple, *n.f.* couple, pair.
coupler, *vb.* couple.
coupole, *n.f.* dome.
coupon, *n.m.* remnant; coupon.
coupure, *n.f.* cut, clipping.
cour, *n.f.* court(yard).
courage, *n.m.* bravery, pluck, courage.
courageux, *adj.* brave.
couramment, *adv.* fluently.
courant, 1. *adj.* current. **peu c.,** unusual. **au c.,** well informed. **2.** *n.m.* stream, current. **c. d'air,** draft.
courbe, *n.f.* curve, sweep.
courber, *vb.* bend, curve.
courbure, *n.f.* curvature.
coureur, *n.m.* runner; womanizer.
courgette, *n.f.* zucchini.
courir, *vb.* run.
couronne, *n.f.* crown, wreath.
couronnement, *n.m.* coronation.
couronner, *vb.* crown.
courrier, *n.m.* mail.
courroie, *n.f.* strap.
courroux, *n.m.* wrath.
cours, *n.m.* course.
course, *n.f.* race, errand.
coursier, *n.m.* messenger.
court, 1. *adj.* short. **2.** *n.m.* (tennis) court.
courtepointe, *n.f.* quilt.
courtier, *n.m.* broker.

courtisan, *n.m.* courtier.

courtois, *adj.* courteous.

courtoisie, *n.f.* courtesy.

couscous, *n.m.* couscous.

cousin, *n.m.* cousin.

coussin, *n.m.* cushion.

coussinet, *n.m.* bearing.

coût, *n.m.* cost.

couteau, *n.m.* knife.

coutellerie, *n.f.* cutlery.

coûter, *vb.* cost.

coûteux, *adj.* expensive, costly.

coutume, *n.f.* custom.

couture, *n.f.* seam. **haute couture,** high fashion.

couturière, *n.f.* dressmaker.

couvée, *n.f.* brood.

couvent, *n.m.* convent.

couver, *vb.* brood, hatch; smolder.

couvercle, *n.m.* lid, cover.

couvert, 1, *n.m.* cover. **2.** *adj.* covered, cloudy.

couverture, *n.f.* blanket, cover; (*pl.*) bedclothes.

couvre-feu, *n.m.* curfew.

couvrir, *vb.* cover.

crabe, *n.m.* crab.

crachat, *n.m.* spit.

cracher, *vb.* spit.

craie, *n.f.* chalk.

craindre, *vb.* fear.

crainte, *n.f.* fear, dread, awe.

craintif, *adj.* fearful.

cramoisi, *adj. and n.m.* crimson.

crampe, *n.f.* cramp.

crampon, *n.m.* clamp, cramp iron.

cramponner, *vb.* **se c.,** cling.

crâne, *n.m.* skull.

crapaud, *n.m.* toad.

craquement, *n.m.* crack.

craquer, *vb.* crack, break down.

crasse, *n.f.* grime.

cratère, *n.m.* crater.

cravate, *n.f.* necktie.

crayon, *n.m.* pencil.

créance, *n.f.* belief. **lettres de c.,** credentials.

créancier, *n.m.* creditor.

créateur *m.,* **créatrice** *f.* **1.** *adj.* creative. **2.** *n.* creator.

création, *n.f.* creation.

créature, *n.f.* creature.

crèche, *n.f.* day-care center.

crédit, *n.m.* credit.

credo, *n.m.* creed.

crédule, *adj.* credulous.

créer, *vb.* create.

crème, *n.f.* cream, custard.

crémerie, *n.f.* dairy store.

créneau, *n.m.* slot.

Créole, *n.m.f.* Creole.

crêpe, *n.f.* pancake; crepe.

crépuscule (-sk-), *n.m.* dusk.

crête, *n.f.* ridge, crest.

crétin, *n.m.* dunce.

cretonne, *n.f.* cretonne.

creuser, *vb.* dig.

creuset, *n.m.* crucible.

creux, *adj. and n.m.* hollow.

crevasse, *n.f.* crevice.

crevé, *adj.* exhausted.

crever, *vb.* burst; die.

crevette, *n.f.* shrimp.

cri, *n.m.* cry, call.

criard, *adj.* garish.

crible, *n.m.* sieve.

crier, *vb.* yell, shout.

crime, *n.m.* crime.

criminel, *adj.* criminal.

crinière, *n.f.* mane.

crise, *n.f.* crisis.

crisper, *vb.* tense, clench.

cristal, *n.m.* crystal.

cristallin, *adj.* crystalline.

cristalliser, *vb.* crystallize.

critère, *n.m.* criterion.

critérium, *n.m.* criterion.

critique, 1. *n.m.f.* critic. **2.** *n.f.* criticism. **3.** *adj.* critical.

critiquer, *vb.* criticize.

croasser, *vb.* croak.

Croatie, *n.f.* Croatia.

croc (-ō), *n.m.* hook.

croche, *n.f.* quaver (music).

crochet, *n.m.* bracket, hook.

crochu, *adj.* hooked.

crocodile, *n.m.* crocodile.

croire, *vb.* believe.

croisade, *n.f.* crusade.

croisé, *n.m.* crusader.

croiser, *vb.* cross.

croiseur, *n.m.* cruiser.

croisière, *n.f.* cruise.

croissance, *n.f.* growth.

croissant, *n.m.* crescent; croissant (pastry).

croître, *vb.* grow.

croix, *n.f.* cross.

croquant, *adj.* crisp.
croque-monsieur, *n.m.* grilled ham and cheese sandwich.
croquer, *vb.* crunch; sketch.
croquet, *n.m.* croquet.
croquis, *n.m.* sketch.
crosse, *n.f.* (golf) club; butt (gun).
crotale, *n.m.* rattlesnake.
crouler, *vb.* fall apart.
croup, *n.m.* croup.
croupir, *vb.* wallow.
croustiller, *vb.* be crispy.
croûte, *n.f.* crust.
croûton, *n.m.* crouton.
croyable, *adj.* believable.
croyance, *n.f.* belief.
croyant, *n.m.* believer.
cru, *adj.* raw.
cruauté, *n.f.* cruelty.
cruche, *n.f.* pitcher.
crucifier, *vb.* crucify.
crucifix, *n.m.* crucifix.
crudités, *n.f.pl.* raw vegetables.
cruel, *adj.* cruel.
cryochirurgie, *n.f.* cryosurgery.
Cuba, *n.m.* Cuba.
Cubain, *n.m.* Cuban.
cubain, *adj.* Cuban.
cube, *n.m.* cube.
cubique, *adj.* cubic.
cueillir, *vb.* pick.
cuiller, *n.f.* spoon. **c. à thé,** teaspoon. **c. à bouche,** tablespoon.
cuillerée, *n.f.* spoonful.
cuir, *n.m.* leather.
cuirassé, *n.m.* battleship.
cuire, *vb.* cook; sting, smart.
cuisine, *n.f.* kitchen, cooking.

cuisinier, *n.m.* cook.
cuisse, *n.f.* thigh.
cuisson, *n.m.* cooking.
cuivre, *n.m.* copper. **c. jaune,** brass.
cul-de-sac, *n.m.* blind alley.
culinaire, *adj.* culinary, cooking.
culotte, *n.f.* breeches, panties.
culpabilité, *n.f.* guilt.
culte, *n.m.* worship; cult.
cultivé, *adj.* cultured.
cultiver, *vb.* cultivate; grow, raise.
culture, *n.f.* culture, cultivation; farming.
culturel, *adj.* cultural.
cure, *n.f.* cure, treatment.
curé, *n.m.* (parish) priest.
curieux, *adj.* curious.
curiosité, *n.f.* curiosity, curio.
curseur, *n.m.* cursor.
cursif, *adj.* cursive.
cuticule, *n.f.* cuticle.
cuve, *n.f.* vat.
cuver, *vb.* ferment.
cuvette, *n.f.* (wash) basin.
cuvier, *n.m.* washtub.
cycle, *n.m.* cycle.
cycliste, *n.m.f.* cyclist.
cyclomoteur, *n.m.* moped.
cyclone, *n.m.* cyclone.
cygne, *n.m.* swan.
cylindre, *n.m.* cylinder.
cylindrique, *adj.* cylindrical.
cymbale, *n.f.* cymbal.
cynique, 1. *n.m.* cynic. 2. *adj.* cynical.
cynisme, *n.m.* cynicism.
cyprès, *n.m.* cypress.
czar, *n.m.* czar.

D

d'abord, *adv.* first, at first.
dactylo, *n.m.f.* typist.
dada, *n.m.* hobby-horse.
daigner, *vb.* deign.
daim, *n.m.* buck.
daine, *n.f.* doe.
dais, *n.m.* canopy.
dalle, *n.f.* slab, flag(stone).
daltonien, *adj.* color-blind.
dame, *n.f.* lady.
damner (dä nä), *vb.* damn.
dancing, *n.m.* dance hall.
Danemark, *n.m.* Denmark.

danger, *n.m.* danger.
dangereux, *adj.* dangerous.
Danois, *n.m.* Dane.
danois, *adj. and n.m.* Danish (language).
dans, *prep.* in, into.
danse, *n.f.* dance.
danser, *vb.* dance.
danseur, *n.m.* dancer.
dard, *n.m.* dart.
date, *n.f.* date (calendar).
dater, *vb.* date.
datte, *n.f.* date (fruit).

dauphin, *n.m.* dolphin.
davantage, *adv.* more, further.
de, *prep.* of, from, by, about; some.
dé, *n.m.* die; thimble.
débacle, *n.f.* downfall.
débarcadère, *n.m.* wharf.
débardeur, *n.m.* tank top.
débarquer, *vb.* land.
débarrasser, *vb.* rid.
débat, *n.m.* debate.
débattre, *vb.* canvass; debate.
débile, *adj.* weak, stupid.
débit, *n.m.* delivery (speech); sale; debit.
débiter, *vb.* sell (retail).
débiteur, *n.m.* debtor.
déblayer, *vb.* clear.
déborder, *vb.* overflow.
déboucher, *vb.* flow (into); uncork.
débourser, *vb.* disburse.
debout, *adv.* up. **être d.,** stand.
débrancher, *vb.* unplug.
débris, *n.m.pl.* wreck, debris.
débrouiller, *vb.* disentangle. **se d.,** manage.
début, *n.m.* beginning, first appearance, debut.
débuter, *vb.* make one's first appearance; begin.
décadence, *n.f.* decay; decadence.
décaféiné, *adj.* decaffeinated.
décalage, *n.m.* gap.
décaler, *vb.* shift.
décapiter, *vb.* behead.
décéder, *vb.* die.
décembre, *n.m.* December.
décence, *n.f.* decency.
décennie, *n.f.* decade.
décent, *adj.* decent.
décentraliser, *vb.* decentralize.
déception, *n.f.* disappointment.
décerner, *vb.* award.
décès, *n.m.* death.
décevoir, *vb.* disappoint.
décharge, *n.f.* discharge.
décharger, *vb.* unload, discharge.
décharné, *adj.* gaunt.
déchausser, *vb.* take off shoes.
déchets (-ā), *n.m.pl.* waste.
déchets nucléaires, *n.m.pl.* nuclear waste.
déchiffrer, *vb.* decipher.
déchirer, *vb.* tear; rend.
déchirure, *n.f.* tear; rent.

décibel, *n.m.* decibel.
décider, *vb.* prevail upon, decide.
décimal, *adj.* decimal.
décisif, *adj.* decisive.
décision, *n.f.* decision.
déclamer, *vb.* recite.
déclaration, *n.f.* statement, declaration.
déclarer, *vb.* state, declare.
déclencher, *vb.* release, set off.
déclic, *n.m.* trigger.
déclin, *n.m.* ebb.
décliner, *vb.* decline.
décoller, *vb.* take off.
décolorer, *vb.* bleach, fade.
décomposer, *vb.* spoil, decompose.
déconcerter, *vb.* baffle, disconcert; embarrass.
décongestionnant, *adj.* decongestant.
déconseiller, *vb.* advise against.
décontracté, *adj.* relaxed.
décor, *n.m.* scenery.
décoratif, *adj.* decorative.
décoration, *n.f.* decoration, trimming.
décorer, *vb.* decorate.
découper, *vb.* carve (meat).
découragé, *adj.* despondent.
découragement, *n.m.* discouragement.
décourager, *vb.* dishearten, discourage.
découverte, *n.f.* discovery.
découvreur, *n.m.* discoverer.
découvrir, *vb.* uncover, detect, discover.
décrépit, *adj.* decrepit.
décret, *n.m.* decree.
décréter, *vb.* enact.
décrire, *vb.* describe.
décrocher, *vb.* unhook.
dédaigneux, *adj.* scornful.
dédain, *n.m.* scorn, disdain.
dedans, *n.m.* inside, within.
dédicace, *n.f.* dedication.
dédier, *vb.* dedicate.
déduction, *n.f.* deduction.
déduire, *vb.* infer, deduce, deduct.
déesse, *n.f.* goddess.
défaillance, *n.f.* weakness.
défaire, *vb.* undo.
défaite, *n.f.* defeat.

défaut, *n.m.* flaw, fault, failure, lack. **à d. de,** for want of.
défavorable, *adj.* unfavorable.
défavoriser, *vb.* put at a disadvantage.
défectueux, *adj.* faulty, defective.
défendeur, *n.m.* defendant.
défendre, *vb.* forbid, defend.
défense, *n.f.* prohibition, plea, defense.
défenseur, *n.m.* advocate, defender.
défensif, *adj.* defensive.
déférer, *vb.* defer.
défi, *n.m.* challenge, defiance.
défiance, *n.f.* mistrust.
déficit (-t), *n.m.* deficit.
défier, *vb.* challenge, defy. **se d. de,** mistrust.
défigurer, *vb.* deface.
défiler, *vb.* march off.
défini, *adj.* definite.
définir, *vb.* define.
définitif, *adj.* final, definitive.
définition, *n.f.* definition.
déformer, *vb.* distort, deform.
défouler, *vb.* let off steam.
défraîchi, *adj.* dingy.
défricher, *vb.* reclaim; clear.
défunt, *adj. and n.m.* deceased.
dégagé, *adj.* breezy.
dégât, *n.m.* damage.
dégénérer, *vb.* degenerate.
dégoût, *n.m.* distaste, disgust.
dégoûtant, *adj.* foul, disgusting.
dégoûter, *vb.* disgust.
dégoutter, *vb.* drip.
dégradation, *n.f.* degradation.
dégrader, *vb.* degrade.
degré, *n.m.* degree, step.
déguisement, *n.m.* disguise.
déguiser, *vb.* disguise.
dehors, *adv.* outdoors, outside. **en d. de,** apart from.
déifier, *vb.* deify.
déité, *n.f.* deity.
déjà, *adv.* already.
déjeter, *vb.* make unsymmetrical.
déjeuner, *n.m. and vb.* lunch, breakfast. **petit d.,** breakfast.
déjouer, *vb.* foil, thwart.
delà, *vb.* beyond. **au d. de,** over, past, beyond.
délabrement, *n.m.* decay.
délabrer, *vb.* ruin, wreck.

délacer, *vb.* unlace.
délai, *n.m.* delay.
délaissement, *n.m.* desertion.
délaisser, *vb.* desert.
délassement, *n.m.* relaxation.
délasser, *vb.* refresh.
délateur, *n.m.* informer.
délavé, *adj.* faded, pallid.
délayer, *vb.* dilute with water.
délectable, *adj.* delicious.
délectation, *n.f.* enjoyment.
délecter, *vb.* delight.
délégation, *n.f.* delegation.
délégué, *n.m.* delegate.
déléguer, *vb.* delegate.
délester, *vb.* relieve of ballast.
délétère, *adj.* harmful; offensive.
délibératif, *adj.* deliberative.
délibération, *n.f.* deliberation.
délibéré, *adj.* deliberate.
délibérer, *vb.* deliberate.
délicat, *adj.* delicate, tactful.
délicatesse, *n.f.* delicacy.
délices, *n.f.pl.* delight.
délicieux, *adj.* delicious.
délié, *adj.* slender; keen.
délier, *vb.* untie.
délimiter, *vb.* mark the limits of.
délinéer, *vb.* delineate.
délinquant, 1. *n.m.* delinquent, offender. **2.** *adj.* delinquent.
délirant, *adj.* delirious.
délire, *n.m.* frenzy.
délirer, *vb.* rave.
délit, *n.m.* offense, crime.
délivrance, *n.f.* rescue, deliverance.
délivrer, *vb.* rescue, set free, deliver.
déloger, *vb.* dislodge.
déloyal, *adj.* disloyal.
déloyauté, *n.f.* disloyalty.
deltaplane, *n.m.* hang glider.
déluge, *n.m.* deluge.
déluré, *adj.* clever, cute.
démagogue, *n.m.* demagogue.
demain, *adv.* tomorrow.
demande, *n.f.* application, request, inquiry, claim. **d. en mariage,** proposal.
demander, *vb.* ask, request. **se d.,** wonder.
demandeur, *n.m.* plaintiff.
démangeaison, *n.f.* itch.
démanger, *vb.* itch.

démanteler, vb. dismantle.
démaquiller, vb. remove makeup.
démarcation, n.f. demarcation.
démarche, n.f. walk; bearing; step.
démarrage, n.m. start.
démarrer, vb. unmoor; start off.
démarreur, n.m. (self-)starter.
démasquer, vb. unmask; expose, reveal.
démêlant, n.m. conditioner.
démêler, vb. disentangle.
démembrement, n.m. dismemberment.
démembrer, vb. dismember.
déménagement, n.m. moving.
déménager, vb. move.
déménageur, n.m. furniture mover.
démence, n.f. insanity.
démener, vb. struggle.
dément, adj. insane.
démenti, n.m. denial.
démentir, vb. deny, refute.
démesuré, adj. measureless, immense.
démettre, vb. se **d. (de),** resign.
demeure, n.f. abode.
demeurer, vb. dwell.
demi, n.m. and adj. half.
demi-cercle, n.m. semicircle.
demi-dieu, n.m. demigod.
demi-frère, n.m. stepbrother.
demi-heure, n.f. half an hour.
démilitariser, vb. demilitarize.
demi-place, n.f. half price; half fare.
demi-saison, adj. between-season.
demi-sœur, n.f. stepsister.
demi-solde, n.f. half-pay.
démission, n.f. resignation.
démobilisation, n.f. demobilization.
démobiliser, vb. demobilize.
démocrate, n.m.f. democrat.
démocratie, n.f. democracy.
démocratique, adj. democratic.
démodé, adj. old-fashioned.
demoiselle, n.f. young lady. **d. d'honneur,** bridesmaid.
démolir, vb. demolish.
démolition, n.f. demolition.
démon, n.m. demon.
démonétiser, vb. demonetize.
démoniaque, adj. demonic.

démonstratif, adj. effusive; demonstrative.
démonstration, n.f. demonstration.
démonter, vb. take down; dismantle.
démontrable, adj. demonstrable.
démontrer, vb. demonstrate.
démoralisation, n.f. demoralization.
démoraliser, vb. demoralize.
démouler, vb. remove from a mold.
démuni, adj. lacking, impoverished.
dénationaliser, vb. denationalize.
dénaturer, vb. denature.
dénégation, n.f. denial.
dénigrer, vb. disparage.
dénivelé, adj. not level.
dénombrement, n.m. enumeration; census.
dénombrer, vb. count.
dénomination, n.f. denomination, designation.
dénommer, vb. name.
dénoncer, vb. report, denounce.
dénonciation, n.f. denunciation.
dénoter, vb. denote.
dénouement, n.m. result, outcome.
dénouer, vb. untie.
denrée, n.f. foodstuff, produce.
dense, adj. dense.
densité, n.f. density.
dent, n.f. tooth. **mal de d.s,** toothache. **brosse à d.s,** toothbrush.
dentaire, adj. dental.
denté, adj. cogged.
dentelle, n.f. lace.
dentifrice, n.m. tooth paste or powder.
dentiste, n.m. dentist.
dentition, n.f. dentition.
denture, n.f. set of natural teeth.
dénuder, vb. denude.
dénué, adj. destitute, bare.
dénuement, n.m. destitution.
dénuer, vb. divest.
déodorant, n.m. deodorant.
dépannage, n.m. emergency repairs.
dépanner, vb. repair; help out.
dépareillé, adj. odd (unmatched).
départ, n.m. departure.

département, *n.m.* department.

départir, *vb.* divide in shares.

dépassé, *adj.* outdated.

dépasser, *vb.* outrun, pass.

dépayser, *vb.* disorient, confuse.

dépêche, *n.f.* dispatch.

dépêcher, *vb.* **se d.,** hurry.

dépeindre, *vb.* portray.

dépendance, *n.f.* annex (to a building).

dépendant, *adj.* dependent.

dépendre, *vb.* depend.

dépens, *n.m.pl.* expenses.

dépense, *n.f.* expenditure, expense.

dépenser, *vb.* spend, expend.

dépérir, *vb.* waste away; decline.

dépeupler, *vb.* depopulate.

déphasé, *adj.* disoriented.

dépiécer, *vb.* dismember.

dépit, *n.m.* spite. **en d. de,** despite.

déplacement, *n.m.* displacement.

déplacé, *adj.* out of place.

déplacer, *vb.* displace, move, shift.

déplaire à, *vb.* displease.

déplaisant, *adj.* displeasing.

déplanter, *vb.* transplant.

déplantoir, *n.m.* trowel.

dépliant, *n.m.* leaflet.

déplier, *vb.* unfold.

déploiement, *n.m.* deployment.

déplorable, *adj.* wretched, deplorable.

déplorer, *vb.* deplore.

déployer, *vb.* deploy.

déplumer, *vb.* pluck.

déportation, *n.f.* deportation.

déportements, *n.m.pl.* misconduct.

déporter, *vb.* deport.

déposant, *n.m.* depositor.

déposer, *vb.* deposit, set down, depose.

dépositaire, *n.m.f.* trustee.

déposséder, *vb.* oust; dispossess.

dépôt, *n.m.* deposit, depot. **d. de vivres,** commissary.

dépotoir, *n.m.* rubbish dump.

dépouille, *n.f.* hide, skin, pelt.

dépouiller, *vb.* strip. **se d. de,** shed.

dépourvu, *adj.* devoid; needy.

dépoussiéreur, *n.m.* vacuum cleaner.

dépravation, *n.f.* depravity.

dépraver, *vb.* deprave.

dépréciation, *n.f.* depreciation.

déprécier, *vb.* depreciate, cheapen.

déprédation, *n.f.* depredation.

dépression, *n.f.* depression.

déprimer, *vb.* depress.

depuis, *adv. and prep.* since. **d. que,** *conj.* since.

députation, *n.f.* delegation.

député, *n.m.* representative, deputy.

déraciné, *adj.* rootless.

déraciner, *vb.* uproot, eradicate.

dérailler, *vb.* derail; talk nonsense.

déraison, *n.f.* unreason.

déraisonnable, *adj.* unreasonable.

dérangement, *n.m.* disturbance.

déranger, *vb.* disturb, trouble.

déraper, *vb.* skid.

derechef, *adv.* once again.

dérégler, *vb.* upset, disorder.

dérider, *vb.* smooth; cheer up.

dérision, *n.f.* derision. **tourner en d.,** deride.

dérisoire, *adj.* ridiculous, derisory.

dérivation, *n.f.* derivation, etymology.

dérive, *n.f.* drift. **à la d.,** adrift.

dériver, *vb.* derive; drift.

dernier, *adj.* last, latter.

dernièrement, *adv.* lately.

dérober, *vb.* rob. **se d.,** steal away.

dérouiller, *vb.* remove the rust from.

dérouler, *vb.* unroll, unfold.

déroute, *n.f.* rout.

dérouter, *vb.* mislead; confuse.

derrière, *n.m., adv. and prep.* behind.

derviche, *n.m.* dervish.

dès, *prep.* since. **d. que,** *conj.* as soon as.

désabuser, *vb.* disillusion.

désaccord, *n.m.* disagreement.

désaccoutumer, *vb.* break of a habit.

désaffecté, *adj.* disused.

désaffecter, *vb.* close down.

désaffection, *n.f.* alienation.

désagréable, *adj.* nasty, distasteful.

désagrégation, *n.f.* disintegration.

désaligné, *adj.* out of alignment.

désaltérer, *vb.* quench (one's) thirst.

désapprobation, *n.f.* disapproval.

désapprouver, *vb.* disapprove.

désarçonner, *vb.* disconcert.
désarmement, *n.m.* disarmament.
désarmer, *vb.* disarm.
désarroi, *n.m.* disorder.
désastre, *n.m.* disaster.
désastreux, *adj.* disastrous.
désavantage, *n.m.* disadvantage.
désaveu, *n.m.* denial.
désavouer, *vb.* disown.
désaxé, *adj. and n.m.* unbalanced (person).
descendance, *n.f.* descent.
descendant, 1. *n.m.* offspring, descendant. **2.** *adj.* downward, descending.
descendre, *vb.* go down, come down, alight, descend.
descente, *n.f.* raid; descent.
descriptif, *adj.* descriptive.
description, *n.f.* description.
désembarquer, *vb.* disembark, unload.
désemparé, *adj.* distraught.
désenchanter, *vb.* disenchant.
désenivrer, *vb.* sober up.
déséquilibre, *n.m.* imbalance.
déséquilibrer, *vb.* throw off balance.
désert, *n.m.* wilderness, desert.
déserter, *vb.* desert.
déserteur, *n.m.* deserter.
désertion, *n.f.* desertion.
désespéré, *adj.* hopeless, forlorn, desperate.
désespérer, *vb.* despair.
désespoir, *n.m.* desperation, despair.
déshabiller, *vb.* undress.
déshériter, *vb.* disinherit.
déshonnête, *adj.* improper, indecent.
déshonneur, *n.m.* disgrace, dishonor.
déshonorant, *adj.* dishonorable.
déshonorer, *vb.* disgrace, dishonor.
déshydrater, *vb.* dehydrate.
désignation, *n.f.* nomination.
désigner, *vb.* appoint, nominate; point out; designate.
désillusion, *n.f.* disillusion.
désinfectant, *n.m.* disinfectant.
désinfecter, *vb.* disinfect, fumigate.
désinfection, *n.f.* disinfection.

désintégration, *n.f.* disintegration.
désintégrer, *vb.* disintegrate.
désintéressé, *adj.* unselfish.
désintéressement, *n.m.* unselfishness.
désintoxication, *n.f.* detoxification.
désinvolte, *adj.* casual.
désir, *n.m.* desire, wish.
désirable, *adj.* desirable.
désirer, *vb.* desire, wish.
désireux, *adj.* desirous.
désistement, *n.m.* withdrawal.
désobéir à, *vb.* disobey.
désobéissance, *n.f.* disobedience.
désobéissant, *adj.* disobedient.
désobligeant, *adj.* disagreeable.
désodorisant, *n.m.* air freshener, deodorant.
désœuvré, *adj.* idle.
désolation, *n.f.* desolation.
désolé, *adj.* disconsolate; desolate.
désoler, *vb.* desolate.
désopilant, *adj.* hilarious.
désordonné, *adj.* disorderly.
désordonner, *vb.* upset, confuse.
désordre, *n.m.* disorder.
désorganisation, *n.f.* disorganization.
désorganiser, *vb.* disorganize.
désorienté, *adj.* disoriented.
désormais, *adv.* henceforth.
despote, *n.m.* despot.
despotique, *adj.* despotic.
despotisme, *n.m.* despotism.
dessécher, *vb.* dry out, parch; drain.
dessein, *n.m.* plan, intent.
desserrer, *vb.* loosen.
dessert, *n.m.* dessert.
desservir, *vb.* serve; clear away.
dessin, *n.m.* drawing, design, sketch.
dessinateur, *n.m.* designer.
dessiner, *vb.* draw, design. **se d.,** loom.
dessous, *n.m.* underside. **en d., au-d. de,** beneath, underneath.
dessus, *n.m.* top. **en d., au-d. de,** above. **de d. de lit,** bedspread.
déstabiliser, *vb.* destabilize.
destin, *n.m.* fate, destiny.
destinataire, *n.m.f.* addressee.
destination, *n.f.* destination. **à d. de,** bound for.

destinée, n.f. destiny.

destiner, vb. destine, intend.

destituer, vb. dismiss.

destructeur, adj. destructive.

destructif, adj. destructive.

destruction, n.f. destruction.

désuet, adj. obsolete.

désuétude, n.f. disuse.

désunion, n.f. disunion.

désunir, vb. disconnect.

détaché, adj. loose.

détachement, n.m. detachment.

détacher, vb. detach. **se d.,** stand out.

détail, n.m. item; particular, detail. **au d.,** at retail.

détaillant, n.m. retailer.

détailler, vb. retail, itemize; detail.

détaxe, n.f. tax refund.

détaxer, vb. reduce the tax on.

détective, n.m. detective.

déteindre, vb. run (of colors).

détendre, vb. release; relax. **se d.,** relax.

détenir, vb. detain.

détente, n.f. **1.** trigger. **2.** (politics) détente.

détention, n.f. custody, detention.

détenu, n.m. prisoner.

détergent, n.m. detergent.

détérioration, n.f. deterioration.

détériorer, vb. deteriorate.

détermination, n.f. determination.

déterminer, vb. determine, fix.

détestable, adj. detestable, hateful.

détester, vb. abhor, loathe, detest.

détonation, n.f. detonation.

détoner, vb. detonate.

détour, n.m. turn; detour.

détourné, adj. devious.

détourner, vb. turn away; divert; avert; embezzle.

détracteur, n.m. critic.

détresse, n.f. trouble, distress.

détriment, n.m. detriment.

détritus, n.m.pl. rubbish.

détroit, n.m. strait.

détruire, vb. destroy.

dette, n.f. debt.

D.E.U.G., n.m. advanced (university) degree.

deuil, n.m. mourning.

deux, adj. and n.m. two. **tous les d.,** both.

deuxième, adj. second.

deux-points, n.m. colon.

dévaler, vb. hurtle down.

dévaliser, vb. rob.

dévaliseur, n.m. robber.

dévaloriser, vb. devalue.

dévaluation, n.f. devaluation.

devancer, vb. be ahead of.

devant, 1. n.m. front. **2.** prep. before, in front of.

devanture, n.f. window, (shop) front.

dévastation, n.f. devastation.

dévaster, vb. devastate.

déveine, n.f. bad luck.

développement, n.m. development.

développer, vb. develop.

devenir, vb. become.

déverser, vb. divert.

dévêtir, vb. undress, disrobe.

déviation, n.f. deviation.

dévider, vb. unwind.

dévier, vb. turn away.

deviner, vb. guess.

devinette, n.f. puzzle, riddle.

devis, n.m. estimate.

dévisager, vb. stare at.

devise, n.f. motto; currency (finance).

dévisser, vb. unscrew.

dévoiler, vb. unveil, disclose, reveal.

devoir, n.m. duty.

devoir, vb. owe; be supposed to; have to; (conditional) ought.

dévorer, vb. devour.

dévot, adj. devout.

dévotion, n.f. devotion.

dévoué, adj. devoted.

dévouement, n.m. devotion.

dévouer, vb. dedicate, devote.

dextérité, n.f. dexterity.

diabète, n.m. diabetes.

diabétique, adj. and n.m.f. diabetic.

diable, n.m. devil.

diablerie, n.f. mischief.

diabolique, adj. diabolic.

diacre, n.m. deacon.

diacritique, adj. diacritic.

diadème, n.m. diadem.

diagnostic, n.m. diagnosis.

diagnostiquer, vb. diagnose.

diagonal, adj. diagonal.

diagramme, *n.m.* diagram.
dialectal, *adj.* dialect.
dialecte, *n.m.* dialect.
dialogue, *n.m.* dialogue.
dialoguer, *vb.* converse, talk together.
diamant, *n.m.* diamond.
diamétral, *adj.* diametric.
diamètre, *n.m.* diameter.
diaphane, *adj.* diaphanous.
diaphragme, *n.m.* diaphragm.
diapositive, *n.f.* slide (photography).
diarrhée, *n.f.* diarrhea.
diathermie, *n.f.* diathermy.
diatribe, *n.f.* diatribe.
dictateur, *n.m.* dictator.
dictature, *n.f.* dictatorship.
dictée, *n.f.* dictation.
dicter, *vb.* dictate.
diction, *n.f.* diction.
dictionnaire, *n.m.* dictionary.
dicton, *n.m.* maxim, proverb.
didactique, *adj.* didactic.
dièse, *adj.* and *n.m.* sharp (music).
diesel, *adj* and *n.m.* diesel.
diète, *n.f.* diet.
diététique, *adj.* dietetic.
Dieu, *n.m.* God.
diffamant, *adj.* libelous.
diffamateur, *n.m.* libeler.
diffamation, *n.f.* libel.
diffamer, *vb.* defame.
différence, *n.f.* difference.
différenciation, *n.f.* differentiation.
différencier, *vb.* differentiate.
différend, *n.m.* difference, dispute.
différent, *adj.* different.
différer, *vb.* defer; differ.
difficile, *adj.* arduous, hard; difficult; fastidious.
difficilement, *adv.* with difficulty.
difficulté, *n.f.* trouble; difficulty.
difficulté psychologique, *n.f.* hangup.
difforme, *adj.* deformed.
difformité, *n.f.* deformity.
diffus, *adj.* diffuse.
diffuser, *vb.* diffuse, broadcast.
diffusion, *n.f.* spread, diffusion; broadcasting.
digérer, *vb.* digest.
digestible, *adj.* digestible.

digestif, 1. *adj.* digestive. **2.** *n.m.* after-dinner liqueur.
digestion, *n.f.* digestion.
digital, *adj.* digital.
digitaline, *n.f.* digitalis.
digne, *adj.* worthy.
dignitaire, *n.m.* dignitary.
dignité, *n.f.* dignity.
digression, *n.f.* digression.
digue, *n.f.* dike, dam.
dilapidation, *n.f.* waste.
dilater, *vb.* expand, dilate.
dilemme, *n.m.* dilemma.
dilettante, *n.m.* amateur.
diligence, *n.f.* diligence.
diligent, *adj.* diligent.
diluer, *vb.* dilute.
dilution, *n.f.* dilution.
dimanche, *n.m.* Sunday.
dimension, *n.f.* dimension.
diminuer, *vb.* lessen, decrease, diminish.
diminutif, *adj.* and *n.m.* diminutive.
diminution, *n.f.* decrease.
dinde, *n.f.* turkey.
dindon, *n.m.* turkey.
dîner, 1. *n.m.* dinner. **2.** *vb.* dine.
dîneur, *n.m.* diner.
dingue, *adj.* (colloquial) crazy.
diphtérie, *n.f.* diphtheria.
diphtongue, *n.f.* diphthong.
diplomate, *n.m.* diplomat.
diplomatie, *n.f.* diplomacy.
diplomatique, *adj.* diplomatic.
diplôme, *n.m.* diploma.
dipsomane, *n.m.f.* dipsomaniac.
dipsomanie, *n.f.* dipsomania.
dire, *vb.* say, tell. **vouloir d.,** mean. **c'est-à-d.,** namely; that is.
direct, *adj.* direct.
directement, *adv.* directly.
directeur, *n.m.* manager, director.
directif, *adj.* guiding.
direction, *n.f.* management, leadership, direction.
directive, *n.f.* instruction.
directorat, *n.m.* directorate.
dirigeable, *adj.* and *n.m.* dirigible.
dirigeant, *adj.* ruling.
diriger, *vb.* manage, boss; steer, direct.
dirigisme, *n.m.* interventionism.
discernable, *adj.* barely visible.

discernement, *n.m.* discernment, judgment.
discerner, *vb.* discern.
disciple, *n.m.* follower, disciple.
disciplinaire, *adj.* disciplinary.
discipline, *n.f.* discipline.
discipliner, *vb.* discipline.
disco, *adj.* disco.
discontinu, *adj.* intermittent.
discontinuer, *vb.* discontinue.
disconvenance, *n.f.* unsuitability.
discordance, *n.f.* discord.
discorde, *n.f.* discord.
discothèque, *n.f.* discotheque.
discourir, *vb.* speak one's views.
discours, *n.m.* speech, oration, talk, discourse.
discourtois, *adj.* discourteous.
discrédit, *n.m.* disrepute.
discréditer, *vb.* disparage.
discret, *adj.* discreet.
discrétion, *n.f.* discretion.
discrimination, *n.f.* discrimination.
disculper, *vb.* exonerate.
discursif, *adj.* discursive.
discussion, *n.f.* argument, discussion.
discutable, *adj.* debatable.
discuter, *vb.* argue, debate, discuss.
disette, *n.f.* famine.
diseur, *n.m.* talker.
disgrâce, *n.f.* disgrace.
disgracier, *vb.* put out of favor.
disjoindre, *vb.* sever, disjoint.
dislocation, *n.f.* dislocation.
disloquer, *vb.* dislocate.
disparaître, *vb.* disappear.
disparate, *adj.* unlike; badly matched.
disparition, *n.f.* disappearance.
disparu, *n.m.* missing person; dead person.
dispendieux, *adj.* expensive.
dispensaire, *n.m.* dispensary.
dispensation, *n.f.* dispensation.
dispense, *n.f.* military exemption.
dispenser, *vb.* dispense.
disperser, *vb.* scatter, disperse.
dispersion, *n.f.* dispersal.
disponible, *adj.* available.
disposé, *adj.* disposed. **d. d'avance,** predisposed. **peu d.,** reluctant.
disposer, *vb.* arrange.

dispositif, *n.m.* device.
disposition, *n.f.* arrangement, disposal, disposition.
disproportionné, *adj.* disproportionate.
dispute, *n.f.* row, fight, quarrel, dispute.
disputer, *vb.* dispute. **se d.,** quarrel.
disquaire, *n.m.* record dealer.
disqualifier, *vb.* disqualify.
disque, *n.m.* disk, record.
disquette, *n.f.* floppy disk, diskette.
dissemblable, *adj.* unlike.
dissemblance, *n.f.* dissimilarity.
disséminer, *vb.* scatter.
dissension, *n.f.* dissension.
dissentiment, *n.m.* dissent.
disséquer, *vb.* dissect.
dissertation, *n.f.* essay.
dissimulation, *n.f.* pretense.
dissimuler, *vb.* dissemble, pretend.
dissipation, *n.f.* dissipation.
dissiper, *vb.* dispel, waste, dissipate.
dissolu, *adj.* dissolute.
dissolution, *n.f.* dissolution.
dissonant, *adj.* discordant.
dissoudre, *vb.* dissolve.
dissuader, *vb.* dissuade.
distance, *n.f.* distance.
distancer, *vb.* outdistance.
distant, *adj.* distant.
distillation (-l-), *n.f.* distillation.
distiller (-l-), *vb.* distill.
distillerie (-l-), *n.f.* distillery.
distinct (-kt), *adj.* distinct.
distinctif, *adj.* distinctive.
distinction, *n.f.* distinction.
distingué, *adj.* distinguished.
distinguer, *vb.* discriminate; make out; distinguish.
distraction, *n.f.* distraction; pastime.
distraire, *vb.* distract, amuse. **se d.,** have fun.
distrait, *adj.* absentminded.
distribuer, *vb.* give out, deal out, distribute.
distributeur, *n.m.* distributor.
distribution, *n.f.* distribution; delivery; cast.
district (-trĕk), *n.m.* district.
dit, *adj.* called.

diurétique, *adj. and n.m.* diuretic.
diurne, *adj.* diurnal.
divaguer, *vb.* ramble.
divan, *n.m.* davenport, couch.
divergence, *n.f.* divergence.
diverger, *vb.* diverge.
divers, *adj.* various.
diversifier, *vb.* diversify.
diversion, *n.f.* diversion.
diversité, *n.f.* diversity.
divertir, *vb.* divert, entertain. **se d.,** enjoy oneself.
divertissement, *n.m.* diversion.
dividende, *n.m.* dividend.
divin, *adj.* divine.
divinateur, *n.m.* soothsayer.
divinité, *n.f.* divinity.
diviser, *vb.* part, divide.
divisible, *adj.* divisible.
division, *n.f.* division.
divorce, *n.m.* divorce.
divorcer, *vb.* divorce.
divulguer, *vb.* divulge.
dix (-s), *adj. and n.m.* ten.
dix-huit (-z-), *adj. and n.m.* eighteen.
dix-huitième (-z-), *adj. and n.m.f.* eighteenth.
dixième (-z-), *adj. and n.m.f.* tenth.
dix-neuf (-z-), *adj. and n.m.* nineteen.
dix-sept (-s-), *adj. and n.m.* seventeen.
dizaine, *n.f.* (group of) ten.
docile, *adj.* docile.
docilité, *n.f.* docility.
docte, *adj.* learned, wise.
docteur, *n.m.* doctor.
doctorat, *n.m.* doctorate.
doctrine, *n.f.* doctrine.
document, *n.m.* document.
documentaliste, *n.m.f.* researcher.
documenter, *vb.* document.
dodo, *n.m.* (colloquial) **faire d.,** go to sleep.
dodu, *adj.* plump.
dogmatique, *adj.* dogmatic.
dogme, *n.m.* dogma.
dogue, *n.m.* watchdog.
doigt (dwä), *n.m.* finger. **d. de pied,** toe.
doit, *n.m.* debit.
doléances, *n.f.pl.* grievances.
dollar, *n.m.* dollar.
domaine, *n.m.* domain, property.

dôme, *n.m.* dome.
domestique, 1. *n.m.f.* servant. **2.** *adj.* domestic.
domicile, *n.m.* residence.
dominant, *adj.* dominant.
domination, *n.f.* sway, domination, dominion.
dominer, *vb.* rule, dominate.
domino, *n.m.* domino.
dommage, *n.m.* injury; damage. **c'est d.,** that's too bad. **quel d.!,** what a pity!
dompter, *vb.* tame, subdue.
don, *n.m.* gift.
donateur, *n.m.* donor.
donation, *n.f.* donation.
donc (-k), *adv.* therefore.
donjon, *n.m.* dungeon.
donne, *n.f.* deal (cards).
donner, *vb.* give.
donneur, *n.m.* giver.
dont, *pron.* whose, of which.
dopage, *n.m.* doping.
doper, *vb.* dope.
dorénavant, *adv.* hereafter.
dorer, *vb.* gild.
dorloter, *vb.* coddle.
dormant, *adj.* dormant; asleep.
dormir, *vb.* sleep.
dortoir, *n.m.* dormitory.
dos, *n.m.* back.
dosage, *n.m.* mixture.
dose, *n.f.* dose.
doser, *vb.* decide the amount.
dossier, *n.m.* record.
dot (-t), *n.f.* dowry.
doter, *vb.* endow.
douaire, *n.m.* dowry.
douane, *n.f.* customs, custom house.
douanier, *n.m.* customs officer.
double, *adj. and n.m.* double. **faire le d. de,** duplicate.
doubler, *vb.* double.
doublure, *n.f.* lining.
doucement, *adv.* gently.
doucereux, *adj.* sugary; oversweet.
douceur, *n.f.* sweetness; gentleness, meekness.
douche, *n.f.* shower bath; douche.
doucher, *vb.* **se d.,** take a shower.
doudoune, *n.f.* anorak.
douer, *vb.* endow.
douille, *n.f.* socket.

douleur, *n.f.* pain, ache; sorrow, grief.

douloureux, *adj.* painful.

doute, *n.m.* doubt.

douter, *vb.* doubt. **se d. de,** suspect.

douteux, *adj.* dubious, doubtful, questionable.

douve, *n.f.* ditch.

doux *m.,* **douce** *f. adj.* soft, sweet, gentle, mild, meek.

douzaine, *n.f.* dozen.

douze, *adj. and n.m.* twelve.

douzième, *adj. and n.m.f.* twelfth.

doyen, *n.m.* dean.

dragée, *n.f.* sugar-coated pill.

dragon, *n.m.* dragon; dragoon.

draguer, *vb.* dredge; try to pick up.

drainage, *n.m.* drainage.

drainer, *vb.* drain.

dramatique, *adj.* dramatic.

dramatiser, *vb.* dramatize.

dramaturge, *n.m.* playwright.

drame, *n.m.* drama.

drap, *n.m.* sheet.

drapeau, *n.m.* flag.

draper, *vb.* drape.

draperie, *n.f.* drapery.

drapier, *n.m.* clothier.

dresser, *vb.* draw up.

dressoir, *n.m.* dresser.

drive, *n.m.* drive (tennis).

drogue, *n.f.* drug.

droguer, *vb.* drug.

droguerie, *n.f.* hardware store.

droguiste, *n.m.* owner or keeper of a hardware store.

droit, 1. *n.m.* right; law; claim. **2.** *adj. and adv.* (up)right, straight, fair. **d. d'auteur,** copyright.

droite, *n.f.* right. **à d.,** (to the) right.

droitier, *n.m.* right-handed person.

droiture, *n.f.* uprightness.

drôle, *adj.* funny.

du *m.,* **de la,** *f.,* **des,** *pl. prep.* some, any.

dû *m.,* **due** *f. adj.* due.

duc, *n.m.* duke.

duché, *n.m.* dukedom.

duchesse, *n.f.* duchess.

ductile, *adj.* ductile.

duel, *n.m.* duel.

duelliste, *n.m.* duelist.

dûment, *adv.* duly.

dune, *n.f.* dune.

duo, *n.m.* duet.

dupe, *n.f.* dupe.

duper, *vb.* trick.

duperie, *n.f.* trickery.

duplicité, *n.f.* duplicity.

dur, *adj.* hard, tough.

durabilité, *n.f.* durability.

durable, *adj.* lasting, durable.

durant, *prep.* during.

durcir, *vb.* harden.

durcissement, *n.m.* hardening.

durée, *n.f.* duration.

durement, *adv.* hard, harshly, strongly.

durer, *vb.* last.

dureté, *n.f.* hardness.

duvet, *n.m.* down.

duveté, *adj.* downy.

dynamique, *adj.* dynamic.

dynamite, *n.f.* dynamite.

dynamo, *n.f.* dynamo.

dynastie, *n.f.* dynasty.

dynastique, *adj.* dynastic.

dysenterie, *n.f.* dysentery.

dyslexie, *n.f.* dyslexia.

dyspepsie, *n.f.* dyspepsia.

E

eau, *n.f.* water. **faire e.,** leak.

eau-de-vie, *n.f.* brandy.

eau-forte, *n.f.* nitric acid.

ébahir, *vb.* amaze.

ébahissement, *n.m.* amazement.

ébarber, *vb.* trim, clip.

ébattre, *vb.* **s'é.,** frolic.

ébauche, *n.f.* outline.

ébaucher, *vb.* outline.

ébène, *n.m.* ebony.

ébéniste, *n.m.* cabinetmaker.

ébénisterie, *n.f.* cabinet work.

éblouir, *vb.* dazzle.

éblouissement, *n.m.* dazzle, amazement.

éboulement, *n.m.* cave-in.

ébouriffer, *vb.* ruffle.

ébranler, *vb.* shake.

ébriété, *n.f.* drunkenness.

ébullition, *n.f.* boiling point.

écaille, *n.f.* scale.

écarlate, *adj. and n.f.* scarlet.

écart, *n.m.* separation. **à l'é.,** aloof.

écarté, *adj.* isolated; lonely.

écartement, *n.m.* gap, separation.

écarter, *vb.* set aside.

ecclésiastique, *adj. and n.m.* ecclesiastic.

écervelé, *adj.* scatterbrained.

échafaud, *n.m.* scaffold.

échafaudage, *n.m.* scaffolding.

échalote, *n.f.* shallot.

échancrer, *vb.* scallop, notch.

échange, *n.m.* exchange.

échangeable, *adj.* exchangeable.

échanger, *vb.* exchange.

échantillon, *n.m.* sample.

échappatoire, *n.f.* loophole.

échappement, *n.m.* exhaust.

échapper, *vb.* escape.

écharde, *n.f.* splinter.

écharpe, *n.f.* scarf; sling.

échasse, *n.f.* stilt.

échauder, *vb.* scald.

échauffer, *vb.* heat up.

échéance, *n.f.* maturity (finance).

échec, *n.m.* failure.

échecs (-shĕ), *n.m.pl.* chess.

échelle, *n.f.* ladder; scale.

échelon, *n.m.* step; echelon.

échevelé, *adj.* dishevelled.

échine, *n.f.* spine.

échiner, *vb.* work like a slave.

écho (-kō), *n.m.* echo.

échoir, *vb.* fall due.

échoppe, *n.f.* booth, stall.

échouer, *vb.* fail. **faire é.,** frustrate.

éclabousser, *vb.* splash.

éclair, *n.m.* flash.

éclairage, *n.m.* lighting.

éclaircie, *n.f.* clearing.

éclaircir, *vb.* clear up.

éclairer, *vb.* (en)lighten, light, clear up, clarify.

éclaireur, *n.m.* scout.

éclat, *n.m.* chip, splinter; burst; brilliance, radiance, glamour.

éclatant, *adj.* bursting; loud; brilliant.

éclatement (de pneu), *n.m.* blowout.

éclater, *vb.* burst out.

éclectique, *adj.* eclectic.

éclipse, *n.f.* eclipse.

éclipser, *vb.* eclipse.

éclore, *vb.* hatch; open, blossom.

écluse, *n.f.* lock.

écœurant, *adj.* sickly, disgusting.

écœurer, *vb.* disgust.

école, *n.f.* school.

écolier, *n.m.* schoolboy.

écologie, *n.f.* ecology.

écologique, *adj.* ecological.

écologiste, *n.m.f.* ecologist; environmentalist.

économe, *adj.* economical.

économie, *n.f.* economy. **é. politique,** economics.

économique, *adj.* economic(al).

économiser, *vb.* economize.

économiste, *n.m.f.* economist.

écope, *n.f.* ladle.

écoper, *vb.* ladle or bail out.

écorce, *n.f.* bark.

écorcher, *vb.* skin.

écorchure, *n.f.* gall.

Écossais, *n.m.* Scotchman, Scotsman.

écossais, *adj.* Scotch, Scottish.

Écosse, *n.f.* Scotland.

écosystème, *n.m.* ecosystem.

écot, *n.m.* share.

écouler, *vb.* drain. **s'é.,** flow, elapse.

écoute, *n.f.* listening.

écouter, *vb.* listen (to).

écouteur, *n.m.* listener.

écran, *n.m.* screen.

écraser, *vb.* crush.

écrémer, *vb.* skim.

écrevisse, *n.f.* crayfish.

écrier, *vb.* **s'é.,** exclaim.

écrin, *n.m.* case, box.

écrire, *vb.* write. **machine à é.,** typewriter.

écrit, *adj.* written.

écriteau, *n.m.* notice.

écritoire, *n.f.* inkstand.

écriture, *n.f.* writing, scripture.

écrivain, *n.m.* writer.

écrou, *n.m.* nut.

écrouler, *vb.* **s'é.,** fall to pieces.

écru, *adj.* natural, off-white.

écu, *n.m.* shield.

écueil, *n.m.* reef; pitfall.

écuelle, *n.f.* bowl, dish.

écume, *n.f.* lather, foam.

écuménique, *adj.* ecumenical.

écureuil, *n.m.* squirrel.

écurie, *n.f.* stable.

écusson, *n.m.* escutcheon.
écuyer (-kwē-), *n.m.* squire.
édenté, *adj.* toothless.
édifice, *n.m.* building.
édifier, *vb.* build; edify.
édit, *n.m.* edict.
éditer, *vb.* publish.
éditeur, *n.m.* publisher.
édition, *n.f.* edition, publishing.
éditorial, *adj.* editorial.
éducateur, *n.m.* educator.
éducation, *n.f.* breeding, education.
éduquer, *vb.* educate, train.
effacer, *vb.* erase, efface.
effarant, *adj.* alarming.
effarer, *vb.* alarm.
effectif, *adj.* effective, actual.
effectivement, *adv.* effectively.
effectuer, *vb.* effect.
efféminé, *adj.* effeminate.
effet, *n.m.* effect; (*pl.*) belongings.
en e., as a matter of fact, indeed.
efficace, *adj.* effective.
efficacité, *n.f.* efficacy.
effigie, *n.f.* effigy.
effleurer, *vb.* skim, graze.
effluves, *n.m.pl.* exhalations.
effondrement, *n.m.* collapse.
effondrer, *vb.* **s'e.,** collapse, sink.
efforcer, *vb.* **s'e.,** endeavor, try hard.
effort, *n.m.* endeavor, strain, exertion, effort.
effrayant, *adj.* fearful.
effrayer, *vb.* frighten, scare, startle.
effréné, *adj.* unrestrained; frantic.
effriter, *vb.* **s'e.,** crumble.
effroi, *n.m.* fright.
effronté, *adj.* brazen.
effronterie, *n.f.* effrontery.
effroyable, *adj.* appalling.
effusion, *n.f.* shedding.
égal, *adj.* even, equal, same.
également, *adv.* equally.
égaler, *vb.* equal.
égaliser, *vb.* equalize.
égalité, *n.f.* equality, evenness.
égard, *n.m.* regard, consideration, esteem. **à l'é. de,** as for. **plein d'é.s,** considerate.
égaré, *adj.* astray.
égarement, *n.m.* aberration.

égarer, *vb.* mislay, bewilder. **s'é.,** go astray, get lost.
égayer, *vb.* cheer up.
église, *n.f.* church.
égoïsme, *n.m.* selfishness, egoism.
égoïste, *adj.* selfish.
égorger, *vb.* kill.
égotisme, *n.m.* egotism.
égout, *n.m.* sewer.
égoutter, *vb.* drain; drip.
égratigner, *vb.* scratch.
égratignure, *n.f.* scratch.
Égypte, *n.m.* Egypt.
Égyptien, *n.m.* Egyptian.
égyptien, *adj.* Egyptian.
éhonté, *adj.* brazen, shameless.
éjecter, *vb.* eject.
élaboration, *n.f.* working out, elaboration; data processing.
élaborer, *vb.* draft, elaborate.
élan, *n.m.* elk; zest.
élancé, *adj.* slim.
élancer, *vb.* **s'é.,** dash.
élargir, *vb.* widen, increase, enlarge.
élasticité, *n.f.* elasticity.
élastique, *adj. and n.m.* elastic.
électeur, *n.m.* voter.
électif, *adj.* elective.
élection, *n.f.* election.
électoral, *adj.* electoral.
électricien, *n.m.* electrician.
électricité, *n.f.* electricity.
électrique, *adj.* electric, electrical.
électrocardiogramme, *n.m.* electrocardiogram.
électrochoc, *n.m.* electric shock treatment.
électrocuter, *vb.* electrocute.
électroménager, *adj.* **appareils é.s,** household appliances.
électron, *n.m.* electron.
électronique, *adj.* electronic.
électrophone, *n.m.* record-player.
élégance, *n.f.* elegance.
élégant, *adj.* elegant, smart, stylish.
élégie, *n.f.* elegy.
élément, *n.m.* element.
élémentaire, *adj.* elementary.
éléphant, *n.m.* elephant.
élevage, *n.m.* breeding.
élévation, *n.f.* elevation.
élève, *n.m.f.* pupil.
élevé, *adj.* lofty.

élever, vb. raise. **s'é.,** arise; soar.
éleveur, n.m. breeder.
élider, vb. elide.
éligibilité, n.f. eligibility.
éligible, adj. eligible.
élimination, n.f. elimination.
éliminer, vb. eliminate.
élire, vb. elect.
élite, n.f. elite.
elle, pron.f. she, her; (pl.) they, them (f.).
elle-même, pron. herself.
ellipse, n.m. ellipse.
élocution, n.f. elocution.
éloge, n.m. praise.
éloigné, adj. remote.
éloignement, n.m. distance.
éloigner, vb. take away. **s'é.,** go away, recede.
élongation, n.f. pulled muscle.
éloquence, n.f. eloquence.
éloquent, adj. eloquent.
élu, adj. chosen.
éluder, vb. evade, elude.
émacié, adj. emaciated.
émail, n.m. enamel.
émancipation, n.f. emancipation.
émanciper, vb. emancipate.
émaner, vb. emanate.
emballage, n.m. wrapping.
emballer, vb. pack.
embarcadère, n.m. wharf.
embarcation, n.f. craft.
embargo, n.m. embargo.
embarquement, n.m. loading, boarding.
embarquer, vb. embark.
embarras, n.m. embarrassment; trouble, fix.
embarrassant, adj. embarrassing, awkward.
embarrasser, vb. embarrass.
embaucher, vb. hire.
embaumé, adj. balmy.
embaumer, vb. perfume; embalm.
embellir, vb. beautify.
embêter, vb. bore, irritate.
emblème, n.m. emblem.
embolie, n.f. embolism.
embouchure, n.f. mouth.
embourber, vb. bog.
embouteillage, n.m. traffic jam.
embranchement, n.m. junction.
embrasser, vb. embrace, kiss.
embrayage, n.m. clutch.

embrayer, vb. let in the clutch.
embrouillement, n.m. tangle, mix-up.
embrouiller, vb. perplex; entangle.
embrun, n.m. spray.
embuscade, n.f. ambush.
émeraude, n.f. emerald.
émerger, vb. emerge.
émerveiller, vb. astonish.
émetteur, n.m. transmitter.
émettre, vb. emit, send forth, issue.
émeute, n.f. riot.
émietter, vb. crumble.
émigrant, n.m. emigrant.
émigration, n.f. emigration.
émigré, n.m. political exile.
émigrer, vb. (e)migrate.
émincer, vb. cut into thin slices.
éminemment, adv. eminently.
éminence, n.f. eminence.
éminent, adj. eminent.
émission, n.f. issue.
emmagasinage, n.m. storage.
emmagasiner, vb. store.
emmener, vb. take away.
émoi, n.m. commotion.
émotif, adj. emotional.
émotion, n.f. emotion, feeling.
émoussé, adj. blunt.
émouvant, adj. moving.
émouvoir, vb. move.
empailler, vb. stuff.
empaler, vb. impale.
empan, n.m. span.
emparer, vb. **s'e. de,** take possession of.
empêchement, n.m. prevention.
empêcher, vb. prevent, stop, hinder, inhibit.
empereur, n.m. emperor.
empester, vb. stink.
empêtrer, vb. entangle.
emphase, n.f. emphasis.
emphatique, adj. emphatic.
empiéter, vb. encroach, trespass.
empire, n.m. empire.
empirer, vb. worsen.
empirique, adj. empirical.
emplette, n.f. purchase. **faire des e.s,** shop.
emplir, vb. fill.
emploi, n.m. employment; use; job.

employé, *n.m.* employee, clerk, (public) servant.

employer, *vb.* employ, use.

employeur, *n.m.* employer.

empoigner, *vb.* grab.

empois, *n.m.* starch.

empoisonné, *adj.* poisonous.

empoisonner, *vb.* poison.

emporter, *vb.* take away. **s'e.,** get angry.

empreinte, *n.f.* print, impression.

empressé, *adj.* solicitous.

empressement, *n.m.* eagerness.

empresser, *vb.* **s'e.,** be eager.

emprise, *n.f.* expropriation; influence.

emprisonnement, *n.m.* imprisonment.

emprisonner, *vb.* imprison.

emprunt, *n.m.* loan.

emprunter, *vb.* borrow from.

emprunteur, *n.m.* borrower.

ému, *adj.* touched, stirred.

émule, *n.* rival, competitor.

émulsion, *n.f.* lotion.

en, 1. *prep.* in, into. **2.** *adv.* thence; of it; some, any.

encadrer, *vb.* frame.

encaisser, *vb.* cash; tolerate.

en-cas, *n.m.* reserve.

enceinte, *adj.f.* pregnant.

encens, *n.m.* incense.

enchaîner, *vb.* chain.

enchantement, *n.m.* enchantment.

enchanter, *vb.* delight, charm, enchant.

enchère, *n.f.* bid. **vente aux e.s,** auction.

enclore, *vb.* fence in, enclose.

enclos, 1. *n.m.* enclosure, **2.** *adj.* shut in.

enclume, *n.f.* anvil.

encoche, *n.f.* notch.

encoignure, *n.f.* corner.

encoller, *vb.* paste.

encombrant, *adj.* cumbersome.

encombré, *adj.* crowded.

encombrement, *n.m.* congestion.

encombrer, *vb.* crowd, clutter, block up.

encontre, *adv.* **à l'e.,** toward, counter (to).

encore, *adv.* still, yet, again.

encourageant, *adj.* encouraging.

encouragement, *n.m.* encouragement.

encourager, *vb.* encourage, urge, promote.

encourir, *vb.* incur.

encre, *n.f.* ink.

encrier, *n.m.* inkwell.

encyclopédie, *n.f.* encyclopedia.

endetté, *adj.* indebted.

endiguer, *vb.* dam up.

endimanché, *adj.* in one's Sunday best.

endive, *n.f.* endive, chicory.

endocrinologie, *n.f.* endocrinology.

endolori, *adj.* painful.

endommager, *vb.* damage.

endormi, *adj.* asleep.

endormir, *vb.* put to sleep. **s'e.,** go to sleep.

endossement, *n.m.* endorsement.

endosser, *vb.* endorse; shoulder.

endroit, *n.m.* place.

enduire, *vb.* smear, daub.

endurance, *n.f.* endurance.

endurant, *adj.* patient.

endurcir, *vb.* harden.

endurcissement, *n.m.* hardening.

énergie, *n.f.* energy.

énergique, *adj.* energetic.

énervant, *adj.* enervating.

énervé, *adj.* nervous.

énerver, *vb.* irritate.

enfance, *n.f.* childhood. **première e.,** infancy.

enfant, *n.m.f.* child.

enfantement, *n.m.* childbirth.

enfanter, *vb.* bear (children).

enfantillage, *n.m.* childishness.

enfantin, *adj.* childish.

enfariner, *vb.* coat with flour.

enfer (-r), *n.m.* hell.

enfermer, *vb.* shut in.

enfiévrer, *vb.* excite, inspire.

enfin, *adv.* finally, at last.

enflammer, *vb.* inflame.

enfler, *vb.* swell.

enflure, *n.f.* swelling.

enfoncer, *vb.* sink.

enfouir, *vb.* bury.

enfourchure, *n.f.* bifurcation; crotch of a tree.

enfreindre, *vb.* violate.

enfuir, *vb.* **s'e.,** run away, flee, elope.

enfumer, *vb.* fill or cover with smoke.

engagé, *adj.* committed.

engageant, *adj.* personable, charming.

engagement, *n.m.* pledge, agreement, engagement.

engager, *vb.* hire, engage. s'e., volunteer.

engelure, *n.f.* chilblain.

engendrer, *vb.* beget.

engin, *n.m.* machine; engine, motor.

englober, *vb.* include.

engloutir, *vb.* devour.

engorgement, *n.m.* choking.

engouement, *n.m.* infatuation.

engouffrer, *vb.* engulf.

engourdir, *vb.* dull.

engrais, *n.m.* fertilizer.

engraisser, *vb.* fatten.

engraver, *vb.* strand or ground (a ship).

engrenage, *n.m.* gear.

engrener, *vb.* engage (gears).

engueuler, *vb.* (colloquial) bawl out.

enhardir, *vb.* make bolder.

enième, *adj.* (colloquial) umpteenth.

énigmatique, *adj.* enigmatic.

énigme, *n.f.* riddle, puzzle, enigma.

enivrant, *adj.* intoxicating.

enivrement, *n.m.* intoxication.

enivrer, *vb.* intoxicate. s'e., get drunk.

enjambée, *n.f.* stride.

enjamber, *vb.* stride.

enjeu, *n.m.* stake.

enjoindre, *vb.* enjoin; call upon.

enjôlement, *n.m.* cajolery.

enjôler, *vb.* cajole.

enjoliver, *vb.* beautify.

enjoué, *adj.* playful.

enjouement, *n.m.* playfulness.

enlacer, *vb.* entwine; interlace; embrace.

enlaidir, *vb.* make or become ugly.

enlevable, *adj.* detachable.

enlèvement, *n.m.* removal, abduction.

enlever, *vb.* take away, remove, abduct.

enliser, *vb.* s'e., sink.

enneigé, *adj.* snow-covered.

ennemi, *adj. and n.m.* enemy.

ennoblir, *vb.* exalt; ennoble.

ennui (-nwē), *n.m.* nuisance, bore, bother; boredom.

ennuyer, *vb.* bore, annoy, vex, bother, irk.

ennuyeux, *adj.* boring, tedious, dull.

énoncer, *vb.* enunciate.

énonciation, *n.f.* enunciation.

énorme, *adj.* enormous.

énormité, *n.f.* enormity.

enquérir, *vb.* inquire.

enquête, *n.f.* inquiry.

enquiquiner, *vb.* irritate.

enraciner, *vb.* root. s'e., take root.

enragé, *adj.* rabid.

enrageant, *adj.* infuriating.

enrager, *vb.* be, go mad. s'e., get angry.

enregistrement, *n.m.* registration, recording; checking.

enregistrer, *vb.* record, register, list; check (luggage).

enrhumer, *vb.* s'e., catch a cold.

enrichir, *vb.* enrich.

enrober, *vb.* coat, envelop.

enrôlement, *n.m.* enlistment, enrollment.

enrôler, *vb.* enlist, enroll.

enroué, *adj.* hoarse.

enrouement, *n.m.* hoarseness.

enrouler, *vb.* s'e., roll up, twist, wind.

enseignant, *n.m.* teacher.

enseigne, *n.f.* sign, ensign.

enseignement, *n.m.* teaching, instruction.

enseigner, *vb.* teach.

ensemble, 1. *n.m.* set. **2.** *adv.* together.

ensevelir, *vb.* bury.

ensoleillé, *adj.* sunny.

ensommeillé, *adj.* sleepy.

ensorceler, *vb.* bewitch.

ensuite, *adv.* then, next, afterwards.

ensuivre, *vb.* s'e., ensue.

entablement, *n.m.* entablature.

entacher, *vb.* taint, besmirch.

entailler, *vb.* hack (notch).

entamer, *vb.* begin.

entassement, *n.m.* accumulation.

entasser, *vb.* heap up.

ente, *n.f.* scion (horticulture).

entendement, *n.m.* understanding, sense.

entendre, *vb.* hear; understand. **s'e.,** get on together.

entendu, *adj.* understood, agreed. **bien e.,** of course.

enténébré, *adj.* gloomy.

entente, *n.f.* understanding, agreement.

entériner, *vb.* ratify.

enterrement, *n.m.* burial.

enterrer, *vb.* bury.

entêté, *adj.* perverse.

entêtement, *n.m.* stubbornness.

entêter, *vb.* **s'e.,** be stubborn, insist.

enthousiasme, *n.m.* enthusiasm.

enthousiaste, 1. *n.m.f.* enthusiast. **2.** *adj.* enthusiastic. **e. de,** keen on.

entichement, *n.m.* infatuation.

entier, *adj.* whole, complete, entire.

entité, *n.f.* entity.

entonner, *vb.* start to sing.

entonnoir, *n.m.* funnel.

entorse, *n.f.* sprain.

entourage, *n.m.* circle of friends; surroundings.

entourer, *vb.* surround, encircle.

entournure, *n.f.* armhole.

entr'acte, *n.m.* intermission.

entr'aide, *n.f.* mutual assistance.

entrailles, *n.f.pl.* bowels.

entrain, *n.m.* zest.

entraînant, *adj.* rousing.

entraîner, *vb.* draw along; involve, entail; coach, train.

entraîneur, *n.m.* coach.

entrant, *adj.* incoming.

entrave, *n.f.* obstacle.

entraver, *vb.* clog.

entre, *prep.* among, between.

entre-clos, *adj.* ajar.

entre-deux, *n.m.* interval.

entrée, *n.f.* admission, entry; main course.

entreface, *n.f.* interface.

entregent, *n.m.* tact; spirit.

entrelacer, *vb.* interlace.

entremets (-mè), *n.m.* (side) dish; dessert.

entremetteur, *n.m.* intermediary.

entreposer, *vb.* store.

entreposeur, *n.m.* warehouseman.

entrepôt, *n.m.* warehouse.

entreprenant, *adj.* enterprising.

entreprendre, *vb.* undertake.

entrepreneur, *n.m.* contractor. **e. de pompes funèbres,** undertaker.

entreprise, *n.f.* concern, undertaking.

entrer (dans), *vb.* enter, come in, go in. **laisser e.,** admit.

entretenir, *vb.* entertain. **s'e.,** converse.

entretien, *n.m.* maintenance; conference; talk, conversation.

entrevoir, *vb.* glimpse.

entrevue, *n.f.* interview.

entr'ouvert, *adj.* ajar.

entr'ouvrir, *vb.* open halfway.

énumération, *n.f.* enumeration.

énumérer, *vb.* enumerate.

envahir, *vb.* invade.

envahissement, *n.m.* invasion.

enveloppe, *n.f.* envelope; wrapping.

envelopper, *vb.* envelop, wrap, enfold.

envergure, *n.f.* scope.

envers, 1. *n.m.* wrong side. **2.** *prep.* toward.

enviable, *adj.* enviable.

envie, *n.f.* envy, desire. **avoir e. de,** want to, feel like.

envier, *vb.* envy.

envieux, *adj.* envious.

environ, *prep. and adv.* around, about; approximately.

environnement, *n.m.* surroundings.

environnementaliste, *n.m.f.* environmentalist.

environner, *vb.* surround.

environs, *n.m.pl.* surroundings.

envisager, *vb.* consider.

envoi, *n.m.* shipment, sending.

envoler, *vb.* **s'e.,** fly away.

envoûter, *vb.* bewitch.

envoyé, *n.m.* envoy.

envoyer, *vb.* send.

enzyme, *n.f.* enzyme.

éon, *n.m.* eon.

épais, *adj.* thick.

épaisseur, *n.f.* thickness.

épaissir, *vb.* thicken.

épancher, *vb.* shed (blood).

épanouir, *vb.* **s'é.,** bloom.

épargne, *n.f.* savings.

épargner, vb. save, spare.
éparpiller, vb. scatter.
épars, adj. scattered, sparse.
éparvin, n.m. spavin.
épatant, adj. (colloq.) grand.
épate, n.f. swagger.
épatement, n.m. amazement.
épater, vb. amaze.
épaule, n.f. shoulder.
épaulette, n.f. epaulette.
épave, n.f. wreck.
épée, n.f. sword.
épeler, vb. spell.
épellation, n.f. spelling.
éperdu, adj. distracted.
éperlan, n.m. smelt.
éperon, n.m. spur.
éperonner, vb. spur.
épervier, n.m. hawk.
épeuré, adj. frightened.
éphémère, adj. ephemeral, fleeting.
épice, n.f. spice.
épicé, adj. spicy.
épicerie, n.f. grocery.
épicier, n.m. grocer.
épidémie, n.f. epidemic.
épiderme, n.m. epidermis.
épidermique, adj. epidermal.
épier, vb. spy.
épigramme, n.f. epigram.
épilatoire, adj. and n.m. depilatory.
épilepsie, n.f. epilepsy.
épileptique, adj. and n.m.f. epileptic.
épilogue, n.m. epilogue.
épinards (-nár), n.m.pl. spinach.
épine, n.f. spine, thorn. **é. dorsale,** spinal column.
épinet, n.f. spinet.
épineux, adj. thorny.
épingle, n.f. pin. **é. à cheveux,** hairpin. **é. anglaise,** safety pin.
épingler, vb. pin.
épique, adj. epic.
épiscopal, adj. Episcopal.
épisode, n.m. episode.
épisodique, adj. episodic.
épistolaire, adj. epistolary.
épitaphe, n.f. epitaph.
épithète, n.f. epithet.
épitomé, n.m. epitome.
épitre, n.f. epistle.
éploré, adj. tearful.

épluche-légumes, n.m. (potato) peeler.
éplucher, vb. peel.
épointé, adj. dull, blunted.
éponge, n.f. sponge.
éponger, vb. sponge up.
épopée, n.f. epic.
époque, n.f. epoch.
épouffé, adj. breathless, panting.
épouiller, vb. delouse.
épouse, n.f. wife.
épouser, vb. marry.
épouseur, n.m. suitor.
épousseter, vb. dust.
époussette, n.f. duster.
époustouflant, adj. staggering.
épouvantable, adj. terrible.
épouvante, n.f. fright.
épouvanter, vb. frighten.
époux, n.m. husband.
épreindre, vb. squeeze.
éprendre, vb. s'é., fall in love.
épreuve, n.f. trial, test; ordeal; proof.
éprouver, vb. experience.
éprouvette, n.f. test tube.
épuisant, adj. exhausting.
épuisement, n.m. exhaustion.
épuiser, vb. exhaust.
épuration, n.f. purification.
épurer, vb. purify.
équanimité (-kwá-), n.f. equanimity.
équateur (-kwá-), n.m. equator.
équation (-kwá-), n.f. equation.
équatorial (-kwá-), adj. equatorial.
équestre, adj. equestrian.
équidistant, adj. equidistant.
équilibre, n.m. poise.
équilibrer, vb. balance.
équilibriste, n. tightrope walker.
équinoxe, n.m. equinox.
équinoxial, adj. equinoctial.
équipage, n.m. crew.
équipe, n.f. team, crew, gang; shift.
équipement, n.m. equipment.
équiper, vb. equip.
équipier, n.m. team member.
équitable, adj. fair.
équitation, n.f. (horse) riding.
équité, n.f. equity.
équivalent, adj. and n.m. equivalent.
équivaloir, vb. equal in value.
équivoque, adj. equivocal.

érable, *n.m.* maple.
éradication, *n.f.* eradication.
éraflure, *n.m.* scratch; graze.
érailler, *vb.* unravel.
ère, *n.f.* era.
érection, *n.f.* erection; construction.
éreintant, *adj.* exhausting.
éreinter, *vb.* exhaust.
erg, *n.m.* erg.
ergoter, *vb.* quibble.
ériger, *vb.* erect.
ermitage, *n.m.* hermitage.
ermite, *n.m.* hermit.
éroder, *vb.* erode.
érosif, *adj.* erosive.
érosion, *n.f.* erosion.
érotique, *adj.* erotic.
errant, *adj.* wandering.
erratique, *adj.* erratic.
errer, *vb.* wander; err.
erreur, *n.f.* mistake, error.
erroné, *adj.* erroneous.
éructation, *n.f.* belch.
éructer, *vb.* belch.
érudit, *adj.* learned, scholarly.
érudition, *n.f.* learning.
éruption, *n.f.* rash, eruption.
érysipèle, *n.m.* erysipelas.
escabeau, *n.m.* stool.
escadrille, *n.f.* (ships) flotilla; (airplanes) squadron.
escadron, *n.m.* squadron.
escalade, *n.f.* climbing; escalation.
escalader, *vb.* scale; escalate.
escalator, *n.m.* escalator.
escale, *n.f.* stopover.
escalier, *n.m.* stairs.
escalope, *n.f.* cutlet.
escamotage, *n.f.* legerdemain.
escamoter, *vb.* evade, get around.
escamoteur, *n.f.* conjurer, magician.
escapade, *n.f.* escapade.
escarcelle, *n.f.* wallet.
escargot, *n.m.* snail.
escarmouche, *n.f.* skirmish.
escarole, *n.f.* chicory, endive.
escarpé, *adj.* abrupt.
escarpement, *n.m.* steepness.
eschare, *n.f.* scab; bedsore.
esclandre, *n.m.* slander.
esclavage, *n.m.* slavery.
esclave, *n.m.f.* slave.
escompte, *n.m.* discount.

escorte, *n.f.* escort.
escorter, *vb.* escort.
escouade, *n.f.* squad.
escrime, *n.f.* fencing.
escrimer, *vb.* fight.
escrimeur, *n.m.* swordsman.
escroc (-ô), *n.m.* swindler.
escroquer, *vb.* swindle.
escroquerie, *n.f.* swindle.
esculent, *adj.* esculent.
espace, *n.m.* space.
espacé, *adj.* at great intervals.
espacer, *vb.* space out.
espadon, *n.m.* swordfish.
espadrille, *n.f.* rope sandal.
Espagne, *n.f.* Spain.
Espagnol, *n.m.* Spaniard.
espagnol, *adj. and n.m.* Spanish.
espalier, *n.m.* espalier.
espèce, *n.f.* species, kind; (*pl.*) cash.
espérance, *n.f.* hope.
espéranto, *n.m.* Esperanto.
espérer, *vb.* hope.
espiègle, *adj.* mischievous.
espièglerie, *n.f.* mischief.
espion, *n.m.* spy.
espionnage, *n.m.* espionage.
espionner, *vb.* spy on.
esplanade, *n.f.* esplanade.
espoir, *n.m.* hope.
esprit, *n.m.* spirit, mind, wit. Saint-E., Holy Ghost.
esquif, *n.m.* skiff.
Esquimau, *m.*, **Esquimaude**, *f.* *n.* Eskimo.
esquimau, *adj.* Eskimo.
esquinancie, *n.m.* quinsy.
esquinter, *vb.* exhaust, tire out.
esquisse, *n.f.* sketch.
esquisser, *vb.* sketch.
esquiver, *vb.* dodge.
essai, *n.m.* essay; attempt; experiment; assay.
essaim, *n.m.* swarm.
essaimer, *vb.* swarm.
essayer, *vb.* try; assay.
essence, *n.f.* gasoline; essence.
essentiel, *adj.* essential.
esseulement, *n.f.* solitude.
essieu, *n.m.* axle.
essor, *n.m.* flight; rapid expansion.
essorer, *vb.* dry.
essoufflé, *adj.* breathless.

essoufflement, *n.m.* breathlessness.

essuie-glace, *n.m.* windshield wiper.

essuyer, *vb.* wipe.

est (-t), *n.m.* east.

estacade, *n.f.* stockade.

estafette, *n.f.* courier.

estafier, *n.m.* bodyguard.

estagnon, *n.m.* oil drum.

estaminet, *n.m.* bar, taproom.

estampe, *n.f.* engraving.

estampille, *n.f.* trademark.

esthète, *n.m.* esthete.

esthéticienne, *n.f.* beautician.

esthétique, *adj.* aesthetic.

estimable, *adj.* estimable.

estimateur, *n.m.* estimator; appraiser.

estimatif, *adj.* estimated.

estimation, *n.f.* estimate.

estime, *n.f.* esteem; estimation.

estimer, *vb.* esteem; estimate, value, rate.

estival, *adj.* of summer.

estivant, *n.m.* summer tourist.

estiver, *vb.* spend the summer.

estoc, *n.m.* tree trunk.

estomac (mä), *n.m.* stomach.

estomper, *vb.* blur. s'e., soften, become blurred.

estourbir, *vb.* kill.

estrade, *n.f.* platform; stage.

estragon, *n.m.* tarragon.

estropié. 1. *n.m.* cripple. **2.** *adj.* crippled.

estropier, *vb.* cripple.

estuaire, *n.m.* estuary.

estudiantin, *adj.* student.

esturgeon, *n.m.* sturgeon.

et, *conj.* and.

étable, *n.f.* barn.

établi, *n.m.* worktable.

établir, *vb.* settle; establish.

établissement, *n.m.* establishment.

étage, *n.m.* floor, story.

étagère, *n.f.* whatnot shelf.

étain, *n.m.* tin.

étal, *n.m.* stall.

étalage, *n.m.* display.

étalager, *vb.* display.

étaler, *vb.* display; spread.

étalon, *n.m.* standard.

étameur, *n.m.* tinsmith.

étamine, *n.f.* coarse muslin; stamen.

étampe, *n.f.* stamp.

étamper, *vb.* stamp.

étanche, *adj.* impervious.

étancher, *vb.* quench; stanch.

étang, *n.m.* pond.

étape, *n.f.* stage.

état, *n.m.* state.

étatisé, *adj.* state-controlled.

état-major, *n.m.* staff.

États-Unis, *n.m.pl.* United States.

été, *n.m.* summer.

éteindre, *vb.* extinguish, put out.

éteint, *adj.* extinguished.

étendage, *n.m.* clotheslines.

étendard, *n.m.* standard.

étendre, *vb.* extend, spread, reach.

étendu, *adj.* extensive.

étendue, *n.f.* extent.

éternel, *adj.* everlasting.

éterniser, *vb.* perpetuate.

éternité, *n.f.* eternity.

éternuement, *n.m.* sneeze.

éternuer, *vb.* sneeze.

éther (-r), *n.m.* ether.

éthéré, *adj.* ethereal.

Éthiopie, *n.f.* Ethiopia.

éthique, *n.f.* ethics.

ethnie, *n.f.* ethnic group.

ethnique, *adj.* ethnic.

étinceler, *vb.* sparkle.

étincelle, *n.f.* spark, sparkle.

étincellement, *n.m.* sparkle, glitter.

étiolement, *n.m.* atrophy.

étioler, *vb.* blanch.

étiqueter, *vb.* label.

étiquette, *n.f.* label, tag; etiquette.

étirer, *vb.* stretch out.

étoffe, *n.f.* stuff, material, cloth.

étoffer, *vb.* stuff.

étoile, *n.f.* star.

étoiler, *vb.* bespangle.

étonnement, *n.m.* astonishment.

étonner, *vb.* astonish.

étouffé, *adj.* braised.

étouffer, *vb.* smother.

étourderie, *n.f.* thoughtlessness.

étourdi, *adj.* thoughtless.

étourdir, *vb.* daze.

étourdissant, *adj.* dazing.

étourdissement, *n.m.* dizziness.

étrange, *adj.* strange.

étranger, *n.m. and adj.* alien.

étranglement, *n.m.* strangulation.
étrangler, *vb.* strangle.
étrave, *n.f.* stem, bow.
être, 1. *n.m.* being. **2.** *vb.* be.
étrécir, *vb.* shrink.
étreindre, *vb.* clasp.
étreinte, *n.f.* clasp; hug, embrace.
étrier, *n.m.* stirrup.
étrille, *n.f.* currycomb.
étroit, *adj.* narrow.
Étrusque, *n.m.f.* Etruscan.
étrusque, *adj.* Etruscan.
étude, *n.f.* study.
étudiant, *n.m.* student.
étudier, *vb.* study.
étui, *n.m.* **1.** case. **2.** needle case.
étuve, *n.f.* steam room.
étymologie, *n.f.* etymology.
étymologique, *adj.* etymological.
eucalyptus, *n.m.* eucalyptus.
eucharistie, *n.f.* eucharist.
eunuque, *n.m.* eunuch.
euphémique, *adj.* euphemistic.
euphémisme, *n.m.* euphemism.
euphonie, *n.f.* euphony.
euphonique, *adj.* euphonic.
euphorie, *n.f.* euphoria.
Europe, *n.f.* Europe.
Européen, *n.m.* European.
européen, *adj.* European.
euthanasie, *n.f.* euthanasia.
eux, *pron. m.pl.* them.
évacuable, *adj.* able to be evacuated.
évacuation, *n.f.* evacuation.
évacuer, *vb.* evacuate.
évader, *vb.* s'é., escape.
évaluateur, *n.m.* appraiser.
évaluation, *n.f.* appraisal.
évaluer, *vb.* evaluate, rate, assess.
évangélique, *adj.* evangelic.
évangéliste, *n.m.* evangelist.
évangile, *n.m.* gospel.
évanouir, *vb.* s'é., fade away; faint.
évanouissement, *n.m.* fainting fit.
évaporation, *n.f.* evaporation.
évaporer, *vb.* evaporate.
évasif, *adj.* evasive.
évasion, *n.f.* escape.
évêché, *n.m.* bishopric.
éveil, *n.m.* alertness.
éveillé, *adj.* sprightly.
éveiller, *vb.* wake.
événement, *n.m.* event.
éventail, *n.m.* fan.

éventrer, *vb.* disembowel.
éventualité, *n.f.* possibility.
éventuel, *adj.* possible.
éventuellement, *adv.* possibly.
évêque, *n.m.* bishop.
éviction, *n.f.* eviction.
évidemment, *adv.* evidently.
évidence, *n.f.* evidence. **en é.,** conspicuous.
évident, *adj.* obvious, evident.
évider, *vb.* scoop out.
évier, *n.m.* sink.
évincer, *vb.* oust.
éviscérer, *vb.* eviscerate, disembowel.
évitable, *adj.* avoidable.
éviter, *vb.* avoid.
évocateur, *adj.* evocative.
évocation, *n.f.* evocation.
évolué, *adj.* mature.
évolution, *n.f.* evolution.
évoquer, *vb.* evoke.
exact (-kt), *adj.* exact, precise.
exactement, *adv.* exactly.
exactitude, *n.f.* precision.
exagération, *n.f.* exaggeration.
exagéré, *adj.* excessive.
exagérer, *vb.* exaggerate.
exaltant, *adj.* exciting.
exaltation, *n.f.* exaltation.
exalté, *adj.* impassioned.
exalter, *vb.* exalt, elate.
examen, *n.m.* examination.
examiner, *vb.* examine.
exaspération, *n.f.* exasperation.
exaspérer, *vb.* exasperate, aggravate.
exaucer, *vb.* grant.
excavateur, *n.m.* steam shovel.
excavation, *n.f.* excavation.
excaver, *vb.* excavate.
excédent, *n.m.* excess; overweight.
excéder, *vb.* exceed.
excellence, *n.f.* excellence; excellency, highness.
excellent, *adj.* excellent.
exceller, *vb.* excel.
excentrique, *adj.* eccentric.
excepté, *prep.* except.
excepter, *vb.* except.
exception, *n.f.* exception.
exceptionnel, *adj.* exceptional.
excès, *n.m.* excess.
excessif, *adj.* excessive, extreme.
exciser, *vb.* excise; cut out.

excitabilité, *n.f.* excitability.
excitable, *adj.* excitable.
excitant, 1. *n.m.* stimulant. **2.** *adj.* stimulating.
exciter, *vb.* excite.
exclamatif, *adj.* exclamatory.
exclamation, *n.f.* exclamation.
exclamer, *vb.* exclaim.
exclure, *vb.* exclude.
exclusif, *adj.* exclusive.
exclusion, *n.f.* exclusion.
excommunication, *n.f.* excommunication.
excommunier, *vb.* excommunicate.
excorier, *vb.* excoriate.
excrément, *n.m.* excrement.
excréter, *vb.* excrete.
excrétion, *n.f.* excretion.
excroissance, *n.f.* (out)growth.
excursion, *n.f.* excursion.
excursionniste, *n.m.f.* excursionist.
excusable, *adj.* excusable.
excuse, *n.f.* plea; excuse.
excuser, *vb.* excuse. **s'e. de,** apologize for.
exécrable, *adj.* atrocious.
exécrer, *vb.* loathe.
exécuter, *vb.* perform; enforce.
exécuteur, *n.m.* executor.
exécutif, *adj. and n.m.* executive.
exécution, *n.f.* performance; enforcement; execution.
exemplaire, 1. *n.m.* copy. **2.** *adj.* exemplary.
exemple, *n.m.* instance, example.
exempt, *adj.* exempt.
exempt de droits, *adj.* duty-free.
exempter, *vb.* exempt.
exemption, *n.f.* exemption.
exerçant, *adj.* practicing.
exercer, *vb.* exercise; drill, train. **s'e.,** practice.
exercice, *n.m.* exercise; drill, practice.
exhalation, *n.f.* exhalation.
exhaler, *vb.* exhale.
exhaustion, *n.f.* exhaust.
exhiber, *vb.* show, present; exhibit.
exhibition, *n.f.* exhibition.
exhortation, *n.f.* exhortation.
exhorter, *vb.* exhort.
exhumer, *vb.* exhume.
exigeant, *adj.* demanding.

exigence, *n.f.* requirement.
exiger, *vb.* require, exact, demand.
exigu, *m.* **exiguë** *ĕ adj.* tiny.
exil (-l), *n.m.* exile.
exilé, *n.m.* exile.
exiler, *vb.* banish.
existant, *adj.* existent.
existence, *n.f.* existence.
exister, *vb.* exist.
exode, *n.m.* exodus.
exonération, *n.f.* exoneration.
exonérer, *vb.* exonerate.
exorbitant, *adj.* exorbitant.
exorciser, *vb.* exorcise.
exotique, *adj.* exotic.
expansible, *adj.* expansible.
expansif, *adj.* expansive.
expansion, *n.f.* expansion.
expatriation, *n.f.* expatriation.
expatrié, *n.m.* exile, expatriate.
expectorant, *adj. and n.m.* expectorant.
expectorer, *vb.* expectorate.
expédient, *n.m.* makeshift.
expédier, *vb.* dispatch.
expéditif, *adj.* expeditious.
expédition, *n.f.* dispatch; expedition, shipment.
expérience, *n.f.* experience; experiment.
expérimental, *adj.* experimental.
expérimentation, *n.f.* experimentation.
expérimenté, *adj.* experienced.
expert, *adj. and n.m.* expert.
expiable, *adj.* expiable.
expiation, *n.f.* atonement.
expier, *vb.* atone for.
expiration, *n.f.* expiration.
expirer, *vb.* expire.
explétif, *n.m. and adj.* expletive.
explicatif, *adj.* explanatory.
explication, *n.f.* explanation.
explicite, *adj.* explicit, clear.
expliquer, *vb.* explain.
exploit, *n.m.* feat, exploit.
exploitation, *n.f.* exploitation; working.
exploiter, *vb.* exploit.
explorateur, *n.m.* explorer.
exploratif, *adj.* exploratory.
exploration, *n.f.* exploration.
explorer, *vb.* explore.
exploser, *vb.* explode.
explosible, *adj.* explosive.

explosif, *adj. and n.m.* explosive.
explosion, *n.f.* blast, explosion.
exportation, *n.f.* export, exportation.
exporter, *vb.* export.
exposé, *n.m.* account, statement.
exposer, *vb.* expound; expose; exhibit.
exposition, *n.f.* exposition; exposure; show, display.
exprès, 1. *n.m.* special delivery. **2.** *adj.* express. **3.** *adv.* on purpose.
express, *n.m.* espresso.
expressif, *adj.* expressive.
expression, *n.f.* expression.
exprimable, *adj.* expressible.
exprimer, *vb.* express.
exproprier, *vb.* expropriate.
expulser, *vb.* expel.
expulsion, *n.f.* expulsion.
expurgation, *n.f.* expurgation.
expurger, *vb.* expurgate.
exquis, *adj.* exquisite.
exsangue, *adj.* bloodless.
exsuder, *vb.* exude.
extase, *n.f.* ecstasy.
extasier, *vb.* s'e. sur, rave about.
extatique, *adj.* ecstatic.
extensif, *adj.* extensive.
extension, *n.f.* extension.
exténuation, *n.f.* extenuation.
exténuer, *vb.* extenuate, exhaust.
extérieur, 1. *n.m.* exterior. **2.** *adj.* exterior, outer.
extérieurement, *adv.* externally.
extermination, *n.f.* extermination.

exterminer, *vb.* exterminate.
externat, *n.m.* day school.
externe, *adj.* external.
exterritorialité, *n.f.* extraterritoriality.
extincteur, *n.m.* fire extinguisher.
extinction, *n.f.* extinction.
extirper, *vb.* extirpate, root out.
extorquer, *vb.* extort.
extorsion, *n.f.* extortion.
extra, *adj.* first-rate.
extra-, *prefix* extra.
extraction, *n.f.* extraction; descent.
extrader, *vb.* extradite.
extradition, *n.f.* extradition.
extra-fin, *adj.* extremely fine.
extraire, *vb.* extract.
extrait, *n.m.* extract; abstract.
extraordinaire, *adj.* extraordinary, unusual.
extraordinairement, *adv.* extraordinarily.
extravagance, *n.f.* extravagance.
extravagant, *adj.* extravagant.
extraverti, *n.m.* extrovert.
extrême, *adj. and n.m.* extreme.
extrémiste, *n.m.f.* extremist.
extrémité, *n.f.* extremity.
extrinsèque, *adj.* extrinsic.
extroverti, *n.m.* extrovert.
extrusion, *n.f.* extrusion.
exubérance, *n.f.* exuberance.
exubérant, *adj.* exuberant.
exultation, *n.f.* exultation.
exulter, *vb.* exult.

F

fable, *n.f.* fable.
fabliau, *n.m.* fabliau.
fabricant, *n.m.* maker, manufacturer.
fabricateur, *n.m.* forger.
fabrication, *n.f.* make.
fabrique, *n.f.* factory.
fabriquer, *vb.* manufacture.
fabuleux, *adj.* fabulous.
fabuliste, *n.m.* fabulist.
fac, *n.f.* (colloquial) university.
façade, *n.f.* front.
face, *n.f.* face. **en f. de,** opposite. **faire f. à,** confront.
facétie, *n.f.* joke, prank.

facétieux, *adj.* facetious.
facette, *n.f.* facet.
fâché, *j.* angry; sorry.
fâcher, *vb.* anger, offend; grieve. **se f.,** get angry.
fâcherie, *n.f.* quarrel, argument.
fâcheux, *adj.* unpleasant.
facial, *adj.* facial.
facile, *adj.* easy.
facilité, *n.f.* fluency; ease.
faciliter, *vb.* facilitate, make easy.
façon, *n.f.* way, manner, fashion. **de f. à,** so as to.
faconde, *n.f.* glibness; fluency.
façonner, *vb.* shape, fashion.

facsimilé, *n.m.* facsimile.

facteur, *n.m.* factor, element; mail carrier.

factice, *adj.* artificial.

factieux, *adj.* factious; quarrelsome.

faction, *n.f.* faction, party.

factionnaire, *n.m.* sentry.

facture, *n.f.* invoice, bill.

facturer, *vb.* bill; send an invoice to.

facultatif, *adj.* optional.

faculté, *n.f.* faculty.

fadaise, *n.f.* nonsense.

fade, *adj.* insipid.

fadeur, *n.f.* insipidity.

fagot, *n.m.* bundle.

faible, *adj.* weak, faint, dim, feeble.

faiblement, *adv.* feebly, weakly.

faiblesse, *n.f.* weakness, frailty; dimness.

faiblir, *vb.* weaken.

faïence, *n.f.* earthenware.

faille, *n.f.* fault.

failli, *adj.* and *n.m.* bankrupt.

faillibilité, *n.f.* fallibility.

faillible, *adj.* fallible.

faillir, *vb.* fail.

faillite, *n.f.* bankruptcy.

faim, *n.f.* hunger.

fainéant, *n.m.* loafer.

faire, *vb.* make, do. **f. part,** inform. **f. mal à,** hurt. **f. voir,** show.

faire-part, *n.m.* announcement.

faisable, *adj.* feasible.

faisan, *n.m.* pheasant.

faisceau, *n.m.* bundle; beam.

fait, *n.m.* fact. **tout à f.,** wholly.

falaise, *n.f.* cliff.

fallacieux, *adj.* fallacious.

falloir, *vb.* be necessary. **comme il faut,** decent.

falot, *n.m.* lamp.

falsificateur, *n.* forger; falsifier.

falsification, *n.f.* falsification.

falsifier, *vb.* falsify.

famélique, *adj.* starving.

fameux, *adj.* famous.

familial, *adj.* family.

familiariser, *vb.* familiarize.

familiarité, *n.f.* familiarity.

familier, *adj.* familiar.

familièrement, *adv.* familiarly.

famille, *n.f.* family, household.

famine, *n.f.* famine.

fanatique, *adj. and n.m.f.* fanatic.

fanatisme, *n.m.* fanaticism.

faner, *vb.* fade.

fanfare, *n.f.* fanfare.

fanfaronnade, *n.f.* boast.

fange, *n.f.* filth; vice.

fantaisie, *n.f.* fancy, fantasy.

fantaisiste, *adj.* eccentric.

fantasme, *n.m.* fantasy.

fantastique, *adj.* fantastic.

fantoche, *n.m.* puppet.

fantôme, *n.m.* phantom, ghost; joke.

faon, *n.m.* fawn.

faramineux, *adj.* phenomenal.

farce, *n.f.* stuffing; farce.

farceur, *n.m.* jokester.

farcir, *vb.* stuff.

fard, *n.m.* facial makeup.

fardeau, *n.m.* burden.

farfelu, *adj.* weird.

farinacé, *adj.* farinaceous.

farine, *n.f.* meal, flour.

farniente, *n.m.* idleness.

farouche, *adj.* fierce; sullen, shy.

fascinant, *adj.* fascinating.

fascination, *n.f.* fascination.

fascine, *n.f.* faggot (of wood).

fasciner, *vb.* fascinate.

fascisme, *n.m.* fascism.

fasciste, *n.m.f.* fascist.

faste, *n.m.* ostentation.

fast-food, *n.m.* fast-food establishment.

fastidieux, *adj.* dull.

fat, *adj.* foppish.

fatal, *adj.* mortal, fatal.

fatalisme, *n.m.* fatalism.

fataliste, *n.m.f.* fatalist.

fatalité, *n.f.* fatality; misfortune.

fatidique, *adj.* fateful.

fatigant, *adj.* tiring.

fatigue, *n.f.* weariness.

fatiguer, *vb.* tire.

fatuité, *n.f.* smugness.

faubourg, *n.m.* suburb.

faubourien, *adj.* suburban.

fauché, *adj.* broke.

faucher, *vb.* mow.

faucheur, *n.m.* reaper, mower.

faucille, *n.f.* sickle.

faucon, *n.m.* hawk.

fauconneau, *n.m.* young falcon.

fauconnerie, *n.f.* falconry.

faufil, *n.m.* basting thread.

faufiler, *vb.* baste.

faune, *n.f.* fauna, wildlife.

faussaire, *n.m.f.* forger; liar.

faussement, *adv.* falsely.

fausser, *vb.* pervert, warp, distort.

fausset, *n.m.* falsetto; spigot, faucet.

fausseté, *n.f.* falseness.

faute, *n.f.* fault, mistake. **f. de,** for want of.

fauteuil, *n.m.* armchair.

fauteur, *n.m.* trouble-maker.

fautif, *adv.* faulty, wrong.

fauve, *adj.* wild.

faux, 1. *n.m.* forgery. **2.** *n.f.* scythe.

faux *m.,* **fausse** *f. adj.* false, wrong; spurious; counterfeit.

faux-filet, *n.m.* sirloin.

faveur, *n.f.* favor. **en f. de,** on behalf of.

favorable, *adj.* conducive, favorable.

favorablement, *adv.* favorably.

favori, *n.m.* whisker.

favori *m.,* **favorite** *f. adj. and n.* favorite.

favoriser, *vb.* favor.

favoritisme, *n.m.* favoritism.

fax, *n.m.* fax (machine).

faxer, *vb.* fax.

fayot, *n.m.* kidney bean.

féal, *adj.* faithful.

fébrile, *adj.* feverish.

fécal, *adj.* fecal.

fécond, *adj.* fertile.

féconder, *vb.* fertilize.

fécondité, *n.f.* fertility.

féculent, *adj.* starchy.

fédéral, *adj.* federal.

fédéraliser, *vb.* federalize.

fédéraliste, *n.m.f. and adj.* federalist.

fédération, *n.f.* confederacy, federation.

fédérer, *vb.* federate.

fée, *n.f.* fairy.

féerie, *n.f.* fairyland.

féerique, *adj.* fairylike.

feindre, *vb.* feign, pretend.

feinte, *n.f.* feint.

fêler, *vb.* crack.

félicitation, *n.f.* congratulation.

félicité, *n.f.* bliss.

féliciter, *vb.* congratulate.

félin, *adj.* feline.

félon, *adj.* disloyal.

fêlure, *n.f.* crack.

femelle, *adj. and n.f.* female.

féminin, *adj.* female, feminine.

féministe, *n.m.f.* feminist.

femme, *n.f.* woman, wife. **f. de chambre,** chambermaid.

fémoral, *adj.* femoral.

fémur, *n.m.* thighbone.

fendille, *n.f.* crack.

fendiller, *vb.* **se f.,** crack.

fendoir, *n.m.* cleaver.

fendre, *vb.* split, rip.

fenêtre, *n.f.* window.

fenil, *n.m.* hayloft.

fenouil, *n.m.* fennel.

fente, *n.f.* crack; rip, split.

féodal, *adj.* feudal.

féodalité, *n.f.* feudalism.

fer (-r), *n.m.* iron. **chemin de f.,** railway. **fil de f.,** wire. **f. à cheval,** horseshoe.

fermail, *n.m.* brooch; clasp.

ferme, *n.f.* farm. **maison de f.,** farmhouse.

ferme, *adj.* firm, steady, fast.

fermement, *adv.* firmly.

ferment, *n.m.* ferment.

fermentation, *n.f.* fermentation.

fermenter, *vb.* ferment.

fermer, *vb.* close. **f. à clef,** lock.

fermeté, *n.f.* firmness.

fermeture, *n.f.* closing.

fermier, *n.m.* farmer.

féroce, *adj.* fierce.

férocité, *n.f.* ferocity.

ferraille, *n.f.* old iron.

ferreux, *adj.* ferrous.

ferrique, *adj.* ferric.

ferroviaire, *adj.* rail(way).

fertile, *adj.* fertile.

fertilisant, *n.m.* fertilizer.

fertilisation, *n.f.* fertilization.

fertiliser, *vb.* fertilize.

fertilité, *n.f.* fertility.

férule, *n.f.* cane, rod.

fervemment, *adv.* fervently.

fervent, *adj.* fervent.

ferveur, *n.f.* fervor.

fesse, *n.f.* buttock.

fessée, *n.f.* spanking.

fesser, *vb.* spank.

festin, *n.m.* feast.

festiner, *vb.* feast.

festival, *n.m.* festival.

feston, *n.m.* festoon.

fête, *n.f.* feast, party. **jour de f.,** holiday.

fêter, *vb.* fete.

fétiche, *n.m.* fetish.

fétide, *adj.* fetid.

feu, *n.m.* fire. **f. de joie,** bonfire. **f. d'artifice,** fireworks. **prendre f.,** catch fire. **coup de f.,** shot.

feu, *adj.* late (deceased).

feuillage, *n.m.* foliage.

feuille, *n.f.* leaf; sheet; foil.

feuillet, *n.m.* leaf.

feuilleter, *vb.* skim (book); roll and turn (pastry).

feuilleton, *n.m.* serial, TV series.

feutre, *n.m.* felt.

fève, *n.f.* bean.

février, *n.m.* February.

fez, *n.m.* fez.

fi, *interj.* fie!

fiable, *adj.* reliable.

fiacre, *n.m.* cab.

fiançailles, *n.f.pl.* engagement, betrothal.

fiancé, *n.m.* fiancé.

fiancer, *vb.* betroth.

fiasco, *n.m.* fiasco.

fibre, *n.f.* fiber.

fibreux, *adj.* fibrous.

ficeler, *vb.* tie up.

ficelle, *n.f.* string, twine.

fiche, *n.f.* slip (of paper).

ficher, *vb.* **se f. de,** care nothing about.

fichier, *n.m.* card index, file.

fichu, *adj.* ruined.

fictif, *adj.* fictitious.

fiction, *n.f.* fiction.

fidèle, *adj.* faithful.

fidélité, *n.f.* fidelity, loyalty, allegiance.

fief, *n.m.* fief.

fiel, *n.m.* gall.

fiente, *n.f.* dung.

fier (-r), *adj.* proud.

fier, *vb.* **se f.,** trust.

fierté, *n.f.* trust.

fièvre, *n.f.* fever.

fiévreux, *adj.* feverish.

fifre, *n.m.* fife(r).

figer, *vb.* coagulate.

figue, *n.f.* fig.

figurant, *n.m.* extra (film).

figuratif, *adj.* figurative.

figure, *n.f.* face; figure.

figurer, *vb.* figure, imagine. **se f.,** fancy.

fil (-l), *n.m.* thread, string. **f. de fer,** wire.

filament, *n.m.* filament.

filature, *n.f.* spinning mill.

file, *n.f.* file.

filer, *vb.* spin.

filet, *n.m.* net.

filial, *adj.* filial.

filière, *n.f.* network.

filin, *n.m.* rope.

fille, *n.f.* daughter. **jeune f.,** girl. **vieille f.,** old maid.

fillette, *n.f.* little girl.

filleul, *n.m.* godson.

film, *n.m.* film.

filmer, *vb.* film.

filou, *n.m.* thief.

fils (fēs), *n.m.* son.

filtrant, *adj.* filtering.

filtration, *n.f.* filtration.

filtre, *n.m.* filter.

filtrer, *vb.* filter.

fin, 1. *n.f.* end. **2.** *adj.* fine; sharp; clever.

final, *adj.* final.

finaliste, *n.m.f.* finalist.

finalité, *n.f.* finality.

finance, *n.f.* finance.

financer, *vb.* finance.

financier, 1. *n.m.* financier. **2.** *adj.* financial.

finasser, *vb.* finesse.

finesse, *n.f.* fineness; slimness.

finir, *vb.* finish.

Finlande, *n.f.* Finland.

Finnois, *n.m.* Finn.

finnois, *adj.* and *n.m.* Finnish.

firmament, *n.m.* firmament.

firme, *n.f.* company.

fisc, *n.m.* tax authorities.

fiscal, *adj.* fiscal.

fissure, *n.f.* fissure.

fiston, *n.m.* (colloquial) son.

fixation, *n.f.* fixation.

fixe, *adj.* set, fixed.

fixer, *vb.* fix, settle; stare at.

fixité, *n.f.* fixity.

flaccidité, *n.f.* flabbiness.

flacon, *n.m.* bottle.

flagellation, *n.f.* flagellation.

flageller, *vb.* flog.

flageolet, *n.m.* kidney bean.
flagrant, *adj.* flagrant.
flair, *n.m.* flair.
flairer, *vb.* smell.
flamand, *adj.* Flemish.
flambant, *adj.* flaming.
flambeau, *n.m.* torch.
flambée, *n.f.* blaze.
flamber, *vb.* blaze.
flamboyant, *adj.* flaming; flamboyant.
flamboyer, *vb.* flame, flare.
flamme, *n.f.* flame.
flan, *n.m.* custard pie.
flanc, *n.m.* side, flank.
flanchet, *n.m.* flank (of beef).
flanelle, *n.f.* flannel.
flâner, *vb.* saunter, stroll; loiter, loaf.
flâneur, *n.m.* idler.
flanquer, *vb.* flank.
flaque, *n.f.* puddle.
flash, *n.m.* flash, news flash.
flasque, *adj.* flabby.
flatter, *vb.* flatter.
flatterie, *n.f.* flattery.
flatteur, *n.m.* flatterer.
fléau, *n.m.* scourge, plague.
flèche, *n.f.* arrow.
fléchir, *vb.* bend.
flegmatique, *adj.* phlegmatic.
flegme, *n.m.* phlegm.
flemmard, *n.m.* lazybones.
flemme, *n.f.* laziness.
flet, *n.m.* flounder.
flétan, *n.m.* halibut.
flétrir, *vb.* wilt, wither.
fleur, *n.f.* flower, blossom, bloom.
fleuret, *n.m.* foil.
fleuri, *adj.* flowery.
fleurir, *vb.* flower, bloom, blossom.
fleuriste, *n.m.* florist.
fleuve, *n.m.* river.
flexibilité, *n.f.* flexibility.
flexible, *adj.* flexible.
flic, *n.m.* (colloquial) cop.
flipper, *n.m.* pinball.
flirt (-t), *n.m.* flirtation.
flirter, *vb.* flirt.
flocon, *n.m.* flake.
flore, *n.f.* flora.
florissant, *adj.* prosperous, flourishing.
flot, *n.m.* wave. **à f.**, afloat.

flottant, *adj.* floating; irresolute.
flotte, *n.f.* fleet.
flottement, *n.m.* fluctuation; wavering.
flotter, *vb.* float.
flou, *adj.* hazy, indistinct.
fluctuation, *n.f.* fluctuation.
fluctuer, *vb.* fluctuate.
fluet *m.*, **fluette** *f.* *adj.* thin, delicate.
fluide, *adj. and n.m.* fluid, liquid.
fluidité, *n.f.* fluidity.
fluor, *n.m.* fluoride.
fluorescent, *adj.* fluorescent.
flûte, *n.f.* flute.
flûté, *adj.* soft; flutelike.
fluvial, *adj.* river.
flux, *n.m.* flow, flux.
fluxion, *n.f.* inflammation.
foi, *n.f.* faith; trust.
foie, *n.m.* liver.
foin, *n.m.* hay.
foire, *n.f.* fair.
fois, *n.f.* time. **à la f.**, at once.
foison, *n.f.* abundance.
foisonner, *vb.* abound.
folâtre, *adj.* frisky.
folâtrer, *vb.* frolic.
folichon, *adj.* playful.
folie, *n.f.* mania, madness, folly.
folklore, *n.m.* folklore.
follement, *adv.* foolishly.
follet, *adj.* merry, playful.
fomenter, *vb.* foment.
foncé, *adj.* dark.
foncer, *vb.* deepen.
fonction, *n.f.* function.
fonctionnaire, *n.m.* official, civil servant.
fonctionnement, *n.m.* operation, working.
fonctionner, *vb.* function, work.
fonctions, *n.f.pl.* office.
fond, *n.m.* bottom, (back)ground. **à f.**, thorough(ly). **au f.**, fundamentally.
fondamental, *adj.* basic, fundamental.
fondateur, *n.m.* founder.
fondation, *n.f.* foundation, establishment.
fondé, *adj.* authentic; (*comm.*) funded.
fondement, *n.m.* foundation.
fonder, *vb.* found.

fonderie, n.f. foundry.
fondre, vb. melt; fuse.
fondrière, n.f. bog.
fonds, n.m. fund.
fondu, adj. melted, molten.
fongus (-s), n.m. fungus.
fontaine, n.f. fountain.
fonte, n.f. melting.
fonts, n.m.pl. font.
foot, n.m. (colloquial) football.
football, n.m. football.
footing, n.m. walking; jogging.
forain, n.m. peddler.
forçat, n.m. convict.
force, n.f. strength, force; emphasis.
forcé, adj. forced; far-fetched.
forcément, adv. of necessity.
forcené, adj. frantic.
forceps, n.m. forceps.
forcer, vb. force, compel.
forcir, vb. thrive.
forer, vb. bore, drill.
forestier, n.m. forest ranger.
foret, n.m. drill.
forêt, n.f. forest.
foreuse, n.f. drill.
forfait, n.m. crime; forfeit; contract.
forfaiture, n.f. mishandling.
forfanterie, n.f. bragging.
forge, n.f. forge.
forger, vb. forge.
forgeron, n.m. blacksmith.
forgeur, n.m. forger; inventor.
formaliser, vb. formalize.
formaliste, adj. formal; precise.
formalité, n.f. formality, ceremony.
formater, vb. format.
formation, n.f. formation, training.
forme, n.f. shape, form.
formel, adj. formal.
former, vb. form, shape.
formidable, adj. tremendous; formidable.
formulaire, n.m. form.
formule, n.f. formula; form.
formuler, vb. formulate, draw up.
fort, 1. n.m. fort. **2.** adj. strong, loud. **3.** adv. hard.
forteresse, n.f. fort(ress).
fortifiant, adj. strengthening.
fortification, n.f. fortification.

fortifier, vb. strengthen.
fortuit, adj. accidental.
fortuité, n.f. fortuitousness.
fortune, n.f. fortune.
fortuné, adj. lucky, fortunate.
fosse, n.f. pit.
fossé, n.m. ditch; dike.
fossette, n.f. dimple.
fossile, n.m. fossil.
fossoyer, vb. dig a trench.
fou m., **folle** f. adj. mad, crazy, demented.
foudre, n.m. thunderbolt.
foudroyant, adj. terrifying, crushing.
foudroyer, vb. crush, blast.
fouet, n.m. whip, lash.
fouetter, vb. flog, whip.
fougère, n.f. fern.
fougue, n.f. ardor.
fougueux, adj. fiery, impetuous.
fouille, n.f. excavation.
fouiller, vb. ransack.
fouillis, n.m. litter, mess.
fouir, vb. dig, burrow.
foulard, n.m. scarf.
foule, n.f. crowd, mob.
fouler, vb. trample.
foulure, n.f. sprain; wrench.
four, n.m. oven.
fourbe, 1. n.m. knave. **2.** adj. scheming.
fourberie, n.f. knavery.
fourbir, vb. polish.
fourche, n.f. fork.
fourchette, n.f. fork.
fourgon, n.m. wagon.
fourmi, n.f. ant.
fourmillement, n.m. swarming; tingling.
fourmiller, vb. mill; swarm.
fourneau, n.m. stove, furnace.
fournée, n.f. batch.
fourniment, n.m. equipment.
fournir de, vb. supply, furnish.
fournisseur, n.m. tradesman.
fournitures, n.f.pl. supplies.
fourrage, n.m. fodder, forage.
fourrager, vb. forage.
fourré, adj. lined (of clothing); thick; wooded.
fourreau, n.m. sheath.
fourrer, vb. thrust in. **se f.,** interfere, meddle.
fourreur, n.m. furrier.

fourrure, *n.f.* fur.
fourvoyer, *vb.* mislead.
foutaise, *n.f.* (colloquial) rubbish.
foyer, *n.m.* focus; hearth. **f. domestique,** home.
frac, *n.m.* dress coat.
fracas, *n.m.* crash; rattle; noise; ado.
fracasser, *vb.* **se f.,** shatter.
fraction, *n.f.* fraction.
fracture, *n.f.* fracture.
fracturer, *vb.* break, fracture.
fragile, *adj.* brittle, delicate, frail, fragile.
fragilité, *n.f.* fragility.
fragment, *n.m.* fragment.
fragmenter, *vb.* divide up.
fraîcheur, *n.f.* freshness, coolness.
fraîchir, *vb.* freshen.
frais, *n.m.pl.* expense(s), cost, fee.
frais *m.,* **fraîche** *f. adj.* fresh, cool.
fraise, *n.f.* strawberry; ruffle.
framboise, *n.f.* raspberry.
franc, 1. *n.m.* franc **2.** *adj.m.,* **franche** *f.* frank, open.
Français, *n.m.* Frenchman.
français, *adj. and n.m.* French.
Française, *n.f.* Frenchwoman.
France, *n.f.* France.
franchement, *adv.* frankly.
franchir, *vb.* clear, cross.
franchise, *n.f.* frankness.
franciser, *vb.* make French.
franc-maçon, *n.m.* Freemason.
franco, *adv.* postage paid.
francophone, *adj.* French-speaking.
francophonie, *n.f.* French-speaking communities.
franc-parler, *n.m.* frankness.
franc-tireur, *n.m.* sniper; freelancer.
frange, *n.f.* fringe.
frangible, *adj.* breakable.
frapper, *vb.* strike, hit, rap, knock. **f. du pied,** stamp.
frasque, *n.f.* prank.
fraternel, *adj.* brotherly.
fraterniser, *vb.* fraternize.
fraternité, *n.f.* brotherhood.
fraude, *n.f.* fraud.
frauder, *vb.* defraud.
fraudeur, *n.m.* smuggler.
frauduleux, *adj.* fraudulent.
frayer, *vb.* open up; rub.

frayeur, *n.f.* fright.
fredaine, *n.f.* prank.
fredonner, *vb.* hum.
frégate, *n.f.* frigate.
frein, *n.m.* brake; check.
freiner, *vb.* brake; restrain.
frelater, *vb.* adulterate.
frêle, *adj.* frail.
frelon, *n.m.* hornet.
frémir, *vb.* tremble. **faire f.,** thrill.
frémissement, *n.m.* shiver; thrill.
frêne, *n.m.* ash (tree).
frénésie, *n.f.* frenzy.
frénétique, *adj.* frantic.
fréquemment, *adv.* often.
fréquence, *n.f.* frequency.
fréquent, *adj.* frequent.
fréquenter, *vb.* frequent, associate with.
frère, *n.m.* brother.
fresque, *n.f.* fresco.
fret, *n.m.* freight.
fréter, *vb.* charter (ship); freight.
frétillant, *adj.* lively.
frétiller, *vb.* wag; quiver.
fretin, *n.m.* young fish.
frette, *n.f.* hoop.
friand, *adj.* dainty; fond (of).
friandise, *n.f.* love of delicacies; candy.
fric, *n.m.* (colloquial) money, dough, bread.
fricoter, *vb.* cook, stew.
friction, *n.f.* friction.
frictionner, *vb.* chafe.
frigidaire, *n.m.* (trademark) refrigerator.
frigide, *adj.* frigid.
frigo, *n.m.* frozen meat; fridge.
frigorifier, *vb.* freeze; refrigerate.
frileux, *adj.* chilly; susceptible to cold.
frime, *n.f.* pretense, sham.
frimer, *vb.* put on an act.
fringant, *adj.* lively, frisky.
friper, *vb.* crush, rumple.
fripier, *n.m.* secondhand clothing dealer.
fripon, 1. *adj.* knavish. **2.** *n.m.* rascal.
friponnerie, *n.f.* roguery.
fripouille, *n.f.* rascal.
frire, *vb.* fry.
frisé, *adj.* curly.

friser, *vb.* curl.

frisoir, *n.m.* (hair) curler.

frisson, *n.m.* shudder, shiver.

frissonnement, *n.m.* shudder, shivering.

frissonner, *vb.* shudder, shiver.

frites, *n.f.pl.* French fries.

friture, *n.f.* frying.

frivole, *adj.* frivolous.

frivolité, *n.f.* frivolity.

froc, *n.m.* (monk's) frock.

froid, *adj. and n.m.* cold. **un peu f.,** chilly. **avoir f.,** be cold.

froideur, *n.f.* coldness.

froissé, *adj.* bruised. **être f. de,** resent.

froissement, *n.m.* crumpling; rustling, jostling.

froisser, *vb.* crease, wrinkle; bruise, hurt.

frôler, *vb.* graze.

fromage, *n.m.* cheese.

froment, *n.m.* wheat.

froncement, *n.m.* puckering, contraction.

froncer, *vb.* pucker. **f. les sourcils,** frown.

frondaison, *n.f.* foliage.

fronde, *n.f.* sling.

fronder, *vb.* sling; censure.

front, *n.m.* forehead.

frontière, *n.f.* boundary, border; frontier.

frottement, *n.m.* rubbing.

frotter, *vb.* rub.

frou-frou, *n.m.* rustle.

fructueux, *adj.* fruitful.

frugal, *adj.* frugal.

frugalité, *n.f.* frugality.

fruit, *n.m.* fruit.

fruiterie, *n.f.* fruit store.

fruitier, *n.m.* fruit seller.

fruste, *adj.* uncultivated.

frustrer, *vb.* frustrate.

fugace, *adj.* fleeting.

fugitif, *adj.* fugitive.

fugue, *n.f.* flight, escape.

fuir, *vb.* flee; shun; leak.

fuite, *n.f.* escape, flight; leak.

fume-cigarette, *n.m.* cigarette holder.

fumée, *n.f.* smoke.

fumer, *vb.* smoke.

fumeur, *n.m.* one who smokes.

fumeux, *adj.* smoky.

fumier, *n.m.* dung.

fumiste, *n.m.* shirker.

fumisterie, *n.f.* con.

funèbre, *adj.* funereal.

funérailles, *n.f.pl.* funeral.

funeste, *adj.* disastrous.

fureter, *vb.* pry.

fureur, *n.f.* fury.

furibond, *adj.* furious.

furie, *n.f.* fury.

furieux, *adj.* furious.

furtif, *adj.* sly.

fuseau, *n.m.* spindle.

fusée, *n.f.* rocket.

fuser, *vb.* melt; spread.

fusible, *n.m.* fuse wire.

fusil, *n.m.* rifle.

fusiller (-zēl yā), *vb.* shoot.

fusion, *n.f.* merger; meltdown.

fusionner, *vb.* merge.

futé, *adj.* cunning, crafty.

futile, *adj.* futile.

futur, *adj. and n.m.* future.

futurologie, *n.f.* futurology.

fuyant, *adj.* passing, transitory; fugitive.

fuyard, *n.* fugitive.

G

gâcher, *vb.* mess.

gâchette, *n.f.* trigger.

gâchis, *n.m.* waste.

gadoue, *n.f.* sludge.

gaffe, *n.f.* blunder.

gage, *n.m.* pledge, wage.

gageure, *n.f.* bet.

gagnant, *n.m.* winner.

gagner, *vb.* earn, gain, win, beat (in a game).

gai, *adj.* cheerful, cheery, merry, gay.

gaieté, *n.f.* mirth, cheer, merriment, gaiety.

gaillard, *adj.* hearty, sound.

gain, *n.m.* gain, profit.

gaine, *n.f.* girdle.

galant, 1. *n.m.* beau. **2.** *adj.* gallant, civil, courteous. **g. homme,** gentleman.

galanterie, *n.f.* courtesy, compliment.

galaxie, *n.f.* galaxy.

galbe, *n.m.* outline, contour.

galère, *n.f.* galley, ship.

galerie, *n.f.* gallery; balcony (theater).

galet, *n.m.* boulder.

galette, *n.f.* flat cake.

Galles, *n.f.pl.* **le pays de G.,** Wales.

Gallois, *n.m.* Welshman.

gallois, *adj. and n.m.* Welsh.

gallon, *n.m.* gallon.

galon, *n.m.* stripe, braid.

galop, *n.m.* gallop.

galoper, *vb.* gallop.

galvaudé, *adj.* worthless.

gambader, *vb.* frolic.

gamin, *n.m.* boy; urchin.

gamme, *n.f.* scale.

gangster (-r), *n.m.* gangster.

gant, *n.m.* glove.

ganterie, *n.f.* glove shop.

garage, *n.m.* garage.

garagiste, *n.m.f.* garage keeper, car mechanic.

garant, *n.m.* sponsor.

garantie, *n.f.* guarantee, pledge.

garantir, *vb.* guarantee, pledge; warrant.

garçon, *n.m.* boy; waiter; bachelor; flight attendant.

garçonnière, *n.f.* bachelor's apartment.

garde, *n.f.* watch, guard; custody. **prendre g. à,** beware of. **avant-g.,** vanguard. **g. du corps,** bodyguard.

garde-boue, *n.m.* fender.

garde-feu, *n.m.* fender (fireplace).

garde-manger, *n.m.* pantry.

garder, *vb.* guard, keep, mind.

garderie, *n.f.* nursery, day-care center.

garde-robe, *n.f.* wardrobe.

gardeur, *n.m.* keeper.

gardien, *n.m.* keeper, guard, watchman, guardian.

gare, 1. *n.f.* station. **2.** *interj.* look out!

garer, *vb.* garage, park.

gargariser, *vb.* se **g.,** gargle.

gargarisme, *n.m.* gargle.

gargouille, *n.f.* gargoyle.

garnement, *n.m.* rascal.

garni, *adj.* furnished; garnished.

garnir, *vb.* trim, garnish.

garnison, *n.f.* garrison.

garniture, *n.f.* fittings.

gars, *n.m.* chap, guy.

gas-oil, *n.m.* diesel (oil).

gaspillage, *n.m.* waste.

gaspiller, *vb.* waste, squander.

gastronomique, *adj.* gastronomic.

gâteau, *n.m.* cake. **g. de miel,** honeycomb. **g. sec,** cookie.

gâter, *vb.* spoil.

gâterie, *n.f.* excessive indulgence.

gâteux, *adj.* senile.

gauche, *adj. and n.f.* left. **à g.,** on *or* to the left. *adj.* awkward, clumsy.

gaucher, *n.m.* left-handed person.

gaucherie, *n.f.* clumsiness.

gaufre, *n.f.* waffle.

gaule, *n.f.* pole.

gaulois, *adj.* Gallic; bawdy.

gausser, *vb.* se **g. de,** mock, banter.

gaver, *vb.* force-feed.

gaz (-z), *n.m.* gas.

gaze, *n.f.* gauze.

gazette, *n.f.* newspaper.

gazeux, *adj.* gassy, gaseous. **boisson gazeuse,** carbonated drink.

gazoduc, *n.m.* gas pipeline.

gazon, *n.m.* turf, lawn.

gazouillement, *n.m.* warble, twitter.

géant, *n.m.* giant.

geindre, *vb.* moan, whine.

gel, *n.m.* frost; gel.

gelé, *adj.* frozen.

gelée, *n.f.* jelly; frost.

geler, *vb.* freeze.

gélule, *n.f.* capsule.

gelures, *n.f.pl.* frostbite.

gémir, *vb.* groan, wail, moan.

gémissement, *n.m.* groan, moan.

gênant, *adj.* troublesome, bothersome.

gencive, *n.f.* gum.

gendarme, *n.m.* policeman.

gendarmerie, *n.f.* police force.

gendre, *n.m.* son-in-law.

gêne, *n.f.* trouble, uneasiness. **être à la g.,** be uneasy.

gêné, *adj.* uneasy.

généalogie, *n.f.* pedigree.

gêner, *vb.* hinder, be in the way; embarrass; bother.

général, *adj. and n.m.* general,

overhead *(comm.)*. **quartier g.,** headquarters.

généraliser, *vb.* generalize.

généralissime, *n.m.* commander-in-chief.

généraliste, *n.m.f.* general practitioner.

généralité, *n.f.* generality.

génération, *n.f.* generation.

généreusement, *adv.* generously.

généreux, *adj.* generous, liberal.

générosité, *n.f.* generosity.

génial, *adj.* of genius, highly original; *(colloquial)* fantastic.

génie, *n.m.* genius; engineer corps. **soldat du g.,** engineer.

genièvre, *n.m.* gin.

génisse, *n.f.* heifer.

genou, *n.m.* knee; *(pl.)* lap.

genre, *n.m.* kind, gender.

gens, *n.m.f.pl.* people, persons, folk.

gentiane, *n.f.* gentian.

gentil *m.*, **gentille** *f.* *adj.* pleasant, nice.

gentilhomme, *n.m.* nobleman; peer.

gentillesse, *n.f.* prettiness, gracefulness.

géographie, *n.f.* geography.

géographique, *adj.* geographical.

géologie, *n.f.* geology.

géométrie, *n.f.* geometry.

géométrique, *adj.* geometric.

gérance, *n.f.* managership.

géranium, *n.m.* geranium.

gérant, *n.m.* manager, director, superintendent.

gerbe, *n.f.* sheaf.

gerçure, *n.f.* chap.

gérer, *vb.* manage.

germain, *adj.* first (of cousins).

germe, *n.m.* germ.

germer, *vb.* sprout.

gésir, *vb.* lie.

geste, *n.m.* gesture.

gesticuler, *vb.* gesticulate.

gestion, *n.f.* management.

ghetto, *n.m.* ghetto.

gibier, *n.m.* game.

giboulée, *n.f.* sudden storm.

gicler, *vb.* spurt.

gifler, *vb.* slap.

gigantesque, *adj.* great, huge.

gigot, *n.m.* leg (of meat).

gigue, *n.f.* leg; jig.

gilet, *n.m.* vest. **g. de dessous,** undershirt.

gingembre, *n.m.* ginger.

girafe, *n.f.* giraffe.

girofle, *n.m.* **clou de g.,** clove.

giron, *n.m.* lap.

gisement, *n.m.* deposit.

gitan, *n.m.* gypsy.

gîte, *n.m.* lodging, bed.

givre, *n.m.* frost.

glabre, *adj.* smooth-shaven.

glaçage, *n.m.* frosting.

glace, *n.f.* ice; ice cream; mirror.

glacé, *adj.* icy, frozen.

glacer, *vb.* freeze.

glacial, *adj.* icy.

glacier, *n.m.* glacier.

glacière, *n.f.* icebox.

glacis, *n.m.* slope.

glaçon, *n.m.* block of ice; ice cube.

glaise, *n.f.* clay.

gland, *n.m.* acorn.

glande, *n.f.* gland.

glaner, *vb.* glean.

glapir, *vb.* yelp; screech.

glas, *n.m.* knell.

glissade, *n.f.* slide, slip.

glissant, *adj.* slippery.

glisser, *vb.* slide, slip. **se g.,** creep, sneak.

global, *adj.* entire.

globe, *n.m.* globe. **g. de l'œil,** eyeball.

globule, *n.m.* corpuscle.

gloire, *n.f.* glory.

glorieux, *adj.* glorious.

glorifier, *vb.* glorify.

glose, *n.f.* criticism; gloss.

glossaire, *n.m.* glossary.

glousser, *vb.* cluck.

glouton, *adj.* gluttonous.

gluant, *adj.* sticky.

goal, *n.m.* goalkeeper.

gobelet, *n.m.* goblet.

gober, *vb.* swallow.

godasse, *n.f.* (colloquial) shoe.

goéland, *n.m.* seagull.

goinfre, *n.m.* glutton.

golfe, *n.m.* gulf.

gomme, *n.f.* gum; eraser.

gommeux, *adj.* gummy.

gond, *n.m.* hinge.

gonflé, *adj.* swollen; full of nerve.

gonfler, *vb.* inflate; swell.

gonfleur, *n.m.* tire pump.
gorge, *n.f.* throat; gorge.
gorger, *vb.* cram.
gosier, *n.m.* throat.
gosse, *n.m.f.* kid (child).
gothique, *adj.* Gothic.
goudron, *n.m.* tar.
gouffre, *n.m.* gulf, abyss.
goujat, *n.m.* boor, cad.
goulu, *adj.* gluttonous.
gourde, *n.f.* flask.
gourer, *vb.* (colloquial) **se g.,** make a mistake.
gourmand, 1. *n.m.* glutton. **2.** *adj.* greedy.
gourmander, *vb.* scold.
gourmandise, *n.f.* greediness.
gourmer, *vb.* curb.
gourmet, *n.m.* epicure.
gourmette, *n.f.* curb (horse).
gourou, *n.m.* guru.
gousse, *n.f.* shell, pod.
goût, *n.m.* taste, relish.
goûter, 1. *n.m.* snack. **2.** *vb.* taste, relish.
goutte, *n.f.* drop; gout.
goutteux, *adj.* gouty.
gouttière, *n.f.* gutter.
gouvernail, *n.m.* rudder, helm.
gouvernante, *n.f.* governess.
gouvernement, *n.m.* government.
gouverner, *vb.* govern, rule, steer.
gouverneur, *n.m.* governor.
grabuge, *n.m.* squabble.
grâce, *n.f.* grace. **faire g. de,** spare.
gracier, *vb.* pardon.
gracieux, *adj.* graceful, gracious.
grade, *n.m.* grade, rank.
gradé, *n.m.* non-commissioned officer.
gradin, *n.m.* step, tier.
graduel, *adj.* gradual.
graduer, *vb.* graduate.
graffiti, *n.m.pl.* graffiti.
grain, *n.m.* grain, seed, berry, kernel. **g. de beauté,** mole.
graine, *n.f.* seed, berry.
graissage, *n.m.* greasing.
graisse, *n.f.* grease, fat.
graisser, *vb.* grease.
grammaire, *n.f.* grammar.
gramme, *n.m.* gram.
grand, *adj.* big, great, tall. **grand'chose,** much.
grandement, *adv.* grandly, greatly.

grandeur, *n.f.* size, height, greatness.
grandiose, *adj.* grand.
grandir, *vb.* grow.
grand-mère, *n.f.* grandmother.
grand-père, *n.m.* grandfather.
grange, *n.f.* barn.
granit (-t), *n.m.* granite.
graphique, *n.m.* chart.
grappe, *n.f.* bunch, cluster.
gras, grasse *f. adj.* fat, stout.
grassement, *adj.* plentifully.
grasset, *adj.* plump.
grassouillet, *adj.* plump.
gratification, *n.f.* bonus.
gratifier, *vb.* bestow.
gratin, *n.m.* cheese topping.
gratis (-s), *adv.* free.
gratitude, *n.f.* gratitude.
gratte-ciel, *n.m.* skyscraper.
gratter, *vb.* scrape, scratch.
gratuit, *adj.* free.
grave, *adj.* grave.
graveleux, *adj.* gritty.
graver, *vb.* engrave.
graveur, *n.m.* engraver.
gravier, *n.m.* gravel.
gravir, *vb.* climb.
gravité, *n.f.* gravity.
graviter, *vb.* gravitate.
gravure, *n.f.* engraving. **g. à l'eau-forte,** etching.
gré, *n.m.* pleasure.
Grec *m.,* **Grecque** *f. n.* Greek (person).
grec, *n.m.* Greek (language).
grec *m.,* **grecque** *f. adj.* Greek.
Grèce, *n.f.* Greece.
gréement, *n.m.* rig.
gréer, *vb.* rig.
greffer, *vb.* graft, transplant.
greffier, *n.m.* clerk.
grêle, 1. *n.f.* hail. **2.** *adj.* thin, slight.
grêler, *vb.* hail.
grêlon, *n.m.* hailstone.
grelotter, *vb.* shiver.
grenade, *n.f.* grenade; pomegranate.
grenier, *n.m.* attic.
grenouille, *n.f.* frog.
grève, *n.f.* strike. **se mettre en g.,** strike.
gréviste, *n.m.f.* striker.

gribouiller, vb. scribble.
grief, n.m. grievance.
grièvement, adv. seriously.
griffe, n.f. claw, clutch.
griffer, vb. seize; scratch.
griffonner, vb. scribble.
grignoter, vb. nibble.
gril, n.m. grill.
grillade, n.f. broiling.
grille, n.f. grate, gate.
grille-pain, n.m. toaster.
griller, vb. broil, roast, toast.
grillon, n.m. cricket.
grimace, n.f. grimace.
grimacer, vb. make faces.
grimer, vb. make up.
grimper, vb. climb.
grincer, vb. creak, grate, grind.
grippe, n.f. flu.
gris, adj. gray; drab; drunk.
griser, vb. get drunk.
grive, n.f. thrush.
grogner, vb. growl, snarl, grumble.
grommeler, vb. mutter.
gronder, vb. scold, nag; roar, rumble.
gros m., **grosse** f. adj. overly large; gross, stout, rough. **en g.,** wholesale.
groseille, n.f. currant.
grossesse, n.f. pregnancy.
grosseur, n.f. size, thickness.
grossier, adj. coarse, crude, gross.
grossièreté, n.f. coarseness.
grossir, vb. magnify, grow.
grossiste, n.m. wholesaler.
grosso modo, adv. roughly.
grotesque, adj. grotesque.

grotte, n.f. cave, grotto.
grouiller, vb. stir, swarm.
groupe, n.m. group, party; cluster.
groupement, n.m. grouping.
grouper, vb. group.
grue, n.f. crane.
gruyère, n.m. Gruyère (cheese).
gué, n.m. ford. **traverser à g.,** wade.
guêpe, n.f. wasp.
guère, adv. hardly.
guérila, n.f. guerrilla warfare.
guérir, vb. cure, heal.
guérison, n.f. cure.
guerre, n.f. war.
guerrier, adj. warlike.
guetter, vb. watch (for).
gueule, n.f. mouth, (colloquial) mouth, face.
gueuler, vb. bawl (out).
gueux, n.m. beggar, tramp.
guichet, n.m. ticket window.
guide, n.m. guide(book).
guider, vb. guide.
guidon, n.m. handlebars.
guignol, n.m. Punch and Judy show; puppet; clown.
guillemets, n.m.pl. quotation marks, inverted commas.
guillotine, n.f. guillotine.
guingan, n.m. gingham.
guirlande, n.f. garland.
guise, n.f. way, manner.
guitare, n.f. guitar.
gymnase, n.m. gymnasium.
gymnastique, n.f. gymnastics.
gynécologie, n.f. gynecology.
gynécologiste, n.m.f. gynecologist.

H

habile, adj. clever, skillful, smart, able.
habileté, n.f. craft, ability.
habillement, n.m. apparel.
habillements masculins, n.m.pl. menswear.
habiller, vb. dress.
habilleur n.m., **habilleuse** f. dresser.
habit, n.m. coat; attire; (pl.) clothes.
habitant, n.m. inhabitant, resident.

habitation, n.f. dwelling.
habiter, vb. inhabit, live.
habitude, n.f. habit, practice. **d'h.,** customarily. **avoir l'h. de,** be accustomed to.
habitué, n.m. regular visitor, regular (client).
habituel, adj. customary, usual.
habituer, vb. get used to.
hâbleur, n.m. boaster.
hache, n.f. ax.
hacher, vb. mince, chop, hack up.

hachette, *n.f.* hatchet.

hachis, *n.m.* hash.

hagard, *adj.* haggard.

haie, *n.f.* hedge.

haillon, *n.m.* rag.

haine, *n.f.* hatred.

haineux, *adj.* hating.

haïr, *vb.* hate.

haïssable, *adj.* hateful.

halage, *n.m.* towage.

hâle, *n.m.* tan; sunburn.

haleine, *n.f.* breath.

haler, *vb.* haul, tow.

hâler, *vb.* tan. **se h.,** become sun-burned.

haleter, *vb.* pant, gasp.

hall, *n.m.* hall.

halle, *n.f.* market.

hallucination, *n.f.* hallucination.

halte, *n.f.* halt.

haltère, *n.m.* dumbbell.

hamac, *n.m.* hammock.

hamburger, *n.m.* hamburger.

hameau, *n.m.* hamlet.

hameçon, *n.m.* hook.

hampe, *n.f.* handle.

hanche, *n.f.* hip.

handicap, *n.m.* handicap.

handicapé, *n.m.* handicapped (person).

hangar, *n.m.* shed.

hanter, *vb.* haunt.

hantise, *n.f.* obsession.

happer, *vb.* snap.

harcèlement, *n.m.* hassle, harassment.

harceler, *vb.* worry, bother; hassle; harass.

hardes, *n.f.pl.* togs.

hardi, *adj.* bold.

hardiesse, *n.f.* boldness.

hareng, *n.m.* herring.

hargneux, *adj.* cross, snarling.

haricot, *n.m.* bean.

harmonie, *n.f.* harmony.

harmonieux, *adj.* harmonious.

harmoniser, *vb.* put in tune, harmonize.

harnacher, *vb.* harness.

harnais, *n.m.* harness.

harpe, *n.f.* harp.

harpin, *n.m.* boat hook.

hasard, *n.m.* chance. **au h.** or **par h.,** at random.

hasarder, *vb.* venture.

hasardeux, *adj.* hazardous, unsafe.

hâte, *n.f.* haste, hurry. **à la h.,** hastily.

hâter, *vb.* hasten, hurry.

hâtif, *adj.* early, hasty.

hausse, *n.f.* rise, increase.

haussement, *n.m.* raising; shrug.

hausser, *vb.* raise; shrug.

haussier, *n.m.* bull (stock exchange).

haut, 1. *n.m.* top. **2.** *adj.* high, loud. **à haute voix,** aloud. **en h.,** up, above.

hautain, *adj.* haughty, lofty, proud.

hautbois, *n.m.* oboe.

haute fidélité, *n.f.* high fidelity.

hautement, *adv.* highly.

hauteur, *n.f.* height; haughtiness. **être à la h. de,** be up to.

hauturier, *adj.* seagoing.

hâve, *adj.* wan, gaunt.

havre, *n.m.* haven.

havresac, *n.m.* knapsack.

hebdo, *n.m.* (colloquial) weekly.

hebdomadaire, *adj.* weekly.

héberger, *vb.* shelter.

hébété, *adj.* dull.

hébreu, 1. *n.m.* Hebrew (language). **2.** *adj.* Hebrew.

hécatombe, *n.f.* slaughter.

hectare, *n.m.* hectare.

hégémonie, *n.f.* hegemony.

hein, *interj.* huh?

hélas (-s), *interj.* alas!

héler, *vb.* call, hail.

hélice, *n.f.* propeller.

hélicoptère, *n.m.* helicopter.

helvétique, *adj.* Swiss.

hématome, *n.m.* bruise.

hémisphère, *n.m.* hemisphere.

hémorragie, *n.f.* hemorrhage.

hennir, *vb.* neigh.

hépatite, *n.f.* hepatitis.

héraut, *n.m.* herald.

herbage, *n.m.* grass, pasture.

herbe, *n.f.* grass, herb; marijuana. **mauvaise h.,** weed.

herbeux, *adj.* grassy.

héréditaire, *adj.* hereditary.

hérésie, *n.f.* heresy.

hérétique, 1. *n.m.f.* heretic. **2.** *adj.* heretic, heretical.

hérisser, *vb.* bristle.

hérisson, *n.m.* hedgehog.

héritage, *n.m.* inheritance.

hériter, *vb.* inherit.

héritier, *n.m.* heir.

hermétique, *adj.* (sealed) tight.

hermine, *n.f.* ermine.

hernie, *n.f.* hernia.

héroïne, *n.f.* heroine; heroin (drug).

héroïque, *adj.* heroic.

héroïsme, *n.m.* heroism.

héros, *n.m.* hero.

hertz, *n.m.* hertz.

hésitation, *n.f.* hesitation.

hésiter, *vb.* hesitate, waver, falter.

hétéroclite, *adj.* heterogeneous.

hétérogène, *adj.* heterogeneous.

hétérosexuel *adj.* heterosexual.

hêtre, *n.m.* beech.

heure, *n.f.* hour; time. **de bonne h.,** early.

heureusement, *adv.* happily, luckily.

heureux, *adj.* glad, happy; lucky, fortunate; successful.

heurt, *n.m.* blow, shock.

heurter, *vb.* collide (with).

heurtoir, *n.m.* (door) knocker.

hexagone, *n.m.* hexagon. **L'h.,** France.

hibou, *n.m.* owl.

hideux, *adj.* hideous.

hier (-r), *adv.* yesterday.

hiérarchie, *n.f.* hierarchy.

hi-fi, *adj. and n.m.* hi-fi.

hilare, *adj.* hilarious.

hilarité, *n.f.* hilarity.

Hindou, *n.m.* Hindu.

hindou, *adj.* Hindu.

hippodrome, *n.m.* race course.

hippopotame, *n.m.* hippopotamus.

hirondelle, *n.f.* swallow.

hispanique, *adj.* Hispanic.

hisser, *vb.* hoist.

histoire, *n.f.* history; story; to-do, fuss.

historien, *n.m.* historian.

historique, *adj.* historic.

hiver (-r), *n.m.* winter.

hiverner (*h.* ..., **s'h.,** hibernate.

hocher, *vb.* shake, nod.

hochet, *n.m.* rattle.

hockey, *n.m.* hockey.

hoirie, *n.f.* inheritance.

hold-up, *n.m.* hold-up.

Hollandais, *n.m.* Hollander, Dutchman.

hollandais, *adj. and n.m.* Dutch.

Hollande, *n.f.* Holland; the Netherlands.

hologramme, *n.m.* hologram.

holographie, *n.f.* holography.

homard, *n.m.* lobster.

homicide, *n.m.* homicide.

hommage, *n.m.* homage.

hommasse, *adj.* mannish.

homme, *n.m.* man. **h. d'affaires,** businessman.

homogène, *adj.* of the same kind, homogeneous.

homologue, *n.m.* counterpart.

homonyme, *n.m.* namesake.

homosexuel, *adj.* homosexual.

Hongrie, *n.f.* Hungary.

Hongrois, *n.m.* Hungarian (person).

hongrois, 1. *n.m.* Hungarian (language). **2.** *adj.* Hungarian.

honnête, *adj.* honest.

honnêteté, *n.f.* honesty, fairness.

honneur, *n.m.* honor, credit.

honorable, *adj.* honorable.

honoraires, *n.m.pl.* fee.

honorer, *vb.* honor.

honorifique, *adj.* honorary.

honte, *n.f.* shame. **avoir h. de,** be ashamed of; **faire h. à.,** shame.

honteux, *adj.* ashamed; shameful.

hôpital, *n.m.* hospital.

hoquet, *n.m.* hiccup.

horaire, *n.m.* timetable.

horde, *n.f.* horde.

horizon, *n.m.* horizon.

horizontal, *adj.* horizontal.

horloge, *n.f.* clock.

horloger, *n.m.* watchmaker.

hormis, *prep.* except.

horreur, *n.f.* horror.

horrible, *adj.* horrible, ghastly.

horrifier, *vb.* horrify.

horrifique, *adj.* hair-raising.

horripiler, *vb.* annoy.

hors, *prep.* except (for).

hors-bord, *n.m.* outboard boat.

hors de, *prep.* out of, outside.

hors-taxe, *adj.* duty-free.

horticole, *adj.* horticultural.

hospice, *n.m.* refuge.

hospitalier, *adj.* hospitable.
hospitaliser, *vb.* hospitalize; shelter.
hospitalité, *n.f.* hospitality.
hostie, *n.f.* (*eccles.*) host.
hostile, *adj.* hostile.
hostilité, *n.f.* hostility.
hôte, *n.m.* host; guest.
hôtel, *n.m.* hotel; mansion. **h. de ville,** city hall.
hôtelier, *n.m.* innkeeper.
hôtesse, *n.f.* hostess.
hôtesse de l'air, *n.f.* stewardess, flight attendant.
hotte, *n.f.* basket carried on back.
houblon, *n.m.* hop (plant).
houe, *n.f.* hoe.
houer, *vb.* hoe.
houille, *n.f.* coal.
houillère, *n.f.* coal mine.
houle, *n.f.* surge.
houleux, *adj.* stormy, rough.
houppe, *n.f.* tuft; powder puff.
hourra, *n.m.* cheer.
housse, *n.f.* covering.
houx, *n.m.* holly.
hublot, *n.m.* porthole.
huer, *vb.* shout, hoot.
huile, *n.f.* oil.
huiler, *vb.* oil.
huileux, *adj.* oily.
huissier, *n.m.* usher.
huit, *adj. and n.m.* eight.
huitième, *adj. and n.m.f.* eighth.
huître, *n.f.* oyster.
humain, *adj.* human; humane.
humanitaire, *adj.* humanitarian.
humanité, *n.f.* humanity.
humble, *adj.* lowly, humble.
humecter, *vb.* moisten.

humer, *vb.* suck up, sniff up.
humeur, *n.f.* humor; mood, temper.
humide, *adj.* damp, humid.
humidité, *n.f.* moisture.
humiliation, *n.f.* humiliation.
humilier, *vb.* humiliate, humble.
humilité, *n.f.* humility.
humoristique, *adj.* humorous.
humour, *n.m.* humor.
hune, *n.f.* (*naut.*) top.
huppe, *n.f.* tuft, crest.
hurlement, *n.m.* noise, howling.
hurler, *vb.* howl, roar, yell.
hutte, *n.f.* hut, shed.
hybride, *adj. and n.m.* hybrid.
hydratant, *adj.* moisturizing.
hydravion, *n.m.* seaplane.
hydroélectrique, *adj.* hydroelectric.
hydrogène, *n.m.* hydrogen.
hyène, *n.f.* hyena.
hygiène, *n.f.* sanitation; hygiene.
hygiénique, *adj.* hygienic.
hymne, *n.m.* hymn; *n.f.* church hymn.
hypermarché, *n.m.* very large supermarket; hypermarket.
hypnotiser, *vb.* hypnotize.
hypocondriaque, *adj. and n.m.f.* hypochondriac.
hypocrisie, *n.f.* hypocrisy.
hypocrite, 1. *n.m.f.* hypocrite. 2. *adj.* hypocritical.
hypothèque, *n.f.* mortgage.
hypothéquer, *vb.* mortgage.
hypothèse, *n.f.* hypothesis.
hystérectomie, *n.f.* hysterectomy.
hystérie, *n.f.* hysteria.
hystérique, *adj.* hysterical.

I

ici, *adv.* here. **d'i.,** hence.
ictère, *n.m.* jaundice.
idéal, *adj. and n.m.* ideal.
idéaliser, *vb.* idealize.
idéalisme, *n.m.* idealism.
idéaliste, *n.m.f.* idealist.
idée, *n.f.* idea, notion.
identification, *n.f.* identification.
identifier, *vb.* identify.
identique, *adj.* identical.
identité, *n.f.* identity.

idéologie, *n.f.* ideology.
idiome, *n.m.* idiom.
idiot, *adj. and n.m.* idiot(ic).
idiotie, *n.f.* idiocy.
idiotisme, *n.m.* idiom.
idolâtrer, *vb.* idolize.
idole, *n.f.* idol.
idyllique, *adj.* idyllic.
if, *n.m.* yew.
ignare, *adj.* ignorant.
ignoble, *adj.* ignoble.

ignorance, *n.f.* ignorance.

ignorant, *adj.* ignorant.

ignorer, *vb.* not know.

il (ēl), *pron.* he, it; (*pl.*) they.

île, *n.f.* island.

illégal (-l-), *adj.* illegal.

illégitime (-l-), *adj.* illegitimate.

illettré (-l-), *adj.* illiterate.

illicite (-l-), *adj.* illicit.

illimité (-l-), *adj.* boundless.

illogique (-l-), *adj.* illogical.

illuminer (-l-), *vb.* light, illuminate.

illusion (-l-), *n.f.* illusion; delusion.

illustration (-l-), *n.f.* illustration.

illustre (-l-), *adj.* illustrious, famous.

illustrer (-l-), *vb.* illustrate.

îlot, *n.m.* small island.

image, *n.f.* picture.

imaginaire, *adj.* fancied, imaginary.

imaginatif, *adj.* imaginative.

imagination, *n.f.* imagination.

imaginer, *vb.* imagine.

imam, *n.m.* imam.

imbattable, *adj.* unbeatable.

imbécile, 1. *n.m.f.* idiot. **2.** *adj.* idiotic.

imbécillité, *n.f.* imbecility; stupidity.

imberbe, *adj.* beardless.

imbiber, *vb.* soak; steep.

imbu, *adj.* imbued; steeped.

imitation, *n.f.* imitation, copy.

imiter, *vb.* imitate, copy; mimic.

immaculé, *adj.* immaculate.

immangeable, *adj.* uneatable.

immatériel, *adj.* incorporeal.

immatriculer, *vb.* matriculate.

immédiat, *adj.* immediate.

immense, *adj.* immense, great, huge.

immensité, *n.f.* immensity.

immerger, *vb.* immerse.

immeuble, *n.m.* real estate.

immigrer, *v.b.* immigrate.

imminent, *adj.* imminent.

immiscer, *vb.* s'i., meddle, interfere.

immixtion, *n.f.* mixing; interference.

immobile, *adj.* motionless.

immobilier, *adj.* property.

immodéré, *adj.* immoderate.

immoler, *vb.* sacrifice. s'i., sacrifice oneself.

immonde, *adj.* filthy.

immoral, *adj.* immoral.

immortaliser, *vb.* immortalize.

immortalité, *n.f.* immortality.

immortel, *adj. and n.m.* immortal.

immuable, *adj.* unchangeable.

immuniser, *vb.* immunize.

immunité, *n.f.* immunity.

impact, *n.m.* impact.

impair, *adj.* odd (number).

impalpable, *adj.* intangible.

impardonnable, *adj.* unforgivable.

imparfait, *adj. and n.m.* imperfect.

impartial, *adj.* impartial.

impasse, *n.f.* dead end.

impassible, *adj.* impassive.

impatience, *n.f.* impatience.

impatient, *adj.* impatient.

impatienter, *vb.* provoke.

impayable, *adj.* invaluable; very funny.

impeccable, *adj.* faultless.

impécunieux, *adj.* impecunious.

impénétrable, *adj.* impenetrable.

impératif, *adj. and n.m.* imperative.

impératrice, *n.f.* empress.

imperceptible, *adj.* imperceptible.

imperfection, *n.f.* imperfection.

impérial, *adj.* imperial.

impérialisme, *n.m.* imperialism.

impérieux, *adj.* domineering.

impérissable, *adj.* imperishable.

imperméabiliser, *vb.* waterproof.

imperméable, 1. *n.m.* raincoat. **2.** *adj.* waterproof.

impersonnel, *adj.* impersonal.

impertinence, *n.f.* impertinence.

impertinent, *adj.* saucy.

impétueux, *adj.* headlong, impetuous.

impie, *adj.* impious.

impitoyable, *adj.* merciless, pitiless, ruthless.

implanter, *vb.* establish; implant.

impliquer, *vb.* involve; imply.

implorer, *vb.* implore, beg.

impoli, *adj.* rude, impolite, discourteous.

impolitesse, *n.f.* discourtesy.

impopulaire, *adj.* unpopular.

importance, *n.f.* significance, importance.

important, *adj.* momentous, important.
importateur, *n.m.* importer.
importation, *n.f.* import.
importer, *vb.* matter; import.
importun, *adj.* tiresome, bothersome; importunate.
importuner, *vb.* pester, keep bothering.
importunité, *n.f.* importunity.
imposable, *adj.* taxable.
imposer, *vb.* impose; tax; enforce.
imposition, *n.f.* imposition.
impossibilité, *n.f.* impossibility.
dans l'i. de, unable to.
impossible, *adj.* impossible.
imposteur, *n.m.* fraud (person), faker, impostor.
imposture, *n.f.* imposture, deception.
impôt, *n.m.* tax, tariff.
impotent, *adj.* weak, infirm.
impôt sur les ventes, *n.m.* sales tax.
imprécis, *adj.* imprecise.
imprégner, *vb.* impregnate, imbue.
imprenable, *adj.* impregnable.
impression, *n.f.* print, impression.
impressionnable, *adj.* sensitive, impressionable.
impressionnant, *adj.* impressive.
impressionner, *vb.* affect.
imprévisible, *adj.* unforeseeable.
imprévoyance, *n.f.* improvidence.
imprévoyant, *adj.* not foresighted.
imprévu, *adj.* unexpected, unforeseen.
imprimante, *n.f.* printer.
imprimé, *n.m.* printed matter.
imprimer, *vb.* impress; print.
imprimerie, *n.f.* printery, printing.
imprimeur, *n.m.* printer.
improbable, *adj.* improbable.
improbité, *n.f.* dishonesty.
improductif, *adj.* unproductive.
impromptu, *adv., adj. and n.m.* impromptu.
impropre, *adv.* improper, unfit.
improviste, *adv.* **à l'i.,** all of a sudden.
imprudence, *n.f.* indiscretion.
impudence, *n.f.* impudence.
impudicité, *n.f.* lewdness.
impuissance, *n.f.* impotence.

impuissant, *adj.* impotent; powerless, helpless.
impulsif, *adj.* impulsive.
impulsion, *n.f.* impulse, spur.
impunément, *adv.* with impunity.
impunité, *n.f.* impunity.
impur, *adj.* impure.
impureté, *n.f.* impurity.
imputer, *vb.* impute.
inabordable, *adj.* inaccessible.
inaccessible, *adj.* inaccessible.
inaccoutumé, *adj.* unusual.
inachevé, *adj.* unfinished.
inactif, *adj.* inactive, indolent.
inadapté, *adj.* maladjusted.
inadmissible, *adj.* unacceptable.
inadvertance, *n.f.* oversight.
inanimé, *adj.* lifeless.
inanité, *n.f.* uselessness.
inaperçu, *adj.* unperceived.
inattaquable, *adj.* unassailable.
inattendu, *adj.* unexpected.
inaugurer, *vb.* inaugurate.
inavouable, *adj.* unavowable, shameful.
incalculable, *adj.* countless, incalculable.
incapable, *adj.* unable.
incapacité, *n.f.* incapacity.
incarcérer, *vb.* imprison.
incarnat, *adj.* flesh-colored, rosy.
incarner, *vb.* embody.
incartade, *n.f.* insult, prank.
incendie, *n.m.* fire.
incendier, *vb.* set fire to.
incertain, *adj.* uncertain.
incertitude, *n.f.* suspense.
incessamment, *adv.* incessantly; immediately.
incessant, *adj.* incessant.
inceste, *n.m.* incest.
incident, *n.m.* incident.
incinérer, *vb.* cremate; incinerate.
incisif, *adj.* incisive.
incision, *n.f.* incision.
inciter, *vb.* incite.
inclinaison, *n.f.* slope.
inclination, *n.f.* bow, nod; propensity.
incliner, *vb.* slant; nod, bow. **s'i.,** lean.
inclure, *vb.* include, enclose.
inclus, *adj.* included. **ci-inclus,** enclosed, herewith.
inclusif, *adj.* inclusive.

incohérent, *adj.* incoherent.
incolore, *adj.* colorless.
incomber, *vb.* devolve upon.
incombustible, *adj.* incombustible.
incommode, *adj.* uncomfortable, inconvenient.
incommoder, *vb.* inconvenience.
incomparable, *adj.* incomparable.
incompatible, *adj.* incompatible.
incompétence, *n.f.* incompetence.
incomplet, *adj.* imperfect, unfinished.
incompréhension, *n.m.* lack of understanding.
incompris, *adj.* unappreciated, not understood.
inconditionnel, *adj.* unquestioning.
inconduite, *n.f.* misconduct.
incongru, *adj.* unseemly.
inconnu, *adj.* unknown.
inconscient, *adj. and n.m.* unconscious.
inconséquent, *adj.* inconsistent.
inconsidéré, *adj.* thoughtless.
inconsistant, *adj.* weak, inconsistent.
inconstant, *adj.* fickle.
incontestable, *adj.* unquestionable.
incontesté, *adj.* unquestioned.
incontinent, 1. *adj.* incontinent. **2.** *adv.* immediately.
incontrôlable, *adj.* not verifiable.
inconvenance, *n.f.* impropriety.
inconvénient, *n.m.* inconvenience.
incorporer, *vb.* embody.
incorrect, *adj.* incorrect.
incrédule, *adj.* incredulous.
incriminer, *vb.* accuse.
incroyable, *adj.* incredible.
incroyant, *n.m.* unbeliever.
inculper, *vb.* charge, accuse.
inculquer, *vb.* instill.
inculte, *adj.* uncultivated; unkempt.
incurable, *adj.* incurable.
incurie, *n.f.* carelessness, neglect.
incursion, *n.f.* incursion.
Inde, *n.f.* India.
indécent, *adj.* indecent.
indécis, *adj.* doubtful, vague, dim.
indéfini, *adj.* indefinite.
indéfinissable, *adj.* nondescript.

indéfrisable, *n.f.* permanent wave.
indélicat, *adj.* indelicate.
indélicatesse, *n.f.* indelicacy; blunder.
indemne, *adj.* unharmed.
indemniser, *vb.* compensate for.
indemnité, *n.f.* indemnity.
indépendance, *n.f.* independence.
indépendant, *adj.* independent.
index (-ks), *n.m.* index; forefinger.
indicateur, *n.m.* timetable; informer.
indicatif, *adj. and n.m.* indicative.
indicatif interurbain, *n.m.* area code.
indication, *n.f.* indication.
indice, *n.m.* sign, proof.
indicible, *adj.* unspeakable, inexpressible.
Indien, *n.m.* Indian.
indien, *adj.* Indian.
indifférence, *n.f.* indifference.
indifférent, *adj.* indifferent.
indigène, *n.m.f.* native.
indigent, *adj.* destitute.
indigeste, *adj.* indigestible.
indignation, *n.f.* indignation, anger.
indigne, *adj.* worthless, unworthy.
indigné, *adj.* indignant.
indigner, *vb.* anger.
indiquer, *vb.* indicate, point out.
indirect, *adj.* indirect.
indiscret, *adj.* indiscreet.
indiscutable, *adj.* indisputable.
indispensable, *adj.* indispensable, essential.
indisposer, *vb.* indispose; set against.
indisposition, *n.f.* ailment.
indistinct, *adj.* indistinct.
individu, *n.m.* individual, person.
individuel, *adj.* individual.
indomptable, *adj.* adamant; unconquerable.
indu, *adj.* undue; not ordinary.
induire, *vb.* induce; infer.
indulgence, *n.f.* indulgence.
indulgent, *adj.* lenient; indulgent.
indûment, *adv.* unduly.
industrie, *n.f.* industry.
industriel, *adj.* industrial.
inébranlable, *adj.* immovable, firm.
inédit, *adj.* unpublished.

inefficace, *adj.* ineffectual.
inégal, *adj.* uneven, unequal.
inégalité, *n.f.* inequality; irregularity.
inepte, *adj.* inept; stupid.
ineptie, *n.f.* inept action.
inépuisable, *n.f.* inexhaustible.
inertie, *n.f.* inertia.
inestimable, *adj.* priceless.
inévitable, *adj.* inevitable.
inexact, *adj.* inexact.
inexécutable, *adj.* impracticable.
inexplicable, *adj.* inexplicable.
inexprimable, *adj.* inexpressible.
infaillible, *adj.* infallible.
infâme, *adj.* infamous.
infamie, *n.f.* infamy.
infanterie, *n.f.* infantry.
infarctus, *n.f.* coronary (thrombosis).
infatigable, *adj.* untiring.
infécond, *adj.* barren, sterile.
infect, *adj.* infected; rotten.
infecter, *vb.* infect.
infection, *n.f.* infection.
inférieur, *adj. and n.m.* inferior, low(er).
infériorité, *n.f.* inferiority.
infernal, *adj.* infernal.
infester, *vb.* infest.
infidèle, *adj.* disloyal, unfaithful, false.
infidélité, *n.f.* infidelity.
infime, *adj.* lowest; tiny.
infini, *adj. and n.m.* infinite.
infinité, *n.f.* infinity.
infinitif, *n.m.* infinitive.
infirme, *adj. and n.m.f.* invalid.
infirmer, *vb.* invalidate; weaken.
infirmière, *n.f.* nurse.
infirmité, *n.f.* infirmity.
inflammation, *n.f.* inflammation.
inflation, *n.f.* inflation.
infliger, *vb.* inflict.
influence, *n.f.* influence.
influent, *adj.* influential.
information, *n.f.* inquiry; (*pl.*) news.
informatique, *n.f.* computer science.
informatiser, *vb.* computerize.
informe, *adj.* shapeless.
informer, *vb.* inform. **i. de,** acquaint with.
infraction, *n.f.* breach.

infructueux, *adj.* fruitless.
infuser, *vb.* infuse. **faire i.,** brew.
ingambe, *adj.* nimble.
ingénieur, *n.m.* engineer.
ingénieux, *adj.* ingenious.
ingéniosité, *n.f.* ingenuity.
ingénu, *adj.* naive; ingenuous.
ingrat, *adj.* ungrateful.
ingrédient, *n.m.* ingredient.
inguérissable, *adj.* incurable.
inhabile, *adj.* awkward; incapable.
inhabituel, *adj.* unusual.
inhalation, *n.f.* inhalation.
inhiber, *vb.* inhibit.
inhospitalier, *adj.* inhospitable.
inhumain, *adj.* cruel, inhuman.
inimitié, *n.f.* enmity.
inique, *adj.* unfair.
initial, *adj.* initial.
initiale, *n.f.* initial.
initialiser, *vb.* format.
initiative, *n.f.* initiative.
initier, *vb.* initiate.
injecté, *adj.* **i. de sang,** bloodshot.
injecter, *vb.* inject.
injection, *n.f.* injection.
injonction, *n.f.* injunction.
injures, *n.f.pl.* abuse.
injurier, *vb.* abuse; insult.
injurieux, *adj.* abusive; insulting, offensive.
injuste, *adj.* unfair.
injustice, *n.f.* injustice.
inlassable, *adj.* untiring.
inné, *adj.* innate.
innocence, *n.f.* innocence.
innocent, *adj.* innocent.
innocenter, *vb.* declare innocent.
innombrable, *adj.* countless.
innovation, *n.f.* innovation.
inoccupé, *adj.* idle; unoccupied.
inoculer, *vb.* inoculate.
inodore, *adj.* odorless.
inoffensif, *adj.* innocuous, harmless.
inondation, *n.f.* flood.
inonder, *vb.* flood.
inopiné, *adj.* unexpected.
inoubliable, *adj.* unforgettable.
inouï, *adj.* unheard-of.
inox(ydable), *adj.* stainless.
inquiet, *adj.* restless, anxious, uneasy.
inquiéter, *vb.* trouble. **s'i.,** worry.
inquiétude, *n.f.* misgiving, worry.

insaisissable, *adj.* imperceptible.
insalubre, *adj.* unhealthy.
inscription, *n.f.* incription, entry.
inscrire, *vb.* inscribe; enter.
insecte, *n.m.* bug, insect.
insensé, *adj.* mad.
insensible, *adj.* insensible, unfeeling.
inséparable, *adj.* inseparable.
insérer, *vb.* insert.
insigne, *n.m.* badge, sign.
insignifiant, *adj.* petty, insignificant.
insinuer, *vb.* hint.
insipide, *adj.* tasteless; dull.
insistance, *n.f.* insistence.
insister, *vb.* insist.
insolation, *n.f.* sunstroke.
insolence, *n.f.* insolence.
insolite, *adj.* unusual.
insomnie, *n.f.* insomnia.
insondable, *adj.* bottomless.
insouciant, *adj.* casual, careless.
insoumis, *adj.* rebellious.
inspecter, *vb.* examine, survey.
inspecteur, *n.m.* inspector.
inspection, *n.f.* inspection.
inspiration, *n.f.* inspiration.
inspirer, *vb.* inspire.
instable, *adj.* temperamental; unsteady, unstable.
installer, *vb.* install.
instamment, *adv.* urgently.
instance, *n.f.* entreaty; instance; authority.
instant, *n.m.* instant. **à l'i.,** at once.
instantané, 1. *n.m.* snapshot. 2. *adj.* instantaneous.
instinct, *n.m.* instinct.
instinctif, *adj.* instinctive.
instituer, *vb.* institute.
institut, *n.m.* institute.
instituteur, *n.m.* teacher.
institution, *n.f.* institution, institute.
institutrice, *n.f.* teacher.
instructeur, *n.m.* teacher.
instructif, *adj.* instructive.
instruction, *n.f.* education, instruction; (*pl.*) directions.
instruire, *vb.* educate, teach, instruct.
instrument, *n.m.* instrument.
instrumentation, *n.f.* orchestration.

insu, *n.m.* **à l'i. de,** unknown to.
insuccès, *n.m.* failure.
insuffisance, *n.f.* deficiency.
insuffisant, *adj.* deficient.
insulaire, 1. *n.m.* islander. 2. *adj.* insular.
insuline, *n.f.* insulin.
insulte, *n.f.* affront, insult.
insulter, *vb.* affront, insult.
insurgé, *adj. and n.m.* insurgent.
insurger, *vb.* **s'i.,** revolt.
insurmontable, *adj.* insuperable.
intact (-kt), *adj.* intact.
intarissable, *adj.* inexhaustible.
intègre, *adj.* upright.
intégrisme, *n.m.* fundamentalism.
intégrité, *n.f.* integrity.
intellect, *n.m.* intellect.
intellectuel, *adj. and n.m.* intellectual.
intelligence, *n.f.* intelligence.
intelligent, *adj.* intelligent.
intelligible, *adj.* intelligible; audible.
intempérie, *n.f.* inclemency (of weather).
intempestif, *adj.* untimely.
intenable, *adj.* unbearable.
intendance, *n.f.* administration.
intendant, *n.m.* director.
intendante, *n.f.* matron.
intense, *adj.* intense.
intensif, *adj.* intensive.
intensité, *n.f.* intensity.
intention, *n.f.* intention.
intentionné, *adj.* intentioned.
intentionnel, *adj.* intentional.
interactif, *adj.* interactive.
intercéder, *vb.* intercede.
intercepter, *vb.* intercept.
interdiction, *n.f.* ban.
interdire, *vb.* forbid.
intéressant, *adj.* interesting.
intéresser, *vb.* interest, concern, affect.
intérêt, *n.m.* interest.
intérieur, *adj. and n.m.* interior.
interjection, *n.f.* interjection.
interlocuteur, *n.m.* speaker; person one is speaking to.
interloquer, *vb.* embarrass.
intermède, *n.m.* interlude.
intermédiaire, 1. *adj.* intermediate. 2. *n.m.f.* intermediary.
interminable, *adj.* interminable.

internat, *n.m.* boarding school.
international, *adj.* international.
interne, 1. *adj.* internal. **2.** *n.m.f.* resident student.
interner, *vb.* intern.
interpellation, *n.f.* questioning.
interpeller, *vb.* ask.
interphone, *n.m.* intercom.
interposer, *vb.* interpose.
interprétation, *n.f.* interpretation.
interprète, *n.m.f.* interpreter.
interpréter, *vb.* interpret.
interrogateur, 1. *n.m.* examiner. **2.** *adj.* questioning.
interrogation, *n.f.* interrogation.
interrogatoire, *n.m.* cross-examination.
interroger, *vb.* question.
interrompre, *vb.* interrupt.
interrupteur, *n.m.* switch.
interruption, *n.f.* break, intermission, interruption.
interurbain, *n.m.* long-distance telephone service.
intervalle, *n.m.* interval.
intervenir, *vb.* interfere.
intervention, *n.f.* interference.
intervertir, *vb.* transpose.
interview, *n.m. or f.* interview.
interviewer, *vb.* interview.
intestin, *n.m.* bowels.
intimation, *n.f.* notification.
intime, *adj.* intimate.
intimer, *vb.* notify.
intimider, *vb.* daunt, intimidate.
intimité, *n.f.* intimacy.
intituler, *vb.* entitle.
intolérance, *n.f.* intolerance.
intonation, *n.f.* intonation.
intoxication, *n.f.* poisoning.
intoxiquer, *vb.* poison; brainwash.
intraitable, *adj.* intractable, difficult to deal with.
intrépide, *adj.* fearless.
intrigant, 1. *adj.* intriguing. **2.** *n.m.* schemer.
intrigue, *n.f.* plot, intrigue.
intriguer, *vb.* intrigue; puzzle.
intrinsèque, *adj.* intrinsic.
introduction, *n.f.* introduction.
introduire, *vb.* introduce, insert.
introuvable, *adj.* unfindable.
intrus, *n.m.* intruder.
introverti, *n.m.* introvert.
intrusion, *n.f.* intrusion; trespass.

intuitif, *adj.* intuitive.
intuition, *n.f.* intuition.
inusité, *adj.* unusual.
inutile, *adj.* useless, needless.
invalide, 1. *n.m.f.* invalid. **2.** *adj.* disabled, invalid.
invalider, *vb.* invalidate.
invasion, *n.f.* invasion.
invectiver, *vb.* abuse, revile.
inventaire, *n.m.* inventory.
inventer, *vb.* invent.
inventeur, *n.m.* inventor.
invention, *n.f.* invention.
inventorier, *vb.* inventory, catalogue.
inverse, *adj.* inverted, inverse.
investigateur, 1. *adj.* searching. **2.** *n.m.* investigator.
investigation, *n.f.* investigation, inquiry.
investir, *vb.* invest.
invétéré, *adj.* inveterate.
invincible, *adj.* invincible.
invisible, *adj.* invisible.
invitation, *n.f.* invitation.
invité, *n.m.* guest.
inviter, *vb.* invite, ask.
involontaire, *adj.* involuntary.
invoquer, *vb.* call upon.
invraisemblable, *adj.* improbable.
iode, *n.m.* iodine.
Irak, *n.m.* Iraq.
Iran, *n.m.* Iran.
iris (-s), *n.m.* iris.
irisé, *adj.* iridescent.
Irlandais, *n.m.* Irishman.
irlandais, *adj.* Irish.
Irlande, *n.f.* Ireland.
ironie, *n.f.* irony.
ironique, *adj.* ironical.
irradier, *vb.* radiate.
irraisonnable, *adj.* irrational.
irrationnel, *adj.* irrational.
irréel, *adj.* unreal.
irréfléchi, *adj.* thoughtless, rash.
irrégulier, *adj.* irregular.
irréligieux, *adj.* irreligious.
irrésistible, *adj.* irresistible.
irrésolu, *adj.* irresolute.
irrespectueux, *adj.* disrespectful.
irrévérence, *n.f.* disrespect.
irrigation, *n.f.* irrigation.
irriguer, *vb.* irrigate.
irritation, *n.f.* irritation.

irriter, *vb.* irritate, anger; provoke.
Islam, *n.m.* Islam.
islamique, *adj.* Islamic.
Islande, *n.f.* Iceland.
isolateur, *adj.* insulating.
isolement, *n.m.* isolation.
isoler, *vb.* isolate.
isoloire, *n.m.* polling booth.
Israël, *n.m.* Israel.
Israélien, *n.m.* Israeli.
israélien, *adj.* Israeli.
Israélite, *n.m.* Jew.
israélite, *adj.* Jewish.
issue, *n.f.* issue, outlet; outcome.

isthme, *n.m.* isthmus.
Italie, *n.f.* Italy.
Italien, *n.m.* Italian (person).
italien, 1. *n.m.* Italian (language). **2.** *adj.* Italian.
italique, 1. *n.m.* italics. **2.** *adj.* italic.
itinéraire, *n.m.* route, itinerary.
ivoire, *n.m.* ivory.
ivre, *adj.* drunk, intoxicated.
ivresse, *n.f.* drunkenness, intoxication.
ivrogne, *n.m.f.* drunkard.
ivrognerie, *n.f.* drunkenness.

J

jaboter, *vb.* prattle.
jacasser, *vb.* chatter.
jachère, *n.f.* fallow.
jacinthe, *n.f.* hyacinth.
jadis (-s), *adv.* formerly.
jaillir, *vb.* gush, spurt.
jaillissement, *n.m.* gush, spurt.
jais, *n.m.* jet (mineral).
jalon, *n.m.* staff; landmark.
jalonner, *vb.* mark out.
jalouser, *vb.* envy.
jalousie, *n.f.* jealousy.
jaloux, *adj.* jealous.
jamais, *adv.* ever; never.
jambe, *n.f.* leg.
jambière, *n.f.* legging.
jambon, *n.m.* ham.
jante, *n.f.* rim.
janvier, *n.m.* January.
Japon, *n.m.* Japan.
Japonais, *n.m.* Japanese (person).
japonais, 1. *n.m.* Japanese (language). **2.** *adj.* Japanese.
japper, *vb.* yelp.
jaquette, *n.f.* jacket.
jardin, *n.m.* garden.
jardinage, *n.m.* gardening.
jardinier, *n.m.* gardener.
jargon, *n.m.* jargon.
jarre, *n.f.* jar.
jarretière, *n.f.* garter.
jaser, *vb.* jabber.
jasmin, *n.m.* jasmine.
jatte, *n.f.* bowl.
jaunâtre, *adj.* yellowish.
jaune, 1. *adj.* yellow. **2.** *n.m.* yolk (of egg).

jaunir, *vb.* turn yellow.
jaunisse, *n.f.* jaundice.
jazz, *n.m.* jazz.
je (ja), *pron.* I.
jeans, *n.m.pl.* jeans.
jésuite, *n.m.* Jesuit.
jet, *n.m.* jet (water, gas).
jetable, *adj.* disposable.
jetée, *n.f.* pier.
jeter, *vb.* throw.
jeton, *n.m.* token.
jeu, *n.m.* play, game. **mettre en j.,** stake.
jeudi, *n.m.* Thursday.
jeune, *adj.* young, youthful.
jeûne, *n.m.* fast.
jeûner, *vb.* fast.
jeunesse, *n.f.* youth.
joaillerie, *n.f.* jewelry.
joaillier, *n.m.* jeweler.
job, *n.m.* (colloquial) job.
jobard, *n.m.* fool.
joie, *n.f.* joy.
joindre, *vb.* join.
joint, *n.m.* joint.
jointure, *n.f.* joint (esp. of the body).
joli, *adj.* pretty.
joliment, *adv.* prettily; awfully.
jonc, *n.m.* rush (plant).
joncher, *vb.* scatter.
jonction, *n.f.* junction.
jongler, *vb.* juggle.
jongleur, *n.m.* juggler.
jonquille, *n.f.* jonquil.
Jordanie, *n.f.* Jordan.

joue, *n.f.* cheek.
jouer, *vb.* play.
jouet, *n.m.* toy.
joueur, *n.m.* player.
joufflu, *adj.* chubby-cheeked, chubby.
joug (-g), *n.m.* yoke.
jouir, *vb.* enjoy.
jouissance, *n.f.* enjoyment.
jouisseur, *n.m.* pleasure-seeker.
jour, *n.m.* day, daylight. **j. de fête,** holiday. **point du j.,** dawn.
journal, *n.m.* newspaper, journal; diary.
journalier, *adj.* daily.
journalisme, *n.m.* journalism.
journaliste, *n.m.f.* journalist.
journée, *n.f.* day.
journellement, *adv.* daily.
joute, *n.f.* joust.
jovialité, *n.f.* jollity.
joyau, *n.m.* jewel.
joyeux, *adj.* joyful.
jubilé, *n.m.* jubilee.
jubiler, *vb.* exult.
judaïsme, *n.m.* Judaism.
judas, *n.m.* peephole.
judiciare, *adj.* judicial; legal.
judicieux, *adj.* wise; judicious.
juge, *n.m.* judge.
jugement, *n.m.* judgment, reason. **mettre en j.,** try.
juger, *vb.* judge.
jugulaire, *adj.* jugular.

Juif *m.,* **Juive** *f. n.* Jew.
juif *m.,* **juive** *f. adj.* Jewish.
juillet, *n.m.* July.
juin, *n.m.* June.
jules, *n.m.* (colloquial) guy.
jumeau *m.,* **jumelle** *f. adj. and n.* twin.
jumeler, *vb.* couple, join.
jumelles, *n.f.pl.* opera glasses.
jument, *n.f.* mare.
jungle, *n.f.* jungle.
jupe, *n.f.* skirt.
jupon, *n.m.* petticoat.
jurer, *vb.* swear.
juridiction, *n.f.* jurisdiction.
juridique, *adj.* judicial, legal.
jurisconsulte, *n.m.f.* jurist; lawyer.
jurisprudence, *n.f.* jurisprudence.
juriste, *n.m.f.* jurist.
juron, *n.m.* oath.
jury, *n.m.* jury.
jus, *n.m.* juice; gravy.
jusque, *prep.* up to. **jusqu'à,** as far as; until. **jusqu'ici,** hitherto.
juste, 1. *adj.* just, fair, right. 2. *adv.* just.
justement, *adv.* precisely, exactly.
justesse, *n.f.* accuracy, precision.
justice, *n.f.* justice, fairness.
justifiant, *adj.* justifying.
justification, *n.f.* justification.
justifier, *vb.* justify.
juteux, *adj.* juicy.
juvénile, *adj.* juvenile.

K

kaki, *adj.* khaki.
kangourou, *n.m.* kangaroo.
karaté, *n.m.* karate.
kasher, *adj.* kosher.
képi, *n.m.* cap.
kermesse, *n.f.* fair.
kidnapper, *vb.* kidnap.
kif, *n.m.* marijuana.
kilogramme, *n.m.* kilogram.
kilohertz, *n.m.* kilohertz.

kilométrage, *n.m.* mileage.
kilomètre, *n.m.* kilometer.
kilométrique, *adj.* kilometric.
kinésithérapeute, *n.m.f.* physiotherapist.
kiosque, *n.m.* kiosk; newsstand; bandstand.
klaxon, *n.m.* car horn.
kyrielle, *n.f.* litany.
kyste, *n.m.* cyst.

L

la, *pron.* her; it *(f.).*
là, *adv.* there.
là-bas, *adv.* yonder, out there.

labeur, *n.m.* labor.
labo, *n.m.* (colloquial) lab.
laboratoire, *n.m.* laboratory.

laborieux, *adj.* industrious, laborious.

labour, *n.m.* plowing.

labourer, *vb.* plow.

labyrinthe, *n.m.* maze.

lac, *n.m.* lake.

lacérer, *vb.* lacerate; tear up.

lacet, *n.m.* shoelace; winding.

lâche, 1. *n.m.f.* coward. **2.** *adj.* cowardly; loose.

lâchement, *adv.* loosely; shamefully.

lâcher, *vb.* loosen; let go. **l. pied,** give ground, flee.

lâcheté, *n.f.* cowardice.

lacis, *n.m.* network.

laconique, *adj.* laconic.

lacrymogène, *adj.* **gaz l.,** tear gas.

lacté, *adj.* milky.

lacune, *n.f.* gap, blank.

ladre, *adj.* stingy, mean.

lagune, *n.f.* lagoon.

laid, *adj.* ugly.

laideron, *n.m.* ugly person.

laideur, *n.f.* ugliness.

lainage, *n.m.* woolen goods.

laine, *n.f.* wool.

laineux, *adj.* woolly; downy.

laïque (lä ēk), *n.m.* layman.

laisse, *n.f.* leash.

laisser, *vb.* let; leave.

laisser-aller, *n.m.* freedom; negligence.

laissez-passer, *n.m.* pass.

lait, *n.m.* milk.

laitage, *n.m.* dairy foods.

laiterie, *n.f.* dairy.

laiteux, *adj.* milky.

laitier, *n.m.* milkman.

laiton, *n.m.* brass.

laitue, *n.f.* lettuce.

lambeau, *n.m.* rag.

lambin, *adj.* slow, dawdling.

lame, *n.f.* blade.

lamé, *adj.* gold- or silver-trimmed.

lamelle, *n.f.* (microscope) slide.

lamentable, *adj.* sad, grievous.

lamentation, *n.f.* lamentation.

lamenter, *vb.* mourn, lament.

laminer, *vb.* laminate.

lampadaire, *n.m.* lamp; street lamp.

lampe, *n.f.* lamp. **l. de poche,** flashlight.

lamper, *vb.* drink, gulp.

lampion, *n.m.* Chinese lantern.

lampiste, *n.m.* lamplighter.

lance, *n.f.* lance.

lancer, *vb.* hurl; launch.

lanceur, *n.m.* pitcher.

lancinant, *adj.* throbbing (of pain).

lande, *n.f.* wasteland; moor.

landau, *n.m.* baby carriage.

langage, *n.m.* language.

langoureux, *adj.* languishing.

langouste, *n.f.* crayfish, crawfish.

langue, *n.f.* tongue; language.

languette, *n.f.* tonguelike strip.

langueur, *n.f.* languor.

languir, *vb.* pine, languish.

languissant, *adj.* languid.

lanière, *n.f.* strap, thong.

lanterne, *n.f.* lantern.

lapider, *vb.* stone; abuse.

lapin, *n.m.* rabbit.

laps, *n.m.* lapse of time.

lapsus (-sys), *n.m.* slip.

laquais, *n.m.* footman, lackey.

laque, *n.f.* shellac; hairspray.

larcin, *n.m.* larceny, theft.

lard, *n.m.* bacon, fat.

larder, *vb.* lard; pierce.

large, *adj.* wide.

largesse, *n.f.* generosity.

largeur, *n.f.* width.

larguer, *vb.* drop, let go.

larme, *n.f.* tear.

larmoyer, *vb.* weep, whimper.

larron, *n.m.* thief.

laryngite, *n.f.* laryngitis.

las, *adj.* weary.

lascif, *adj.* lewd, wanton.

laser, *n.m.* laser.

lasser, *vb.* weary.

lassitude, *n.f.* weariness.

latéral, *adj.* lateral.

Latin, *n.m.* Latin (person).

latin, 1. *n.m.* Latin (language). **2.** *adj.* Latin.

latitude, *n.f.* latitude.

latte, *n.f.* lath.

laurier, *n.m.* bay, laurel.

lavabo, *n.m.* lavatory.

lavage, *n.m.* washing.

lavande, *n.f.* lavender.

lavandière, *n.f.* laundress.

lavement, *n.m.* enema.

laver, *vb.* wash.

lavette, *n.f.* dishrag.

laxatif, *n.m.* laxative.

le (lə) *m.*, **la** *f.*, **les** *pl.* **1.** *art.* the. **2.** *pron.* him, her, it.

lécher, *vb.* lick.

lèche-vitrines, *n.m.* window shopping.

leçon, *n.f.* lesson.

lecteur, *n.m.* reader.

lecture, *n.f.* reading.

légal, *adj.* lawful, legal.

légaliser, *vb.* legalize.

légalité, *n.f.* legality.

légataire, *n.m.* legatee.

légation, *n.f.* legation.

légendaire, *adj.* legendary.

légende, *n.f.* legend; inscription.

léger, *adj.* light.

légèreté, *n.f.* lightness.

légion, *n.f.* legion.

législateur, *n.m.* legislator.

législatif, *adj.* legislative.

législation, *n.f.* legislation.

législature, *n.f.* legislature.

légitime, *adj.* legitimate, lawful.

legs, *n.m.* bequest.

léguer, *vb.* bequeath.

légume, *n.m.* vegetable.

lendemain, *n.m.* the next day.

lent, *adj.* slow.

lenteur, *n.f.* slowness.

lentille, *n.f.* lentil; lens.

léopard, *n.m.* leopard.

lèpre, *n.f.* leprosy.

lépreux, 1. *adj.* leprous. **2.** *n.m.* leper.

lequel, *pron.* which, who.

les, *pron.* them.

lesbien, *adj.* lesbian.

lesbienne, *n.f.* lesbian.

léser, *vb.* wrong, hurt.

lésine, *n.f.* stinginess.

lésion, *n.f.* wrong; lesion.

lessive, *n.f.* laundry.

lessiveuse, *n.f.* washing machine.

lest (-t), *n.m.* ballast.

leste, *adj.* nimble, clever.

lettre, *n.f.* letter.

lettré, *adj.* lettered, literate.

leucémie, *n.f.* leukemia.

leur, 1. *pron.* to them; **le leur, la leur,** theirs. **2. leur** *m.f.*, **leurs** *pl.* *adj.* their.

leurre, *n.m.* lure, trap.

leurrer, *vb.* lure.

levain, *n.m.* yeast; leaven.

levée, *n.m.* embankment, levee.

lever, *vb.* raise. **se l.,** get up.

levier, *n.m.* lever.

lèvre, *n.f.* lip.

lévrier, *n.m.* greyhound.

lexique, *n.m.* lexicon.

lézard, *n.m.* lizard.

lézarde, *n.f.* crevice.

liaison, *n.f.* connection, linkage.

liant, *adj.* supple; affable.

liasse, *n.f.* file; wad.

Liban, *n.m.* Lebanon.

libelle, *n.m.* libel.

libeller, *vb.* draw up, word.

libéral, *adj.* liberal.

libérateur, *n.m.* rescuer.

libérer, *vb.* free.

liberté, *n.f.* freedom, liberty.

libertin, 1. *adj.* wanton. **2.** *n.* libertine.

libraire, *n.m.* bookseller.

librairie, *n.f.* bookstore.

libre, *adj.* free.

libre-échange, *n.m.* free trade.

Libye, *n.f.* Libya.

licence, *n.f.* license.

licencié, *n.m.* licensee; holder of university degree.

licencier, *v.b.* dismiss, lay off.

licencieux, *adj.* licentious.

licite, *adj.* lawful.

licorne, *n.f.* unicorn.

licou, *n.m.* halter.

lie, *n.f.* dreg.

liège, *n.m.* cork.

lien, *n.m.* bond, link, tie.

lier, *vb.* bind, tie, link.

lierre, *n.m.* ivy.

lieu, *n.m.* place. **au l. de,** instead of.

lieu-commun, *n.m.* commonplace.

lieue, *n.f.* league (distance).

lieutenant, *n.m.* lieutenant.

lièvre, *n.m.* hare.

ligne, *n.f.* line.

lignée, *n.f.* offspring.

ligoter, *vb.* bind up.

ligue, *n.f.* league.

liguer, *vb.* league.

lilas, *n.m.* lilac.

limaçon, *n.m.* snail.

lime, *n.f.* file; lime (fruit).

limer, *vb.* file.

limier, *n.m.* bloodhound.

limitation, *n.f.* limitation.

limitation des naissances, *n.f.* birth control, contraception.

limite, n.f. limit, border.

limiter, vb. limit, confine.

limoger, vb. dismiss.

limon, n.m. mud, slime.

limonade, n.f. lemon soda.

limoneux, adj. muddy.

limpide, adj. clear, limpid.

lin, n.m. flax.

linceul, n.m. shroud.

linéaire, adj. lineal.

linge, n.m. linen; wash.

lingerie, n.f. linen goods; under-wear.

linguistique, adj. linguistic.

linon, n.m. lawn (sheer linen).

linteau, n.m. lintel.

lion, n.m. lion.

lippu, adj. thick-lipped.

liqueur, n.f. liquid; liqueur.

liquidation, n.f. liquidation; settling.

liquide, adj. and n.m. liquid, fluid.

liquider, vb. liquidate.

liquoreux, adj. sweet.

lire, vb. read.

lis (-s), n.m. lily.

liséré, n.m. piping, border.

liseur, n.m. reader.

liseuse, n.f. bookmark.

lisible, adj. legible.

lisière, n.f. edge.

lisse, adj. smooth.

lisser, vb. smooth.

liste, n.f. list, roll.

lit, n.m. bed.

litanie, n.f. litany.

lit-cage, n.m. (folding) cot.

lit de la mer, n.m. seabed.

literie, n.f. bedding.

litière, n.f. litter.

litige, n.m. litigation.

litigieux, adj. litigious.

litre, n.m. liter.

littéraire, adj. literary.

littéral, adj. literal.

littérature, n.f. literature.

littoral, n.m. coast.

liturgie, n.f. liturgy.

livide, adj. livid.

livraison, n.f. delivery. **l. contre remboursement,** C.O.D.

livre, n.f. pound.

livre, n.m. book.

livre de poche, n.m. paperback.

livrée, n.f. livery.

livrer, vb. deliver.

livresque, adj. bookish, from books.

livreur, n.m. delivery man.

local, adj. local.

localiser, vb. locate.

localité, n.f. locality.

locataire, n.m.f. tenant.

location, n.f. renting.

loch (-k), n.m. log.

locomotive, n.f. locomotive.

locuste, n.f. locust.

locution, n.f. locution, phrase.

loge, n.f. box.

logement, n.m. lodging.

loger, vb. lodge.

logiciel, n.m. software.

logique, 1. n.f. logic. **2.** adj. logical.

logis, n.m. dwelling.

loi, n.f. law.

loin, adv. far, away.

lointain, adj. distant.

loir, n.m. dormouse.

loisible, adj. optional, allowable.

loisir, n.m. leisure.

Londres, n.m. London.

long m., **longue** f. adj. long.

longe, n.f. leash; loin (of veal).

longer, vb. go along.

longeron, n.m. beam, girder.

longitude, n.f. longitude.

longtemps, adv. long.

longueur, n.f. length.

look, n.m. (colloquial) look, image.

lopin, n.m. small piece, plot.

loquace, adj. talkative.

loque, n.f. morsel, rag.

loquet, n.m. latch.

loqueteux, adj. tattered.

lorgner, vb. glance at; ogle.

lorgnon, n.m. glasses.

loriot, n.m. oriole.

lors, adv. then. **l. de,** at the time of.

lorsque, conj. when.

losange, n.m. diamond, lozenge.

lot, n.m. lot, prize.

loterie, n.f. raffle, lottery.

lotion, n.f. lotion.

lotir, vb. divide, apportion.

loto, n.m. lotto, lottery.

louable, adj. praiseworthy.

louage, n.m. hire.

louange, n.f. praise.

louche, adj. shady.

loucher, *vb.* squint.
louer, *vb.* praise; hire, rent.
loueur, *n.m.* one who rents.
loup, *n.m.* wolf.
loupe, *n.f.* magnifying glass.
louper, *vb.* (colloquial) spoil, botch.
loup-garou, *n.m.* werewolf.
lourd, *adj.* heavy.
lourdaud, *n.m.* clod.
lourdeur, *n.f.* heaviness; dullness.
lorve, *n.f.* she-wolf.
loyal, *adj.* loyal.
loyauté, *n.f.* loyalty.
loyer, *n.m.* rent.
lubricité, *n.f.* lewdness.
lubrifier, *vb.* lubricate.
lucarne, *n.f.* attic window.
lucide, *adj.* lucid.
lucidité, *n.f.* clearness.
luciole, *n.f.* firefly.
lueur, *n.f.* gleam.
luge, *n.f.* sled.
lugubre, *adj.* doleful, dismal, lugubrious.
lui, *pron.* he; to him, to her.
lui-même, *pron.* himself, itself.
luire, *vb.* gleam.
luisant, *adj.* shiny.
lumière, *n.f.* light.

lumineux, *adj.* luminous.
lunaire, *adj.* lunar.
lunatique, *adj.* whimsical.
lunch, *n.m.* buffet lunch.
lundi, *n.m.* Monday.
lune, *n.f.* moon. **l. de miel,** honeymoon. **clair de l.,** moonlight.
lunetier, *n.m.* optician.
lunettes, *n.f.pl.* glasses.
lustre, *n.m.* chandelier; luster; five-year period.
lustrer, *vb.* polish, gloss.
luth, *n.m.* lute.
lutiner, *vb.* tease.
lutte, *n.f.* strife, struggle, contest.
lutter, *vb.* struggle, contend.
luxe, *n.m.* luxury.
Luxembourg, *n.m.* Luxembourg.
luxer, *vb.* dislocate.
luxueux, *adj.* luxurious.
luxure, *n.f.* lust.
luzerne, *n.f.* alfalfa.
lycée, *n.m.* high school.
lycéen, *n.m.* high-school student.
lymphatique, *adj.* lymphatic.
lynchage, *n.m.* lynching.
lyncher, *vb.* lynch.
lyre, *n.f.* lyre.
lyrique, *adj.* lyric.
lys, *n.m.* lily.

M

M. (abbr. for **Monsieur**), *n.m.* Mr.
macabre, *adj.* macabre, ghastly.
macadam, *n.m.* macadam.
macédoine, *n.f.* salad; mixture.
macérer, *vb.* macerate, soak.
mâcher, *vb.* chew.
machin, *n.m.* thing, gadget.
machinal, *adj.* mechanical.
machination, *n.f.* plot, scheme.
machine, *n.f.* machine. **m. à copier,** copier. **m. à écrire,** typewriter.
machiner, *vb.* plot.
machiniste, *n.m.f.* machinist.
macho, *adj.* (colloquial) macho.
mâchoire, *n.f.* jaw.
mâchonner, *vb.* mumble; munch.
maçon, *n.m.* mason.
maculer, *vb.* spot, blot.
Madame, *n.f.* Madam, Mrs.
madeleine, *n.f.* light cake.
Mademoiselle, *n.f.* Miss.

Madone, *n.f.* Madonna.
mafia, *n.f.* mafia.
magasin, *n.m.* store.
magazine, *n.m.* magazine.
mages, *n.m.pl.* Magi, Wise Men.
Maghreb, *n.m.* North Africa.
magicien, *n.m.* magician.
magie, *n.f.* magic.
magique, *adj.* magic.
magistral, *adj.* masterly, authoritative.
magistrat, *n.m.* magistrate.
magistrature, *n.f.* judiciary.
magnanime, *adj.* magnanimous.
magnat, *n.m.* magnate.
magnétique, *adj.* magnetic.
magnétophone, *n.m.* tape recorder.
magnétoscope, *n.m.* video-recorder.
magnificence, *n.f.* magnificence.

magnifique, *adj.* magnificent.

magouille, *n.f.* scheming.

mahométan, *adj.* Mohammedan.

mai, *n.m.* May.

maigre, *adj.* lean, thin, meager.

maigrir, *vb.* lose weight.

maille, *n.f.* stitch; mesh.

maillot, *n.m.* shorts; T-shirt. **m. de bain,** bathing suit.

main, *n.f.* hand. **sous la m.,** handy.

main-d'œuvre, *n.f.* manpower.

maintenant, *adv.* now. **dès m.,** henceforth.

maintenir, *vb.* maintain.

maintien, *n.m.* upkeep; behavior.

maire, *n.m.* mayor.

mairie, *n.f.* city hall.

mais, *conj.* but.

maïs, (mä ēs), *n.m.* corn.

maison, *n.f.* house.

maisonnée, *n.f.* household.

maître, *n.m.* master, teacher.

maîtresse, *n.f.* mistress, teacher.

maîtrise, *n.f.* mastery.

maîtriser, *vb.* master, overcome.

majesté, *n.f.* majesty.

majestueux, *adj.* majestic.

majeur, *adj.* major.

majordome, *n.m.* majordomo.

majorer, *vb.* increase price, overprice.

majoritaire, *adj.* majority.

majorité, *n.f.* majority.

majuscule, *n.f.* capital.

mal, 1. *n.m.* harm, ill, evil. 2. *adv.* badly. **faire m. à,** hurt. **avoir m. à,** have a pain in.

malade, 1. *n.m.f.* sick person, patient. 2. *adj.* sick.

maladie, *n.f.* disease, illness, sickness.

maladif, *adj.* sickly.

maladresse, *n.f.* awkwardness.

maladroit, *adj.* awkward.

malaise, *n.m.* discomfort.

malappris, *adj.* ill-bred.

malaria, *n.f.* malaria.

malavisé, *adj.* indiscreet, ill-advised.

Malaisie, *n.f.* Malaysia.

malchance, *n.f.* bad luck, mishap.

maldonne, *n.f.* misdeal.

mâle, *adj. and n.m.* male.

malédiction, *n.f.* curse.

maléfice, *n.m.* witchery, evil spell.

malencontre, *n.f.* unlucky incident.

malencontreux, *adj.* unlucky.

malentendu, *n.m.* misunderstanding.

malfaiteur, *n.m.* malefactor.

malfamé, *adj.* ill-famed.

malgré, *prep.* despite.

malhabile, *adj.* awkward, dull.

malheur, *n.m.* misfortune, accident.

malheureux, *adj.* unfortunate; unhappy, miserable.

malhonnête, *adj.* dishonest.

malhonnêteté, *n.f.* dishonesty.

malice, *n.f.* mischief, malice.

malicieux, *adj.* malicious, roguish.

malin *m.,* **maligne** *f. adj.* sharp, sly; malignant.

malingre, *adj.* sickly, puny.

malintentionné, *adj.* ill-disposed.

malle, *n.f.* trunk.

mallette, *n.f.* small suitcase.

malnutrition, *n.f.* malnutrition.

malotru, *n.m.* boor, lout.

malpropre, *adj.* messy.

malpropreté, *n.f.* messiness.

malsain, *adj.* unhealthy.

malséant, *adj.* improper.

Malte, *n.f.* Malta.

maltraiter, *vb.* misuse.

malveillant, *adj.* malevolent.

malvenu, *adj.* without any right.

malversation, *n.f.* embezzlement.

maman, *n.f.* mamma.

mamelle, *n.f.* udder.

mamelon, *n.m.* nipple; hillock.

mamie, *n.f.* (colloquial) granny.

mammifère, *n.m.* mammal.

manche, *n.m.* handle. *f.* sleeve. **La M.,** the English Channel.

manchette, *n.f.* cuff.

manchon, *n.m.* muff.

manchot, *n.m.* one-armed person.

mandarine, *n.f.* tangerine.

mandat, *n.m.* warrant, writ, mandate. **m.-poste,** money order.

mandataire, *n.m.* agent, proxy.

mander, *vb.* send for, inform.

manège, *n.m.* horsemanship.

manette, *n.f.* handle, lever; joystick.

mangeable, *adj.* eatable.

mangeoire, *n.f.* manger.

manger, *vb.* eat.

maniable, *adj.* manageable; easygoing.

maniaque, 1. *n.m.f.* maniac. **2.** *adj.* maniac, maniacal.

manie, *n.f.* mania.

manier, *vb.* handle; wield.

manière, *n.f.* manner.

maniéré, *adj.* affected.

manière de vivre, *n.f.* life style.

manif (-f), *n.f.* (colloquial) demo.

manifestation, *n.f.* demonstration.

manifeste, 1. *n.m.* manifesto, petition. **2.** *adj.* manifest, evident, overt.

manifester, *vb.* manifest, show.

manigance, *n.f.* trick, intrigue.

manipuler, *adj.* manipulate.

manivelle, *n.f.* crank; winch.

mannequin, *n.m.* dummy; model.

manœuvre, *n.f.* maneuver.

manoir, *n.m.* country house, estate.

manquant, 1. *adj.* missing. **2.** *n.m.* absentee.

manque, *n.m.* lack.

manquer, *vb.* miss, lack; fail.

mansarde, *n.f.* attic.

mansuétude, *n.f.* mildness, kindness.

manteau, *n.m.* cloak, coat.

manucure, *n.m.f.* manicurist.

manuel, *adj. and n.m.* manual.

manufacture, *n.f.* manufacture.

manuscrit, *adj. and n.m.* manuscript.

manutention, *n.f.* management.

maquereau, *n.m.* mackerel; (colloquial) pimp.

maquette, *n.f.* preliminary sketch or model.

maquillage, *n.m.* makeup.

maquis, *n.m.* scrub land; Resistance fighters.

maquisard, *n.* Resistance fighter.

marais, *n.m.* marsh.

marasme, *n.m.* slump.

marâtre, *n.f.* stepmother.

maraude, *n.f.* marauding.

marbre, *n.m.* marble.

marchand, *n.m.* merchant.

marchander, *vb.* bargain, haggle.

marchandises, *n.f.pl.* goods.

marche, *n.f.* march, step.

marché, *n.m.* market, bargain. **bon m.,** cheap.

marchepied, *n.m.* runningboard.

marcher, *vb.* walk, step, march; run (machine).

marcheur, *n.m.* pedestrian.

mardi, *n.m.* Tuesday.

mare, *n.f.* pool.

marécage, *n.m.* bog.

marécageux, *adj.* marshy.

maréchal, *n.m.* marshal.

marée, *n.f.* tide.

mareyeur, *n.m.* fish seller.

marge, *n.f.* margin.

margarine, *n.f.* margarine.

margelle, *n.f.* edge, brink.

marguerite, *n.f.* daisy.

mari, *n.m.* husband.

mariage, *n.m.* marriage.

marié, 1. *n.m.* bridegroom. **2.** *adj.* married.

mariée, *n.f.* bride.

marie-jeanne, *n.f.* marijuana.

marier, *vb.* marry.

marijuana, *n.f.* marijuana.

marin, 1. *n.m.* sailor. **2.** *adj.* marine. **fusilier m.,** marine.

marinade, *n.f.* mixture for pickling.

marine, *n.f.* navy.

mariner, *vb.* pickle.

marionnette, *n.f.* puppet.

maritime, *adj.* marine.

marmite, *n.f.* pot.

marmiter, *vb.* blast (with gunfire?)

marmonner, *vb.* mumble.

marmot, *n.m.* kid, brat.

marmotter, *vb.* mumble.

Maroc (-k), *n.m.* Morocco.

marocain, *adj. and n.m.* Moroccan.

maroquinerie, *n.f.* leather goods.

marotte, *n.f.* fad.

marque, *n.f.* brand, mark.

marquer, *vb.* mark.

marqueur, *n.m.* marker, scorekeeper.

marquis, *n.m.* marquis.

marraine, *n.f.* godmother; sponsor.

marrant, *adj.* funny.

marron, *n.m.* chestnut; brown.

marronier, *n.m.* chestnut tree.

mars (-s), *n.m.* March.

marteau, *n.m.* hammer.

marteler, vb. hammer.
martial, adj. warlike.
martre, n.f. marten.
martyr, n.m. martyr.
martyre, n.m. martyrdom.
marxisme, n.m. Marxism.
mascarade, n.f. masquerade.
mascotte, n.f. mascot.
masculin, adj. masculine.
maso, n.m. (colloquial) masochist.
masochiste, n.m.f. masochist.
masque, n.m. mask.
masquer, vb. mask.
massacre, n.m. slaughter.
massage, n.m. massage.
masse, n.f. mass.
masser, vb. mass; massage.
massif, adj. massive, solid.
massue, n.f. club.
mastiquer, vb. chew.
mat (-t), adj. dull.
mât (mä), n.m. mast.
matelas, n.m. mattress.
matelot, n.m. sailor.
matérialiser, vb. materialize.
matérialisme, n.m. materialism.
matérialiste, n.m.f. materialist.
  adj. materialistic.
matériaux, n.m.pl. stuff, materials.
matériel, adj. material, real.
maternel, adj. native; maternal.
maternité, n.f. maternity.
mathématique, adj. mathematical.
mathématiques, n.f.pl. mathematics.
maths, n.f.pl. (colloquial) math.
matière, n.f. matter. **table des m.s,**
  index.
matin, n.m. morning.
mâtin, n.m. big dog.
matinal, adj. early.
matinée, n.f. morning.
matineux, adj. rising early.
matois, adj. cunning, sly.
matou, n.m. tomcat.
matraque, n.f. heavy club.
matrice, n.f. womb.
matricule, n.f. roster, registration.
matriculer, vb. enroll, register.
matrimonial, adj. marital.
mâture, n.f. masts (of boats).
maturité, n.f. maturity.
maudire, vb. curse.
maudit, adj. cursed, miserable.
maugréer, vb. curse, grumble.

maussade, adj. glum, sullen, cross.
mauvais, adj. bad.
maxime, n.f. maxim.
maximum, n.m. maximum.
mayonnaise, n.f. mayonnaise.
mazout, n.m. (fuel) oil.
me (mə), pron. me; myself.
méandre, n.m. winding.
mec, n.m. (colloquial) guy.
mécanicien, n.m. mechanic, engineer.
mécanique, adj. mechanical.
mécaniser, vb. mechanize.
mécanisme, n.m. mechanism, machinery.
mécano, n.m. mechanic.
méchamment, adv. maliciously.
méchanceté, n.f. wickedness, malice.
méchant, adj. wicked, malicious.
mèche, n.f. lock (hair); wick, fuse.
mécompte, n.m. error; disappointment.
méconnaissable, adj. unrecognizable.
méconnaître, vb. fail to recognize.
mécontent, adj. discontented.
mécontentement, n.m. discontent.
mécontenter, vb. dissatisfy.
mécréant, n.m. unbeliever.
médaille, n.f. medal.
médaillon, n.m. locket.
médecin, n.m. physician.
médecine, n.f. medicine.
médiateur, n.m. mediator; ombudsman (in France).
médiation, n.f. mediation.
médiatique, adj. media.
médical, adj. medical.
médicament, n.m. medicine.
médicinal, adj. medicinal.
médiéval, adj. medieval.
médiocre, adj. mediocre.
médiocrité, n.f. mediocrity.
médire, vb. slander, defame.
médisance, n.f. slander.
méditation, n.f. meditation.
méditer, vb. meditate; muse, brood.
Méditerranée, n.f. the Mediterranean.
méditerranéen, adj. Mediterranean.
médium, n.m. medium.

méduse, n.f. jellyfish.
méduser, vb. stupefy.
méfait, n.m. crime, misdeed.
méfiance, n.f. distrust.
méfiant, adj. distrustful.
méfier, vb. **se m. de,** distrust.
mégarde, n.f. heedlessness.
mégère, n.f. vixen, shrew.
mégot, n.m. cigarette butt.
meilleur, adj. better, best.
mélancolie, n.f. melancholy.
mélancolique, adj. melancholy.
mélange, n.m. mixture.
mélasse, n.f. molasses.
mêlée, n.f. struggle.
mêler, vb. mix. **se m. de,** meddle in.
mélèze, n.m. larch.
melliflu, adj. sweet, honeyed.
mélo, 1. n.m. melodrama. **2.** adj. melodramatic.
mélodie, n.f. melody.
mélodieux, adj. melodious.
mélodique, adj. melodic.
mélodrame, n.m. melodrama.
mélomane, n.m. lover of music.
melon, n.m. melon.
membrane, n.f. membrane.
membre, n.m. member, limb.
membrure, n.f. frame, limbs.
même, 1. adj. same, very; self. **moi-m.,** myself; **lui-m.,** himself, etc. **2.** adv. even. **de m.,** likewise. **tout de m.,** notwithstanding. **mettre à m. de,** enable to.
mémé, n.f. (colloquial) granny.
mémento, n.m. memento, notebook.
mémoire, n.f. memory; memoir.
mémorable, adj. memorable.
mémorandum, n.m. memorandum.
mémorial, n.m. memorial; memoirs.
menaçant, adj. threatening.
menace, n.f. threat.
menacer, vb. threaten.
ménage, n.m. household.
ménagement, n.m. discretion.
ménager, 1. n.m. manager. **2.** vb. manage.
ménagère, n.f. housewife, housekeeper.
ménagerie, n.f. menagerie.
mendiant, n.m. beggar.
mendicité, n.f. begging.

mendier, vb. beg.
menées, n.f.pl. schemes.
mener, vb. lead.
ménestrel, n.m. minstrel.
ménétrier, n.m. country fiddler.
meneur, n.m. leader, ringleader.
méningite, n.f. meningitis.
ménopause, n.f. menopause.
menottes, n.f.pl. handcuffs.
mensonge, n.m. falsehood, lie.
mensonger, adj. false, deceptive.
mensualité, n.f. remittance paid monthly.
mensuel, adj. monthly.
mensurable, adj. measurable.
menterie, n.f. lie.
menteur, n.m. liar.
menthe, n.f. mint.
mention, n.f. mention.
mentionner, vb. mention.
mentir, vb. lie.
menton, n.m. chin.
menu, 1. n.m. menu. **2.** adj. little, minute.
menuet, n.m. minuet.
menuiserie, n.f. woodwork.
menuisier, n.m. carpenter.
méprendre, vb. **se m.,** be mistaken.
mépris, n.m. contempt, scorn.
méprisable, adj. mean, contemptible.
méprisant, adj. contemptuous.
méprise, n.f. mistake, misunderstanding.
mépriser, vb. scorn, despise.
mer (-r), n.f. sea. **mal de m.,** seasickness.
mercantile, adj. mercantile.
mercenaire, adj. and n.m. mercenary.
mercerie, n.f. haberdashery.
merci, n.m. thanks; mercy.
mercredi, n.m. Wednesday.
mercure, n.m. mercury.
mère, n.f. mother.
méridien, n.m. meridian.
méridional, adj. southern.
meringue, n.f. meringue.
méritant, adj. meritorious.
mérite, n.m. merit, desert.
mériter, vb. merit, deserve.
méritoire, adj. meritorious.
merle, n.m. blackbird.

merveille, *n.f.* marvel.

merveilleux, *adj.* wonderful, marvelous.

mésalliance, *n.f.* misalliance.

mésallier, *vb.* marry badly.

mésaventure, *n.f.* accident, mishap.

Mesdames, *pl.* of **Madame.**

Mesdemoiselles, *pl.* of **Mademoiselle.**

mésestime, *n.f.* low opinion or repute.

mésintelligence, *n.f.* difficulty, discord.

mesquin, *adj.* shabby, mean, stingy.

mesquinerie, *n.f.* meanness.

message, *n.m.* message.

messager, *n.m.* messenger.

messe, *n.f.* Mass.

Messie, *n.m.* Messiah.

Messieurs, *pl.* of **Monsieur.**

mesurage, *n.m.* measurement.

mesure, *n.f.* measure. **à m. que,** as.

mesuré, *adj.* measured, cautious.

mesurer, *vb.* measure.

métairie, *n.f.* small farm.

métal, *n.m.* metal.

métallique, *adj.* metallic.

métallurgie, *n.f.* metallurgy.

métamorphose, *n.f.* transformation.

métaphore, *n.f.* metaphor.

métaphysique, 1. *n.f.* metaphysics. **2.** *adj.* metaphysical.

métayer, *n.m.* small farmer.

météo, *n.f.* weather report.

météore, *n.m.* meteor.

météorologie, *n.f.* meteorology.

métèque, *n.m.* alien.

méthode, *n.f.* method.

méthodique, *adj.* methodical, systematic.

méticuleux, *adj.* meticulous.

métier, *n.m.* loom; craft, trade.

métis, *adj.* hybrid, crossbred.

métrage, *n.m.* measurement.

mètre, *n.m.* meter.

métrique, *adj.* metric.

métro, *n.m.* subway.

métropole, *n.f.* metropolis; native land.

métropolitain, *adj.* metropolitan.

mets, *n.m.* food, dish.

mettable, *adj.* wearable.

metteur, *n.m.* **m. en scène,** play director.

mettre, *vb.* put, place, set. **se m. à,** begin.

meuble, *n.m.* piece of furniture; (*pl.*) furniture.

meubler, *vb.* furnish, outfit.

meule, *n.f.* stack.

meunier, *n.m.* miller.

meurtre, *n.m.* murder.

meurtrier, *n.m.* murderer.

meurtrière, *n.f.* murderess.

meurtrir, *vb.* bruise.

meurtrissure, *n.f.* bruise.

meute, *n.f.* dog pack; mob.

Mexicain, *n.m.* Mexican.

mexicain, *adj.* Mexican.

Mexique, *n.m.* Mexico.

mezzanine, *n.f.* mezzanine.

mi, *adj.* mid, half.

miaou, *n.m.* mew.

miauler, *vb.* mew.

mica, *n.m.* mica.

miche, *n.f.* loaf of bread.

micro, *n.m.* microphone, mike; micro.

microbe, *n.m.* microbe.

microfiche, *n.f.* microfiche.

microforme, *n.f.* microform.

micro-ondes, *n.m.* microwave oven.

microphone, *n.m.* microphone.

micropuaquette, *n.f.* (micro)chip.

microprocesseur, *n.m.* microprocessor.

microscope, *n.m.* microscope.

microscopique, *adj.* microscopic.

midi, *n.m.* noon; south.

midinette, *n.f.* young saleswoman.

mie, *n.f.* crumb.

miel, *n.m.* honey.

mielleux, *adj.* honeyed, sweet.

mien, *pron.* **le mien, la mienne,** mine.

miette, *n.f.* crumb.

mieux, *adv.* better, best.

mièvre, *adj.* affected.

mignard, *adj.* dainty, mincing.

mignon, 1. *adj.* delicate, dainty. **2.** *n.m.* darling.

migraine, *n.f.* headache.

migration, *n.f.* migration.

mijoter, *vb.* cook slowly, simmer.

mil (mēl), *n.m.* thousand.

milice, *n.f.* militia.

milieu, *n.m.* middle, center; environment.

militaire, *adj.* military.

militant, *adj.* militant.

militarisme, *n.m.* militarism.

militer, *vb.* militate.

mille (-l), 1. *n.m.* mile. **2.** *adj.* and *n.m.f.* thousand.

millénaire, *n.m.* millenium.

millet, *n.m.* millet.

milliard, *n.m.* billion.

millier (-l-), *n.m.* thousand.

milligramme (-l-), *n.m.* milligram.

millimètre, *n.m.* millimeter.

million (-l-), *n.m.* million.

millionnaire (-l-), *adj.* and *n.m.f.* millionaire.

mime, *n.m.* mime, mimic.

mimique, *adj.* mimic.

minable, *adj.* shabby, poor.

minauder, *vb.* simper.

mince, *adj.* slender, slight, thin.

minceur, *n.f.* slimness.

mine, *n.f.* mine; mien; lead.

miner, *vb.* mine; wear away; weaken.

minerai, *n.m.* ore.

minéral, *adj.* and *n.m.* mineral.

minet, *n.m.* (colloquial) kitty.

mineur, 1. *n.m.* miner. **2.** *adj.* and *n.m.* minor.

miniature, *n.f.* miniature.

miniaturiser, *vb.* miniaturize.

minibus, *n.m.* minibus.

minier, *adj.* of mines.

minime, *adj.* very small.

minimum, *n.m.* minimum.

mini-ordinateur, *n.m.* minicomputer.

ministère, *n.m.* ministry, department, board.

ministériel, *adj.* ministerial.

ministre, *n.m.* minister. **premier m.,** prime minister, premier.

Minitel, *n.m.* (trademark) Minitel (videotext terminal and service).

minorité, *n.f.* minority.

minotier, *n.m.* miller.

minuit, *n.m.* midnight.

minuscule, *adj.* minute.

minute, *n.f.* minute.

minuterie, *n.f.* time switch.

minutie, *n.f.* trifle; care with details.

minutieux, *adj.* minute.

mioche, *n.m.f.* urchin.

miracle, *n.m.* miracle.

miraculeux, *adj.* miraculous.

mirage, *n.m.* mirage.

mirer, *vb.* aim at, look at.

mirifique, *adj.* wonderful.

miroir, *n.m.* mirror.

miroiter, *vb.* glisten.

misanthrope, 1. *n.m.f.* misanthrope. **2.** *adj.* misanthropic.

mise, *n.f.* putting; mode. **m. en scène,** setting.

miser, *vb.* bid.

misérable, *adj.* miserable, wretched, squalid.

misère, *n.f.* misery.

miséreux, *adj.* poor, miserable.

miséricorde, *n.f.* mercy.

miséricordieux, *adj.* merciful.

misogyne, 1. *n.m.f.* misogynist. **2.** *adj.* woman-hating; misogynist.

missel, *n.m.* missal.

missile, *n.m.* missile.

mission, *n.f.* mission.

missionnaire, *adj.* and *n.m.f.* missionary.

missive, *n.f.* missive.

mistral, *n.m.* mistral wind.

mitaine, *n.f.* mitten.

mite, *n.f.* moth.

mi-temps, *n.f.* half-time, part-time.

miteux, *adj.* shabby.

mitiger, *vb.* moderate.

mitoyen, *adj.* midway; jointly owned.

mitrailleuse, *n.f.* machine gun.

mixage, *n.m.* (sound) mixing.

mixte, *adj.* mixed, joint.

Mlle. (abbr. for **Mademoiselle**), *n.f.* Miss.

Mme. (abbr. for **Madame**), *n.f.* Mrs.

mobile, *adj.* movable.

mobilier, *adj.* movable.

mobilisation, *n.f.* mobilization.

mobiliser, *vb.* mobilize.

mobilité, *n.f.* mobility; instability.

moche, *adj.* ugly.

modalité, *n.f.* mode.

mode, *n.f.* fashion, mode; mood; *pl.* millinery. **à la m.,** fashionable.

modèle, *n.m.* model, pattern.

modeler, *vb.* model, shape.

modelliste, *n.m.f.* dress designer.

modem, *n.m.* modem.
modérateur, *n.m.* moderator.
modération, *n.f.* moderation.
modéré, *adj.* moderate.
modérer, *vb.* check, moderate.
moderne, *adj.* modern.
moderniser, *vb.* modernize.
modernité, *n.f.* modernity.
modeste, *adj.* modest.
modestie, *n.f.* modesty.
modicité, *n.f.* small quantity.
modification, *n.f.* alteration.
modifier, *vb.* modify, qualify.
modique, *adj.* moderate, unimportant.
modiste, *n.f.* milliner.
modulation, *n.f.* modulation.
module, *n.m.* module.
moduler, *vb.* modulate.
moelle, *n.f.* marrow.
moelleux (mwä lУ), *adj.* mellow, soft.
mœurs (-s), *n.f.pl.* manner(s), custom.
moi, 1. *n.m.* ego. **2.** *pron.* me.
moignon, *n.m.* stump.
moi-même, *pron.* myself; I myself.
moindre, *adj.* less, lesser, least.
moine, *n.m.* monk.
moineau, *n.m.* sparrow.
moins, *adv.* less, least. **au m.,** at least. **à m. que,** unless.
moire, *n.f.* watered silk.
mois, *n.m.* month.
moisi, *adj.* moldy.
moisir, *vb.* mold.
moisissure, *n.f.* mold.
moisson, *n.f.* harvest, crop.
moissonner, *vb.* reap, harvest.
moissonneur, *n.m.* harvester.
moissonneuse, *n.f.* reaping machine.
moite, *adj.* moist.
moiteur, *n.f.* dampness.
moitié, *n.f.* half. **à m.,** half.
molaire, *adj. and n.f.* molar.
môle, *n.m.* pier.
molécule, *n.f.* molecule.
molester, *vb.* molest.
mollah, *n.m.* mullah.
mollasse, *adj.* flabby, soft.
mollesse, *n.f.* softness; weakness.
mollet, 1. *adj.* soft. **œufs m.s,** soft-boiled eggs. **2.** *n.m.* calf of leg.
molletière, *n.f.* legging.

molleton, *n.m.* heavy flannel.
mollir, *vb.* soften, slacken.
mollusque, *n.m.* mollusk.
môme, *n.m.f.* (colloquial) kid.
moment, *n.m.* moment.
momentané, *adj.* momentary.
mon, ma, *m.f.,* **mes** *pl. adj.* my.
monacal, *adj.* pertaining to monks.
Monaco, *n.m.* Monaco.
monarchie, *n.f.* monarchy.
monarchiste, *n.m.f.* monarchist.
monarque, *n.m.* monarch.
monastère, *n.m.* monastery.
monastique, *adj.* monastic.
monceau, *n.m.* pile.
mondain, *adj.* worldly.
monde, *n.m.* world; people. **tout le m.,** everybody, everyone. **mettre au m.,** bear.
mondial, *adj.* worldwide.
monétaire, *adj.* monetary.
moniteur, *n.m.* monitor.
monnaie, *n.f.* change; money, currency. **Hôtel de la M.,** mint.
monnayer, *vb.* mint.
monocle, *n.m.* monocle.
monogramme, *n.m.* monogram.
monologue, *n.m.* monologue.
monologuer, *vb.* soliloquize.
monoplan, *n.m.* monoplane.
monopole, *n.m.* monopoly.
monopoliser, *vb.* monopolize.
monosyllabe, *n.m.* monosyllable.
monosyllabique, *adj.* monosyllabic.
monotone, *adj.* monotonous.
monotonie, *n.f.* monotony, dullness.
monseigneur, *n.m.* title of honor; My Lord.
Monsieur, *n.m.,* gentleman, sir; Mr.
monstre, *n.m.* monster.
monstrueux, *adj.* monstrous.
monstruosité, *n.f.* monstrosity.
mont, *n.m.* mountain, hill.
montage, *n.m.* carrying up; setting; (film) editing.
montagnard, *n.m.* mountaineer.
montagne, *n.f.* mountain.
montagneux, *adj.* mountainous.
montant, *n.m.* amount.
mont-de-piété, *n.m.* pawnshop.
monté, *adj.* mounted; supplied.
montée, *n.f.* ascent, rise, climb.

monter, vb. go up, mount, climb, rise.
montre, n.f. watch; display. **m.-bracelet**, wristwatch.
montrer, vb. show.
montreur, n.m. showman.
montueux, adj. hilly.
monture, n.f. mount; setting.
monument, n.m. monument.
monumental, adj. monumental.
moquer, vb. **se m. de**, make fun of, mock, laugh at.
moquerie, n.f. mockery, ridicule.
moquette, n.f. wall-to-wall carpeting.
moqueur, adj. mocking.
moral, adj. ethical, moral.
morale, n.f. morals, morality. **m.** morale.
moraliser, vb. moralize.
moraliste, n.m.f. moralist.
moralité, n.f. morals, morality.
morbide, adj. morbid.
morceau, n.m. piece, bit, morsel. **gros m.**, lump, chunk.
morceler, vb. cut up.
mordant, adj. pointed.
mordiller, vb. nibble.
mordre, vb. bite.
morfondre, vb. chill.
morgue, n.f. morgue.
moribond, adj. dying.
morne, adj. bleak, dismal, dreary.
morose, adj. morose.
morosité, n.f. moroseness.
morphine, n.f. morphine.
morphinomane, n. drug addict.
morphologie, n.f. morphology.
mors, n.m. horse's bit.
morse, n.m. walrus.
morsure, n.f. bite.
mort, 1. n.m. dummy; dead man. 2. n.f. death. 3. adj. dead.
mortaise, n.f. mortise.
mortalité, n.f. mortality.
mortel, adj. deadly, mortal.
morte-saison, n.f. off season.
mortier, n.m. mortar.
mortifier, vb. mortify.
mort-né, adj. stillborn.
mortuaire, adj. mortuary.
morue, n.f. cod.
mosaïque (-à ĕk), n.f. mosaic.
Moscou, n.m. Moscow.
mosquée, n.f. mosque.

mot, n.m. word; cue.
motard, n.m. biker; motorcycle cop.
motel, n.m. motel.
moteur, n.m. motor.
motif, n.m. motive.
motion, n.f. motion.
motiver, vb. motivate, justify.
motocyclette, n.f. motorcycle.
motocycliste, n.m. motorcyclist.
motorisé, adj. having transportation.
motte, n.f. clod.
mou m., **molle** f. adj. soft.
mouchard, n.m. spy.
moucharder, vb. spy.
mouche, n.f. fly.
moucher, vb. blow the nose.
moucheron, n.m. gnat.
moucheté, adj. spotted.
moucheture, n.f. spot.
mouchoir, n.m. handkerchief.
moudre, vb. grind.
moue, n.f. pout, wry face.
mouette, n.f. gull.
moufette, n.f. skunk.
moufle, n.f. mitten.
mouillage, n.m. wetting.
mouillé, adj. wet.
mouiller, vb. soak.
moulage, n.m. cast (from mold).
moule, 1. n.m. mold. 2. n.f. mussel.
mouler, vb. mold.
mouleur, n.m. molder.
moulin, n.m. mill.
moulinette, n.f. vegetable shredder.
moulure, n.f. molding.
mourant, adj. dying.
mourir, vb. die.
mouron, n.m. pimpernel.
mousquetaire, n.m. musketeer.
mousse, n.f. moss; foam, lather.
mousseline, n.f. muslin.
mousser, vb. foam, froth.
mousseux, adj. foaming.
mousson, n.m. monsoon.
moustache, n.f. mustache, whisker.
moustiquaire, n.f. mosquito net.
moustique, n.m. mosquito.
moutarde, n.f. mustard.
mouton, n.m. sheep; mutton.
moutonner, vb. curl; make woolly.
mouture, n.f. grinding.

mouvant, *adj.* moving, shifting.

mouvement, *n.m.* movement, stir.

mouvoir, *vb.* move.

moyen, 1. *n.m.* means; medium. 2. *adj.* middle, average.

moyennant, *prep.* by means of.

moyenne, *n.f.* average.

Moyen Orient, *n.m.* Middle East.

muabilité, *n.f.* changeability.

mucilage, *n.m.* mucilage.

mue, *n.f.* molting; changing (esp. of voice).

muer, *vb.* molt (animals); break, change (voice).

muet *m.,* **muette** *f. adj.* dumb, mute.

mufle, *n.m.* cad.

mugir, *vb.* roar, bellow.

mugissement, *n.m.* roaring, bellowing.

muguet, *n.m.* lily of the valley.

mulâtre, *adj. and n.m.f.* mulatto.

mulet, *n.m.* mule.

muletier, *n.m.* muleteer.

mulot, *n.m.* field mouse.

multinational, *adj.* multinational.

multiple, *adj.* multiple, manifold.

multiplicande, *n.m.* multiplicand.

multiplication, *n.f.* multiplication.

multiplicité, *n.f.* multiplicity.

multiplier, *vb.* multiply.

multitude, *n.f.* multitude.

municipal, *adj.* municipal.

municipalité, *n.f.* municipality.

munificence, *n.f.* munificence, liberality.

munificent, *adj.* very generous.

munir, *vb.* provide, supply.

munitionner, *vb.* provision, supply.

munitions, *n.f.pl.* ammunition.

muqueux, *adj.* mucous.

mur, *n.m.* wall.

mûr, *adj.* ripe, mature.

muraille, *n.f.* wall.

mural, *adj.* mural.

mûre, *n.f.* blackberry.

mûrier, *n.m.* mulberry tree.

mûrir, *vb.* ripen, mature.

murmure, *n.m.* murmur.

murmurer, *vb.* murmur.

musarder, *vb.* waste time, dawdle.

muscade, *n.f.* nutmeg.

muscle, *n.m.* muscle.

musculaire, *adj.* muscular.

musculeux, *adj.* muscular.

muse, *n.f.* muse.

museau, *n.m.* muzzle.

musée, *n.m.* museum.

museler, *vb.* muzzle; gag.

muselière, *n.f.* muzzle.

muser, *vb.* trifle, dawdle.

musette, *n.f.* lunchbag; accordion.

musical, *adj.* musical.

musicien, 1. *adj.* musical. 2. *n.m.* musician.

musique, *n.f.* music.

musulman, *adj. and n.m.* Mohammedan.

mutabilité, *n.f.* mutability.

mutation, *n.f.* change, replacement.

mutilation, *n.f.* mutilation.

mutiler, *vb.* mutilate, mangle, mar.

mutin, *adj.* refractory, mutinous.

mutiner, *vb.* **se m.,** mutiny, revolt.

mutinerie, *n.f.* mutiny.

mutisme, *n.m.* muteness, lack of speech.

mutuel, *adj.* mutual.

myope, *adj.* nearsighted.

myopie, *n.f.* nearsightedness.

myosotis, *n.m.* forget-me-not.

myriade, *n.f.* myriad.

myrrhe, *n.f.* myrrh.

myrte, *n.m.* myrtle.

mystère, *n.m.* mystery.

mystérieux, *adj.* mysterious, weird.

mysticisme, *n.m.* mysticism.

mystification, *n.f.* hoax.

mystifier, *vb.* mystify.

mystique, *adj.* mystic.

mythe, *n.m.* myth.

mythique, *adj.* mythical.

mythologie, *n.f.* mythology.

N

nabot, *n.m.* dwarf.

nacre, *n.f.* mother-of-pearl.

nacré, *adj.* pearly.

nage, *n.f.* act of swimming.

nageoire, *n.f.* fin.

nager, *vb.* swim.

nageur, *n.m.* swimmer.

naguère, *adv.* a short time ago.

naïf (nä ēf) *m.,* **naïve** *f. adj.* naive.

nain, *adj.* and *n.m.* dwarf.

naissance, *n.f.* birth.

naissant, *adj.* beginning; newborn.

naître, *vb.* be born.

naïveté (nä ēv-), *n.f.* simplicity.

nantir, *vb.* give as security; furnish.

nantis, *n.m.pl.* the well-to-do.

nantissement, *n.m.* pledge, guarantee.

naphte, *n.m.* naphtha.

nappe, *n.f.* tablecloth.

narcisse, *n.m.* daffodil.

narcotique, *adj.* narcotic.

narguer, *vb.* defy, flout.

narine, *n.f.* nostril.

narrateur, *n.m.* narrator, storyteller.

narration, *n.f.* narrative, recital.

narrer, *vb.* narrate, relate.

nasal, *adj.* nasal.

naseau, *n.m.* nostril.

nasiller, *vb.* talk with a nasal voice.

nasse, *n.f.* fish trap.

natal, *adj.* native.

natalité, *n.f.* birthrate.

natation, *n.f.* swimming.

natif, *adj.* and *n.m.* native.

nation, *n.f.* nation.

national, *adj.* national.

nationalisation, *n.f.* nationalization.

nationaliser, *vb.* nationalize.

nationalisme, *n.m.* nationalism.

nationalité, *n.f.* nationality.

nativité, *n.f.* nativity.

naturaliser, *vb.* naturalize; (of animals) stuff.

naturalisme, *n.m.* naturalism, naturalness.

naturaliste, *n.m.f.* naturalist.

nature, *n.f.* nature.

naturel, 1. *adj.* nature. **2.** *adj.* natural.

naufrage, *n.m.* shipwreck.

naufragé, *adj.* shipwrecked.

nauséabond, *adj.* nauseous, offensive.

nausée, *n.f.* nausea.

nautique, *adj.* nautical.

nautisme, *n.m.* water sports.

naval, *adj.* naval.

navet, *n.m.* turnip.

navette spatiale, *n.f.* space shuttle.

navigable, *adj.* navigable.

navigateur, *n.m.* navigator, seaman.

navigation, *n.f.* seafaring, navigation.

naviguer, *vb.* sail, navigate.

navire, *n.m.* ship.

navrant, *adj.* distressing, causing grief.

navrer, *vb.* wound; grieve.

né, *adj.* born.

néanmoins, *adv.* yet, nevertheless, however.

néant, *n.m.* nothing(ness).

nébuleux, *adj.* cloudy; worried.

nécessaire, *adj.* requisite, necessary.

nécessité, *n.f.* necessity. **n. préalable,** prerequisite.

nécessiter, *vb.* make necessary or imperative.

nécessiteux, *adj.* needy.

nécrologe, *n.m.* obituary.

néerlandais, *adj.* Dutch (language).

nef, *n.f.* nave.

néfaste, *adj.* ill-omened, unlucky.

négatif, *adj.* negative.

négation, *n.f.* negation; negative word.

négative, *n.f.* negative argument or opinion.

négligé, 1. *adj.* neglected, sloppy. **2.** *n.m.* state of undress.

négligeable, *adj.* negligible.

négligence, *n.f.* neglect.

négligent, *adj.* negligent.

négliger, *vb.* overlook, neglect.

négoce, *n.m.* commerce, trade.

négociable, *adj.* negotiable.

négociant, *n.m.* merchant.

négociation, *n.f.* negotiation.

négocier, *vb.* negotiate.

nègre, *adj.* and *n.m.* black, Negro.

négresse, *n.f.* a black woman.

neige, *n.f.* snow.

neiger, *vb.* snow.

neigeux, *adj.* snowy.

néon, *n.m.* neon.

néophyte, *n.m.* neophyte, convert.

Néo-Zélandais, *n.* New Zealander.

néphrite, *n.f.* nephritis.

nerf (nĕr), *n.m.* nerve.

nerveux, *adj.* nervous.
nervosité, *n.f.* nervousness.
net (-t) *m.*, **nette** *f. adj.* net, clear; clean, neat.
netteté, *n.f.* clearness, neatness.
nettoyer, *vb.* clean, scour.
nettoyeur, *n.m.* one who or that which cleans.
neuf, *adj. and n.m.* nine.
neuf *m.*, **neuve** *f. adj.* brand-new.
neutraliser, *vb.* counteract.
neutralité *n.f.* neutrality.
neutre, *adj. and n.m.* neutral.
neutron, *n.m.* neutron.
neuvième, *adj. and n.m.f.* ninth.
neveu, *n.m.* nephew.
névralgie, *n.f.* neuralgia.
névrite, *n.f.* neuritis.
névrose, *n.f.* neurosis.
névrosé, *adj. and n.m.* neurotic.
nez, *n.m.* nose.
ni, *conj.* nor. **ni . . . ni . . .**, neither . . . nor . . .
niais, *adj.* foolish.
niaiserie, *n.f.* silliness, trifle.
niche, *n.f.* alcove.
nichée, *n.f.* brood.
nicher, *vb.* se **n.**, nestle.
nickel, *n.m.* nickel.
nicotine, *n.f.* nicotine.
nid, *n.m.* nest.
nièce, *n.f.* niece.
nielle, *n.f.* wheat blight.
nier, *vb.* deny.
nigaud, *n.m.* fool, simpleton.
nihilisme, *n.m.* nihilism.
nimbe, *n.m.* halo.
n'importe, *interj.* never mind.
nippes, *n.f.pl.* old clothes.
nitrate, *n.m.* nitrate.
niveau, *n.m.* level. **au n. de**, level with.
niveler, *vb.* make level; survey.
nivellement, *n.m.* leveling; surveying.
noble, 1. *n.m.* nobleman, peer. 2. *adj.* noble.
noblesse, *n.f.* nobility.
noce, *n.f.* wedding. **faire la n.**, revel.
noceur, *n.m.* gay blade.
nocif, *adj.* harmful.
noctambule, *n.m.f.* sleep-walker; noctambulist.
nocturne, *adj.* nocturnal.

Noël (nō ĕl), *n.m.* Christmas; carol.
nœud (nœ), *n.m.* knot.
noir, *adj. and n.m.* black.
noircir, *vb.* blacken.
noisetier, *n.m.* hazel (tree).
noisette, 1. *n.f.* hazelnut. 2. *adj.* light reddish brown.
noix, *n.f.* nut, walnut.
nolis, *n.m.* freight.
nom, *n.m.* name; noun.
nomade, *adj.* wandering, roaming.
nombre, *n.m.* number.
nombrer, *vb.* number.
nombreux, *adj.* numerous, manifold.
nombril, *n.m.* navel.
nominal, *adj.* nominal.
nominatif, *adj. and n.m.* nominative.
nomination, *n.f.* nomination, appointment.
nommément, *adv.* particularly, namely.
nommer, *vb.* name; nominate, appoint.
non, *adv.* no. **n. plus**, neither.
non-aligné, *adj.* non-aligned.
nonchalamment, *adv.* carelessly, nonchalantly.
nonchalant, *adj.* nonchalant.
non-combattant, *adj. and n.m.* non-combatant.
nonne, *n.f.* nun.
nonobstant, *prep.* in spite of, notwithstanding.
nonpareil, *adj.* unequaled.
non-sens, *n.m.* nonsense.
nord, *n.m.* north.
normal, *adj.* normal.
normand, *adj.* Norman; equivocal.
Normandie, *n.f.* Normandy.
norme, *n.f.* norm.
Norvège, *n.f.* Norway.
Norvégien, *n.m.* Norwegian (person).
norvégien, 1. *n.m.* Norwegian (language). 2. *adj.* Norwegian.
nostalgie, *n.f.* nostalgia.
notabilité, *n.f.* notability.
notable, 1. *n.m.* notable. 2. *adj.* remarkable, notable.
notaire, *n.m.* lawyer, notary.
notamment, *adv.* particularly.
notation, *n.f.* notation.
note, *n.f.* note, bill; grade.

noter, vb. note.
notice, n.f. notice, review.
notification, n.f. notification.
notifier, vb. notify.
notion, n.f. notion.
notoire, adj. notorious.
notoriété, n.f. notoriety.
notre sg., **nos** pl. adj. our.
nôtre, pron. **le n.,** ours.
nouer, vb. tie.
noueux, adj. knotty.
nouilles, n.f.pl. noodles.
nounours, n.m. teddy bear.
nourrice, n.f. (wet) nurse.
nourricier, adj. nourishing; of nursing.
nourrir, vb. feed, nourish, foster.
nourrisson, n.m. infant.
nourriture, n.f. food, nourishment.
nous, pron. we, us, ourselves.
nouveau m., **nouvelle** f. adj. new, fresh. **de n.,** anew.
nouveauté, n.f. novelty.
nouvel an, n.m. new year.
nouvelle, n.f. news.
nouvellement, adv. recently, newly.
Nouvelle-Zélande, n.f. New Zealand.
novembre, n.m. November.
novice, n.m.f. novice.

noviciat, n.m. novitiate.
noyade, n.f. drowning.
noyau, n.m. kernel, nucleus.
noyauter, vb. infiltrate.
noyer, vb. drown.
noyer, n.m. walnut (tree).
nu, adj. naked, bare.
nuage, n.m. cloud; gloom.
nuageux, adj. cloudy.
nuance, n.m. shade, degree.
nucléaire, adj. nuclear.
nudité, n.f. bareness.
nuée, n.f. cloud; swarm.
nuire, vb. injure, harm.
nuisible, adj. injurious, hurtful.
nuit, n.f. night.
nul, adj. no, none; void. **nulle part,** nowhere.
nullement, adv. not at all.
nullité, n.f. nonentity.
numéraire, n.m. cash.
numéral, adj. and n.m. numeral.
numérique, adj. numerical.
numéro, n.m. number.
nu-pieds, adj. barefoot.
nuptial, adj. bridal.
nuque, n.f. nape.
nu-tête, adj. bareheaded.
nutritif, adj. nutritious.
nutrition, n.f. nutrition.
nylon, n.m. nylon.
nymphe, n.f. nymph.

O

oasis (-s), n.f. oasis.
obéir, vb. obey.
obéissance, n.f. obedience.
obéissant, adj. obedient.
obélisque, n.m. obelisk.
obérer, vb. burden with debt.
obèse, adj. obese.
obésité, n.f. obesity.
objecter, vb. object.
objecteur, n.m. **o. de conscience,** conscientious objector.
objectif, adj. and n.m. objective.
objection, n.f. objection.
objet, n.m. object.
obligation, n.f. obligation.
obligatoire, adj. compulsory, mandatory, binding.
obligeance, n.f. obligingness.
obliger, vb. oblige, accommodate.

oblique, adj. slanting; devious.
oblitération, n.f. obliteration.
oblitérer, vb. obliterate.
oblong, adj. oblong.
obnubilé, adj. obsessed.
obscène, adj. filthy, obscene.
obscénité, n.f. obscenity.
obscur, adj. obscure, dark, dim.
obscurcir, vb. darken, obscure.
obscurcissement, n.m. darkening; state of being obscure.
obscurément, adv. obscurely.
obscurité, n.f. darkness, dimness, obscurity.
obséder, vb. harass, haunt.
obsèques, n.f.pl. funeral.
obséquieusement, adv. obsequiously.
obséquieux, adj. obsequious.

observance, *n.f.* observance.

observateur, *n.m.* observer.

observation, *n.f.* observation, remark.

observer, *vb.* observe, watch.

obsession, *n.f.* obsession.

obstacle, *n.m.* obstacle, bar.

obstétrical, *adj.* obstetrical.

obstétrique, *n.f.* obstetrics.

obstination, *n.f.* stubbornness.

obstiné, *adj.* obstinate, stubborn.

obstiner, *vb.* s'o., persist.

obstruction, *n.f.* obstruction.

obstruer, *vb.* obstruct, stop up.

obtempérer, *vb.* obey.

obtenir, *vb.* obtain, get.

obtention, *n.f.* obtaining.

obtus, *adj.* obtuse, dull, stupid.

obus (-s), *n.m.* shell.

obusier, *n.m.* howitzer.

occasion, *n.f.* opportunity, chance; bargain.

occasionnel, *adj.* occasional.

occasionner, *vb.* cause, bring about.

occident, *n.m.* west.

occidental, *adj.* western.

occulte, *adj.* occult.

occupant, *n.m.* occupant, tenant.

occupation, *n.f.* pursuit; occupation.

occupé, *adj.* busy.

occuper, *vb.* occupy, busy. s'o. de, attend to.

occurrence, *n.f.* occurrence.

océan, *n.m.* ocean.

océanique, *adj.* oceanic.

ocre, *n.f.* ochre.

octane, *n.m.* octane.

octave, *n.f.* octave.

octobre, *n.m.* October.

octroyer, *vb.* grant.

oculaire, *adj.* ocular.

oculiste, *n.m.f.* oculist.

ode, *n.f.* ode.

odeur, *n.f.* odor, scent, perfume.

odieux, *adj.* hateful, obnoxious, odious.

odorant, *adj.* having a fragrant odor.

odorat, *n.m.* (sense of) smell.

œil, *n.m., pl.* **yeux,** eye. **coup d'o.,** glance.

œillade, *n.f.* wink, quick look.

œillère, *n.f.* eyetooth.

œillet, *n.m.* carnation.

œuf, *n.m.* egg.

œuvre, *n.f.* work.

offensant, *adj.* offensive.

offense, *n.f.* offense.

offenser, *vb.* offend.

offenseur, *n.m* offender.

offensif, *adj.* offensive.

offensive, *n.f.* offensive.

offensivement, *adv.* offensively.

office, *n.m.* office, pantry; (church) service.

officiant, *n.m.* one who officiates.

officiel, *adj.* official.

officier, 1. *n.m.* officer; mate. **2.** *vb.* officiate.

officieux, *adj.* officious.

offrande, *n.f.* offering.

offre, *n.f.* offer.

offrir, *vb.* offer, present.

offusquer, *vb.* obscure, shadow; irritate.

ogive, *n.f.* warhead.

ogre, *n.m.* ogre.

oie, *n.f.* goose.

oignon (ô nYON), *n.m.* onion; bulb.

oindre, *vb.* anoint.

oiseau, *n.m.* bird.

oiselet, *n.m.* small bird.

oiseux, *adj.* idle, empty, useless.

oisif, *adj.* idle.

oisillon, *n.m.* young bird.

oisiveté, *n.f.* idleness.

oléagineux, *adj.* oily.

oléoduc, *n.m.* oil pipeline.

olivâtre, *adj.* olive-colored.

olive, *n.f.* olive.

olivier, *n.m.* olive tree.

olympique, *adj.* Olympic.

ombilical, *adj.* umbilical.

ombrage, *n.m.* shade.

ombragé, *adj.* shady.

ombrager, *vb.* shade.

ombrageux, *adj.* suspicious, doubtful.

ombre, *n.f.* shade, shadow.

ombrelle, *n.f.* parasol.

ombreux, *adj.* shady.

omelette, *n.f.* omelet.

omettre, *vb.* omit.

omission, *n.f.* omission.

omnibus (-s), *n.m.* bus.

omnipotent, *adj.* omnipotent.

omoplate, *n.f.* shoulder blade.

on, *pron.* one (indef. subj.).

once, *n.f.* ounce.
oncle, *n.m.* uncle.
onction, *n.f.* unction.
onctueux, *adj.* unctuous.
onde, *n.f.* wave.
ondé, *adj.* wavy.
on-dit, *n.m.* rumor.
ondoyer, *vb.* wave.
ondulation, *n.f.* wave. **o. permanente,** permanent wave.
onduler, *vb.* wave.
onéreux, *adj.* burdensome.
ongle, *n.m.* (finger)nail.
onglée, *n.f.* numb feeling.
onguent, *n.m.* salve, ointment.
onomatopée, *n.f.* onomatopœia.
onze, *adj. and n.m.* eleven.
onzième, *adj. and n.m.f.* eleventh.
opacité, *n.f.* opacity.
opale, *n.f.* opal.
opaque, *adj.* opaque.
opéra, *n.m.* opera.
opérateur, *n.m.* operator; cameraman.
opération, *n.f.* operation; transaction.
opératoire, *adj.* operative.
opéré, *n.m.* patient undergoing surgery.
opérer, *vb.* operate.
opérette, *n.f.* operetta.
opiner, *vb.* hold or express an opinion.
opiniâtre, *adj.* stubborn.
opiniâtreté, *n.f.* stubbornness.
opinion, *n.f.* opinion.
opium, *n.m.* opium.
opportun, *adj.* timely.
opportunité, *n.f.* timeliness.
opposant, *n.m.* opponent.
opposé, *adj.* opposite, averse.
opposer, *vb.* oppose. **s'o. à,** oppose, resist.
opposition, *n.f.* opposition.
oppresser, *vb.* weigh heavily on.
oppresseur, *n.m.* oppressor.
oppressif, *adj.* oppressive.
oppression, *n.f.* oppression.
opprimer, *vb.* oppress.
opprobre, *n.m.* disgrace, infamy.
opter, *vb.* select, decide.
opticien, *n.m.* optician.
optimisme, *n.m.* optimism.
optimiste, 1. *adj.* optimistic. **2.** *n.m.f.* optimist.

option, *n.f.* option.
optique, *adj.* optic.
opulence, *n.f.* opulence, riches.
opuscule, *n.m.* small work.
or, 1. *n.m.* gold. **2.** *conj.* now.
oracle, *n.m.* oracle.
orage, *n.m.* storm.
orageusement, *adv.* turbulently, stormily.
orageux, *adj.* stormy.
oraison, *n.f.* prayer, oration.
oral, *adj.* oral.
orange, *n.f.* orange.
oranger, *n.m.* orange tree.
orateur, *n.m.* speaker, orator.
oratoire, *adj.* oratorical. **art o.,** oratory.
orbe, *n.m.* orb, sphere.
orbite, *n.m.* orbit; socket (as of eye).
orchestre (-k-), *n.m.* orchestra, band.
orchestrer (-k-), *vb.* orchestrate.
orchidée, *n.f.* orchid.
ordinaire, *adj. and n.m.* ordinary.
ordinal, *adj. and n.m.* ordinal.
ordinateur, *n.m.* computer.
ordonnance, *n.f.* prescription; ordinance, decree.
ordonné, *adj.* orderly, tidy.
ordonner, *vb.* order, ordain, bid, command.
ordre, *n.m.* order. **de premier o.,** first-rate.
ordure, *n.f.* filth, garbage, refuse.
ordurier, *adj.* foul.
oreille, *n.f.* ear.
oreiller, *n.m.* pillow.
oreillons, *n.m.pl.* mumps.
orfèvrerie, *n.f.* gold or silver jewelry.
organdi, *n.m.* organdy.
organe, *n.m.* organ (body).
organigramme, *n.m.* flow chart, organization chart.
organique, *adj.* organic.
organisateur, 1. *n.m.* organizer. **2.** *adj.* organizing.
organisation, *n.f.* organization, arrangement.
organiser, *vb.* organize.
organisme, *n.m.* organism.
organiste, *n.m.f.* organist.
orgasme, *n.m.* orgasm, climax.
orge, *n.f.* barley.

orgelet, *n.m.* sty (of eye).
orgie, *n.f.* orgy.
orgue, *n.m.* organ (instrument).
orgueil, *n.m.* pride.
orgueilleux, *adj.* proud, haughty.
Orient, *n.m.* Orient, East.
Oriental, *n.m.* Oriental.
oriental, *adj.* Oriental, eastern.
orientation, *n.f.* positioning.
orienté, *adj.* slanted.
orienter, *vb.* orient.
orifice, *n.m.* orifice, hole.
originaire, *adj.* original, native.
originairement, *adv.* originally.
original, 1. *n.m.* eccentric person.
2. *adj.* original.
originalement, *adv.* originally; unusually.
originalité, *n.f.* originality.
origine, *n.f.* origin, source.
originel, *adj.* original.
oripeau, *n.m.* tinsel.
orme, *n.m.* elm.
orné, *adj.* ornate.
ornement, *n.m.* ornament, adornment, trimming.
ornemental, *adj.* ornamental.
ornementation, *n.f.* ornamentation.
orner, *vb.* adorn, trim.
ornière, *n.f.* rut, track.
ornithologie, *n.f.* ornithology.
orphelin, *n.m.* orphan.
orphelinat, *n.m.* orphanage.
orphéon, *n.m.* choral group.
orteil, *n.m.* toe.
orthodoxe, *adj.* orthodox.
orthodoxie, *n.f.* orthodoxy.
orthographe, *n.f.* spelling, orthography.
orthographier, *vb.* spell.
ortie, *n.f.* nettle.
os, *n.m.* bone.
oscillant, *adj.* oscillating.
oscillation, *n.f.* sway.
osciller, *vb.* fluctuate, oscillate.
osé, *adj.* attempted, bold.
oser, *vb.* dare.
osier, *n.m.* willow.
ossature, *n.f.* bony structure, skeleton.
ossements, *n.m.pl.* human remains.
osseux, *adj.* bony.

ossifier, *vb.* ossify.
ostensible, *adj.* ostensible.
ostentation, *n.f.* ostentation.
ostraciser, *vb.* ostracize.
otage, *n.m.* hostage.
ôter, *vb.* take off; take away.
otite, *n.f.* ear infection.
ou, *conj.* or. **ou . . . ou . . .,** either . . . or . . .
où, *adv.* where.
ouailles, *n.f.pl.* religious congregation.
ouate, *n.f.* cotton; padding.
ouater (wä-), *vb.* pad.
oubli, *n.m.* forgetfulness; oblivion.
oublier, *vb.* forget.
oubliettes, *n.f.pl.* dungeon.
oublieux, *adj.* forgetful.
ouest (wĕst), *n.m.* west.
oui (wē), *adv.* yes.
ouï-dire, *n.m.* gossip, hearsay.
ouïe, *n.f.* hearing; gill.
ouïr, *vb.* hear.
ouragan, *n.m.* hurricane.
ourler, *vb.* hem.
ourlet, *n.m.* hem.
ours (-s), *n.m.* bear. **o. blanc,** polar bear.
ourson, *n.m.* bear cub.
outil, *n.m.* tool, implement.
outillage, *n.m.* quantity of tools, equipment.
outiller, *vb.* supply with tools.
outrage, *n.m.* outrage.
outrageant, *adj.* outrageous.
outrager, *vb.* outrage, affront.
outrance, *n.f.* extreme degree. **à o.** to the very end.
outre, *adv. and prep.* beyond. **en o.,** besides, furthermore.
outré, *adj.* excessive, extreme.
outrecuidant, *adj.* excessively bold and forward.
outre-mer, *adv.* across the seas.
outrer, *vb.* overdo, irritate.
ouvert, *adj.* open.
ouverture, *n.f.* opening, gap; overture.
ouvrable, *adj.* work, workable.
ouvrage, *n.m.* work.
ouvrer, *vb.* work.
ouvreuse, *n.f.* usher or usherette.
ouvrier, *n.m.* workman; *pl.* labor.

ouvrir, vb. open.

ouvroir, n.m. workroom or workshop.

ovaire, n.m. ovary.

ovale, adj. and n.m. oval.

ovation, n.f. ovation.

overdose, n.f. overdose.

ovni, n.m. UFO.

ovule, n.f. egg.

oxyder, vb. oxidize.

oxygène, n.m. oxygen.

ozone, n.f. ozone.

P

pacage, n.m. land used for pasture.

pacemaker, n.m. pacemaker.

pacificateur, 1. adj. pacifying. **2.** n.m. peacemaker.

pacification, n.f. peacemaking.

pacifier, vb. pacify, appease, soothe.

pacifique, adj. pacific, peaceful, peaceable.

pacifisme, n.m. pacifism.

pacotille, n.f. small wares.

pacte, n.m. covenant, pact.

pactiser, vb. make a pact, compromise.

pagaie, n.f. paddle.

pagaille, n.f. mess.

pagale, n.f. disorder, rush.

paganisme, n.m. paganism.

pagayer, vb. paddle.

pagayeur, n.m. paddler.

page, 1. n.m. page (boy). **2.** n.f. page (in book).

pages centrales, n.f.pl. centerfold.

pagination, n.f. pagination.

paginer, vb. number pages.

pagode, n.f. pagoda.

paie, n.f. pay.

paiement, payement, n.m. payment.

païen, adj. and n.m. pagan, heathen.

paillard, adj. lewd, indecent.

paillasse, n.f. mattress of straw; ticking.

paillasson, n.m. (door)mat.

paille, n.f. straw; defect (in gems).

paillette, n.f. spangle; defect.

pain, n.m. bread, loaf. **petit p.,** roll.

pair, 1. n.m. peer. **2.** adj. even (number), equal.

paire, n.f. pair.

pairesse, n.f. peeress.

pairie, n.f. peerage.

paisible, adj. peaceful.

paître, vb. graze.

paix, n.f. peace.

Pakistan, n.m. Pakistan.

palabre, n.f. palaver.

palais, n.m. palace; palate.

palan, n.m. gear for hoisting.

palatal, adj. palatal.

pale, n.f. blade; paddle.

pâle, adj. pale.

palefrenier, n.m. groom.

Palestine, n.f. Palestine.

palet, n.m. quoit.

paletot, n.m. overcoat.

palette, n.f. palette.

pâleur, n.f. paleness.

palier, n.m. stair landing.

pâlir, vb. grow pale or dim.

palissade, n.f. paling, fence.

pâlissant, adj. becoming pale.

palliatif, n.m. palliative; stopgap measure.

palmarès, n.m. list of winners.

palme, n.f. palm.

palmier, n.m. palm (tree).

palpable, adj. palpable.

palper, vb. touch, feel.

palpitant, adj. fluttering, palpitating.

palpiter, vb. flutter, beat, palpitate.

paludéen, adj. marshy.

paludisme, n.m. malaria.

pâmer, vb. **se p.,** faint.

pamphlet, n.m. pamphlet; satire.

pamphlétaire, n.m. pamphleteer.

pamplemousse, n.m. grapefruit.

pan, n.m. side, piece, flap.

panacée, n.f. panacea.

panache, n.m. plume; spirit.

panais, n.m. parsnip.

pancarte, n.f. sign, placard.

pandit, n.m. pundit.

pané, adj. dotted with bread crumbs.

panier, n.m. basket.

panique, adj. and n.f. panic.

panne, *n.f.* fat; accident, break-down.
panneau, *n.m.* panel.
panoplie, *n.f.* outfit; display.
panorama, *n.m.* panorama.
panse, *n.f.* paunch, cud.
pansement, *n.m.* dressing.
panser, *vb.* groom; dress.
pantalon, *n.m.* trousers.
panteler, *vb.* pant, gasp.
panthère, *n.f.* panther.
pantomime, *n.f.* pantomime.
pantoufle, *n.f.* slipper.
pantoufler, *vb.* act silly.
paon (pän), *n.m.* peacock.
papa, *n.m.* daddy.
papal, *adj.* papal.
papauté, *n.f.* papacy.
pape, *n.m.* pope.
paperasse, *n.f.* waste paper; official documents.
paperassier, *adj.* scribbling, petty.
papeterie, *n.f.* stationery.
papetier, *n.m.* stationer.
papier, *n.m.* paper.
papier à notes, *n.m.* notepaper.
papier à tapisser, *n.m.* wallpaper.
papier peint, *n.m.* wallpaper.
papillon, *n.m.* butterfly.
papillonner, *vb.* flutter, trifle.
papoter, *vb.* prate, prattle.
pâque, *n.f.* Passover.
paquebot, *n.m.* small liner, packet.
pâquerette, *n.f.* daisy.
Pâques, *n.m.* Easter.
paquet, *n.m.* package, parcel, bundle; deck (cards).
par, *prep.* by; through.
parabole, *n.f.* parabola; parable.
parachever, *vb.* perfect.
parachute, *n.m.* parachute.
parade, *n.f.* parade, procession.
parader, *vb.* parade, show off.
paradis, *n.m.* paradise.
paradoxal, *adj.* paradoxical.
paradoxe, *n.m.* paradox.
paraffine, *n.f.* paraffin.
parage, *n.m.* ancestry, descent; locality.
parages, *n.m.pl.* vicinity.
paragraphe, *n.m.* paragraph.
paraître, *vb.* appear, seem.
parallèle, *adj. and n.m.f.* parallel.
paralyser, *vb.* paralyze.
paralysie, *n.f.* paralysis.

paralytique, *adj. and n.m.f.* paralytic.
paramètre, *n.m.* parameter.
parangon, *n.m.* model, paragon.
paranoïa, *n.f.* paranoia.
paraphraser, *vb.* paraphrase.
parapluie, *n.m.* umbrella.
parasite, *n.m.* parasite.
parasol, *n.m.* parasol.
paratonnerre, *n.m.* lightning rod.
paravent, *n.m.* screen.
parc (-k), *n.m.* park.
parcelle, *n.f.* part, instalment.
parce que, *conj.* because.
parchemin, *n.m.* parchment.
parcimonie, *n.f.* parsimony.
parcomètre, *n.m.* parking meter.
parcourir, *vb.* run through.
parcours, *n.m.* course, journey.
par-dessous, *adv. and prep.* under(neath).
pardessus, *n.m.* overcoat.
par-dessus, *adv. and prep.* above, over.
pardon, 1. *n.m.* pardon, forgiveness. **2.** *interj.* sorry!
pardonner, *vb.* forgive, pardon.
pardonneur, *n.m.* pardoner.
pare-balles, *adj.* bullet-proof.
pare-boue, *n.m.* mudguard.
pare-brise, *n.m.* windshield.
pare-chocs, *n.m.* bumper.
pareil, *adj.* like.
parent, *n.m.* relative; (*pl.*) parents.
parenté, *n.f.* relationship.
parenthèse, *n.f.* parenthesis.
parer, *vb.* attire, deck out; parry.
paresse, *n.f.* sloth.
paresser, *vb.* laze, waste time.
paresseux, *adj.* lazy.
parfaire, *vb.* complete, finish up.
parfait, *adj.* perfect.
parfois, *adv.* sometimes.
parfum, *n.m.* perfume.
parfumé, *adj.* fragrant.
parfumer, *vb.* perfume.
parfumerie, *n.f.* perfumery.
pari, *n.m.* bet.
paria, *n.m.* outcast.
parier, *vb.* bet.
parieur, *n.m.* one who bets.
Parisien, *n.m.* Parisian.
parisien, *adj.* Parisian.
parité, *n.f.* equality, parity.
parjure, *n.m.* perjury.

parjurer, vb. **se p.,** commit perjury.
parking, n.m. parking lot.
parlant, adj. speaking, chatty.
parlement, n.m. parliament.
parlementaire, adj. parliamentary.
parlementer, vb. parley.
parler, vb. talk, speak.
parleur, n.m. one who speaks or talks.
parloir, n.m. parlor.
parmi, prep. among.
parodie, n.f. parody.
parodier, vb. parody, imitate.
paroi, n.f. wall lining.
paroisse, n.f. parish.
paroissial, adj. parochial.
parole, n.f. speech, word. **prendre la p.,** take the floor.
paroxysme, n.m. peak.
parquer, vb. park, enclose.
parquet, n.m. floor.
parqueterie, n.f. parquetry.
parrain, n.m. godfather.
parsemer, vb. spread, strew.
part, n.f. share, part. **de la p. de,** on behalf of. **quelque p.,** somewhere. **nulle p.,** nowhere. **faire p. à,** share; inform.
partage, n.m. partition, sharing, share.
partager, vb. share, divide.
partance, n.f. going, sailing.
partant, n.m. one who leaves.
partenaire, n.m.f. partner.
parti, n.m. party.
partial, adj. partial.
partialité, n.f. bias, partiality.
participant, adj. and n.m. participant.
participation, n.f. participation, share.
participe, n.m. participle.
participer, vb. partake, take part.
particularité, n.f. peculiarity.
particule, n.f. particle.
particulier, adj. particular; private; peculiar, special.
partie, n.f. part, party.
partiel, adj. partial.
partir, vb. depart, leave, go (come) away, sail.
partisan, n.m. partisan, follower.
partitif, adj. partitive.
partition, n.f. score (music).

partout, adv. everywhere, throughout. **p. où,** wherever.
parure, n.f. ornament.
parution, n.f. publication, appearance.
parvenir, vb. reach.
parvenu, n.m. upstart.
pas, 1. n.m. step, pace. **faux p.,** slip. **2.** adv. not. **p. du tout,** not at all.
passable, adj. fair.
passage, n.m. aisle, passage, alley.
passager, 1. n.m. passenger. **2.** adj. passing, fugitive.
passant, n.m. passer-by.
passavant, n.m. permit.
passe, n.f. passing, permit.
passé, adj. and n.m. past.
passe-partout, n.m. skeleton key; passport.
passeport, n.m. passport.
passer, vb. pass; go by; spend; strain. **se p. de,** go without.
passereau, n.m. sparrow.
passerelle, n.f. bridge.
passe-temps, n.m. pastime.
passible, adj. capable of feeling.
passif, adj. and n.m. passive.
passion, n.f. passion.
passionné, adj. passionate.
passionnel, adj. concerning or due to passion.
passionner, vb. interest, excite. **se p.,** be eager or excited over.
passoire, n.f. device for straining.
pastel, n.m. crayon.
pastèque, n.f. watermelon.
pasteur, n.m. pastor.
pasteuriser, vb. pasteurize.
pastille, n.f. lozenge, cough drop.
pastis, n.m. aniseed liquor.
pastoral, adj. pastoral.
pataud, adj. awkward.
patauger, vb. flounder.
pâte, n.f. paste, dough, batter.
pâté, n.m. block; pie.
patelin, n.m. (colloquial) village.
patenôtre, n.f. (Lord's) prayer.
patent, adj. patent, evident.
patente, n.f. license.
patenter, vb. license.
paterne, adj. paternal.
paternel, adj. paternal.
paternité, n.f. fatherhood.
pâteux, adj. pasty, thick, muddy.
pathétique, adj. pathetic.

pathologie, n.f. pathology.

patience, n.f. patience.

patient, adj. and n.m. patient.

patienter, vb. wait.

patin, n.m. skate.

patiner, vb. skate.

patineur, n.m. skater.

patinoire, n.f. skating rink.

pâtir, vb. suffer.

pâtisserie, n.f. pastry.

patois, n.m. dialect; gibberish.

pâtre, n.m. shepherd.

patriarche, n.m. patriarch.

patricien, adj. and n.m. patrician.

patrie, n.f. native country, homeland.

patrimoine, n.m. patrimony.

patriote, n.m.f. patriot.

patriotique, adj. patriotic.

patriotisme, n.m. patriotism.

patron, n.m. employer, boss; model, pattern; patron.

patronat, n.m. management, employers.

patronner, vb. patronize, support.

patrouille, n.f. patrol.

patrouiller, vb. patrol.

patte, n.f. paw, leg; flap.

pâturage, n.m. pasture.

pâture, n.f. fodder; pasture.

paume, n.f. palm.

paumé, 1. n.m. loser. **2.** adj. lost.

paupière, n.f. eyelid.

pause, n.f. pause.

pauvre, adj. poor.

pauvreté, n.f. poverty.

pavaner, vb. se p., swagger, strut.

pavé, n.m. pavement.

paver, vb. pave.

pavillon, n.m. pavilion.

pavot, n.m. poppy.

payant, adj. paying, profitable.

paye, n.f. payment, salary.

payement, n.m. payment.

payer, vb. pay, settle.

payeur, n.m. payer.

pays, n.m. country.

paysage, n.m. landscape, scenery.

paysager, adj. of the country, rural.

paysan, n.m. peasant.

Pays-Bas, les, n.m.pl. Holland; the Netherlands.

péage, n.m. toll, tollgate.

peau, n.f. skin, hide.

pêche, n.f. peach; fishing.

péché, n.m. sin.

pécher, vb. sin.

pêcher, 1. vb. fish. **2.** n.m. peach tree.

pêcherie, n.f. fishing place.

pécheur m., **pécheresse** f. **1.** n. sinner. **2.** adj. sinful.

pêcheur, n.m. fisherman.

pécule, n.m. savings.

pécuniaire, adj. pecuniary.

pédagogie, n.f. pedagogy.

pédale, n.f. pedal.

pédalo, n.m. pedal boat.

pédant, adj. and n.m. pedant, pedantic.

pédanterie, n.f. pedantry.

pédé(raste), n.m. homosexual.

pédestre, adj. pedestrian.

pédiatre, n.m. pediatrician.

pédicure, n.m. podiatrist.

pègre, n.f. underworld.

peigne, n.m. comb.

peigner, vb. comb.

peignoir, n.m. dressing-gown.

peindre, vb. paint, portray, depict.

peine, n.f. pain; penalty. **à p.,** hardly, barely; **faire de la p. à,** pain, vb.; **valoir la p. de,** be worth while to; **se donner la p.,** take the trouble.

peiner, vb. labor; grieve.

peintre, n.m. painter.

peinture, n.f. paint, painting.

péjoratif, adj. pejorative.

pelage, n.m. coat.

pelé, adj. bald, uncovered.

pêle-mêle, adv. pell-mell.

peler, vb. peel, pare.

pèlerin, n.m. pilgrim.

pèlerinage, n.m. pilgrimage.

pèlerine, n.f. cape.

pélican, n.m. pelican.

pelle, n.f. shovel.

pelletier, n.m. furrier.

pellicule, n.f. film.

pelote, n.f. ball, pellet.

peloton, n.m. ball; group of soldiers.

pelouse, n.f. lawn.

peluche, n.f. **animal en p.,** stuffed animal.

pelure, n.f. peel.

pénal, adj. penal.

pénalité, n.f. penalty.

penaud, *adj.* sheepish.

penchant, *n.m.* bent, liking, tendency.

pencher, *vb.* tilt, lean, droop. **se p.,** bend.

pendaison, *n.f.* hanging (execution).

pendant, *prep.* during; pending. **p. que,** as, while.

pendentif, *n.m.* pendant.

penderie, *n.f.* wardrobe.

pendiller, *vb.* dangle.

pendre, *vb.* hang.

pendule, *n.m.* pendulum. *n.f.* clock.

pénétrable, *adj.* penetrable.

pénétrant, *adj.* keen.

pénétration, *n.f.* penetration.

pénétrer, *vb.* penetrate, pervade.

pénible, *adj.* painful.

pénicilline, *n.f.* penicillin.

péninsule, *n.f.* peninsula.

pénis, *n.m.* penis.

pénitence, *n.f.* penance.

pénitencier, *n.m.* penitentiary.

pénitent, *adj. and n.m.* penitent.

penne, *n.f.* feather.

pénombre, *n.f.* gloom, shadow.

pensée, *n.f.* thought; pansy.

penser, *vb.* think.

penseur, *n.m.* thinker.

pensif, *adj.* thoughtful, pensive.

pension, *n.f.* board; pension.

pensionnaire, *n.m.f.* boarder.

pensionnat, *n.m.* boarding school.

pente, *n.f.* slope, slant.

Pentecôte, *n.f.* Whitsun, Pentecost.

pénurie, *n.f.* penury, scarcity.

pépé, *n.m.* (colloquial) grandpa.

pépier, *vb.* chirp.

pépin, *n.m.* pip, kernel; (colloquial) problem.

pépinière, *n.f.* nursery (plants).

pépite, *n.f.* nugget.

perçant, *adj.* sharp.

perce, *n.f.* boring tool.

percée, *n.f.* opening; breakthrough.

perce-neige, *n.f.* snowdrop.

percepteur, *n.m.* tax collector.

perception, *n.f.* perception; collecting.

percer, *vb.* pierce, bore.

percevoir, *vb.* collect, amass; perceive.

perche, *n.f.* pole, perch.

percher, *vb.* se p., perch.

perchoir, *n.m.* perch.

perclus, *adj.* lame, crippled.

percolateur, *n.m.* percolator.

percussion, *n.f.* percussion.

percuter, *vb.* hit, strike.

perdition, *n.f.* perdition.

perdre, *vb.* lose; waste.

perdrix, *n.f.* partridge.

père, *n.m.* father.

péremptoire, *adj.* peremptory.

perfection, *n.f.* perfection.

perfectionnement, *n.m.* improvement, finishing.

perfectionner, *vb.* perfect, finish.

perfectionniste, *adj. and n.m.f.* perfectionist.

perfide, *adj.* treacherous.

perfidie, *n.f.* treachery.

perforation, *n.f.* perforation.

perforer, *vb.* perforate, drill.

péricliter, *vb.* collapse.

péridural, *adj.* **anesthésie p.,** epidural.

péril (-I), *n.m.* peril, danger.

périlleux, *adj.* perilous, dangerous.

périmé, *adj.* outdated, expired.

périmètre, *n.m.* perimeter.

période, *n.f.* period, term, stage.

périodique, *adj.* periodic.

péripétie, *n.f.* shift of luck.

périphérique, *adj.* outlying, peripheral.

périr, *vb.* perish.

périscope, *n.m.* periscope.

périssable, *adj.* perishable.

perle, *n.f.* pearl, bead.

perlé, *adj.* pearly, perfect.

permanence, *n.f.* permanence.

permanent, *adj.* permanent.

perméable, *adj.* permeable.

permettre, *vb.* permit, allow.

permis, *n.m.* permit, license.

permission, *n.f.* permission; leave (of absence), furlough.

permissionnaire, *n.m.f.* one having a permit; one on leave.

permuter, *vb.* change, exchange.

pernicieux, *adj.* pernicious.

pérorer, *vb.* harangue, argue.

Pérou, *n.m.* Peru.

perpendiculaire, *adj.* perpendicular.

perpétrer, *vb.* commit.

perpétuel, *adj.* perpetual.

perpétuer, *vb.* perpetuate.

perplexe, *adj.* perplexed, undecided.

perplexité, *n.f.* perplexity.

perquisition, *n.f.* exploration, search.

perron, *n.m.* flight of steps.

perroquet, *n.m.* parrot.

perruque, *n.f.* wig.

persan, *adj. and n.m.* Persian.

perse, *adj.* Persian.

persécuter, *vb.* persecute.

persécution, *n.f.* persecution.

persévérance, *n.f.* perseverance.

persévérant, *adj.* persevering, resolute.

persévérer, *vb.* persevere.

persienne, *n.f.* blind, shutter.

persifler, *vb.* banter, ridicule.

persil, *n.m.* parsley.

Persique, *adj.* le golfe P., the Persian Gulf.

persistance, *n.f.* persistence.

persistant, *adj.* persistent.

persister, *vb.* persist.

personnage, *n.m.* personage; character.

personnalité, *n.f.* personality.

personne, 1. *n.f.* person. **2.** *pron.* nobody.

personnel, 1. *n.m.* personnel, staff. **2.** *adj.* personal.

personnifier, *vb.* personify.

perspective, *n.f.* perspective, prospect.

perspicace, *adj.* discerning.

perspicacité, *n.f.* insight.

persuader, *vb.* persuade, convince; induce.

persuasif, *adj.* persuasive.

perte, *n.f.* loss, waste; (*pl.*) casualties.

pertinence, *n.f.* pertinence.

pertinent, *adj.* relevant, pertinent.

perturbateur, *n.m.* agitator, disturber.

perturbation, *n.f.* disruption.

perturber, *vb.* disturb.

pervenche, *n.f.* periwinkle.

pervers, *adj.* perverse, contrary.

pervertir, *vb.* pervert.

pesant, *adj.* heavy, ponderous.

pesanteur, *n.f.* weight, dullness.

peser, *vb.* weigh.

pessimisme, *n.m.* pessimism.

pessimiste, *n.m.f.* pessimist.

peste, *n.f.* pestilence; nuisance.

pester, *vb.* **p. contre,** curse against.

pestilence, *n.f.* pestilence, plague, nuisance.

pétale, *n.m.* petal.

pétanque, *n.f.* bowling.

pétiller, *vb.* twinkle, crackle.

petit, 1. *adj.* little, small, petty. **2.** *n.m.* cub.

petite-fille, *n.f.* granddaughter.

petitesse, *n.f.* smallness, pettiness.

petit-fils (-fēs), *n.m.* grandson.

petit-gris, *n.m.* fur of the squirrel.

pétition, *n.f.* petition.

pétitionner, *vb.* request, ask.

petits-enfants, *n.m.pl.* grandchildren.

petits-pois, *n.m.pl.* peas.

pétrifiant, *adj.* petrifying.

pétrifier, *vb.* petrify or (se p.) become petrified.

pétrin, *n.m.* (colloquial) jam, fix.

pétrir, *vb.* knead, mold.

pétrole, *n.m.* petroleum, kerosene.

pétulance, *n.f.* petulance.

peu, 1. *n.m.* little; few. **2.** *adv.* not. **p. à p.,** gradually.

peuplade, *n.f.* tribe, clan.

peuple, *n.m.* people.

peupler, *vb.* people.

peuplier, *n.m.* poplar.

peur, *n.f.* fear. **avoir p.,** be afraid. **de p. que . . . ne,** lest.

peureux, *adj.* shy, timid.

peut-être, *adv.* perhaps, maybe.

phallocrate, *n.m.* macho.

phallocratie, *n.f.* machismo.

phantasme, *n.m.* fantasy.

phare, *n.m.* beacon, lighthouse; headlight.

pharmacie, *n.f.* drugstore, pharmacy.

pharmacien, *n.m.* druggist.

phase, *n.f.* phase.

phénix, *n.m.* phoenix; superior person.

phénoménal, *adj.* phenomenal.

phénomène, *n.m.* phenomenon; freak.

philanthrope, *n.m.* philanthropist.

philanthropie, *n.f.* philanthropy.
philatélie, *n.f.* stamp collecting.
Philippines, *n.f.pl.* the Philippines.
philosophe, *n.m.f.* philosopher.
philosophie, *n.f.* philosophy.
philosophique, *adj.* philosophical.
phobie, *n.f.* phobia.
phonéticien, *n.m.* phonetician.
phonétique, *adj. and n.f.* phonetic, phonetics.
phonographe, *n.m.* phonograph.
phoque, *n.m.* seal.
phosphorescent, *adj.* luminous.
photo, *n.f.* photograph.
photocopie, *n.f.* photocopy.
photocopieur, *n.m.* photocopier.
photographe, *n.m.f.* photographer.
photographie, *n.f.* photograph; photography.
phrase, *n.f.* sentence.
phtisie, *n.f.* consumption.
phtisique, *adj. and n.m.* consumptive.
physicien, *n.m.* physical scientist.
physionomie, *n.f.* looks, expression.
physique, 1. *n.f.* physics. 2. *adj.* physical.
piailler, *vb.* peep, squeal.
pianiste, *n.m.f.* pianist.
piano, *n.m.* piano.
pic, *n.m.* peak.
pichet, *n.m.* jug.
pick-up, *n.m.* phonograph.
picoter, *vb.* prick, peck.
pièce, *n.f.* piece; coin; patch; room. **p. de théâtre**, play.
pied, *n.m.* foot. **aller à p.**, walk. **coup de p.**, kick.
pied-à-terre, *n.m.* temporary quarters.
piédestal, *n.m.* pedestal.
pied-noir, *n.m.* Algerian-born French person.
piège, *n.m.* snare, trap.
pierre, *n.f.* stone.
pierreries, *n.f.pl.* jewelry, gems.
pierreux, *adj.* full of stone or grit.
pierrot, *n.m.* clown in pantomine.
piété, *n.f.* piety.
piétiner, *vb.* trample; mark time.
piéton, *n.m.* pedestrian.
piètre, *adj.* pitiful, mean, wretched.

pieu, *n.m.* stake, pile.
pieuvre, *n.f.* octopus.
pieux, *adj.* pious.
pigeon, *n.m.* pigeon, dove.
piger, *vb.* (colloquial) understand.
pigiste, *n.m.f.* freelance(r).
pile, *n.f.* stack; battery.
piler, *vb.* crush; beat someone.
pilier, *n.m.* pillar, column.
pillage, *n.m.* plundering.
piller, *vb.* plunder.
pilotage, *n.m.* piloting; driving piles.
pilote, *n.m.f.* pilot.
piloter, *vb.* pilot, lead.
pilule, *n.f.* pill.
piment, *n.m.* chili.
pimenter, *vb.* flavor, season.
pimpant, *adj.* stylish, smart.
pin, *n.m.* pine.
pinacle, *n.m.* pinnacle.
pinard, *n.m.* (colloquial) (cheap) wine.
pince, *n.f.* clip; (*pl.*) pliers.
pinceau, *n.m.* paintbrush.
pince-nez, *n.m.* eyeglasses.
pincer, *vb.* pinch, nip.
pinte, *n.f.* pint.
pioche, *n.f.* pickax.
piocher, *vb.* dig.
piocheur, *n.m.* digger.
pion, *n.m.* pawn, peon.
pioncer, *vb.* nap, sleep.
pionnier, *n.m.* pioneer.
pipe, *n.f.* pipe.
pipeline, *n.m.* pipeline.
piper, *vb.* catch, decoy, trick.
piquant, *adj.* sharp. **mot p.**, quip.
pique, *n.f.* spade.
pique-nique, *n.m.* picnic.
piquer, *vb.* prick, sting.
piquet, *n.m.* picket, peg, stake.
piqûre, *n.f.* prick, sting, puncture.
pirate, *n.m.f.* pirate.
pirate de l'air, *n.m.f.* hijacker.
piraterie, *n.f.* piracy.
pire, *adj.* worse, worst.
pirouette, *n.f.* pirouette.
pis, *adv.* worse, worst.
piscine, *n.f.* pool.
pissenlit, *n.m.* dandelion.
pistache, *n.f.* pistachio.
piste, *n.f.* track.
pistolet, *n.m.* pistol.

piston, *n.m.* piston; strings (influence).

pistonner, *vb.* help, push; pull strings for.

pitance, *n.f.* meager amount, as of food.

piteux, *adj.* pitiful.

pitié, *n.f.* pity, mercy.

pitoyable, *adj.* pitiful, miserable.

pitre, *n.m.* clown.

pittoresque, *adj.* picturesque, colorful.

pivoine, *n.f.* peony.

pivot, *n.m.* pivot.

pivoter, *vb.* turn, pivot, revolve.

pizza, *n.f.* pizza.

placard, *n.m.* closet; poster.

placarder, *vb.* post, display.

place, *n.f.* place, room.

placement, *n.m.* investment; placing.

placer, *vb.* invest; place.

placet, *n.m.* petition, demand.

placide, *adj.* placid.

placidité, *n.f.* placidness.

plafond, *n.m.* ceiling.

plafonner, *vb.* reach one's ceiling.

plage, *n.f.* beach.

plagiaire, *n.m.f.* one who plagiarizes.

plagiat, *n.m.* plagiarism.

plagier, *vb.* plagiarize.

plaid, *n.m.* plaid.

plaider, *vb.* plead.

plaideur, *n.m.* pleader.

plaidoirie, *n.f.* lawyer's speech.

plaie, *n.f.* wound, sore.

plaignant, *n.m.* plaintiff.

plaindre, *vb.* pity. **se p.,** complain.

plaine, *n.f.* plain.

plainte, *n.f.* complaint.

plaintif, *adj.* mournful.

plaire, *vb.* please. **s'il vous plaît,** if you please.

plaisance, *n.f.* pleasure, ease.

plaisant, *adj.* joking.

plaisanter, *vb.* joke.

plaisanterie, *n.f.* joke.

plaisir, *n.m.* pleasure.

plan, *n.m.* plan; plane; schedule, scheme. **premier p.,** foreground.

planche, *n.f.* board, shelf, plank. **planche à roulettes,** *n.f.* skateboard.

plancher, *n.m.* floor.

planer, *vb.* glide; hover.

planétaire, 1. *adj.* planetary. **2.** *n.m.* planetarium.

planète, *n.f.* planet.

planeur, *n.m.* glider (plane).

planifier, *vb.* plan.

plantation, *n.f.* plantation.

plante, *n.f.* plant; sole.

planter, *vb.* plant.

planteur, *n.m.* planter.

planton, *n.m.* military orderly.

plantureux, *adj.* fertile, rich.

plaque, *n.f.* plate, slab. **p. de projection,** lantern-slide.

plaquer, *vb.* plate; abandon.

plaquette, *n.f.* booklet; plaque.

plastic, *n.m.* plastic explosive.

plastique, *adj.* plastic.

plastiquer, *adj.* blow up.

plastronner, *vb.* pose, strut jauntily.

plat, 1. *n.m.* dish, platter. **2.** *adj.* flat. **œuf sur le p.,** fried egg.

platane, *n.m.* plane-tree.

plat-bord, *n.m.* gunwale.

plateau, *n.m.* plateau; tray.

plate-bande, *n.f.* flower bed.

plate-forme, *n.f.* platform.

platine, 1. *n.f.* platen, plate; turntable. **2.** *n.m.* platinum.

platitude, *n.f.* flatness.

plâtras, *n.m.* rubbish, rubble.

plâtre, *n.m.* plaster; cast (*med.*).

plausible, *adj.* plausible.

plébéien, *adj.* ignoble.

plébiscite, *n.m.* plebiscite.

plein, *adj.* full; crowded.

pleinement, *adv.* fully.

plénier, *adj.* complete, plenary.

plénitude, *n.f.* fullness.

pléthore, *n.f.* overabundance, plethora.

pleurer, *vb.* cry, weep, lament, mourn.

pleurésie, *n.f.* pleurisy.

pleurnicher, *vb.* complain, whine.

pleurs, *n.m.pl.* tears, weeping.

pleutre, *n.m.* cad, coward.

pleuvoir, *vb.* rain.

pli, *n.m.* envelope; fold, pleat, crease.

pliable, *adj.* pliable.

pliant, *n.m.* folding chair.

plier, *vb.* fold, bend.

plissement, *n.m.* fold, folding.

plisser, *vb.* pleat.

plomb, *n.m.* lead.

plomberie, *n.f.* plumbing.

plombier, *n.m.* plumber.

plongeoir, *n.m.* diving board.

plongeon, *n.m.* plunge, dive.

plonger, *vb.* plunge, dive, dip.

plongeur, *n.m.* diver; dishwasher.

plouf, *interj. and n.m.* splash, plop.

ploutocrate, *n.m.* plutocrat.

ployer, *vb.* incline, bend.

pluie, *n.f.* rain.

pluie radioactive, *n.f.* fallout.

plumage, *n.m.* feathers.

plume, *n.f.* pen; feather.

plumeau, *n.m.* feather duster.

plumer, *vb.* pluck.

plumet, *n.m.* plume.

plumeux, *adj.* feathery.

plumier, *n.m.* pen or pencil case.

plupart, *n.f.* greater part, majority.
  pour la p., mostly.

pluralité, *n.f.* plurality.

pluriel, *adj. and n.m.* plural.

plus, *adv.* more, most. **ne . . . p.,** no
  more. **non p.,** neither. **en p.,** extra.

plusieurs, *adj. and pron.* several.

plus-que-parfait, *n.m.* pluperfect.

plus-value, *n.f.* profit.

plutôt, *adv.* rather.

pluvieux, *adj.* rainy, wet.

pneu, *n.m.* tire.

pneumatique, *abbr.* **pneu,** *n.m.*
  tire.

pneumonie, *n.f.* pneumonia.

pochade, *n.f.* hasty sketch.

poche, *n.f.* pocket.

pocher, *vb.* poach.

pocheter, *vb.* pocket.

pochette, *n.f.* little pocket; handkerchief.

pochoir, *n.m.* stencil.

poêle, *n.m.* stove.

poème, *n.m.* poem.

poésie, *n.f.* poem, poetry.

poète, *n.m.* poet.

poétique, *adj.* poetic.

poids (pwä), *n.m.* weight.

poignant, *adj.* poignant, keen.

poignard, *n.m.* dagger.

poignarder, *vb.* stab.

poigne, *n.f.* grip, power.

poignée, *n.f.* handful; handle.

poignet, *n.m.* wrist; cuff.

poil (pwäl), *n.m.* hair.

poilu, 1. *adj.* hairy. **2.** *n.m.* French
  soldier.

poinçon, *n.m.* punch.

poing, *n.m.* fist.

point, *n.m.* point, dot, period;
  stitch. **p. de vue,** point of view. **p.
  du jour,** dawn. **ne . . . p.,** none. **être
  sur le p. de,** be about to. **au p.,** in
  focus. **deux p.s,** colon. **p. d'interrogation,** question mark.

pointage, *n.m.* pointing; *(mil.)*
  sighting.

pointe, *n.f.* point, tip, touch (small
  amount).

pointer, *vb.* point, aim; check in.

pointeur, *n.m.* pointer, checker.

pointillage, *n.m.* dotting.

pointiller, *vb.* dot; tease.

pointilleux, *adj.* fussy, precise.

pointu, *adj.* pointed.

pointure, *n.f.* size (shoe).

point-virgule, *n.m.* semicolon.

poire, *n.f.* pear.

poireau, *n.m.* leek.

poireauter, *vb.* hang around.

poirier, *n.m.* pear tree.

pois, *n.m.* pea; dot.

poison, *n.m.* poison.

poisser, *vb.* make gluey or sticky.

poisson, *n.m.* fish.

poissonnerie, *n.f.* fish store.

poissonneux, *adj.* filled with fish.

poissonnier, *n.m.* fish dealer.

poitrinaire, *adj. and n.m.f.* consumptive.

poitrine, *n.f.* chest.

poivre, *n.m.* pepper.

poivrer, *vb.* spice with pepper.

poivrier, *n.m.* pepper plant.

poivron, *n.m.* pepper.

poix, *n.f.* pitch.

polaire, *adj.* polar.

pôle, *n.m.* pole.

polémique, *n.f.* argument.

poli, 1. *adj.* civil, polite. **2.** *n.m.* polish.

police, *n.f.* police; (insurance) policy.

policer, *vb.* refine.

polichinelle, *n.m.* Punch (puppet).

policier, *n.m.* policeman. **roman p.,**
  detective story.

polir, *vb.* polish.

polisseur, *n.m.* polisher.

polisson, 1. *n.m.* gamin, scamp. **2.** *adj.* running wild.

polissonnerie, *n.f.* naughty action or remark.

politesse, *n.f.* good manners.

politicien, *n.m.f.* politician, political schemer.

politique, 1. *n.f.* policy, politics. **2.** *adj.* politic, political.

polka, *n.f.* polka.

pollen, *n.m.* pollen.

polluer, *vb.* pollute.

pollution, *n.f.* pollution.

Pologne, *n.f.* Poland.

Polonais, *n.m.* Pole.

polonais, *adj. and n.m.* Polish.

poltron, 1. *adj.* craven, cowardly. **2.** *n.m.* coward.

poltronnerie, *n.f.* cowardly behavior.

polycopier, *vb.* duplicate.

polygame, 1. *n.m.f.* polygamist. **2.** *adj.* polygamous.

polygamie, *n.f.* polygamy.

polygone, *n.m.* polygon.

polyvalent, *adj.* varied, versatile.

pommade, *n.f.* pomade, salve.

pomme, *n.f.* apple. **p. de terre,** potato.

pommeau, *n.m.* pommel.

pommette, *n.f.* cheekbone.

pommier, *n.m.* apple tree.

pompe, *n.f.* pump; pomp.

pomper, *vb.* pump.

pompeux, *adj.* pompous.

pompier, *n.m.* fireman.

pompiste, *n.m.f.* gas station attendant.

pompon, *n.m.* pompom, tuft.

ponce, *n.f.* pumice.

ponctualité, *n.f.* punctuality.

ponctuation, *n.f.* punctuation.

ponctuel, *adj.* punctual.

ponctuer, *vb.* punctuate.

pondre, *vb.* lay (eggs).

poney, *n.m.* pony.

pont, *n.m.* bridge; deck.

pontife, *n.m.* pontiff.

pont-levis, *n.m.* drawbridge.

ponton, *n.m.* pontoon.

pop, *adj. and n.m.* pop (music).

popeline, *n.f.* poplin.

popote, *n.f.* mess (military).

populace, *n.f.* mob.

populaire, *adj.* popular.

populariser, *vb.* popularize.

popularité, *n.f.* popularity.

population, *n.f.* population.

populeux, *adj.* populous.

porc, *n.m.* pig, pork.

porcelaine, *n.f.* china.

porc-épic, *n.m.* porcupine.

porche, *n.m.* porch.

porcherie, *n.f.* pigpen.

pore, *n.m.* pore.

poreux, *adj.* porous.

porno, *adj.* porn.

pornographie, *n.f.* pornography.

port, *n.m.* port, harbor; carrying; postage.

portable, *adj.* wearable.

portail, *n.m.* portal.

portant, *adj.* **bien/mal p.,** in good/ill health.

portatif, *adj.* portable.

porte, *n.f.* door, gate.

porte-affiches, *n.m.* billboard.

porte-avions, *n.m.* aircraft carrier.

portée, *n.f.* range, import, scope, reach; litter. **hors de p.,** out of reach.

portefaix, *n.m.* porter.

portefeuille, *n.m.* wallet, case, portfolio.

portemanteau, *n.m.* cloak rack.

portement, *n.m.* carrying.

porte-monnaie, *n.m.* purse.

porte-parole, *n.m.* spokesman.

porter, *vb.* carry, bear; wear. **se p.,** be (in health).

porte-rame, *n.m.* oarlock.

porteur, *n.m.* porter, bearer.

portier, *n.m.* doorman, porter.

portière, *n.f.* door-curtain.

portion, *n.f.* portion, share.

portique, *n.m.* portico, porch.

porto, *n.m.* port wine.

portrait, *n.m.* portrait.

portraitiste, *n.m.f.* painter of portraits.

Portugais, *n.m.* Portuguese (person).

portugais, 1. *n.m.* Portuguese (language). **2.** *adj.* Portuguese.

Portugal, *n.m.* Portugal.

pose, *n.f.* pose, attitude.

posé, *n.f.* poised, set.

poser, *vb.* place, stand, set, lay. **se p.,** settle, alight.

poseur, *n.m.* person or thing that places or applies; affected person.

positif, *adj.* and *n.m.* positive.

position, *n.f.* stand, place, position.

positiviste, *n.m.f.* positivist.

posologie, *n.f.* dosage.

posséder, *vb.* own, possess.

possesseur, *n.m.* possessor.

possessif, *adj.* and *n.m.* possessive.

possession, *n.f.* possession.

possibilité, *n.f.* possibility.

possible, *adj.* possible. **tout son p.,** one's utmost.

postal, *adj.* postal.

poste, *n.f.* mail. **mettre à la p.,** mail. **p. restante,** general delivery.

poste, *n.m.* post. **p. d'essence,** gas station. **p. de secours,** first-aid station.

poster, *vb.* post (letter); place.

postérieur, *adj.* rear, posterior.

postérité, *n.f.* posterity.

posthume, *adj.* posthumous.

postiche, *adj.* false, unnecessary.

postier, *n.m.* postal worker.

post-scriptum, *n.m.* postscript.

postulant, *n.m.* applicant.

postuler, *vb.* apply for.

posture, *n.f.* posture.

pot, *n.m.* pot, pitcher, jar.

potable, *adj.* drinkable.

potage, *n.m.* soup.

potager, *adj.* vegetable.

potasse, *n.f.* potash.

pot-au-feu, *n.m.* stew.

pot-de-vin, *n.m.* tip, bribe.

pote, *n.m.* (colloquial) buddy.

poteau, *n.m.* post.

potée, *n.f.* potful.

potelé, *adj.* chubby.

potence, *n.f.* gallows.

potentat, *n.m.* potentate.

potentiel, *adj.* and *n.m.* potential.

poterie, *n.f.* pottery.

poterne, *n.f.* postern.

potier, *n.m.* potter.

potins, *n.m.pl.* gossip.

potion, *n.f.* potion.

potiron, *n.m.* pumpkin.

pou, *n.m.* louse.

poubelle, *n.f.* garbage can.

pouce, *n.m.* thumb; inch.

pouding, *n.m.* pudding.

poudre, *n.f.* powder.

poudrer, *vb.* powder.

poudreux, *adj.* full of powder or dust.

poudrier, *n.m.* compact (cosmetic).

poudroyer, *vb.* be dusty.

pouilleux, *adj.* infested with lice.

poulailler, *n.m.* henhouse.

poulain, *n.m.* colt.

poule, *n.f.* hen, chicken.

poulet, *n.m.* chicken.

poulette, *n.f.* pullet.

poulie, *n.f.* pulley.

poulpe, *n.m.* octopus.

pouls, *n.m.* pulse.

poumon, *n.m.* lung.

poupe, *n.f.* poop (of ship).

poupée, *n.f.* doll.

poupin, *adj.* smart, chic.

pour, *prep.* for; in order to. **p. que,** so that.

pourboire, *n.m.* tip, gratuity.

pourceau, *n.m.* hog.

pour-cent, *n.m.* percent.

pourcentage, *n.m.* percentage.

pourchasser, *vb.* pursue.

pourfendeur, *n.m.* killer, bully.

pourparlers, *n.m.pl.* discussion, parley.

pourpoint, *n.m.* doublet.

pourpre, *adj.* purple.

pourquoi, *adv.* why.

pourri, *adj.* rotten.

pourrir, *vb.* rot, spoil.

pourriture, *n.f.* rot.

poursuite, *n.f.* pursuit.

poursuivant, *n.m.* one who sues or prosecutes.

poursuivre, *vb.* pursue; sue, prosecute.

pourtant, *adv.* however.

pourvoi, *n.m.* appeal (at court).

pourvoir, *vb.* provide, supply. **p. à,** cater to.

pourvoyeur, *n.m.* caterer, purveyor.

pourvu que, *conj.* provided that.

pousse, *n.f.* shoot, sprouting.

poussée, *n.f.* push.

pousser, *vb.* push, urge, drive, grow.

poussette, *n.f.* stroller.

poussier, *n.m.* coal dust.

poussière, *n.f.* dust.

poussiéreux, *adj.* dusty.

poussin, *n.m.* newly hatched chick.
poussoir, *n.m.* push-button.
poutre, *n.f.* beam.
pouvoir, 1. *vb.* be able, can, may. **2.** *n.m.* power.
prairie, *n.f.* meadow.
praline, *n.f.* burnt almond.
praticable, *adj.* practicable.
praticien, *n.m.* practitioner.
pratique, 1. *n.f.* practice, exercise. **2.** *adj.* practical.
pratiquement, *adv.* practically, virtually.
pratiquer, *vb.* practice, exercise.
pré, *n.m.* meadow.
préalable, *adj.* preliminary.
préambule, *n.m.* preamble.
préau, *n.m.* yard, as of a prison.
préavis, *n.m.* advance notice.
précaire, *adj.* precarious.
précaution, *n.f.* precaution, discretion.
précédent, *n.m.* precedent.
précéder, *vb.* precede; come (go) before.
précepte, *n.m.* precept.
précepteur, *n.m.* tutor.
prêche, *n.m.* sermon.
prêcher, *vb.* preach.
précieux, *adj.* precious, valuable.
préciosité, *n.f.* preciosity.
précipice, *n.m.* precipice.
précipitamment, *adv.* headlong.
précipitation, *n.f.* hurry.
précipité, *adj.* hasty.
précipiter, *vb.* precipitate. **se p.,** rush, hasten.
précis, *adj.* precise, exact, accurate.
précisément, *adv.* precisely, definitely, just so.
préciser, *vb.* specify.
précision, *n.f.* accuracy, precision.
précité, *adj.* previously cited.
précoce, *adj.* precocious.
précocité, *n.f.* precociousness.
précompter, *vb.* deduct in advance.
préconçu, *adj.* preconceived.
préconiser, *vb.* extol, praise.
préconnaissance, *n.f.* foreknowledge.
précurseur, *n.m.* precursor.
prédécesseur, *n.m.* predecessor.

prédestination, *n.f.* predestination.
prédicateur, *n.m.* preacher.
prédiction, *n.f.* prediction.
prédilection, *n.f.* preference, predilection.
prédire, *vb.* foretell, predict.
prédisposer, *vb.* predispose.
prédisposition, *n.f.* predisposition.
prédominant, *adj.* predominant.
prééminence, *n.f.* preeminence.
préfabriquer, *adj.* prefabricated.
préface, *n.f.* preface.
préfecture, *n.f.* prefecture, district.
préférable, *adj.* preferable.
préférence, *n.f.* preference.
préférer, *vb.* prefer.
préfet, *n.m.* prefect.
préfixe, *n.m.* prefix.
préfixer, *vb.* fix in advance.
prégnant, *adj.* pregnant.
préhistorique, *adj.* prehistoric.
préjudice, *n.m.* injury.
préjudiciel, *adj.* interlocutory (as in law).
préjugé, *n.m.* prejudice.
préjuger, *vb.* prejudge.
prélasser, *vb.* **se p.,** bask, lounge.
prélat, *n.m.* prelate.
prélèvement, *n.m.* deduction in advance.
prélever, *vb.* deduct previously.
préliminaire, *adj.* preliminary.
prélude, *n.m.* prelude.
prématuré, *adj.* premature.
préméditation, *n.f.* premeditation.
préméditer, *vb.* premeditate.
prémices, *n.f.pl.* first fruits, first works.
premier, *adj.* first, foremost; early; former.
prémisse, *n.f.* premise.
prémonition, *n.f.* premonition.
prémunir, *vb.* warn, take precautions.
prendre, *vb.* take.
preneur, *n.m.* buyer.
prénom, *n.m.* given name.
prénommé, *adj.* previously named.
préoccupation, *n.f.* care, worry.
préoccuper, *vb.* worry.
prépaiement, *n.m.* prepayment.
préparatifs, *n.m.pl.* preparation.
préparation, *n.f.* preparation.

préparatoire, adj. preparatory.
préparer, vb. prepare.
prépondérance, n.f. preponderance.
prépondérant, adj. preponderant.
préposé, n.m. one in charge.
préposition, n.f. preposition.
préretraite, n.f. early retirement.
prérogative, n.f. prerogative.
près, 1. adv. near. **2.** prep. **p. de,** near. **de p.,** nearby.
présage, n.m. omen.
présager, vb. (fore)bode.
presbyte, adj. far-sighted.
presbytère, n.m. parsonage, presbytery.
prescription, n.f. prescription.
prescrire, vb. prescribe.
préséance, n.f. precedence.
présélection, n.f. triage.
présence, n.f. presence; attendance.
présent, adj. and n.m. present.
présentable, adj. presentable.
présentation, n.f. presentation, introduction.
présentement, adv. now, at present.
présenter, vb. present; introduce. **se p. à l'esprit,** come to mind.
préservatif, n.m. condom.
préservation, n.f. preservation.
préserver, vb. preserve.
présidence, n.f. presidency.
président, n.m. president, chairman.
présidente, n.f. chairwoman.
présidentiel, adj. presidential.
présider, vb. preside.
présomptif, adj. apparent, presumed.
présomptueux, adj. presumptuous.
presque, adv. almost, nearly.
presqu'île, n.f. peninsula.
pressage, n.m. pressing.
pressant, adj. urgent.
presse, n.f. press; crowd.
pressé, adj. hurried.
pressentiment, n.m. foreboding, misgiving.
pressentir, vb. foresee.
presse-papiers, n.m. paperweight.
presser, vb. press; urge; hurry.
pressing, n.m. dry cleaner.

pression, n.f. pressure.
pressoir, n.m. machine or device for squeezing.
pressurer, vb. squeeze, put pressure on.
prestance, n.f. imposing appearance.
prestation, n.f. allowance; performance.
preste, adj. dexterous, nimble.
prestesse, n.f. vivacity, nimbleness.
prestige, n.m. prestige; illusion.
prestigieux, adj. enchanting.
présumer, vb. presume.
présupposer, vb. presuppose.
prêt, 1. n.m. loan. **2.** adj. ready.
prêtable, adj. lendable.
prétendant, n.m. claimant.
prétendre, vb. claim.
prétendu, adj. supposed, so-called.
prétentieux, adj. pretentious.
prétention, n.f. claim.
prêter, vb. lend.
prêteur, n.m. lender.
prétexte, n.m. pretext.
prétexter, vb. pretend, feign.
prêtre, n.m. priest.
prêtresse, n.f. priestess.
preuve, n.f. proof.
preux, adj. and n.m. gallant, brave.
prévalence, n.f. attentiveness, obligingness.
prévenant, adj. considerate.
prévenir, vb. prevent; warn.
préventif, 1. adj. preventive. **2.** n.m. deterrent.
prévention, n.f. bias; prevention.
prévenu, adj. partial, biased.
prévision, n.f. forecast, expectation, prediction.
prévoir, vb. foresee.
prévôt, n.m. provost.
prévoyance, n.f. foresight.
prévoyant, adj. farseeing, prudent.
prier, vb. beg; pray.
prière, n.f. prayer.
prieur, n.m. prior.
prieuré, n.m. priory.
primaire, adj. primary.
primauté, n.f. preeminence, primacy.
prime, 1. n.f. premium; subsidy. **2.** adj. first; accented.

primé, *adj.* prize-winning.

primer, *vb.* outdo, excel.

primeur, *n.f.* freshness, earliness.

primitif, *adj.* primitive; original.

primordial, *adj.* primordial.

prince, *n.m.* prince.

princesse, *n.f.* princess.

princier, *adj.* princely.

principal, *adj.* chief, main, principal.

principauté, *n.f.* principality.

principe, *n.m.* principle.

printanier, *adj.* of spring.

printemps, *n.m.* spring.

priorité, *n.f.* priority.

prisable, *adj.* estimable.

prise, *n.f.* grasp, hold, grip. **p. de courant,** (electric) plug.

prisée, *n.f.* appraisal.

priser, *vb.* appraise; prize; take (drugs).

priseur, *n.m.* auctioneer, appraiser.

prisme, *n.m.* prism.

prison, *n.f.* jail, prison.

prisonnier, *n.m.* prisoner.

privation, *n.f.* privation, want, hardship.

privé, *adj.* private.

priver, *vb.* deprive.

privilège, *n.m.* privilege, license.

privilégier, *vb.* license.

prix, *n.m.* price, charge, fare; prize; award.

prix-courant, *n.m.* list of prices.

probabilité, *n.f.* probability, chances.

probable, *adj.* likely, probable.

probant, *adj.* convincing.

probité, *n.f.* probity.

problématique, *adj.* problematical.

problème, *n.m.* problem.

procédé, *n.m.* procedure, process.

procéder, *vb.* proceed.

procédure, *n.f.* proceeding.

procès, *n.m.* trial; (law)suit.

procession, *n.f.* procession.

processionnel, *adj.* processional.

processus, *n.m.* process.

procès-verbal, *n.m.* minutes (of meeting).

prochain, 1. *n.m.* neighbor. **2.** *adj.* next.

prochainement, *adv.* soon.

proche, *adj.* near, close.

Proche-Orient, *n.m.* Near East.

proclamation, *n.f.* proclamation.

proclamer, *vb.* proclaim.

procréation, *n.f.* procreation.

procurer, *vb.* procure, get.

procureur, *n.m.* prosecuting attorney.

prodigalement, *adv.* prodigally.

prodigalité, *n.f.* extravagance.

prodige, *n.m.* prodigy.

prodigieux, *adj.* wondrous.

prodigue, *adj.* extravagant, lavish, profuse.

prodiguer, *vb.* lavish.

producteur, *n.m.* producer.

productif, *adj.* productive.

production, *n.f.* production.

productivité, *n.f.* productivity.

produire, *vb.* produce, yield, breed.

produit, *n.m.* product, commodity.

proéminence, *n.f.* prominence.

proéminent, *adj.* prominent, standing out.

prof, *n.m.* teacher.

profane, *adj.* profane.

profaner, *vb.* misuse, debase, profane.

proférer, *vb.* say, utter.

professer, *vb.* profess.

professeur, *n.m.* professor, teacher.

profession, *n.f.* profession.

professionnel, *adj.* professional.

professoral, *adj.* professorial.

professorat, *n.m.* professorship; teaching.

profil (-l), *n.m.* profile.

profiler, *vb.* show a profile of.

profit, *n.m.* profit.

profitable, *adj.* profitable.

profiter, *vb.* profit.

profiteur, *n.m.* profiteer.

profond, *adj.* deep, profound; in-depth.

profondeur, *n.f.* depth.

profus, *adj.* profuse.

profusion, *n.f.* profusion, excess.

progéniture, *n.f.* offspring.

programmation, *n.f.* programming.

programme, *n.m.* program.

progrès, *n.m.* progress, advance.

progresser, *vb.* progress.

progressif, *adj.* progressive.

progressiste, *n.m.* progressive.

prohiber, *vb.* prohibit.

prohibitif, *adj.* prohibitive.

prohibition, *n.f.* prohibition.

proie, *n.f.* prey.

projecteur, *n.m.* projector.

projectile, *n.m.* missile.

projection, *n.f.* projection.

projet, *n.m.* project, plan. **p. de loi,** bill.

projeter, *vb.* project, plan.

prolétaire, *adj. and n.m.* proletarian.

prolétariat, *n.m.* proletariat.

prolifération, *n.f.* proliferation.

prolifique, *adj.* prolific.

prolixe, *adj.* verbose.

prologue, *n.m.* prologue.

prolongation, *n.f.* extension, prolongation.

prolonger, *vb.* extend, prolong.

promenade, *n.f.* excursion; walk; ride.

promener, *vb.* take out. **se p.,** take a walk (ride).

promeneur, *n.m.* walker.

promesse, *n.f.* promise.

promettre, *vb.* promise.

promiscuité, *n.f.* promiscuity; crowding.

promontoire, *n.m.* promontory.

promoteur, *n.m.* promoter.

promotion, *n.f.* promotion.

promouvoir, *vb.* promote.

prompt, *adj.* prompt.

promptitude, *n.f.* quickness.

promulguer, *vb.* promulgate.

prôner, *vb.* lecture to, praise.

pronom, *n.m.* pronoun.

prononcer, *vb.* pronounce, utter; deliver.

prononciation, *n.f.* pronunciation.

pronostic, *n.m.* prognosis; prediction.

propagande, *n.f.* propaganda.

propagandiste, *n.m.f.* propagandist.

propagateur, *n.m.* propagator.

propagation, *n.f.* propagation.

propager, *vb.* propagate.

propension, *n.f.* inclination, propensity.

prophète, *n.m.* prophet.

prophétie, *n.f.* prophecy.

prophétique, *adj.* prophetic.

prophétiser, *vb.* prophesy.

propice, *adj.* favorable. **peu p.,** unfavorable.

propitiation, *n.f.* propitiation, conciliation.

proportion, *n.f.* proportion.

proportionné, *adj.* proportionate.

proportionnel, *adj.* proportional.

proportionner, *vb.* keep in proportion.

propos, *n.m.* subject; discourse. **à p.,** relevant. **à p. de,** with regard to.

proposable, *adj.* suitable, appropriate.

proposer, *vb.* propose; move. **se p. de,** intend, mean.

proposition, *n.f.* proposal, proposition.

propre, *adj.* proper; clean, neat; own. **peu p.,** unfit.

propreté, *n.f.* cleanliness, neatness.

propriétaire, *n.m.f.* proprietor.

propriété, *n.f.* property (landed), estate.

propulser, *vb.* push, propel.

propulseur, *n.m.* propeller.

propulsion, *n.f.* propulsion.

proroger, *vb.* postpone, extend time limit.

prosaïque (-zä ĕk), *adj.* prosaic.

prosaïsme, *n.m.* prosaicness, dullness.

prosateur, *n.m.* writer of prose.

proscription, *n.f.* proscription.

proscrire, *vb.* outlaw, proscribe.

proscrit, *adj. and n.m.* exile(d); forbidden.

prose, *n.f.* prose.

prosodie, *n.f.* prosody.

prospecter, *vb.* search, as for gold.

prospecteur, *n.m.* prospector.

prospectus (-s), *n.m.* leaflet, pamphlet.

prospère, *adj.* prosperous.

prospérer, *vb.* flourish, thrive, prosper.

prospérité, *n.f.* prosperity.

prosterner, *vb.* prostrate.

prostituée, *n.f.* prostitute.

prostitution, *n.f.* prostitution.

protagoniste, *n.m.f.* main character.

protecteur, 1. n.m. protector; patron. **2.** adj. protective.

protecteur du citoyen, n.m. ombudsman (in Quebec).

protection, n.f. protection.

protectorat, n.m. protectorate.

protéger, vb. protect; patronize, foster.

protéine, n.f. protein.

protestant, adj. and n.m. Protestant.

protestantisme, n.m. Protestantism.

protestation, n.f. protest.

protester, vb. protest.

protêt, n.m. protest.

prothèse, n.f. artificial aid, as a denture.

protocole, n.m. protocol.

prototype, n.m. prototype.

protubérance, n.f. protuberance.

proue, n.f. prow, front.

prouesse, n.f. prowess.

prouver, vb. prove.

provenance, n.f. place of origin; product.

provençal, 1. adj. of Provence. **2.** n.m. language of Provence.

provende, n.f. provender, foodstuffs.

provenir, vb. come from.

proverbe, n.m. proverb, saying.

proverbial, adj. proverbial.

providence, n.f. providence.

providentiel, adj. providential.

province, n.f. province.

provincial, adj. and n.m. provincial.

provincialisme, n.m. provincialism.

proviseur, n.m. principal, headmaster.

provision, n.f. supply, store, provision.

provisoire, adj. temporary.

provocateur, n.m. one who provokes action.

provocation, n.f. provocation.

provoquer, vb. provoke.

proximité, n.f. closeness, proximity.

prude, 1. n.f. prude. **2.** adj. prudish.

prudence, n.f. caution, prudence.

prudent, adj. cautious, prudent.

pruderie, n.f. prudishness.

prune, n.f. plum.

pruneau, n.m. prune.

prunelle, n.f. pupil (of eye).

prunier, n.m. plum tree.

Prusse, n.f. Prussia.

Prussien, n.m. Prussian (person).

prussien, adj. Prussian.

psalmiste, n.m. psalmist.

psaume, n.m. psalm.

psautier, n.m. psalm book.

pseudonyme, n.m. pseudonym.

psychanalyse (-k-), n.f. psychoanalysis.

psychédélique (-k-), adj. psychedelic.

psychiatre (-k-), n.m. psychiatrist.

psychiatrie (-k-), n.f. psychiatry.

psychique (-k-), adj. psychic.

psychologie (-k-), n.f. psychology.

psychologique (-k-), adj. psychological.

psychologue (-k-), n.m.f. psychologist.

psychose (-k-), n.f. psychosis.

psychothérapie (-k-), n.f. psychotherapy.

puant, adj. foul; shameful.

pub, n.f. advertising; advertisement.

puberté, n.f. puberty.

public, 1. adj. m., **publique** f. public. **2.** n.m. public; audience (theater).

publication, n.f. publication.

publiciste, n.m.f. publicist.

publicité, n.f. publicity, advertisement(s).

publier, vb. publish, issue.

puce, n.f. flea.

pucelle, n.f. young girl, virgin.

pudeur, n.f. modesty.

pudiband, adj. prudish.

pudique, adj. modest.

puer, vb. smell, have an offensive odor.

puéril (-l), adj. childish.

pugiliste, m. boxer.

puîné, adj. younger (of a brother or sister).

puis, adv. then.

puisard, n.m. cesspool.

puisatier, n.m. well-digger.

puiser, vb. draw up, derive.

puisque, conj. since, as.

puissamment, *adv.* very, powerfully.

puissance, *n.f.* power.

puissant, *adj.* potent, powerful, mighty.

puits (pwē), *n.m.* well; shaft.

pull(-over), *n.m.* sweater.

pulluler, *vb.* breed abundantly, multiply.

pulmonaire, *adj.* pulmonary.

pulpe, *n.f.* pulp.

pulpeux, *adj.* pulpy.

pulsar, *n.m.* pulsar.

pulsation, *n.f.* pulsation, beating.

pulvérisateur, *n.m.* vaporizer, spray.

pulvériser, *vb.* spray; pulverize.

punaise, *n.f.* bedbug; thumbtack.

punir, *vb.* punish.

punitif, *adj.* punitive.

punition, *n.f.* punishment.

pupille (-l), *n.m.f.* ward; pupil (of the eye).

pupitre, *n.m.* desk.

pur, *adj.* pure.

purée, *n.f.* mash.

purement, *adv.* purely, solely.

pureté, *n.f.* purity.

purgatoire, *n.m.* purgatory.

purge, *n.f.* purge.

purger, *vb.* purge.

purification, *n.f.* purification.

purifier, *vb.* purify, cleanse.

puritain, *adj. and n.m.* Puritan.

pur-sang, *n.m.* thoroughbred.

purulent, *adj.* purulent.

pusillanime, *adj.* fainthearted.

pustule, *n.f.* pimple.

putain, *n.f.* (colloquial) whore.

putois, *n.m.* skunk; polecat.

putréfier, *vb.* corrupt, rot, spoil.

putride, *adj.* putrid.

putsch, *n.m.* putsch.

puzzle, *n.m.* jigsaw (puzzle).

pygmée, *n.m.* Pygmy.

pyjama, *n.m.* pajamas.

pyramidal, *adj.* pyramidal, overwhelming.

pyramide, *n.f.* pyramid.

Pyrénées, *n.f.pl.* the Pyrenees.

Q

quadragénaire (kw-), *n.m.* person in his forties.

quadrangle (kw-), *n.m.* quadrangle.

quadrillé, *adj.* checked, ruled off.

quadriphonique (kw-), *adj.* quadraphonic.

quadrupède (kw-), *n.m. and adj.* quadruped.

quadruple (kw-), *adj.* quadruple.

quai, *n.m.* pier, dock; (station) platform.

qualification, *n.f.* qualification.

qualifier, *vb.* qualify.

qualité, *n.f.* quality, nature, grade.

quand, *adv.* when.

quant à, *prep.* as to, as for.

quantité, *n.f.* amount, quantity.

quarantaine, *n.f.* quarantine.

quarante, *adj. and n.m.* forty.

quart, *n.m.* fourth, quarter.

quartier, *n.m.* district, quarter. **q. général,** headquarters.

quartz (kw-), *n.m.* quartz.

quasar (kw-), *n.m.* quasar.

quasi, *adv.* nearly, quasi.

quasiment, *adv.* almost.

quatorze, *adj. and n.m.* fourteen.

quatrain, *n.m.* quatrain.

quatre, *adj. and n.m.* four.

quatre-vingt-dix, *adj. and n.m.* ninety.

quatre-vingts, *adj. and n.m.* eighty.

quatrième, *adj. and n.m.f.* fourth.

quatuor (kw-), *n.m.* quartet.

que, 1. *pron.* whom, which, that. **2.** *conj.* that, than.

quel, *adj.* which, what; of what kind.

quelconque, *adj.* of any kind, ordinary.

quelque, *adj.* some, any. **q. chose,** something. **q. part,** somewhere.

quelquefois, *adv.* sometimes.

quelques, *adj.* a few.

quelques-uns, *pron.* a few.

quelqu'un, *pron.* somebody.

querelle, *n.f.* quarrel.

quereller, *vb.* quarrel (with); scold.

querelleur, 1. *n.m.* quarreler. **2.** *adj.* inclined to quarrel.

question, *n.f.* question; issue, matter.

questionner, *vb.* question.

quête, *n.f.* quest, seeking.

quêter, *vb.* seek, look for.

queue (kœ), *n.f.* tail; line. **faire la q.,** stand in line.

qui, 1. *interr. pron.* who, whom. **2.** *rel. pron.* who, which. **q. que,** whoever.

quiconque, *pron.* whoever.

quiétude, *n.f.* quiet, tranquility.

quignon, *n.m.* large piece of bread.

quincaillerie, *n.f.* hardware.

quinine, *n.f.* quinine.

quinquagénaire, *n.m.* person in his fifties.

quintal, *n.m.* unit of weight (100 kilograms).

quinte, *n.f.* **q. de toux,** coughing fit.

quintuple, *n.m.* five times.

quinze, *adj. and n.m.* fifteen.

quinzième, *adj. and n.m.f.* fifteenth.

quiproquo, *n.m.* misunderstanding.

quittance, *n.f.* receipt.

quitte, *adj.* free, quit, released.

quitter, *vb.* quit, leave.

quoi, *pron. and interj.* what.

quoique, *conj.* though.

quote-part, *n.f.* quota.

quotidien, *adj.* daily.

R

rabâcher, *vb.* keep repeating.

rabais, *n.m.* reduction.

rabaisser, *vb.* diminish, lower.

rabattre, *vb.* put down, suppress, quell.

rabbin, *n.m.* rabbi.

rabbinique, *adj.* rabbinical.

rabot, *n.m.* plane.

raboter, *vb.* plane, perfect.

raboteux, *adj.* rugged.

rabougri, *adj.* puny, stunted.

raccommodage, *n.m.* fixing, mending.

raccommoder, *vb.* mend.

raccompagner, *vb.* take back.

raccorder, *vb.* join, bring together.

raccourci, *n.m.* shortcut.

raccourcir, *vb.* shorten, curtail.

raccourcissement, *n.m.* shortening, curtailing.

raccrocher, *vb.* hook up, hang up; recover.

race, *n.f.* race.

rachat, *n.m.* redemption.

racheter, *vb.* redeem.

rachitique, *adj.* rickety, affected with rickets.

rachitisme, *n.m.* rickets.

racine, *n.f.* root.

raciste, *n.m.f.* racist.

racket, *n.m.* racketeering.

raclage, *n.m.* action of scraping.

racler, *vb.* scrape.

racoler, *vb.* recruit, esp. by fraud.

racontars, *n.m.pl.* gossip.

raconter, *vb.* tell, narrate, recount.

raconteur, *n.m.* story-teller.

radar, *n.m.* radar.

radeau, *n.m.* raft.

radiant, *adj.* radiant.

radiateur, *n.m.* radiator.

radiation, *n.f.* radiation.

radical, *adj. and n.m.* radical.

radier, *vb.* radiate; erase.

radieux, *adj.* radiant, beaming, glorious.

radio, *n.f.* radio; wireless; x-ray.

radio-actif, *adj.* radioactive.

radiocassette, *n.f.* radio and cassette player.

radiodiffuser, *vb.* broadcast.

radio-émission, *n.f.* broadcast.

radiogramme, *n.m.* radiogram.

radiographie, *n.f.* radiography.

radiophonique, *adj.* radio.

radis, *n.m.* radish.

radium, *n.m.* radium.

radoter, *vb.* babble, drivel.

radoub, *n.m.* refitting (of ship).

radoucir, *vb.* quiet, soften, appease.

rafale, *n.f.* blast, gust, squall.

raffermir, *vb.* make stronger or more secure.

raffinement, *n.m.* refinement.

raffiner, *vb.* refine.

raffinerie, *n.f.* refinery.

raffoler, vb. dote on, be mad about.
rafistoler, vb. mend, patch.
rafle, n.f. (police) raid.
rafler, vb. carry off.
rafraîchir, vb. refresh.
rafraîchissement, n.m. refreshment.
rage, n.f. rage, fury; rabies.
rager, vb. be angry, rage.
rageur, n.m. irritable person.
ragot, n.m. nasty gossip.
ragoût, n.m. stew.
ragoûtant, adj. tasty, pleasing.
ragréer, vb. refinish, renovate.
raid, n.m. raid.
raide, adj. stiff; taut; steep.
raideur, n.f. stiffness.
raidir, vb. stiffen.
raie, n.f. streak; part (in hair).
raifort, n.m. horseradish.
rail, n.m. rail.
railler, vb. make fun of.
raillerie, n.f. jesting.
railleur, n.m. scoffer, jester.
rainure, n.f. groove.
rais, n.m. ray, spoke.
raisin, n.m. grape(s). **r. sec**, raisin.
raison, n.f. reason, judgment. **avoir r.**, be right.
raisonnable, adj. reasonable, rational.
raisonnement, n.m. reason; argument.
raisonner, vb. reason.
rajeunir, vb. rejuvenate.
rajuster, vb. readjust.
râle, n.m. rail (bird); rattle in throat.
ralentir, vb. slacken, slow down.
râler, vb. rattle (in dying); groan.
rallier, vb. rally.
rallonger, vb. make an addition to, lengthen.
rallye, n.m. rally.
ramadam, n.m. Ramadan.
ramage, n.m. flower pattern; chirping; babble.
ramassé, adj. thick-set, dumpy.
ramasser, vb. pick up.
ramasseur, n.m. collector.
rame, n.f. oar.
rameau, n.m. branch.
ramener, vb. bring (take) back.
rameneur, vb. restorer.

ramer, vb. row.
rameur, n.m. rower.
ramifier, vb. divide into branches, ramify.
ramille, n.f. twig.
ramollir, vb. soften; weaken.
rampe, n.f. banister; ramp.
ramper, vb. crawl, creep.
rance, 1. adj. rancid. 2. n.m. rancidness.
rancœur, n.f. rancor.
rançon, n.f. ransom.
rancune, n.f. grudge, spite, rancor. **garder de la r.**, bear a grudge.
rancunier, adj. rancorous, bitter.
randonnée, n.f. walk, hike, ride.
rang, n.m. row; rank.
rangée, n.f. file, row.
ranger, vb. rank, array, (ar)range.
ranimer, vb. revive.
rapace, adj. predatory; greedy.
rapatrier, vb. repatriate.
râpe, n.f. file, rasp.
râper, vb. grate.
rapide, 1. n.m. rapid. 2. adj. rapid, fast, quick.
rapidité, n.f. rapidity.
rapiécer, vb. patch.
rapière, n.f. rapier.
rapin, n.m. art student, pupil.
rapiner, vb. plunder, rob.
rappel, n.m. recall, repeal; reminder.
rappeler, vb. recall, remind. **se r.**, remember.
rapport, n.m. report; relation.
rapporter, vb. bring back; report. **se r. à**, relate to, refer to.
rapporteur, n.m. (court) reporter; tattle-tale.
rapprochement, n.m. bringing close, junction.
rapprocher, vb. bring together. **se r. de**, approximate.
rapt, n.m. rape, kidnapping.
raquette, n.f. racket; snowshoe.
rare, adj. scarce, rare.
raréfier, vb. rarefy.
rarement, adv. seldom.
rareté, n.f. rarity, uniqueness, scarcity.
ras, adj. smooth-shaven; open.
raser, vb. shave.
rasoir, n.m. razor.
rassasier, vb. cloy, sate.

rassemblement, *n.m.* rally.

rassembler, *vb.* gather, congregate; muster.

rasseoir, *vb.* reseat. **se r.,** be seated again.

rasséréner, *vb.* clear up (weather).

rassis, *adj.* stale.

rassurer, *vb.* reassure, comfort.

rat, *n.m.* rat.

ratatiner, *vb.* shrivel, shrink.

rate, *n.f.* spleen.

raté, *adj.* failed.

râteau, *n.m.* rake.

râteler, *vb.* rake.

râtelier, *n.m.* rack.

rater, *vb.* miss.

ratière, *n.f.* rat trap.

ratifier, *vb.* ratify.

ration, *n.f.* ration.

rationnel, *adj.* rational.

rationnement, *n.m.* rationing.

rationner, *vb.* ration.

ratissoire, *n.f.* scraper, rake.

rattacher, *vb.* fasten.

rattraper, *vb.* overtake, catch up with.

rature, *n.f.* erasure.

raturer, *vb.* erase, blot out.

rauque, *adj.* hoarse; raucous.

ravage, *n.m.* havoc.

ravager, *vb.* lay waste.

ravaler, *vb.* restore.

ravauder, *vb.* mend, patch.

ravi, *adj.* delighted.

ravigoter, *vb.* enliven, refresh.

ravin, *n.m.* ravine.

ravir, *vb.* ravish; delight.

ravissant, *adj.* ravishing, charming; ravenous.

ravissement, *n.m.* rapture.

ravisseur, *n.m.* ravisher, robber.

ravitailler, *vb.* resupply, refuel.

raviver, *vb.* revive.

rayé, *adj.* striped.

rayer, *vb.* streak; cross out.

rayon, *n.m.* ray, beam; shelf. **r. x,** x-ray.

rayonnant, *adj.* beaming.

rayonne, *n.f.* rayon.

rayonnement, *n.m.* radiation; radiance.

rayonner, *vb.* radiate, beam.

rayure, *n.f.* streak, blemish.

raz-de-marée, *n.m.* tidal wave.

re-, ré-, *prefix.* re-, again.

réabonnement, *n.m.* renewal of subscription.

réabonner, *vb.* renew, resubscribe.

réacteur, *n.m.* jet engine.

réaction, *n.f.* reaction. **avion à r.,** jet-plane.

reactionnaire, *adj. and n.m.f.* reactionary.

réadapter, *vb.* readjust.

réagir, *vb.* react.

réalisable, *adj.* realizable.

réalisateur, *n.m.* director; producer.

réalisation, *n.f.* attainment, carrying out.

réaliser, *vb.* realize; produce; direct. **se r.,** materialize.

réaliste, 1. *n.m.f.* realist. **2.** *adj.* realist, realistic.

réalité, *n.f.* reality.

réassurer, *vb.* reinsure.

rébarbatif, *adj.* forbidding.

rebattre, *vb.* repeat, beat again.

rebattu, *adj.* trite.

rebelle, 1. *n.m.f.* rebel. **2.** *adj.* rebel, rebellious.

rebeller, *vb.* **se r.,** rebel.

rébellion, *n.f.* rebellion.

rebondi, *adj.* plump.

rebondir, *vb.* bounce.

rebondissement, *n.m.* new development.

rebord, *n.m.* border, edge.

rebuffade, *n.f.* rebuff, rebuke.

rebut, *n.m.* trash, refuse, junk, rubbish.

rebuter, *vb.* rebuke, discard.

récalcitrant, *adj.* stubborn.

receler, *vb.* accept stolen goods; hide.

récemment, *adv.* recently.

recensement, *n.m.* census.

recenser, *vb.* make a census.

récent, *adj.* recent.

réceptacle, *n.m.* receptacle.

récepteur, *n.m.* receiver.

réceptif, *adj.* receptive.

réception, *n.f.* reception; receipt.

récession, *n.f.* recession.

recette, *n.f.* recipe; receipt; (*pl.*) returns.

receveur, *n.m.* conductor; receiver.

recevoir, *vb.* receive, get; entertain.

réchapper, *vb.* escape, get out.

recharge, *n.f.* refill.

réchaud, *n.m.* food warmer, chafing dish.
réchauffer, *vb.* warm again; excite.
recherche, *n.f.* inquiry, (re)search; quest.
rechercher, *vb.* seek again, investigate.
rechigner, *vb.* balk.
rechute, *n.f.* relapse.
récif, *n.m.* reef.
récipient, *n.m.* container.
réciproque, *adj.* mutual.
récit, *n.m.* account.
réciter, *vb.* recite, tell.
réclamation, *n.f.* complaint.
réclame, *n.f.* advertisement.
réclamer, *vb.* claim, demand.
reclus, 1. *adj.* withdrawn, secluded. 2. *n.m.* recluse.
réclusion, *n.f.* (solitary) confinement.
recoin, *n.m.* recess, corner.
récolte, *n.f.* crop, harvest.
récolter, *vb.* harvest, gather.
recommandable, *adj.* advisable.
recommandation, *n.f.* recommendation.
recommander, *vb.* recommend; register (letter).
recommencer, *vb.* start again.
récompense, *n.f.* reward.
récompenser, *vb.* reward.
réconcilier, *vb.* reconcile.
reconduire, *vb.* accompany, show out, dismiss.
réconfort, *n.m.* comfort.
reconnaissance, *n.f.* recognition; gratitude.
reconnaissant, *adj.* grateful.
reconnaître, *vb.* recognize; admit, acknowledge.
reconstituer, *vb.* rebuild, restore.
recourir, *vb.* resort.
recours, *n.m.* resort, recourse. **avoir r. à,** resort to; appeal to.
recouvrement, *n.m.* recovery.
recouvrer, *vb.* recover, retrieve.
recouvrir, *vb.* re-cover, cover completely.
récréation, *n.f.* amusement.
récréer, *vb.* entertain. **se r.,** amuse oneself.
recroqueviller, *vb.* **se r.,** curl up, huddle up.

recrudescence, *n.f.* fresh outbreak.
recrue, *n.f.* recruit.
recruter, *vb.* recruit.
rectangle, *n.m.* rectangle.
recteur, *n.m.* rector.
rectificatif, *n.m.* correction.
rectifier, *vb.* rectify, correct.
reçu, *n.m.* receipt.
recueil, *n.m.* collection, compilation.
recueillir, *vb.* gather, collect, glean.
recul, *n.m.* kick, recoil.
reculade, *n.f.* backing, retreat.
reculer, *vb.* recoil, draw back, go back.
récupérer, *vb.* recover, get back; rehabilitate.
récuser, *vb.* challenge; reject.
recycler, *vb.* recycle.
rédacteur, *n.m.* editor.
rédaction, *n.f.* editorial staff.
reddition, *n.f.* surrendering.
rédemption, *n.f.* redemption.
redevance, *n.f.* rental charge, license fee.
rédiger, *vb.* draw up.
redingote, *n.f.* frock-coat.
redire, *vb.* repeat, echo, reveal.
redoubler, *vb.* intesify, increase; repeat (class).
redoutable, *adj.* redoubtable, alarming.
redouter, *vb.* dread.
redresser, *vb.* straighten.
réduction, *n.f.* reduction, decrease, cut.
réduire, *vb.* reduce. **se r. à,** amount to.
réduit, *n.m.* retreat, hovel.
réel, *adj.* real, actual.
réfection, *n.f.* reconstruction; refreshments.
réfectoire, *n.m.* dining-room.
référence, *n.f.* reference.
référer, *vb.* refer.
refermer, *vb.* close up or again.
réfléchir, *vb.* reflect, consider, ponder.
reflet, *n.m.* reflection.
refléter, *vb.* reflect.
réflexe, *adj. and n.m.* reflex.
réflexion, *n.f.* reflection, consideration, thought.

refluer, *vb.* return to source, ebb.
reflux, *n.m.* ebb.
refondre, *vb.* cast again; remodel, improve.
réformateur, 1. *adj.* reforming. **2.** *n.m.* reformer, crusader.
réforme, *n.f.* reform, reformation.
réformer, *vb.* reform.
refoulement, *n.m.* forcing back, retreat.
refouler, *vb.* drive back, repel.
réfractaire, *adj.* refractory.
réfrigérant, *n.m.* refrigerator.
réfrigérer, *vb.* put under refrigeration.
refroidir, *vb.* chill, cool.
refroidissement, *n.m.* cooling, refrigeration, chill.
refuge, *n.m.* refuge.
réfugié, *n.m.* refugee.
réfugier, *vb.* se r., take refuge.
refus, *n.m.* refusal, denial.
refuser, *vb.* refuse, withhold, deny.
réfutation, *n.f.* rebuttal.
réfuter, *vb.* disprove, refute.
regagner, *vb.* regain, recover.
regain, *n.m.* regrowth, renewal.
régal, *n.m.* feast, repast.
régaler, *vb.* entertain, treat.
regard, *n.m.* look.
regarder, *vb.* look (at); concern.
régence, *n.f.* regency.
régénérer, *vb.* regenerate.
régent, *adj. and n.m.* regent.
régenter, *vb.* direct, dominate.
régie, *n.f.* management, control; control room.
régime, *n.m.* diet; government; direction.
régiment, *n.m.* regiment.
région, *n.f.* area, region.
régional, *adj.* regional.
régir, *vb.* rule.
régisseur, *n.m.* (stage) manager.
registre, *n.m.* register, record.
réglage, *n.m.* adjusting, tuning.
règle, *n.f.* rule; ruler.
règlement, *n.m.* regulation; settlement.
réglementaire, *adj.* according to regulations.
régler, *vb.* regulate; rule; settle.
règne, *n.m.* reign.
régner, *vb.* reign.
régression, *n.f.* regression.

regret, *n.m.* regret.
regrettable, *adj.* regrettable.
regretter, *vb.* regret, be sorry for.
régulariser, *vb.* regularize.
régularité, *n.f.* regularity.
régulateur, *n.m.* regulator.
régulier, *adj.* regular.
réhabiliter, *vb.* rehabilitate.
rehausser, *vb.* enhance.
rein, *n.m.* kidney; (*pl.*) loins; back.
reine, *n.f.* queen.
réinsertion, *n.f.* reintegration, rehabilitation.
réintégrer, *vb.* return to, reinstate.
réitérer, *vb.* reiterate.
rejet, *n.m.* rejection.
rejeter, *vb.* reject.
rejeton, *n.m.* plant shoot; offspring.
rejoindre, *vb.* rejoin; catch up with, overtake.
réjouir, *vb.* rejoice, delight, cheer up.
réjouissance, *n.f.* festivity.
relâche, *n.m.* respite; (theater) closing.
relâché, *adj.* loose.
relâcher, *vb.* relax, slacken.
relais, *n.m.* relay.
relance, *n.f.* boost.
relater, *vb.* relate.
relatif, *adj.* relative.
relation, *n.f.* relation, connection.
relaxation, *n.f.* relaxation, release.
relayer, *vb.* relay.
reléguer, *vb.* relegate, banish.
relève, *n.f.* (*mil.*) relief, replacement.
relèvement, *n.m.* bearing.
relever, *vb.* lift; relieve; point out.
relief, *n.m.* relief. **mettre en r.,** emphasize.
relier, *vb.* bind; link.
relieur, *n.m.* binder, esp. of books.
religieuse, *n.f.* nun.
religieux, *adj.* religious.
religion, *n.f.* religion.
reliquaire, *n.m.* receptacle for relic.
relique, *n.f.* relic.
relire, *vb.* reread.
reliure, *n.f.* binding.
reluire, *vb.* shine, glisten.
remanier, *vb.* redo, modify.
remarquable, *adj.* remarkable; noticeable.

remarque, *n.f.* remark.

remarquer, *vb.* remark; notice.

rembarrer, *vb.* drive back; put in one's place.

remblai, *n.m.* embankment.

rembourrer, *vb.* stuff.

remboursement, *n.m.* refund.

rembourser, *vb.* repay, refund.

remède, *n.m.* remedy, cure.

remédiable, *adj.* remediable.

remédier, *vb.* remedy.

remerciement, *n.m.* thanks.

remercier, *vb.* thank.

remettre, *vb.* put back; restore; remit; pardon. **se r.,** recover.

réminiscence, *n.f.* reminiscence.

remise, *n.f.* discount; delivery.

rémission, *n.f.* remmission.

remontant, *n.m.* tonic.

remonte-pente, *n.m.* ski lift.

remontrance, *n.f.* remonstrance.

remontrer, *vb.* show anew, point out error.

remords (-môr), *n.m.* remorse.

remorquer, *vb.* tow.

remorqueur, *n.m.* tug(boat).

rémouleur, *n.m.* sharpener, grinder.

remous, *n.m.* eddy.

rempart, *n.m.* bulwark, rampart.

remplaçant, *n.m.* substitute.

remplacer, *vb.* replace, substitute.

rempli, *adj.* tuck, hitch.

remplier, *vb.* take a tuck in.

remplir, *vb.* fill; carry out; crowd.

remporter, *vb.* take away, bring back; win.

remuer, *vb.* stir. **se r.,** bustle.

rémunérer, *vb.* pay.

renaissance, *n.f.* rebirth, revival.

renaître, *vb.* be reborn, get new life.

renard, *n.m.* fox; sly person.

rencontre, *n.f.* meeting, encounter. **aller à la r. de,** go to meet.

rencontrer, *vb.* meet; come across.

rendement, *n.m.* output.

rendez-vous, *n.m.* date, appointment.

rendre, *vb.* give back; repay; surrender. **se r. compte de,** realize.

rendu, *adj.* tired out, all in.

rêne, *n.f.* rein.

rené, *adj.* born-again.

renégat, *adj. and n.m.* renegade.

renfermé, *adj.* withdrawn.

renfermer, *vb.* enclose.

renfler, *vb.* swell, inflate.

renforcer, *vb.* reinforce.

renfort, *n.m.* reinforcement, aid.

renfrogner, *vb.* **se r.,** scowl, frown.

rengaine, *n.f.* often-told story.

renifler, *vb.* sniff.

renne, *n.m.* reindeer.

renom, *n.m.* renown, repute.

renommée, *n.f.* fame, renown.

renoncer, *vb.* renounce, give up, forego.

renonciation, *n.f.* renunciation.

renouement, *n.m.* renewing, retying.

renouer, *vb.* tie up (again).

renouveau, *n.m.* springtime.

renouveler, *vb.* renew, renovate.

renouvellement, *n.m.* renewal.

rénover, *vb.* renovate.

renseignements, *n.m.pl.* information.

renseigner, *vb.* inform. **se r.,** inquire.

rentable, *adj.* profitable.

rente, *n.f.* income; interest; annuity.

rentier, *n.m.* one who lives off interest on investments.

rentrée, *n.f.* return.

rentrer, *vb.* go back, go home.

renversant, *adj.* amazing, overwhelming.

renverser, *vb.* overthrow, overturn; reverse.

renvoi, *n.m.* dismissal; return.

renvoyer, *vb.* send back, return; dismiss.

repaire, *n.m.* den, animal's lair.

repaître, *vb.* feed, feast.

répandre, *vb.* diffuse, scatter, spill.

répandu, *adj.* prevalent, widespread.

reparaître, *vb.* reappear.

réparateur, *n.m.* restorer, repairer.

réparation, *n.f.* repair; amends.

réparer, *vb.* repair; make up for, make amends for.

repartie, *n.f.* reply, quick retort.

repartir, *vb.* leave again; retort.

répartir, *vb.* apportion, allot, distribute.

repas, *n.m.* meal.

repasser, vb. press; pass; look over.

repentir, 1. n.m. repentance. **2.** vb. **se r.**, repent.

répercussion, n.f. repercussion.

répercuter, vb. reverberate, echo.

repère, n.m. guiding mark.

repérer, vb. spot, locate.

répertoire, n.m. list, repertory.

répéter, vb. repeat; rehearse.

répétition, n.f. repetition; rehearsal.

répit, n.m. respite.

replacer, vb. replace.

replier, vb. fold again or up.

réplique, n.f. rejoinder; cue.

répliquer, vb. rejoin.

répondant, n.m. respondent, bail.

répondeur, n.m. answering machine.

répondre, vb. answer, reply. **r. de**, vouch for.

réponse, n.f. answer, reply.

report, n.m. (in bookkeeping) amount brought forward.

reportage, n.m. reporting.

reporter, 1. n.m. reporter. **2.** vb. carry or take back.

repos, n.m. rest.

reposer, vb. rest, repose.

repousser, vb. push back, repel; spurn.

repoussoir, n.m. foil.

répréhensible, adj. objectionable.

répréhension, n.f. reprehension, censure.

reprendre, vb. take back; resume.

représailles, n.f.pl. retaliation.

représentant, n.m. representative.

représentatif, adj. representative.

représentation, n.f. representation, performance.

représenter, vb. represent.

répressif, adj. repressive.

répression, n.f. repression.

réprimande, n.f. reproof, rebuke, reprimand.

réprimander, vb. chide, reprove, reprimand.

réprimer, vb. quell.

reprise, n.f. recovery; turn; darn. **à plusieurs r.s**, repeatedly.

repriser, vb. darn.

réprobation, n.f. reprobation.

reproche, n.m. reproach.

reprocher, vb. reproach.

reproduction, n.f. reproduction.

reproduction exacte, n.f. clone.

reproduire, vb. reproduce.

réprouver, vb. censure.

reptile, n.m. reptile.

républicain, adj. and n.m. republican.

république, n.f. republic.

répudier, vb. repudiate.

répugnance, n.f. repugnance.

répulsion, n.f. repulsion.

réputation, n.f. reputation.

réputer, vb. consider, esteem.

requête, n.f. request, plea.

requin, n.m. shark.

requis, adj. required, necessary.

réquisition, n.f. requisition.

rescousse, n.f. rescue.

réseau, n.m. network.

réserve, n.f. reserve, reservation; qualification. **de r.**, spare, extra.

réservé, adj. aloof, reticent.

réserver, vb. reserve.

réserviste, n.m.f. reservist (mil.).

réservoir, n.m. tank, reservoir.

résidant, adj. resident.

résidence, n.f. residence, dwelling.

résider, vb. reside.

résidu, n.m. residue.

résignation, n.f. resignation.

résigner, vb. resign.

résiliation, n.f. cancelling.

résine, n.f. resin.

résistance, n.f. endurance, resistance.

résister, vb. resist.

résolu, adj. resolute.

résolument, adv. resolutely.

résolution, n.f. resolution.

résonnance, n.f. resonance.

résonnant, adj. resonant.

résonner, vb. resound.

résorber, vb. **se r.**, be reduced, be absorbed.

résoudre, vb. resolve, solve.

respect (-spè), n.m. respect.

respectable, adj. decent, respectable.

respecter, vb. respect.

respectif, adj. respective.

respectueux, adj. respectful.

respiration, n.f. respiration, breathing.

respirer, vb. breathe.

resplendir, vb. gleam resplendently.

responsabilité, n.f. responsibility.

responsable, adj. responsible; accountable, liable.

ressaisir, vb. regain possession.

ressasser, vb. keep going over.

ressemblance, n.f. likeness.

ressembler, vb. resemble. se r., look alike.

ressentiment, n.m. resentment.

ressentir, vb. feel, resent, show.

resserrer, vb. tighten, compress.

ressort, n.m. spring; elasticity.

ressortir, vb. stand out.

ressortissant, n.m. national, citizen.

ressource, n.f. resort, resource.

ressusciter, vb. revive, resuscitate.

restant, n.m. remainder.

restaurant, n.m. restaurant.

restaurateur, n.m. restorer; restaurant owner.

restauration, n.f. restoration; catering.

restaurer, vb. restore.

reste, n.m. remainder, rest, remnant.

rester, vb. remain, stay.

restituer, vb. give back, restore.

restoroute, n.m. restaurant along highway.

restreindre, vb. restrict.

restrictif, adj. restrictive.

restriction, n.f. restriction.

résultat, n.m. outcome, upshot, result.

résulter, vb. result.

résumé, n.m. summing up.

résumer, vb. sum up.

résurrection, n.f. resurrection; revival.

rétablir, vb. restore, reestablish. se r., recover.

rétablissement, n.m. recovery.

retard, n.m. delay. en r., late; slow.

retarder, vb. delay, retard; be slow.

retenir, vb. retain; keep; hold (back); detain. se r. de, refrain from.

rétentif, adj. retentive.

retentir, vb. resound.

retentissant, adj. reechoing.

retenue, n.f. deduction; detention; reticence.

réticence, n.f. silence, reticence.

retirer, vb. withdraw. se r., retire, retreat.

retombées, n.f.pl. fallout.

rétorquer, vb. retort.

retoucher, vb. retouch, alter.

retour, n.m. return. de r., back.

retourner, vb. go back, return; invert. se r., turn around.

retrait, n.m. contraction, retraction.

retraite, n.f. retreat; privacy.

retrancher, vb. cut off, curtail.

retransmettre, vb. broadcast.

rétrécir, vb. shrink, contract.

rétribution, n.f. salary, recompense.

rétroactif, adj. retroactive; retrospective.

rétrograde, adj. reactionary; backward-looking.

retrousser, vb. turn up.

retrouver, vb. find; recover.

rétroviseur, n.m. rear-view mirror.

réunion, n.f. meeting, convention, reunion.

réunir, vb. unite. se r., assemble.

réussi, adj. successful.

réussir, vb. succeed.

réussite, n.f. successful outcome.

revanche, n.f. revenge. en r., in return.

rêve, n.m. dream.

réveil, n.m. awaking; revival.

réveille-matin, n.m. alarm clock.

réveiller, vb. wake (up), rouse, arouse.

réveillon, n.m. Christmas Eve; New Year's Eve.

révélateur, 1. adj. revealing. **2.** n.m. revealer.

révélation, n.f. revelation.

révéler, vb. disclose, reveal.

revenant, n.m. ghost, specter.

revendeur, n.m. retailer, old-clothes dealer.

revendication, n.f. claim, demand.

revendiquer, vb. claim.

revenir, vb. come back, return, recur; amount to.

revenu, n.m. income, revenue.

rêver, vb. dream.

réverbère, n.m. street lamp.

réverbérer, vb. reverberate.

révéremment, adv. reverently.

révérence, *n.f.* reverence; bow, curtsy.

révérend, *adj.* reverend.

révérer, *vb.* revere.

rêverie, *n.f.* dreaming, reverie.

revers, *n.m.* reverse, wrong side; lapel.

revêtir, *vb.* clothe; assume.

rêveur, 1. *n.m.* dreamer. **2.** *adj.* pensive.

revirement, *n.m.* change of mind, reversal.

réviser, *vb.* revise.

réviseur, *n.m.* reviser, inspector.

révision, *n.f.* revision, review.

revivre, *vb.* revive.

révocation, *n.f.* revocation, annulment.

revoir, *vb.* see again. **au r.,** good-bye.

révolte, *n.f.* revolt.

révolter, *vb.* **se r.,** revolt.

révolu, *adj.* past.

révolution, *n.f.* revolution, turn.

révolutionnaire, *adj. and n.m.f.* revolutionary.

revolver, *n.m.* revolver.

révoquer, *vb.* revoke.

revue, *n.f.* review, magazine.

rez-de-chaussée, *n.m.* ground floor.

rhétorique, *n.f.* rhetoric.

rhinocéros, *n.m.* rhinoceros.

Rhône, *n.m.* Rhone.

rhubarbe, *n.f.* rhubarb.

rhum, *n.m.* rum.

rhumatisme, *n.m.* rheumatism.

rhume, *n.m.* cold.

ricaner, *vb.* laugh objectionably.

riche, *adj.* rich, wealthy.

richesse, *n.f.* wealth.

ricocher, *vb.* ricochet, spring back.

rictus, *n.m.* grin; grimace.

ride, *n.f.* wrinkle, ripple.

rideau, *n.m.* curtain.

rider, *vb.* ripple, wrinkle.

ridicule, 1. *n.m.* ridicule. **2.** *adj.* ridiculous.

ridiculiser, *vb.* ridicule.

rien, *pron.* nothing.

rieur, *n.m.* laugher.

rigide, *adj.* rigid.

rigidité, *n.f.* rigidity.

rigole, *n.f.* ditch, gutter.

rigoler, *vb.* laugh.

rigolo *m.,* **rigolote** *f. adj.* funny.

rigoureux, *adj.* rigorous.

rigueur, *n.f.* rigor.

rime, *n.f.* rhyme.

rimer, *vb.* rhyme.

rince-doigts, *n.m.* finger bowl.

rincer, *vb.* rinse.

ringard, *adj.* old-fashioned.

ripaille, *n.f.* feasting, revelry.

riposte, *n.f.* retort.

rire, 1. *n.m.* laugh, laughter. **2.** *vb.* laugh.

ris, *n.m.* laugh; reef in a sail; sweetbread.

risée, *n.f.* laugh, mocking.

risible, *adj.* laughable.

risque, *n.m.* risk.

risquer, *vb.* risk.

risque-tout, *n.m.* daredevil.

rissoler, *vb.* brown, as in cooking.

rite, *n.m.* rite.

rituel, *adj.* ritual.

rivage, *n.m.* shore, bank.

rival, *adj. and n.m.* rival.

rivaliser, *vb.* compete, rival.

rivalité, *n.f.* rivalry.

rive, *n.f.* bank.

river, *vb.* clinch.

riverain, *n.m.* local resident.

rivet, *n.m.* rivet.

rivière, *n.f.* river.

rixe, *n.f.* brawl.

riz, *n.m.* rice.

rizière, *n.f.* rice field.

robe, *n.f.* dress, gown, frock, robe.

robinet, *n.m.* faucet, tap.

robot, *n.m.* robot.

robuste, *adj.* hardy, strong, robust.

roc, *n.m.* rock.

rocailleux, *adj.* rocky, rough.

roche, *n.f.* rock.

rocher, *n.m.* rock.

rocheux, *adj.* rocky.

rock, *adj.* rock (music).

rôder, *vb.* prowl.

rôdeur, *n.m.* prowler.

rogner, *vb.* pare, trim down.

rognon, *n.m.* kidney.

rogue, *adj.* proud, arrogant.

roi, *n.m.* king.

rôle, *n.m.* role, part.

Romain, *n.m.* Roman (person).

romain, *adj.* Roman.

roman, *n.m.* novel.

romance, *n.f.* ballad.
romancier, *n.m.* novelist.
romanesque, *adj.* romantic.
roman-feuilleton, *n.m.* serial.
romanichel, *n.m.* gypsy.
romantique, *adj.* romantic.
romarin, *n.m.* rosemary.
rompre, *vb.* break.
ronce, *n.f.* bramble.
rond, **1.** *n.m.* round; circle. **2.** *adj.* round.
ronde, *n.f.* round, patrol.
rondelle, *n.f.* washer; slice.
rondeur, *n.f.* roundness.
rond-point, *n.m.* traffic circle.
ronflement, *n.m.* snoring, roar.
ronfler, *vb.* snore.
ronger, *vb.* gnaw; fret.
rongeur, *adj. and n.m.* rodent.
ronronner, *vb.* purr, murmur.
rosace, *n.f.* rose window.
rosaire, *n.m.* rosary.
rosbif, *n.m.* roast beef.
rose, **1.** *n.f.* rose. **2.** *adj.* pink.
rosé, *adj.* pinkish.
roseau, *n.m.* reed.
rosée, *n.f.* dew.
rosier, *n.m.* rosebush.
rossignol, *n.m.* nightingale.
rôt, *n.m.* roast (meat).
rotation, *n.f.* rotation.
rotatoire, *adj.* rotary.
roter, *vb.* belch.
rôti, *n.m.* roast.
rôtir, *vb.* roast.
rôtisserie, *n.f.* grillroom.
rotondité, *n.f.* rotundity.
rotule, *n.f.* kneecap.
roturier, *adj.* commonplace, vulgar.
rouage, *n.m.* gearwheel, part, cog.
roublardise, *n.f.* cunningness.
roucouler, *vb.* coo.
roue, *n.f.* wheel.
roué, **1.** *n.m.* rake, debauchee. **2.** *adj.* crafty.
rouge, **1.** *n.m.* rouge. **2.** *adj.* red. **r. foncé,** maroon.
rouge-gorge, *n.m.* robin.
rougeole, *n.f.* measles.
rougeur, *n.f.* flush, blush.
rougir, *vb.* blush.
rouille, *n.f.* rust.
rouiller, *vb.* rust.
rouir, *vb.* soak.

rouleau, *n.m.* roll, roller, scroll, coil.
roulement, *n.m.* rolling, winding; rotation.
rouler, *vb.* roll, wind.
roulette, *n.f.* little wheel, caster.
roulis, *n.m.* roll.
Roumain, *n.m.* Romanian (person).
roumain, **1.** *n.m.* Romanian (language). **2.** *adj.* Romanian.
Roumanie, *n.f.* Romania.
rouquin, *n.m.* redhead.
rousseur, *n.f.* redness. **tache de r.,** freckle.
roussir, *vb.* scorch.
route, *n.f.* road, way, course, route. **en r.,** under way. **en r. pour,** on the way to.
routine, *n.f.* routine.
routinier, *adj.* routine.
roux, *adj. and n.m.* red, reddish-brown.
royal, *adj.* royal, regal.
royaliste, *adj. and n.m.f.* royalist.
royaume, *n.m.* kingdom.
royauté, *n.f.* royalty.
ruban, *n.m.* ribbon, tape.
rubéole, *n.f.* German measles.
rubis, *n.m.* ruby.
rubrique, *n.f.* red ocher; heading.
ruche, *n.f.* hive.
rude, *adj.* rough, gruff, harsh; rugged.
rudement, *adv.* terribly (hard).
rudesse, *n.f.* harshness.
rudiment, *n.m.* rudiment, element.
rudimentaire, *adj.* rudimentary.
rudoyer, *vb.* bully.
rue, *n.f.* street, road.
ruée, *n.f.* rush.
ruelle, *n.f.* lane, alley.
ruer, *vb.* **se r.,** rush.
rugby, *n.m.* Rugby.
rugbyman, *n.m.* Rugby player.
rugir, *vb.* roar.
rugissement, *n.m.* roar.
rugueux, *adj.* rugged, harsh.
ruine, *n.f.* ruin.
ruiner, *vb.* ruin.
ruineux, *adj.* ruinous.
ruisseau, *n.m.* brook, creek; gutter.

ruisseler, *vb.* stream, flow.
rumeur, *n.f.* rumor; noise.
ruminant, *adj. and n.m.* ruminant.
ruminer, *vb.* chew the cud.
rupture, *n.f.* break, rupture.
rural, *adj.* rural.
ruse, *n.f.* trick; cunning.
rusé, *adj.* sly, cunning.
Russe, *n.m.f.* Russian (person).

russe, 1. *n.m.* Russian (language).
2. *adj.* Russian.
Russie, *n.f.* Russia.
rusticité, *n.f.* rusticity, uncouthness.
rustique, *adj.* rustic.
rustre, *adj. and n.m.* boor, boorish.
rythme, *n.m.* rhythm.
rythmique, *adj.* rhythmical.

S

sabbat, *n.m.* Sabbath.
sable, *n.m.* sand.
sablé, *n.m.* shortbread biscuit.
sabler, *vb.* sand; quaff.
sablier, *n.m.* sandbox; sandman; hourglass.
sablonneux, *adj.* sandy.
sablonnière, *n.f.* sand pit.
sabord, *n.m.* porthole.
sabot, *n.m.* hoof; wooden shoe.
sabotage, *n.m.* sabotage.
saboter, *vb.* sabotage.
saboteur, *n.m.* saboteur; awkward bungler.
sabre, *n.m.* saber.
sac, *n.m.* sack, bag. **s. à main,** pocketbook. **s. à air,** airbag.
saccade, *n.f.* jerk.
saccager, *vb.* ransack, sack, plunder.
saccharine, *n.f.* saccharin.
sacerdoce, *n.m.* priesthood.
sachet, *n.m.* sachet; packet.
sacre, *n.m.* consecration, coronation.
sacré, *adj.* sacred.
sacrement, *n.m.* sacrament.
sacrer, *vb.* crown, consecrate; curse.
sacrifice, *n.m.* sacrifice.
sacrifier, *vb.* sacrifice.
sacrilège, *n.m.* sacrilege.
sacristain, *n.m.* sexton.
sac tyrolien, *n.m.* backpack.
sadique, *adj.* sadistic.
sadisme, *n.m.* sadism.
sagace, *adj.* shrewd.
sagacité, *n.f.* sagacity.
sage, 1. *n.m.* sage. **2.** *adj.* wise, good.
sage-femme, *n.f.* midwife.
sagesse, *n.f.* wisdom.

Sahara, *n.m.* Sahara (desert).
saignant, *adj.* rare (meat).
saignée, *n.f.* bleeding.
saigner, *vb.* bleed.
saillant, *adj.* prominent, projecting.
saillie, *n.f.* projection.
saillir, *vb.* protrude.
sain, *adj.* healthy, sound, wholesome. **s. d'esprit,** sane.
saindoux, *n.m.* lard.
saint, 1. *n.m.* saint. **2.** *adj.* holy.
Saint-Esprit, *n.m.* Holy Ghost.
sainteté, *n.f.* holiness.
saisie, *n.f.* seizure.
saisir, *vb.* seize, grasp, snatch, grab.
saisissement, *n.m.* chill; seizure.
saison, *n.f.* season.
salade, *n.f.* salad.
saladier, *n.m.* salad bowl or dish.
salaire, *n.m.* wages, earnings, pay.
salarié, 1. *adj.* salaried. **2.** *n.m.* person earning a salary.
sale, *adj.* dirty.
salé, *adj.* salty.
saler, *vb.* salt.
saleté, *n.f.* dirt.
salière, *n.f.* saltcellar.
salin, *adj.* salt, salty.
salir, *vb.* get dirty.
salive, *n.f.* saliva.
salle, *n.f.* (large) room, hall, auditorium, (hospital) ward. **s. de classe,** classroom. **s. de bain,** bathroom.
salon, *n.m.* parlor.
salopette, *n.f.* overalls.
saltimbanque, *n.m.f.* charlatan; buffoon, acrobat.
salubre, *adj.* healthful.
salubrité, *n.f.* healthfulness.

saluer, vb. bow, greet, salute.

salut, n.m. bow, salute; salvation.

salutaire, adj. wholesome, beneficial.

salutation, n.f. greeting.

salve, n.f. salvo, salute.

samedi, n.m. Saturday.

SAMU, n.m. paramedics.

sanctifier, vb. hallow.

sanction, n.f. sanction.

sanctionner, vb. sanction, countenance.

sanctuaire, n.m. sanctuary.

sandale, n.f. sandal.

sang, n.m. blood.

sang-froid, n.m. calmness, composure.

sanglant, adj. bloody.

sangler, vb. strap, fasten.

sanglier, n.m. (wild) boar.

sanglot, n.m. sob.

sangloter, vb. sob.

sangsue, n.f. leech.

sanguin, adj. pertaining to blood.

sanguinaire, adj. bloodthirsty.

sanitaire, adj. sanitary.

sans, prep. without, out of. **s. doute,** without doubt. **s. plomb,** unleaded. **s. repos,** restless. **s. valeur,** worthless. **s. nom,** nameless.

sans-souci, adj. carefree, careless.

santé, n.f. health.

Saoudien, n.m. Saudi (person).

Saoudien, adj. Saudi Arabian.

saoul (soo), adj. drunk.

saper, vb. sap, weaken.

saphir, n.m. sapphire.

sapin, n.m. fir.

sarcasme, n.m. sarcasm.

sarcastique, adj. sarcastic.

sarcler, vb. weed, root out.

Sardaigne, n.f. Sardinia.

sardine, n.f. sardine.

sardonique, adj. sardonic.

satanique, adj. satanic.

satellite, n.m. satellite.

satin, n.m. satin.

satire, n.f. satire.

satiriser, vb. satirize.

satisfaction, n.f. satisfaction.

satisfaire, vb. satisfy.

satisfaisant, adj. satisfactory.

saturer, vb. saturate.

satyre, n.m. satyr.

sauce, n.f. sauce. **s. piquante,** hot sauce.

saucisse, n.f. sausage.

saucisson, n.m. (slicing) sausage.

sauf, 1. prep. but. **2.** adj. safe. **sain et s.,** safe and sound.

sauf-conduit, n.m. safe-conduct.

sauge, n.f. sage.

saugrenu, adj. absurd, preposterous.

saule, n.f. willow.

saumon, n.m. salmon.

saumure, n.f. brine.

saut, n.m. spring, jump.

saute, n.f. wind shift.

sauter, vb. spring, jump, leap, skip. **faire s.,** blow up.

sauterelle, n.f. grasshopper.

sautiller, vb. hop.

sauvage, 1. n.m.f. savage. **2.** adj. wild, savage.

sauvegarde, n.f. safeguard.

sauvegarder, vb. safeguard; (computers) save, back up.

sauve-qui-peut, n.m. stampede, panic.

sauver, vb. save. **se s.,** run away.

sauvetage, n.m. salvage.

sauveteur, n.m. rescuer, saver.

sauveur, n.m. savior; Savior.

savane, n.f. prairie.

savant, 1. n.m. scholar. **2.** adj. learned.

saveur, n.f. flavor, savor, zest.

savoir, 1. vb. know, be aware, have knowledge. **vouloir s.,** wonder. **2.** n.m. knowledge.

savoir-faire, n.m. poise, ability.

savoir-vivre, n.m. breeding, manners.

savon, n.m. soap.

savonner, vb. soap, lather.

savourer, vb. relish.

savoureux, adj. tasty.

saxo(phone), n.m. sax(ophone).

scabreux, adj. improper; risky.

scalper, vb. scalp.

scandale, n.m. scandal.

scandaleux, adj. scandalous.

scandaliser, vb. shock.

scander, vb. scan.

Scandinave, n.m.f. Scandinavian (person).

scandinave, adj. Scandinavian.

Scandinavie, n.f. Scandinavia.

scaphandre, *n.m.* diving suit; space suit.

scarabée, *n.m.* beetle.

scarlatine, *n.f.* scarlet fever.

sceau, *n.m.* seal.

scélérat, *n.m.* villain, criminal, knave, ruffian.

sceller, *vb.* seal.

scénario, *n.m.* scenario.

scène, *n.f.* scene; stage.

scénique, *adj.* scenic.

scepticisme, *n.m.* skepticism.

sceptique, 1. *n.m.f.* skeptic. **2.** *adj.* skeptical.

sceptre, *n.m.* scepter.

schéma, *n.m.* diagram.

schématique, *adj.* digrammatic; oversimplified.

schisme, *n.m.* schism.

schizophrène (sk-), *adj.* schizophrenia.

sciatique, *n.f.* sciatica.

scie, *n.f.* saw.

science, *n.f.* science.

science-fiction, *n.f.* science fiction.

scientifique, 1. *adj.* scientific. **2.** *n.m.f.* scientist.

scier, *vb.* saw.

scinder, *vb.* divide.

scintiller, *vb.* twinkle.

scission, *n.f.* cutting, division.

sclérose, *n.f.* sclerosis.

scolaire, *adj.* scholastic. **système s.,** school system.

scolastique, *adj.* scholastic.

scooter, *n.m.* (motor) scooter.

score, *n.m.* score.

Scotch, *n.m.* Scotish whisky; (trademark) Scotch tape.

scout (-t), *n.m.* scout.

scrofule, *n.f.* scrofula.

scrupule, *n.m.* scruple.

scrupuleux, *adj.* scrupulous.

scruter, *vb.* scan, scrutinize.

scrutin, *n.m.* ballot, poll.

sculpter (-lt-), *vb.* carve.

sculpteur (-lt-), *n.m.* sculptor.

sculpture (-lt-), *n.f.* sculpture.

se (sə), *pron.* himself, herself, itself, oneself, themselves, each other.

séance, *n.f.* sitting; session; meeting.

séant, *adj.* sitting, proper.

seau, *n.m.* pail, bucket.

sec *m.,* **sèche** *f.* *adj.* dry.

sécession, *n.f.* secession.

sèche-cheveux, *n.m.* hair dryer.

sécher, *vb.* dry.

sécheresse, *n.f.* dryness, drought.

séchoir, *n.m.* dryer.

second (-g-), *adj.* second.

secondaire (-g-), *adj.* secondary.

seconde (-g-), *n.f.* second.

seconder (-g-), *vb.* second, help.

secouer, *vb.* shake, rouse.

secourir, *vb.* relieve, succor, help.

secours, *n.m.* help, relief. **premiers s.,** first aid. **poste de s.,** first-aid station. **au s.!,** help!

secousse, *n.f.* jar, shock.

secret, *adj. and n.m.* secret.

secrétaire, *n.m.f.* secretary.

sécréter, *vb.* secrete.

sécrétion, *n.f.* secretion.

sectaire, *adj.* sectarian.

secte, *n.f.* sect.

secteur, *n.m.* district, sector.

section, *n.f.* section.

sectionner, *vb.* cut into sections.

Sécu, *n.f.* Social Security.

séculaire, *adj.* secular.

séculier, *adj.* secular, lay.

sécuriser, *vb.* make (someone) feel secure.

sécurité, *n.f.* safety.

sédatif, *adj. and n.m.* sedative.

sédentaire, *adj.* sedentary, stationary.

séditieux, *adj.* seditious.

sédition, *n.f.* sedition.

séduction, *n.f.* seduction.

séduire, *vb.* seduce, attract, allure.

séduisant, *adj.* attractive.

segment, *n.m.* segment.

ségrégation, *n.f.* segregation.

seigle, *n.m.* rye.

seigneur, *n.m.* lord, peer.

seigneurie, *n.f.* lordship.

sein, *n.m.* bosom, breast.

séisme, *n.m.* earthquake.

seize, *adj. and n.m.* sixteen.

seizième, *adj. and n.m.f.* sixteenth.

séjour, *n.m.* stay. **lieu de s.,** resort.

séjourner, *vb.* sojourn.

sel, *n.m.* salt.

sélection, *n.f.* selection.

self(-service), *n.m.* self-service.

selle, *n.f.* saddle.

seller, *vb.* saddle.

sellette, *n.f.* little stool or saddle.
selon, *prep.* according to.
seltz, *n.m.* eau de s., soda water.
semailles, *n.f.pl.* sowing.
semaine, *n.f.* week; weekly pay.
semblable, *adj.* similar, alike.
semblant, *n.m.* show; appearance. faire s., make believe.
sembler, *vb.* seem, appear.
semelle, *n.f.* sole (shoe).
semence, *n.f.* seed.
semer, *vb.* sow.
semestre, *n.m.* semester.
semeur, *n.m.* sower.
sémillance, *n.f.* briskness, liveliness.
séminaire, *n.m.* seminar; seminary.
semi-remorque, *n.f.* semitrailer.
sémitique, *adj.* Semitic.
semoncer, *vb.* lecture, scold.
semoule, *n.f.* semolina.
sénat, *n.m.* senate.
sénateur, *n.m.* senator.
sénile, *adj.* senile.
sénilité, *n.f.* senility.
sens (-s), *n.m.* meaning, sense; direction.
sensation, *n.f.* sensation, feeling.
sensationnel, *adj.* sensational.
sensé, *adj.* sensible.
sensibiliser, *vb.* make sensitive.
sensibilité, *n.f.* sensitivity.
sensible, *adj.* sensitive; conscious (of).
sensitif, *adj.* oversensitive.
sensualisme, *n.m.* sensualism.
sensualité, *n.f.* sensuality.
sensuel, *adj.* sensual.
sentence, *n.f.* sentence.
sentencieux, *adj.* sententious.
senteur, *n.f.* smell.
sentier, *n.m.* path.
sentiment, *n.m.* feeling.
sentimental, *adj.* sentimental.
sentimentalité, *n.f.* sentimentality.
sentinelle, *n.f.* sentry.
sentir, *vb.* feel; smell.
séparable, *adj.* separable.
séparation, *n.f.* separation, parting.
séparatiste, *adj.* separatist.
séparé, *adj.* separate.
séparer, *vb.* separate, segregate. se s., part.
sept (sèt), *adj. and n.m.* seven.

septembre, *n.m.* September.
septième (sèt-), *adj. and n.m.f.* seventh.
septique, *adj.* septic.
sépulcre, *n.m.* sepulcher.
sépulture, *n.f.* burial (place).
sequelles, *n.f.pl.* after-effects, aftermath.
séquence, *n.f.* sequence.
séquestrer, *vb.* withdraw.
serein, *adj.* serene, placid.
sérénade, *n.f.* serenade.
sérénité, *n.f.* serenity.
serf, 1. *n.m.* serf. **2.** *adj.* in serfdom or the like.
sergent, *n.m.* sergeant.
série, *n.f.* series.
sérieux, 1. *adj.* serious, sober, grave. **2.** *n.m.* gravity.
serin, *n.m.* canary.
seringue, *n.f.* syringe.
serment, *n.m.* oath.
sermon, *n.m.* sermon.
sermonner, *vb.* lecture, preach.
séropositif, *adj.* HIV-positive.
serpent, *n.m.* snake, serpent.
serpenter, *vb.* wind, wander.
serpillière, *n.f.* floor-cloth.
serre, *n.f.* greenhouse; claw.
serré, *adj.* tight.
serre-joint, *n.m.* clamp.
serrer, *vb.* tighten, squeeze, press; crowd; shake (hands). **s. dans ses bras,** hug.
serrure, *n.f.* lock.
sérum, *n.m.* serum.
servage, *n.m.* servitude.
servant, 1. *adj.* serving. **2.** *n.m.* server; gunner.
servante, *n.f.* maid.
serveuse, *n.f.* waitress.
serviable, *adj.* helpful.
service, *n.m.* service, favor. **être de s.,** be on duty.
serviette, *n.f.* napkin; towel; briefcase.
servile, *adj.* menial.
servilité, *n.f.* servility.
servir, *vb.* serve. **se s. de,** use. **ne s. à rien,** be of no use.
serviteur, *n.m.* attendant, servant.
servitude, *n.f.* slavery.
session, *n.f.* session.
seuil, *n.m.* threshold.
seul, *adj.* alone, only, single.

seulement, *adv.* only, solely.

sève, *n.f.* sap.

sévère, *adj.* severe, stern.

sévérité, *n.f.* severity, rigor.

sévir, *vb.* punish, rage.

sevrer, *vb.* wean, withhold.

sexe, *n.m.* sex; sex organ(s).

sexisme, *n.m.* sexism.

sexiste, *adj.* sexist.

sexuel, *adj.* sexual.

seyant, *adj.* becoming, suitable.

shampooing, *n.m.* shampoo.

short, *n.m.* (pair of) shorts.

shrapnel, *n.m.* shrapnel.

si, 1. *adv.* so, so much; yes. **si . . . que,** however (+*adj.*). **2.** *conj.* if, whether.

Sicile, *n.f.* Sicily.

sida, SIDA, *n.m.* AIDS.

sidérurgie, *n.f.* iron and steel industry.

siècle, *n.m.* century.

siège, *n.m.* seat; siege.

siéger, *vb.* sit, convene, reside.

sien, *pron.* **le sien, la sienne,** his, hers, its.

sieste, *n.f.* siesta.

siffler, *vb.* whistle, hiss.

sifflerie, *n.f.* hissing, whistling.

sifflet, *n.m.* whistle.

sigle, *n.m.* abbreviation, acronym.

signal, *n.m.* signal.

signalement, *n.m.* description, details.

signaler, *vb.* point out.

signataire, *n.m.f.* signatory.

signature, *n.f.* signature.

signe, *n.m.* sign. **s. de la tête,** nod. **faire s. à,** beckon.

signer, *vb.* sign. **se s.,** cross oneself.

significatif, *adj.* significant, meaningful.

signification, *n.f.* significance, meaning.

signifier, *vb.* signify, mean.

silence, *n.m.* silence.

silencieux, *adj.* noiseless, silent.

silex, *n.m.* flint.

silhouette, *n.f.* outline, silhouette.

silicium, *n.m.* silicon.

sillage, *n.m.* wake, course.

sillon, *n.m.* furrow.

sillonner, *vb.* plow.

similaire, *adj.* similar.

simple, *adj.* plain, simple, mere; no-frills.

simplicité, *n.f.* simplicity.

simplifier, *vb.* simplify.

simpliste, *adj.* simplistic.

simulacre, *n.m.* pretense, sham.

simulation, *n.f.* simulation.

simuler, *vb.* pretend.

simultané, *adj.* simultaneous.

sincère, *adj.* candid, sincere.

sincérité, *n.f.* candor, sincerity.

singe, *n.m.* monkey; imitator.

singer, *vb.* imitate, ape.

singularité, *n.f.* singularity; peculiar trait.

singulier, *adj.* and *n.m.* singular; peculiar, strange.

sinistre, 1. *n.m.* disaster, damage. **2.** *adj.* sinister.

sinistré, *n.m.* disaster victim. **2.** *adj.* disaster-stricken.

sinon, *conj.* otherwise.

sinueux, *adj.* winding, sinuous.

sirène, *n.f.* siren; mermaid.

sirop, *n.m.* syrup.

siroter, *vb.* sip.

site, *n.m.* site.

sitôt, *adv.* as soon (as).

situation, *n.f.* situation; position, location, office.

situer, *vb.* situate, locate.

six (sès), *adj.* and *n.m.* six.

sixième (-z-), *adj.* and *n.m.f.* sixth.

ski, *n.m.* ski. **faire du s.,** ski.

skieur, *n.m.* skier.

Slave, 1. *adj.* Slavonic. **2.** *n.m.f.* Slav.

slip, *n.m.* underpants, panties.

SMIC, *n.m.* minimum wage.

smoking, *n.m.* dinner jacket, tuxedo.

snak(-bar), *n.m.* snackbar.

snob, *n.m.* snob.

sobre, *adj.* temperate, sober.

sobriété, *n.f.* moderation, temperance.

sobriquet, *n.m.* nickname.

soc, *n.m.* plowshare.

sociable, *adj.* sociable.

social, *adj.* social.

socialisme, *n.m.* socialism.

socialiste, *adj.* and *n.m.f.* socialist.

société, *n.f.* society; company.

sociologie, *n.f.* sociology.

sociologue, *n.m.f.* sociologist.

sœur, n.f. sister.
sofa, n.m. sofa.
soi-disant, adj. so-called.
soie, n.f. silk; bristle.
soierie, n.f. silk goods.
soif, n.f. thirst. **avoir s.,** be thirsty.
soigné, adj. trim. **mal s.,** sloppy.
soigner, vb. tend, look after, take care of.
soigneux, adj. careful.
soi-même, pron. oneself.
soin, n.m. care. **prendre s. de,** take care of.
soir, n.m. evening. **hier s.,** last night. **ce s.,** tonight. **le s.,** at night.
soirée, n.f. evening.
soit, vb. so be it. **s . . . s.,** whether . . . or. **s. que,** whether.
soixantaine, n.f. about sixty.
soixante (-s-), adj. and n.m. sixty.
soixante-dix, adj. and n.m. seventy.
sol, n.m. earth, soil, ground.
solaire, adj. solar.
soldat, n.m. soldier.
solde, n.m. balance.
sole, n.f. sole (fish).
solécisme, n.m. solecism.
soleil, n.m. sun, sunshine. **coucher du s.,** sunset. **lever du s.,** sunrise.
solennel, adj. solemn.
solenniser, vb. solemnize.
solennité, n.f. solemnity.
solex, n.m. (trademark) moped.
solidaire, adj. jointly binding.
solidariser, vb. **se s.,** unite, join together.
solidarité, n.f. joint responsibility.
solide, adj. and n.m. solid.
solidifier, vb. solidify.
solidité, n.f. solidity.
soliloque, n.m. soliloquy.
soliste, n.m.f. soloist.
solitaire, adj. lonely, lonesome.
solitude, n.f. solitude.
solliciter, vb. solicit, ask, apply.
sollicitude, n.f. solicitude.
soluble, adj. soluble.
solution, n.f. solution.
solvable, adj. solvent.
sombre, adj. dark, dim, gloomy, somber.
sombrer, vb. sink.
sommaire, n.m. summary.
sommation, n.f. appeal, summons.

somme, 1. n.f. amount, sum. **2.** n.m. nap.
sommeil, n.m. sleep. **avoir s.,** be sleepy.
sommeiller, vb. doze, slumber.
sommer, vb. summon.
sommet, n.m. top, peak, summit.
somnifère, n.m. sleeping pill.
somnolence, n.f. drowsiness.
somnolent, adj. drowsy, sleepy.
somptueux, adj. lavish, sumptuous.
son m., **sa** f., **ses** pl. adj. his, her, its.
son, n.m. sound, ring; bran.
sonate, n.f. sonata.
sondage, n.m. (opinion) poll.
sonde, n.f. sounding line; probe; catheter; feeding tube.
sonder, vb. fathom; probe.
songe, n.m. dream.
songer, vb. think of, dream.
songeur, 1. adj. dreamy, thoughtful. **2.** n.m. dreamer.
sonner, vb. sound, ring, strike.
sonnerie, n.f. ringing.
sonnette, n.f. bell.
sonore, adj. sonorous.
sonorisation, n.f. public address system.
sophiste, n.m.f. sophist.
sophistiqué, adj. sophisticated.
soprano, n.m. soprano.
sorbet, n.m. sorbet.
sorcellerie, n.f. sorcery.
sorcier, n.m. wizard.
sorcière, n.f. witch.
sordide, adj. sordid.
sort, n.m. lot.
sorte, n.f. sort, kind. **de s. que,** so that.
sortie, n.f. exit, way out.
sortilège, n.m. sorcery.
sortir, vb. go (come, get) out.
sot m., **sotte** f. adj. silly, stupid, foolish, dumb.
sottise, n.f. foolishness.
sou, n.m. cent. **sans le s.,** penniless.
soubassement, n.m. basement.
soubresaut, n.m. bound, jerk.
souche, n.f. stub, stump.
souci, n.m. care, worry, concern.
soucier, vb. **se s. (de),** care, worry (about).
soucieux, adj. anxious.

soucoupe, *n.f.* saucer. **s. volante,** flying saucer.

soudain, *adj.* sudden.

soudaineté, *n.f.* suddenness.

soude, *n.f.* soda.

souder, *vb.* solder, fuse.

souffle, *n.m.* breath.

souffler, *vb.* blow.

soufflet, *n.m.* bellows; blow, slap.

souffleter, *vb.* slap one's face.

souffrance(s), *n.f. (pl.)* misery, pain, suffering.

souffrir, *vb.* suffer, bear.

soufre, *n.m.* sulphur.

souhait, *n.m.* wish.

souhaiter, *vb.* wish for.

souiller, *vb.* soil, defile.

souillure, *n.f.* stain, dirt.

soûl (sōō), *adj.* drunk.

soulager, *vb.* relieve, alleviate.

soûler, *vb.* fill with food and drink, inebriate.

soulèvement, *n.m.* uprising.

soulever, *vb.* lift, raise, arouse.

soulier, *n.m.* shoe.

souligner, *vb.* underline.

soumettre, *vb.* submit, subdue.

soumis, *adj.* obedient, submissive.

soumission, *n.f.* submission.

soupape, *n.f.* valve.

soupçon, *n.m.* suspicion.

soupçonner, *vb.* suspect.

soupçonneux, *adj.* suspicious.

soupe, *n.f.* soup.

souper, *vb.* supper.

soupir, *n.m.* sigh.

soupirant, *n.m.* suitor.

soupirer, *vb.* sigh. **s. après,** yearn for.

souple, *adj.* flexible.

souplesse, *n.f.* suppleness, pliability.

source, *n.f.* source; spring.

sourcil, *n.m.* eyebrow.

sourciller, *vb.* frown.

sourcilleux, *adj.* haughty, disdainful.

sourd, *adj.* deaf.

sourd-muet, *n.m.* deaf mute.

souriant, *adj.* cheerful.

souricière, *n.f.* (mouse)trap.

sourire, *n.m. and vb.* smile.

souris, *n.f.* mouse.

sournois, *adj.* sly.

sous, *prep.* under.

souscription, *n.f.* subscription.

souscrire, *vb.* subscribe.

sous-entendre, *vb.* imply.

sous-estimer, *vb.* underestimate.

sous-louer, *vb.* sublet.

sous-marin, *n.m.* submarine.

sous-produit, *n.m.* by-product.

soussigné, *adj.* undersigned.

sous-sol, *n.m.* basement.

sous-titre, *n.m.* subtitle.

soustraction, *n.f.* subtraction.

soustraire, *vb.* subtract.

sous-traitant, *n.m.* subcontractor.

sous-vêtements, *n.m.pl.* underwear.

soutane, *n.f.* cassock.

soute, *n.f.* storeroom.

soutenir, *vb.* support, uphold, maintain; claim; back up.

soutenu, *adj.* steady.

souterrain, *adj.* underground.

soutien, *n.m.* support.

soutien-gorge, *n.m.* brassiere.

souvenance, *n.f.* recall, recollection.

souvenir, 1. *n.m.* remembrance, memory. **2.** *vb.* **se s. de,** remember.

souvent, *adv.* often.

souverain, *n.m.* ruler, sovereign.

souveraineté, *n.f.* sovereignty.

Soviétique, *n.m.f.* Soviet citizen.

soviétique, *adj.* Soviet.

soyeux, *adj.* silky.

spacieux, *adj.* spacious.

spasme, *n.m.* spasm.

spatial, *adj.* space.

spatule, *n.f.* spatula.

spécial, *adj.* special.

spécialiser, *vb.* specialize.

spécialiste, *n.m.f.* specialist.

spécialité, *n.f.* specialty.

spécifier, *vb.* specify.

spécifique, *adj.* specific.

spécimen, *n.m.* specimen.

spectacle, *n.m.* sight, show.

spectaculaire, *adj.* spectacular.

spectateur, *n.m.* spectator.

spectre, *n.m.* ghost; spectrum.

spéculation, *n.f.* speculation.

spéculer, *vb.* speculate.

sphère, *n.f.* sphere.

spinal, *adj.* spinal.

spiral, *adj.* spiral.

spirale, *n.f.* spiral.

spirite, *n.m.f.* spiritualist.
spiritisme, *n.m.* spiritualism.
spirituel, *adj.* spiritual; witty.
spiritueux, *adj.* pertaining to alcohol.
splendeur, *n.f.* splendor.
splendide, *adj.* splendid.
spolier, *vb.* plunder, pillage.
spontané, *adj.* spontaneous.
spontanéité, *n.f.* spontaneity.
sporadique, *adj.* sporadic.
sport, *n.m.* sport.
sportif, *adj.* sporting, athletic, sports.
spot, *n.m.* spot(light).
squatter, 1. *n.m.* squatter. 2. *vb.* squat in.
squelette, *n.m.* skeleton.
stabiliser, *vb.* stabilize.
stabilité, *n.f.* stability.
stable, *adj.* stable, steady.
stage, *n.m.* training or instruction period.
stagflation, *n.f.* stagflation.
stagiaire, *n.m.f.* trainee.
stagnant, *adj.* stagnant.
stalle, *n.f.* stall.
stance, *n.f.* stanza.
standard, *n.m.* switchboard.
standardiste, *n.m.f.* phone operator.
starter, *n.m.* (car) choke.
station, *n.f.* stand, stop, station (subway).
stationnaire, *adj.* stationary.
stationnement, *n.m.* parking.
stationner, *vb.* park.
station-service, *n.f.* gas/service station.
statique, *adj.* static.
statistique, *n.f.* statistics.
statue, *n.f.* statue.
statuer, *vb.* decree, decide.
stature, *n.f.* stature.
statut, *n.m.* statute.
steak, *n.m.* steak.
sténographe, *n.m.f.* stenographer.
sténographie, *n.f.* stenography.
stéréo, *n.f. and adj.* stereo.
stéréophonique, *adj.* stereophonic.
stérile, *adj.* barren.
stérilet, *n.m.* coil, IUD.
stériliser, *vb.* sterilize.
stéthoscope, *n.m.* stethoscope.

stigmatiser, *vb.* mark, stigmatize.
stimulant, *n.m.* stimulus.
stimuler, *vb.* stimulate.
stipuler, *vb.* stipulate.
stoïque, *adj. and n.m.f.* stoic.
stop, *n.m.* stop sign; hitchhiking.
store, *n.m.* (window) shade, blind.
strapontin, *n.m.* folding seat.
stratagème, *n.m.* stratagem.
stratégie, *n.f.* strategy.
stratégique, *adj.* strategic.
stressant, *adj.* stressful.
strict (-kt), *adj.* severe, strict.
strier, *vb.* mark, streak, groove.
structure, *n.f.* structure.
stuc, *n.m.* stucco.
studieux, *adj.* studious.
stupéfait, *adj.* astounded.
stupéfiant, *n.m.* narcotic, dope.
stupéfier, *vb.* astound.
stupeur, *n.f.* amazement.
stupide, *adj.* stupid.
stupidité, *n.f.* stupidity.
style, *n.m.* style.
styler, *vb.* train, teach.
stylet, *n.m.* stiletto.
stylographe, stylo, *n.m.* fountain pen.
suavité, *n.f.* suavity.
subalterne, *adj. and n.m.f.* junior (rank).
subdiviser, *vb.* subdivide.
subir, *vb.* undergo, bear.
subit, *adj.* sudden.
subjectif, *adj.* subjective.
subjonctif, *adj. and n.m.* subjunctive.
subjuguer, *vb.* subdue, overcome.
sublime, *adj.* sublime, exalted.
submerger, *vb.* submerge, flood.
subordonné, *adj. and n.m.* subordinate.
subordonner, *vb.* subordinate.
suborner, *n.f.* bribing.
subreptice, *adj.* surreptitious.
subséquent, *adj.* subsequent.
subside, *n.m.* subsidy.
subsister, *vb.* subsist, live.
substance, *n.f.* substance.
substantiel, *adj.* substantial.
substantif, *n.m.* noun.
substituer, *vb.* substitute.
substitution, *n.f.* substitution.
subtil (-l), *adj.* subtle.
subtilité, *n.f.* subtlety.

subvenir, vb. provide.
subvention, n.f. grant, subsidy.
subventionner, vb. subsidize.
subversif, adj. subversive.
suc, n.m. juice.
succéder à, vb. succeed, follow.
succès, n.m. success, hit.
successeur, n.m. successor.
successif, adj. successive.
succession, n.f. succession.
succion, n.f. suction.
succomber, vb. succumb.
succursale, n.f. branch office.
sucer, vb. suck.
sucre, n.m. sugar.
sucrer, vb. add sugar.
sucreries, n.f.pl. sweets.
sud (-d), n.m. south.
sudation, n.f. sweating.
sud-est, n.m. southeast.
sud-ouest, n.m. southwest.
Suède, n.f. Sweden.
Suédois, n.m. Swede (person).
suédois, adj. and n.m. Swedish.
suer, vb. sweat.
sueur, n.m. sweat.
suffire, vb. suffice.
suffisance, n.f. adequacy; conceit.
suffisant, adj. sufficient, adequate; conceited.
suffixe, n.m. suffix.
suffoquer, vb. suffocate.
suffrage, n.m. suffrage.
suggérer, vb. suggest.
suggestion, n.f. suggestion.
suicide, n.m. suicide.
suicider, vb. **se s.,** kill oneself.
suie, n.f. soot.
suif, n.m. tallow.
suinter, vb. seep.
Suisse, 1. n.m. Swiss (person). **2.** n.f. Switzerland.
suisse, adj. Swiss.
suite, n.f. sequence; retinue; (pl.) results, aftermath. **et ainsi de s.,** and so on. **tout de s.,** at once.
suivant, 1. n.m. follower. **2.** adj. next, following, subsequent. **3.** prep. by, according to.
suivi, adj. followed, coherent.
suivre, vb. follow; attend. **faire s.,** forward.
sujet, 1. n.m. subject; topic. **2.** adj. subject. **s. à,** liable to.

sujétion, n.f. subjection, slavery.
superbe, adj. superb, magnificent.
super(carburant), n.m. high-octane gasoline.
superette, n.f. small supermarket.
superficie, n.f. surface.
superficiel, adj. superficial, shallow.
superflu, adj. superfluous.
supérieur, adj. and n.m. superior, higher, upper; senior.
supériorité, n.f. superiority.
superlatif, adj. and n.m. superlative.
supermarché, n.m. supermarket.
superpuissance, n.f. superpower.
superstar, n.f. superstar.
superstitieux, adj. superstitious.
superstition, n.f. superstition.
suppléant, adj. and n.m. assistant, substitute.
suppléer, vb. substitute.
supplément, n.m. supplement.
supplémentaire, adj. extra. **heures s.s,** overtime.
supplice, n.m. punishment, torture.
supplier, vb. beseech, entreat, beg, supplicate.
support, n.m. support, stand.
supportable, adj. tolerable.
supporter, vb. support; bear, stand, endure.
supposer, vb. suppose, assume.
supposition, n.f. assumption, conjecture, supposition.
suppôt, n.m. implement, tool, agent.
suppression, n.f. suppression.
supprimer, vb. suppress, put down; take out.
supputation, n.f. computation.
supputer, vb. compute.
suprématie, n.f. supremacy.
suprême, adj. supreme.
sur, prep. on, upon, over.
sûr, adj. safe, sure, secure.
surabonder, vb. be very abundant.
suranné, adj. out-of-date.
surcharge, n.f. excess load.
surcharger, vb. overload.
surcroît, n.m. addition.
surdité, n.f. deafness.
suret, adj. sour.

sureté, *n.f.* safety, security, reliability.

surf, *n.m.* surf.

surface, *n.f.* surface, area.

surgélateur, *n.m.* deep freeze.

surgir, *vb.* spring up, arise.

surhumain, *adj.* superhuman.

surintendant, *n.m.* superintendent.

sur-le-champ, *adv.* at once, immediately.

surlendemain, *n.m.* two days later.

surmener, *vb.* overwork.

surmonter, *vb.* overcome, surmount.

surnager, *vb.* float.

surnaturel, *adj. and n.m.* supernatural.

surnom, *n.m.* nickname.

surpasser, *vb.* surpass.

surpeuplé, *adj.* overpopulated.

surplis, *n.m.* surplice.

surplomber, *vb.* overhang.

surplus, *n.m.* surplus, excess.

surprendre, *vb.* surprise.

surprise, *n.f.* surprise.

sursaut, *n.m.* start.

sursauter, *vb.* give a start.

sursis, *n.m.* delay, putting off.

surtaxe, *n.f.* surtax.

surtout, 1. *n.m.* overcoat. 2. *adv.* above all.

surveillance, *n.f.* supervision, watch.

surveillant, *n.m.* superintendent.

surveiller, *vb.* supervise, watch over.

survenir, *vb.* happen.

survêtement, *n.m.* track suit.

survie, *n.f.* survival.

survivance, *n.f.* survival.

survivre, *vb.* survive.

susceptible, *adj.* susceptible; liable.

susciter, *vb.* arouse, provoke.

suspect (-kt), *adj.* suspicious.

suspecter, *vb.* suspect.

suspendre, *vb.* suspend, hang, sling.

suspens, *adv.* en s., in suspense.

suspense, *n.m.* suspense.

suspension, *n.f.* suspension.

suspicion, *n.f.* suspicion.

sustenter, *vb.* sustain, bulwark.

svelte, *adj.* slender, slim.

sweat-shirt (swèt shœrt), *n.m.* sweatshirt.

syllabe, *n.f.* syllable.

sylphide, *n.f.* sylph.

sylvestre, *adj.* sylvan, woody.

sylviculture, *n.f.* forestry.

symbole, *n.m.* symbol.

symboliser, *vb.* symbolize.

symétrie, *n.f.* symmetry.

sympa, *adj.* nice.

sympathie, *n.f.* sympathy. **avoir de la s. pour**, like.

sympathique, *adj.* congenial, likeable.

sympathiser, *vb.* sympathize.

symphonie, *n.f.* symphony.

symptôme, *n.m.* symptom.

synchroniser, *vb.* synchronize.

syncape, *n.f.* blackout.

syndic, *n.m.f.* association/union representative.

syndical, *adj.* of a trade union.

syndicat, *n.m.* syndicate. **s. ouvrier**, trade union.

syndiqué, *n.m.* (trade) union member.

syndrome, *n.m.* syndrome.

synonyme, *n.m.* synonym.

syntaxe, *n.f.* syntax.

synthèse, *n.f.* synthesis.

synthétique, *adj.* synthetic.

Syrie, *n.f.* Syria.

Syrien, *adj.* Syrian (person).

syrien, *adj.* Syrian.

systématique, *adj.* systematic.

système, *n.m.* system.

T

tabac (-bâ), *n.m.* tobacco.

tabagie, *n.f.* smoking.

tabernacle, *n.m.* tabernacle.

table, *n.f.* table. **t. des matières**, index.

tableau, *n.m.* picture. **t. noir**, blackboard.

tabler, *vb.* count on, depend.

tablette, *n.f.* tablet.

tableur, *n.m.* spreadsheet.

tablier, *n.m.* apron.

tabou, *n.m.* taboo.

tabouret, *n.m.* stool.

tache, *n.f.* spot, stain, blot, smear.

tâche, *n.f.* task; assignment.

tacher, *vb.* spot, stain, blot.

tâcher, *vb.* try.

tacite, *adj.* tacit, silent.

taciturne, *adj.* unspeaking.

tact (-kt), *n.m.* tact.

tacticien, *n.m.* tactician.

tactique, 1. *adj.* of tactics, tactical. **2.** *n.f.* tactics.

taffetas, *n.m.* taffeta.

taie, *n.f.* **t. d'oreiller,** pillowcase.

taillade, *n.f.* slash.

taille, *n.f.* waist, figure; size.

tailler, *vb.* trim, cut.

tailleur, *n.m.* tailor.

taire, *vb.* keep quiet. **se t.,** be silent.

talent, *n.m.* ability, talent.

talon, *n.m.* heel; (check) stub.

talus, *n.m.* slope.

tambour, *n.m.* drum.

tambourin, *n.m.* tambourine.

tamis, *n.m.* sieve.

tampon, *n.m.* plug, pad. **t. hygiénique,** tampon.

tamponner, *vb.* plug; run together.

tan, *n.m.* tan (leather).

tandis que, *conj.* while, whereas.

tangible, *adj.* tangible.

tanguer, *vb.* cover with pitch.

tant, *adv.* so much, so many. **t. que,** as long as.

tante, *n.f.* aunt.

tantième, *n.m.* part, percentage.

tantôt, *adv.* presently, soon.

tapage, *n.m.* din.

tapageur, *adj.* rowdy.

taper, *vb.* pat, knock, tap; type.

tapir, se, *vb.* squat, cower, lurk.

tapis, *n.m.* carpet, rug.

tapisserie, *n.f.* tapestry.

tapissier, *n.m.* upholsterer.

taquiner, *vb.* tease.

taquinerie, *n.f.* teasing.

tard, *adv.* late.

tarder, *vb.* delay.

tardif, *adj.* slow, tardy, late.

tare, *n.f.* defect.

tarière, *n.f.* auger.

tarif, *n.m.* scale of charges; rate; fare. **t. douanier,** tariff.

tartan, *n.m.* plaid.

tarte, *n.f.* pie.

tartine, *n.f.* slice of bread.

tartre, *n.m.* tartar.

tas, *n.m.* heap, pile.

tasse, *n.f.* cup.

tasser, *vb.* pack, fill up.

tâter, *vb.* feel.

tâtonner, *vb.* grope.

taudis, *n.m.* hovel, slum.

taupe, *n.f.* mole.

taureau, *n.m.* bull.

taux, *n.m.* rate.

taverne, *n.f.* tavern.

taxe, *n.f.* tax. **t. (à la) valeur ajoutée,** value-added tax.

taxer, *vb.* tax, assess.

taxi, *n.m.* cab, taxi.

Tchécoslovaquie, *n.f.* Czechoslovakia.

te (ta), *pron.* you, yourself.

technicien, *n.m.* technician.

technique, 1. *n.f.* technique. **2.** *adj.* technical.

technologie, *n.f.* technology.

teindre, *vb.* dye.

teint, *n.m.* complexion.

teinte, *n.f.* tint, shade.

teinter, *vb.* tint, stain.

teinture, *n.f.* dye.

teinturier, *n.m.* dry-cleaner; dyer.

tel, *adj.* such.

télé, *n.f.* TV.

télécommande, *n.f.* remote control.

télécommunitions, *n.f.pl.* telecommunications.

télécopie, *n.f.* fax.

télécopieur, *n.m.* fax machine.

télédistribution, *n.f.* cable TV.

télégramme, *n.m.* telegram.

télégraphe, *n.m.* telegraph.

télégraphie, *n.f.* telegraphy. **t. sans fil,** *abbr.* T.S.F., radio, wireless.

télégraphier, *vb.* telegraph.

téléguider, *vb.* operate by remote control, radio-control.

télématique, *n.f.* computer communications.

téléphone, *n.m.* telephone. **coup de t.,** telephone call.

téléphoner, *vb.* telephone.

télescope, *n.m.* telescope.

télescoper, *vb.* crash, run together.

téléspectateur, *n.m.* TV viewer.

téléviseur, *n.m.* TV set.
télévision, *n.f.* television.
télex, *n.m.* telex.
tellement, *adv.* so much.
téméraire, *adj.* rash.
témoignage, *n.m.* testimony; token.
témoigner, *vb.* testify.
témoin, *n.m.* witness.
tempe, *n.f.* temple (anatomy).
tempérament, *n.m.* temper, temperament.
tempérance, *n.f.* temperance.
tempérant, *adj.* temperate.
température, *n.f.* temperature.
tempéré, *adj.* temperate.
tempérer, *vb.* moderate, calm, lessen.
tempête, *n.f.* storm, tempest.
tempétueux, *adj.* tempestuous.
temple, *n.m.* temple.
temporaire, *adj.* temporary.
temporiser, *vb.* temporize, evade.
temps (tän), *n.m.* time; weather.
tenace, *adj.* tenacious.
ténacité, *n.f.* tenacity.
tenailles, *n.f.pl.* tongs.
tendance, *n.f.* tendency, trend, leaning.
tendre, 1. *adj.* tender, fond, loving. **2.** *vb.* tend, extend.
tendresse, *n.f.* tenderness, fondness.
tendu, *adj.* tense; uptight.
ténèbres, *n.f.pl.* gloom, darkness.
ténébreux, *adj.* dismal.
teneur, *n.m.* t. de livres, bookkeeper.
tenir, *vb.* hold.
tennis (-s), *n.m.* tennis.
ténor, *n.m.* tenor.
tension, *n.f.* strain; stress.
tentacule, *n.m.* tentacle.
tentatif, *adj.* tentative.
tentation, *n.f.* temptation.
tentative, *n.f.* attempt.
tente, *n.f.* tent; awning.
tenter, *vb.* tempt, try, attract.
tenture, *n.f.* wallcovering.
tenue, *n.f.* rig; conduct, manners.
ténuité, *n.f.* tenuity, unimportance.
térébenthine, *n.f.* turpentine.
terme, *n.m.* term, period; end.
terminaison, *n.f.* ending.

terminal, *adj. and n.m.* terminal.
terminer, *vb.* end.
terminologie, *n.f.* terminology.
terminus, *n.m.* terminus.
terne, *adj.* drab, dull, dim, dingy.
ternir, *vb.* tarnish, dull.
terrain, *n.m.* ground(s).
terrasse, *n.f.* terrace.
terrasser, *vb.* heap up, embank; knock down, conquer.
terre, *n.f.* earth, ground, land. pomme de t., potato. à t., ashore.
terrestre, *adj.* earthly.
terreur, *n.f.* terror, fright, fear.
terrible, *adj.* terrible, awful; (colloquial) terrific.
terrifier, *vb.* terrify.
terrine, *n.f.* terrine, pâté.
territoire, *n.m.* territory.
terroir, *n.m.* soil.
terroriser, *vb.* terrorize.
terrorisme, *n.m.* terrorism.
tertre, *n.m.* mound.
tesson, *n.m.* broken piece, fragment.
testament, *n.m.* testament, will.
testateur, *n.m.* testator.
tester, *vb.* test.
testicule, *n.m.* testicle.
tête, *n.f.* head. tenir t. à, cope with.
téter, *vb.* suck.
téton, *n.m.* breast.
têtu, *adj.* stubborn.
texte, *n.m.* text.
textile, *adj.* textile.
textuel, *adj.* textual.
texture, *n.f.* texture.
Thaïlande, *n.f.* Thailand.
thé, *n.m.* tea.
théâtral, *adj.* theatrical.
théâtre, *n.m.* theater.
théière, *n.f.* teapot.
thème, *n.m.* theme.
théologie, *n.f.* theology.
théorie, *n.f.* theory.
théorique, *adj.* theoretical.
thérapie, *n.f.* therapy.
thermomètre, *n.m.* thermometer.
thermostat, *n.m.* thermostat.
thésauriser, *vb.* hoard.
thèse, *n.f.* thesis.
thon, *n.m.* tuna.
thym, *n.m.* thyme.
ticket, *n.m.* check, ticket, coupon.
tiède, *adj.* lukewarm.

tiédir, vb. make or become cool.
tien, pron. **le tien, la tienne**, yours.
tiers, n.m. third.
Tiers Monde, n.m. Third World.
tige, n.f. stem, stalk.
tigre, n.m. tiger.
tilleul, n.m. linden, lime tree.
timbre, n.m. stamp. **t.-poste**, postage stamp.
timbrer, vb. stamp.
timide, adj. timid, shy, coy, bashful.
timidité, n.f. timidity.
timoré, adj. timorous.
tintamarre, n.m. racket.
tinter, vb. ring, knell, tinkle.
tir, n.m. shooting, firing.
tirage, n.m. printing, print; circulation, edition.
tirailleur, n.m. sharpshooter.
tire, n.f. pull, yank.
tire-bouchon, n.m. corkscrew.
tirer, vb. draw, pull; shoot.
tiret, n.m. blank; dash.
tiroir, n.m. drawer.
tisane, n.f. drink, herbal tea.
tisser, vb. weave.
tisserand, n.m. weaver.
tissu, n.m. web; cloth, fabric.
titre, n.m. title, right.
titrer, vb. invest with a title.
titulaire, n.m. incumbent.
toast (-t), n.m. toast.
toaster, vb. toast.
toi, pron. you.
toile, n.f. web; canvas; linen.
toilette, n.f. toilet; dressing, dress.
toison, n.f. fleece.
toit, n.m. roof.
toiture, n.f. roofing.
tolérance, n.f. tolerance.
tolérer, vb. tolerate, bear.
tomate, n.f. tomato.
tombe, n.f. grave.
tombeau, n.m. tomb.
tombée, n.f. fall, decline.
tomber, vb. fall. **laisser t.**, drop.
tome, n.m. volume.
ton, n.m. tone, pitch.
ton m., **ta** f., **tes** pl. adj. your.
tonalité, n.f. dial tone, tone, key.
tondeuse, n.f. (lawn) mower.
tondre, vb. shear; mow.
tonique, adj. and n.m. tonic.
tonne, n.f. ton; barrel.

tonneau, n.m. cask, barrel.
tonner, vb. thunder.
tonnerre, n.m. thunder.
topaze, n.f. topaz.
topographie, n.f. topography.
torche, n.f. torch.
tordre, vb. twist, wrench, wring. **se t.**, writhe.
torpeur, n.f. torpor.
torpille, n.f. torpedo.
torrent, n.m. torrent.
torride, adj. torrid.
torse, n.m. torso.
tort, n.m. wrong. **avoir t.**, be wrong.
tortiller, vb. twist, wiggle.
tortionnaire, n.m.f. torturer.
tortu, adj. crooked.
tortue, n.f. turtle, tortoise.
torture, n.f. torture.
torturer, vb. torture.
tôt, adv. soon, early.
total, adj. and n.m. total.
totalisateur, n.m. adding machine.
totaliser, vb. total, add up.
totalitaire, adj. totalitarian.
totalité, n.f. entirety.
toubib (-b) n.m. (colloquial) doctor.
touchant, prep. concerning.
touche, n.f. key.
toucher, **1.** n.m. touch. **2.** vb. touch; collect; affect; border on.
touffe, n.f. tuft, bunch.
touffu, adj. bushy.
toujours, adv. always, still, ever, yet.
toupie, n.f. top (child's toy).
tour, **1.** n.m. turn; trick; stroll. **faire le t. de**, go around. **2.** n.f. tower.
tourbe, n.f. rabble.
tourbillon, n.m. whirl. **t. d'eau**, whirlpool. **t. de vent**, whirlwind.
tourbillonner, vb. whirl.
tourelle, n.f. turret.
touriste, n.m.f. tourist.
tourment, n.m. torment.
tourmenter, vb. torment.
tournage, n.m. (film) shooting.
tourne-disques, n.m. record player.
tournedos, n.m. beefsteak.
tournée, n.f. round.
tourner, vb. turn, revolve, spin.
tournesol, n.m. sunflower.

tournevis, *n.m.* screwdriver.

tournoi, *n.m.* tournament.

tournure, *n.f.* figure; turn of phrase.

tousser, *vb.* cough.

tout, 1. *adj.m.,* **toute** *f.,* **tous** *m.pl.,* **toutes** *f.pl.* all, each, every. **2.** *pron.* everything. **tous les deux,** both. **t. d'un coup,** all at once. **t. de même,** all the same. **pas du t.,** not at all.

toutefois, *adv.* however.

tout-puissant, *adj.* almighty.

toux, *n.f.* cough.

toxicomane, *n.m.f.* drug addict.

toxique, *adj.* toxic.

tracasser, *vb.* worry.

trace, *n.f.* trace, step, track, footprint.

tracer, *vb.* outline, trace.

tracteur, *n.m.* tractor.

traction, *n.f.* traction.

tradition, *n.f.* tradition.

traditionnel, *adj.* traditional.

traducteur, *n.m.* translator.

traduction, *n.f.* translation.

traduire, *vb.* translate.

trafic, *n.m.* traffic.

trafiquer, *vb.* traffic; carry on dealings.

tragédie, *n.f.* tragedy.

tragique, *adj.* tragic.

trahir, *vb.* betray.

trahison, *n.f.* treason.

train, *n.m.* train.

traînard, *n.m.* loiterer, dawdler.

traîne, *n.f.* train of dress.

traîneau, *n.m.* sled, sleigh.

traîner, *vb.* drag, haul.

traire, *vb.* milk.

trait, *n.m.* feature; draft; shot. **t. d'union,** hyphen.

traité, *n.m.* treaty.

traitement, *n.m.* treatment. **t. de données,** data processing. **t. de texte,** word processing.

traiter, *vb.* treat, deal; process.

traiteur, *n.m.* caterer.

traître, *n.m.* traitor.

traîtrise, *n.f.* treachery.

trajet, *n.m.* crossing.

trame, *n.f.* web (woof); plan, plot.

tramer, *vb.* devise.

tramway, *n.m.* streetcar.

tranchant, *adj.* sharp, crisp.

tranche, *n.f.* slice.

tranchée, *n.f.* trench.

trancher, *vb.* cut.

tranquille (-l-), *adj.* quiet. **laisser t.,** leave alone.

tranquilliser (-l-), *vb.* soothe, make tranquil.

tranquillité (-l-), *n.f.* quiet, stillness.

transaction, *n.f.* transaction.

transe, *n.f.* fright, fear.

transférer, *vb.* transfer.

transformer, *vb.* transform.

transfuser, *vb.* transfuse.

transfusion, *n.f.* transfusion.

transitif, *adj.* transitive.

transition (-z-), *n.f.* transition.

transitoire (-z-), *adj.* transitory.

transmettre, *vb.* transmit, convey, send.

transmetteur, *n.m.* transmitter.

transmission, *n.f.* transmission.

transparent, *adj.* transparent.

transpiration, *n.f.* perspiration.

transpirer, *vb.* perspire.

transplanter, *vb.* transplant.

transport, *n.m.* transfer, transport, transportation; bliss, ecstasy. **t.s en commun,** mass transport.

transporter, *vb.* transport, transfer, convey.

transposer, *vb.* transpose.

transsexuel, *adj.* transsexual.

traumatiser, *vb.* traumatize.

travail, *n.m.* work, job, labor.

travailler, *vb.* work.

travailleur, 1. *n.m.* worker, laborer. **2.** *adj.* industrious.

travée, *n.f.* span.

travers, *n.m.* breadth. **à t.,** across, through. **de t.,** askance, awry.

traversée, *n.f.* crossing.

traverser, *vb.* cross.

traversin, *n.m.* bolster.

travesti, *adj.* transvestite.

travestir, *vb.* disguise.

trébucher, *vb.* stumble, trip.

trèfle, *n.m.* clover; club (cards).

treillis, *n.m.* denim.

treize, *adj. and n.m.* thirteen.

tréma, *n.m.* dieresis.

tremblement, *n.m.* trembling. **t. de terre,** earthquake.

trembler, *vb.* tremble, shake, quake.

trembloter, *vb.* quiver.

trémousser, vb. flutter.

trempe, n.f. temper, cast.

tremper, vb. soak, drench, temper.

trentaine, n.f. about thirty.

trente, adj. and n.m. thirty.

trépasser, vb. die.

trépied, n.m. tripod, trivet.

très, adv. very.

trésor, n.m. treasure, treasury; darling.

trésorier, n.m. treasurer.

tressaillement, n.m. thrill; start.

tressaillir, vb. thrill; start.

tresse, n.f. braid.

tresser, vb. braid.

tréteau, n.m. trestle.

trêve, n.f. truce.

tri, n.m. sorting, selection.

triangle, n.m. triangle.

tribade, n.f. lesbian.

tribu, n.f. tribe.

tribulation, n.f. tribulation.

tribut, n.m. tribute.

tributaire, adj. tributary.

tricher, vb. cheat.

tricherie, n.f. cheating.

tricolore, adj. three-colored; (French) blue, white, red; (fig.) France.

tricot, n.m. knitting; undershirt; sweater.

tricoter, vb. knit.

trier, vb. sort.

trimestre, n.m. term.

trimestriel, adj. quarterly.

trinquer, vb. touch glasses in making a toast.

triomphant, adj. triumphant.

triomphe, n.m. triumph.

triompher, vb. triumph.

triple, adj. and n.m. triple.

tripoter, vb. fiddle with, dabble in; bother.

triste, adj. sad.

tristesse, n.f. sadness.

trivial, adj. trivial.

trivialité, n.f. triviality.

troc, n.m. barter.

trois, adj. and n.m. three.

troisième, adj. and n.m.f. third.

trompe, n.f. horn, trumpet; elephant's trunk.

trompe l'œil, n.m. trompe l'œil style of painting.

tromper, vb. deceive, cheat. **se t.,** be wrong, make a mistake.

tromperie, n.f. deceit.

trompette, n.f. trumpet.

trompeur, adj. deceitful.

tronc, n.m. trunk.

trône, n.m. throne.

trop, adv. too; too much, too many.

trophée, n.m. trophy.

tropical, adj. tropical.

tropique, n.m. tropic.

troquer, vb. barter, dicker, trade.

trot, n.m. trot.

trotter, vb. trot.

trottiner, vb. trot, jog.

trottoir, n.m. sidewalk.

trou, n.m. hole.

trouble, n.m. disturbance, riot.

troublé, adj. anxious, worried.

troubler, vb. perturb.

trouer, vb. pierce, bore.

trouille, n.f. (colloquial) **avoir la t.,** be scared to death.

troupe, n.f. troop.

troupeau, n.m. herd, flock, drove.

troupier, n.m. soldier, trooper.

trousseau, n.m. bunch; outfit.

trousser, vb. truss up, turn up.

trouvaille, n.f. discovery; find.

trouver, vb. find. **se t.,** be located.

truc, n.m. trick; thing.

truelle, n.f. trowel.

truite, n.f. trout.

truquer, vb. fake.

trust, n.m. trust.

T.S.F., n.f. radio.

tu, pron. you.

tube, n.m. tube, pipe.

tuberculeux, adj. tuberculous.

tuberculose, n.f. tuberculosis.

tuer, vb. kill.

tuerie, n.f. slaughter, massacre.

tueur, n.m. killer.

tuile, n.f. tile.

tulipe, n.f. tulip.

tuméfier, vb. make swollen.

tumulte, n.m. tumult, turmoil, uproar.

tunique, n.f. tunic.

Tunisie, n.f. Tunisia.

Tunisien, n.m. Tunisian (person).

tunisien, adj. Tunisian.

tunnel, n.f. tunnel.

Turc *m.*, **Turque** *f. n.* Turk.
turc, *n.m.* Turkish (language).
turc *m.*, **turque** *f. adj.* Turkish.
Turquie, *n.f.* Turkey.
tutelle, *n.f.* tutelage, protection.
tuteur, *n.m.* guardian.
tutoyer, *vb.* address familiarly as "tu."

tuyau, *n.f.* pipe; hose.
tympan, *n.m.* eardrum.
type, *n.m.* type; fellow, guy.
typique, *adj.* typical.
tyran, *n.m.* tyrant.
tyrannie, *n.f.* tyranny.
tyranniser, *vb.* tyrannize.
tzigane, *n.m.f.* gypsy.

U

ubiquité, *n.f.* ubiquity.
ulcère, *n.m.* ulcer.
ultérieur, *adj.* ulterior, further.
ultime, *adj.* ultimate, last.
un *m.*, **une** *f.* **1.** *art. a.* **2.** *adj. and n.* one.
unanime, *adj.* unanimous.
unanimité, *n.f.* unanimity.
uni, *adj.* united; plain; even.
unifier, *vb.* unify.
uniforme, *adj. and n.m.* uniform.
union, *n.f.* union.
unique, *adj.* unique; only.
unir, *vb.* unite.
unisexuel, *adj.* unisex.
unisson, *n.m.* unison.
unité, *n.f.* unit, unity.
univers, *n.m.* universe.
universel, *adj.* universal.
université, *n.f.* university, college.
urbain, *adj.* urban.

urbanisme, *n.m.* city planning.
urgence, *n.f.* urgency, emergency.
urgent, *adj.* urgent, pressing.
urine, *n.f.* urine.
urne, *n.f.* urn; ballot box.
urticaire, *n.f.* hives.
usage, *n.m.* use; custom.
usager, *adj.* for daily use.
usé, *adj.* shabby, worn-out.
user, *vb.* wear out.
usine, *n.f.* factory.
ustensile, *n.f.* utensil.
usuel, *adj.* usual.
usure, *n.f.* wear and tear; usury; interest.
usurper, *vb.* usurp.
utile, *adj.* helpful, useful.
utilisation, *n.f.* use.
utiliser, *vb.* use.
utilité, *n.f.* utility.
utopie, *n.f.* utopia.

V

vacance, *n.f.* vacancy; *(pl.)* vacation.
vacarme, *n.m.* uproar.
vaccin, *n.m.* vaccine.
vacciner, *vb.* vaccinate.
vache, *n.f.* cow.
vaciller (-l-), *vb.* waver.
vacuité, *n.f.* emptiness, vacuity.
vagabond, *adj.* vagrant.
vagabonder, *vb.* roam, tramp.
vagin, *n.m.* vagina.
vague, **1.** *n.f.* wave. **2.** *adj.* vague.
vaguer, *vb.* wander.
vaillant, *adj.* valiant, brave, gallant.
vain, *adj.* idle; vain, futile.
vaincre, *vb.* defeat.
vainqueur, *n.m.* victor.

vaisseau, *n.m.* ship.
vaisselle, *n.f.* dishes.
valable, *adj.* valid; worthwhile.
valeur, *n.f.* valor; value, worth; *(pl.)* securities.
valeureux, *adj.* brave, valorous.
valide, *adj.* valid.
valise, *n.f.* suitcase.
vallée, *n.f.* valley.
vallon, *n.m.* valley, vale.
valoir, *vb.* be worth. v. **mieux**, be better.
valorisé, *adj.* valued.
valoriser, *vb.* add value to.
valse, *n.f.* waltz.
vandale, *n.m.f.* vandal.
vanille, *n.f.* vanilla.
vanité, *n.f.* conceit, vanity.

vaniteux, adj. vain.

vantard, adj. boastful.

vanter, vb. extol. **se v.,** boast, brag.

vapeur, 1. n.m. steamship. **2.** n.f. vapor, steam.

vaporisateur, n.f. vaporizer, spray.

variation, n.f. variation, change.

varicelle, n.f. chicken pox.

varier, vb. vary.

variété, n.f. variety.

variole, n.f. smallpox.

vase, n.m. vase, jar, pot.

vasectomie, n.f. vasectomy.

vaseux, adj. slimy; hazy.

vassal, n.m. vassal.

vaste, adj. vast, spacious.

vaurien, n.m. worthless person, idler.

veau, n.m. calf.

vedette, n.f. (movie) star.

végéter, vb. vegetate.

véhicule, n.m. vehicle.

veille, n.f. eve, day before.

veiller, vb. watch over, sit up.

veine, n.f. vein; luck.

véliplanchiste, n.m.f. windsurfer.

vélo, n.m. bike.

vélomoteur, n.m. moped.

velours, n.m. velvet. **v. côtelé,** corduroy.

velouté, adj. like velvet.

velu, adj. hairy.

vendange, n.f. vintage.

vendeur, n.m. seller; clerk, salesman.

vendre, vb. sell.

vendredi, n.m. Friday.

vénéneux, adj. poisonous.

vénérer, vb. venerate.

vengeance, n.f. revenge.

venger, vb. avenge. **se v.,** get revenge.

venimeux, adj. poisonous.

venin, n.m. poison.

venir, vb. come. **v. de,** have just. **... à v.,** forthcoming.

vent, n.m. wind.

vente, n.f. sale.

venteux, adj. windy.

ventilateur, n.m. fan.

ventiler, vb. ventilate.

ventre, n.m. belly.

venue, n.f. advent, arrival.

vêpres, n.f.pl. vespers.

ver (-r), n.m. worm.

veracité, n.f. veracity.

véranda, n.f. porch.

verbe, n.m. verb.

verbeux, adj. wordy, verbose.

verdeur, n.f. greenness, sharpness; vigor.

verdict (-kt), n.m. verdict.

verdir, vb. make or become green.

verdure, n.f. greenery.

verge, n.f. rod.

verger, n.m. orchard.

verglas, n.m. sleet.

vérification, n.f. check.

vérifier, vb. check, confirm.

véritable, adj. genuine, real.

vérité, n.f. truth.

vermine, n.f. vermin.

vermouth, n.m. vermouth.

vernir, vb. varnish.

vernis, n.m. varnish.

vérole, n.f. **petite v.,** smallpox.

verre, n.m. glass.

verrou, n.m. bolt.

verrouiller, vb. bolt.

vers, 1. n.m. verse. **2.** prep. toward.

verse, adj. **tomber à v.,** pour.

verser, vb. pour; shed.

versifier, vb. versify.

version, n.f. version, translation.

vert, adj. green.

vertèbre, n.f. vertebra.

vertical, adj. upright, vertical.

vertige, n.m. dizziness.

vertigineux, adj. dizzy.

vertu, n.f. virtue.

vertueux, adj. virtuous.

verveux, adj. lively, animated.

vessie, n.f. bladder.

veste, n.f. jacket.

vestiaire, n.m. cloak-room.

vestibule, n.m. hall, lobby.

vestige, n.m. vestige, remains.

veston, n.m. jacket, coat.

vêtement, n.m. garment; (pl.) clothes.

vétéran, n.m. veteran.

vétérinaire, n.m.f. veterinary.

vêtir, vb. clothe.

véto, n.m. veto.

veuf, n.m. widower.

veuve, n.f. widow.

vexation, n.f. vexation.

vexer, vb. vex.

viaduc, n.m. viaduct.

viande, *n.f.* meat.
vibrant, *adj.* vibrant, vibrating.
vibration, *n.f.* vibration.
vibrer, *vb.* vibrate.
vicaire, *n.m.* vicar.
vice, *n.m.* vice.
vice-roi, *n.m.* viceroy.
vicieux, *adj.* depraved, wrong.
vicomte, *n.m.* viscount.
victime, *n.f.* victim.
victoire, *n.f.* victory.
victorieux, *adj.* victorious.
victuailles (věk tYǐ), *n.f.pl.* provisions.
vidange, *n.f.* emptying, cleaning.
vide, 1. *n.m.* emptiness, vacuum, blank, gap. **2.** *adj.* empty, void, vacant, blank.
vidéocassette, *n.f.* videocassette.
vidéodisque, *n.m.* videodisc.
vider, *vb.* empty, drain.
vie, *n.f.* life.
vieil, *adj.* old.
vieillard, *n.m.* old man.
vieille, 1. *n.f.* old woman. **2.** *adj.f.* old.
vieillesse, *n.f.* old age.
vieillir, *vb.* age.
Vienne, *n.f.* Vienna.
vierge, *n.f.* virgin.
Viêt-nam, Vietnam, *n.m.* Vietnam.
Vietnamien, *(m.),* **Vietnamienne** *(f) n.* Vietnamese (person).
vietnamien, *n.m.* and *adj.* Vietnamese.
vieux, *adj.m.* old.
vif *m.,* **vive** *f. adj.* lively, quick, brisk, bright, vivacious.
vif-argent, *n.m.* quicksilver.
vigie, *n.f.* lookout man or station.
vigilance, *n.f.* vigilance.
vigilant, *adj.* watchful.
vigne, *n.f.* vine; vineyard.
vigneron, *n.m.* wine grower.
vignoble, *n.m.* vineyard.
vigoureux, *adj.* lusty, hardy, vigorous.
vigueur, *n.f.* vigor, force.
vil (-l), *adj.* vile.
vilain, *adj.* ugly, mean, wicked.
village (-l-), *n.m.* village.
ville (-l), *n.f.* city, town.
villégiature (-l-), *n.f.* country holiday.

vin, *n.m.* wine.
vinaigre, *n.m.* vinegar.
vindicatif, *adj.* vindictive.
vingt (văN), *adj.* and *n.m.* twenty.
vingtaine (văN-), *n.f.* score; about twenty.
vingtième (văN-), *adj.* and *n.m.f.* twentieth.
viol, *n.m.* rape, violation.
violateur, *n.m.* violator.
violation, *n.f.* violation.
violemment, *adv.* violently.
violence, *n.f.* violence.
violent, *adj.* violent.
violer, *vb.* violate.
violet, *adj.* purple, violet.
violette, *n.f.* violet.
violon, *n.m.* violin.
violoncelle, *n.m.* cello.
vipère, *n.f.* viper.
virement, *n.m.* transfer.
virgule, *n.f.* comma.
viril (-l), *adj.* manly.
virilité, *n.f.* manhood.
virtuel, *adj.* virtual.
virtuose, *n.m.f.* virtuoso.
virus (-s), *n.m.* virus.
vis (-s), *n.f.* screw.
visa, *n.m.* visa.
visage, *n.m.* face.
vis-à-vis, *adv.* opposite, across from.
viser, *vb.* aim.
visibilité, *n.f.* visibility.
visible, *adj.* visible.
visière, *n.f.* visor; keenness.
vision, *n.f.* vision.
visionnaire, *adj.* and *n.m.f.* visionary.
visite, *n.f.* call, visit.
visiter, *vb.* visit.
visiteur, *n.m.* visitor.
visqueux, *adj.* viscous, sticky.
visser, *vb.* screw.
visuel, *adj.* visual.
vital, *adj.* vital.
vitalité, *n.f.* vitality.
vitamine, *n.f.* vitamin.
vite, *adv.* quick, fast.
vitesse, *n.f.* speed, rate; gear. **changer de v.,** shift gears.
viticole, *adj.* wine.
viticulteur, *n.m.* wine grower.
vitrail, *n.m.* (church) window.

vitre, *n.f.* pane.

vitrine, *n.f.* display case, shop window.

vitupération, *n.f.* vituperation.

vivace, *adj.* long-lived; perennial (of plant).

vivacité, *n.f.* vivacity.

vivant, *adj.* alive.

vivement, *adv.* quickly, smartly, vividly.

vivre, *vb.* live.

vocabulaire, *n.m.* vocabulary.

vocal, *adj.* vocal.

vocation, *n.f.* vocation.

vodka, *n.f.* vodka.

vœu (vœ), *n.m.* vow.

vogue, *n.f.* vogue.

voguer, *vb.* sail.

voici, *vb.* here is, behold.

voie, *n.f.* track, road. **v. d'eau,** leak.

voilà, *vb.* there is; behold.

voile, *n.m.* veil; sail.

voiler, *vb.* veil, hide.

voilure, *n.f.* sails.

voir, *vb.* see. **faire v.,** show.

voirie, *n.m.* dump; highway maintenance.

voisin, 1. *n.m.* neighbor. **2.** *adj.* nearby, adjoining.

voisinage, *n.m.* neighborhood.

voisiner, *vb.* act like a neighbor.

voiture, *n.f.* car; carriage. **en v.!,** all aboard!

voix, *n.f.* voice.

vol, *n.m.* flight; theft, robbery; rip-off.

volage, *adj.* fickle.

volaille, *n.f.* fowl, poultry.

volant, *n.m.* steering wheel.

volatil, *adj.* volatile.

volcan, *n.m.* volcano.

volcanique, *adj.* volcanic.

volée, *n.f.* flight, covey; herd.

voler, *vb.* fly; steal, rob; rip off.

volet, *n.m.* shutter, blind.

voleur, *n.m.* thief, robber.

vol frété, *n.m.* charter flight.

volontaire, 1. *n.m.f.* volunteer. **2.** *adj.* voluntary, volunteer.

volonté, *n.f.* will.

volontiers, *adv.* gladly, willingly.

voltigement, *n.m.* flutter.

voltiger, *vb.* flutter; hover.

volubilité, *n.f.* volubility, glibness.

volume, *n.m.* volume.

volumineux, *adj.* bulky.

volupté, *n.f.* pleasure, voluptuousness.

vomir, *vb.* vomit.

vorace, *adj.* voracious.

votant, *n.m.* voter.

vote, *n.m.* vote.

voter, *vb.* vote.

votre *sg.,* **vos** *pl. adj.* your.

vôtre, *pron.* **le v.,** yours.

vouer, *vb.* vow.

vouloir, *vb.* want, wish, will. **v. dire,** mean. **v. savoir,** wonder. **v. bien,** be willing. **en v. à,** bear a grudge against.

vous, *pron.* you, yourself.

voûte, *n.f.* vault.

voûter, *vb.* arch.

vouvoyer, *vb.* address politely as "vous."

voyage, *n.m.* journey, trip.

voyager, *vb.* travel.

voyageur, *n.m.* traveler, passenger.

voyageur de banlieue, *n.m.* commuter.

voyant, 1. *n.m.* clairvoyant. **2.** *adj.* gaudy, flashy.

voyelle, *n.f.* vowel.

vrai, *adj.* true, real.

vraisemblable, *adj.* probable, likely.

vraisemblance, *n.f.* probability.

vue, *n.f.* view, sight.

vue d'ensemble, *n.f.* overview.

vulcaniser, *vb.* vulcanize.

vulgaire, *adj.* vulgar, rude.

vulgariser, *vb.* popularize.

vulgarité, *n.f.* vulgarity.

vulnérable, *adj.* vulnerable.

W, X, Y, Z

wagon, *n.m.* coach, car.

wagon-lits, *n.m.* sleeping car.

wagon-restaurant, *n.m.* diner, dining-car.

walkman, *n.m.* (trademark) Walkman.

Wallon, *n.m. and adj.* Walloon.

watt, *n.m.* watt.

week-end, *n.m.* weekend.
whisky, *n.m.* whiskey.
xénophobe (ks-), *n.m.f. and adj.* xenophobic (person).
xérès (ks-), *n.m.* sherry.
xylophone (ks-), *n.m.* xylophone.
y, *adv.* there, in it, to it.
yacht, *n.m.* yacht.
yaourt, *n.m.* yogurt.
yoga, *n.m.* yoga.
Yougoslave, *n.m.f.* Yugoslav (person).
yougoslave, *adj.* Yugoslav.
Yougoslavie, *n.f.* Yugoslavia.
yuppie, *n.m.f.* yuppie.

zèbre, *n.m.* zebra.
zèle, *n.m.* zeal.
zélé, *adj.* zealous.
zénith, *n.m.* zenith.
zéro, *n.m.* zero.
zeste, *n.m.* peel, zest.
zézayer, *vb.* lisp.
zibeline, *n.f.* sable.
zigzaguer, *vb.* zigzag.
zinc, *n.m.* zinc; (bar) counter.
zone, *n.f.* zone, district; slum.
zodiaque, *n.m.* zodiac.
zoologie, *n.f.* zoology.
zoologique, *adj.* zoological. **jardin z.,** zoo.

A

a, *art.* un *m.,* une *f.*

aardvark, *n.* aardvark *m.*

aback, *adv.* déconcerté.

abacus, *n.* abaque *m.*

abandon, *vb.* abandonner.

abandon, *n.* abandon *m.*

abandoned, *adj.* abandonné.

abandonment, *n.* abandon *m.*

abase, *vb.* abaisser, avilir.

abasement, *n.* abaissement *m.,* avilissement *m.*

abash, *vb.* déconcerter.

abate, *vb.* diminuer.

abatement, *n.* diminution *f.*

abbess, *n.* abbesse *f.*

abbey, *n.* abbaye *f.*

abbot, *n.* abbé *m.*

abbreviate, *vb.* abréger.

abbreviation, *n.* abréviation *f.*

abdicate, *vb.* abdiquer.

abdication, *n.* abdication *f.*

abdomen, *n.* abdomen *m.*

abdominal, *adj.* abdominal.

abduct, *vb.* enlever.

abduction, *n.* enlèvement *m.*

abductor, *n.* ravisseur *m.*

aberrant, *adj.* aberrant, égaré.

aberration, *n.* égarement *m.*

abet, *vb.* aider, encourager, appuyer.

abetment, *n.* encouragement *m.,* appui *m.*

abettor, *n.* aide *m.,* complice *m.*

abeyance, *n.* suspension *f.*

abhor, *vb.* détester.

abhorrence, *n.* aversion extrême *f.,* horreur *f.*

abhorrent, *adj.* odieux, répugnant (à).

abide, *vb.* (tolerate) supporter; (remain) demeurer; (**a. by the law**) respecter la loi.

abiding, *adj.* constant, durable.

ability, *n.* talent *m.*

abject, *adj.* abject.

abjuration, *n.* abjuration *f.*

abjure, *vb.* abjurer, renoncer à.

abjurer, *n.* personne *(f.)* qui abjure.

ablative, *adj.* *and n.* ablatif *m.*

ablaze, *adj.* en feu, en flammes.

able, *adj.* capable; (**to be a.**) pouvoir.

able-bodied, *adj.* fort, robuste.

able-bodied seaman, *n.* marin *(m.)* de première classe.

ablution, *n.* ablution *f.*

ably, *adv.* capablement.

abnegate, *vb.* nier.

abnegation, *n.* abnégation *f.*

abnormal, *adj.* anormal.

abnormality, *n.* irrégularité *f.*

abnormally, *adv.* anormalement.

aboard, **1.** *adv.* (*naut.*) à bord; (**all a.**) en voiture. **2.** *prep.* à bord de.

abode, *n.* demeure *f.*

abolish, *vb.* abolir.

abolishment, *n.* abolissement *m.*

abolition, *n.* abolition *f.*

abominable, *adj.* abominable.

abominate, *vb.* abominer.

abomination, *n.* abomination *f.*

aboriginal, *adj.* aborigène, primitif.

aborigines, *n.* aborigènes *m.pl.*

abort, *vb.* faire avorter.

abortion, *n.* avortement *m.*

abortive, *adj.* abortif, manqué.

abound, *vb.* abonder (en).

about, **1.** *adv.* (approximately) à peu près; (around) autour *m.;* (**to be a. to**) être sur le point de. **2.** *prep.* (concerning) au sujet de; (near) auprès de; (around) autour de.

about-face, *n.* volte-face *f.*

above, **1.** *adv.* au-dessus. **2.** *prep.* (higher than) au-dessus de; (more than) plus de.

aboveboard, **1.** *adj.* ouvert, franc. **2.** *adv.* ouvertement, franchement.

abrasion, *n.* abrasion *f.*

abrasive, *adj.* abrasif.

abreast, *adv.* de front.

abridge, *vb.* abréger.

abridgment, *n.* abrégé *m.,* réduction *f.*

abroad, *adv.* à l'étranger.

abrogate, *vb.* abroger.

abrogation, *n.* abrogation *f.*

abrupt, *adj.* brusque; (steep) escarpé.

abruptly, *adv.* brusquement, subitement.

abruptness, n. brusquerie f., précipitation f.
abscess, n. abcès m.
abscond, vb. disparaître, se dérober.
absence, n. absence f.
absent, adj. absent.
absentee, n. absent m., manquant m.
absinthe, n. absinthe f.
absolute, adj. absolu.
absolutely, adv. absolument.
absoluteness, n. pouvoir absolu m.; arbitraire m.
absolution, n. absolution f.
absolutism, n. absolutisme m.
absolve, vb. absoudre.
absorb, vb. absorber.
absorbed, adj. absorbé, préoccupé.
absorbent, n. and adj. absorbant m.
absorbing, adj. absorbant, préoccupant.
absorption, n. absorption f.
abstain from, vb. s'abstenir de.
abstemious, adj. abstème.
abstinence, n. abstinence f.
abstract, 1. n. (book) extrait m. **2.** adj. abstrait.
abstracted, adj. détaché, pensif.
abstraction, n. abstraction f.
abstruse, adj. caché, abstrus.
absurd, adj. absurde.
absurdity, n. absurdité f.
absurdly, adv. absurdement.
abundance, n. abondance f.
abundant, adj. abondant.
abundantly, adv. abondamment.
abuse, 1. n. (misuse) abus m.; (insult) injures f.pl. **2.** vb. abuser de, injurier.
abusive, adj. (insulting) injurieux.
abusively, adv. abusivement, injurieusement.
abut, vb. s'embrancher (sur) aboutir (à).
abutment, n. contrefort m.; (of a bridge) culée f.
abysmal, adj. exécrable.
abyss, n. abîme m.
academic, adj. académique.
academic freedom, n. liberté (f.) de l'enseignement.
academy, n. académie f.

acanthus, n. acanthe f.
accede, vb. consentir.
accelerate, vb. accélérer.
acceleration, n. accélération f.
accelerator, n. accélérateur m.
accent, n. accent m.
accentuate, vb. accentuer.
accept, vb. accepter.
acceptability, n. acceptabilité f.
acceptable, adj. acceptable.
acceptably, adv. agréablement.
acceptance, n. acceptation f.
access, n. accès m.
accessible, adj. accessible.
accession, n. accession f.
accessory, n. and adj. accessoire m.
accident, n. accident m.
accidental, adj. accidentel.
accidentally, adv. accidentellement, par hasard.
acclaim, vb. acclamer.
acclamation, n. acclamation f.
acclimate, vb. acclimater.
acclivity, n. montée f., rampe f.
accolade, n. accolade f.
accommodate, vb. (lodge) loger; (oblige) obliger.
accommodating, adj. accommodant, obligeant.
accommodation, n. (lodging) logement m.
accompaniment, n. accompagnement m.
accompanist, n. accompagnateur m., accompagnatrice f.
accompany, vb. accompagner.
accomplice, n. complice m.f.
accomplish, vb. accomplir.
accomplished, adj. accompli, achevé.
accord, n. accord m.
accordance, n. conformité f.
accordingly, adv. (correspondingly) à l'avenant; (therefore) donc.
according to, prep. selon.
accordion, n. accordéon m.
accost, vb. aborder.
account, n. (comm.) compte m.; (narrative) récit m.
accountable, adj. responsable de.
accountant, n. comptable m.
account for, vb. rendre compte de.
accounting, n. comptabilité f.

accouter, vb. habiller, équiper.
accouterments, n. équipements m.pl., accoutrements m.pl.
accredit, vb. accréditer.
accretion, n. accroissement m.
accrual, n. accroissement m.
accrue, vb. provenir.
accrued interest, n. intérêt (m.) cumulé.
accumulate, vb. entasser.
accumulation, n. entassement m.
accumulative, adj. (thing) qui s'accumule, (person) qui accumule.
accumulator, n. accumulateur m., accumulatrice f.
accuracy, n. précision f.
accurate, adj. précis.
accursed, adj. maudit, exécrable.
accusation, n. accusation f.
accusative, n. and adj. accusatif m.
accuse, vb. accuser.
accused, n. and adj. accusé m., accusée f.
accuser, n. accusateur m., accusatrice f.
accustom, vb. accoutumer.
accustomed, adj. accoutumé, habituel.
ace, n. as m.
acerbity, n. acerbité f., âpreté f.
acetate, n. acétate m.
acetic acid, n. acide (m.) acétique.
acetylene, n. acétylène m.
ache, 1. n. douleur f. 2. vb. faire mal à.
achieve, vb. accomplir.
achievement, n. accomplissement m.
acid, adj. and n. acide m.
acidify, vb. acidifier.
acidity, n. acidité f.
acidosis, n. acidose f.
acid test, n. épreuve (f.) concluante.
acidulous, adj. acidulé.
acknowledge, vb. reconnaître; (a. receipt of) accuser réception de.
acme, n. comble m., apogée m.
acne, n. acné f.
acolyte, n. acolyte m.
acorn, n. gland m.
acoustics, n. acoustique f.
acquaint, vb. informer (de); (be a.ed with) connaître.
acquaintance, n. connaissance f.

acquainted, adj. connu, familier (avec).
acquiesce in, vb. acquiescer à.
acquiescence, n. acquiescement m.
acquire, vb. acquérir.
acquirement, n. acquis m., acquisition f.
acquisition, n. acquisition f.
acquisitive, adj. porté à acquérir.
acquit, vb. acquitter.
acquittal, n. acquittement m.
acre, n. arpent m., acre f.
acreage, n. superficie f.
acrid, adj. âcre.
acrimonious, adj. acrimonieux.
acrimony, n. acrimonie f., aigreur f.
acrobat, n. acrobate m.f.
acrobatic, n. acrobatie f.
across, 1. prep. à travers; (on the other side of) de l'autre côté de. 2. adv. en travers.
acrostic, n. acrostiche m.
acrylic, n. acrylique f.
act, 1. n. acte m. 2. vb. (do) agir; (play) jouer; (behave) se conduire.
acting, 1. n. (theater) jeu m.; feinte f. 2. adj. (taking the place of) suppléant; (comm.) gérant.
actinism, n. actinisme m.
actinium, n. actinium m.
action, n. action f.
activate, vb. activer.
activation, n. activation f.
activator, n. activateur m.
active, adj. actif.
activity, n. activité f.
actor, n. acteur m.
actress, n. actrice f.
actual, adj. réel.
actuality, n. réalité f., actualité f.
actually, adv. réellement, véritablement; en effet.
actuary, n. actuaire m.
actuate, vb. mettre en action, animer.
acumen, n. finesse f., pénétration f.
acupuncture, n. acuponcture f.
acute, adj. (geom.) aigu m., aiguë f.; (mind) fin.
acutely, adv. vivement, d'une manière poignante.
acuteness, n. finesse f., vivacité f.
ad, n. annonce f.
adage, n. adage m., proverbe m.

adamant, adj. indomptable.
Adam's apple, n. pomme (f.) d'A-dam.
adapt, vb. adapter.
adaptability, n. faculté (f.) d'a-daptation.
adaptable, adj. adaptable.
adaptation, n. adaptation f.
adapter, n. qui adapte.
adaptive, adj. adaptable.
add, vb. (join) ajouter; (arith.) additionner.
adder, n. vipère f.
addict, n. toxicomane, m.f.
addicted, adj. adonné (à).
addition, n. addition f.
additional, adj. additionel.
additive, n. additif m.
addle, 1. vb. corrompre, rendre couvi (of eggs). **2.** adj. couvi, pourri.
address, 1. n. (on letters, etc.) adresse f.; (speech) discours m. **2.** vb. (a letter) adresser; (a person) adresser la parole à.
addressee, n. destinataire m.f.
adduce, vb. alléguer, avancer.
adenoid, adj. and n. adénoïde f.
adeptly, vb. habilement, adeptement.
adeptness, n. habileté f.
adequacy, n. suffisance f.
adequate, adj. suffisant.
adequately, adv. suffisamment, convenablement.
adhere, vb. adhérer.
adherence, n. adhérence f., attachement m.
adherent, n. adhérent m.
adhesion, n. adhésion f.
adhesive, adj. adhésif.
adhesiveness, n. propriété d'ad-hérer f.
ad hoc, adj. improvisé.
adieu, n. (pl.) adieu, adieu m.
adjacent, adj. adjacent.
adjective, n. adjectif m.
adjoin, vb. adjoindre, être contigu (à).
adjourn, vb. ajourner, tr.; s'a-journer, intr.
adjournment, n. ajournement m.
adjudicate, vb. juger.
adjunct, n. and adj. adjoint m., accessoire m.

adjust, vb. ajuster, arranger, régler.
adjuster, n. ajusteur m.
adjustment, n. ajustement m., accommodement m.
adjutant, n. capitaine (m.) adjudant major.
ad-lib, vb. improviser.
administer, vb. administrer.
administration, n. administration f.
administrative, adj. administratif.
administrator, n. administrateur m.
admirable, adj. admirable.
admirably, adv. admirablement.
admiral, n. amiral m.
admiralty, n. amirauté f.
admiration, n. admiration f.
admire, vb. admirer.
admirer, n. admirateur m.
admiringly, adv. avec admiration.
admissible, adj. admissible.
admission, n. (entrance) entrée f.; (confession) aveu m.
admit, vb. (let in) laisser entrer; (confess) avouer.
admittance, n. entrée f.
admittedly, adv. de l'aveu de tout le monde.
admixture, n. mélange m.
admonish, vb. réprimander.
admonition, n. admonition f., avertissement m.
ad nauseam, adv. à n'en plus finir.
ado, n. fracas m.
adolescence, n. adolescence f.
adolescent, adj. and n. adolescent m.f.
adopt, vb. adopter.
adoption, n. adoption f.
adorable, adj. adorable.
adoration, n. adoration f.
adore, vb. adorer.
adorn, vb. orner.
adornment, n. ornement m.
adrenal glands, n.pl. capsules (f.pl.) surrénales.
adrenalin, n. adrénaline f.
Adriatic (Sea), n. Adriatique f.
adrift, adv. (naut.) à la dérive.
adroit, adj. adroit.
adulate, vb. aduler.
adulation, n. adulation f.
adult, adj. and n. adulte m.f.

adulterant, n. adultérant m.
adulterate, vb. adultérer; (of wines, milk, etc.) frelater.
adulterer, n. adultère m.
adulteress, n. femme adultère f.
adultery, n. adultère m.
advance, 1. n. (motion forward) avancement m.; (progress) progrès m.; (pay) avances f.pl.; (in a.) d'avance. **2.** vb. avancer.
advanced, adj. avancé.
advancement, n. avancement m., progrès m.
advantage, n. avantage m.
advantageous, adj. avantageux.
advantageously, adv. avantageusement.
advent, n. venue f.; (eccles.) Avent m.
adventitious, adj. adventice, fortuit.
adventure, n. aventure f.
adventurer, n. aventurier m.
adventurous, adj. aventureux.
adventurously, adv. aventureusement.
adverb, n. adverbe m.
adverbial, adj. adverbial.
adversary, n. adversaire m.
adverse, adj. adverse.
adversely, adv. défavorablement, d'une manière hostile.
adversity, n. adversité f.
advert, vb. faire allusion (à).
advertise, vb. annoncer; (a. a product) faire de la réclame pour un produit.
advertisement, n. publicité f., réclame f.; (in a paper) annonce f.; (on a wall) affiche f.
advertiser, n. annonceur m.
advertising, n. publicité f., annonce (newspaper) f.
advice, n. conseil m.; (comm.) avis m.
advisability, n. convenance f., utilité f.
advisable, adj. recommandable.
advisably, adv. convenablement.
advise, vb. conseiller.
advisedly, adv. de propos délibéré.
advisement, n. délibération.
advocacy, n. défense f., plaidoyer m.
advocate, 1. n. (law) avocat m.;

aegis, n. égide f.
aerate, vb. aérer.
aeration, n. aération f.
aerial, adj. aérien.
aerially, adv. d'une manière aérienne.
aerie, n. aire f.
aerobics, n. aérobic m.
aerodynamic, adj. aérodynamique.
aerogram, n. aérogramme m.
aeronautics, n. aéronautique f.
aerosol, n. atomiseur m.
aerospace, adj. aérospatial.
aesthetic, adj. esthétique.
afar, adv. loin, de loin.
affability, n. affabilité f.
affable, adj. affable.
affably, adv. affablement.
affair, n. affaire f.
affect, vb. (move) toucher; (concern) intéresser; (pretend) affecter.
affectation, n. affectation f.
affected, adj. maniéré.
affecting, adj. touchant, émouvant.
affection, n. affection f.
affectionate, adj. affectueux.
affectionately, adv. affectueusement.
afferent, adj. afférent.
affiance, vb. fiancer.
affidavit, n. attestation (sous serment) f.
affiliate, vb. affilier.
affiliation, n. affiliation f.
affinity, n. affinité f.
affirm, vb. affirmer.
affirmation, n. affirmation f.
affirmative, adj. affirmatif.
affirmatively, adv. affirmativement.
affix, vb. apposer.
afflict, vb. affliger (de).
affliction, n. affliction f.
affluence, n. affluence f., opulence f.
affluent, adj. affluent, opulent.
afford, vb. (have the means to) avoir les moyens de.
affray, n. bagarre f., tumulte m.
affront, 1. n. affront m. **2.** vb. insulter.

afield, *adv.* aux champs, en campagne; (**go far a.**) aller très loin.

afire, *adv.* en feu.

afloat, *adv.* à flot, en train.

aforementioned, *adj.* mentionné plus haut, susdit.

aforesaid, *adj.* susdit, ledit.

afraid, *pred. adj.* (be afraid) avoir peur.

afresh, *adv.* de nouveau.

Africa, *n.* Afrique *f.*

African, **1.** *n.* Africain *m.* **2.** *adj.* africain.

aft, *adv.* à l'arrière.

after, **1.** *adv. and prep.* après. **2.** *conj.* après que.

aftereffect, *n.* effet *m.*

aftermath, *n.* suites *f. pl.*

afternoon, *n.* après-midi *m.* or *f.*

aftershave, *n.* lotion après-rasage *f.*

afterthought, *n.* réflexion *(f.)* tardive.

afterward, *adv.* ensuite.

again, *adv.* de nouveau, encore; (**a. and a.**) maintes et maintes fois.

against, *prep.* contre.

agape, *adv.* bouche bée.

agate, *n.* agate *f.*

age, **1.** *n.* âge *m.* **2.** *vb.* vieillir.

aged, *adj.* vieux, âgé.

ageism, *n.* attitude *(f.)* discriminative basée sur l'âge.

ageless, *adj.* qui ne vieillit jamais.

agency, *n. (comm.)* agence *f.*

agenda, *n.* ordre du jour *m.*; agenda *m.*

agent, *n.* agent *m.*

agglutinate, *vb.* agglutiner.

agglutination, *n.* agglutination *f.*

aggrandize, *vb.* agrandir.

aggrandizement, *n.* agrandissement *m.*

aggravate, *vb.* (intensify) aggraver; (exasperate) exaspérer.

aggravation, *n.* aggravation *f.*, agacement *m.*

aggregate, *n.* masse *f.*

aggregation, *n.* agrégation *f.*, assemblage *m.*

aggression, *n.* agression *f.*

aggressive, *adj.* agressif.

aggressively, *adv.* agressivement.

aggressiveness, *n.* caractère *(m.)* agressif.

aggressor, *n.* agresseur *m.*

aggrieved, *adj.* affligé.

aghast, *adj.* consterné.

agile, *adj.* agile.

agility, *n.* agilité *f.*

agitate, *vb.* agiter.

agitation, *n.* agitation *f.*

agitator, *n.* agitateur *m.*

agnostic, *n. and adj.* agnostique *m.*

ago, *adv.* il y a (always precedes).

agonized, *adj.* torturé, déchirant.

agony, *n.* (anguish) angoisse *f.*; (death agony) agonie *f.*

agrarian, *adj.* agraire, agrarien.

agree, *vb.* être d'accord.

agreeable, *adj.* agréable.

agreeably, *adv.* agréablement.

agreement, *n.* accord *m.*

agriculture, *n.* agriculture *f.*

ahead, **1.** *adv. and interj.* en avant. **2.** *prep.* (a. of) en avant de.

aid, **1.** *n.* aide *f.*; (**first a.**) premiers secours; (**first-a.station**) poste de secours. **2.** *vb.* aider.

aide, *n.* aide *m.*, assistant *m.*

AIDS, *n.* SIDA *m.*

ail, *vb. intr.* être souffrant.

ailing, *adj.* malade.

ailment, *n.* indisposition *f.*

aim, **1.** *n.* (fig.) but *m.* **2.** *vb.* viser.

aimless, *adj.* sans but.

aimlessly, *adv.* sans but, à la dérive.

air, **1.** *n.* air *m.*; (a. force) aviation *f.*; (by a. mail) par avion; (in the open a.) en plein air. **2.** *vb.* aérer.

airbag, *n.* (in automobiles) sac à air *m.*

air base, *n.* champ *(m.)* d'aviation.

airborne, *adj.* par voie de l'air.

air-condition, *vb.* climatiser.

air conditioner, *n.* climatiseur *m.*

air conditioning, *n.* climatisation *f.*

aircraft, *n.* avion *m.pl.*; (a. carrier) porte-avions *m.*

air gun, *n.* fusil à vent.

airing, *n.* aérage *m.*, tour *m.*

airline, *n.* ligne *(f.)* aérienne.

airliner, *n.* avion *m.*

air mail, *n.* poste *(f.)* aérienne.

airplane, *n.* avion *m.*

air pollution, *n.* pollution *(f.)* de l'air.

airport, *n.* aéroport *m.*

air pressure, *n.* pression (*f.*) d'air.

air raid, *n.* raid (*m.*) aérien.

airsick, *adj.* (**to be a.**) avoir le mal d'air.

airtight, *adj.* imperméable à l'air, étanche.

air-traffic controller, *n.* aiguilleur (*m.*) du ciel.

airy, *adj.* (**well-aired**) aéré; (light) léger.

aisle, *n.* (passageway) passage *m.*; (*arch.*) bas côté *m.*

ajar, *adv.* entr'ouvert.

akin, *adj.* allié (à), parent (de).

alacrity, *n.* empressement *m.*

alarm, *n.* alarme *f.*

alarmist, *n.* alarmiste *m.*

alas, *interj.* hélas.

albeit, *conj.* bien que.

albino, *n.* albinos *m.*

album, *n.* album *m.*

alcohol, *n.* alcool *m.*

alcoholic, *adj.* alcoolique, alcoolisé.

alcove, *n.* (recess) niche *f.*; (sleeping alcove) alcôve *f.*

ale, *n.* bière *f.*

alert, *adj.* alerte.

alfalfa, *n.* luzerne *f.*

algebra, *n.* algèbre *f.*

Algeria, *n.* Algérie *f.*

algorithm, *n.* algorithme *m.*

alias, **1.** *n.* nom d'emprunt *m.* **2.** *adv.* autrement nommé, dit.

alibi, *n.* alibi *m.*

alien, *adj.* étranger.

alienate, *vb.* aliéner.

alight, *vb.* (descend) descendre; (stop after descent) s'abattre.

align, *vb.* aligner.

alike, **1.** *adj.* semblable; (**be a.**) se ressembler. **2.** *adv.* également.

alimentary canal, *n.* canal (*m.*) alimentaire.

alimony, *n.* pension (*f.*) alimentaire.

alive, *adj.* vivant.

alkali, *n.* alcali *m.*

alkaline, *adj.* alcalin.

all, **1.** *adj.* tout *m.sg.*, toute *f.sg.*, tous *m.pl.*, toutes *f.pl.* **2.** *adv. and pron.* (everything) tout; (**above a.**) surtout; (**a. at once**) tout d'un coup; (**a. the same**) tout de même; (**that's a.**) c'est tout; (**not at a.**) pas

du tout; (everybody) tous; (**a. of you**) vous tous.

allay, *vb.* apaiser.

allegation, *n.* allégation *f.*

allege, *vb.* alléguer.

allegiance, *n.* fidélité *f.*

allegory, *n.* allégorie *f.*

allergy, *n.* allergie *f.*

alleviate, *vb.* soulager.

alley, *n.* (in town) ruelle *f.*; (**blind a.**) cul-de-sac *m.*

alliance, *n.* alliance *f.*

allied, *adj.* allié.

alligator, *n.* alligator *m.*

all-night, *adj.* qui dure toute la nuit.

allocate, *vb.* assigner.

allot, *vb.* (grant) accorder; (distribute) répartir.

allotment, *n.* partage *m.*, lot *m.*

all-out, **1.** *adj.* total. **2.** *adv.* à fond.

allow, *vb.* (permit) permettre; (admit) admettre; (grant) accorder; (**a. for**) tenir compte de.

allowance, *n.* (money granted) allocation *f.*; (food) tolérance *f.*; (tolerance) tolérance *f.*; (pension) rente *f.*; (**weekly a.**) semaine *f.*

alloy, *n.* alliage *m.*

all right, *adv.* très bien.

allude to, *vb.* faire allusion à.

allure, *vb.* séduire.

allusion, *n.* allusion *f.*

ally, **1.** *n.* allié *m.* **2.** *vb.* allier.

almanac, *n.* almanach *m.*

almighty, *adj.* tout-puissant.

almond, *n.* amande *f.*

almost, *adv.* presque.

alms, *n.* aumône *f.*

aloft, *adv.* en haut.

alone, *adj.* seul; (**let a.**) laisser tranquille.

along, **1.** *prep.* le long de. **2.** *adv.* (**come a.!**) venez donc!

alongside, *prep.* le long de.

aloof, **1.** *adv.* à l'écart. **2.** *adj.* réservé.

aloud, *adv.* à haute voix.

alpaca, *n.* alpaga (fabric) *m.*; alpaca (animal) *m.*

alphabet, *n.* alphabet *m.*

alphabetical, *adj.* alphabétique.

alphabetize, *vb.* alphabétiser.

Alps, *n.pl.* Alpes *f.pl.*

already, *adv.* déjà.

also, *adv.* aussi.
altar, *n.* autel *m.*
alter, *vb.* changer.
alteration, *n.* modification *f.*
altercation, *n.* altercation *f.*, dispute *f.*
alternate, 1. *n.* remplaçant *m.* **2.** *adj.* alternatif. **3.** *vb.* alterner.
alternative, *n.* alternative *f.*
alternator, *n.* alternateur *m.*
although, *conj.* bien que.
altitude, *n.* altitude *f.*
altogether, *adv.* tout à fait.
altruism, *n.* altruisme *m.*
alum, *n.* alun *m.*
aluminum, *n.* aluminium *m.*
Alzheimer's (disease), *n.* maladie (*f.*) d'Alzheimer.
always, *adv.* toujours.
amalgam, *n.* amalgame *n.*
amalgamate, *vb.* amalgamer; (computer) fusionner.
amass, *vb.* amasser.
amateur, *n.* amateur *m.*
amaze, *vb.* étonner.
amazement, *n.* stupeur *f.*
amazing, *adj.* étonnant.
ambassador, *n.* ambassadeur *m.*, ambassadrice *f.*
amber, *n.* ambre *m.*
ambidextrous, *adj.* ambidextre.
ambiguity, *n.* ambiguïté *f.*
ambiguous, *adj.* ambigu *m.*, ambiguë *f.*
ambition, *n.* ambition *f.*
ambitious, *adj.* ambitieux.
ambivalent, *adj.* ambigu, ambivalent.
amble, *vb.* errer.
ambulance, *n.* ambulance *f.*
ambulatory, *adj.* ambulatoire.
ambush, *n.* embuscade *f.*
ameliorate, *vb.* améliorer.
amenable, *adj.* responsable, soumis (à), sujet (à).
amend, *vb.* amender.
amendment, *n.* amendement *m.*
amenity, *n.* aménité *f.*, agrément *m.*
America, *n.* Amérique *f.*; **(North A.)** A. du Nord; **(South A.)** A. du Sud.
American, 1. *n.* Américain *m.* **2.** *adj.* américain.
amethyst, *n.* améthyste *f.*

amiable, *adj.* aimable.
amicable, *adj.* amical.
amid, *prep.* au milieu de.
amidships, *adv.* par le travers.
amiss, *adv.* de travers.
amity, *n.* amitié *f.*
ammonia, *n.* ammoniaque *f.*
ammunition, *n.* munitions (*f.pl.*) de guerre.
amnesia, *n.* amnésie *f.*
amnesty, *n.* amnistie *f.*
amniocentesis, *n.* amniocentèse *f.*
amoeba, *n.* amibe *f.*
among, *prep.* parmi, entre.
amoral, *adj.* amoral.
amorous, *adj.* amoureux.
amorphous, *adj.* amorphe.
amortize, *vb.* amortir.
amount, 1. *n.* (sum) somme *f.*; (quantity) quantité *f.* **2.** *vb.* **(a. to)** (sum) se monter à; (summary) se réduire à.
amp, *n.* (colloquial) amp(ère) *m.*
ampere, *n.* ampère *m.*
amphibian, *n.* amphibie *m.*
amphibious, *adj.* amphibie.
amphitheater, *n.* amphithéâtre *m.*
ample, *adj.* ample.
amplify, *vb.* amplifier.
amplifier, *n.* amplificateur *m.*
amputate, *vb.* amputer.
amputee, *n.* amputé *m.*
amuse, *vb.* amuser.
amusement, *n.* amusement *m.*
an, *art.* un *m.*, une *f.*
anachronism, *n.* anachronisme *m.*
analog, *adj.* analogique.
analogous, *adj.* analogue.
analogy, *n.* analogie *f.*
analysis, *n.* analyse *f.*
analyst, *n.* analyste *m.f.*
analytic, *adj.* analytique.
analyze, *vb.* analyser.
anarchy, *n.* anarchie *f.*
anathema, *n.* anathème *m.*
anatomy, *n.* anatomie *f.*
ancestor, *n.* ancêtre *m.*
ancestral, *adj.* d'ancêtres, héréditaire.
ancestry, *n.* aïeux, *m.*
anchor, 1. *vb.* ancrer. **2.** *n.* ancre *f.*
anchorperson, *n.* présentateur *m.*, présentatrice *f.*
anchorage, *n.* mouillage *m.*, ancrage *m.*

anchovy, *n.* anchois *m.*

ancient, *adj.* ancien *m.,* ancienne *f.*

ancillary, *adj.* auxiliaire.

and, *conj.* et.

anecdote, *n.* anecdote *f.*

anemia, *n.* anémie *f.*

anesthetic, *adj. and n.* anesthésique *m.*

anesthetist, *n.* anesthésiste *m.f.*

anew, *adv.* de nouveau.

angel, *n.* ange *m.*

anger, *n.* colère *f.*

angle, 1. *n.* angle *m.;* **(at an a.)** en biais. **2.** *vb.* (fish) pêcher à la ligne.

Anglican, *adj. and n.* anglican.

angry, *adj.* fâché; **(to get a.)** se fâcher.

anguish, *n.* angoisse *f.*

angular, *adj.* anguleux.

aniline, *n.* aniline *f.*

animal, *n. and adj.* animal *m.*

animate, *vb.* animer.

animated, *adj.* animé.

animated cartoon, *n.* dessin animé *m.*

animation, *n.* animation *f.*

animosity, *n.* animosité *f.*

anise, *n.* anis *m.*

ankle, *n.* cheville *f.*

annals, *n.pl.* annales *f.pl.*

annex, *n.* (to a building) dépendance *f.*

annexation, *n.* annexion *f.*

annihilate, *vb.* anéantir.

anniversary, *n.* anniversaire *m.*

annotate, *vb.* annoter.

annotation, *n.* annotation *f.*

announce, *vb.* annoncer.

announcement, *n.* annonce *f.*

announcer, *n.* speaker *m.*

annoy, *vb.* (vex) contrarier; (bore) ennuyer.

annoyance, *n.* contrariété *f.*

annual, *adj.* annuel.

annuity, *n.* annuité *f.,* rente annuelle *f.*

annul, *vb.* annuler.

anode, *n.* anode *f.*

anoint, *vb.* oindre.

anomalous, *adj.* anomal, irrégulier.

anonymous, *adj.* anonyme.

another, *adj. and pron.* un autre *m.,* une autre *f.;* **(one a.)** l'un l'autre.

answer, 1. *vb.* répondre. **2.** *n.* réponse *f.*

answerable, *adj.* responsable (de), susceptible de réponse.

ant, *n.* fourmi *f.*

antacid, *n.* antiacide.

antagonism, *n.* antagonisme *m.*

antagonist, *n.* antagoniste *m.*

antagonistic, *adj.* en opposition (à), hostile (à), opposé (à).

antagonize, *vb.* s'opposer à.

antarctic, *adj.* antarctique.

antecedent, *adj. and n.* antécédent *m.*

antedate, *vb.* antidater.

antelope, *n.* antilope *f.*

antenna, *n.* antenne *f.*

anterior, *adj.* antérieur.

anteroom, *n.* antichambre *m. or f.*

anthem, *n.* (national) hymne national *m.*

anthology, *n.* anthologie *f.*

anthracite, *n.* anthracite *m.*

anthrax, *n.* anthrax *m.*

anthropology, *n.* anthropologie *f.*

antiaircraft, *adj.* contre-avion, antiaérien.

antibiotic, *n.* antibiotique *m.*

antibody, *n.* anticorps *m.*

antic, *n.* bouffonnerie *f.*

anticipate, *vb.* (advance) anticiper; (expect) s'attendre à; (foresee) prévoir.

anticipation, *n.* anticipation *f.*

anticlerical, *adj.* anticlérical.

anticlimax, *n.* anticlimax *m.*

antidote, *n.* antidote *m.*

antifreeze, *n.* antigel *m.*

antihistamine, *n.* antihistaminique *m.*

antimony, *n.* antimoine *m.*

antinuclear, *adj.* antinucléaire.

antipathy, *n.* antipathie *f.*

antiquated, *adj.* desuet, vieilli.

antique, *n.* antique *m.;* **(a. dealer)** antiquaire *m.*

antiquity, *n.* antiquité *f.*

anti-Semite, *n.* antisémite *m.*

anti-Semitic, *adj.* antisémite.

antiseptic, *n. and adj.* antiseptique *m.*

antisocial, *adj.* antisocial.

antithesis, *n.* antithèse *f.*

antitoxin, *n.* antitoxine *f.*

antler, *n.* andouiller *m.*

anus, n. anus m.

anvil, n. enclume f.

anxiety, n. anxiété f.

anxious, adj. inquiet m., inquiète f.

any, 1. adj. (in questions, for "some") du m.sg., de la f.sg., des pl.; (not . . . a.) ne . . . pas de; (no matter which) n'importe quel; (every) tout. **2.** pron. (**a. of it** or **them,** with verb) en.

anybody, pron. (somebody) quelqu'un; (somebody, implying negation) personne; (not . . . a.) ne . . . personne; (no matter who) n'importe qui.

anyhow, adv. en tout cas; d'une manière quelconque.

anyone, pron. see anybody.

anything, pron. (something) quelque chose; (something, implying negation) rien; (not . . . a.) ne . . . rien; (no matter what) n'importe quoi.

anyway, adv. see anyhow.

anywhere, adv. n'importe où.

apart, 1. adv. à part. **2.** prep. (**a. from**) en dehors de.

apartheid, n. apartheid m.

apartment, n. appartement m.

apathetic, adj. apathique.

apathy, n. apathie f.

ape, 1. n. singe m. **2.** vb. singer.

aperture, n. ouverture f.

apex, n. sommet m.

aphorism, n. aphorisme m.

aphrodisiac, n. and adj. aphrodisiaque.

apiary, n. rucher m.

apiece, adv. chacun.

apocalypse, n. apocalypse f.

apogee, n. apogée m.

apologetic, adj. use verb s'excuser.

apologist, n. apologiste m.

apologize for, vb. s'excuser de.

apology, n. excuses f.pl.

apoplectic, adj. apoplectique.

apoplexy, n. apoplexie f.

apostate, n. apostat m.

apostle, n. apôtre m.

apostolic, adj. apostolique.

apostrophe, n. apostrophe f.

appall, vb. épouvanter.

apparatus, n. appareil m.

apparel, n. habillement m.

apparent, adj. apparent.

apparition, n. apparition f.

appeal, 1. n. appel m. **2.** vb. (**a. to**) en appeler à.

appear, vb. (become visible) apparaître; (seem) sembler.

appearance, n. (apparition) apparition f.; (semblance) apparence f.; (aspect) aspect m.

appease, vb. apaiser.

appeaser, n. personne qui apaise.

appellant, n. appelant m.

appellate, adj. d'appel.

append, vb. attacher; apposer, ajouter.

appendage, n. accessoire m., apanage m.

appendectomy, n. appendectomie f.

appendicitis, n. appendicite f.

appendix, n. appendice m.

appetite, n. appétit m.

appetizer, n. (drink) apéritif m.

appetizing, adj. appétissant.

applaud, vb. applaudir.

applause, n. applaudissements m.pl.

apple, n. pomme f.

applesauce, n. compote (f.) de pommes.

appliance, n. appareil m.

applicable, adj. applicable.

applicant, n. postulant m.

application, n. (request) demande f.

applied, adj. appliqué.

apply, vb. (**a. to somebody**) s'adresser à; (**a. for a job**) solliciter; (put on) appliquer; (**a. oneself**) s'appliquer.

appoint, vb. (a person) nommer; (time, place) désigner.

appointment, n. (meeting) rendez-vous m.; (**make an a. with**) donner un rendezvous à; (nomination) nomination f.

apportion, vb. répartir.

apposition, n. apposition f.

appraisal, n. évaluation f.

appraise, vb. priser.

appreciable, adj. appréciable.

appreciate, vb. apprécier.

appreciation, n. appréciation f.

apprehend, vb. saisir.

apprehension, n. (seizure) arresta-

tion *f.*; (understanding) compréhension *f.*; (fear) appréhension *f.*
apprehensive, *adj.* craintif.
apprentice, *n.* apprenti *m.*
apprenticeship, *n.* stage *m.*
apprise, *vb.* prévenir, informer.
approach, 1. *n.* approche *f.*; (make a.s to) faire des avances à. **2.** *vb.* s'approcher de.
approachable, *adj.* abordable, accessible.
approbation, *n.* approbation *f.*
appropriate, 1. *adj.* convenable. **2.** *vb.* s'approprier.
appropriation, *n.* appropriation *f.*
approval, *n.* approbation *f.*
approve, *vb.* approuver.
approximate, 1. *adj.* approximatif. **2.** *vb.* se rapprocher (de).
approximately, *adv.* approximativement, à peu près.
approximation, *n.* approximation *f.*
appurtenance, *n.* appartenance *f.*, dépendance *f.*
apricot, *n.* abricot *m.*
April, *n.* avril *m.*
apron, *n.* tablier *m.*
apropos, *adj.* à propos.
apse, *n.* abside *f.*
apt, *adj.* (likely to) sujet à; (suitable for) apte à; (appropriate) à propos; (clever) habile.
aptitude, *n.* aptitude *f.*
aqualung, *n.* scaphandre autonome *m.*
aquarium, *n.* aquarium *m.*
Aquarius, *n.* le Verseau.
aquatic, *adj.* aquatique.
aqueduct, *n.* aqueduc *m.*
aqueous, *adj.* aqueux.
aquiline, *adj.* aquilin.
Arab, 1. *n.* Arabe *m.f.* **2.** *adj.* arabe.
Arabic, *adj. and n.* arabe *m.*
arable, *adj.* arable, labourable.
arbiter, *n.* arbitre *m.*
arbitrary, *adj.* arbitraire.
arbitrate, *vb.* arbitrer.
arbitration, *n.* arbitrage *m.*
arbitrator, *n.* arbitre *m.*
arbor, *n.* (bower) berceau *f.*
arboreal, *adj.* arboricole.
arc, *n.* arc *m.*
arcade, *n.* arcade *f.*

arch, 1. *n.* arc *m.*; (of bridge) arche *f.* **2.** *adj.* espiègle.
archaeology, *n.* archéologie *f.*
archaic, *adj.* archaïque.
archbishop, *n.* archevêque *m.*
archdiocese, *n.* archidiocèse *m.*
archduke, *n.* archiduc *m.*
archenemy, *n.* ennemi (*m.*) de toujours.
archer, *n.* archer *m.*
archery, *n.* tir à l'arc *m.*
archetype, *n.* achétype *m.*, modèle *m.*
archipelago, *n.* archipel *m.*
architect, *n.* architecte *m.*
architectural, *adj.* architectural.
architecture, *n.* architecture *f.*
archives, *n.* archives *f.pl.*
archway, *n.* voûte *f.*, passage (sous une voûte) *m.*
arctic, *adj.* arctique.
ardent, *adj.* ardent.
ardor, *n.* ardeur *f.*
arduous, *adj.* difficile.
area, *n.* (geom.) aire *f.*; (locality) région *f.*; (surface) surface *f.*
area code, *n.* indicatif (*m.*) interurbain.
arena, *n.* arène *f.*
Argentina, *n.* Argentine *f.*
argentine, *adj.* argentin.
argue, *vb.* (reason) argumenter; (indicate) prouver; (discuss) discuter.
argument, *n.* (reasoning) argument *m.*; (dispute) discussion *f.*
argumentative, *adj.* disposé à argumenter, raisonneur.
aria, *n.* air *m.*, chanson *f.*
arid, *adj.* aride.
arise, *vb.* (move upward) s'élever; (originate from) provenir de.
aristocracy, *n.* aristocratie *f.*
aristocrat, *n.* aristocrate *m.f.*
aristocratic, *adj.* aristocratique.
arithmetic, *n.* arithmétique *f.*
ark, *n.* arche *f.*
arm, 1. *n.* (limb) bras *m.*; (weapon) arme *f.* **2.** *vb.* armer.
armament, *n.* armement *m.*
armchair, *n.* fauteuil *m.*
armed forces, *n.* forces armées *f.pl.*
armed robbery, *n.* vol (*m.*) à main armée.

armful, n. brassée f.

armhole, n. emmanchure f., entournure f.

armistice, n. armistice m.

armor, n. armure f.

armory, n. (drill hall) salle (f.) d'exercice.

armpit, n. aisselle f.

armrest, n. accoudoir m.

arms, n. armes f.pl.

army, n. armée f.

arnica, n. arnica f.

aroma, n. arome m.

aromatic, adj. aromatique.

around, 1. adv. autour de. **2.** prep. autour de.

arouse, vb. (stir) soulever; (awake) réveiller; (anger, passion) exciter.

arraign, vb. accuser, poursuivre en justice.

arrange, vb. arranger.

arrangement, n. arrangement m.

array, 1. n. (military) rangs m.pl.; (display) étalage m. **2.** vb. ranger.

arrear, n. arriéré m.

arrest, 1. n. (capture) arrestation f.; (military) arrêts m.pl.; (halt) arrêt m. **2.** vb. arrêter.

arrival, n. arrivée f.

arrive, vb. arriver.

arrogance, n. arrogance f.

arrogant, adj. arrogant.

arrogate, vb. usurper; (a. to oneself) s'arroger.

arrow, n. flèche f.

arrowhead, n. pointe (f.) de flèche; (plant) sagittaire f.

arsenal, n. arsenal m.

arsenic, n. arsenic m.

arson, n. crime d'incendie m.

art, n. art m.; (fine a.s) beaux-arts.

artefact, n. objet fabriqué m.

arterial, adj. artériel.

arteriosclerosis, n. artériosclérose f.

artery, n. artère f.

artesian well, n. puits artésien m.

artful, adj. (crafty) artificieux; (skillful) adroit.

arthritis, n. arthrite f.

artichoke, n. artichaut m.

article, n. article m.

articulate, vb. articuler.

articulation, n. articulation f.

artifice, n. artifice m.

artificial, adj. artificiel.

artificiality, n. nature artificielle f.

artillery, n. artillerie f.

artisan, n. artisan m.

artist, n. artiste m.

artistic, adj. artistique.

artistry, n. habileté f.

artless, adj. ingénu, naïf.

as, 1. adv. comme; (as . . . as) aussi . . . que; (as much as) autant que; (such as) tel que. **2.** conj. (so . . . as) de façon à; (while) pendant que; (since) puisque; (progress) à mesure que. **3.** prep. (as to) quant à.

asbestos, n. asbeste m.

ascend, vb. monter.

ascendancy, n. ascendant m.

ascendant, adj. ascendant, supérieur.

ascent, n. montée f.; (of a mountain) ascension f.

ascertain, vb. s'assurer (de).

ascetic, n. ascétique m.

ascribe, vb. attribuer.

ash, n. cendre f.; (tree) frêne m.

ashamed, adj. honteux; (be a. of) avoir honte de.

ashen, adj. cendré, gris pâle.

ashore, adv. à terre; (go a.) débarquer.

ashtray, n. cendrier m.

Ash Wednesday, n. mercredi (m.) des cendres.

Asia, n. Asie f.

Asian, 1. n. Asiatique m.f. **2.** adj. asiatique.

aside, adv. de côté.

ask, vb. demander à; (invite) inviter.

askance, adv. de travers, obliquement.

askew, adv. and adj. de travers.

asleep, adj. endormi.

asp, n. aspic m.

asparagus, n. asperges f.pl.

aspect, n. aspect m.

asperity, n. aspérité f., rudesse f.

aspersion, n. aspersion f.

asphalt, n. asphalte m.

asphyxia, n. asphyxie f.

asphyxiate, vb. asphyxier.

aspirant, n. aspirant m.

aspirate, vb. aspirer.

aspiration, n. aspiration f.

aspirator, n. aspirateur m.

aspire, vb. aspirer.

aspirin, n. aspirine f.

ass, n. âne m., ânesse f.

assail, vb. assaillir.

assailable, adj. attaquable.

assailant, n. assaillant m.

assassin, n. assassin m.

assassinate, vb. assassiner.

assassination, n. assassinat m.

assault, n. assaut m.

assay, 1. n. essai m., vérification f., épreuve f. **2.** vb. essayer.

assemblage, n. assemblage m.

assemble, vb. assembler, tr.; s'assembler, intr.

assembly, n. assemblée f.

assent, 1. n. assentiment m. **2.** vb. consentir.

assert, vb. affirmer.

assertion, n. assertion f.

assertive, adj. assertif.

assertiveness, n. qualité d'être assertif.

assess, vb. (tax) taxer; (evaluate) évaluer.

assessor, n. assesseur m.

assets, n.pl. (comm.) actif m.; (property) biens m.pl.

asseverate, vb. affirmer solennellement.

asseveration, n. affirmation f.

assiduous, adj. assidu.

assiduously, adv. assidûment.

assign, vb. assigner.

assignable, adj. assignable, transférable.

assignation, n. assignation f., rendez-vous m.

assignment, n. (law) cession f.; (school) tâche f., devoir m.

assimilate, vb. assimiler, tr.; s'assimiler, intr.

assimilation, n. assimilation f.

assimilative, adj. assimilatif, assimilateur.

assistance, n. aide f.

assistant, n. aide m.f.

assist in, vb. aider à.

associate, vb. associer, tr.; s'associer, intr.

association, n. association f.

assonance, n. assonance f.

assort, vb. assortir.

assorted, adj. assorti.

assortment, n. assortiment m.

assuage, vb. adoucir, apaiser.

assume, vb. (take) prendre; (appropriate) s'arroger; (feign) simuler; (suppose) supposer.

assuming, adj. prétentieux, arrogant.

assumption, n. supposition f.; (eccles.) Assomption f.

assurance, n. assurance f.

assure, vb. assurer.

assured, adj. assuré.

assuredly, adv. assurément.

aster, n. aster m.

asterisk, n. astérisque m.

astern, adv. à l'arrière, de l'arrière.

asteroid, n. astéroïde m.

asthma, n. asthme m.

astigmatism, n. astigmatisme m.

astir, adj. agité, debout.

astonish, vb. étonner.

astonishment, n. étonnement m.

astound, vb. stupéfier.

astral, adj. astral.

astray, adj. égaré; (go a.) s'égarer.

astride, adv. à califourchon.

astringent, n. and adj. astringent m.

astrology, n. astrologie f.

astronaut, n. astronaute m.

astronomy, n. astronomie f.

astute, adj. fin.

asunder, adv. (apart) écartés; (to pieces) en morceaux.

asylum, n. asile m.

asymmetry, n. asymétrie f.

at, prep. (time, place, price) à; (someone's house, shop, etc.) chez.

ataxia, n. ataxie f.

atheist, n. athée m.f.

athlete, n. athlète m.f.

athletic, adj. athlétique.

athletics, n. sports m.pl.

athwart, adv. de travers.

Atlantic, adj. atlantique.

Atlantic Ocean, n. océan Atlantique m.

atlas, n. atlas m.

atmosphere, n. atmosphère f.

atmospheric, adj. atmosphérique.

atoll, n. atoll m.

atom, n. atome m.

atomic, adj. atomique.

atomic bomb, n. bombe atomique f.

atomic energy, *n.* énergie atomique *f.*

atomic theory, *n.* théorie atomique *f.*

atomic warfare, *n.* guerre atomique *f.*

atomic weight, *n.* poids atomique *m.*

atonal, *adj.* atonal.

atone for, *vb.* expier.

atonement, *n.* expiation *f.*

atrocious, *adj.* atroce.

atrocity, *n.* atrocité *f.*

atrophy, *n.* atrophie *f.*

atropine, *n.* atropine *f.*

attach, *vb.* attacher.

attaché, *n.* attaché *m.*

attaché case, *n.* mallette *f.*, attaché-case *m.*

attachment, *n.* attachement *m.*; (device) accessoire *m.*

attack, 1. *n.* attaque *f.* **2.** *vb.* attaquer.

attacker, *n.* agresseur *m.*

attain, *vb.* atteindre.

attainable, *adj.* qu'on peut atteindre.

attainment, *n.* (realization) réalisation *f.*; (knowledge) connaissance *f.*

attempt, *n.* tentative *f.*

attend, *vb.* (give heed to) faire attention à; (medical) soigner; (serve) servir; (meeting) assister à; (lectures) suivre; (see to) s'occuper de.

attendance, *n.* service *m.*; présence *f.*

attendant, *n.* serviteur *m.*; (retinue) suite *f.*

attention, *n.* attention *f.*; (pay a. to) faire attention à.

attentive, *adj.* attentif.

attentively, *adv.* attentivement.

attenuate, *vb.* atténuer.

attest, *vb.* attester.

attic, *n.* grenier *m.*

attire, 1. *n.* costume *m.* **2.** *vb.* parer, *tr.*; se parer, *intr.*

attitude, *n.* attitude *f.*

attorney, *n.* avoué *m.*

attract, *vb.* attirer.

attraction, *n.* attraction *f.*

attractive, *adj.* attrayant.

attributable, *adj.* attribuable, imputable.

attribute, 1. *n.* attribut *m.* **2.** *vb.* attribuer, imputer (à).

attrition, *n.* attrition *f.*; (war of a.) guerre (*f.*) d'usure.

attune, *vb.* accorder, mettre à l'unisson.

auburn, *adj.* châtain roux.

auction, *n.* vente (*f.*) aux enchères.

auctioneer, *n.* commissaire-priseur *m.*

audacious, *adj.* audacieux.

audacity, *n.* audace *f.*

audible, *adj.* intelligible.

audience, *n.* (listeners) auditoire *m.*; (interview) audience *f.*

audiovisual, *adj.* audiovisuel.

audiovisual aids, *n.* supports audiovisuels *m.pl.*

audit, 1. *vb.* vérifier (des comptes). **2.** *n.* vérification (des comptes) *f.*

audition, *n.* audition *f.*

auditor, *n.* vérificateur *m.*, censeur *m.*

auditorium, *n.* salle *f.*

auditory, *adj.* auditif.

auger, *n.* tarière *f.*

augment, *vb.* augmenter.

augur, *vb.* augurer.

August, *n.* août *m.*

aunt, *n.* tante *f.*

au pair, *n.* jeune fille (*f.*) au pair.

aura, *n.* atmosphère *f.*

auspice, *n.* auspice *m.*

auspicious, *adj.* de bon augure.

austere, *adj.* austère.

austerity, *n.* austérité *f.*

Australia, *n.* Australie *f.*

Australian, 1. *n.* Australien *m.* **2.** *adj.* australien.

Austria, *n.* Autriche *f.*

Austrian, 1. *n.* Autrichien *m.* **2.** *adj.* autrichien.

authentic, *adj.* authentique.

authenticate, *vb.* authentiquer, valider.

authenticity, *n.* authenticité *f.*

author, *n.* auteur *m.*

authoritarian, *adj.* autoritaire.

authoritative, *adj.* autoritaire.

authoritatively, *adv.* avec autorité, en maître.

authority, n. autorité f.
authorization, n. autorisation f.
authorize, vb. autoriser.
austistic, adj. autistique.
auto, n. auto f.
autobiography, n. autobiographie f.
autocracy, n. autocratie f.
autocrat, n. autocrate m.
autograph, 1. n. autographe m. **2.** vb. autographier.
autoimmune, adj. auto-immune.
automatic, adj. automatique.
automatically, adv. automatiquement.
automation, n. automatisation f.
automobile, n. automobile f.
automotive, adj. automoteur.
autonomously, adv. d'une manière autonome.
autonomy, n. autonomie f.
autopsy, n. autopsie f.
autumn, n. automne m.
auxiliary, adj. auxiliaire.
avail, vb. servir; **(be of no a.)** ne servir à rien.
available, adj. disponible.
avalanche, n. avalanche f.
avarice, n. avarice f.
avariciously, adv. avec avarice.
avenge, vb. venger.
avenger, n. vengeur m., vengeresse f.
avenue, n. avenue f.
average, 1. n. moyenne f. **2.** adj. moyen.
averse, adj. opposé.
aversion, n. aversion f.
avert, vb. détourner.
aviary, n. volière f.
aviation, n. aviation f.

aviator, n. aviateur m.
aviatrix, n. aviatrice f.
avid, adj. avide.
avocado, n. avocat m.
avocation, n. distraction f., profession f., métier m.
avoid, vb. éviter.
avoidable, adj. évitable.
avoidance, n. action d'éviter f.
avow, vb. avouer.
avowal, n. aveu m.
avowed, adj. avoué, confessé.
avowedly, adv. de son propre aveu, ouvertement.
await, vb. attendre.
awake, vb. éveiller, tr.; s'éveiller, intr.
awaken, vb. see awake.
award, 1. n. (prize) prix m.; (law) sentence f. **2.** vb. décerner.
aware, adj. **(be a.)** savoir; **(not to be a.)** ignorer.
awash, adv. dans l'eau.
away, adv. loin; **(go a.)** s'en aller; **(a. from)** absent de.
awe, n. crainte f.
awesome, adj. inspirant du respect.
awful, adj. affreux.
awhile, adv. pendant quelque temps.
awkward, adj. (clumsy) gauche; (embarrassing) embarrassant.
awning, n. tente f.
awry, adv. de travers.
ax, n. hache f.
axiom, n. axiome m.
axis, n. axe m.
axle, n. essieu m.
ayatollah, n. ayatollah m.
azure, 1. n. azur m. **2.** adj. azuré.

B

babble, vb. babiller.
babbler, n. babillard m.
babe, n. enfant m.f.
baboon, n. babouin m.
baby, n. bébé m.
babyish, adj. enfantin.
baby-sit, vb. garder les enfants.
baby-sitter, n. baby-sitter m.f.
bachelor, n. célibataire m.; **(B. of**

Arts/Science) licencié(e) ès lettres/sciences.
bacillus, n. bacille m.
back, 1. n. dos m. **2.** vb. **(b. up, go b.)** reculer; (uphold) soutenir. **3.** adv. en arrière.
backache, n. mal de/aux reins m.
backbone, n. épine dorsale f.
backer, n. partisan m.

backfire, *vb.* (car) pétarader; (plans) mal tourner.

background, *n.* fond *m.*, arrière-plan *m.*

backhand, *adj.* donné avec le revers de la main.

backing, *n.* soutien *m.*

backlash, *n.* contrecoup *m.*, répercussion *f.*

backlog, *n.* réserve *f.*

back out, *vb.* se retirer.

backpack, *n.* sac à dos *m.*

backside, *n.* derrière *m.*

backstage, *adv.* dans les coulisses.

backup, (computer) **1.** *n.* sauvegarde *f.* **2.** *adj.* de sauvegarde.

backward, *adj.* en arrière.

backwardness, *n.* retard *m.*

backwards, *adv.* en arrière.

backwater, **1.** *n.* eau stagnante *f.* **2.** *vb.* aller en arrière (dans l'eau).

backwoods, *n.* forêts vierges *f.pl.*

backyard, *n.* arrière-cour *f.*

bacon, *n.* porc (*m.*) salé et fumé, lard *m.*

bacteria, *n.* bactéries *f.pl.*

bacteriologist, *n.* bactériologue *m.f.*

bacteriology, *n.* bactériologie *f.*

bacterium, *n.* bactérie *f.*

bad, *adj.* mauvais; (wicked) méchant.

badge, *n.* insigne *m.*

badger, *vb.* ennuyer.

badly, *adv.* mal.

badness, *n.* mauvaise qualité *f.*; (wickedness) méchanceté *f.*

baffle, *vb.* déconcerter.

bafflement, *n.* confusion *f.*

bag, *n.* sac *m.*; (suitcase) valise *f.*

baggage, *n.* bagage *m.*

baggage cart, *n.* (airport) chariot *m.*

baggage claim, *n.* bulletin (*m.*) de bagage.

baggy, *adj.* bouffant.

bagpipe, *n.* cornemuse *f.*

Bahamas, *n.* les Bahamas *f.pl.*

bail, **1.** *n.* (law) caution *f.* **2.** *vb.* (**b. out water**) vider (l'eau).

bailiff, *n.* huissier *m.*

bait, *n.* appât *m.*

bake, *vb.* faire cuire au four, *tr.*

baker, *n.* boulanger *m.*

bakery, *n.* boulangerie *f.*

baking, *n.* boulangerie *f.*

baking powder, *n.* levure *f.*

baking soda, *n.* bicarbonate (*m.*) de sodium.

balance, **1.** *n.* (equilibrium) équilibre *m.*; (bank) solde *m.* (account, scales) balance *f.* **2.** *vb.* balancer, *tr.*

balance sheet, *n.* bilan *m.*

balcony, *n.* balcon *m.*; (theater) galerie *f.*

bald, *adj.* chauve.

baldness, *n.* calvitie *f.*; (fig.) sécheresse *f.*

bale, *n.* balle *f.*

balk, *vb.* frustrer.

balky, *adj.* regimbé.

ball, *n.* (games, bullet) balle *f.*; (round object) boule *f.*; (dance) bal *m.*

ballad, *n.* (song) romance *f.*; (poem) ballade *f.*

ballast, *n.* lest *m.*

ball bearing, *n.* roulement (*m.*) à billes.

ballerina, *n.* ballerine *f.*

ballet, *n.* ballet *m.*

ballistic, *adj.* balistique; (**b. missile**) engin (*m.*) balistique.

balloon, *n.* ballon *m.*

ballot, *n.* scrutin *m.*; (**b. box**) urne *f.*

ballpoint pen, *n.* stylo (*m.*) à bille.

ballroom, *n.* salon de bal *m.*

balm, *n.* baume *m.*

balmy, *adj.* embaumé; doux.

balsa, *n.* balsa *f.*

balsam, *n.* baume *m.*

balustrade, *n.* balustrade *f.*

bamboo, *n.* bambou *m.*

ban, **1.** *n.* ban *m.* **2.** *vb.* mettre au ban, *tr.*

banal, *adj.* banal.

banana, *n.* banane *f.*

band, *n.* bande *f.*; (music) orchestre *m.*

bandage, *n.* bandage *m.*

Band-Aid, *n.* pansement adhésif *m.*

bandanna, *n.* foulard *m.*

bandbox, *n.* carton (de modiste) *m.*

bandit, *n.* bandit *m.*

bandmaster, *n.* chef de musique *m.*

bandsman, *n.* musicien *m.*

bandstand, *n.* kiosque *m.*

bandwagon, *n.* (**jump on the b.**)

(fig.) monter dans le train en marche.

baneful, *adj.* pernicieux.

bang, 1. *n.* coup *m.;* **(b.s)** frange *f.* **2.** *vb.* frapper.

banish, *vb.* bannir.

banishment, *n.* bannissement *m.*

banister, *n.* rampe *f.*

banjo, *n.* banjo *m.*

bank, *n.* banque *f.;* (river) rive *f.*

bank account, *n.* compte (*m.*) en banque.

bankbook, *n.* livret de banque *m.*

banker, *n.* banquier *m.*

banking, *n.* banque *f.,* affaires de banque *f.pl.*

bank note, *n.* billet de banque *m.*

bankrupt, *adj. and n.* failli *m.*

bankruptcy, *n.* faillite *f.*

bank statement, *n.* relevé (*m.*) de compte.

banner, *n.* bannière *f.*

banquet, *n.* banquet *m.*

banter, 1. *n.* badinage *m.* **2.** *vb.* badiner, railler.

baptism, *n.* baptême *m.*

baptismal, *adj.* baptismal.

Baptist, *n.* Baptiste *m.*

baptistery, *n.* baptistère *m.*

baptize, *vb.* baptiser.

bar, *n.* (drinks) bar *m.;* (metal) barre *f.;* (law) barreau *m.*

barb, *n.* barbillon *m.*

barbarian, barbarous, *adj. and n.* barbare *m.f.*

barbarism, *n.* barbarie *f.;* *(gramm.)* barbarisme *m.*

barbecue, *n.* barbecue *m.*

barbed wire, *n.* fil (*m.*) de fer barbelé.

barbell, *n.* haltère *m.*

barber, *n.* coiffeur *m.*

barbiturte, *n.* barbiturique *m.*

bar code, *n.* code (*m.*) à barres.

bare, 1. *adj.* nu. **2.** *vb.* découvrir.

bareback, *adv.* à dos nu.

barefoot, *adv.* nu-pieds.

barely, *adv.* à peine.

bareness, *n.* nudité *f.*

bargain, 1 *n.* marché *m.* **2.** *vb.* marchander.

barge, *n.* chaland *m.*

barium, *n.* barium *m.*

bark, 1. *n.* (tree) écorce *f.;* (dog) aboiement *m.* **2.** *vb.* (dog) aboyer.

barley, *n.* orge *f.*

barmaid, *n.* serveuse *f.*

barman, *n.* barman *m.*

barn, *n.* (grain) grange *f.;* (livestock) étable *f.*

barnacle, *n.* (shellfish) anatife *m.;* (goose) barnache *f.*

barnyard, *n.* basse-cour *f.*

barometer, *n.* baromètre *m.*

barometric, *adj.* barométrique.

baron, *n.* baron *m.*

baroness, *n.* baronne *f.*

baronial, *adj.* baronnial, seigneurial.

baroque, *adj.* baroque.

barracks, *n.* caserne *f.*

barrage, *n.* barrage *m.*

barred, *adj.* barré, empêché, exclus, défendu.

barrel, *n.* tonneau *m.*

barren, *adj.* stérile.

barrenness, *n.* stérilité *f.*

barricade, *n.* barricade *f.*

barrier, *n.* barrière *f.*

barring, *prep.* sauf.

barroom, *n.* buvette *f.,* comptoir *m.,* bar *m.*

bartender, *n.* barman *m.*

barter, 1. *n.* troc *m.* **2.** *vb.* échanger, troquer.

base, 1. *n.* base *f.* **2.** *adj.* bas *m.,* basse *f.* **3.** *vb.* baser, fonder.

baseball, *n.* baseball *m.*

baseboard, *n.* moulure de base *f.*

basement, *n.* sous-sol *m.*

baseness, *n.* bassesse *f.*

bash, *vb.* frapper.

bashful, *adj.* timide.

bashfully, *adv.* timidement, modestement.

bashfulness, *n.* timidité *f.,* modestie *f.*

basic, *adj.* fondamental.

basil, *n.* basilic *m.*

basin, *n.* (wash) cuvette *f.;* (river) bassin *m.*

basis, *n.* base *f.*

bask, se chauffer, *intr.*

basket, *n.* (with handle) panier *m.;* (without handle) corbeille *f.*

basketball, *n.* basket(ball) *m.*

Basque, 1. *n.* Basque *m.f.* **2.** *adj.* basque.

bass, *n.* (music) basse *f.;* (fish) bar *m.*

bassinet, n. bercelonnette f.

bassoon, n. basson m.

bastard, n. bâtard m.; (law) enfant naturel m.; (vulgar) salaud m.

baste, vb. (cooking) arroser; (sewing) faufiler.

bat, n. (animal) chauve-souris f.; (baseball) batte f.

batch, n. fournée f.

bate, vb. rabattre, diminuer.

bath, n. bain m.

bathe, vb. se baigner.

bather, n. baigneur m.

bathing, n. baignade f.

bathing cap, n. bonnet (m.) de bain.

bathing suit, n. maillot (m.) de bain.

bathrobe, n. peignoir (m.) de bain.

bathroom, n. salle (f.) de bain.

bathtub, n. baignoire f.

baton, n. bâton m.

battalion, n. bataillon m.

batter, n. (cooking) pâte f.

battery, n. (military) batterie f.; (electric) pile f.

battle, 1. n. bataille f. **2.** vb. lutter.

battlefield, n. champ (m.) de bataille.

battleship, n. cuirassé m.

bauxite, n. bauxite f.

bawdy, adj. paillard.

bawl, vb. brailler.

bay, n. (geography) baie f.; (plant) laurier m.

bayonet, n. baïonnette f.

bazaar, n. bazar m.

be, vb. être.

beach, n. plage f.

beachhead, n. (haut de) plage f.

beacon, n. phare m.

bead, n. perle f.

beading, n. ornement de grains m.

beady, adj. comme un grain, couvert de grains.

beak, n. bec m.

beaker, n. gobelet m., coupe f.

beam, 1. n. (construction) poutre f.; (light) rayon m. **2.** vb. rayonner.

beaming, adj. rayonnant.

bean, n. haricot m.

bear, 1. n. ours m.; (teddy b.) our-

son m. **2.** vb. (carry) porter; (endure) supporter; (birth) enfanter.

bearable, adj. supportable.

beard, n. barbe f.

bearded, adj. barbu.

beardless, adj. imberbe.

bearer, n. porteur m.

bearing, n. (person) maintien m.; (machinery) coussinet m.; (naut.) relèvement m.

bearskin, n. peau (f.) d'ours.

beast, n. bête f.

beat, 1. vb. battre. **2.** n. battement m.

beaten, adj. battu.

beatify, vb. béatifier.

beating, n. battement m., rossée f.

beau, n. galant m.

beautician, n. esthéticien(ne) m.(f.).

beautiful, adj. beau (bel) m., belle f.

beautifully, adv. admirablement.

beautify, vb. embellir.

beauty, n. beauté f.

beauty mark, n. grain (m.) de beauté.

beauty parlor, n. salon (m.) de beauté.

beaver, n. castor m.

becalm, vb. calmer, apaiser; (naut.) abriter.

because, conj. parce que.

beckon, vb. faire signe (à).

become, vb. devenir.

becoming, adj. convenable; (dress) seyant.

bed, n. lit m.

bedbug, n. punaise f.

bedclothes, n. couvertures f.pl.

bedding, n. literie f.

bedfellow, n. camarade de lit m.

bedizen, vb. parer, attifer.

bedlam, n. chahut m.

bedraggled, adj. débraillé.

bedridden, adj. alité.

bedrock, n. roche solide f.

bedroom, n. chambre (f.) à coucher.

bedside, n. bord du lit m.

bedspread, n. dessus (m.) de lit.

bedstead, n. bois de lit m.

bedtime, n. heure (f.) de se coucher.

bee, n. abeille f.

beef, n. bœuf m.

beefsteak, n. bifteck m.

beefy, adj. musclé, costaud.

beehive, n. ruche f.

beeper, n. récepteur (m.) de poche

beer, n. bière f.

beeswax, n. cire jaune f.

beet, n. betterave f.

beetle, n. scarabée m.

befall, vb. arriver (à).

befit, vb. convenir (à).

befitting, adj. convenable.

before, 1. adv. (place) en avant; (time) avant. **2.** prep. (place) devant; (time) avant. **3.** conj. avant que.

beforehand, adv. d'avance.

befriend, vb. aider; traiter en ami.

befuddle, vb. embrouiller, déconcerter.

beg, vb. (of beggar) mendier; (ask) prier.

beget, vb. engendrer, produire.

beggar, n. mendiant m.

beggarly, adj. chétif, misérable.

begin, vb. commencer.

beginner, n. commençant m.

beginning, n. commencement m.

begrudge, vb. envier, donner à contrecoeur.

beguile, vb. tromper, séduire.

behalf, n. **(on b. of)** de la part de; **(in b. of)** en faveur de.

behave, vb. se conduire.

behavior, n. conduite f.

behead, vb. décapiter.

behind, 1. adv. and prep. derrière. **2.** n. derrière m.

behold, 1. vb. voir. **2.** interj. voici.

beige, adj. beige.

being, n. être m.

bejewel, vb. orner de bijoux.

belated, adj. attardé.

belch, vb. éructer, roter.

belfry, n. clocher m., beffroi m.

Belgian, 1. n. Belge m.f. **2.** adj. belge.

Belgium, n. Belgique f.

belie, vb. démentir.

belief, n. croyance f.; (confidence) confiance f.

believable, adj. croyable.

believe, vb. croire.

believer, n. croyant m.

belittle, vb. rabaisser.

bell, n. (house) sonnette f.; (church) cloche f.

bellboy, n. chasseur m.

bell buoy, n. bouée sonore f.

belligerence, n. belligérance f.

belligerent, adj. and n. belligérant m.

belligerently, adv. d'une manière belligérante.

bellow, vb. mugir.

bellows, n. soufflet m.

bell-tower, n. clocher m.

belly, n. ventre m.

belongings, n. effets m.pl., affaires f.pl.

belong to, vb. appartenir à.

beloved, adj. and n. chéri m.

below, 1. adv. en bas. **2.** prep. au-dessous de.

belt, n. ceinture f.

beltway, n. périphérique m.

bemused, adj. perplexe.

bemoan, vb. lamenter.

bench, n. banc m.

bend, vb. plier; (curve) courber, tr.

beneath, see below.

benediction, n. bénédiction f.

benefactor, n. bienfaiteur m.

benefactress, n. bienfaitrice f.

beneficent, adj. bienfaisant.

beneficial, adj. salutaire.

beneficiary, n. bénéficiaire m.

benefit, n. (favor) bienfait m.; (advantage) bénéfice m.

Benelux, n. Bénélux m.

benevolence, n. bienveillance f.

benevolent, adj. bienveillant.

benevolently, adv. bénévolement.

benign, adj. bénin m., bénigne f.

benignity, n. bénignité f.

bent, n. penchant m.

benzene, n. benzène m.

benzine, n. benzine f.

bequeath, vb. léguer.

bequest, n. legs m.

berate, vb. gronder.

bereave, vb. priver (de).

bereavement, n. privation f., perte f., deuil m.

beriberi, n. béribéri m.

Bermuda, n. Bermudes f.pl.

berry, n. baie f.

berserk, adj. fou m., folle f.

berth, n. couchette f.

beseech, vb. supplier.

beseechingly, adv. en suppliant.

beset, vb. attaquer, presser, assiéger.

beside, prep. à côté de.

besides, adv. en outre.

besiege, vb. assiéger.

besieged, adj. assiégé.

besieger, n. assiégeant m.

besmirch, vb. tacher, salir.

best, 1. adj. (le) meilleur. 2. adv. (le) mieux.

bestial, adj. bestial.

bestir, vb. remuer.

best man, n. garçon d'honneur (at weddings) m.

bestow, vb. accorder.

bestowal, n. dispensation f.

best-seller, n. best-seller m., succès de librairie.

bet, 1. n. pari m. 2. vb. parier.

betake (oneself), vb. se rendre.

betray, vb. trahir.

betroth, vb. fiancer.

betrothal, n. fiançailles f.pl.

better, 1. adj. meilleur. 2. adv. mieux.

between, prep. entre.

bevel, 1. adj. en biseau. 2. vb. biaiser.

beverage, n. boisson f.

bevy, n. essaim m.

bewail, vb. lamenter, pleurer.

beware of, vb. prendre garde à.

bewilder, vb. égarer.

bewildered, adj. égaré, dérouté(e).

bewildering, adj. déconcertant.

bewilderment, n. égarement m.

bewitch, vb. ensorceler.

beyond, 1. adv. au delà. 2. prep. au delà de.

biannual, adj. semestriel.

bias, n. (slant) biais m.; (prejudice) prévention f.

bib, n. bavette f.

Bible, n. Bible f.

biblical, adj. biblique.

bibliography, n. bibliographie f.

bicarbonate, n. bicarbonate m.

bicentennial, n. and adj. bicentenaire m.

biceps, n. biceps m.

bicker, vb. se quereller, se chamailler.

bicycle, 1 n. bicyclette f. 2. vb. faire de la bicyclette.

bicyclist, n. cycliste m.

bid, 1. n. (auction) enchère f.; (bridge) appel m. 2. vb. (order) ordonner; (invite) inviter; (auction) faire une offre.

bidder, n. enchérisseur m.

bide, vb. (live) demeurer; (wait) attendre.

biennial, adj. biennal.

bier, n. corbillard m., civière f.

bifocal, 1. adj. bifocal. 2. n. lunettes bifocales f.pl.

big, adj. grand.

bigamy, n. bigamie f.

big business, n. les grandes affaires f.pl.

bigot, n. bigot m.

bigotry, n. bigoterie f.

bike, n. vélo m.

bilateral, adj. bilatéral.

bile, n. bile f.

bilingual, adj. bilingue.

bilious, adj. bilieux.

bill, n. (restaurant) addition f.; (hotel, profession) note f.; (shop, public utility, etc.) facture f.; (money) billet (m.) de banque; (poster) affiche f.; (politics) projet (m.) de loi; (**b. of fare**) carte (f.) du jour; (bird) bec m.

billboard, n. panneau (m.) d'affichage.

billet, n. (mil.) billet de logement m.

billfold, n. portefeuille m.

billiard balls, n. billes f.pl.

billiards, n. billard m.

billion, n. (U.S.) milliard m., (Britain) billion m.

bill of health, n. patente (f.) de santé.

bill of lading, n. connaissement m.

bill of sale, n. lettre de vente f., acte (m.) de propriété.

billow, n. grande vague f., lame f.

billy-goat, n. bouc m.

bimetallic, adj. bimétallique.

bimonthly, adj. and adv. bimensuel.

bin, n. coffre m.

bind, vb. lier; (books) relier m.

bindery, n. atelier de reliure m.

binding, 1. n. (book) reliure f. 2. adj. obligatoire.

binoculars, n. jumelles f.pl.

biochemistry, n. biochimie f.

biodegradable, adj. sujet à la putréfaction.

biofeedback, n. biofeedback m., information (f.) reçue par un organisme pendant un processus biologique.

biographer, n. biographe m.

biographical, adj. biographique.

biography, n. biographie f.

biological, adj. biologique.

biologically, adv. biologiquement.

biology, n. biologie f.

biorhythm, n. biorythme m.

bipartisan, adj. représentant les deux partis.

biped, n. bipède m.

birch, n. bouleau m.

bird, n. oiseau m.

birdlike, adj. comme un oiseau.

bird of prey, n. oiseau de proie m.

bird's-eye view, n. vue (f.) à vol d'oiseau.

birth, n. naissance f.

birth certificate, n. acte (m.) de naissance.

birth control, n. contrôle (m.) des naissances.

birthday, n. anniversaire (m.) de naissance, fête f.

birthmark, n. tache (f.) de naissance.

birthplace, n. lieu (m.) de naissance.

birth rate, n. natalité f.

birthright, n. droit (m.) d'aînesse.

biscuit, n. (hard) biscuit m.; (soft) petit pain (m.) au lait.

bisect, vb. couper en deux.

bisexual, adj. bis(s)exuel.

bishop, n. évêque m.

bishopric, n. évêché m.

bismuth, n. bismuth m.

bison, n. bison m.

bit, n. (piece) morceau m.; (a bit of) un peu (de); (harness) mors m.; (computer) unité unique d'information f.

bitch, n. chienne f.; (vulgar) garce f., salope f.

bite, 1. n. morsure f. **2.** vb. mordre.

biting, adj. mordant.

bitter, adj. amer.

bitterly, adv. amèrement, avec amertume.

bitterness, n. amertume f.

bivouac, n. bivouac m.

biweekly, adj. and adv. tous les quinze jours.

blab, vb. jaser.

black, adj. noir.

Black, n. and adj. (for person) noir m.; noire f.

blackberry n. mûre (f.) de ronce.

blackbird, n. merle m.

blackboard, n. tableau (m.) noir.

black currant, n. cassis m.

blacken, vb. noircir.

black eye, n. œil poché m.

blackguard, n. gredin m., polisson m., salaud m.

blackmail, 1. n. chantage m. **2.** vb. faire chanter.

black market, n. marché noir m.

blackout, n. panne (f.) d'electricité; (med.) syncope f.

blacksmith, n. forgeron m.

bladder, n. vessie f.

blade, n. (sword, knife) lame f.; (grass) brin m.

blame, 1. n. blâme m. **2.** vb. blâmer.

blameless, adj. innocent, sans tache.

blanch, vb. blanchir, palir.

bland, adj. doux m., douce f.; (insipid) fade.

blank, 1. n. (space) blanc m.; (void) vide m.; (printing) tiret m. **2.** adj. (page) blanc m., blanche f.; (empty) vide.

blanket, n. couverture f.

blare, 1. n. son (de la trompette) m., rugissement m. **2.** vb. retentir, intr.

blaspheme, vb. blasphémer.

blasphemer, n. blasphémateur m.

blasphemous, adj. blasphématoire.

blasphemy, n. blasphème m.

blast, n. (wind) rafale f.; (mine) explosion f.

blatant, adj. criard, bruyant.

blaze, 1. n. flambée f. **2.** vb. flamber.

blazer, n. blazer m.

blazing, adj. enflammé, flamboyant.

bleach, vb. décolorer, tr.

bleak, adj. morne.

bleakness, *n.* froidure *f.*
bleat, *vb.* bêler.
bleed, *vb.* saigner.
blemish, *n.* défaut *m.*
blend, 1. *n.* mélange *m.* 2. *vb.* mêler, *tr.*
blended, *adj.* mélangé.
blender, *n.* mixeur *m.*, mixer *m.*
bless, *vb.* bénir.
blessed, *adj.* béni.
blessing, *n.* bénédiction *f.*
blight, 1. *vb.* flétrir, détruire, nieller, brouir. 2. *n.* brouissure *f.*, flétrissure *f.*
blind, 1. *n.* store *m.* 2. *adj.* aveugle; **(b. alley)** cul-de-sac *m.*
blindfold, *adj. and adv.* les yeux bandés.
blinding, *adj.* aveuglant.
blindly, *adv.* aveuglément.
blindness, *n.* cécité *f.*
blink, *vb.* clignoter.
bliss, *n.* béatitude *f.*
blissful, *adj.* bienheureux.
blissfully, *adv.* heureusement.
blister, *n.* ampoule *f.*
blithe, *adj.* gai, joyeux.
blizzard, *n.* tempête (*f.*) de neige.
bloat, *vb.* boursoufler.
bloated, *adj.* gonflé.
bloc, *n.* bloc *m.*
block, 1. *n.* bloc *m.*; (houses) pâté *m.* 2. *vb.* bloquer.
blockade, *n.* blocus *m.*
blond, *adj. and n.* blond *m.*
blood, *n.* sang *m.*
blood-curdling, *adj.* à tourner le sang.
bloodhound, *n.* limier *m.*
bloodless, *adj.* exsangue, sans effusion de sang.
blood plasma, *n.* plasma (*m.*) du sang.
blood poisoning, *n.* empoisonnement (*m.*) du sang.
blood pressure, *n.* tension artérielle *f.*
bloodshed, *n.* effusion (*f.*) de sang.
bloodshot, *adj.* injecté de sang.
bloodthirsty, *adj.* sanguinaire.
bloody, *adj.* sanglant.
bloom, 1. *n.* fleur *f.* 2. *vb.* fleurir.
blooming, 1. *n.* floraison *f.* 2. *adj.* fleurissant.

blossom, *see* bloom.
blot, 1. *n.* tache *f.* 2. *vb.* (spot) tacher; (dry ink) sécher l'encre.
blotch, *n.* tache *f.*
blotchy, *adj.* couvert de taches.
blotter, *n.* buvard *m.*
blouse, *n.* blouse *f.*
blow, 1. *n.* coup *m.* 2. *vb.* souffler; **(b. out)** éteindre; **(b. over)** passer; **(b. up)** faire sauter, *tr.*
blowout, *n.* éclatement (*m.*) de pneu.
blowtorch, *n.* chalumeau *m.*
blubber, 1. *vb.* pleurer comme un veau. 2. *n.* graisse de baleine *f.*
bludgeon, 1. *n.* matraque *f.* 2. *vb.* donner des coups de matraque.
blue, *adj.* bleu; **(have the b.s)** avoir le cafard.
blue jeans, *n.* blue jeans *m.pl.*
blueprint, *n.* dessin négatif *m.*
bluff, *n.* bluff *m.*
bluffer, *n.* bluffeur *m.*
blunder, *n.* bévue *f.*
blunderer, *n.* maladroit *m.*
blunt, *adj.* (blade) émoussé; (person) brusque.
bluntly, *adv.* brusquement.
bluntness, *n.* brusquerie *f.*
blur, *vb.* (smear) barbouiller.
blurb, *n.* résumé *m.*; publicitaire.
blurt, *vb.* **(b. out)** lâcher, dire.
blush, 1. *n.* rougeur *f.* 2. *vb.* rougir.
bluster, *n.* fanfaronnade *f.*
boar, *n.* (wild) sanglier *m.*
board, *n.* (plank) planche *f.*; (daily meals) pension *f.*; (boat) bord *m.*; (politics) ministère *m.*; (administration) conseil *m.*
boarder, *n.* pensionnaire *m.f.*
boarding house, *n.* pension *f.*
boarding pass, *n.* carte (*f.*) d'embarquement.
boarding school, *n.* internat *m.*, pensionnat *m.*
boast (of), *vb.* se vanter (de).
boaster, *n.* vantard *m.*
boastful, *adj.* vantard.
boastfulness, *n.* vantardise *f.*
boat, *n.* bateau *m.*
boathouse, *n.* abri (*m.*) à bateaux.
boatswain, *n.* maître d'équipage *m.*
bob, *vb.* (hair) couper court.
bobbin, *n.* bobine *f.*

bode, *vb.* présager.

bodice, *n.* corsage *m.*

bodily, *adj.* corporel.

body, *n.* corps *m.*

bodyguard, *n.* garde *(f.)* du corps.

bog, 1. *n.* marécage *m.* **2.** *vb.* embourber.

bogus, *adj.* bidon.

Bohemia, *n.* (geographical) Bohême *f.*; *(fig.)* bohème *f.*

Bohemian, 1. *n.* (geographical) Bohémien *m.*; *(fig.)* bohème *m.f.* **2.** *adj.* (geographical) bohémien; *(fig.)* bohème.

boil, 1. *vb.* bouillir, *intr.*; faire bouillir, *tr.* **2.** *n.* *(med.)* furoncle *m.*, clou *m.*

boiler, *n.* chaudière *f.*

boisterous, *adj.* (person) bruyant.

boisterously, *adv.* bruyamment.

bold, *adj.* hardi.

boldface, *adj.* (type) caractères gras *m.pl.*

boldly, *adv.* hardiment, avec audace.

boldness, *n.* hardiesse *f.*

Bolivia, *n.* Bolivie *f.*

bologna, *n.* saucisson *(m.)* de Bologne.

bolster, *n.* traversin *f.*

bolster up, *vb.* soutenir.

bolt, 1. *n.* verrou *m.* **2.** *vb.* verrouiller.

bomb, *n.* bombe *f.*

bombard, *vb.* bombarder.

bombardier, *n.* bombardier *m.*

bombardment, *n.* bombardement *m.*

bombastic, *adj.* pompeux.

bomber, *n.* avion *(m.)* de bombardement; bombardier *m.*

bombproof, *adj.* à l'épreuve des bombes.

bombshell, *n.* bombe *f.*

bombsight, *n.* viseur *(m.)* de lancement.

bona fide, *adj.* véritable.

bonbon, *n.* bonbon *m.*

bond, *n.* lien *m.*; (law, finance) obligation *f.*

bondage, *n.* servitude *f.*

bonded, *adj.* entreposé.

bone, *n.* os *m.*

boneless, *adj.* sans os.

bonfire, *n.* feu *(m.)* de joie.

bonnet, *n.* chapeau *m.*

bonus, *n.* gratification *f.*

boo, *vb.* huer.

book, 1. *n.* livre *m.* **2.** *vb.* (ticket) prendre, (space) réserver.

bookbindery, *n.* atelier *(m.)* de reliure.

bookcase, *n.* bibliothèque *f.*

bookkeeper, *n.* teneur *(m.)* de livres.

bookkeeping, *n.* comptabilité *f.*

booklet, *n.* opuscule *m.*, brochure *f.*

bookseller, *n.* libraire *m.*; (secondhand) bouquiniste *m.*

bookstore, bookshop, *n.* librairie *f.*

boom, 1. *n.* grondement *m.*; (in numbers) forte augmentation. **2.** *vb.* gronder; prospérer.

boon, *n.* bienfait *m.*, don *m.*

boor, *n.* rustre *m.*

boorish, *adj.* rustre.

boost, *vb.* (push) pousser; (praise) louer.

boot, 1. *n.* bottine *f.*, botte *f.* **2.** *vb.* initialiser.

bootblack, *n.* cireur *m.*

booth, *n.* (fair) baraque *f.*; (telephone) cabine *f.*

booty, *n.* butin *m.*

booze, *n.* boissons *(f.pl.)* alcooliques.

border, *n.* bord *m.*; (of country) frontière *f.*

borderline, *adj.* touchant (à), avoisinant.

bore, *vb.* (make a hole) forer; (annoy) ennuyer.

boredom, *n.* ennui *m.*

boric acid, *n.* acide borique *m.*

boring, *adj.* ennuyeux.

born, 1. *adj.* né. **2.** *vb.* (be b.) naître.

born-again, *adj.* rené.

borough, *n.* (administration) circonscription électorale *f.*; (large village) bourg *m.*

borrower, *n.* emprunteur *m.*

borrow from, *vb.* emprunter à.

Bosnia, *n.* Bosnie *f.*

bosom, *n.* sein *m.*

boss, 1. *n.* patron *m.* **2.** *vb.* diriger.

bossy, *adj.* comme un patron, impérieux.

botanical, *adj.* botanique.

botany, *n.* botanique *f.*

botch, 1. *n.* ravaudage *m.* **2.** *vb.* ravauder, faire une mauvaise besogne.

both, *adj. and pron.* tous (les) deux *m.,* toutes (les) deux *f.*

bother, 1. *n.* ennui *m.* **2.** *vb.* gêner.

bothersome, *adj.* gênant.

bottle, *n.* bouteille *f.*

bottleneck, *n.* (traffic) bouchon *m.*

bottom, *n.* fond *m.*

bottomless, *adj.* sans fond.

bough, *n.* branche *f.*

bouillon, *n.* bouillon *m.*

boulder, *n.* galet *m.*

boulevard, *n.* boulevard *m.*

bounce, *vb.* (ball) rebondir.

bound, 1. *n.* (limit) borne *f.;* (jump) bond *m.* **2.** *vb.* (limit) borner; (jump) bondir.

boundary, *n.* frontière *f.*

bound for, *adj.* en route pour.

boundless, *adj.* sans bornes, illimité.

boundlessly, *adv.* sans bornes.

bounteous, *adj.* généreux, bienfaisant.

bounty, *n.* largesse *f.;* (premium) prime *f.*

bouquet, *n.* bouquet *m.*

bourgeois, *adj.* bourgeois.

bout, *n.* (fever) accès *m.*

bovine, *n.* bovine *f.; adj.* bovin.

bow, *n.* (weapon) arc *m.;* (violin) archet *m.;* (curtsy) révérence *f.;* (ship) avant *m.*

bow, *vb.* incliner, *tr.*

bowels, *n.* entrailles *f.pl.*

bowl, 1. *n.* bol *m.* **2.** *vb.* jouer aux boules.

bowlegged, *adj.* à jambes arquées.

bowler, *n.* joueur *(m.)* de boule.

bowling, *n.* jeu *(m.)* de boules.

box, 1. *n.* boîte *f.;* (theater) loge *f.* **2.** *vb.* boxer.

boxcar, *n.* wagon *(m.)* de marchandises.

boxer, *n.* boxeur *m.*

boxing, *n.* boxe *f.*

box office, *n.* bureau *(m.)* de location.

boy, *n.* garçon *m.*

boycott, *vb.* boycotter.

boyfriend, *n.* (petit) ami *m.*

boyhood, *n.* première jeunesse *f.*

boyish, *adj.* enfantin, puéril.

boyishly, *adv.* comme un gamin.

bra, *n.* soutien-gorge *m.*

brace, 1. *vb.* fortifier. **2.** *n.* vilebrequin (tool) *m.,* paire *f.,* couple *m.*

bracelet, *n.* bracelet *m.*

bracket, *n.* (wall) console *f.;* (printing) crochet *m.*

brag, *vb.* se vanter.

braggart, *n.* fanfaron *m.*

braid, *n.* (hair) tresse *f.;* (sewing) galon *m.*

Braille, *n.* braille *m.*

brain, *n.* cerveau *m.;* **(b.s)** cervelle *f.*

brainwash, *vb.* faire un lavage de cerveau à.

brainy, *adj.* intelligent.

brake, *n.* frein *m.*

bramble, *n.* ronce *f.*

bran, *n.* son *m.*

branch, *n.* branche *f.*

brand, *n.* marque *f.*

brandish, *vb.* brandir.

brand-new, *adj.* tout neuf.

brandy, *n.* eau-de-vie *f.*

brash, *adj.* impertinent.

brass, *n.* cuivre *(m.)* jaune.

brassiere, *n.* soutien-gorge *f.*

brat, *n.* gosse *m.f.*

bravado, *n.* bravade *f.*

brave, *adj.* courageux.

bravery, *n.* courage *m.*

brawl, *n.* rixe *f.*

brawn, *n.* partie charnue *f.,* muscles *m.pl.*

bray, *vb.* braire.

brazen, *adj.* (person) effronté.

Brazil, *n.* Brésil *m.*

breach, *n.* infraction *f.;* *(mil.)* brèche *f.*

bread, *n.* pain *m.*

breadcrumbs, *n.* chapelure *f.*

breadth, *n.* largeur *f.*

breadwinner, *n.* soutien *(m.)* de la famille.

break, 1. *n.* rupture *f.;* (pause) interruption *f.;* (rest) pause *f.* **2.** *vb.* rompre, briser, casser.

breakable, *adj.* cassable.

breakage, *n.* cassure *f.,* rupture *f.*

breakdown, *n.* panne *f.;* dépression *f.;* analyse *f.*

breakfast, n. (petit) déjeuner m.
breakwater, n. brise-lames m., jetée f.
breast, n. poitrine f., sein m.
breath, n. haleine f.; (fig., wind) souffle m.
Breathalyzer, n. alcootest m.
breathe, vb. respirer.
breathless, adj. (out of breath) essoufflé.
breathlessly, adv. hors d'haleine.
breathtaking, adj. à vous couper le souffle.
bred, adj. élevé.
breeches, n. pantalon m.sg.
breed, vb. produire; (livestock) élever.
breeder, n. (raiser) éleveur m.
breeding, n. (manners) éducation f.; (animals) élevage m.
breeze, n. brise f.
breezy, adj. (windy) venteux; (manner) dégagé.
Breton, 1. n. Breton m. **2.** adj. breton.
brevity, n. brièveté f.
brew, vb. (beer) brasser; (tea) faire infuser, tr.
brewery, n. brasserie f.
briar, n. ronce f.
bribe, vb. corrompre.
briber, n. corrupteur m.
bribery, n. corruption f.
brick, n. brique f.
bricklaying, n. maçonnerie f.
bricklike, adj. comme une brique.
bridal, adj. nuptial.
bride, n. mariée f.
bridegroom, n. marié m.
bridesmaid, n. demoiselle (f.) d'honneur.
bridge, n. pont m.; (boat) passerelle f.; (cards) bridge m.
bridged, adj. lié.
bridgehead, n. tête de pont f.
bridle, n. bride f.
brief, 1. vb. bref m., brève f. **2.** n. dossier m. **3.** vb. donner des instructions à.
briefcase, n. serviette f.
briefly, adv. brièvement.
briefness, n. brièveté f.
brier, n. bruyère f., ronces f.pl.
brig, n. brick m.
brigade, n. brigade f.

bright, adj. vif m., vive f.; intelligent.
brighten, vb. faire briller, tr.
brightness, n. éclat m.
brilliance, n. éclat m.
brilliant, adj. brillant.
brim, n. bord m.
brine, n. saumure f.
bring, vb. (thing) apporter; (person) amener; (b. about) amener, causer; (b. up) élever.
brink, n. bord m.
briny, adj. salé.
brisk, adj. vif m., vive f.
brisket, n. (meat) poitrine f.
briskly, adv. vivement.
briskness, n. vivacité f.
bristle, n. soie f.
bristly, adj. hérissé (de), poilu.
British, adj. britannique.
British Empire, n. Empire Britannique m.
British Isles, n. Iles Britanniques f.pl.
brittle, adj. fragile.
broad, adj. large.
broadcast, 1. vb. diffuser. **2.** n. émission f.
broadcaster, n. speaker m.
broadcloth, n. drap (m.) fin.
broaden, vb. élargir.
broadly, adv. largement.
broadminded, adj. large d'esprit.
broadside, n. côte f., bordée f.
brocade, n. brocart m.
brocaded, adj. de brocart.
broccoli, n. brocoli m.
brochure, n. brochure f.
broil, vb. griller.
broiler, n. gril m.
broke, adj. fauché.
broken-hearted, adj. qui a le coeur brisé.
broker, n. courtier m.; (stock-b.) agent (m.) de change.
brokerage, n. courtage m.
bronchial, adj. bronchique.
bronchitis, n. bronchite f.
bronze, n. bronze m.
brooch, n. broche f.
brood, 1. n. couvée f. **2.** vb. couver.
brook, n. ruisseau m.
broom, n. balai m.
broomstick, n. manche (m.) à balai.

broth, n. bouillon m.

brothel, n. bordel m., maison mal famée f.

brother, n. frère m.

brotherhood, n. fraternité f.

brother-in-law, n. beau-frère m.

brotherly, adj. fraternel.

brow, n. front m.

browbeat, vb. intimider.

brown, adj. brun.

browse, vb. (animals) brouter; (books) feuilleter (des livres).

bruise, 1. n. meurtrissure f. **2.** vb. meurtrir.

bruised, adj. couvert de bleus.

brunette, adj. and n. brune f.

brunt, n. choc m.

brush, 1. n. brosse f.; **(paint-b.)** pinceau m. **2.** vb. brosser.

brushwood, n. broussailles f.pl.

brusque, adj. brusque.

brusquely, adv. brusquement.

Brussels, n. Bruxelles f.

brutal, adj. brutal.

brutality, n. brutalité f.

brutalize, vb. abrutir.

brute, n. brute f.

bubble, 1. n. bulle f. **2.** vb. bouillonner.

buck, n. daim m.; (male) mâle m.; (colloquial) dollar m.

bucket, n. seau m.

buckle, n. boucle f.

buckram, n. bougran m.

buckshot, n. chevrotine f.

buckwheat, n. sarrasin m., blé noir m.

bud, 1. n. bourgeon m. **2.** vb. bourgeonner.

budding, adj. en herbe.

buddy, n. copain m., pote m.

budge, vb. bouger.

budget, n. budget m.

buffalo, n. buffle m.

buffer, n. tampon m.; (computer) mémoire (f.) tampon.

buffet, n. (sideboard) buffet m.

buffoon, n. bouffon m.

bug, 1. n. insecte m.; (computer) erreur f. **2.** v. embêter; mettre des micros dans.

bugle, n. clairon m.

build, vb. bâtir.

builder, n. (buildings) entrepreneur m.; (ships) constructeur m.

building, n. bâtiment m.

bulb, n. (electricity) ampoule f.; (botany) bulbe m.

Bulgaria, n. Bulgarie f.

bulge, n. bosse f.

bulimia, n. boulimie f.

bulk, n. masse f.

bulkhead, n. cloison étanche f.

bulky, adj. volumineux.

bull, n. taureau m.

bulldog, n. bouledogue m.

bulldozer, n. machine à refouler f.

bullet, n. balle f.

bulletin, n. bulletin m.

bulletproof, adj. à l'épreuve des balles.

bullfight, n. corrida f.

bullfighting, n. tauromachie f.

bullfinch, n. bouvreuil m.

bullion, n. lingot m.

bully, 1. n. brute f., tyran m. **2.** vb. rudoyer.

bulwark, n. rempart m.

bum, n. fainéant m.

bumblebee, n. bourdon m.

bump, 1. n. (blow) coup m.; (protuberance) bosse f. **2.** vb. cogner.

bumper, n. (auto) pare-chocs m.

bumpy, adj. cahoteux.

bun, n. brioche f.

bunch, n. (flowers) bouquet m.; (grapes) grappe f.; (keys) trousseau m.

bundle, n. paquet m.

bungalow, n. bungalow m.

bungle, vb. bousiller.

bunion, n. cor m.

bunk, n. couchette f.; (colloquial) foutaises f.pl.

bunny, n. lapin m.

bunting, n. drapeaux m.pl.

buoy, n. bouée f.

buoyant, adj. qui a du ressort.

burden, n. fardeau m.

burdensome, adj. onéreux.

bureau, n. (office) bureau m.; (chest of drawers) commode f.

bureaucracy, n. bureaucratie f.

bureaucrat, n. bureaucrate m.f.

burglar, n. cambrioleur m.

burglarize, vb. cambrioler.

burglary, n. vol (m.) avec effraction, cambriolage.

Burgundy, n. Bourgogne f.

burial, n. enterrement m.

burlap, n. gros canevas m.
burly, adj. corpulent.
Burma, n. Birmanie f.
burn, vb. brûler.
burner, n. bec m.
burning, adj. brûlant.
burnish, vb. brunir, polir.
burp, vb. roter.
burrow, n. terrier m.
burst, vb. éclater.
bury, vb. enterrer.
bus, n. autobus m.
bush, n. buisson m.; (land) brousse f.
bushel, n. boisseau m.
bushy, adj. buissonneux; (hair) touffu.
busily, adv. activement.
business, n. affaire f.; (comm.) affaires f.pl.
businesslike, adj. pratique.
businessman, n. homme (m.) d'affaires.
businesswoman, n. femme (f.) d'affaires.
bust, n. buste m.
bustle, vb. se remuer.
busy, adj. occupé.
busybody, n. officieux m.
but, conj. mais; (only) ne . . . que; (except) sauf.
butane, n. butane m.
butcher, n. boucher m.
butchery, n. tuerie f., massacre m.
butler, n. maître (m.) d'hôtel.

butt, n. bout m.; (of jokes) plastron m.; (of cigarette) mégot m.; (colloquial) derrière m.
butter, n. beurre m.
buttercup, n. bouton (m.) d'or.
butterfly, n. papillon m.
buttermilk, n. babeurre m.
butterscotch, n. caramel (m.) au beurre.
buttock, n. fesse f.
button, n. bouton m.
buttonhole, n. boutonnière f.
buttress, n. contrefort m.; (flying b.) arc-boutant m.
buxom, adj. (of women) aux formes rebondies.
buy, vb. acheter.
buyer, n. acheteur m.
buzz, 1. n. bourdonnement m. 2. vb. bourdonner.
buzzard, n. buse f.
buzzer, n. trompe f., sirène f.
by, prep. (through) par; (near) près de.
by-and-by, adv. bientôt.
bye(-bye), interj. au revoir, salut.
bygone, adj. passé, d'autrefois.
bylaw, n. règlement local m.
by-pass, 1. n. route (f.) d'évitement. 2. vb. faire un détour.
by-product, n. sous-produit m.
bystander, n. spectateur m.
byte, n. unité fondamentale de données f.; octet m.
byway, n. sentier détourné m.

C

cab, n. (taxi) taxi m.; (horse) fiacre m.
cabaret, n. cabaret m.
cabbage, n. chou m.
cabin, n. (hut) cabane f.; (boat) cabine f.
cabinet, n. cabinet m.
cabinetmaker, n. ébéniste m.
cable, 1. n. câble m. 2. vb. câbler.
cable car, n. téléphérique m.
cablegram, n. câblogramme m.
caboose, n. fourgon m.
cachet, n. cachet m.
cackle, 1. n. caquet m. 2. vb. caqueter.
cacophony, n. cacophonie f.

cactus, n. cactus m.
cad, n. mufle m.
cadaver, n. cadavre m.
cadaverous, adj. cadavérique.
cadence, n. cadence f.
cadet, n. cadet m.
cadmium, n. cadmium m.
cadre, n. cadre m.
Caesarean (section), n. césarienne f.
café, n. café, (-restaurant) m.
cafeteria, n. restaurant m.
caffeine, n. caféine f.
cage, n. cage f.
caged, adj. mis en cage.
cagey, adj. méfiant.

caisson, *n.* caisson *m.*

cajole, *vb.* cajoler.

cake, *n.* gâteau *m.*

calamitous, *adj.* calamiteux, désastreux.

calamity, *n.* calamité *f.*

calcify, *vb.* calcifier.

calcium, *n.* calcium *m.*

calculable, *adj.* calculable.

calculate, *vb.* calculer.

calculating, *adj.* qui fait des calculs.

calculation, *n.* calcul *m.*

calculator, *n.* calculatrice *f.*

calculus, *n.* calcul *m.*

caldron, *n.* chaudron *m.*

calendar, *n.* calendrier *m.*

calender, *n.* calandre *f.*

calf, *n.* veau *m.*

calfskin, *adj.* en peau de veau.

caliber, *n.* calibre *m.*

calico, *n.* calicot *m.*

calisthenic, *adj.* callisthénique.

calisthenics, *n.* callisthénie *f.*

calk, *vb.* ferrer à glace.

call, 1. *n.* appel *m.;* (visit) visite *f.* **2.** *vb.* appeler; **(c. on)** faire visite à.

calligraphy, *n.* calligraphie *f.*

calling, *n.* vocation *f.,* profession *f.*

calling card, *n.* carte de visite *f.*

callously, *adv.* d'une manière insensible.

callousness, *n.* insensibilité *f.*

callow, *adj.* blanc-bec.

callus, *n.* callosité *f.*

calm, 1. *adj.* calme. **2.** *vb.* calmer.

calmly, *adv.* calmement.

calmness, *n.* calme *m.,* tranquillité *f.*

caloric, *adj.* calorique.

calorie, *n.* calorie *f.*

calorimeter, *n.* calorimètre *m.*

calumniate, *vb.* calomnier.

calumny, *n.* calomnie *f.*

Calvary, *n.* Calvaire *m.*

calve, *vb.* vêler.

calyx, *n.* calice *m.*

camaraderie, *n.* camaraderie *f.*

Cambodia, *n.* Cambodge *m.*

cambric, *n.* batiste *f.*

camcorder, *n.* camescope *m.*

camel, *n.* chameau *m.*

camellia, *n.* camélia *m.*

camel's hair, *n.* poil *(m.)* de chameau.

cameo, *n.* camée *m.*

camera, *n.* appareil photographique *m.*

Cameroons, *n.* la République fédérale du Cameroun.

camouflage, *vb.* camoufler.

camouflaged, *adj.* camouflé.

camouflaging, *n.* camouflant.

camp, 1. *n.* camp *m.;* (holiday camp) camping *m.* **2.** *vb.* camper.

campaign, *n.* campagne *f.*

camper, *n.* qui fait du camping; (vehicle) camping-car *m.*

camphor, *n.* camphre *m.*

camphor ball, *n.* balle *(f.)* de camphre.

campsite, *n.* (terrain *m.* de) camping.

campus, *n.* terrains *(m.pl.)* de l'université.

can, 1. *n.* (food) boîte *f.;* (general) bidon *m.* **2.** *vb.* (be able) pouvoir; (put in a can) conserver.

Canada, *n.* Canada *m.*

Canadian, 1. *n.* Canadien *m.* **2.** *adj.* canadien.

canal, *n.* canal *m.*

canalize, *vb.* canaliser.

canapé, *n.* canapé *m.*

canard, *n.* canard *m.*

canary, *n.* serin *m.*

Canary Islands, *n.* Îles Canaries *f.pl.*

cancel, *vb.* annuler; (erase) biffer.

cancellation, *n.* annulation *f.*

cancer, *n.* cancer *m.*

candelabrum, *n.* candélabre *m.*

candid, *adj.* sincère.

candidacy, *n.* candidature *f.*

candidate, *n.* candidat *m.*

candidly, *adv.* franchement.

candidness, *n.* candeur *f.*

candied, *adj.* candi.

candle, *n.* bougie *f.;* (church) cierge *m.*

candler, *n.* fabricant *(m.)* de chandelles.

candlestick, *n.* chandelier *m.*

candor, *n.* sincérité *f.*

candy, *n.* bonbon *m.*

cane, *n.* canne *f.*

canine, *adj.* canin.

canister, *n.* boîte à thé *f.*

canker, *n.* chancre *m.*

cankerworm, *n.* ver rongeur *m.*

canned, *adj.* conservé en boîtes (de fer blanc).

canner, *n.* travailleur dans une conserverie *m.*

cannery, *n.* conserverie *f.*

cannibal, *adj. and n.* cannibale *m.f.*

canning, *n.* mise en conserve, en boîtes (de fer blanc) *f.*

cannon, *n.* canon *m.*

cannonade, *n.* cannonade *f.*

cannoneer, *n.* canonier *m.*

cannot, *vb.* ne peut pas.

canny, *adj.* avisé, rusé.

canoe, *n.* canot *m.*

canon, *n.* chanoine *m.;* (rule) canon *m.*

canonical, *adj.* canonique.

canonize, *vb.* canoniser.

can opener, *n.* ouvre-boîte *m.*

canopy, *n.* dais *m.*

cant, *n.* hypocrisie *f.*

can't, *vb.* ne peut pas.

cantaloupe, *n.* melon *m.,* cantaloup *m.*

cantankerous, *adj.* grincheux.

canteen, *n.* cantine *f.;* bidon *m.*

canter, 1. *n.* petit galop *f.* 2. *vb.* aller au petit galop.

cantonment, *n.* cantonnement *m.*

canvas, *n.* toile *f.*

canvass, 1. *n.* sollicitation *f.* 2. *vb.* solliciter; (discuss) débattre.

canyon, *n.* gorge *f.,* défilé *m.*

cap, *n.* bonnet *m.;* (peaked) casquette *f.*

capability, *n.* capacité *f.*

capable, *adj.* capable.

capably, *adv.* capablement.

capacious, *adj.* ample, spacieux.

capacity, *n.* capacité *f.*

caparison, 1. *n.* caparaçon *m.* 2. *vb.* caparaçonner.

cape, *n.* (geography) cap *m.;* (cloak) cape *f.*

caper, 1. *n.* bond *m.;* (plant) câpre *f.* 2. *vb.* bondir.

capillary, *adj.* capillaire.

capital, 1. *n.* (finance) capital *m.;* (city) capitale *f.;* (letter) majuscule *f.;* (architecture) chapiteau *m.* 2. *adj.* capital.

capitalism, *n.* capitalisme *m.*

capitalist, *n.* capitaliste *m.f.*

capitalistic, *adj.* capitaliste.

capitalization, *n.* capitalisation *f.*

capitalize, *vb.* capitaliser.

capitulate, *vb.* capituler.

capon, *n.* chapon *m.*

caprice, *n.* caprice *m.*

capricious, *adj.* capricieux.

capriciously, *adv.* capricieusement.

capriciousness, *n.* caractère capricieux *m.,* humeur fantasque *f.*

capsize, *vb.* chavirer, *intr.;* faire chavirer, *tr.*

capsule, *n.* capsule *f.*

captain, *n.* capitaine *m.*

caption, *n.* en-tête *m.*

captious, *adj.* chicaneur.

captivate, *vb.* captiver.

captivating, *adj.* séduisant.

captive, *adj. and n.* captif *m.*

captivity, *n.* captivité *f.*

captor, *n.* capteur *m.*

capture, 1. *n.* capture *f.* 2. *vb.* capturer.

car, *n.* (auto) voiture *f.;* (train) wagon *m.*

caracul, *n.* caracul *m.*

carafe, *n.* carafe *f.*

caramel, *n.* caramel *m.*

carat, *n.* carat *m.*

caravan, *n.* caravane *f.*

caraway, *n.* carvi *m.,* cumin *(m.)* (des prés).

carbide, *n.* carbure *m.*

carbine, *n.* carabine *f.*

carbohydrate, *n.* carbohydrate *m.*

carbon, *n.* carbone *m.*

carbon dioxide, *n.* acide carbonique *m.*

carbon monoxide, *n.* oxyde de carbone *m.*

carbon paper, *n.* papier carbone *m.*

carbuncle, *n.* escarboucle *f.,* (med.) charbon *m.*

carburetor, *n.* carburateur *m.*

carcass, *n.* carcasse *f.*

carcinogenic, *adj.* cancérogène *f.*

card, *n.* carte *f.*

cardboard, *n.* carton *m.*

cardiac, *adj.* cardiaque.

cardigan, *n.* gilet de tricot *m.*

cardinal, *adj.* cardinal *m.*

care, 1. *n.* (worry) souci *m.;* (attention) attention *f.;* **(take c.!)** faites attention!; (charge) soin *m.;* **(take c. of)** prendre soin de. 2. *vb.* (c.

about) se soucier de; **(c. for)** aimer; (look after) soigner.

careen, vb. caréner.

career, n. carrière f.

carefree, adj. insouciant.

careful, adj. soigneux.

carefully, adv. soigneusement, attentivement.

carefulness, n. soin m., attention f.

careless, adj. insouciant.

carelessly, adv. nonchalamment, négligemment.

carelessness, n. insouciance f., négligence f.

caress, 1. n. caresse f. **2.** vb. caresser.

caretaker, n. concierge m.f.

cargo, n. cargaison f.

Caribbean, n. the C. (sea) la mer des Caraïbes; **the C.** (islands) les Antilles.

caricature, n. caricature f.

caries, n. carie f.

carillon, n. carillon m.

carload, n. voiturée f.

carnage, n. carnage m.

carnal, adj. charnel.

carnation, n. œillet m.

carnival, n. carnaval m.

carnivorous, adj. carnivore.

carol, n. **(Xmas c.)** noël m.

carouse, vb. faire la fête.

carousel, n. carrousel m.

carpenter, n. charpentier m.

carpet, n. tapis m.

carpeting, n. pose de tapis f.

car pool, n. groupe (m.) de personnes qui voyagent régulièrement ensemble en auto.

carriage, n. (vehicle) voiture f.; (bearing) maintien m.; (transport) transport m.

carrier, n. porteur m., messager m.

carrier pigeon, n. pigeon voyageur m.

carrot, n. carotte f.

carry, vb. porter; **(c. on)** continuer; **(c. out)** exécuter; **(c. through)** mener à bonne fin.

cart, n. charrette f.

cartage, n. charriage m., transport m.

cartel, n. cartel m.

carter, n. charretier m.

cartilage, n. cartilage m.

carton, n. carton m.

cartoon, n. dessin satirique m., (cinema) dessin (m.) animé.

cartoonist, n. caricaturiste m.

cartridge, n. cartouche f.

carve, vb. (art) sculpter; (meat) découper.

carver, n. découpeur m., sculpteur m.

carving, n. découpage m., sculpture f.

cascade, n. cascade f.

case, n. (instance, state of things) cas m.; (law) cause f.; (packing) caisse f.; (holder) étui m.; **(in any c.)** en tout cas.

cash, 1. n. espèces f.pl.; (C.O.D.) livraison (f.) contre remboursement. **2.** vb. **(c. a check)** toucher.

cashew, n. noix (f.) de cajou.

cashier, n. caissier m.

cashmere, n. cachemire m.

cash register, n. caisse f.

casing, n. revêtement m., enveloppe f.

casino, n. casino m.

cask, n. tonneau m.

casket, n. cassette f.

casserole, n. casserole f.

cassette, n. cassette f.

cast, 1. n. (throw) coup m.; (characteristic) trempe f.; (theater) distribution f.; **(c. from mold)** moulage m.; (hue) nuance f.; (med.) plâtre m. **2.** vb. (throw) jeter; (metal) couler.

castaway, n. naufragé m.; rejeté m.

caste, n. caste f.

caster, n. fondeur m.

castigate, vb. châtier, punir.

cast iron, n. fonte f.

castle, n. château m.

castoff, adj. abandonné.

castrate, vb. châtrer.

casual, adj. (accidental) casuel; (person) insouciant.

casually, adv. fortuitement, en passant.

casualness, n. nonchalance f.

casualties, n. (mil.) pertes f.pl.

cat, n. chat m., chatte f.

cataclysm, n. cataclysme m.

catacomb, n. catacombe f.

catalogue, n. catalogue m.

catalyst, n. catalyseur m.

catapult, *n.* catapulte *f.*
cataract, *n.* cataracte *f.*
catarrh, *n.* catarrhe *m.*
catastrophe, *n.* catastrophe *f.*
catch, *vb.* attraper; (seize, understand) saisir; **(c. up)** se rattraper.
catcher, *n.* qui attrape.
catchword, *n.* mot d'ordre *m.*
catchy, *adj.* (musical air) facile à retenir; (question) insidieuse.
catechism, *n.* catéchisme *m.*
catechize, *vb.* catéchiser.
categorical, *adj.* catégorique.
category, *n.* catégorie *f.*
cater, *vb.* pourvoir à.
caterpillar, *n.* chenille *f.*
catgut, *n.* corde *(f.)* à boyau.
catharsis, *n.* catharsis *f., (med.)* purgation *f.*
cathartic, *adj.* cathartique, purgatif.
cathedral, *n.* cathédrale *f.*
cathode, *n.* cathode *f.*
Catholic, *adj.* catholique.
Catholic Church, *n.* Église catholique *f.*
Catholicism, *n.* catholicisme *m.*
cat nap, *n.* somme *m.*
catsup, *n.* sauce piquante *f.*
cattle, *n.* bétail m., bestiaux *m.pl.*
cattleman, *n.* éleveur de bétail *m.*
catty, *adj.* méchant.
catwalk, *n.* coursive *f.*
caucus, *n.* comité *(m.)* local ou electoral.
cauliflower, *n.* chou-fleur *m.*
causation, *n.* causation *f.*
cause, *n.* cause *f.*
causeway, *n.* chaussée *f.*
caustic, *adj.* caustique.
cauterize, *vb.* cautériser.
cautery, *n.* cautère *m.*
caution, 1. *n.* prudence *f.* 2. *vb.* avertir.
cautious, *adj.* prudent.
cavalcade, *n.* cavalcade *f.*
cavalier, *adj. and n.* cavalier *m.*
cavalry, *n.* cavalerie *f.*
cave, *n.* caverne *f.*
cave-in, *n.* effondrement *m.*
cavern, *n.* caverne *f.*
caviar, *n.* caviar *m.*
cavity, *n.* cavité *f.*
cavort, *vb.* cabrioler.
CD, *n.* compact disc *m.*

cease, *vb.* cesser (de).
ceaseless, *adj.* incessant, continuel.
cedar, *n.* cèdre *m.*
cede, *vb.* céder.
cedilla, *n.* cédille *f.*
ceiling, *n.* plafond *m.*
celebrant, *n.* célébrant *m.*
celebrate, *vb.* célébrer.
celebration, *n.* célébration *f.*
celebrity, *n.* célébrité *f.*
celerity, *n.* célérité *f.*, vitesse *f.*
celery, *n.* céleri *m.*
celestial, *adj.* céleste.
celibacy, *n.* célibat *m.*
celibate, *adj.* célibataire.
cell, *n.* cellule *f.*
cellar, *n.* cave *f.*
cellist, *n.* violoncelliste *m.f.*
cello, *n.* violoncelle *m.*
cellophane, *n.* cellophane *f.*
cellular, *adj.* cellulaire.
celluloid, *n.* celluloïd *m.*
cellulose, *n.* cellulose *f.*
Celtic, *adj.* celtique.
cement, 1. *n.* ciment *m.* 2. *vb.* cimenter.
cemetery, *n.* cimetière *m.*
censor, 1. *n.* censeur *m.* 2. *vb.* censurer.
censorious, *adj.* critique, hargneux.
censorship, *n.* censure *f.*
censure, *n.* censure *f.*
census, *n.* recensement *m.*
cent, *n.* cent *m.*; **(per c.)** pour cent.
centenary, centennial, *adj. and n.* centenaire *n.*
center, *n.* centre *m.*
centerfold, *n.* pages centrales *f.pl.*
centerpiece, *n.* pièce de milieu *f.*
centigrade, *adj.* centigrade.
centigrade thermometer, *n.* thermomètre centigrade *m.*
centipede, *n.* mille-pattes *m.*
central, *adj.* central.
Central America, *n.* Amérique *(f.)* Centrale.
central heating, *n.* chauffage *(m.)* central.
centralize, *vb.* centraliser.
century, *n.* siècle *m.*
century plant, *n.* agave *(m.)* d'Amérique.
ceramic, *adj.* céramique.

ceramics, *n.* céramique *f.*

cereal, *adj.* and *n.* céréale *f.*

cerebral, *adj.* cérébral.

ceremonial, *adj.* and *n.* cérémonial *m.*

ceremonious, *adj.* cérémonieux.

ceremony, *n.* cérémonie *f.*

certain, *adj.* certain.

certainly, *adv.* certainement.

certainty, *n.* certitude *f.*

certificate, *n.* certificat *m.;* (**birth c.**) acte (*m.*) de naissance.

certification, *n.* certification *f.*

certified, *adj.* certifié, diplômé, breveté.

certifier, *n.* (personne) qui certifie.

certify, *vb.* certifier.

certitude, *n.* certitude *f.*

cervical, *adj.* cervical.

cervix, *n.* col (du l'utérus *m.*)

cessation, *n.* cessation *f.,* suspension *f.*

cession, *n.* cession *f.*

cesspool, *n.* fosse (*f.*) d'aisances.

Chad, *n.* Tchad *m.*

chafe, *vb.* frictionner.

chaff, 1. *n.* menue paille *f.;* (colloquial) blague *f.* **2.** *vb.* blaguer.

chafing dish, *n.* réchaud *m.*

chagrin, *n.* chagrin *m.*

chain, *n.* chaîne *f.*

chain reaction, *n.* réaction caténaire *f.*

chain store, *n.* succursale (*f.*) de grand magasin.

chair, *n.* chaise *f.;* (**arm-c.**) fauteuil *m.*

chairman, *n.* président *m.*

chairmanship, *n.* présidence *f.*

chairperson, *n.* président *m.,* présidente *f.*

chairwoman, *n.* présidente *f.*

chalice, *n.* calice *m.*

chalk, *n.* craie *f.*

chalky, *adj.* de craie, calcaire.

challenge, 1. *n.* défi *m.* **2.** *vb.* défier; (dispute) contester.

challenger, *n.* qui fait un défi, prétendant *m.*

chamber, *n.* chambre *f.*

chamberlain, *n.* chambellan *m.*

chambermaid, *n.* femme de chambre *f.*

chamber music, *n.* musique de chambre *f.*

chameleon, *n.* caméléon *m.*

chamois, *n.* chamois *m.*

champ, *vb.* ronger, mâcher.

champagne, *n.* champagne *m.*

champion, *n.* champion *m.*

championship, *n.* championnat *m.*

chance, *n.* chance *f.;* (**by c.**) par hasard; (**take a c.**) prendre un risque.

chancel, *n.* sanctuaire *m.,* choeur *m.*

chancellery, *n.* chancellerie *f.*

chancellor, *n.* chancelier *m.*

chancy, *adj.* risqué.

chandelier, *n.* lustre *m.*

change, 1. *n.* changement *m.;* (money) monnaie *f.;* (exchange) change *m.* **2.** *vb.* changer.

changeability, *n.* variabilité *f.*

changeable, *adj.* changeant.

changer, *n.* changeur *m.*

channel, *n.* canal *m.;* (**the English C.**) la Manche *f.;* (television) chaîne *f.*

chant, 1. *n.* chant *m.* **2.** *vb.* chanter.

chaos, *n.* chaos *m.*

chaotic, *adj.* chaotique.

chap, *n.* (on skin) gerçure *f.;* (young man) gars *m.*

chapel, *n.* chapelle *f.*

chaperon, *n.* (person) duègne *f.,* chaperon *m.*

chaplain, *n.* aumônier *m.*

chapman, *n.* colporteur *m.*

chapped, *adj.* gercé.

chapter, *n.* chapitre *m.*

char, *vb.* carboniser.

character, *n.* caractère *m.;* (in fiction) personnage *m.;* (role) rôle *m.*

characteristic, 1. *n.* trait caractéristique *m.* **2.** *adj.* caractéristique.

characteristically, *adv.* d'une manière caractéristique.

characterization, *n.* action de caractériser *f.*

characterize, *vb.* caractériser.

charcoal, *n.* charbon (*m.*) de bois.

charge, 1. *n.* (guns, legal, office) charge *f.;* (price) prix *m.;* (care) soin *m.* **2.** *vb.* charger; (**c. with**) charger de; (price) demander.

charger, *n.* grand plat *m.;* cheval de bataille *m.*

chariot, *n.* char *m.,* chariot *m.*

charioteer, n. conducteur de chariot m.

charisma, n. charisme m.

charitable, adj. charitable.

charitableness, n. bienveillance f.

charitably, adv. charitablement.

charity, n. charité f.

charlatan, n. charlatan m.

charlatanism, n. charlatanisme m.

charm, 1. n. charme m. **2.** vb. charmer.

charmer, n. charmeur m., enchanteur m.

charming, adj. charmant.

charred, adj. carbonisé.

chart, n. (map) carte f.; (graph) graphique m.

charter, 1. n. charte f. **2.** vb. (boat) affréter.

charter flight, n. vol frété m.; charter m.

charwoman, n. femme (f.) de journée; femme (f.) de ménage.

chase, 1. n. chasse f. **2.** vb. chasser.

chaser, n. chasseur m.; ciseleur m.

chasm, n. abîme m.

chassis, n. chassis m.

chaste, adj. chaste.

chasten, vb. châtier, corriger.

chasteness, n. pureté f.

chastise, vb. châtier.

chastisement, n. châtiment m.

chastity, n. chasteté f.

chat, 1. n. causette f. **2.** vb. causer.

chateau, n. château m.

chattel, n. bien m., meuble m.

chatter, 1. n. bavardage m. **2.** vb. bavarder.

chatterbox, n. bavard m.

chatty, adj. bavard.

chauffeur, n. chauffeur m.

chauvinist, adj. (male) phallocrate; (nationalist) chauvin m.

cheap, adj. (inexpensive) bon marché; (mean) de peu de valeur.

cheapen, vb. déprécier.

cheaply, adv. à bon marché.

cheapness, n. bon marché m., bas prix m.; basse qualité f.

cheat, vb. tromper; (at games) tricher.

cheater, n. tricheur m., trompeur m.

check, 1. n. (restraint) frein m.; (verification) vérification f.; (stub) ticket m.; (bill) addition f.; (bank draft) chèque m. **2.** vb. (stop) arrêter; (restrain) modérer; (verify) vérifier; (luggage) enregistrer.

checker, n. enregistreur m., contrôleur m.

checkbook, n. chéquier m., carnet (m.) de chèques.

checkers, n. jeu de dames m.

checkmate, 1. n. échec et mat m. **2.** vb. mater.

checkroom, n. vestiaire m.

cheek, n. joue f.

cheer, 1. n. (applause) hourra m. **2.** vb. (acclaim) acclamer; (c. up, tr.) réjouir.

cheerful, adj. gai.

cheerfully, adv. gaiement, de bon cœur.

cheerfulness, n. gaieté f., bonne humeur f.

cheerless, adj. triste, morne, sombre.

cheery, adj. gai, joyeux.

cheese, n. fromage m.

cheesecloth, n. gaze f.

cheesy, adj. fromageux.

cheetah, n. guépard m.

chef, n. chef m.

chemical, adj. chimique.

chemically, adv. chimiquement.

chemist, n. chimiste m.f.

chemistry, n. chimie f.

chemotherapy, n. chimiothérapie f.

chenille, n. chenille f.

cherish, vb. chérir.

cherry, n. cerise f.

cherub, n. chérubin m.

chess, n. échecs m.pl.

chessman, n. pièce f.

chest, n. (box) coffre m.; (body) poitrine f.; (c. of drawers) commode f.

chestnut, n. châtaigne f.

chevron, n. chevron m.

chew, vb. mâcher.

chewer, n. mâcheur m.

chic, adj. chic, élégant, smart.

chicanery, n. chicane f., chicanerie f.

chick, n. poussin m.

chicken, n. poulet m.

chicken-hearted, adj. peureux.

chicken-pox, n. varicelle f.

chickpea, *n.* pois *(m.)* chiche.
chicle, *n.* chiclé *m.*
chicory, *n.* chicorée *f.*
chide, *vb.* gronder, réprimander.
chief, 1. *n.* chef *m.* **2.** *adj.* principal; **(c. executive)** directeur général.
chiefly, *adv.* surtout, principalement.
chieftain, *n.* chef de clan *m.*
chiffon, *n.* chiffon *m.*
chilblain, *n.* engelure *f.*
child, *n.* enfant *m.f.*
childbirth, *n.* enfantement *m.;* accouchement *m.*
childhood, *n.* enfance *f.*
childish, *adj.* enfantin.
childishness, *n.* puérilité *f.,* enfantillage *m.*
childless, *adj.* sans enfant.
childlessness, *n.* l'état d'être sans enfants.
childlike, *adj.* comme un enfant, en enfant.
Chile, *n.* Chili *m.*
Chilean, 1. *n.* Chilien *m.* **2.** *adj.* chilien.
chili, *n.* piment *m.*
chill, 1. *n.* froid *m.;* (shiver) frisson *m.* **2.** *vb.* refroidir.
chilliness, *n.* froid *m.,* frisson *m.*
chilly, *adj.* un peu froid.
chime, 1. *n.* carillon *m.* **2.** *vb.* carillonner.
chimney, *n.* cheminée *f.*
chimney sweep, *n.* ramoneur *m.*
chimpanzee, *n.* chimpanzé *m.*
chin, *n.* menton *m.*
China, *n.* Chine *f.*
china, *n.* (ware) porcelaine *f.*
chinchilla, *n.* chinchilla *m.*
Chinese, 1. *n.* (person) Chinois *m.;* (language) chinois *m.* **2.** *adj.* chinois.
chink, *n.* fente *f.,* crevasse *f.*
chintz, *n.* perse *f.*
chip, 1. *n.* éclat *m.;* (potato c.s) chips *m.pl.* **2.** *vb.* ébrecher.
chipmunk, *n.* tamias *m.*
chiropractor, *n.* chiropracteur *m.*
chirp, *vb.* pépier, gazouiller.
chisel, 1. *vb.* ciseler. **2.** *n.* ciseau *m.*
chitchat, *n.* bavardage *m.*
chivalrous, *adj.* chevaleresque.
chivalry, *n.* chevalerie *f.*
chive, *n.* ciboulette *f.*

chloride, *n.* chlorure *m.*
chlorine, *n.* chlore *m.*
chloroform, *n.* chloroforme *m.*
chlorophyll, *n.* chlorophylle *m.*
chockfull, *adj.* plein comme un œuf.
chocolate, *n.* chocolat *m.*
choice, *n.* choix *m.*
choir, *n.* chœur *m.*
choke, *vb.* étouffer.
choker, *n.* foulard *m.*
cholera, *n.* choléra *m.*
choleric, *adj.* cholérique.
cholesterol, *n.* cholestérol *m.*
choose, *vb.* choisir.
choosy, *adj.* exigeant.
chop, 1. *n.* (meat) côtelette *f.* **2.** *vb.* couper.
chopper, *n.* couperet *m.*
choppy, *adj.* (sea) clapoteux.
chopstick, *n.* baguette *f.,* bâtonnet *m.*
choral, *adj.* choral.
chord, *n.* (music) accord *m.*
chore, *n.* travail *(m.)* de ménage.
choreography, *n.* chorégraphie *f.*
chorister, *n.* choriste *m.,* enfant de chœur *m.*
chortle, *vb.* glousser de joie.
chorus, *n.* chœur *m.;* (of song) refrain *m.*
chowder, *n.* (sorte de) bouillabaisse *f.*
Christ, *n.* le Christ *m.*
christen, *vb.* baptiser.
Christendom, *n.* chrétienté *f.*
christening, *n.* baptême *m.*
Christian, 1. *n.* Chrétian *m.* **2.** *adj.* chrétien.
Christianity, *n.* christianisme *m.*
Christmas, *n.* Noël *m.;* **(C. Day)** jour *(m.)* de Noël; **(C. Eve)** veille *(f.)* de Noël; **(C. tree)** sapin *(m.)* de Noël.
chromatic, *adj.* chromatique.
chromium, *n.* chrome *m.*
chromosome, *n.* chromosome *m.*
chronic, *adj.* chronique.
chronically, *adv.* d'une manière chronique.
chronicle, *n.* chronique *f.*
chronological, *adj.* chronologique.
chronologically, *adv.* chronologiquement.
chronology, *n.* chronologie *f.*

chrysalis, *n.* chrysalide *f.*

chrysanthemum, *n.* chrysanthème *m.*

chubby, *adj.* joufflu.

chuck, *n.* petite tape *f.*, gloussement (de volaille) *m.*

chuckle, *vb.* rire tout bas.

chug, 1. *n.* souffle *m.* (d'une machine à vapeur). **2.** *vb.* souffler.

chum, *n.* camarade *m.*, copain *m.*

chummy, *adj.* familier, intime.

chunk, *n.* gros morceau *m.*

chunky, *adj.* en gros morceaux.

church, *n.* église *f.*

churchman, *n.* homme (*m.*) d'église, ecclésiastique *m.*

churchyard, *n.* cimetière *m.*

churn, *vb.* baratter.

chute, *n.* glissière *f.*

chutney, *n.* chutney *m.*

cicada, *n.* cigale *f.*

cider, *n.* cidre *m.*

cigar, *n.* cigare *m.*

cigarette, *n.* cigarette *f.*

cilia, *n.* cils *m.pl.*

ciliary, *adj.* ciliaire.

cinch, *n.* (it's a c.) c'est facile.

cinchona, *n.* quinquina *m.*

cinder, *n.* cendre *f.*

Cinderella, *n.* Cendrillon *f.*

cinema, *n.* cinéma *m.*

cinematic, *adj.* cinématographique.

cinnamon, *n.* cannelle *f.*

cipher, *n.* chiffre *m.*; (nought) zéro *m.*

circle, 1. *n.* cercle *m.* **2.** *vb.* entourer (de).

circuit, *n.* circuit *m.*

circuitous, *adj.* détourné, sinueux.

circuitously, *adv.* d'une manière détournée, par des détours.

circular, *adj.* circulaire.

circularize, *vb.* envoyer des circulaires.

circulate, *vb.* circuler, *intr.;* faire circuler, *tr.*

circulation, *n.* circulation *f.;* (newspaper) tirage *m.*

circulator, *n.* circulateur *m.*

circulatory, *adj.* circulaire, circulatoire.

circumcise, *vb.* circoncire.

circumcision, *n.* circoncision *f.*

circumference, *n.* circonférence *f.*

circumflex, *n.* accent (*m.*) circonflexe.

circumlocution, *n.* circonlocution *f.*

circumscribe, *vb.* circonscrire.

circumspect, *adj.* circonspect.

circumstance, *n.* (condition) circonstance *f.;* (financial) moyens *m.pl.*

circumstantial, *adj.* circonstancié.

circumstantially, *adv.* en détail.

circumvent, *vb.* circonvenir.

circumvention, *n.* circonvention *f.*

circus, *n.* cirque *m.*

cirrhosis, *n.* cirrhose *f.*

cistern, *n.* citerne *f.*

citadel, *n.* citadelle *f.*

citation, *n.* citation *f.*

cite, *vb.* citer.

citizen, *n.* citoyen *m.*

citizenry, *n.* tous les citoyens *m.pl.*

citizenship, *n.* droit (*m.*) de cité.

citric acid, *n.* acide citrique *m.*

citrus fruit, *n.* agrume *m.*

city, *n.* ville *f.;* cité *f.*

city hall, *n.* hôtel (*m.*) de ville.

city planning, *n.* urbanisme *m.*

civic, *adj.* civique.

civics, *n.* instruction (*f.*) civique.

civil, *adj.* civil; (polite) poli; (**c. servant**) fonctionnaire *m.*

civilian, *n.* civil *m.*

civility, *n.* civilité *f.*, politesse *f.*

civilization, *n.* civilisation *f.*

civilize, *vb.* civiliser.

civilized, *adj.* civilisé.

civil rights, *n.* droits (*m.pl.*) de l'homme.

civil servant, *n.* fonctionnaire *m.*

civil service, *n.* administration (civile) *f.*

civil war, *n.* guerre civile *f.*

clad, *adj.* habillé, vêtu.

claim, 1. *n.* (demand) demande *f.;* (right) droit *m.* **2.** *vb.* (demand) réclamer, prétendre; (insist) soutenir.

claimant, *n.* réclamateur *m.*, prétendant *m.*

clairvoyance, *n.* clairvoyance *f.*

clairvoyant, *n.* voyant *m.*

clam, *n.* palourde *f.*, mollusque *m.*

clamber, *vb.* grimper.

clammy, *adj.* visqueux, moite.

clamor, *n.* clameur *f.*

clamorous, *adj.* bruyant.

clamp, 1. *n.* (metal) crampon *m.;* (carpentry) serre-joint *m.* **2.** *vb.* cramponner, serrer.

clan, *n.* clan *m.,* clique *f.,* coterie *f.*

clandestine, *adj.* clandestin.

clandestinely, *adv.* clandestinement.

clang, 1. *n.* cliquetis *m.,* son métallique *m.* **2.** *vb.* résonner.

clangor, *n.* cliquetis *m.*

clannish, *adj.* de clan.

clap, *vb.* (applaud) applaudir.

clapboard, *n.* bardeau *m.*

clapper, *n.* claqueur *m.,* battant (of a bell) *m.*

claque, *n.* claque *f.*

claret, *n.* vin rouge *(m.)* de Bordeaux.

clarification, *n.* clarification *f.*

clarify, *vb.* (lit.) clarifier; *(fig.)* éclaircir.

clarinet, *n.* clarinette *f.*

clarinetist, *n.* clarinettiste *m.f.*

clarion, *n.* clairon *m.*

clarity, *n.* clarté *f.*

clash, 1. *vb.* choquer, *tr.;* s'entrechoquer, *intr.* **2.** *n.* choc *m.*

clasp, 1. *n.* agrafe *f.;* (embrace) étreinte *f.* **2.** *vb.* agrafer, étreindre.

class, *n.* classe *f.*

classic, classical, *adj.* classique.

classicism, *n.* classicisme *m.*

classifiable, *adj.* classifiable.

classification, *n.* classification *f.*

classified, *adj.* (information) secret.

classified ad, *n.* petite annonce *f.*

classify, *vb.* classifier, classer.

classmate, *n.* camarade *(m.)* de classe.

classroom, *n.* salle *(f.)* de classe.

clatter, *n.* bruit *m.*

clause, *n.* clause *f.*

claustrophobia, *n.* claustrophobie *f.*

claw, *n.* griffe *f.*

claw-hammer, *n.* marteau à dent *m.*

clay, *n.* argile *f.,* glaise *f.*

clean, 1. *adj.* propre. **2.** *vb.* nettoyer.

clean-cut, *adj.* net, fin.

cleaner, *n.* **(dry-c.)** teinturier *m.*

cleaning, *n.* nettoyage *m.*

cleanliness, cleanness, *n.* propreté *f.*

cleanse, *vb.* nettoyer, curer.

cleanser, *n.* chose qui nettoie *f.,* détersif *m.,* cureur *m.*

clear, 1. *adj.* clair. **2.** *vb.* **(c. up)** déblayer; (profit) gagner; (get over) franchir; (weather, *intr.*) s'éclaircir.

clearance sale, *n.* vente *f.,* liquidation *f.*

clear-cut, *adj.* nettement dessiné.

clearing, *n.* (open place) clairière *f.,* éclaircissement *m., (comm.)* acquittement *m.,* (woods) éclaircie *f.*

clearing house, *n.* banque de virement *f.,* chambre de compensation *f.*

clearly, *adv.* clairement, nettement, évidemment.

clearness, *n.* clarté *f.,* netteté *f.*

cleat, *n.* fer *m., (naut.)* taquet *m.*

cleavage, *n.* fendage *m.,* scission *f.*

cleave, *vb.* (split) fendre; (adhere) adhérer.

cleaver, *n.* fendeur (person) *m.;* fendoir *m.,* couperet (instrument) *m.*

cleft, *n.* fente *f.*

clemency, *n.* clémence *f.*

clench, *vb.* serrer.

clergy, *n.* clergé *m.*

clergyman, *n.* ecclésiastique *m.*

clerical, *adj.* (clergy) clérical; (business) de bureau.

clericalism, *n.* cléricalisme *m.*

clerk, *n.* (business) employé *m.;* (store) commis *m.;* (law, *eccles.*) clerc *m.*

clerkship, *n.* place de clerc *f.,* place de commis *f.*

clever, *adj.* habile.

cleverly, *adv.* habilement.

cleverness, *n.* adresse *f.*

clew, *n.* fil *m.*

cliché, *n.* cliché *m.*

click, 1. *n.* cliquetis *m.,* déclic *m.;* (computer) clic *m.* **2.** *vb.* cliqueter; (computer) cliquer.

client, *n.* client *m.*

clientele, *n.* clientèle *f.*

cliff, *n.* falaise *f.*

climactic, *adj.* arrivé à son apogée.

climate, *n.* climat *m.*

climatic, *adj.* climatique.

climax, *n.* comble *m.*

climb, 1. *n.* montée *f.* **2.** *vb.* monter, grimper.

climber, *n.* grimpeur *m.*, ascensioniste *m.*

clinch, *vb.* river; (settle) conclure.

cling, *vb.* s'accrocher.

clinging, *adj.* qui se cramponne, qui s'accroche (à).

clinic, *n.* clinique *f.*

clinical, *adj.* clinique.

clinically, *adv.* d'une manière clinique.

clink, *vb.* tinter, cliqueter.

clip, 1. *vb.* couper. **2.** *n.* pince *f.*; **(paper c.)** trombone *m.*

clipper, *n.* rogneur *m.*, tondeuse (instrument) *f.*, *(naut.)* fin voilier *m.*

clipping, *n.* coupure *f.*

clique, *n.* clique *f.*

cloak, *n.* manteau *m.*; **(c. room)** vestiaire *m.*

clobber, *vb.* rosser.

clock, *n.* horloge *f.*; **(two o'c.)** deux heures.

clockwise, *adv.* dans le sens des aiguilles d'une montre.

clockwork, *n.* mouvement (*m.*) d'horlogerie.

clod, *n.* motte (*f.*) de terre; (person) lourdaud *m.*

clog, 1. *vb.* entraver. **2.** *n.* sabot *m.*

cloister, *n.* cloître *m.*

clone, *n.* reproduction exacte *f.*

close, 1. *adj.* (closed) fermé; (narrow) étroit; (near) proche; (secret) réservé. **2.** *vb.* fermer. **3.** *adv.* tout près. **4.** *prep.* **(c. to)** près de.

closely, *adv.* de près, étroitement.

closeness, *n.* proximité *f.*, lourdeur (of weather) *f.*, réserve *f.*

closet, *n.* (room) cabinet *m.*; (clothes) placard *m.*

close-up, *n.* gros plan *m.*

closure, *n.* fermeture *f.*

clot, *n.* (blood) caillot *m.*

cloth, *n.* étoffe *f.*

clothe, *vb.* vêtir (de); habiller *m.*

clothes, *n.* habits *m.pl.*

clothes hanger, *n.* cintre *m.*

clothespin, *n.* pince *f.*

clothier, *n.* drapier *m.*, tailleur *m.*

clothing, *n.* vêtements *m.pl.*

cloud, *n.* nuage *m.*

cloudburst, *n.* trombe *f.*, rafale (*f.*) de pluie.

cloudiness, *n.* état nuageux *m.*, obscurité *f.*

cloudless, *adj.* sans nuage.

cloudy, *adj.* nuageux, couvert.

clout, *n.* **1.** (blow) gifle *f.*, tape *f.*; (power) pouvoir *m.* **2.** *vb.* gifler, taper.

clove, *n.* clou (*m.*) de girofle; **(c. of garlic)** gousse (*f.*) d'ail.

clover, *n.* trèfle *m.*

clown, *n.* bouffon *m.*

clownish, *adj.* rustre, grossier, de paysan.

cloy, *vb.* rassasier.

cloying, *adj.* écœurant.

club, 1. *n.* (society) club *m.*, société *f.*, cercle *m.*; (stick) massue *f.*; (golf) crosse *f.*; (cards) trèfle *m.* **2.** *vb.* matraquer.

clubfoot, *n.* pied bot *m.*

clue, *n.* fil *m.*

clump, *n.* (trees) bosquet *m.*; massif *m.*

clumsiness, *n.* gaucherie *f.*, maladresse *f.*

clumsy, *adj.* gauche.

cluster, 1. *n.* (people) groupe *m.*; (fruit) grappe *f.*; (flowers, trees) bouquet *m.* **2.** *vb.* se grouper.

clutch, 1. *n.* (claw) griffe *f.*; (auto) embrayage *m.* **2.** *vb.* saisir.

clutter, 1. *vb.* encombrer. **2.** *n.* désordre *m.*

coach, 1. *n.* (carriage) carrosse *m.*; (train) wagon *m.*; (sports) entraîneur *m.* **2.** *vb.* (sports) entraîner; (school) donner des leçons particulières à.

coachman, *n.* cocher *m.*

coagulate, *vb.* se coaguler.

coagulation, *n.* coagulation *f.*

coal, *n.* charbon (*m.*) de terre, houille *f.*

coalesce, *vb.* se fondre, se fusionner, s'unir.

coalition, *n.* coalition *f.*

coal tar, *n.* goudron (*m.*) de houille.

coarse, *adj.* grossier.

coarsen, *vb.* rendre plus grossier.

coarseness, *n.* grossièreté *f.*

coast, 1. *n.* côte *f.* **2.** *vb.* (bicycle) descendre en roue libre.

coastal, *adj.* de la côte, littoral.

coaster, *n.* caboteur *m.*; dessous de carafe *m.*

coast guard, *n.* garde-côtes *m.*

coastline, *n.* littoral *m.*

coat, 1. *n.* (man) pardessus *m.*; (woman) manteau *m.*; (paint) couche *f.* **2.** *vb.* **(c. with)** revêtir de.

coating, *n.* couche *f.*, enduit *m.*, étoffe pour habits *f.*

coat of arms, *n.* écusson *m.*

coax, *vb.* cajoler.

cob, *n.* épi *m.*

cobalt, *n.* cobalt *m.*

cobbler, *n.* savetier *m.*, cordonnier *m.*

cobblestone, *n.* pavé *m.*

cobra, *n.* cobra *m.*

cobweb, *n.* toile *(f.)* d'araignée.

cocaine, *n.* cocaïne *f.*

cock, 1. *n.* (fowl) coq *m.*; (male) mâle *m.* **2.** *vb.* faire de l'œil.

cocker spaniel, *n.* épagneul cocker *m.*

cockeyed, *adj.* louche.

cockhorse, *n.* dada *m.*

cockpit, *n.* poste *(m.)* de pilotage.

cockroach, *n.* blatte *f.*, cafard *m.*

cocksure, *adj.* sûr et certain.

cocktail, *n.* cocktail *m.*; **(fruit c.)** macédoine *f.* (de fruits).

cocky, *adj.* suffisant.

cocoa, *n.* cacao *m.*

coconut, *n.* noix *(f.)* de coco.

cocoon, *n.* cocon *m.*

cod, *n.* morue *f.*

coddle, *vb.* dorloter.

code, *n.* code *m.*

codeine, *n.* codéine *f.*

codfish, *n.* morue *f.*

codify, *vb.* codifier.

cod-liver oil, *n.* huile *(f.)* de foie de morue.

coeducation, *n.* enseignement mixte *m.*

coequal, *adj.* égal.

coerce, *vb.* contraindre.

coercion, *n.* coercition *f.*, contrainte *f.*

coercive, *adj.* coercitif.

coexist, *vb.* coexister.

coffee, *n.* café *m.*

coffee break, *n.* pause-café *f.*

coffee pot, *n.* cafetière *f.*

coffee shop, *n.* cafétéria *f.*

coffee table, *n.* table *(f.)* basse.

coffer, *n.* coffre *m.*

coffin, *n.* cercueil *m.*

cog, *n.* dent *f.*

cogent, *adj.* puissant, fort.

cogitate, *vb.* méditer, penser.

cognac, *n.* cognac *m.*

cognizance, *n.* connaissance *f.*

cognizant, *adj.* instruit, (law) compétent.

cogwheel, *n.* roue *(f.)* d'engrenage.

cohabit, *vb.* vivre en concubinage.

coherent, *adj.* cohérent.

cohesion, *n.* cohésion *f.*

cohesive, *adj.* cohésif.

cohort, *n.* cohorte *f.*

coiffure, *n.* coiffure *f.*

coil, *n.* rouleau *m.*

coin, *n.* pièce *(f.)* de monnaie.

coinage, *n.* monnayage *m.*, monnaie *f.*

coincide, *vb.* coïncider.

coincidence, *n.* coïncidence *f.*

coincident, *adj.* coïncident.

coincidental, *adj.* coïncident, d'accord (avec).

coincidentally, *adv.* par coïncidence.

colander, *n.* passoire *f.*

cold, 1. *n.* (temperature) froid *m.*; *(med.)* rhume *m.* **2.** *adj.* froid; **(it is c.)** il fait froid; **(feel c.)** avoir froid; **(catch c.)** attraper un rhume.

cold-blooded, *adj.* de sang froid.

coldly, *adv.* froidement.

coldness, *n.* froideur *f.*

cold sore, *n.* bouton *(m.)* de fièvre.

colic, *n.* colique *f.*

collaborate, *vb.* collaborer.

collaboration, *n.* collaboration *f.*

collaborator, *n.* collaborateur *m.*

collapse, 1. *n.* effondrement *m.*; *(med.)* affaissement *m.* **2.** *vb.* s'effondrer; *(med.)* s'affaisser.

collapsible, *adj.* pliant.

collar, *n.* col *m.*; (dog) collier *m.*

collarbone, *n.* clavicule *f.*

collate, *vb.* collationner, comparer.

collateral, *adj. and n.* collatéral *m.*

collation, *n.* collation *f.*, comparaison *f.*, repas froid *m.*

colleague, *n.* collègue *m.f.*

collect, *vb.* rassembler.

collection, *n.* collection *f.*; (money) collecte *f.*

collective, *adj.* collectif.

collectively, *adv.* collectivement.

collector, *n.* (art) collectionneur *m.*; (tickets) contrôleur *m.*

college, *n.* collège *m.*; (higher education) université *f.*

collegiate, *adj.* de collège, collégial.

collide, *vb.* se heurter (contre).

collie, *n.* colley *m.*

colliery, *n.* houillère *f.*, mine *(f.)* de charbon.

collision, *n.* collision *f.*

colloquial, *adj.* familier.

colloquialism, *n.* expression de style familier *f.*

colloquially, *adv.* en style familier.

colloquy, *n.* colloque *m.*, entretien *m.*

collusion, *n.* collusion *f.*, connivence *f.*

colon, *n.* (*gramm.*) deux points *m.pl.*

colonel, *n.* colonel *m.*

colonial, *adj.* colonial.

colonist, *n.* colon *m.*

colonization, *n.* colonisation *f.*

colonize, *vb.* coloniser.

colony, *n.* colonie *f.*

color, 1. *n.* couleur *f.* 2. *vb.* colorer, *tr.*

color-blind, *adj.* daltonien.

coloration, *n.* coloris *m.*

colored, *adj.* coloré, de couleur, colorié.

colorful, *adj.* coloré, pittoresque.

coloring, *n.* coloris *m.*, couleur *f.*; (skin) teint *m.*

colorless, *adj.* sans couleur, incolore, terne.

colossal, *adj.* colossal.

colt, *n.* poulain *m.*

colter, *n.* coutre *m.*

column, *n.* colonne *f.*

columnist, *n.* journaliste (qui a sa rubrique à lui) *m.*

coma, *n.* coma *m.*

comb, 1. *n.* peigne *m.* 2. *vb.* peigner.

combat, 1. *n.* combat *m.* 2. *vb.* combattre.

combatant, *adj. and n.* combattant *m.*

combative, *adj.* combatif.

combination, *n.* combinaison *f.*

combination lock, *n.* serrure *(f.)* à combinaisons.

combine, *vb.* combiner, *tr.*

combustible, *adj. and n.* combustible *m.*

combustion, *n.* combustion *f.*

come, *vb.* venir; (c. about) arriver; (c. across) rencontrer; (c. away) partir; (c. back) revenir; (c. down) descendre; (c. in) entrer; (c. off) se détacher; (c. out) sortir; (c. up) monter; (c. upon) tomber sur.

comedian, *n.* comédien *m.*

comedienne, *n.* comédienne *f.*

comedy, *n.* comédie *f.*

comely, *adj.* avenant.

comet, *n.* comète *f.*

comfort, 1. *n.* (mental) consolation *f.*; (material) confort *m.* 2. *vb.* consoler.

comfortable, *adj.* commode.

comfortably, *adv.* confortablement, commodément.

comforter, *n.* consolateur *m.*; (quilt) édredon *m.*

comfortingly, *adv.* d'une manière réconfortante.

comfortless, *adj.* sans consolation, inconsolable, désolé.

comic, comical, *adj.* comique.

comic strip, *n.* bande *(f.)* dessinée.

coming, *n.* venue *f.*, arrivée *f.*, approche *f.*

comma, *n.* virgule *f.*

command, 1. *n.* commandement *m.* 2. *vb.* commander (à).

commandeer, *vb.* réquisitionner.

commander, *n.* commandant *m.*

commander in chief, *n.* généralissime *m.*

commandment, *n.* commandement *m.*

commando, *n.* commando *m.*

commemorate, *vb.* commémorer.

commemoration, *n.* célébration *f.*, commémoration *f.*

commemorative, *adj.* commémoratif.

commence, *vb.* commencer.

commencement, *n.* (school) distribution *(f.)* des diplômes.

commend, *vb.* (entrust) recommander; (praise) louer.

commendable, *adj.* louable, recommandable.

commendably, *adv.* d'une manière louable.

commendation, *n.* louange *f.*

commensurate, *adj.* proportionné.

comment, 1. *n.* commentaire *m.* **2.** *vb.* commenter.

commentary, *n.* commentaire *m.*; reportage *m.*

commentator, *n.* commentateur *m.*

commerce, *n.* commerce *m.*

commercial, 1. *adj.* commercial. **2.** *n.* annonce (*f.*) publicitaire; spot *m.*

commercialism, *n.* commercialisme *m.*

commercialize, *vb.* commercialiser.

commercially, *adv.* commercialement.

commiserate, *vb.* plaindre, avoir pitié de.

commissary, *n.* (person) commissaire *m.*; (supply store) dépôt (*m.*) de vivres.

commission, *n.* (assignment) commande *f.*; (officer) brevet *m.*; (committee, percentage) commission *f.*

commissioner, *n.* commissaire *m.*

commit, *vb.* commettre; (c. oneself) s'engager.

commitment, *n.* engagement *m.*

committee, *n.* comité *m.*

commodious, *adj.* spacieux.

commodity, *n.* produit *m.*, commodité *f.*, denrée *f.*

common, *adj.* commun; (vulgar) vulgaire.

common law, *n.* droit coutumier *m.*

commonly, *adv.* communément, ordinairement.

Common Market, *n.* Marché (*m.*) commun.

commonness, *n.* vulgarité *f.*

commonplace, 1. *n.* lieu-commun *m.* **2.** *adj.* banal.

common sense, *n.* bon sens *m.*

commonwealth, *n.* état *m.*

commotion, *n.* agitation *f.*

communal, *adj.* communal.

commune, *n.* commune *f.*

communicable, *adj.* communicable.

communicant, *n.* communiant *m.*

communicate, *vb.* communiquer.

communication, *n.* communication *f.*

communicative, *adj.* communicatif.

communion, *n.* communion *f.*

communiqué, *n.* communiqué *m.*

communism, *n.* communisme *m.*

communist, *adj. and n.* communiste *m.f.*

communistic, *adj.* communiste.

community, *n.* communauté *f.*

commutation, *n.* commutation *f.*

commutation ticket, *n.* carte (*f.*) d'abonnement

commute, *vb.* changer; (law) commuer; faire la navette.

commuter, *n.* voyageur (*m.*) de banlieue.

compact, 1. *n.* (agreement) accord *m.*; (cosmetic) poudrier *m.* **2.** *adj.* compact.

compact disc, *n.* disque (*m.*) compact.

compact disc player, *n.* lecteur (*m.*) de disque compact.

compactness, *n.* compacité *f.*

companion, *n.* compagnon *m.*, compagne *f.*

companionable, *adj.* sociable.

companionship, *n.* camaraderie *f.*

company, *n.* compagnie *f.*

comparable with, *adj.* comparable à.

comparative, *adj. and n.* comparatif *m.*

comparatively, *adv.* comparativement, relativement.

compare, *vb.* comparer.

comparison, *n.* comparaison *f.*

compartment, *n.* compartiment *m.*

compass, *n.* (naut.) boussole *f.*; (geom.) compas *m.*

compassion, *n.* compassion *f.*

compassionate, *adj.* compatissant.

compassionately, *adv.* avec compassion.

compatible, *adj.* compatible.

compatriot, *n.* compatriote *m.f.*

compel, vb. forcer.

compelling, adj. irrésistible.

compendium, n. abrégé m., résumé m.

compensate, vb. compenser.

compensation, n. compensation f.

compensatory, adj. compensateur.

compete, vb. rivaliser.

competence, n. compétence f.

competent, adj. capable.

competently, adv. convenablement, avec compétence.

competition, n. concurrence f.

competitive, adj. concurrentiel; de compétition.

competitor, n. concurrent m.

compile, vb. compiler.

complacency, n. contentement (m.) de soi-même.

complacent, adj. content de soi-même.

complacently, adv. avec un air (un ton) suffisant.

complain, vb. se plaindre.

complainer, n. plaignant m., réclameur m.

complainingly, adv. d'une manière plaignante.

complaint, n. plainte f.

complement, n. complément m.

complementary, adj. complémentaire.

complete, adj. complet.

completely, adv. complètement, tout à fait.

completeness, n. état complet m., perfection f.

completion, n. achèvement m.

complex, adj. and n. complexe m.

complexion, n. teint m.

complexity, n. complexité f.

compliance, n. acquiescement m.

compliant, adj. complaisant, accommodant.

complicate, vb. compliquer.

complicated, adj. compliqué.

complication, n. complication f.

complicity, n. complicité f.

compliment, n. compliment m.

complimentary, adj. flatteur, de félicitation; (ticket) de faveur.

comply with, vb. se conformer à.

component, n. composant m., élément m.

comport, vb. s'accorder (avec), convenir (à).

compose, vb. composer; (c. oneself) se calmer.

composed, adj. composé, calme, tranquille.

composer, n. compositeur m.

composite, adj. composé.

composition, n. composition f.

compost, n. compost m., terreau m.

composure, n. calme m., tranquillité f., sang-froid m.

compote, n. compote f.

compound, 1. adj. and n. composé m. **2.** vb. aggraver.

compound fracture, n. fracture (f.) compliquée.

compound interest, n. interêt (m.) composé.

comprehend, vb. comprendre.

comprehensible, adj. compréhensible, intelligible.

comprehension, n. compréhension f.

comprehensive, adj. compréhensif.

compress, 1. n. compresse f. **2.** vb. comprimer, tr.

compressed, adj. comprimé.

compression, n. compression f.

compressor, n. compresseur m.

comprise, vb. comprendre.

compromise, 1. n. compromis m. **2.** vb. compromettre.

compromiser, n. comprometteur m.

compulsion, n. contrainte f.

compulsive, adj. coercitif, obligatoire; (psychological) compulsif; (liar, smoker) invétéré.

compulsory, adj. obligatoire.

compunction, n. componction f., scrupule m.

computation, n. supputation f.

compute, vb. supputer.

computer, n. ordinateur m.

computerize, vb. informatiser.

computer programmer, n. programmeur m.

computer science, n. informatique f.

comrade, n. camarade m.f.

comradeship, n. camaraderie f.

con, vb. rouler, escroquer.

concave, adj. concave.

conceal, vb. cacher.

concealment, n. action (f.) de cacher.

concede, vb. concéder.

conceit, n. vanité f.

conceited, adj. vaniteux, suffisant.

conceivable, adj. concevable.

conceivably, adv. d'une manière concevable.

conceive, vb. concevoir.

concentrate, vb. concentrer, tr.

concentration, n. concentration f.

concentration camp, n. camp (m.) de concentration.

concept, n. concept m.

conception, n. conception f.

concern, 1. n. (what pertains to one) affaire f.; (comm.) entreprise f.; (solicitude) souci m. **2.** vb. concerner; **(c. oneself with)** s'intéresser à; **(be c.ed about)** s'inquiéter de.

concerning, prep. concernant.

concert, n. concert m.

concerted, adj. concerté.

concerto, n. concerto m.

concession, n. concession f.

conciliate, vb. concilier.

conciliation, n. conciliation f.

conciliator, n. conciliateur m.

conciliatory, adj. conciliant, conciliatoire.

concise, adj. concis.

concisely, adv. avec concision, succinctement.

conciseness, n. concision f.

conclave, n. conclave m.

conclude, vb. conclure.

conclusion, n. conclusion f.

conclusive, adj. concluant.

conclusively, adv. d'une manière concluante.

concoct, vb. préparer.

concoction, n. mélange m.

concomitant, 1. adj. concomitant. **2.** n. accessoire m.

concord, n. concorde f.

concordat, n. concordat m.

concourse, n. concours m., affluence f.

concrete, 1. n. béton m. **2.** adj. concret.

concretely, adv. d'une manière concrète.

concreteness, n. état concret m.

concubine, n. concubine f.

concur, vb. (events) concourir; (persons) être d'accord.

concurrence, n. assentiment m., concours m.

concurrent, adj. concourant.

concussion, n. secousse f., ébranlement m.

condemn, vb. condamner.

condemnable, adj. condamnable.

condemnation, n. condamnation f.

condensation, n. condensation f.

condense, vb. condenser, tr.

condenser, n. condenseur m.

condescend, vb. condescendre.

condescendingly, adv. avec condescendance

condescension, n. condescendance f.

condiment, n. condiment m., assaisonnement m.

condition, 1. n. condition f. **2.** vb. conditionner.

conditional, adj. and n. conditionnel m.

conditionally, adv. conditionnellement.

conditioner, n. (hair) après-shampooing m.

condolence, n. condoléance f.

condole with, vb. faire ses condoléances à.

condom, n. préservatif m.

condominium, n. condominium m.

condone, vb. approuver (tacitement).

conducive, adj. favorable.

conduct, 1. n. conduite f. **2.** vb. conduire.

conductivity, n. conductivité f.

conductor, n. conducteur m.; (bus) receveur m.; (rail) chef (m.) de train; (music) chef (m.) d'orchestre.

conduit, n. conduit m., tuyau m.

cone, n. cône m.

confection, n. confection f.; (sweet) bonbon m.

confectioner, n. confiseur m.

confectionery, n. confiserie f.

confederacy, confederation, n. confédération f.

confederate, *adj. and n.* confédéré *m.*

confer, *vb.* conférer.

conference, *n.* (meeting) entretien *m.;* (congress) congrès *m.*

confess, *vb.* avouer; *(eccles.)* confesser, *tr.*

confession, *n.* confession *f.*

confessional, *n.* confessional *m.*

confessor, *n.* confesseur *m.*

confetti, *n.* confetti *m.*

confidant, *n.* confident *m.*

confidante, *n.* confidente *f.*

confide, *vb.* confier (à), *tr.*

confidence, *n.* (trust) confiance *f.;* (secret) confidence *f.*

confident, *adj.* confiant.

confidential, *adj.* confidentiel.

confidentially, *adv.* confidentiellement.

confidently, *adv.* avec confiance.

configure, *vb.* (computer) configurer.

confine, *vb.* (banish) confiner; (limit) limiter.

confinement, *n.* détention *f.*

confirm, *vb.* confirmer.

confirmation, *n.* confirmation *f.*

confirmed, *adj.* invétéré, incorrigible.

confiscate, *vb.* confisquer.

confiscation, *n.* confiscation *f.*

conflagration, *n.* conflagration *f.,* incendie *m.*

conflict, *n.* conflit *m.*

conflicting, *adj.* contradictoire.

conform, *vb.* conformer, *tr.*

conformation, *n.* conformation *f.,* conformité *f.*

conformer, *n.* conformiste *m.*

conformist, *n.* conformiste *m.*

conformity, *n.* conformité *f.*

confound, *vb.* confondre; **(c. him!)** que le diable l'emporte!

confront, *vb.* confronter.

confrontation, *n.* confrontation *f.*

confuse, *vb.* confondre.

confusing, *adj.* peu clair.

confusion, *n.* confusion *f.*

congeal, *vb.* congeler, *tr.*

congealment, *n.* congélation *f.*

congenial, *adj.* (person) sympathique; (thing) convenable.

congenital, *adj.* congénital.

congenitally, *adv.* d'une manière congénitale.

congested, *adj.* (area) surpeuplé; (road) bloqué; (medical) congestionné.

congestion, *n.* *(med.)* congestion *f.;* (traffic) encombrement *m.*

conglomerate, *adj.* conglomeré.

conglomeration, *n.* conglomération *f.*

congratulate, *vb.* féliciter (de).

congratulation, *n.* félicitation *f.*

congratulatory, *adj.* de félicitation.

congregate, *vb.* rassembler, *tr.*

congregation, *n.* assemblée *f.*

congress, *n.* congrès *m.*

congressional, *adj.* congressionnel.

congressman, -woman, *n.* membre *(m.)* du congrès.

conic, *adj.* conique.

conjecture, *n.* conjecture *f.*

conjugal, *adj.* conjugal.

conjugate, *vb.* conjuguer.

conjugation, *n.* conjugaison *f.*

conjunction, *n.* conjonction *f.*

conjunctive, *adj.* conjonctif.

conjunctivitis, *n.* conjonctivite *f.*

conjure, *vb.* conjurer.

conk, *vb.* **(c. out)** (colloquial) tomber en panne.

con man, *n.* arnaqueur *m.*

connect, *vb.* joindre.

connection, *n.* connexion *f.;* (social) relations *f.pl.;* (train) correspondance *f.*

connivance, *n.* connivence *f.*

connive, *vb.* conniver (à).

connoisseur, *n.* connaisseur *m.*

connotation, *n.* connotation *f.*

connote, *vb.* signifier, vouloir dire.

connubial, *adj.* conjugal, du mariage.

conquer, *vb.* conquérir.

conquerable, *adj.* qui peut être vaincu, domptable.

conqueror, *n.* conquérant *m.*

conquest, *n.* conquête *f.*

conscience, *n.* conscience *f.*

conscientious, *adj.* consciencieux.

conscientiously, *adv.* consciencieusement.

conscious, *adj.* conscient.

consciously, adv. sciemment, en parfaite connaissance.
consciousness, n. conscience f.
conscript, adj. and n. conscrit m.
conscription, n. conscription f.
consecrate, vb. consacrer.
consecration, n. consécration f.
consecutive, adj. consécutif.
consecutively, adv. consécutivement, de suite.
consensus, n. consensus m., assentiment général m.
consent, 1. n. consentement m. **2.** vb. consentir.
consequence, n. conséquence f.
consequent, adj. conséquent.
consequential, adj. conséquent, logique.
consequently, adv. par conséquent.
conservation, n. conservation f.; (c. area) zone (f.) classée.
conservationist, n. défenseur (m.) de l'environnement.
conservatism, n. conservatisme m.
conservative, adj. (politics) conservateur; (comm.) prudent.
conservatively, adv. d'une manière conservatrice.
conservatory, n. conservatoire f.
conserve, vb. conserver.
consider, vb. considérer.
considerable, adj. considérable.
considerably, adv. considérablement.
considerate, adj. prévenant, attentionné.
considerately, adv. avec égards, avec indulgence.
consideration, n. considération f.
considering, prep. vu que, attendu que.
consign, vb. consigner.
consignment, n. expédition f., consignation f.
consistency, n. consistance f.
consistent, adj. consistant; (c. with) conforme à.
consist of, vb. consister en.
consolation, n. consolation f.
console, vb. consoler.
consolidate, vb. consolider.
consommé, n. consommé m.
consonant, n. consonne f.

consort, 1. n. compagnon m., époux m. **2.** vb. s'associer (à).
conspicuous, adj. en évidence.
conspicuously, adv. visiblement, éminemment.
conspicuousness, n. éclat m., position éminente f.
conspiracy, n. conspiration f.
conspirator, n. conspirateur m.
conspire, vb. conspirer.
conspirer, n. conspirateur m.
constancy, n. constance f., fermeté f.
constant, adj. constant.
constantly, adv. constamment.
constellation, n. constellation f.
consternation, n. consternation f.
constipate, vb. constiper.
constipation, n. constipation f.
constituency, n. circonscription électorale f.
constituent, adj. constituant.
constitute, vb. constituer.
constitution, n. constitution f.
constitutional, adj. constitutionnel.
constrain, vb. contraindre.
constrained, adj. contraint.
constraint, n. contrainte f., gêne f.
constrict, vb. resserrer.
constriction, n. resserrement f.
construct, vb. construire.
construction, n. construction f.
constuction worker, n. ouvrier (m.) de bâtiment.
constructive, adj. constructif.
constructively, adv. constructivement, par induction.
constructor, n. constructeur m.
construe, vb. interpréter.
consul, n. consul m.
consular, adj. consulaire.
consulate, n. consulat m.
consult, vb. consulter.
consultant, n. conseiller m., consultant m.
consultation, n. consultation f.
consume, vb. consommer.
consumer, n. consommateur m.
consumer goods, n. biens (m.pl.) de consommation.
consumerism, n. protection (f.) des consommateurs.
consummate, 1. adj. consommé. **2.** vb. consommer.

consummation, n. consommation f.

consumption, n. consommation f.; (med.) phtisie f.

consumptive, adj. poitrinaire, tuberculeux.

contact, n. contact m.

contact lenses, n. lentilles (f.pl.) (de contact), verres (m.pl.) de contact.

contagion, n. contagion f.

contagious, adj. contagieux.

contain, vb. contenir.

container, n. récipient m.

contaminate, vb. contaminer.

contaminated, adj. contaminé.

contamination, n. contamination f.

contemplate, vb. contempler.

contemplation, n. contemplation f.

contemplative, adj. contemplatif.

contemporary, adj. contemporain.

contempt, n. mépris m.

contemptible, adj. méprisable.

contemptuous, adj. méprisant.

contemptuously, adv. avec mépris, dédaigneusement.

contend, vb. (struggle) lutter; (maintain) soutenir.

contender, n. compétiteur m.

content, n. (satisfaction) contentement m.; (c.s) contenu m.

contented with, adj. content de.

contention, n. contention f., lutte f.

contentment, n. contentement m.

contents, n.pl. (of text) contenu m.; (table of c.) table (f.) des matières.

contest, 1. n. (struggle) lutte f.; (competition) concours m. **2.** vb. contester.

contestable, adj. contestable.

contestant, n. concurrent m., disputant m.

context, n. contexte m.

contiguous, adj. contigu m., contiguë f.

continence, n. continence f., retenue f.

continent, adj. and n. continent m.

continental, adj. continental.

contingency, n. contingence f.; (c. plan) plan (m.) d'urgence.

contingent, adj. contingent; **(be c. upon)** dépendre de.

continual, adj. continuel.

continuance, n. continuation f.

continuation, n. continuation f.; (of story) suite f.; (after interruption) reprise f.

continue, vb. continuer.

continuity, n. continuité f.

continuous, adj. continu.

continuously, adv. continûment, sans interruption.

contort, vb. tordre, défigurer.

contortion, n. torsion f.; contorsion f.

contortionist, n. contortionniste m.f.

contour, n. contour m.

contraband, n. contrebande f.

contraception, n. limitation des naissances f., contraception f.

contraceptive, n. contraceptif m.

contract, 1. n. contrat m. **2.** vb. contracter, tr.

contracted, adj. contracté, resserré.

contraction, n. contraction f.

contractor, n. entrepreneur m.

contradict, vb. contredire.

contradictable, adj. qui peut être contredit f.

contradiction, n. contradiction f., démenti m.

contradictory, adj. contradictoire.

contraption, n. machin m.

contrary, adj. and n. contraire m.; **(on the c.)** au contraire.

contrast, 1. n. contraste m. **2.** vb. mettre en contraste, tr.; contraster, intr.

contravene, vb. contrevenir à.

contribute, vb. contribuer.

contribution, n. contribution f.

contributive, adj. contributif.

contributor, n. contribuant m.

contributory, adj. contribuant.

contrite, adj. contrit, pénitent.

contrition, n. contrition f.

contrivance, n. combinaison f., invention f., artifice m.

contrive, vb. inventer, imaginer, arranger.

control, 1. n. autorité f.; (machinery) commande f. **2.** vb. gouverner; (check) contrôler.

controllable, *adj.* vérifiable, gouvernable.
controller, *n.* contrôleur *m.*
control panel, *n.* tableau *(m.)* de commande.
control room, *n.* salle *(f.)* des commandes.
controversial, *adj.* de controverse, polémique.
controversy, *n.* controverse *f.*
contusion, *n.* contusion *f.*
conundrum, *n.* devinette *f.*, énigme *f.*
convalescence, *n.* convalescence *f.*
convalescent, *adj.* convalescent.
convector, *n.* radiateur *m.* (à convexion).
convene, *vb.* assembler, *tr.*
convenience, *n.* convenance *f.*; (comfort) commodité *f.*
convenient, *adj.* commode.
conveniently, *adv.* commodément.
convent, *n.* couvent *m.*
convention, *n.* convention *f.*
conventional, *adj.* conventionnel.
conventionally, *adv.* par convention.
converge, *vb.* converger.
convergence, *n.* convergence *f.*
convergent, *adj.* convergent.
conversant, *adj.* versé (dans), familier (avec).
conversation, *n.* conversation *f.*
conversational, *adj.* de conversation.
conversationalist, *n.* causeur *m.*
converse, **1.** *vb.* converser. **2.** *adj and n.* inverse.
conversely, *adv.* réciproquement.
conversion, *n.* conversion *f.*
convert, *vb.* convertir, *tr.*
converter, *n.* convertisseur *m.*
convertible, *adj.* convertible (of things), convertissable (of persons), décapotable (of car).
convex, *adj.* convexe.
convey, *vb.* (transport) transporter; (transmit) transmettre.
conveyance, *n.* transport *m.*
conveyor, *n.* transporteur *m.*, conducteur (électrique) *m.*; **(c. belt)** tapis (*m.*) roulant.
convict, **1.** *n.* forçat *m.* **2.** *vb.* condamner.
conviction, *n.* (condemnation) condamnation *f.*; (persuasion) conviction *f.*
convince, *vb.* convaincre.
convincing, *adj.* convaincant.
convincingly, *adv.* d'une manière convaincante.
convivial, *adj.* jovial, joyeux.
convocation, *n.* convocation *f.*
convoke, *vb.* convoquer.
convoluted, *adj.* compliqué.
convoy, *n.* convoi *m.*
convulse, *vb.* convulser, bouleverser.
convulsion, *n.* convulsion *f.*
convulsive, *adj.* convulsif.
coo, *vb.* roucouler.
cook, **1.** *n.* cuisinier *m.* **2.** *vb.* cuire, *intr.*; faire cuire, *tr.*
cookbook, *n.* livre *(m.)* de cuisine.
cookie, *n.* gâteau sec *m.*
cooking, *n.* cuisine *f.*
cool, **1.** *adj.* frais *m.*, fraîche *f.* **2.** *vb.* rafraîchir.
cooler, *n.* rafraîchissoir *m.*, réfrigérant *m.*, (motor) radiateur *m.*
coolness, *n.* fraîcheur *f.*
coop, **1.** *n.* cage (*f.*) à poules. **2.** *vb.* (c. up) enfermer.
cooperate, *vb.* coopérer.
cooperation, *n.* coopération *f.*
cooperative, **1.** *n.* coopérative *f.* **2.** *adj.* coopératif.
cooperatively, *adv.* d'une manière coopérative.
co-opt, *vb.* coopter.
coordinate, *vb.* coordonner.
coordination, *n.* coordination *f.*
coordinator, *n.* coordinateur *m.*
co-ownership, *n.* copropriété *f.*
cop, **1.** *n.* (slang) flic *m.* **2.** *vb.* (colloquial) attraper, pincer.
cope with, *vb.* tenir tête à.
copier, *n.* machine à copier *f.*
copious, *adj.* copieux.
copiously, *adv.* copieusement.
copiousness, *n.* abondance *f.*
copper, *n.* cuivre *m.*
copperplate, *n.* cuivre plané *m.*; taille-douce *f.*
copulate, *vb.* s'accoupler.
copy, **1.** *n.* (duplicate) copie *f.*; (book) exemplaire *m.* **2.** *vb.* copier.
copyist, *n.* copiste *m.*, imitateur *m.*
copyright, *n.* droit *(m.)* d'auteur.

coquetry, n. coquetterie f.
coquette, n. coquette f.
coral, n. corail m.; pl. coraux.
cord, n. corde f.
cordial, adj. and n. cordial m.
cordiality, n. cordialité f.
cordially, adv. cordialement.
cordon, n. cordon m.
cordovan, adj. cordovan.
corduroy, n. velours côtelé m.
core, n. cœur m.
coriander, n. coriandre.
cork, n. (botany) liège m.; (stopper) bouchon m.
corkscrew, n. tire-bouchon m.
corn, n. maïs m.; (c. on the cob) épi (m.) de maïs.
cornea, n. cornée f.
corner, n. coin m.
cornerstone, n. pierre angulaire f.
cornet, n. cornet m.
cornetist, n. cornettiste m.
cornstarch, n. farine (f.) de maïs.
cornice, n. corniche f.
cornucopia, n. corne (f.) d'abondance.
corny, adj. rebattu.
corollary, n. corollaire m.
coronary, adj. coronaire.
coronation, n. couronnement m.
coroner, n. coroner m.
coronet, n. (petite) couronne f.
corporal, n. (mil.) caporal m.
corporate, adj. de corporation.
corporation, n. société f. (anonyme).
corps, n. corps m.
corpse, n. cadavre m.
corpulent, adj. corpulent, gros.
corpuscle, n. corpuscule m.
corral, n. corral m.
correct, 1. adj. correct. 2. vb. corriger.
correction, n. correction f.
corrective, 1. adj. correctif. 2. n. correctif m.
correctly, adv. correctement, justement.
correctness, n. correction f.
correlate, vb. être en corrélation, intr.; mettre en corrélation, tr.
correlation, n. corrélation f.
correspond, vb. correspondre.
correspondence, n. correspondance f.

correspondent, n. correspondant m.
corridor, n. couloir m.
corroborate, vb. corroborer.
corroboration, n. corroboration f., confirmation f.
corroborative, adj. corroboratif.
corrode, vb. corroder.
corrosion, n. corrosion f.
corrosive, adj. corrosif.
corrugate, vb. rider, plisser.
corrugated, adj. ondulé.
corrupt, 1. adj. corrompu. 2. vb. corrompre.
corruptible, adj. corruptible.
corruption, n. corruption f.
corruptive, adj. corruptif.
corsage, n. corsage m.
corset, n. corset m.
Corsica, n. Corse f.
cortege, n. cortège m.
cortisone, n. cortisone f.
corvette, n. corvette f.
cosmetic, adj. and n. cosmétique m.
cosmic, adj. cosmique.
cosmic rays, n. rayons cosmiques m.pl.
cosmonaut, n. cosmonaute m.f.
cosmopolitan, adj. and n. cosmopolite m.f.
cosmos, n. cosmos m.
Cossack, n. cosaque m.
cost, 1. n. coût m. 2. vb. coûter.
costliness, n. haut prix m., somptuosité f.
cost-effective, adj. rentable.
cost price, n. prix (m.) de revient.
co-star, n. partenaire m.f.
costly, adj. coûteux.
costume, n. costume m.
costume jewelry, n. bijoux (m.pl.) de fantaisie.
costumer, n. costumier m.
cot, n. (berth) couchette f.; (folding) lit-cage m.
coterie, n. coterie f., clique f.
cotillion, n. cotillon m.
cottage, n. chaumière f.
cottage industry, n. activité (f.) artisanale.
cotton, n. coton m.
cottonseed, n. graine (f.) de coton.
couch, n. divan m.

cougar, *n.* couguar *m.*

cough, 1. *n.* toux *f.* **2.** *vb.* tousser.

could, *vb.* pouvait, pourrait.

council, *n.* conseil *m.*

councilman, -woman, *n.* conseiller *m.*, conseillère *f.*

counsel, 1. *n.* conseil *m.* **2.** *vb.* conseiller.

counselor, *n.* conseiller *m.*

count, **1.** *n.* (calculation) compte *m.*; (title) comte *m.* **2.** *vb.* compter; **(c. on)** compter sur.

countenance, *n.* expression *f.*

counter, 1. *n.* (shop) comptoir *m.* **2.** *adv.* **(c. to)** à l'encontre de.

counteract, *vb.* neutraliser.

counterattack, *n.* action contraire *f.*

counterattack, 1. *n.* contre-attaque *f.* **2.** *vb.* contreattaquer.

counterbalance, 1. *n.* contrepoids *m.* **2.** *vb.* contre-balancer.

counterclockwise, *adj. and adv.* dans le sens inverse des aiguilles d'une montre.

counterfeit, 1. *adj.* (money) faux *m.*, fausse *f.* **2.** *vb.* contrefaire.

countermand, *vb.* contremander.

counteroffensive, *n.* contre-offensive *f.*

counterpart, *n.* contre-partie *f.*, homologue *m.*

counterproductive, *adj.* qui produit l'effet contraire.

countersign, *vb.* contresigner.

countess, *n.* comtesse *f.*

countless, *adj.* innombrable.

country, *n.* (nation) pays *m.*; (opposed to town) campagne *f.*; (native c.) patrie *f.*

countryman, *n.* (of same c.) compatriote *m.f.*; (rustic) campagnard *m.*

countryside, *n.* campagne *f.*

county, *n.* comté *m.*

coupé, *n.* coupé *m.*

couple, 1. *n.* couple *f.* **2.** *vb.* coupler.

coupon, *n.* coupon *m.*

courage, *n.* courage *m.*

courageous, *adj.* courageux.

courier, *n.* courrier *m.*

course, *n.* cours *m.*; **(of c.)** bien entendu; (route) route *f.*; (meal) service *m.*

court, 1. *n.* cour *f.*; (tennis) court. **2.** *vb.* faire la cour à.

courteous, *adj.* courtois.

courtesy, *n.* courtoisie *f.*

courthouse, *n.* palais (*m.*) de justice.

courtier, *n.* courtisan *m.*

courtly, *adj.* de cour, élégant, courtois.

courtmartial, *n.* conseil (*m.*) de guerre.

courtroom, *n.* salle (*f.*) d'audience.

courtship, *n.* cour *f.*

courtyard, *n.* cour *f.*

cousin, *n.* cousin *m.*, cousine *f.*

cove, *n.* anse *f.*, crique *f.*

covenant, *n.* pacte *m.*

cover, 1. *n.* (book, comm., blanket) couverture *f.*; (pot) couvercle *m.*; (shelter) abri *m.*; (envelope) pli *m.*; (mil.) couvert *m.* **2.** *vb.* couvrir.

coverage, *n.* couverture *f.*

coveralls, *n.* bleus (*m.pl.*) de travail.

cover charge, *n.* couvert *m.*

covering, *n.* couverture *f.*, enveloppe *f.*

covert, *adj.* secret; voilé.

cover-up, *n.* tentative (*f.*) pour étouffer une affaire.

covet, *vb.* convoiter.

covetous, *adj.* avide, avaricieux.

cow, *n.* vache *f.*

coward, *n.* and *n.* lâche *m.f.*

cowardice, *n.* lâcheté *f.*

cowardly, *adv.* lâche.

cowboy, *n.* cowboy *m.*

cower, *vb.* se blottir.

cow hand, *n.* vacher *m.*

cowhide, *n.* peau (*f.*) de vache.

cowshed, *n.* étable *f.*

coxswain, *n.* patron (*m.*) de chaloupe, barreur *m.*

coy, *adj.* faussement timide.

cozy, *adj.* confortable, douillet.

crab, 1. *n.* crabe *m.* **2.** *vb.* rouspéter.

crab apple, *n.* pomme sauvage *f.*

crack, 1. *n.* (fissure) fente *f.*; (noise) craquement *m.* **2.** *vb. tr.* (glass, china) fêler; (nuts) casser; (noise) faire craquer. **3.** *vb. intr.* (split) se fendiller; (noise) craquer.

cracked, adj. fendu, fêlé.

cracker, n. biscuit m.

cracking, n. craquement m., claquement m.

crackle, 1. n. crépitement m. **2.** vb. crépiter.

crackup, n. crach m.

cradle, n. berceau m.

craft, n. (skill) habileté f.; (trade) métier m.; (boat) embarcation f.

craftsman, n. artisan m.

craftsmanship, n. habileté f., technique f., art m.

crafty, adj. rusé, astucieux.

crag, n. rocher à pic m., rocher escarpé m.

cram, vb. remplir, farcir.

cramp, n. (med.) crampe f.; (mechanical) crampon m.

cranberry, n. canneberge f., airelle f.

crane, n. grue f.

cranium, n. crâne m.

crank, n. manivelle f.

cranky, adj. d'humeur difficile.

cranny, n. crevasse f., fente f.

craps, n. (slang) jeu de dés m.

crapshooter, n. (slang) joueur aux dés m.

crash, 1. n. (noise) fracas m.; (accident) accident m. **2.** vb. tomber avec fracas, intr.

crash landing, n. atterrissage (m.) forcé.

crass, adj. grossier.

crate, n. caisse f.

crater, n. cratère m.

crave, vb. désirer ardemment.

craven, adj. lâche, poltron.

craving, n. désir ardent m., besoin impérieux m.

crawl, vb. (reptiles) ramper; (persons) se traîner.

crayfish, n. (freshwater) écrevisse f.; (saltwater) langouste f.

crayon, n. pastel m., crayon m.

craze, n. engouement m.

crazed, adj. fou, dément.

crazy, adj. fou m., folle f.

creak, vb. grincer.

creaky, adj. qui crie, qui grince.

cream, n. crème f.

cream cheese, n. fromage (m.) frais.

creamery, n. crèmerie f.

creamy, adj. crémeux, de crème.

crease, 1. n. pli m. **2.** vb. froisser, tr.

create, vb. créer.

creation, n. création f.

creative, adj. créateur m., créatrice f.

creator, n. créateur m., créatrice f.

creature, n. créature f.

credence, n. créance f., croyance f.

credentials, n. lettres (f.pl.) de créance; (student, servant) certificat m.

credibility, n. crédibilité f.

credible, adj. croyable.

credit, n. crédit m.; (merit) honneur m.

creditable, adj. estimable.

creditably, adv. honorablement.

credit card, n. carte (f.) de crédit.

creditor, n. créancier m.

credo, n. credo m.

credulity, n. crédulité f.

credulous, adj. crédule.

creed, n. (belief) croyance f., (theology) credo m.

creek, n. ruisseau m.

creep, vb. (reptiles, insects, plants) ramper; (persons) se glisser.

creepy, adj. qui fait frissonner.

cremate, vb. incinérer.

crematorium, n. four (m.) crématoire.

crematory, n. crématorium m.

Creole, n. créole m.f.

creosote, n. créosote f.

crepe, n. crêpe m.

crescent, n. croissant m.

crest, n. crête f.

crestfallen, adj. abattu, découragé.

Crete, n. Crète f.

cretin, n. crétin m.

cretonne, n. cretonne f.

crevice, n. crevasse f.

crew, n. (boat) équipage m.; (gang) équipe f.

crew cut, n. les cheveux (m.pl.) en brosse.

crib, n. (child's bed) lit (m.) d'enfant; (manger) mangeoire f.

cricket, n. (insect) grillon m.; (game) cricket m.

crier, n. crieur m., huissier m.

crime, n. crime m.

criminal, adj. criminel.

criminologist, n. criminologue m.f.

criminology, n. criminologie f.

crimson, adj. and n. cramoisi m.

cringe, vb. faire des courbettes, se tapir, s'humilier.

crinkle, 1. n. pli m.; sinuosité f. 2. vb. serpenter, former en zigzag.

cripple, 1. n. estropié m. 2. vb. estropier.

crisis, n. crise f.

crisp, adj. (food) croquant; (manner) tranchant.

crispness, n. frisure f.

crisscross, 1. adj. and adv. entrecroisé. 2. vb. (s')entrecroiser.

criterion, n. critérium f.

critic, n. critique m.

critical, adj. critique.

criticism, n. critique f.

criticize, vb. critiquer.

critique, n. critique f.

croak, vb. (frogs) coasser; (crows, persons) croasser.

Croatia, n. Croatie f.

crochet, 1. vb. broder au crochet. 2. n. crochet m.

crock, n. pot (m.) de terre.

crockery, n. faïence f.

crocodile, n. crocodile m.

crocodile tears, n. larmes (f.pl.) de crocodile.

croissant, n. croissant m.

crone, n. vieille femme f.

crony, n. vieux camarade m., compère m.

crook, n. escroc m.; (thief) voleur m.

crooked, adj. tortu.

croon, vb. chantonner, fredonner.

crop, 1. n. (farming) récolte f. 2. vb. (c. up) surgir.

croquet, n. (jeu de) croquet m.

croquette, n. croquette f.

cross, 1. n. croix f. 2. adj. maussade. 3. vb. croiser, tr.; (c. oneself) se signer; (c. out) rayer; (go across) traverser.

crossbreed, n. race croisée f.

cross-examine, vb. contreexaminer.

cross-eyed, adj. louche.

cross-fertilization, n. croisement m.

crossfire, n. feux croisés m.pl.

cross-purpose, n. opposition f., contradiction f., malentendu m.

cross section, n. coupe (f.) en travers.

crossword puzzle, n. mots croisés m.pl.

crotch, n. (tree) fourche f.; (trousers) fourchet m.

crouch, vb. s'accroupir.

croup, n. croupe f.; (med.) croup m.

croupier, n. croupier m.

crouton, n. crouton m.

crow, 1. n. (bird) corneille f.; (cock-c.) chant (m.) du coq. 2. vb. chanter.

crowd, 1. n. foule f. 2. vb. serrer, tr.; (c. with) remplir de.

crowded, adj. (streets, etc.) encombré.

crown, 1. n. couronne f.; (of head) sommet m.; (of hat) calotte f. 2. vb. couronner.

crown prince, n. prince héritier m.

crow's-foot, n. patte d'oie (near the eye) f.; (naut.) araignée f.

crucial, adj. crucial.

crucible, n. creuset m.

crucifix, n. crucifix m.

crucifixion, n. crucifixion f., crucifiement m.

crucify, vb. crucifier.

crude, adj. (unpolished) grossier; (metals, etc.) brut.

crudeness, n. crudité f.

cruel, adj. cruel.

cruelty, n. cruauté f.

cruet, n. burette f.

cruise, n. croisière f.

cruiser, n. croiseur f.

crumb, n. (small piece) miette f.; (not crust) mie f.

crumble, vb. émietter, tr.

crumple, vb. chiffonner, tr.

crunch, 1. vb. croquer, broyer. 2. n. grincement m.

crusade, n. croisade f.

crusader, n. croisé m.

crush, 1. vb. écraser. 2. n. presse f., foule f.; (a c. on) le béguin pour.

crust, n. croûte f.

crustacean, adj. crustacé.

crusty, adj. couvert d'une croûte; (fig.) bourru, maussade.

crutch, n. béquille f.

cry, 1. n. cri m. **2.** vb. (shout) crier; (weep) pleurer.

crybaby, n. pleurnicheur m.

crying, adj. criant.

cryosurgery, n. cryochirurgie f.

crypt, n. crypte f.

cryptic, adj. occulte, secret.

cryptography, n. cryptographie f.

crystal, n. cristal m.

crystalline, adj. cristallin.

crystallize, vb. cristalliser, tr.

cub, n. petit m. (d'un animal).

Cuba, n. Cuba m.

Cuban, 1. n. Cubain m. **2.** adj. cubain.

cubbyhole, n. retraite f., cachette f., placard m.

cube, n. cube m.

cubic, adj. cubique.

cubicle, n. compartiment m., cabine f.

cubic measure, n. mesures (f.pl.) de volume.

cubism, n. cubisme m.

cuckold, 1. n. cocu m. **2.** vb. cocufier, faire cocu.

cuckoo, n. coucou m.; (fig.) niais m.

cucumber, n. concombre m.

cud, n. bol alimentaire m., panse f., chique (of tobacco) m.

cuddle, vb. serrer (dans ses bras), tr.

cudgel, 1. n. bâton m., gourdin m., trique f. **2.** vb. bâtonner.

cue, n. (theater) réplique f.; (hint) mot m.

cuff, n. poignet m.

cuff link, n. bouton (m.) de manchette.

cuisine, n. cuisine f.

cul-de-sac, n. cul de sac m., impasse f.

culinary, adj. culinaire, de cuisine.

cull, vb. cueillir, recueillir.

culminate, vb. culminer.

culmination, n. point culminant m.

culpable, adj. coupable.

culprit, n. coupable m.f.

cult, n. culte m.

cultivate, vb. cultiver.

cultivated, adj. cultivé.

cultivation, n. culture f.

cultivator, n. cultivateur m.

cultural, adj. culturel.

culture, n. culture f.

cumbersome, adj. encombrant.

cumulative, adj. cumulatif.

cunning, 1. n. (guile) ruse f.; (skill) adresse f. **2.** adj. rusé; (attractive) charmant.

cup, n. tasse f.

cupboard, n. armoire f.

cupidity, n. cupidité f.

curable, adj. guérissable.

curator, n. conservateur m.

curb, 1. n. (horse) gourmette f.; (pavement) bord m. **2.** vb. (horse) gourmer; (fig.) brider.

curbstone, n. garde-pavé m.

curd, n. lait caillé m.

curdle, vb. cailler.

cure, 1. n. (healing) guérison f.; (remedy) remède m. **2.** vb. guérir.

curfew, n. couvre-feu m.

curio, n. curiosité f.

curiosity, n. curiosité f.

curious, adj. curieux.

curl, 1. n. boucle f. **2.** vb. friser.

curler, n. bigoudi m.

curly, adj. frisé.

currant, n. groseille f.

currency, n. monnaie f.

current, 1. adj. and n. courant m.

current affairs, n. actualités f.pl.

currently, adv. actuellement.

curriculum, n. programme (m.) d'études., plan (m.) d'études.

curry, 1. n. (food) cari m. **2.** vb. (c. favor with) chercher à s'attirer les bonnes grâces de.

curse, 1. n. (malediction) malédiction f.; (oath) juron m.; (scourge) fléau m. **2.** vb. maudire; (swear) jurer.

cursed, adj. maudit.

cursor, n. curseur m.

cursory, adj. rapide, superficiel.

curt, adj. brusque.

curtail, vb. raccourcir.

curtain, n. rideau m.

curtsy, n. révérence f.

curvature, n. courbure f.

curve, 1. n. courbe f. **2.** vb. courber, tr.

cushion, n. coussin m.

cuspidor, n. crachoir m.

custard, n. crème f.

custodian, n. gardien m.
custody, n. (care) garde f.; (arrest) détention f.
custom, n. coutume f.
customary, adj. habituel.
customer, n. client m.
customize, vb. personnaliser.
customized, adj. fait sur demande.
custom-made, adj. fait sur mesure.
customs, n. douane f.
customs-officer, n. douanier m.
cut, 1. n. (wound) coupure f.; (clothes, hair) coupe f.; (reduction) réduction f. **2.** vb. couper.
cutaneous, adj. cutané.
cute, adj. gentil m., gentille f.
cut glass, n. cristal m.
cuticle, n. cuticule f.
cutlery, n. coutellerie f.
cutlet, n. côtelette f.
cutout, n. découpage m., coupe f.
cutter, n. coupeur m., coupeuse f.
cutthroat, n. coupe-jarret m.
cutting, 1. n. incision f. **2.** adj. incisif, tranchant.
cyanide, n. cyanure m.
cybernetics, n. cybernétique f.
cyclamate, n. cyclamate m.
cycle, 1. n. cycle m. **2.** vb. faire de la bicyclette.
cyclist, n. cycliste m.
cyclone, n. cyclone m.
cyclotron, n. cyclotron m.
cylinder, n. cylindre m.
cylindrical, adj. cylindrique.
cymbal, n. cymbale f.
cynic, n. cynique m.
cynical, adj. cynique.
cynicism, n. cynisme m.
cypress, n. cyprès m.
czar, n. tsar m.
Czechoslovakie, n. Tchécoslovaquie f.
cyst, n. kyste m.

D

dab, 1. n. coup léger m., tape f. **2.** vb. toucher légèrement.
dabble, vb. humecter, faire l'amateur.
dad, n. papa m.
daddy, n. papa m.
daffodil, n. narcisse m.
daffy, adj. niais, sot.
dagger, n. poignard m.
dahlia, n. dahlia m.
daily, adj. quotidien.
daintiness, n. délicatesse f.
dainty, adj. délicat.
dairy, n. laiterie f.
dairyman, n. crémier m.
dais, n. estrade f.
daisy, n. marguerite f.
dale, n. vallon m., vallée f.
dam, n. digue f.
damage, 1. n. dommage m. **2.** vb. endommager.
damaging, adj. nuisible.
damask, n. damas m.
damnation, n. damnation f.
damp, adj. humide.
dampen, vb. humecter.
dampness, n. humidité f., moiteur f.
damsel, n. demoiselle f., jeune fille f.
dance, 1. n. danse f. **2.** vb. danser.
dancer, n. danseur m.
dandelion, n. pissenlit m.
dandruff, n. pellicules f.pl.
dandy, 1. n. dandy m. **2.** adj. élégant.
Dane, n. Danois m.
danger, n. danger m.
dangerous, adj. dangereux.
dangle, vb. pendiller, intr.
Danish, 1. n. Danois m. **2.** adj. danois.
dank, adj. humide et froid.
dapper, adj. pimpant, petit et vif.
dappled, adj. pommelé.
dare, vb. oser.
daredevil, n. casse-cou m.
daring, adj. audacieux.
dark, adj. sombre.
darken, vb. obscurcir, tr.
dark horse, n. tocard m.
darkness, n. obscurité f.
darkroom, n. chambre noire f.
darling, adj. and n. chéri m.
darn, 1. n. reprise f. **2.** vb. repriser.
darning needle, n. aiguille à repriser f.

dart, 1. *n.* dard *m.*; (sewing) pince *f.* **2.** *vb.* se précipiter.

dash, 1. *n.* (energy) fougue *f.*; (pen) trait *m.* **2.** *vb.* (throw) lancer; (destroy) détruire; (rush) se précipiter.

dashboard, *n.* tableau *(m.)* de bord.

dashing, *adj.* fougueux, brillant, superbe.

data, *n.* données *f.pl.*

database, *n.* base *(f.)* de données.

data processing, *n.* élaboration *f.*, traitement *(m.)* de données.

date, 1. *n.* date *f.*; (appointment) rendez-vous *m.*; (fruit) datte *f.* **2.** *vb.* dater.

dated, *adj.* démodé.

date line, *n.* ligne *(f.)* de changement de date.

daub, 1. *n.* barbouillage *m.* **2.** *vb.* barbouiller.

daughter, *n.* fille *f.*

daughter-in-law, *n.* belle-fille *f.*

daunt, *vb.* intimider.

dauntless, *adj.* intrépide, indomptable.

dauntlessly, *adv.* d'une manière intrépide.

davenport, *n.* divan *m.*

dawdle, *vb.* flâner, muser.

dawn, *n.* aube *f.*

day, *n.* jour *m.*; (span of day) journée *f.*

day care, *n.* garderie *f.*

daydream, *n.* rêverie *f.*

daylight, *n.* lumière *(f.)* du jour.

daylight-saving time, *n.* l'heure *(f.)* d'été.

daytime, *n.* jour *m.* journée *f.*

daze, *vb.* étourdir.

dazzle, *vb.* éblouir.

deacon, *n.* diacre *m.*

dead, *adj.* mort.

deaden, *vb.* amortir.

dead end, *n.* cul-de-sac *m.*, impasse *f.*

dead letter, *n.* lettre morte *f.*

deadline, *n.* ligne *(f.)* de délimitation, date *(f.)* de limite.

deadlock, *n.* impasse *f.*

deadly, *adj.* mortel.

deadpan, *adj.* impassible.

deadwood, *n.* bois mort *m.*

deaf, *adj.* sourd.

deafen, *vb.* assourdir.

deaf-mute, *adj.* sourd-muet.

deafness, *n.* surdité *f.*

deal, 1. *n.* (business) affaire *f.*; (great d.) beaucoup; (cards) donne *f.* **2.** *vb.* (d. with) traiter; (d. out) distribuer.

dealer, *n.* marchand *m.*

dealings, *n.* relations *f.pl.*

dean, *n.* doyen *m.*

dear, *adj. and n.* cher *m.*

dearly, *adv.* chèrement.

dearth, *n.* disette *f.*

death, *n.* mort *f.*

death certificate, *n.* acte *(m.)* de décès.

deathless, *adj.* impérissable.

deathly, *adj.* mortel.

death penalty, *n.* peine *(f.)* de mort.

debacle, *n.* débâcle *f.*

debase, *vb.* avilir.

debatable, *adj.* discutable.

debate, 1. *n.* débat *m.* **2.** *vb.* discuter.

debater, *n.* orateur parlementaire *m.*, argumentateur *m.*

debauch, 1. *n.* débauche *f.* **2.** *vb.* débaucher, corrompre.

debenture, *n.* obligation *f.*

debilitate, *vb.* débiliter, affaiblir.

debility, *n.* débilité *f.*

debit, *n.* débit *m.*

debonair, *adj.* courtois et jovial.

debris, *n.* débris *m.pl.*

debt, *n.* dette *f.*

debtor, *n.* débiteur *m.*

debunk, *vb.* dégonfler.

debut, *n.* début *m.*

debutante, *n.* débutante *f.*

decade, *n.* décennie *f.*

decadence, *n.* décadence *f.*

decadent, *adj.* décadent.

decaffeinated, *adj.* décaféiné.

decalcomania, *n.* décalcomanie *f.*

decanter, *n.* carafe *f.*

decapitate, *vb.* décapiter.

decay, 1. *n.* décadence *f.*; (state of ruin) délabrement *m.*; (teeth) carie *f.* **2.** *vb.* tomber en décadence.

deceased, *adj.* défunt.

deceit, *n.* tromperie *f.*

deceitful, *adj.* trompeur.

deceive, *vb.* tromper.

deceiver, *n.* imposteur *m.*

December, n. décembre m.
decency, n. décence f.
decent, adj. décent.
decentralization, n. décentralisation f.
decentralize, vb. décentraliser.
deception, n. tromperie f., duperie f.
deceptive, adj. décevant, trompeur.
decibel, n. décibel m.
decide, vb. décider.
decided, adj. décidé, prononcé.
decidedly, adv. décidément.
deciduous, adj. à feuillage caduc.
decimal, adj. décimal.
decimal point, n. virgule f.
decimate, vb. décimer.
decipher, vb. déchiffrer.
decision, n. décision f.
decisive, adj. décisif.
deck, n. (boat) pont m.; (cards) jeu m.
deck chair, n. chaise (f.) longue.
deck hand, n. matelot (m.) de pont.
declaim, vb. déclamer.
declamation, n. déclamation f.
declaration, n. déclaration f.
declarative, adj. explicatif, (law) déclaratif.
declare, vb. déclarer.
declension, n. déclinaison f.
decline, vb. décliner.
decode, vb. déchiffrer, décoder.
decoder, n. décodeur m.
décolleté, adj. décolleté.
decompose, vb. décomposer, tr.
decongestant, adj. décongestionnant.
decor, n. décor m.
decorate, vb. décorer.
decoration, n. décoration f.
decorative, adj. décoratif.
decorator, n. décorateur m.
decorous, adj. bienséant, convenable.
decorum, n. décorum m.
decoy, 1. n. leurre m. 2. vb. leurrer.
decrease, 1. n. diminution f. 2. vb. diminuer.
decree, n. décret m.
decrepit, adj. décrépit.
decry, vb. décrier, dénigrer.
dedicate, vb. dédier.

dedication, n. dédicace f.
deduce, vb. déduire.
deduct, vb. déduire.
deduction, n. déduction f.
deductive, adj. déductif.
deed, n. action f.; (law) acte (m.) notarié.
deem, vb. juger.
deep, adj. profond.
deepen, vb. approfondir, tr.
deep freeze, n. surgélateur m.
deeply, adv. profondément.
deep-rooted, adj. enraciné.
deep-seated, adj. profond.
deer, n. cerf m.
deerskin, n. peau (f.) de daim.
deface, vb. défigurer.
defamation, n. diffamation f.
defame, vb. diffamer.
default, n. défaut m.
defeat, 1. n. défaite f. 2. vb. vaincre.
defeatism, n. défaitisme m.
defect, 1. n. défaut m. 2. vb. passer à l'ennemi.
defection, n. défection f.
defective, adj. défectueux.
defend, vb. défendre.
defendant, n. défendeur m.; (in court) accusé m., prévenu m.
defender, n. défenseur m.
defense, n. défense f.
defenseless, adj. sans défense.
defensible, adj. défendable, soutenable.
defensive, adj. défensif.
defer, vb. (put off) différer; (show deference) déférer.
deference, n. déférence f.
deferential, adj. plein de déférence, respectueux.
defiance, n. défi m.
defiant, adj. de défi.
deficiency, n. insuffisance f.
deficient, adj. insuffisant.
deficit, n. déficit m.
defile, vb. souiller.
define, vb. définir.
definite, adj. défini.
definitely, adv. d'une manière déterminée.
definition, n. définition f.
definitive, adj. définitif.
deflate, vb. dégonfler.
deflation, n. dégonflement m.

deflect, vb. faire dévier, détourner.

deforestation, n. déforestation f.

deform, vb. déformer.

deformity, n. difformité f.

defraud, vb. frauder.

defray, vb. payer.

defrost, vb. déglacer.

defroster, n. déglaceur m.

deft, adj. adroit.

defunct, adj. défunt.

defy, vb. défier.

degenerate, vb. dégénérer.

degeneration, n. dégénérescence f.

degradation, n. dégradation f.

degrade, vb. dégrader.

degree, n. degré m.; (university) diplôme m.

dehydrate, vb. déshydrater.

de-ice, vb. dégivrer.

deify, vb. déifier.

deign, vb. daigner.

deity, n. divinité f.

dejected, adj. abattu.

dejection, n. abattement m.

delay, 1. n. retard m. **2.** vb. retarder, tr.; tarder, intr.

delectable, adj. délectable.

delegate, 1. n. délégué m. **2.** vb. déléguer.

delegation, n. délégation f.

delete, vb. rayer, biffer; (computer) effacer.

deletion, n. suppression f., rature f.

deliberate, 1. adj. délibéré. **2.** vb. délibérer.

deliberately, adv. (carefully) de propos délibéré; (on purpose) exprès.

deliberation, n. délibération f.

deliberative, adj. délibératif.

delicacy, n. délicatesse f.

delicate, adj. délicat.

delicatessen, n. charcuterie f.

delicious, adj. délicieux.

delight, 1. n. délices f.pl. **2.** vb. enchanter.

delightful, adj. charmant.

delineate, vb. esquisser, dessiner.

delinquency, n. délit m.

delinquent, adj. and n. délinquant m.

delirious, adj. délirant.

delirium, n. délire m.

deliver, vb. délivrer; (speech) prononcer.

deliverance, n. délivrance f.

delivery, n. (child) accouchement m.; (speech) débit m.; (goods) livraison f.; (letters) distribution f.; (general d.) poste restante f.

delouse, vb. épouiller.

delta, n. delta m.

delude, vb. tromper.

deluge, n. déluge m.

delusion, n. illusion f.

deluxe, adv. de luxe.

delve, vb. creuser, pénétrer.

demagogue, n. démagogue m.

demand, 1. n. demande f. **2.** vb. demander; (as right) exiger.

demanding, adj. exigeant.

demarcation, n. démarcation f.

demean, vb. (d. oneself) s'avilir, s'abaisser.

demeanor, n. maintien m.

demented, adj. fou m., folle f.

demerit, n. démérite m.

demigod, n. demi-dieu m.

demilitarize, vb. démilitariser.

demise, n. décès m., mort f.

demo, n. démonstration f.

demobilization, n. démobilisation f.

demobilize, vb. démobiliser.

democracy, n. démocratie f.

democrat, n. démocrate m.f.

democratic, adj. démocratique.

demolish, vb. démolir.

demolition, n. démolition f.

demon, n. démon m.

demonstrable, adj. démonstrable.

demonstrate, vb. démontrer.

demonstration, n. démonstration f.

demonstrative, adj. démonstratif.

demonstrator, n. démonstrateur m.

demoralize, vb. démoraliser.

demote, vb. réduire à un grade inférieur.

demur, vb. hésiter, s'opposer à.

demure, adj. posé, d'une modestie affectée.

den, n. antre m., repaire m.

denaturalize, vb. dénaturaliser.

denature, vb. dénaturer.

denial, n. dénégation f.; (refusal) refus m.

denim, n. treillis m.
Denmark, n. Danemark m.
denomination, n. dénomination f.; (religion) confession f.
denominator, n. dénominateur m.
denote, vb. dénoter.
denouement, n. dénouement m.
denounce, vb. dénoncer.
dense, adj. dense; (stupid) bête.
density, n. densité f.
dent, n. bosselure f.
dental, adj. dentaire; (gramm.) dental.
dentifrice, n. dentifrice m.
dentist, n. dentiste m.
dentistry, n. art (m.) du dentiste, dentisterie f.
denture, n. dentier m., râtelier m.
denude, vb. dénuder.
denunciation, n. dénonciation f.
deny, vb. nier.
deodorant, n. désodorisant m.
deodorize, vb. désodoriser, désinfecter.
depart, vb. partir, s'en aller, quitter.
department, n. département m.; (government) ministère m.; (d. store) grand magasin m.
departmental, adj. départemental.
departure, n. départ m.
dependability, n. confiance (f.) que l'on inspire.
dependable, adj. digne de confiance.
dependence, n. dépendance f., confiance f.
dependent, 1. adj. dépendant. 2. n. personne (f.) à charge.
depend on, vb. dépendre de; (rely) compter sur.
depict, vb. peindre.
depiction, n. description f.
deplete, vb. épuiser.
deplorable, adj. déplorable.
deplore, vb. déplorer.
depopulate, vb. dépeupler.
deport, vb. déporter.
deportation, n. déportation f.
deportment, n. maintien f.
depose, vb. déposer.
deposit, 1. n. dépôt m. 2. vb. déposer.
depositor, n. déposant m.

depository, n. dépôt m., dépositaire m.
depot, n. dépôt m., gare f.
deprave, vb. dépraver, corrompre.
depravity, n. dépravation f., corruption f.
deprecate, vb. désapprouver, s'opposer à.
depreciate, vb. déprécier.
depreciation, n. dépréciation f.
depredation, n. déprédation f., pillage m.
depress, vb. (lower) abaisser; (fig.) abattre.
depressed, adj. abattu, bas.
depression, n. dépression f.; (personal) abattement m.; (comm.) crise f.
deprivation, n. privation f.
deprive, vb. priver.
depth, n. profondeur f.
depth charge, n. grenade (f.) sous-marine.
deputy, n. délégué m.; (politics) député m.
derail, vb. dérailler.
derange, vb. déranger.
deranged, adj. dérangé, troublé.
derelict, 1. n. vaisseau abandonné m., épave f. 2. adj. abandonné, délaissé.
dereliction, n. abandon m.
deride, vb. tourner en dérision.
derision, n. dérision f.
derisive, adj. dérisoire.
derisory, adj. dérisoire.
derivation, n. dérivation f., origine f.
derivative, n. dérivatif m.
derive, vb. dériver.
dermatology, n. dermatologie f.
derogatory, adj. dérogatoire.
derrick, n. grue f.
descend, vb. descendre.
descendant, n. descendant m.
descent, n. descente f.
describe, vb. décrire.
description, n. description f.
descriptive, adj. descriptif.
desecrate, vb. profaner.
desensitize, vb. désensibiliser.
desert, 1. n. (place) désert m.; (merit) mérite m. 2. vb. déserter.
deserter, n. déserteur m.

desertion, n. abandon m.; (military) désertion f.

deserve, vb. mériter.

deserving, adj. méritoire, de mérite.

design, 1. n. (project) dessein m.; (architecture) projet m. **2.** vb. dessiner; (d. for) destiner à.

designate, vb. désigner.

designation, n. désignation f.

designedly, adv. à dessein.

designer, n. dessinateur m.

designing, adj. intrigant, artificieux.

desirable, adj. désirable.

desire, 1. n. désir m. **2.** vb. désirer.

desirous, adj. désireux.

desist, vb. cesser.

desk, n. (office) bureau m.; (school) pupitre m.

desolate, adj. désolé.

desolation, n. désolation f.

despair, 1. n. désespoir m. **2.** vb. désespérer.

desperado, n. désespéré m., cerveau brûlé m.

desperate, adj. désespéré.

desperation, n. désespoir m.

despicable, adj. méprisable.

despise, vb. mépriser.

despite, prep. en dépit de.

despondent, adj. découragé.

despot, n. despote m.

despotic, adj. despotique.

despotism, n. despotisme m.

dessert, n. dessert m.

destination, n. destination f.

destine, vb. destiner.

destiny, n. destin m.

destitute, adj. (deprived) dénué; (poor) indigent.

destitution, n. destitution f.

destroy, vb. détruire.

destroyer, n. destructeur m.; (naval) contre-torpilleur m.

destructible, adj. destructible.

destruction, n. destruction f.

destructive, adj. destructif.

desultory, adj. à bâtons rompus, décousu.

detach, vb. détacher.

detachment, n. détachement m.

detail, n. détail m.

detain, vb. retenir; (in prison) détenir.

detect, vb. découvrir.

detection, n. découverte f.

detective, n. agent (m.) de la police secrète; (d. novel) roman policier.

detente, n. détente f.

detention, n. détention f.

deter, vb. détourner, empêcher (de), dissuader (de).

detergent, n. détersif m.

deteriorate, vb. détériorer, tr.

deterioration, n. détérioration f.

determination, n. détermination f.

determine, vb. déterminer.

determined, adj. déterminé.

determinism, n. déterminisme m.

deterrence, n. préventif m.

deterrent, n. and adj. préventif m.

detest, vb. détester.

dethrone, vb. détrôner.

detonate, vb. détoner.

detour, n. détour m.

detract, vb. enlever, ôter (à), dénigrer, déroger (à).

detriment, n. détriment m., préjudice m.

detrimental, adj. préjudiciable, nuisible (à).

devaluate, vb. dévaluer, déprécier.

devaluation, n. dévaluation f.

devastate, vb. dévaster.

devastating, adj. dévastateur, (news) accablant.

develop, vb. développer, tr.

developer, n. (photography) révélateur m.

developing nation, n. nation (f.) en voie de développement.

development, n. développement m.

deviant, 1. adj. anormal. **2.** n. déviant m.

deviate, vb. dévier, s'écarter (de).

deviation, n. déviation f., écart m.

device, n. expédient m.

devil, n. diable m.

devilish, adj. diabolique.

devious, adj. détourné.

devise, vb. (plan) combiner; (plot) tramer.

devitalize, vb. dévitaliser.

devoid, adj. dépourvu.

devolution, n. décentralisation f.

devote, vb. consacrer.

devoted, *adj.* dévoué.

devotee, *n.* dévot *m.*, dévote *f.*, adepte *m.f.*

devotion, *n.* (religious) dévotion *f.*; (to person or thing) dévouement *m.*

devour, *vb.* dévorer.

devout, *adj.* dévot.

dew, *n.* rosée *f.*

dewy, *adj.* de rosée.

dexterity, *n.* dextérité *f.*

dexterous, *adj.* adroit.

diabetes, *n.* diabète *m.*

diabolic, *adj.* diabolique.

diadem, *n.* diadème *m.*

diagnose, *vb.* diagnostiquer.

diagnosis, *n.* diagnose *f.*

diagnostic, *adj.* diagnostique.

diagonal, *adj.* diagonal.

diagonally, *adv.* diagonalement.

diagram, *n.* diagramme *m.*

dial, 1. *n.* cadran *m.* **2.** *vb.* **(d. a number)** composer.

dialect, *n.* dialecte *m.*

dialogue, *n.* dialogue *m.*

dial tone, *n.* tonalité *f.*

diameter, *n.* diamètre *m.*

diametrical, *adj.* diamétral.

diamond, *n.* diamant *m.*; (shape) losange *m.*; (cards) carreau *m.*

diaper, *n.* (babies) couche *f.*

diaphragm, *n.* diaphragme *m.*

diarrhea, *n.* diarrhée *f.*

diary, *n.* journal *m.*

diathermy, *n.* diathermie *f.*

diatribe, *n.* diatribe *f.*

dice, *n.* dés *m.pl.*

dicker, *vb.* marchander.

dictaphone, *n.* machine à dicter *f.*

dictate, *vb.* dicter.

dictation, *n.* dictée *f.*

dictator, *n.* dictateur *m.*

dictatorial, *adj.* dictatorial.

dictatorship, *n.* dictature *f.*

diction, *n.* diction *f.*

dictionary, *n.* dictionnaire *m.*

didactic, *adj.* didactique.

die, 1. *n.* dé *m.* **2.** *vb.* mourir.

die-hard, *n.* intransigeant *m.*, ultra *m.*

diesel, *n.* diesel *m.*

diet, *n.* régime *m.*

dietary, *adj.* diététique.

dietetics, *n.* diététique *f.*

dietitian, *n.* diététicien *m.*

differ, *vb.* différer.

difference, *n.* différence *f.*

different, *adj.* différent.

differential, *adj.* différentiel.

differentiate (between), *vb.* faire une différence (entre).

difficult, *adj.* difficile.

difficulty, *n.* difficulté *f.*

diffident, *adj.* hésitant, timide.

diffuse, *adj.* diffus.

diffusion, *n.* diffusion *f.*

dig, *vb.* bêcher; (hole) creuser.

digest, *vb.* digérer.

digestible, *adj.* digestible.

digestion, *n.* digestion *f.*

digestive, *adj. and n.* digestif *m.*

digit, *n.* chiffre *m.*

digital, *adj.* (in watches, etc.) digital, numérique.

digitalis, *n.* digitaline *f.*

dignified, *adj.* plein de dignité.

dignify, *vb.* honorer, élever.

dignitary, *n.* dignitaire *m.*

dignity, *n.* dignité *f.*

digress, *vb.* faire une digression.

digression, *n.* digression *f.*

dike, *n.* (ditch) fossé *m.*; (dam) digue *f.*

dilapidated, *adj.* délabré.

dilapidation, *n.* délabrement *m.*

dilate, *vb.* dilater, *tr.*

dilatory, *adj.* dilatoire, lent, négligent.

dilemma, *n.* dilemme *m.*

dilettante, *n.* dilettante *m.*, amateur *m.*

diligence, *n.* diligence *f.*

diligent, *adj.* diligent.

dill, *n.* aneth *m.*

dilute, *vb.* diluer.

dim, 1. *adj.* (light, sight) faible; (color) terne. **2.** *vb.* réduire, baisser.

dime, *n.* un dixième de dollar *m.*

dimension, *n.* dimension *f.*

diminish, *vb.* diminuer.

diminution, *n.* diminution *f.*

diminutive, 1. *adj.* tout petit. **2.** *n.* (*gramm.*) diminutif *m.*

dimness, *n.* (weakness) faiblesse *f.*; (darkness) obscurité *f.*

dimple, *n.* (face) fossette *f.*

din, *n.* tapage *m.*

dine, *vb.* dîner.

diner, dining-car, *n.* wagon-restaurant *m.*

dingy, *adj.* défraîchi.

dining room, *n.* salle (*f.*) à manger.

dinner, *n.* dîner *m.*; (**d. jacket**) smoking *m.*

dinosaur, *n.* dinosaurie *f.*

diocese, *n.* diocèse *m.*

dint, *n.* (**by d. of**) à force de.

dip, *vb.* plonger.

diphtheria, *n.* diphtérie *f.*

diphthong, *n.* diphtongue *f.*

diploma, *n.* diplôme *m.*

diplomacy, *n.* diplomatie *f.*

diplomat, *n.* diplomate *m.*

diplomatic, *adj.* diplomatique.

dipper, *n.* cuiller (*f.*) à pot.

dire, *adj.* affreux.

direct, 1. *vb.* (guide) diriger; (address) adresser; (film) réaliser; (play) mettre en scène. **2.** *adj.* direct.

direct current, *n.* courant continu *m.*

direction, *n.* direction *f.*; (orders) instructions *f.pl.*

directional, *adj.* de direction.

directive, 1. *n.* directif *m.* **2.** *adj.* dirigeant.

directly, *adv.* directement.

directness, *n.* rectitude *f.*; (frankness) franchise *f.*

director, *n.* directeur *m.*, (theater) metteur (*m.*) en scène, (cinema, TV) réalisateur *m.*

directorate, *n.* conseil (*m.*) d'administration.

directory, *n.* annuaire *m.*

dirge, *n.* chant funèbre *m.*

dirigible, *adj. and n.* dirigeable *m.*

dirt, *n.* saleté *f.*

dirty, 1. *adj.* sale. **2.** *vb.* salir.

disability, *n.* incapacité *f.*

disable, *vb.* mettre hors de combat, *tr.*

disabled, *adj.* invalide.

disabuse, *vb.* désabuser.

disadvantage, *n.* désavantage *m.*

disagree, *vb.* être en désaccord.

disagreeable, *adj.* désagréable.

disagreement, *n.* désaccord *m.*

disappear, *vb.* disparaître.

disappearance, *n.* disparition *f.*

disappoint, *vb.* désappointer.

disappointing, *adj.* décevant.

disappointment, *n.* déception *f.*

disapproval, *n.* désapprobation *f.*

disapprove, *vb.* désapprouver.

disarm, *vb.* désarmer.

disarmament, *n.* désarmement *m.*

disarray, *n.* désarroi *m.*, désordre *m.*

disassemble, *vb.* démonter, désassembler.

disaster, *n.* désastre *m.*

disastrous, *adj.* désastreux.

disavow, *vb.* désavouer.

disavowal, *n.* désaveu *m.*

disband, *vb.* congédier, *tr.*; se débander, *intr.*

disbar, *vb.* rayer du tableau des avocats.

disbelief, *n.* incrédulité *f.*

disbelieve, *vb.* ne pas croire, refuser de croire.

disburse, *vb.* débourser.

disc, *n.* disque *m.*

discard, *vb.* mettre de côté.

discern, *vb.* discerner.

discerning, *adj.* judicieux, éclairé.

discernment, *n.* discernement *m.*

discharge, 1. *n.* décharge *f.*; (mil.) congé *m.* **2.** *vb.* décharger; (mil.) congédier.

disciple, *n.* disciple *m.*

disciplinarian, *n.* disciplinaire *m.*

disciplinary, *adj.* disciplinaire.

discipline, *n.* discipline *f.*

disclaim, *vb.* désavouer, nier.

disclaimer, *n.* désaveu *m.*

disclose, *vb.* révéler.

disclosure, *n.* révélation *f.*

disco, *adj.* disco.

discolor, *vb.* décolorer.

discoloration, *n.* décoloration *f.*

discomfiture, *n.* défaite *f.*, déroute *f.*

discomfort, *n.* malaise *m.*

disconcert, *vb.* déconcerter.

disconnect, *vb.* désunir; (electric) débrancher.

disconnected, *adj.* (electricity) hors circuit.

disconsolate, *adj.* désolé.

discontent, *n.* mécontentement *m.*

discontented, *adj.* mécontent.

discontinue, *vb.* discontinuer.

discord, *n.* discorde *f.*

discordant, *adj.* discordant, en désaccord.

discotheque, *n.* discothèque *f.*

discount, 1. *n.* escompte *m.;* (reduction) remise *f.* **2.** *vb.* ne pas tenir compte de.

discourage, *vb.* décourager.

discouragement, *n.* découragement *m.*

discourse, *n.* discours *m.*

discourteous, *adj.* impoli.

discourtesy, *n.* impolitesse *f.*

discover, *vb.* découvrir.

discoverer, *n.* découvreur *m.*

discovery, *n.* découverte *f.*

discredit, 1. *n.* discrédit *m.* **2.** *vb.* discréditer.

discreditable, *adj.* déshonorant, peu honorable.

discreet, *adj.* discret.

discrepancy, *n.* contradiction *f.*

discretion, *n.* discrétion *f.*

discriminate, *vb.* distinguer.

discrimination, *n.* discernement *m.,* jugement *m.*

discursive, *adj.* discursif, sans suite.

discuss, *vb.* discuter.

discussion, *n.* discussion *f.*

disdain, *n.* dédain *m.*

disdainful, *adj.* dédaigneux.

disease, *n.* maladie *f.*

diseased, *adj.* malade.

disembark, *vb.* débarquer.

disembody, *vb.* dépouiller du corps.

disenchantment, *n.* désenchantement *m.*

disengage, *vb.* dégager.

disentangle, *vb.* démêler.

disfavor, *vb.* défavoriser.

disfigure, *vb.* défigurer, enlaidir.

disfranchise, *vb.* priver du droit de vote.

disgorge, *vb.* dégorger.

disgrace, *n.* disgrâce *f.*

disgraceful, *adj.* honteux.

disgruntled, *adj.* mécontent, de mauvaise humeur.

disguise, 1. *n.* déguisement *m.* **2.** *vb.* déguiser.

disgust, 1. *n.* dégout *m.* **2.** *vb.* dégouter.

disgusting, *adj.* dégoûtant.

dish, *n.* plat *m.;* **(wash the d.s)** laver la vaisselle.

dishcloth, *n.* torchon *m.*

dishearten, *vb.* décourager.

disheveled, *adj.* échevelé.

dishonest, *adj.* malhonnête.

dishonesty, *n.* malhonnêteté *f.*

dishonor, *n.* déshonneur *m.*

dishonorable, *adj.* (action) déshonorant.

dishwasher, *n.* lave-vaisselle *m.*

disillusion, *n.* désillusion *f.*

disinclined, *adj.* **(be d. to)** décourager.

disinfect, *vb.* désinfecter.

disinfectant, *n.* désinfectant *m.*

disinherit, *vb.* déshériter.

disintegrate, *vb.* désagréger.

disinterested, *adj.* désintéressé.

disjointed, *adj.* désarticulé, disloqué.

disk, *n.* disque *m.;* **(floppy d.)** disquette *f.;* **(d. drive)** lecteur *(m.)* de disquettes.

diskette, *n.* disquette *f.*

dislike, 1. *n.* aversion *f.* **2.** *vb.* ne pas aimer.

dislocate, *vb.* disloquer.

dislodge, *vb.* déloger.

disloyal, *adj.* infidèle.

disloyalty, *n.* infidélité *f.,* perfidie *f.*

dismal, *adj.* sombre.

dismantle, *vb.* dépouiller (de).

dismay, *n.* consternation *f.*

dismember, *vb.* démembrer.

dismiss, *vb.* congédier.

dismissal, *n.* renvoi *m.*

dismount, *vb.* descendre.

disobedience, *n.* désobéissance *f.*

disobedient, *adj.* désobéissant.

disobey, *vb.* désobéir à.

disorder, *n.* désordre *m.*

disorderly, *adj.* désordonné.

disorganize, *vb.* désorganiser.

disorient, *vb.* désorienter.

disown, *vb.* désavouer.

disparage, *vb.* déprécier, dénigrer.

disparaging, *adj.* désobligeant.

disparate, *adj.* disparate.

disparity, *n.* inégalité *f.*

dispassionate, *adj.* calme.

dispatch, 1. *n.* (business) expédition *f.;* (speed) promptitude *f.;* (message) dépêche *f.* **2.** *vb.* expédier.

dispatcher, n. expéditeur m.

dispel, vb. dissiper.

dispensable, adj. dont on peut se passer.

dispensary, n. dispensaire m.

dispensation, n. dispensation f.

dispense, vb. distribuer, dispenser.

dispersal, n. dispersion f.

disperse, vb. disperser.

dispirited, adj. découragé.

displace, vb. déplacer.

displaced person, n. réfugié m.

displacement, n. déplacement m.

display, 1. n. (show) exposition f.; (shop, ostentation) étalage m. **2.** vb. étaler.

display window, n. vitrine f.

displease, vb. déplaire à.

disposable, adj. disponible, jetable.

disposal, n. disposition f.

dispose, vb. disposer.

disposition, n. disposition f.; (character) caractère m.

dispossess, vb. déposséder, exproprier.

disproportion, n. disproportion f.

disproportionate, adj. disproportionné.

disprove, vb. réfuter.

disputable, adj. contestable, disputable.

dispute, 1. n. (discussion) discussion f.; (quarrel) dispute f. **2.** vb. (se) disputer.

disqualify, vb. (sports) disqualifier.

disregard, vb. ne tenir aucun compte de.

disrepair, n. délabrement m.

disreputable, adj. déshonorant, honteux.

disrespect, n. irrévérence f.

disrespectful, adj. irrespectueux.

disrobe, vb. déshabiller, dévêtir.

disrupt, vb. faire éclater, rompre.

dissatisfaction, n. mécontentement m.

dissatisfy, vb. mécontenter.

dissect, vb. disséquer.

dissemble, vb. dissimuler.

disseminate, vb. disséminer.

dissension, n. dissension f.

dissent, 1. vb. différer. **2.** n. dissentiment m.

dissertation, n. dissertation f., discours m.

disservice, n. mauvais service rendu m.

dissimilar, adj. dissemblable.

dissipate, vb. dissiper.

dissipated, adj. dissipé.

dissipation, n. dissipation f.

dissociate, vb. désassocier, dissocier.

dissolute, adj. dissolu.

dissolution, n. dissolution f.

dissolve, vb. dissoudre, tr.

dissonance, n. dissonance f., désaccord m.

dissonant, adj. dissonant.

dissuade, vb. dissuader.

distance, n. distance f.

distant, adj. distant.

distaste, n. dégoût m.

distasteful, adj. désagréable.

distemper, 1. n. maladie (f.) des chiens. **2.** vb. peindre en détrempe.

distend, vb. dilater, gonfler.

distended, adj. dilaté.

distill, vb. distiller.

distillation, n. distillation f.

distiller, n. distillateur m.

distillery, n. distillerie f.

distinct, adj. distinct.

distinction, n. distinction f.

distinctive, adj. distinctif.

distinctly, adv. distinctement, clairement.

distinguish, vb. distinguer.

distinguished, adj. distingué.

distort, vb. déformer.

distract, vb. (divert) distraire; (upset) affoler.

distracted, adj. affolé, bouleversé.

distraction, n. (diversion) distraction f.; (madness) folie f.

distraught, adj. affolé, éperdu, hors de soi.

distress, 1. n. détresse f. **2.** vb. affliger.

distressing, adj. affligeant, pénible, désolant.

distribute, vb. distribuer.

distribution, n. distribution f.

distributor, n. distributeur m.

district, n. (region) contrée f.; (administration) district m.; (town) quartier m.

district attorney, *n.* procureur *(m.)* de la République.

distrust, 1. *n.* méfiance *f.* 2. *vb.* se méfier de.

distrustful, *adj.* méfiant.

disturb, *vb.* déranger.

disturbance, *n.* dérangement *m.*

disunite, *vb.* désunir.

disuse, *n.* désuétude *f.*

ditch, *n.* fossé *m.*

ditto, *adv.* idem, de même.

diva, *n.* diva *f.*

divan, *n.* divan *m.*

dive, *vb.* plonger.

dive bomber, *n.* avion *(m.)* de bombardement qui fait des vols piqués.

diver, *n.* plongeur *m.*

diverge, *vb.* diverger.

divergence, *n.* divergence *f.*

divergent, *adj.* divergent.

diverse, *adj.* divers.

diversion, *n.* (amusement) divertissement *m.*; (turning aside) détournement *m.*

diversity, *n.* diversité *f.*

divert, *vb.* (turn aside) détourner; (amuse) divertir.

divest, *vb.* ôter, dépouiller, priver.

divide, *vb.* diviser.

divided, *adj.* divisé, séparé.

dividend, *n.* dividende *m.*

divine, *adj.* divin.

diving, *n.* plongée *f.*; **(d. board)** plongeoir *m.*; **(d. suit)** tenue *(f.)* de plongée.

divinity, *n.* divinité *f.*

divisible, *adj.* divisible.

division, *n.* division *f.*

divisive, *adj.* qui divise, qui sépare.

divorce, 1. *n.* divorce *m.* 2. *vb.* divorcer.

divorcee, *n.* divorcé *m.*, divorcée *f.*

divulge, *vb.* divulguer.

dizziness, *n.* vertige *m.*

dizzy, *adj.* pris de vertige.

do, *vb.* faire; **(how d. you d.?)** comment allez-vous?

docile, *adj.* docile.

dock, *n.* bassin *m.*

docket, *n.* registre *m.*, bordereau *m.*

dockyard, *n.* chantier *(m.)* de construction de navires.

doctor, *n.* (academic) docteur *m.*; (med.) médecin *m.*

doctorate, *n.* doctorat *m.*

doctrinaire, *adj.* doctrinaire.

doctrine, *n.* doctrine *f.*

document, *n.* document *m.*

documentary, *adj.* documentaire.

documentation, *n.* documentation *f.*

dodge, *vb.* esquiver, éluder.

doe, *n.* daine *f.*, biche *f.*

doeskin, *n.* peau *(f.)* de daim.

dog, *n.* chien *m.*

dogfight, *n.* combat *(m.)* de chiens, mêlée générale *f.*

dogged, *adj.* obstiné, tenace.

doggerel, *n.* poésie burlesque *f.*

doghouse, *n.* chenil *m.*

dogma, *n.* dogme *m.*

dogmatic, *adj.* dogmatique.

dogmatism, *n.* dogmatisme *m.*

doily, *n.* petit napperon *m.*

do-it-yourself, *n.* bricolage *m.*

doldrum, *n.* (naut.) zone des calmes *f.*; cafard *m.*

dole, 1. *n.* pitance *f.*; aumône *f.* 2. *vb.* distribuer parcimonieusement.

doleful, *adj.* lugubre.

doll, *n.* poupée *f.*

dollar, *n.* dollar *m.*

dolorous, *adj.* douloureux.

dolphin, *n.* dauphin *m.*

domain, *n.* domaine *m.*

dome, *n.* dôme *m.*

domestic, *adj.* domestique.

domesticate, *vb.* domestiquer, apprivoiser.

domicile, *n.* domicile *m.*

dominance, *n.* dominance *f.*, prédominance *f.*

dominant, *adj.* dominant.

dominate, *vb.* dominer.

domination, *n.* domination *f.*

domineer, *vb.* se montrer tyrannique.

domineering, *adj.* impérieux.

dominion, *n.* domination *f.*; (territory) possessions *f.pl.*

domino, *n.* domino *m.*

don, *vb.* endosser, revêtir.

donate, *vb.* donner.

donation, *n.* donation *f.*

done, *vb.* fait.

donkey, *n.* âne *m.*

don't, *vb.* ne faites pas!, ne fais pas!

doodle, vb. griffonner.

doom, vb. condamner.

doomsday, n. (jour du) jugement dernier m.

door, n. porte f.; **(d.-keeper)** concierge m.f.

doorbell, n. sonnette f.

doorman, n. portier m.

doorstep, n. seuil m., pas (m.) de la porte.

doorway, n. (baie de) porte f., encadrement (m.) de la porte.

dope, 1. n. stupéfiant m. 2. vb. doper.

dormant, adj. endormi, assoupi.

dormer, n. lucarne f.

dormitory, n. maison (f.) d'étudiants.

dosage, n. dosage m.

dose, n. dose f.

dossier, n. dossier m.

dot, n. point m.

dotage, n. radotage m.

dote, vb. radoter; **(d. on)** aimer excessivement.

dot-matrix printer, n. imprimante (f.) matricielle.

double, 1. adj. and n. double m. 2. vb. doubler.

double-bass, n. contre basse f.

double-breasted, adj. croisé.

double-cross, vb. duper, tromper.

double-dealing, n. duplicité f.

double room, n. chambre (f.) pour deux personnes.

double time, n. pas gymnastique m.

doubly, adv. doublement.

doubt, 1. n. doute m. 2. vb. douter (de).

doubtful, adj. douteux.

doubtless, adv. sans doute.

dough, n. pâte f.; (colloquial) fric m.

doughnut, n. pet (m.) de nonne, beignet m.

dour, adj. austère.

douse, vb. plonger, tremper.

dove, n. colombe f.

dowager, n. douairière f.

dowdy, adj. sans élégance, qui manque de chic.

dowel, 1. n. goujon m. 2. vb. goujonner.

down, 1. n. duvet m. 2. adv. en bas. 3. prep. (along) le long de.

downcast, adj. (look) baissé.

downfall, n. chute f.

downgrade, vb. déclasser.

downhearted, adj. découragé, déprimé.

downhill, 1. n. descente f. 2. adj. en pente, incliné.

downpour, n. averse f.

downright, adv. tout à fait.

downstairs, adv. en bas.

downtown, adv. en ville.

downtrodden, adj. opprimé, piétiné.

downward, adj. descendant.

downy, adj. duveteux.

dowry, n. dot f.

doze, vb. sommeiller.

dozen, n. douzaine f.

drab, adj. (color) gris; (dull) terne.

draft, 1. n. (drawing) dessin m.; (mil.) conscription f.; (air) courant (m.) d'air. 2. vb. (mil.) appeler sous le drapeau.

draftee, n. conscrit m.

draftsman, n. dessinateur m.

drafty, adj. plein de courants d'air.

drag, vb. traîner.

dragnet, n. drague f., seine f., chalut m.

dragon, n. dragon m.

dragon-fly, n. libellule f.

drain, vb. drainer, tr.; s'écouler, intr.

drainage, n. drainage m.

dram, n. drachme f., goutte f.

drama, n. drame m.

dramatic, adj. dramatique.

dramatics, n. théâtre m.

dramatist, n. dramaturge m.

dramatize, vb. dramatiser.

dramaturgy, n. dramaturgie f.

drape, vb. draper.

drapery, n. draperie f.

drastic, adj. drastique.

draw, vb. (pull) tirer; (sketch) dessiner.

drawback, n. inconvénient m.

drawbridge, n. pont-levis m.

drawer, n. tiroir m.

drawing, n. dessin m.

drawl, 1. n. voix (f.) traînante. 2. vb. traîner la voix.

dray, n. camion m.

drayman, n. camionneur m.
dread, 1. n. crainte f. **2.** vb. redouter.
dreadful, adj. affreux.
dreadfully, adv. terriblement, affreusement.
dream, n. rêve m.
dreamer, n. rêveur m.
dreamy, adj. rêveur m., rêveuse f.
dreary, adj. morne.
dredge, vb. draguer.
dreg, n. lie f.
drench, vb. tremper.
dress, 1. n. robe f. **2.** vb. habiller, tr.; s'habiller, intr.
dresser, n. commode f.
dressing, n. toilette f.; (surgical) pansement m.
dressing gown, n. robe (f.) de chambre, peignoir m.
dressmaker, n. couturière f.
dress rehearsal, n. répétition générale f.
dressy, adj. chic.
dribble, vb. baver.
drier, n. sécheur m., dessécheur f.
drift, vb. (boat) dériver; (person) se laisser aller.
drifter, n. personne (f.) sans but.
driftwood, n. bois flottant m.
drill, 1. n. (tool) foret m.; (exercise) exercice m. **2.** vb. (hole) forer; (exercise) exercer, tr.; faire l'exercice, intr.
drink, 1. n. boisson f. **2.** vb. boire.
drinkable, adj. potable.
drip, 1. vb. dégoutter. **2.** n. goutte f.
dripping, 1. n. dégouttement m. **2.** adj. ruisselant.
drive, 1. n. promenade (f.) en voiture; (energy) énergie f. **2.** vb. (auto, animals) conduire; (force) pousser.
drivel, n. bave f.
driver, n. (auto) chauffeur m.
driver's license, n. permis (m.) de conduire.
driveway, n. allée f.
driving, n. conduite f.
drizzle, 1. n. bruine f. **2.** vb. bruiner.
dromedary, n. dromadaire m.
drone, 1. n. abeille mâle f.; bourdonnement m. **2.** vb. bourdonner.
drool, vb. baver.

droop, vb. pencher.
drop, 1. n. goutte f.; (fall) chute f. **2.** vb. tomber, intr.; laisser tomber, tr.
dropout, n. étudiant qui quitte l'école avant de recevoir son diplôme m.
dropper, n. compte-gouttes m.
dropsy, n. hydropisie f.
drought, n. sécheresse f.
drove, n. troupeau m.
drown, vb. noyer, tr.
drowse, vb. s'assoupir.
drowsiness, n. somnolence f.
drowsy, adj. somnolent.
drudge, vb. s'éreinter.
drudgery, n. corvée f.
drug, n. drogue f.
drug addict, n. toxicomane m.f.
druggist, n. pharmacien m.
drugstore, n. pharmacie f.
drum, n. tambour m.; (ear) tympan m.
drum major, n. tambour-major m.
drummer, n. tambour m.
drumstick, n. baguette (f.) de tambour.
drunk, adj. ivre.
drunkard, n. ivrogne m.
drunkenness, n. ivresse f.; (habitual) ivrognerie f.
dry, 1. adj. sec m., sèche f. **2.** vb. sécher.
dry-clean, vb. nettoyer à sec.
dry cleaner, n. teinturier m.
dry dock, 1. n. cale sèche f. **2.** vb. mettre en cale sèche.
dry goods, n. articles (m.pl.) de nouveauté.
dryness, n. sécheresse f.
dual, adj. double.
dualism, n. dualisme m.
dubbed, adj. doublé.
dubious, adj. douteux.
duchess, n. duchesse f.
duchy, n. duché m.
duck, n. canard m.
duckling, n. caneton m.
duct, n. conduit m.
ductile, adj. ductile.
dud, 1. adj. incapable. **2.** n. obus qui a raté m.
due, adj. dû m., due f.
duel, n. duel m.

duelist, n. duelliste m.

duet, n. duo m.

duffel bag, n. sac (m.) pour les vêtements de rechange.

duffel coat, n. duffel-coat m.

dugout, n. abri-caverne f.

duke, n. duc m.

dukedom, n. duché m.

dulcet, adj. doux, suave.

dull, adj. (boring) ennuyeux; (blunt) émoussé.

dullard, n. lourdaud m.

dullness, n. (monotony) monotonie f.

duly, adv. dûment.

dumb, adj. muet m., muette f.; (stupid) sot m., sotte f.

dumbfound, vb. abasourdir, interdire.

dumbfounded, adj. sidéré.

dumbwaiter, n. monte-plats m.

dummy, n. (dressmaking) mannequin m.; (cards) mort m.

dump, 1. n. voirie f. **2.** vb. déposer; (computer) vider, transférer.

dumpling, n. boulette (de pâte) f.

dumpy, adj. boulot.

dun, vb. importuner, talonner.

dunce, n. crétin m.

dunce cap, n. bonnet d'âne m.

dune, n. dune f.

dung, n. fiente f.; (agriculture) fumier m.

dungaree, n. salopette f., bleus m.pl.

dungeon, n. cachot m.

dupe, 1. n. dupe f. **2.** vb. duper.

duplex, adj. double.

duplicate, 1. n. double m. **2.** vb. faire le double de.

duplication, n. duplication f.

duplicity, n. duplicité f.

durability, n. durabilité f.

durable, adj. durable.

duration, n. durée f.

duress, n. contrainte f., coercition f.

during, prep. pendant.

dusk, n. crépuscule m.

dusky, adj. sombre.

dust, 1. n. poussière f. **2.** vb. épousseter.

dustpan, n. ramasse-poussière m.

dust storm, n. tourbillon (m.) de poussière.

dusty, adj. poussiéreux.

Dutch, adj. and n. hollandais m.

Dutchman, n. Hollandais m.

dutiful, adj. respectueux, fidèle.

dutifully, adv. avec soumission.

duty, n. (moral, legal) devoir m.; (tax) droit m.; (be on d.) être de service.

duty-free, adj. exempt de droits, hors-taxe.

dwarf, adj. and n. nain m.

dwell, vb. demeurer.

dwindle, vb. diminuer.

dye, 1. n. teinture f. **2.** vb. teindre.

dyer, n. teinturier m.

dyestuff, n. matière colorante f.

dynamic, adj. dynamique.

dynamics, n. dynamique f.

dynamite, n. dynamite f.

dynamo, n. dynamo f.

dynasty, n. dynastie f.

dysentery, n. dysenterie f.

dyslexia, n. dyslexie f.

dyspepsia, n. dyspepsie f.

dyspeptic, adj. dyspeptique.

E

each, 1. adj. chaque. **2.** pron. chacun m., chacune f.; (e. other) l'un l'autre.

eager, adj. ardent.

eagerly, adv. ardemment, avidement.

eagerness, n. empressement m.

eagle, n. (bird) aigle m.; (mil.) aigle f.

eaglet, n. aiglon m.

ear, n. oreille f.

earache, n. mal d'oreille m.

eardrum, n. tympan m.

earl, n. comte m.

early, 1. adj. (of morning) matinal; (first) premier. **2.** adv. de bonne heure; tôt.

earmark, 1. n. marque distinctive f. **2.** vb. marquer, assigner.

earn, vb. gagner.

earnest, adj. sérieux.

earnestly, *adv.* sérieusement, sincèrement.

earnestness, *n.* gravité *f.*, sérieux *m.*

earnings, *n.* salaire *m.*

earphone, *n.* casque (téléphonique) *m.*

earring, *n.* boucle (*f.*) d'oreille.

earshot, *n.* portée de voix *f.*

earth, *n.* terre *f.*

earthenware, *n.* poterie *f.*, argile cuite *f.*, faïence *f.*

earthly, *adj.* terrestre.

earthquake, *n.* tremblement (*m.*) de terre.

earthworm, *n.* ver de terre *m.*

earthy, *adj.* terreux.

ease, 1. *n.* aise *f.*; (with e.) avec facilité. **2.** *vb.* calmer, détendre.

easel, *n.* chevalet *m.*

easily, *adv.* facilement.

easiness, *n.* facilité *f.*

east, *n.* est *m.*; (the E.) l'Orient *m.*

Easter, *n.* Pâques *m.*

easterly, *adj.* d'est, vers l'est.

eastern, *adj.* de l'est, oriental.

eastward, *adv.* vers l'est.

easy, *adj.* facile; (of manners) aisé.

easy chair, *n.* fauteuil *m.*

easygoing, *adj.* insouciant, peu exigeant, accommodant.

eat, *vb.* manger.

eaves, *n.* avant-toit *m.*

eavesdrop, *vb.* écouter aux portes.

ebb, *n.* (water) reflux *m.*; (decline) déclin *m.*

ebony, *n.* ébène *f.*

ebullient, *adj.* bouillonnant.

eccentric, *adj.* excentrique.

eccentricity, *n.* excentricité *f.*

ecclesiastic, *adj. and n.* ecclésiastique *m.*

ecclesiastical, *adj.* ecclésiastique.

echelon, *n.* échelon *m.*

echo, *n.* écho *m.*

eclipse, *n.* éclipse *f.*

ecological, *adj.* écologique.

ecology, *n.* écologie *f.*

economic, *adj.* économique.

economical, *adj.* (person) économe.

economics, *n.* économie (*f.*) politique.

economist, *n.* économiste *m.f.*

economize, *vb.* économiser.

economy, *n.* économie *f.*

ecosystem, *n.* écosystème *m.*

ecru, *n.* écru *m.*

ecstasy, *n.* (religious) extase *f.*; (*fig.*) transport *m.*

ecumenical, *adj.* œcuménique.

eczema, *n.* eczéma *m.*

eddy, *n.* remous *m.*

edge, *n.* bord *m.*; (blade) fil *m.*

edging, *n.* pose *f.*, bordure *f.*

edgy, *adj.* d'un air agacé.

edible, *adj.* comestible.

edict, *n.* édit *m.*

edifice, *n.* édifice *m.*

edify, *vb.* édifier.

edit, *vb.* (text) corriger; (report) préparer; (film) monter.

edition, *n.* édition *f.*

editor, *n.* (text) correcteur *m.*, éditeur *m.*; (paper) rédacteur *m.*

editorial, *n.* éditorial *m.*

educate, *vb.* (upbringing) élever; (knowledge) instruire.

education, *n.* éducation *f.*; (schooling) instruction *f.*

educational, *adj.* pédagogique; scolaire.

educator, *n.* éducateur *m.*

eel, *n.* anguille *f.*

eerie, *adj.* inquiétant.

efface, *vb.* effacer.

effect, 1. *n.* effet *m.* **2.** *vb.* effectuer.

effective, *adj.* (having effect) efficace; (in effect) effectif.

effectively, *adv.* efficacement, effectivement.

effectiveness, *n.* efficacité *f.*

effectual, *adj.* efficace.

effeminate, *adj.* efféminé.

effervesce, *vb.* être en effervescence, pétiller d'animation.

effervescent, *adj.* gazeux.

effete, *adj.* épuisé, caduc.

efficacious, *adj.* efficace.

efficacy, *n.* efficacité *f.*

efficiency, *n.* (person) compétence *f.*; (machine) rendement *m.*

efficient, *adj.* (person) capable.

efficiently, *adv.* efficacement, avec compétence.

effigy, *n.* effigie *f.*

effort, *n.* effort *m.*

effortless, *adj.* sans effort.

effrontery, *n.* effronterie *f.*

effulgent, *adj.* resplendissant.

effusive, *adj.* démonstratif.

egalitarian, *adj.* égalitaire.

egg, *n.* œuf *m.;* **(boiled e.)** œuf à la coque; **(fried e.)** œuf sur le plat; **(poached e.)** œuf poché; **(scrambled e.)** œuf brouillé.

eggplant, *n.* aubergine *f.*

egg shell, *n.* coquille *(f.)* d'œuf.

ego, *n.* moi *m.*

egoism, *n.* égoïsme *m.*

egotism, *n.* égotisme *m.*

egotist, *n.* égotiste *m.*

Egypt, *n.* Égypte *m.*

Egyptian, 1. *n.* Égyptien *m.* **2.** *adj.* égyptien.

eiderdown, *n.* édredon *m.*

eight, *adj. and n.* huit *m.*

eighteen, *adj. and n.* dix-huit *m.*

eighteenth, *adj.* and *n.* dix-huitième *m.f.*

eighth, *adj.* and *n.* huitième *m.f.*

eightieth, *adj.* and *n.* quatre-vingtième *m.f.*

eighty, *adj.* and *n.* quatre-vingts *m.*

Eire, *n.* République *(f.)* d'Irlande.

either, 1. *adj.* (each of two) chaque; (one or other) l'un ou l'autre. **2.** *pron.* chacun; l'un ou l'autre. **3.** *conj.* (e... or) ou... ou . . .

ejaculate, *vb.* éjaculer, prononcer.

eject, *vb.* (throw) jeter.

ejection, *n.* jet *m.,* éjection *f.,* expulsion *f.*

eke, *vb.* suppléer à, subsister pauvrement.

elaborate, 1. *adj.* minutieux. **2.** *vb.* élaborer.

elapse, *vb.* (time) s'écouler.

elastic, *adj. and n.* élastique *m.*

elasticity, *n.* élasticité *f.*

elate, *vb.* exalter, transporter.

elated, *adj.* exalté.

elation, *n.* exaltation *f.*

elbow, *n.* coude *m.*

elbowroom, *n.* aisance *(f.)* des coudes.

elder, *adj. and n.* aîné *m.*

elderberry, *n.* baie de sureau *f.*

elderly, *adj.* d'un certain âge.

eldest, *adj.* aîné.

elect, 1. *vb.* élire. **2.** *adj.* **(the president e.)** le président élu.

election, *n.* élection *f.*

electioneer, *vb.* faire une campagne électorale.

elective, *adj.* électif.

electorate, *n.* électorat *m.,* les votants *m.pl.*

electric, electrical, *adj.* électrique.

electric chair, *n.* fauteuil électrique *m.*

electric eel, *n.* anguille électrique *f.*

electrician, *n.* électricien *m.*

electricity, *n.* électricité *f.*

electrocardiogram, *n.* électrocardiogramme *m.*

electrocute, *vb.* électrocuter.

electrode, *n.* électrode *f.*

electrolysis, *n.* électrolyse *f.*

electron, *n.* électron *m.*

electronic, *adj.* électronique.

electronics, *n.* électronique *f.*

electroplate, 1. *vb.* plaquer. **2.** *adj.* plaqué.

elegance, *n.* élégance *f.*

elegant, *adj.* élégant.

elegiac, *adj.* élégiaque.

elegy, *n.* élégie *f.*

element, *n.* élément *m.*

elemental, elementary, *adj.* élémentaire.

elephant, *n.* éléphant *m.*

elephantine, *adj.* éléphantin.

elevate, *vb.* élever.

elevation, *n.* élévation *f.*

elevator, *n.* ascenseur *m.*

eleven, *adj. and n.* onze *m.*

eleventh, *adj. and n.* onzième *m.f.*

elf, *n.* elfe *m.,* lutin *m.*

elfin, *adj.* d'elfe.

elicit, *vb.* tirer, faire jaillir.

eligibility, *n.* éligibilité *f.*

eligible, *adj.* éligible.

eliminate, *vb.* éliminer.

elimination, *n.* élimination *f.*

elixir, *n.* élixir *m.*

elk, *n.* élan *m.*

ellipse, *n.* ellipse *f.*

elm, *n.* orme *m.*

elocution, *n.* élocution *f.*

elongate, *vb.* allonger, étendre.

elope, *vb.* s'enfuir.

eloquence, *n.* éloquence *f.*

eloquent, *adj.* éloquent.

eloquently, *adv.* d'une manière éloquente.

else, 1. *adj.* autre; **(someone e.)**

quelqu'un d'autre; (**everyone e.**) tous les autres. **2.** *adv.* autrement.
elsewhere, *adv.* ailleurs.
elucidate, *vb.* élucider, éclaircir.
elude, *vb.* éluder.
elusive, *adj.* évasif, insaisissable.
emaciated, *adj.* émacié.
emanate, *vb.* émaner.
emancipate, *vb.* émanciper.
emancipation, *n.* émancipation *f.*
emancipator, *n.* émancipateur *m.*
emasculate, *vb.* émasculer.
embalm, *vb.* embaumer.
embankment, *n.* levée *f.*
embargo, *n.* embargo *m.*
embark, *vb.* embarquer, *tr.*
embarkation, *n.* embarquement *m.*
embarrass, *vb.* embarrasser.
embarrassing, *adj.* embarrassant.
embarrassment, *n.* embarras *m.*
embassy, *n.* ambassade *f.*
embed, *vb.* encastrer.
embellish, *vb.* embellir.
embellishment, *n.* embellissement *m.*
ember, *n.* braise *f.*, charbon ardent *m.*
embezzle, *vb.* détourner.
embitter, *vb.* aigrir, envenimer.
emblazon, *vb.* blasonner.
emblem, *n.* emblème *m.*
emblematic, *adj.* emblématique.
embody, *vb.* incarner, incorporer.
emboss, *vb.* graver en relief, travailler en bosse.
embrace, **1.** *n.* étreinte *f.* **2.** *vb.* embrasser.
embroider, *vb.* broder.
embroidery, *n.* broderie *f.*
embroil, *vb.* embrouiller.
embryo, *n.* embryon *m.*
embryology, *n.* embryologie *f.*
embryonic, *adj.* embryonnaire.
emerald, *n.* émeraude *f.*
emerge, *vb.* émerger.
emergency, *n.* circonstance (*f.*) critique; (**e. exit**) sortie (*f.*) de secours; (**e. landing**) atterrissage (*m.*) forcé.
emergent, *adj.* émergent.
emery, *n.* émeri *m.*
emetic, *n.* émétique *m.*
emigrant, *n.* émigrant *m.*
emigrate, *vb.* émigrer.
emigration, *n.* émigration *f.*

eminence, *n.* éminence *f.*
eminent, *adj.* éminent.
emissary, *n.* émissaire *m.*
emission control, *n.* appareil (*m.*) pour limiter l'émission de vapeurs nuisibles.
emit, *vb.* émettre.
emollient, *adj.* émollient.
emolument, *n.* traitement *m.*
emotion, *n.* émotion *f.*
emotional, *adj.* émotif; (**excitable**) émotionnable.
emperor, *n.* empereur *m.*
emphasis, *n.* (impressiveness) force *f.*; (stress) accent *m.*
emphasize, *vb.* mettre en relief, souligner.
emphatic, *adj.* (manner) énergique.
empire, *n.* empire *m.*
empirical, *adj.* empirique.
employ, *vb.* employer.
employee, *n.* employé *m.*
employer, *n.* patron *m.*
employment, *n.* emploi *m.*
employment agency, *n.* agence (*f.*) de placement.
empower, *vb.* autoriser.
empress, *n.* impératrice *f.*
emptiness, *n.* vide *m.*
empty, **1.** *adj.* vide. **2.** *vb.* vider.
emulate, *vb.* émuler.
emulsion, *n.* émulsion *f.*
enable, *vb.* mettre à même (de).
enact, *vb.* (law) décréter; (play) jouer.
enactment, *n.* promulgation *f.*, acte législatif *m.*
enamel, *n.* émail *m.*, *pl.* émaux.
enamored, *adj.* (**be e. of**) être épris de.
encamp, *vb.* camper, faire camper.
encampment, *n.* campement *m.*
encased, *adj.* (**e. in**) enfermé dans.
encephalitis, *n.* encéphalite *f.*
encephalon, *n.* encéphale *m.*
enchant, *vb.* enchanter.
enchanting, *adj.* ravissant.
enchantment, *n.* enchantement *m.*
encircle, *vb.* entourer.
enclose, *vb.* enclore; (in letter) joindre.
enclosure, *n.* enclos *m.*; (in letter) pièce (*f.*) jointe.
encompass, *vb.* entourer.

encounter, vb. rencontrer.

encourage, vb. encourager.

encouragement, n. encouragement m.

encroach, vb. empiéter.

encumber, vb. encombrer.

encyclical, n. encyclique f.

encyclopedia, n. encyclopédie f.

end, 1. n. fin f.; (extremity) bout m.; (aim) but m. **2.** vb. finir.

endanger, vb. mettre en danger.

endear, vb. rendre cher.

endearing, adj. attachant.

endearment, n. charme m., attrait m.

endeavor, 1. n. effort m. **2.** vb. s'efforcer.

endemic, adj. endémique.

ending, n. terminaison f.

endive, n. chicorée f., endive f.

endless, adj. sans fin.

endocrine gland, n. glande endocrine f.

endorse, vb. (sign) endosser; (support) appuyer.

endorsement, n. (signing) endossement m.; (approval) approbation f.

endow, vb. doter.

endowment, n. dotation f., fondation f.

endurance, n. résistance f.

endure, vb. supporter.

enduring, adj. durable.

enema, n. lavement m.

enemy, adj. and n. ennemi m.

energetic, adj. énergique.

energy, n. énergie f.

enervate, vb. énerver, affaiblir.

enervation, n. affaiblissement m.

enfold, vb. envelopper.

enforce, vb. imposer; (law) exécuter.

enforcement, n. exécution f.

enfranchise, vb. affranchir, accorder le droit de vote.

engage, vb. engager, tr.; (become e.d. to be married) se fiancer.

engaged, adj. occupé, pris; fiancé.

engagement, n. engagement m.; (marriage) fiançailles f.pl.

engaging, adj. attrayant, séduisant.

engender, vb. engendrer.

engine, n. machine f.; (train) locomotive f.; (motor) moteur m.

engineer, n. (profession) ingénieur m.; (engine operator) mécanicien m.; (mil.) soldat (m.) du génie.

engineering, n. génie m., ingénierie f.

England, n. Angleterre f.

English, adj. and n. anglais m.

Englishman, n. Anglais m.

Englishwoman, n. Anglaise f.

engrave, vb. graver.

engraver, n. graveur m.

engraving, n. gravure f.

engross, vb. (absorb) absorber.

engrossing, adj. absorbant.

engulf, vb. engouffrer.

enhance, vb. rehausser.

enigma, n. énigme f.

enigmatic, adj. énigmatique.

enjoin, vb. enjoindre.

enjoy, vb. jouir de; (e. oneself) s'amuser.

enjoyable, adj. agréable.

enjoyment, n. plaisir m.

enlace, vb. enlacer.

enlarge, vb. agrandir, tr.

enlargement, n. agrandissement m.

enlarger, n. agrandisseur m., amplificateur m.

enlighten, vb. éclairer.

enlightenment, n. éclaircissement m.; (the E.) le Siècle (m.) des Lumières.

enlist, vb. enrôler, tr.

enlisted man, n. gradé m.

enlistment, n. enrôlement m.

enliven, vb. animer.

enmesh, vb. engrener, embarrasser.

enmity, n. inimitié f.

ennoble, vb. anoblir.

ennui, n. ennui m.

enormity, n. énormité f.

enormous, adj. énorme.

enough, adj. and adv. assez (de).

enrage, vb. faire enrager.

enrapture, vb. ravir, enchanter.

enrich, vb. enrichir.

enroll, vb. enrôler, s'inscrire.

enrollment, n. inscription f.

ensemble, n. ensemble m.

enshrine, vb. enchâsser.

ensign, n. (navy) enseigne m.

enslave, vb. asservir.
ensnare, vb. prendre au piège.
ensue, vb. s'ensuivre.
entail, vb. (involve) entraîner; (law) substituer.
entangle, vb. empêtrer.
enter, vb. entrer (dans).
enterprise, n. entreprise f.
enterprising, adj. entreprenant.
entertain, vb. (amuse) amuser; (receive) recevoir.
entertainment, n. amusement m.
enthrall, vb. captiver, ensorceler.
enthusiasm, n. enthousiasme m.
enthusiast, n. enthousiaste f.
enthusiastic, adj. enthousiaste.
entice, vb. attirer.
entire, adj. entier.
entirely, adv. entièrement.
entirety, n. totalité f.
entitle, vb. donner droit à; (book) intituler.
entity, n. entité f.
entomb, vb. enterrer, ensevelir.
entrails, n. entrailles f.pl.
entrain, vb. embarquer en chemin de fer.
entrance, 1. n. entrée f. **2.** vb. enchanter.
entrant, n. débutant m., inscrit m.
entrap, vb. attraper, prendre au piège.
entreat, vb. supplier.
entreaty, n. instance f.
entrench, vb. retrancher.
entrust to, vb. confier à.
entry, n. (entrance) entrée f.; (recording) inscription f.
enumerate, vb. énumérer.
enumeration, n. énumération f.
enunciate, vb. énoncer.
enunciation, n. énonciation f.
envelop, vb. envelopper.
envelope, n. enveloppe f.
enviable, adj. enviable.
envious, adj. envieux.
environment, n. milieu m.; (ecology) environnement m.
environmentalist, n. écologiste m.f.; environnementaliste m.
environmental protection, n. protection (f.) de l'environnement.
environs, n. environs m.pl., alentours m.pl.
envisage, vb. envisager.

envoy, n. envoyé m.
envy, 1. n. envie f. **2.** vb. envier.
enzyme, n. enzyme m.
eon, n. éon m.
ephemeral, adj. éphémère.
epic, 1. n. épopée f. **2.** adj. épique.
epicure, n. gourmet m.
epidemic, n. épidémie f.
epidermis, n. épiderme m.
epigram, n. épigramme f.
epilepsy, n. épilepsie f.
epilogue, n. épilogue m.
episode, n. épisode m.
epistle, n. épître f.
epitaph, n. épitaphe f.
epithet, n. épithète f.
epitome, n. épitomé m., résumé m.
epitomize, vb. résumer, abréger.
epoch, n. époque f.
equable, adj. uniforme, régulier.
equal, 1. adj. égal; **2.** vb. égaliser.
equality, n. égalité f.
equalize, vb. égaliser, tr.
equanimity, n. tranquillité (f.) d'esprit, équanimité f., sérénité f.
equate, vb. égaler, mettre en équation.
equation, n. équation f.
equator, n. équateur m.
equatorial, adj. équatorial.
equestrian, adj. équestre.
equidistant, adj. équidistant.
equilateral, adj. équilatéral.
equilibrium, n. équilibre m.
equinox, n. équinoxe m.
equip, vb. équiper.
equipment, n. équipement m.
equitable, adj. équitable, juste.
equity, n. équité f., action f.
equivalent, adj. and n. équivalent m.
equivocal, adj. équivoque.
equivocate, vb. équivoquer.
era, n. ère f.
eradicate, vb. déraciner.
eradicator, n. effaceur m., grattoir m.
erase, vb. effacer.
eraser, n. gomme f.
erasure, n. rature f.
erect, adj. droit.
erection, n. érection f., construction f.
erectness, n. attitude droite f.
ermine, n. hermine f.

erode, vb. éroder, ronger.
erosion, n. érosion f.
erosive, adj. érosif.
erotic, adj. érotique.
err, vb. errer.
errand, n. course f.
errant, adj. errant.
erratic, adj. irrégulier, excentrique.
erring, adj. égaré, dévoyé.
erroneous, adj. erroné.
error, n. erreur f.
erudite, adj. érudit.
erudition, n. érudition f.
erupt, vb. entrer en éruption.
eruption, n. éruption f.
escalate, vb. escalader.
escalator, n. escalier roulant m.
escapade, n. escapade f.
escape, 1. n. fuite f. **2.** vb. échapper.
escapism, n. évasion f., échappement m.
eschew, vb. éviter, s'abstenir.
escort, 1. n. (mil.) escorte f.; (to a lady) cavalier m. **2.** vb. escorter.
esculent, adj. comestible.
escutcheon, n. écusson m.
Eskimo, 1. n. Esquimau m., Esquimaude f. **2.** adj. esquimau m., esquimaude f.
esoteric, adj. ésotérique.
especially, adj. surtout, particulièrement.
espionage, n. espionnage m.
espousal, n. adoption f., adhésion (à) f.
espouse, vb. épouser, embrasser (une cause).
esquire, n. écuyer m.; titre honorifique d'un "gentleman" m.
essay, 1. n. essai m.; (school) composition f. **2.** vb. essayer.
essayist, n. essayiste m.
essence, n. essence f.
essential, adj. essentiel.
essentially, adv. essentiellement.
establish, vb. établir.
establishment, n. établissement m.; (the E.) l'ordre (m.) établi.
estate, n. (condition, class) état m.; (wealth) biens m.pl.; (land) propriété f.
esteem, 1. n. estime f. **2.** vb. estimer.
estimable, adj. estimable.

estimate, 1. n. estimation f.; (comm.) devis m. **2.** vb. estimer.
estimation, n. (opinion) jugement m., estimation f.
estrange, vb. aliéner.
estuary, n. estuaire m.
etching, n. gravure (f.) à l'eau-forte.
eternal, adj. éternel.
eternity, n. éternité f.
ether, n. éther m.
ethereal, adj. éthéré.
ethical, adj. moral.
ethics, n. éthique f.
Ethiopia, n. Éthiopie f.
ethnic, adj. ethnique.
etiquette, n. étiquette f.
Etruscan, 1. n. Étrusque m.f. **2.** adj. étrusque.
etymology, n. étymologie f.
eucalyptus, n. eucalyptus m.
eugenic, adj. eugénésique.
eugenics, n. eugénisme m., eugénique f.
eulogize, vb. faire l'éloge de.
eulogy, n. panégyrique m.
eunuch, n. eunuque m.
euphonious, adj. mélodieux, euphonique.
euphoria, n. euphorie f.
eurocheque, n. eurochèque m.
Europe, n. Europe f.
European, 1. n. Européen m. **2.** adj. européen.
European Community, n. Communauté (f.) européenne.
euthanasia, n. euthanasie f.
evacuate, vb. évacuer.
evacuee, n. évacué m.
evade, vb. éluder.
evaluate, vb. évaluer.
evaluation, n. évaluation f.
evanescent, adj. évanescent, éphémère.
evangelist, n. évangéliste m.
evaporate, vb. évaporer, tr.
evaporation, n. évaporation f.
evasion, n. subterfuge m.
evasive, adj. évasif.
eve, n. veille f.
even, 1. adj. égal; (number) pair. **2.** adv. même.
evening, n. soir m.; (span of e.) soirée f.
evenness, n. égalité f.

event, n. événement m.; (eventuality) cas m.
eventful, adj. mouvementé.
eventual, adj. (ultimate) définitif; (contingent) éventuel.
eventually, adv. en fin de compte, un jour ou l'autre.
ever, adv. (at all times) toujours; (at any time) jamais.
everglade, n. région marécageuse (de la Floride) f.
evergreen, adj. à feuilles persistantes, toujours vert.
everlasting, adj. éternel.
every, adj. (each) chaque; (all) tous les m.; toutes les f.
everybody, everyone, pron. tout le monde; chacun.
everyday, adj. de tous les jours.
everything, pron. tout.
everywhere, adv. partout.
evict, vb. évincer.
eviction, n. éviction f., expulsion f.
evidence, n. évidence f.; (proof) preuve f.
evident, adj. évident.
evidently, adv. évidemment.
evil, 1. n. mal m. 2. adj. mauvais.
evince, vb. démontrer.
eviscerate, vb. éviscérer.
evoke, vb. évoquer.
evolution, n. évolution f.
evolutionist, n. évolutionniste m.f.
evolve, vb. évoluer, développer.
ewe, n. agnelle f.
exacerbate, vb. exacerber.
exact, adj. exact.
exacting, adj. (person) exigeant.
exactly, adv. exactement.
exaggerate, vb. exagérer.
exaggerated, adj. exagéré.
exaggeration, n. exagération f.
exalt, vb. exalter; (raise) élever.
exaltation, n. exaltation f.
examination, n. examen m.
examine, vb. examiner.
example, n. exemple m.
exasperate, vb. exaspérer.
exasperation, n. exaspération f.
excavate, vb. creuser.
exceed, vb. excéder.
exceedingly, adv. extrêmement.
excel, vb. exceller, intr.
excellence, excellency, n. excellence f.

excellent, adj. excellent.
excelsior, n. copeaux (m.pl.) d'emballage.
except, 1. vb. excepter. 2. prep. excepté, sauf.
exception, n. exception f.
exceptional, adj. exceptionnel.
excerpt, n. extrait m.
excess, n. excès m.; (surplus) excédent m.
excessive, adj. excessif.
exchange, 1. n. échange m.; (money) change m. 2. vb. échanger.
exchangeable, adj. échangeable.
excise, n. contribution indirecte f., régie f.
excitable, adj. émotionnable, excitable.
excite, vb. exciter.
excitement, n. agitation f.
exciting, adj. passionnant.
exclaim, vb. s'écrier.
exclamation, n. exclamation f.
exclamation point or **mark,** n. point (m.) d'exclamation.
exclude, vb. exclure.
exclusion, n. exclusion f.
exclusive, adj. exclusif; (stylish) sélect.
excommunicate, vb. excommunier.
excommunication, n. excommunication f.
excoriate, vb. excorier, écorcher.
excrement, n. excrément m.
excruciating, adj. atroce, affreux.
exculpate, vb. disculper, exonérer.
excursion, n. excursion f.
excusable, adj. excusable.
excuse, 1. n. excuse f. 2. vb. excuser.
execrable, adj. exécrable, abominable.
execute, vb. exécuter.
execution, n. exécution f.
executioner, n. bourreau m.
executive, adj. and n. exécutif m., cadre m.
executive mansion, n. maison présidentielle f.
executor, n. exécuteur m.
exemplary, adj. exemplaire.
exemplify, vb. expliquer par des exemples.

exempt, 1. *adj.* exempt. **2.** *vb.* exempter.

exercise, 1. *n.* exercice *m.* **2.** *vb.* exercer.

exercise bike, *n.* vélo *(m.)* d'appartement.

exert, *vb.* employer; (**e. oneself**) s'efforcer de.

exertion, *n.* effort *m.*

exhale, *vb.* exhaler.

exhaust, 1. *n.* (machines) échappement *m.* **2.** *vb.* épuiser.

exhausted, *adj.* épuisé.

exhaustion, *n.* épuisement *m.*

exhaustive, *adj.* complet, approfondi.

exhibit, *vb.* (pictures, etc.) exposer; (show) montrer.

exhibition, *n.* exposition *f.*

exhibitionism, *n.* exhibitionnisme *m.*

exhilarate, *vb.* égayer.

exhort, *vb.* exhorter.

exhortation, *n.* exhortation *f.*

exhume, *vb.* exhumer.

exigency, *n.* exigence *f.*

exile, 1. *n.* exil *m.*; (person) exilé *m.* **2.** *vb.* exiler.

exist, *vb.* exister.

existence, *n.* existence *f.*

existent, *adj.* existant.

exit, 1. *n.* sortie *f.* **2.** *vb.* sortir.

exit ramp, *n.* bretelle *(f.)* d'accès.

exodus, *n.* exode *m.*

exonerate, *vb.* exonérer.

exorbitant, *adj.* exorbitant.

exorcise, *vb.* exorciser.

exotic, *adj.* exotique.

expand, *vb.* étendre, *tr.*; (dilate) dilater, *tr.*

expanse, *n.* étendue *f.*

expansion, *n.* expansion *f.*

expansive, *adj.* expansif.

expatiate, *vb.* discourir.

expatriate, *vb.* expatrier.

expect, *vb.* s'attendre à; (await) attendre.

expectancy, *n.* attente *f.*

expectant, *adj.* (**e. mother**) future maman *f.*

expectation, *n.* attente *f.*; (hope) espérance *f.*

expectorate, *vb.* expectorer.

expediency, *n.* convenance *f.*

expedient, *n.* expédient *m.*

expedite, *vb.* activer, accélérer.

expedition, *n.* expédition *f.*

expel, *vb.* expulser.

expend, *vb.* (money) dépenser; (use up) épuiser.

expenditure, *n.* dépense *f.*

expense, *n.* dépense *f.*; (expenses) frais *m.pl.*

expensive, *adj.* coûteux, cher.

expensively, *adv.* coûteusement.

experience, 1. *n.* expérience *f.* **2.** *vb.* éprouver.

experienced, *adj.* expérimenté.

experiment, *n.* expérience *f.*

experimental, *adj.* expérimental.

expert, *adj. and n.* expert *m.*

expiate, *vb.* expier.

expiration, *n.* expiration *f.*

expire, *vb.* expirer.

explain, *vb.* expliquer.

explanation, *n.* explication *f.*

explanatory, *adj.* explicatif.

expletive, *n.* explétif *m.*

explicit, *adj.* explicite.

explode, *vb.* (burst) éclater, *intr.*

exploit, 1. *n.* exploit *m.* **2.** *vb.* exploiter.

exploitation, *n.* exploitation *f.*

exploration, *n.* exploration *f.*

exploratory, *adj.* exploratif.

explore, *vb.* explorer.

explorer, *n.* explorateur *m.*

explosion, *n.* explosion *f.*

explosive, *adj. and n.* explosif *m.*

exponent, *n.* interprète *m.*

export, 1. *n.* (exportation) exportation *f.*; (exported object) article *(m.)* d'exportation. **2.** *vb.* exporter.

exportation, *n.* exportation *f.*

expose, *vb.* exposer.

exposé, *n.* exposé *m.*

exposition, *n.* exposition *f.*

expository, *adj.* expositoire.

expostulate, *vb.* faire des remontrances à.

exposure, *n.* exposition *f.*

expound, *vb.* exposer.

express, 1. *adj.* exprès. **2.** *vb.* exprimer.

expression, *n.* expression *f.*

expressive, *adj.* expressif.

expressly, *adv.* expressément.

expressman, *n.* agent *(m.)* de messageries.

expropriate, vb. exproprier.
expulsion, n. expulsion f.
expunge, vb. effacer, rayer.
expurgate, vb. expurger, épurer.
exquisite, adj. exquis.
extant, adj. existant.
extemporaneous, adj. improvisé, impromptu.
extend, vb. étendre; (prolong) prolonger.
extension, n. extension f.
extensive, adj. étendu.
extensively, adv. largement, considérablement.
extent, n. étendue f.; **(to some e.)** jusqu'à un certain point.
extenuate, vb. (tire out) exténuer; (diminish) atténuer.
extenuating circumstances, n. circonstances (f.pl.) atténuantes.
exterior, adj. and n. extérieur m.
exterminate, vb. exterminer.
extermination, n. extermination f.
external, adj. externe.
extinct, adj. éteint.
extinction, n. extinction f.
extinguish, vb. éteindre.
extol, vb. vanter.
extort, vb. extorquer.
extortion, n. extorsion f.
extortioner, n. extorqueur m.
extra, adj. (additional) supplémentaire; (spare) de réserve.

extra-, prefix. (outside of) en dehors de; (intensive) extra-.
extract, 1. n. extrait m. **2.** vb. extraire.
extraction, n. extraction f.
extradite, vb. extrader.
extramarital, adj. extra-conjugal.
extraneous, adj. étranger à.
extraordinary, adj. extraordinaire.
extravagance, n. extravagance f.; (money) prodigalité f.
extravagant, adj. extravagant; (money) prodigue.
extravaganza, m. œuvre fantaisiste f.
extreme, adj. and n. extrême m.
extremity, n. extrémité f.
extricate, vb. dégager, tirer.
extrovert, n. extroverti m.
exuberant, adj. exubérant.
exude, vb. exsuder.
exult, vb. exulter.
exultant, adj. exultant, joyeux.
eye, n. œil m. pl. yeux.
eyeball, n. globe (m.) de l'œil.
eyebrow, n. sourcil m.
eyeglass, n. lorgnon m.
eyeglasses, n. lunettes f.pl.
eyelash, n. cil m.
eyelet, n. œillet m.
eyelid, n. paupière f.
eye shadow, n. fard (m.) à paupières.
eyesight, n. vue f.
eyewitness n. témoin oculaire m.

F

fable, n. fable f.
fabric, n. (structure) édifice m.; (cloth) tissu m.
fabricate, vb. fabriquer.
fabrication, n. fabrication f.
fabulous, adj. fabuleux.
façade, n. façade f.
face, 1. n. figure f. **2.** vb. faire face à.
facet, n. facette f.
facetious, adj. facétieux.
face value, n. valeur nominale f.
facial, adj. facial.
facile, adj. facile.
facilitate, vb. faciliter.
facility, n. facilité f.

facing, n. revêtement m., revers m.
facsimile, n. fac-similé m.; (document) télécopie f., fax m.; **(f. machine)** télécopieur m.
fact, n. fait m.; **(as a matter of f.)** en effet.
faction, n. faction f.
factor, n. facteur m.
factory, n. fabrique f., usine f.
factual, adj. effectif, positif.
faculty, n. faculté f.
fad, n. marotte f.
fade, vb. intr. se faner; (color) se décolorer; **(f. away)** s'évanouir.
fail, vb. manquer; (not succeed) échouer.

failing, 1. n. manquement m. **2.** adj. faiblissant. **3.** prep. au défaut de.

faille, n. faille f.

failure, n. (lack) défaut m.; (want of success) insuccès m.

faint, 1. adj. faible. **2.** vb. s'évanouir.

faintly, adv. faiblement, timidement, légèrement.

fair, 1. n. foire f. **2.** adj. (beautiful) beau m., belle f.; (blond) blond; (honest) juste; (pretty good) passable.

fairly, adv. honnêtement, impartialement.

fairness, n. (honesty) honnêteté f.

fairy, n. fée f.

fairyland, n. pays (m.) des fées.

fairy tale, n. conte (m.) de fées.

faith, n. foi f.

faithful, adj. fidèle.

faithless, adj. infidèle.

fake, vb. truquer.

faker, n. truqueur m.

falcon, n. faucon m.

falconry, n. fauconnerie f.

fall, 1. n. chute f.; (autumn) automne m. **2.** vb. tomber.

fallacious, adj. fallacieux.

fallacy, n. fausseté f.

fallen, adj. tombé, déchu.

fallible, adj. faillible.

fallout, n. pluie radioactive f.

fallow, adj. en jachère.

false, adj. faux m., fausse f.

falsehood, n. mensonge m.

falseness, n. fausseté f.

falsetto, n. and adj. fausset m.

falsification, n. falsification f.

falsify, vb. falsifier.

falter, vb. hésiter.

fame, n. renommée f.

famed, adj. célèbre, renommé, fameux.

familiar, adj. familier.

familiarity, n. familiarité f.

familiarize, vb. familiariser.

family, n. famille f.

famine, n. (food) disette f.; (general) famine f.

famished, adj. affamé.

famous, adj. célèbre.

fan, n. éventail m.; (mechanical) ventilateur m.; (of person) admirateur m.

fanatic, adj. and n. fanatique m.

fanatical, adj. fanatique.

fanaticism, n. fanatisme m.

fan belt, n. courroie (f.) de ventilateur.

fanciful, adj. fantastique, fantaisiste.

fancy, 1. n. fantaisie f. **2.** vb. se figurer; avoir envie de.

fanfare, n. fanfare f.

fang, n. croc (of a dog) m., crochet (of a snake) m.

fantastic, adj. fantastique.

fantasy, n. fantaisie f.

far, adj. loin; (so f.) jusqu'ici; (as f. as) autant que; (much) beaucoup; (by f.) de beaucoup.

faraway, adj. lointain.

farce, n. farce f.

farcical, adj. bouffon.

fare, 1. n. (price) prix m.; (food) chère f. **2.** vb. aller.

Far East, n. Extrême-Orient m.

farewell, interj. and n. adieu m.

far-fetched, adj. forcé.

far-flung, adj. très étendu, vaste.

farina, n. farine f.

farm, n. ferme f.

farmer, n. fermier m.

farmhouse, n. maison (f.) de ferme.

farming, n. culture f.

farmyard, n. cour de ferme f.

far-reaching, adj. de grande envergure.

far-sighted, adj. clairvoyant.

farther, 1. adj. plus éloigné. **2.** adv. plus loin.

farthest, adj. and adv. le plus lointain.

fascinate, vb. fasciner.

fascination, n. fascination f.

fascism, n. fascisme m.

fashion, n. mode f.; (manner) manière f.

fashionable, adj. à la mode.

fast, 1. n. jeûne m. **2.** adj. (speedy) rapide; (firm) ferme; (of clock) en avance. **3.** vb. jeûner. **4.** adv. (quickly) vite; (firmly) ferme.

fasten, vb. attacher, tr.

fastener, n. fermeture f.

fastening, n. attache f.

fastidious, *adj.* difficile.
fat, *adj.* gras *m.*, grasse *f.*
fatal, *adj.* fatal; (deadly) mortel.
fatality, *n.* fatalité *f.*
fatally, *adv.* fatalement, mortellement.
fate, *n.* destin *m.*
fateful, *adj.* fatal.
father, *n.* père *m.*
fatherhood, *n.* paternité *f.*
father-in-law, *n.* beau-père *m.*
fatherland, *n.* patrie *f.*
fatherless, *adj.* sans père.
fatherly, *adj.* paternel.
fathom, 1. *n.* (naut.) brasse *f.* 2. *vb.* sonder.
fatigue, *n.* fatigue *f.*
fatten, *vb.* engraisser.
fatty, *adj.* graisseux.
fatuous, *adj.* sot.
faucet, *n.* robinet *m.*
fault, *n.* (mistake) faute *f.*; (defect) défaut *m.*
faultfinding, *n.* disposition (*f.*) à critiquer.
faultless, *adj.* sans défaut.
faultlessly, *adv.* d'une manière impeccable.
faulty, *adj.* défectueux.
fauna, *n.* faune *f.*
favor, 1. *n.* faveur *f.* 2. *vb.* favoriser.
favorable, *adj.* favorable.
favored, *adj.* favorisé.
favorite, *adj. and n.* favori *m.*, favorite *f.*
favoritism, *n.* favoritisme *m.*
fawn, *n.* faon *m.*
fax, 1. *n.* (document) télécopie *f.*, fax *m.*; (**f. machine**) télécopieur *m.* 2. *vb.* télécopier, faxer.
faze, *vb.* bouleverser.
fear, 1. *n.* crainte *f.* 2. *vb.* craindre.
fearful, *adj.* (person) craintif; (thing) effrayant.
fearless, *adj.* intrépide.
fearlessness, *n.* intrépidité *f.*
fearsome, *adj.* redoutable.
feasible, *adj.* faisable.
feast, *n.* fête *f.*; (banquet) festin *m.*
feat, *n.* exploit *m.*
feather, *n.* plume *f.*
feathered, *adj.* emplumé.
featherweight, *n.* poids (*m.*) plume.

feathery, *adj.* plumeux.
feature, *n.* trait *m.*
February, *n.* février *m.*
fecund, *adj.* fécond.
federal, *adj.* fédéral.
federation, *n.* fédération *f.*
fedora, *n.* chapeau mou *m.*
fee, *n.* (for professional services) honoraires *m.pl.*; (school) frais *m.pl.*
feeble, *adj.* faible.
feeble-minded, *adj.* d'esprit faible.
feebleness, *n.* faiblesse *f.*
feed, 1. *n.* nourriture *f.* 2. *vb.* nourrir, *tr.*
feedback, *n.* action (*f.*) de contrôle en retour.
feel, *vb.* sentir, *tr.*; (touch) tâter.
feeling, *n.* sentiment *m.*
feign, *vb.* feindre.
feint, *n.* feinte *f.*
felicitate, *vb.* féliciter.
felicitous, *adj.* heureux.
felicity, *n.* félicité *f.*
feline, *adj.* félin.
fell, *adj.* funeste.
fellow, *n.* (general) homme *m.*, garçon *m.*; (companion) compagnon *m.*
fellowship, *n.* camaraderie *f.*; (university) bourse (*f.*) universitaire.
fellow traveler, *n.* compagnon (*m.*) de route.
felon, *n.* criminel *m.*
felony, *n.* crime *m.*
felt, *n.* feutre *m.*
female, 1. *n.* (person) femme *f.*; (animals, plants) femelle *f.* 2. *adj.* féminin, femelle.
feminine, *adj.* féminin.
femininity, *n.* féminité *f.*
fence, 1. *n.* clôture *f.* 2. *vb.* (enclose) enclore; (sword, foil) faire de l'escrime.
fencer, *n.* escrimeur *m.*
fencing, *n.* escrime *f.*
fender, *n.* garde-boue *m.*; (fireplace) garde-feu *m.*
ferment, *vb.* fermenter.
fermentation, *n.* fermentation *f.*
fern, *n.* fougère *f.*
ferocious, *adj.* féroce.
ferociously, *adv.* d'une manière féroce.
ferocity, *n.* férocité *f.*

ferry, n. passage (m.) en bac; (f. boat) bac m.
fertile, adj. fertile.
fertility, n. fertilité f.
fertilization, n. fertilisation f.
fertilize, vb. fertiliser.
fervency, n. ardeur f.
fervent, adj. fervent.
fervently, adv. ardemment.
fervid, adj. fervent.
fervor, n. ferveur f.
fester, vb. suppurer.
festival, n. fête f.
festive, adj. de fête.
festivity, n. réjouissance f.
festoon, 1. n. feston m. 2. vb. festonner.
fetal, adj. foetal.
fetch, vb. (go and get) aller chercher; (bring) apporter.
fetching, adj. attrayant.
fete, n. fête f.
fetid, adj. fétide.
fetish, n. fétiche m.
fetlock, n. fanon m.
fetter, 1. n. lien m., chaîne f. 2. vb. enchaîner.
fetus, n. fœtus m.
feud, n. inimitié f.; (historical) fief m.
feudal, adj. féodal.
feudalism, n. régime féodal m.
fever, n. fièvre f.
feverish, adj. fiévreux.
feverishly, adv. fébrilement, fiévreusement.
few, 1. adj. peu de; (a f.) quelques. 2. pron. peu; (a f.) quelques-uns.
fiancé, n. fiancé m.
fiasco, n. fiasco m.
fiat, n. décret m.
fib, n. petit mensonge m.
fiber, n. fibre f.
fiberboard, n. fibre (m.) de bois.
fiberglass, n. fibre (m.) de verre.
fibrous, adj. fibreux.
fickle, adj. volage.
fickleness, n. inconstance f.
fiction, n. fiction f.; (literature) romans m.pl.
fictional, adj. de romans.
fictitious, adj. fictif, imaginaire.
fictitiously, adv. d'une manière factice.

fiddle, 1. n. violon m. 2. vb. jouer du violon.
fiddlesticks, interj. quelle blague!
fidelity, n. fidélité f.
fidget, vb. se remuer.
field, n. champ m.
fiend, n. démon m.
fiendish, adj. diabolique, infernal.
fierce, adj. féroce.
fiery, adj. ardent.
fiesta, n. fête f.
fife, n. fifre m.
fifteen, adj. and n. quinze m.
fifteenth, adj. and n. quinzième m.f.
fifth, adj. and n. cinquième m.f.
fifty, adj. and n. cinquante m.
fig, n. figue f.
fight, 1. n. combat m.; (struggle) lutte f.; (quarrel) dispute f. 2. vb. combattre; se disputer.
fighter, n. combattant m.
figment, n. invention f.
figurative, adj. figuré.
figuratively, adv. au figuré.
figure, 1. n. figure f.; (of body) ligne f.; (math.) chiffre m. 2. vb. figurer; calculer.
figured, adj. à dessin.
figurehead, n. homme de paille m.
figure of speech, n. façon (f.) de parler.
figurine, n. figurine f.
filament, n. filament m.
filch, vb. escamoter.
file, 1. n. (tool) lime f.; (row) file f.; (papers) liasse f.; (for papers, etc.) classeur m.; (compil.) fichier m.; (f.s) archives f.pl. 2. vb. (tool) limer; (papers) classer; (f. off) défiler.
filial, adj. filial.
filigree, n. filigrane m.
filing cabinet, n. classeur m.
filings, n. limaille f.
fill, vb. remplir, tr.
fillet, n. (band) bandeau m.; (meat, fish) filet m.
filling, n. remplissage m., (food) farce f.; (tooth) plombage m.
filling station, n. station-service f.
film, n. (cinema) film m.; (photo) pellicule f.
filmy, adj. couvert d'une pellicule.
filter, 1. n. filtre m. 2. vb. filtrer.

filth, n. ordure f.

filthy, adj. immonde; obscène.

fin, n. nageoire f.

final, adj. final.

finale, n. finale m.

finalist, n. finaliste m.

finality, n. finalité f.

finalize, vb. mettre au point.

finally, adv. finalement, enfin.

finance, 1. n. finance f. **2.** vb. financer.

financial, adj. financier.

financier, n. financier m.

find, vb. trouver.

findings, n. conclusions f.pl., verdict m.

fine, 1. n. amende f. **2.** adj. (beautiful) beau m., belle f.; (pure, thin) fin. **3.** vb. mettre à l'amende.

fine arts, n. beaux arts m.pl.

finery, n. parure f.

finesse, 1. n. finesse f. **2.** vb. finasser.

finger, n. doigt m.

finger bowl, n. rince-bouche m.

fingernail, n. ongle m.

fingerprint, n. empreinte digitale f.

finicky, adj. affété.

finish, vb. finir.

finished, adj. fini, achevé.

finite, adj. fini.

Finland, n. Finlande f.

Finn, n. Finlandais, Finnois m.

Finnish, 1. n. finnois m. **2.** adj. finlandais, finnois.

fir, n. sapin m.

fire, 1. n. feu m.; (burning of house, etc.) incendie m. **2.** vb. (weapon) tirer.

fire alarm, n. avertisseur (m.) d'incendie.

firearm, n. arme (f.) à feu.

firecracker, n. pétard m.

firedamp, n. grisou m.

fire engine, n. pompe (f.) à incendie.

fire escape, n. échelle (f.) de sauvetage.

fire extinguisher, n. extincteur m.

firefly, n. luciole f.

fireman, n. pompier m.

fireplace, n. cheminée f.

fireproof, adj. à l'épreuve du feu.

fireside, n. coin du feu m.

firewood, n. bois (m.) de chauffage.

fireworks, n. feu (m.) d'artifice.

firing squad, n. peloton (m.) d'exécution.

firm, 1. n. maison (f.) de commerce. **2.** adj. ferme.

firmness, n. fermeté f.

first, 1. adj. premier. **2.** adv. d'abord.

first aid, n. premiers secours m.pl.

first-class, adj. de premier ordre.

firsthand, adj. de première main.

first-rate, adj. de premier ordre.

fiscal, adj. fiscal.

fish, 1. n. poisson m. **2.** vb. pêcher.

fisherman, n. pêcheur m.

fishery, n. pêcherie f.

fishhook, n. hameçon m.

fishing, n. pêche f.

fishmonger, n. marchand (m.) de poisson.

fishwife, n. marchande (f.) de poisson.

fishy, adj. de poisson; (slang) louche.

fission, n. fission f.

fissure, n. fente f.

fist, n. poing m.

fistic, adj. au poing.

fit, 1. n. accès m. **2.** adj. (suitable) convenable; (capable) capable; **(f. for)** propre à. **3.** vb. (befit) convenir à; (clothes) aller à; (adjust) ajuster, tr.

fitful, adj. agité, irrégulier.

fitness, n. à-propos m.; (person) aptitude f.; (medical) forme (f.) physique.

fitting, 1. n. ajustage m. **2.** adj. convenable.

five, adj. and n. cinq m.

fix, 1. n. embarras m. **2.** vb. fixer; (repair) réparer.

fixation, n. fixation f.

fixed, adj. fixe.

fixture, n. object (m.) d'attache.

fizzy, adj. pétillant, gazeux.

flabbergasted, adj. sidéré.

flabby, adj. flasque.

flaccid, adj. flasque.

flag, n. drapeau m.; (stone) dalle f.

flagellate, vb. flageller.

flagging, 1. n. relâchement m. **2.** adj. qui s'affaiblit.

flagon, n. flacon m.

flagpole, n. mât de drapeau m.

flagrant, adj. flagrant.

flagrantly, adv. d'une manière flagrante.

flagship, n. vaisseau amiral m.

flagstone, n. dalle f.

flail, 1. n. fléau m. **2.** vb. battre au fléau.

flair, n. flair m.

flake, 1. n. (snow) flocon m. **2.** vb. s'écailler.

flamboyant, adj. flamboyant.

flame, 1. n. flamme f. **2.** vb. flamboyer.

flame thrower, n. lanceur (m.) de flammes.

flaming, adj. flamboyant.

flamingo, n. flamant m.

flank, n. flanc m.

flannel, n. flanelle f.

flap, 1. n. (wing) coup m.; (pocket) patte f.; (table) battant m. **2.** vb. battre.

flare, vb. flamboyer.

flare-up, 1. n. emportement m. **2.** vb. s'emporter.

flash, 1. n. éclair m. **2.** vb. briller, clignoter.

flashback, n. retour (m.) en arrière.

flashcube, n. flash-cube m.

flashiness, n. faux brillant m., éclat superficiel m.

flashlight, n. (lighthouse) feu (m.) à éclats; (pocket) lampe (f.) de poche.

flashy, adj. voyant.

flask, n. gourde f.

flat, 1. n. appartement m.; (tire) pneu (m.) crevé. **2.** adj. plat m., platte f.

flatcar, n. wagon en plateforme m.

flatness, n. (evenness) égalité f.; (dullness) platitude f.

flatten, vb. aplatir.

flatter, vb. flatter.

flatterer, n. flatteur m.

flattery, n. flatterie f.

flattop, n. porte-avion m.

flaunt, vb. parader, étaler.

flautist, n. flûtiste m.f.

flavor, n. (taste) saveur f.; (fragrance) arome m.

flavoring, n. assaisonnement m.

flavorless, adj. fade.

flaw, n. défaut m.

flawless, adj. sans défaut, parfait.

flawlessly, adv. d'une manière impeccable.

flax, n. lin m.

flay, vb. écorcher.

flea, n. puce f.

fleck, 1. n. tache f. **2.** vb. tacheter.

fledgling, n. oisillon m.

flee, vb. s'enfuir.

fleece, 1. n. toison f. **2.** vb. voler.

fleecy, adj. laineux, moutonneux.

fleet, n. flotte f.

fleeting, adj. fugitif.

Flemish, adj. flamand.

flesh, n. chair f.

fleshy, adj. charnu.

flex, vb. fléchir.

flexibility, n. flexibilité f.

flexible, adj. flexible.

flick, 1. n. petit coup m. **2.** vb. donner un petit coup à.

flicker, 1. n. lueur (f.) vacillante. **2.** vb. trembloter.

flier, n. aviateur m.

flight, n. (flying) vol m.; (fleeing) fuite f.

flight attendant, n. hôtesse (f.) de l'air.

flighty, adj. étourdi.

flimsy, adj. sans solidité.

flinch, vb. reculer, broncher.

fling, 1. n. jeter. **2.** vb. (have a f.) faire la fête.

flint, n. (lighter) pierre (f.) à briquet; (mineral) silex m.

flip, vb. donner un petit coup à.

flippant, adj. léger.

flippantly, adv. légèrement.

flirt, vb. flirter.

flirtation, n. flirt m.

float, vb. flotter.

flock, 1. n. troupeau m. **2.** vb. accourir.

flog, vb. fouetter.

flood, n. inondation f.

floodgate, n. écluse f.

floodlight, n. lumière (f.) à grand flots.

floor, n. plancher m.; (take the f.) prendre la parole; (story) étage m.

flooring, n. plancher m., parquet m.

floorwalker, n. inspecteur du magasin m.
flop, 1. vb. faire plouf, s'effondrer. **2.** n. fiasco m.
floral, adj. floral.
florid, adj. fleuri, vermeil.
florist, n. fleuriste m.f.
flounce, 1. n. volant m. **2.** vb. se démener.
flounder, n. flet m.
flour, n. farine f.
flourish, vb. prospérer.
flow, vb. couler.
flower, 1. n. fleur f. **2.** vb. fleurir.
flowerpot, n. pot à fleurs m.
flowery, adj. fleuri.
flu, n. grippe f.
fluctuate, vb. osciller.
fluctuation, n. fluctuation f.
flue, n. tuyau (m.) de cheminée.
fluency, n. facilité f.
fluent, adj. (be a f. speaker of . . .) parler . . . couramment.
fluid, adj and n. fluide m.
fluidity, n. fluidité f.
flunk, vb. coller, recaler.
flunkey, n. laquais m.
fluorescent lamp, n. lampe fluorescente f.
fluoride, n. fluorure f.
fluoroscope, n. fluoroscope m.
flurry, 1. n. agitation f. **2.** vb. agiter.
flush, n. (redness) rougeur f.; (plumbing) chasse f.
flustered, adj. énervé.
flute, n. flûte f.
flutter, 1. n. (bird) voltigement m.; (agitation) agitation f. **2.** vb. s'agiter; (heart) palpiter.
flux, n. flux m.
fly, 1. n. mouche f.; (on pants) braguette f. **2.** vb. voler.
foam, n. écume f.
focal, adj. focal.
focus, 1. n. foyer m.; (in f.) au point. **2.** vb. (photo) mettre au point.
fodder, n. fourrage m.
foe, n. ennemi m.
fog, n. brouillard m.
foggy, adj. brumeux.
foil, n. (sheet) feuille f.; (set-off) repoussoir m.; (fencing) fleuret m.
foist, vb. fourrer.

fold, 1. n. pli m. **2.** vb. plier.
folder, n. (booklet) prospectus m.
foliage, n. feuillage m.
folio, n. in-folio m.
folk, n. gens m.f.pl.
folklore, n. folk-lore m.
folksong, n. chanson (f.) folklorique.
follicle, n. follicule m.
follow, vb. suivre.
follower, n. disciple m.
folly, n. folie f.
foment, vb. fomenter.
fond, adj. tendre; (be f. of) aimer.
fondant, n. fondant m.
fondle, vb. caresser.
fondly, adv. tendrement.
fondness, n. tendresse f.
font, n. fonte f.
food, n. nourriture f.
foodstuff, n. comestible m.
fool, n. sot m., sotte f.; (jester) bouffon m.
foolhardiness, n. témérité f.
foolhardy, adj. téméraire.
foolish, adj. sot m., sotte f.
foolproof, adj. infaillible.
foolscap, n. papier écolier m.
foot, n. pied m.
footage, n. métrage m.
football, n. football m., ballon m.
foothill, n. colline basse f.
foothold, n. point d'appui m.
footing, n. pied m.; point d'appui m.
footlights, n. rampe f.
footnote, n. note f.
footsore, adj. empreinte de pas f.; aux pieds endoloris.
footstep, n. pas m.
footstool, n. tabouret m.
footwork, n. jeu de pieds m.
fop, n. fat m.
for, 1. prep. pour. **2.** conj. car.
forage, 1. n. fourrage m. **2.** vb. fourrager.
foray, n. razzia f.
forbear, vb. (avoid) s'abstenir de; (be patient) montrer de la patience.
forbearance, n. patience f.
forbid, vb. défendre (à).
forbidding, adj. menaçant.
force, 1. n. force f. **2.** vb. forcer.
forced, adj. forcé.

forceful, *adj.* énergique.

forcefulness, *n.* énergie *f.*, vigueur *f.*

forceps, *n.* forceps *m.*

forcible, *adj.* forcé.

ford, 1. *n.* gué *m.* **2.** *vb.* traverser à gué.

fore, 1. *adj.* antérieur, de devant. **2.** *n.* avant *m.*

fore and aft, *adv.* de l'avant à l'arrière.

forearm, *n.* avant-bras *m.*

forebears, *n.* ancêtres *m.pl.*

forebode, *vb.* présager.

foreboding, 1. *n.* mauvais augure *m.*, pressentiment *m.* **2.** *adj.* qui présage le mal.

forecast, 1. *n.* prévision *f.* **2.** *vb.* prévoir.

forecaster, *n.* pronostiqueur *m.*

forecastle, *n.* gaillard *m.*

foreclose, *vb.* exclure, forclore.

forefather, *n.* ancêtre *m.*

forefinger, *n.* index *m.*

forefront, *n.* premier rang *m.*

foregone, *adj.* décidé d'avance.

foreground, *n.* premier plan *m.*

forehead, *n.* front *m.*

foreign, *adj.* étranger.

foreign aid, *n.* aide *(f.)* aux pays étrangers.

foreigner, *n.* étranger *m.*

foreleg, *n.* jambe antérieure *f.*

foreman, *n.* contremaître *m.*

foremost, *adj.* premier.

forenoon, *n.* matinée *f.*

forensic, *adj.* judiciaire.

forerunner, *n.* avant-coureur *m.*

foresee, *vb.* prévoir.

foreseeable, *adj.* prévisible.

foreshadow, *vb.* présager.

foresight, *n.* prévoyance *f.*

forest, *n.* forêt *f.*

forestall, *vb.* anticiper, devancer.

forester, *n.* forestier *m.*

forestry, *n.* sylviculture *f.*

foretaste, *n.* avant-goût *m.*

foretell, *vb.* prédire.

forever, *adv.* pour toujours.

forevermore, *adv.* à jamais.

forewarn, *vb.* prévenir.

foreword, *n.* avant-propos *m.*

forfeit, *vb.* forfaire.

forfeiture, *n.* perte *(f.)* par confiscation, forfaiture *f.*

forgather, *vb.* se réunir.

forge, 1. *n.* forge *f.* **2.** *vb.* forger; (signature, money) contrefaire.

forger, *n.* faussaire *m.*, falsificateur *m.*

forgery, *n.* faux *m.*

forget, *vb.* oublier.

forgetful, *adj.* oublieux.

forget-me-not, *n.* myosotis *m.*

forgive, *vb.* pardonner (à).

forgiveness, *n.* pardon *m.*

forgo, *vb.* renoncer à.

fork, *n.* fourchette *f.;* (tool, road) fourche *f.*

forlorn, *adj.* (hopeless) désespéré; (forsaken) abandonné.

form, 1. *n.* forme *f.;* (blank) formule *f.* **2.** *vb.* former.

formal, *adj.* formel.

formaldehyde, *n.* formaldéhyde *f.*

formality, *n.* formalité *f.*

formally, *adv.* formellement.

format, 1. *n.* format *m.* **2.** *vb.* formater.

formation, *n.* formation *f.*

formative, *adj.* formatif.

former, 1. *adj.* précédent; (with latter) premier. **2.** *pron.* le premier.

formerly, *adv.* autrefois, jadis, auparavant.

formidable, *adj.* formidable.

formless, *adj.* informe.

formula, *n.* formule *f.*

formulate, *vb.* formuler.

formulation, *n.* formulation *f.*

forsake, *vb.* abandonner.

forsythia, *n.* forsythie *f.*

fort, *n.* fort *m.*

forte, *n.* fort *m.*

forth, *adv.* en avant; **(and so f.)** et ainsi de suite.

forthcoming, *adv.* à venir.

forthright, 1. *adj.* tout droit. **2.** *adv.* carrément, nettement.

forthwith, *adv.* sur-le-champ, tout de suite.

fortieth, *adj. and n.* quarantième *m.f.*

fortification, *n.* fortification *f.*

fortify, *vb.* fortifier, renforcer.

fortissimo, *adv.* fortissimo.

fortitude, *n.* courage *m.*

fortnight, *n.* quinzaine *f.*

fortress, *n.* forteresse *f.*

fortuitous, *adj.* fortuit.

fortunate, adj. heureux.

fortune, n. fortune f.

fortuneteller, n. diseur (m.) de bonne aventure.

forty, adj. and n. quarante m.

forum, n. (Roman) forum m.

forward, 1. adj. en avant; (advanced) avancé; (bold) hardi. **2.** adv. en avant. **3.** vb. (letter) faire suivre.

forwardness, n. empressement m.; effronterie f.

fossil, n. fossile m.

fossilize, vb. fossiliser.

foster, vb. nourrir.

foster child, n. enfant (m.) adopté.

foul, adj. (dirty) sale; (disgusting) dégoûtant; (obscene) ordurier; (abominable) infâme.

found, vb. fonder.

foundation, n. fondation f.; (theory) fondement m.

founder, n. fondateur m.

foundling, n. enfant trouvé.

foundry, n. fonderie f.

fountain, n. fontaine f.

fountainhead, n. source f.

fountain pen, n. stylo(-graphe) m.

four, adj. and n. quatre m.

four-in-hand, n. attelage à quatre m.

fourscore, adj. quatre-vingts.

foursome, n. à quatre.

fourteen, adj. and n. quatorze m.

fourth, adj. and n. quatrième m.f.; (fraction) quart m.

fourth estate, n. quatrième état m.

fowl, n. volaille f.

fox, n. renard m.

foxglove, n. digitale f.

foxhole, n. renardière f.

fox terrier, n. fox-terrier m.

fox trot, n. fox-trot m.

foxy, adj. rusé.

foyer, n. foyer m.

fracas, n. fracas m.

fraction, n. fraction f.

fracture, n. fracture f.

fragile, adj. fragile.

fragment, n. fragment m.

fragmentary, adj. fragmentaire.

fragrance, n. parfum m.

fragrant, adj. parfumé.

frail, adj. frêle.

frailty, n. faiblesse f.

frame, n. (picture) cadre m.; (structure) structure f.

frame-up, 1. n. coup monté m. **2.** vb. monter un coup.

framework, n. charpente f.

France, n. France f.

franchise, n. droit (m.) électoral.

frank, adj. franc m., franche f.

frankfurter, n. saucisse (f.) de Francfort.

frankincense, n. encens m.

frankly, adv. franchement.

frankness, n. franchise f.

frantic, adj. frénétique.

fraternal, adj. fraternel.

fraternally, adv. fraternellement.

fraternity, n. fraternité f.

fraternization, n. fraternisation f.

fraternize, vb. fraterniser.

fratricide, n. fratricide m.

fraud, n. fraude f.; (person) imposteur m.

fraudulent, adj. frauduleux.

fraudulently, adv. frauduleusement.

fraught, adj. chargé (de), plein, gros.

fray, 1. n. bagarre f. **2.** vb. érailler.

freak, n. (whim) caprice m.; (abnormality) phénomène m.

freckle, n. tache de rousseur f.

freckled, adj. taché de rousseur.

free, 1. adj. libre; (without cost) gratuit. **2.** vb. libérer, affranchir.

freedom, n. liberté f.

freelance, 1. n. journaliste ou politicien indépendant m. **2.** vb. faire du journalisme indépendant.

freestone, n. pêche (f.) dont la chair n'adhère pas au noyau.

free verse, n. vers libre m.

free will, n. libre arbitre m.

freeze, vb. geler; (food) surgeler.

freezer, n. glacière f.; congélateur m.

freezing point, n. point (m.) de congélation.

freight, n. fret m.

freightage, n. frètement m.

freighter, n. affréteur m.

French, adj. and n. français m.

French fries, n. frites f.pl.

French leave, n. filer à l'anglaise.

Frenchman, n. Français m.

French toast, n. tranche de pain frite f.

Frenchwoman, n. Française f.

frenzied, adj. affolé, frénétique.

frenzy, n. frénésie f.

frequency, n. fréquence f.

frequent, 1. adj. fréquent. **2.** vb. fréquenter.

frequently, adv. fréquemment.

fresco, n. fresque f.

fresh, adj. frais m., fraîche f.; (new, recent) nouveau; nouvel m., nouvelle f.; (impudent) culotté.

freshen, vb. rafraîchir.

freshman, n. étudiant (m.) de première année.

freshness, n. fraîcheur f.

fresh-water, adj. d'eau douce.

fret, vb. ronger, tr.

fretful, adj. chagrin.

fretfully, adv. avec irritation.

fretfulness, n. irritabilité f.

friar, n. moine m., frère religieux m.

fricassee, n. fricassée f.

friction, n. friction f.

Friday, n. vendredi m.

fridge, n. frigo m.

friend, n. ami m., amie f.

friendless, adj. sans amis.

friendliness, n. disposition (f.) amicale.

friendly, adj. amical.

friendship, n. amitié f.

fright, n. effroi m.

frighten, vb. effrayer.

frightening, adj. effrayant.

frightful, adj. affreux.

frigid, adj. glacial.

Frigid Zone, n. zone glaciale f.

frill, 1. n. volant m.; affectation f. **2.** vb. plisser.

frilly, adj. froncé, ruché.

fringe, n. frange f.

fringe benefits, n. avantages (m.pl.) sociaux.

frisk, vb. fouiller.

frisky, adj. folâtre.

frivolity, n. frivolité f.

frivolous, adj. frivole.

frivolousness, n. frivolité f.

frizzy, adj. crépu.

frock, n. robe f.; (monk's) froc m.

frog, n. grenouille f.

frolic, vb. folâtrer.

from, prep. de; (time) depuis.

front, n. front m.; (front part) devant m.; (**in f. of**) devant.

frontage, n. étendue de devant f.

frontal, adj. frontal, de face.

frontier, n. frontière f.

frost, n. gelée f.

frostbite, n. gelure f.

frosting, n. glaçage m.

frosty, adj. gelé, glacé.

froth, 1. n. écume f. **2.** vb. écumer.

frowzy, adj. mal tenu, peu soigné.

frozen, adj. gelé; (food) surgelé.

fructify, vb. fructifier.

frugal, adj. frugal.

frugality, n. frugalité f.

fruit, n. fruit m.

fruitful, adj. fructueux.

fruition, n. réalisation f., fructification f.

fruitless, adj. infructueux.

frustrate, vb. faire échouer.

frustration, n. frustration f.

fry, vb. frire, intr.; faire frire, tr.

fryer, n. casserole f.

fuchsia, n. fuchsia m.

fudge, 1. n. espèce de fondant américain. **2.** interj. bah!

fuel, n. combustible m.

fugitive, adj. fugitif.

fugue, n. fugue f.

fulcrum, n. pivot m., point d'appui m.

fulfill, vb. accomplir.

fulfillment, n. accomplissement m.

full, adj. plein.

fullback, n. arrière m.

full dress, adj. en tenue de cérémonie.

fullness, n. plénitude f.

fully, adv. pleinement.

fulminate, vb. fulminer.

fulmination, n. fulmination f.

fumble, vb. tâtonner.

fume, n. fumée f.

fumigate, vb. désinfecter.

fumigator, n. fumigateur m.

fun, n. (amusement) amusement m.; (**have f.**) s'amuser; (joke) plaisanterie f.; (**make f. of**) se moquer de.

function, n. fonction f.; (social occasion) cérémonie f.

functional, adj. fonctionnel.

functionary, n. fonctionnaire m.
fund, n. fonds m.
fundamental, adj. fondamental.
fundamentalist, n. intégriste m.
fundamentalism, n. intégrisme m.
funeral, n. funérailles f.pl.
funereal, adj. funèbre, funéraire.
fungicide, n. fongicide m.
fungus, n. fongus m.
funk, n. (be in a f.) être déprimé.
funnel, n. entonnoir m.; (smoke-stack) cheminée f.
funny, adj. drôle.
fur, n. fourrure f.
furious, adj. furieux.
furlong, n. furlong m.
furlough, n. permission f.
furnace, n. fourneau m.
furnish, vb. fournir; (house) meubler.
furnishings, n. ameublement m.
furniture, n. meubles m.pl.
furor, n. fureur f.
furred, adj. fourré.
furrier, n. fourreur m.

furrow, n. sillon m.
furry, adj. qui ressemble à la fourrure.
further, 1. adj. ultérieur. 2. adv. (distance) plus loin; (extent) davantage.
furtherance, n. avancement m.
furthermore, adv. en outre.
fury, n. furie f.
fuse, vb. fondre.
fuselage, n. fuselage m.
fusillade, n. fusillade f.
fusion, n. fusion f., fusionnement m.
fuss, n. (make a f.) faire des histoires.
fussy, adj. difficile.
futile, adj. futile.
futility, n. futilité f.
future, 1. n. avenir m.; (gramm.) futur m. 2. adj. futur.
futurity, n. avenir m.
futurology, n. futurologie f.
fuzz, n. duvet m., flou m.
fuzzy, adj. flou, frisotté.

G

gab, vb. jaser.
gabardine, n. gabardine f.
gable, n. pignon m.
gadabout, n. coureur m.
gadfly, n. taon m.
gadget, n. truc m.
Gaelic, adj. gaélique.
gaffe, n. gaffe f.
gag, 1. vb. bâillonner. 2. n. blague f., bobard m.; bâillon m.
gaiety, n. gaieté f.
gaily, adv. gaiement.
gain, 1. n. gain m. 2. vb. gagner.
gainful, adj. profitable, rémunérateur.
gainfully, adv. profitablement.
gainsay, vb. contredire.
gait, n. allure f.
gal, n. (colloquial) femme f.
galaxy, n. galaxie f., assemblée brillante f.
gale, n. grand vent m.
gall, n. (bile) fiel m.; (sore) écorchure f.

gallant, adj. (brave) vaillant; (with ladies) galant.
gallantly, adv. galamment.
gallantry, n. vaillance f., galanterie f.
gall bladder, n. vésicule biliaire f.
galleon, n. galion m.
gallery, n. galerie f.
galley, n. galère f., (naut.) cuisine f., (typographic) galée f.
galley proof, n. épreuve en première f.
Gallic, adj. gaulois, français.
gallivant, vb. courailler.
gallon, n. gallon m.
gallop, 1. n. galop m. 2. vb. galoper.
gallows, n. potence f.
gallstone, n. calcul biliaire m.
galore, adv. à foison, à profusion.
galosh, n. galoche f., caoutchouc m.
galvanize, vb. galvaniser.
Gambia, n. Gambie f.
gamble, 1. n. jeu (m.) de hasard. 2. vb. jouer.

gambler, n. joueur m.

gambling, n. jeu m.

gambol, 1. n. gambade f. **2.** vb. gamboler.

game, n. jeu m.; (hunting) gibier m.

gamely, adv. courageusement, crânement.

gameness, n. courage m., crânerie f.

gamin, n. gamin m.

gamut, n. gamme f.

gamy, adj. giboyeux.

gander, n. jars m.

gang, n. bande f.; (workers) équipe f.

gangling, adj. dégingandé.

gangplank, n. passerelle f.

gangrene, n. gangrène f.

gangrenous, adj. gangreneux.

gangster, n. gangster m.

gangway, n. passage m.

gap, n. (opening) ouverture f.; (empty space) vide m.

gape, vb. rester bouche bée.

garage, n. garage m.

garb, n. vêtement m., costume m. **2.** vb. vêtir, habiller.

garbage, n. ordures f.pl.

garble, vb. tronquer, altérer.

garden, n. jardin m.

gardener, n. jardinier m.

gardenia, n. gardénia m.

gargle, 1. n. gargarisme m. **2.** vb. se gargariser.

gargoyle, n. gargouille f.

garish, adj. voyant.

garland, n. guirlande f.

garlic, n. ail m.

garment, n. vêtement m.

garner, vb. mettre en grenier.

garnet, n. grenat m.

garnish, vb. garnir.

garnishee, n. tiers-saisi m.

garnishment, n. saisie-arrêt f.

garret, n. mansarde f.

garrison, n. garnison f.

garrote, 1. n. garrotte f. **2.** vb. garrotter.

garrulous, adj. bavard, loquace.

garter, n. jarretière f.

gas, n. gaz m.; (auto) essence f. **(g. station)** station-service f.

gaseous, adj. gazeux.

gash, 1. n. coupure f., entaille f. **2.** vb. couper, entailler.

gasket, n. garcette f.

gasless, adj. sans gaz.

gas mask, n. masque à gaz m.

gasohol, n. essence (f.) fabriquée avec de l'alcool.

gasoline, n. essence f.

gasp, vb. (astonishment) sursauter; (lack of breath) haleter.

gassy, adj. gazeux; (talkative) bavard.

gastric, adj. gastrique.

gastric juice, n. suc gastrique m.

gastritis, n. gastrite f.

gastronomically, adv. d'une manière gastronomique.

gastronomy, n. gastronomie f.

gate, n. (city) porte f.; (with bars) barrière f.; (wrought-iron) grille f.

gateway, n. porte f., entrée f.

gather, vb. rassembler, tr.; recueillir, tr.

gathering, n. rassemblement m.

gaudily, adv. de manière voyante.

gaudiness, n. éclat criard m., ostentation f.

gaudy, adj. voyant.

gaunt, adj. décharné.

gauntlet, n. gantelet m.

gauze, n. gaze f.

gavel, n. marteau m.

gavotte, n. gavotte f.

gawky, adj. dégingandé.

gay, 1. adj. gai; (homosexual) homosexuel. **2.** n. homosexuel m.

gaze, vb. regarder fixement.

gazelle, n. gazelle f.

gazette, n. gazette f.

gazetteer, n. gazetier m., répertoire géographique m.

gear, n. (implements, device) appareil m.; (machines) engrenage m.; (in g.) engrené; (g. change) changement (m.) de vitesse.

gearing, n. engrenage m.

gearshift, n. changement (m.) de vitesse.

gel, n. gel m.

gelatin, n. gélatine f.

gelatinous, adj. gélatineux.

geld, vb. châtrer.

gelding, n. animal châtré m.

gem, n. pierre (f.) précieuse.

gender, n. genre m.

gene, n. gène m.

genealogical, adj. généalogique.

genealogy, n. généalogie f.
general, adj. and n. général m.
generality, n. généralité f.
generalization, n. généralisation f.
generalize, vb. généraliser.
generally, adv. généralement.
general practitioner, n. généraliste m.
generalship, n. stratégie f.
generate, vb. engendrer, générer.
generation, n. génération f.
generator, n. (electricity) groupe (m.) électrogène.
generic, adj. générique.
generosity, n. générosité f.
generous, adj. généreux.
generously, adv. généreusement.
genetic, adj. génétique.
genetics, n. génétique f.
genial, adj. sympathique.
geniality, n. jovialité f., bienveillance f.
genially, adv. affablement.
genital, adj. génital.
genitals, n. organes génitaux m.pl.
genitive, n. and adj. génitif m.
genius, n. génie m.
genocide, n. génocide m.
genre, n. genre m.
genteel, adj. de bon ton.
gentian, n. gentiane f.
gentile, n. gentil m.
gentility, n. prétention (f.) à la distinction.
gentle, adj. doux m., douce f.
gentleman, n. monsieur m., pl. messieurs; (character) galant homme m.
gentlemanly, adj. comme il faut, bien élevé.
gentlemen's agreement, n. convention verbale f.
gentleness, n. douceur f.
gently, adv. doucement.
gentry, n. petite noblesse f.
genuflect, vb. faire des génuflexions.
genuine, adj. véritable.
genuinely, adv. véritablement.
genuineness, n. authenticité f.
genus, n. genre m.
geographer, n. géographe m.
geographical, adj. géographique.
geography, n. géographie f.
geometric, adj. géométrique.

geometry, n. géométrie f.
geopolitics, n. géopolitique f.
geranium, n. géranium m.
geriatric, adj. gériatrique.
germ, n. germe m.
German, 1. n. (person) Allemand m.; (language) allemand m. **2.** adj. allemand.
germane, adj. approprié.
Germanic, adj. allemand, germanique.
German measles, n. rougeole bénigne f.
Germany, n. Allemagne f.
germicide, n. microbicide m.
germinal, adj. germinal.
germinate, vb. germer.
gestate, vb. enfanter.
gestation, n. gestation f.
gesticulate, vb. gesticuler.
gesticulation, n. gesticulation f.
gesture, n. geste m.
get, vb. (obtain) obtenir; (receive) recevoir; (take) prendre; (become) devenir; (arrive) arriver; **(g. in)** entrer; **(g. off)** descendre; **(g. on,** agree) s'entendre; **(g. on,** go up) monter; **(g. out)** sortir; **(g. up)** se lever.
getaway, n. fuite f.
geyser, n. geyser m.
Ghana, n. Ghana m.
ghastly, adj. horrible.
ghetto blaster, n. stéréo (f.) portable.
ghost, n. (specter) revenant m.; (Holy G.) Saint-Esprit m.
ghost writer, n. collaborateur anonyme m., nègre m.
ghoul, n. goule f., vampire m.
giant, n. géant m.
gibberish, n. baragouin m.
gibbon, n. gibbon m.
gibe, 1. n. raillerie f. **2.** vb. railler.
giblet, n. abatis (de volaille) m.
Gibraltar, n. Gibraltar.
giddy, adj. étourdi.
gift, n. don m.; (present) cadeau m.
gifted, adj. doué.
gigantic, adj. géant, gigantesque.
giggle, vb. rire nerveusement, glousser.
gigolo, n. gigolo m.
gild, vb. dorer.
gill, n. (of fish) ouïes f.pl.

gilt, 1. n. dorure f. **2.** adj. doré.

gilt-edged, adj. doré sur tranche.

gimcrack, 1. n. camelote f. **2.** adj. de camelote.

gimlet, n. vrille f.

gimmick, n. truc m.

gin, n. genièvre m.

ginger, n. gingembre m.

ginger ale, n. boisson (f.) gazeuse au gingembre.

gingerly, adv. avec précaution.

gingersnap, n. biscuit (m.) au gingembre.

gingham, n. guingan m.

giraffe, n. girafe f.

gird, vb. ceindre.

girder, n. support m.

girdle, n. gaine f.

girl, n. jeune fille f.

girlfriend, n. petite amie f.

girlish, adj. de jeune fille.

girth, n. sangle f., circonférence f., corpulence f.

gist, n. fond m., essence f.

give, vb. donner; (**g. back**) rendre; (**g. in**) céder; (**g. out**) distribuer; (**g. up**) renoncer à.

give-and-take, adv. donnant donnant.

given, adj. donné.

given name, n. prénom m.

giver, n. donneur m.

gizzard, n. gésier m.

glace, adj. glacé.

glacial, adj. glaciaire.

glacier, n. glacier m.

glad, adj. heureux.

gladden, vb. réjouir.

glade, n. clairière f., éclaircie f.

gladiolus, n. glaïeul m.

gladly, adv. volontiers.

gladness, n. joie f.

Gladstone bag, n. sac américain m.

glamour, n. éclat m.

glance, 1. n. coup (m.) d'œil. **2.** vb. jeter un coup d'œil.

gland, n. glande f.

glandular, adj. glandulaire.

glare, 1. n. (light) clarté f.; (stare) regard m. enflammé. **2.** vb. (shine) briller; (look) jeter des regards enflammés.

glaring, adj. éclatant, flagrant, voyant, manifeste.

glass, n. verre m.

glass-blowing, n. soufflage m.

glasses, n. lunettes f.pl.

glassful, n. verre m., verrée f.

glassware, n. verrerie f.

glassy, adj. vitreux.

glaucoma, n. glaucome m.

glaze, 1. n. lustre m. **2.** vb. vitrer.

glazier, n. vitrier m.

gleam, 1. n. lueur f. **2.** vb. luire.

glean, vb. glaner.

glee, n. allégresse f.

glee club, n. chœur d'hommes m.

gleeful, adj. joyeux, allègre.

glen, n. vallon m., ravin m.

glib, adj. spécieux, facile.

glide, vb. glisser; (plane) planer.

glider, n. planeur m.

glimmer, 1. n. faible lueur f. **2.** jeter une faible lueur.

glimmering, adj. faible, vacillant.

glimpse, 1. vb. entrevoir. **2.** n. aperçu m.

glint, 1. n. éclair m., reflet m. **2.** vb. entreluire, étinceler.

glisten, vb. briller.

glitter, vb. étinceler.

gloat, vb. se régaler de.

global, adj. global.

globe, n. globe m.

globetrotter, n. globe trotter m.

globular, adj. globulaire, globuleux.

globule, n. globule m.

glockenspiel, n. glockenspiel m.

gloom, n. (darkness) ténèbres f.pl.; (sadness) tristesse f.

gloomy, adj. sombre.

glorification, n. glorification f.

glorify, vb. glorifier.

glorious, adj. glorieux; (weather) radieux.

glory, n. gloire f.

gloss, n. lustre m., vernis m., glose f. **2.** vb. lustrer, glacer.

glossary, n. glossaire m.

glossy, adj. lustré, glacé.

glove, n. gant m.

glow, 1. n. (light) lumière f.; (heat) chaleur f. **2.** vb. briller.

glower, vb. (**g. at**) lancer des regards mauvais à.

glowing, adj. embrasé, rayonnant.

glowingly, adv. en termes chaleureux.

glowworm, n. ver luisant m.

glucose, *n.* glucose *f.*

glue, 1. *n.* colle (*f.*) forte. **2.** *vb.* coller.

glum, *adj.* maussade.

glumness, *n.* air maussade *m.*, tristesse *f.*

glut, 1. *n.* assouvissement *m.*, excès *m.*, pléthore *f.* **2.** *vb.* assouvir, rassasier, gorger.

glutinous, *adj.* glutineux.

glutton, *n.* gourmand *m.*

gluttonous, *adj.* gourmand, goulu.

glycerin, *n.* glycérine *f.*

gnarl, *n.* loupe *f.*, nœud *m.*

gnash, *vb.* grincer.

gnat, *n.* moucheron *m.*

gnaw, *vb.* ronger.

gnu, *n.* gnou *m.*

go, *vb.* aller; (**g. away**) s'en aller; (**g. back**) retourner; (**g. by**) passer; (**g. down**) descendre; (**g. in**) entrer; (**g. on**) continuer; (**g. out**) sortir; (**g. up**) monter; (**g. without**) se passer de.

goad, 1. *n.* aiguillon *m.* **2.** *vb.* aiguillonner, piquer.

goal, *n.* but *m.*

goat, *n.* chèvre *f.*

goatee, *n.* barbiche *f.*

goatherd, *n.* chevrier *m.*

goatskin, *n.* peau (*f.*) de chèvre.

gobble, *vb.* avaler goulûment, dévorer.

gobbler, *n.* avaleur *m.*; dindon *m.*

go-between, *n.* intermédiaire *m.*

goblet, *n.* gobelet *m.*

goblin, *n.* gobelin *m.*, lutin *m.*

God, *n.* Dieu *m.*

godchild, *n.* filleul *m.*

goddess, *n.* déesse *f.*

godfather, *n.* parrain *m.*

godless, *adj.* athée, impie, sans Dieu.

godlike, *adj.* comme un dieu, divin.

godly, *adj.* dévot, pieux, saint.

godmother, *n.* marraine *f.*

godsend, *n.* aubaine *f.*, bienfait du ciel *m.*

Godspeed, *interj.* bon voyage!

go-getter, *n.* homme (*m.*) d'affaires énergique, arriviste *m.*

goggles, *n.* lunettes (*f.pl.*) protectrices.

goiter, *n.* goitre *m.*

gold, *n.* or *m.*

gold brick, *n.* attrape-niais *m.*

golden, *adj.* d'or.

goldenrod, *n.* solidage *m.*

golden rule, *n.* règle (*f.*) par excellence.

gold-filled, *adj.* aurifié, en (or) doublé.

goldfinch, *n.* chardonneret *m.*

goldfish, *n.* poisson rouge *m.*

gold leaf, *n.* feuille d'or *f.*, or battu *m.*

gold-plated, *adj.* plaqué or.

goldsmith, *n.* orfèvre *m.*

gold standard, *n.* étalon or *m.*

golf, *n.* golf *m.*

gondola, *n.* gondole *f.*

gondolier, *n.* gondolier *m.*

gone, *adj.* disparu, parti.

gong, *n.* gong *m.*

gonorrhea, *n.* gonorrhée *f.*, blennorrhagie *f.*

good, 1. *adj.* bon *m.*, bonne *f.* **2.** *n.* bien *m.*; (**goods**) marchandises *f.pl.*

good-bye, *n. and interj.* adieu *m.*

Good Friday, *n.* Vendredi Saint *m.*

good-hearted, *adj.* qui a bon cœur, compatissant.

good-humored, *adj.* de bonne humeur, plein de bonhomie.

good-looking, *adj.* beau, joli.

good-natured, *adj.* au bon naturel, accommodant.

goodness, *n.* bonté *f.*

good will, *n.* bonne volonté *f.*

goody-goody, *n.* petit saint *m.*

goose, *n.* oie *f.*

gooseberry, *n.* groseille verte *f.*

gooseflesh, *n.* chair (*f.*) de poule.

gooseneck, *n.* col (*m.*) de cygne.

goose step, *n.* pas (*m.*) d'oie.

gore, 1. *n.* (dress) chanteau *m.*, soufflet *m.*; (blood) sang coagulé *m.* **2.** *vb.* corner.

gorge, *n.* gorge *f.*

gorgeous, *adj.* splendide.

gorilla, *n.* gorille *m.*

gory, *adj.* sanglant, ensanglanté.

gosh, *interj.* mince (alors).

gosling, *n.* oison *m.*

gospel, *n.* évangile *m.*

gossamer, *n.* filandre *f.*, gaze légère *f.*

gossip, 1. n. bavardage m. **2.** vb. bavarder.

Gothic, adj. gothique.

gouge, 1. n. gouge f. **2.** vb. gouger.

gourd, n. gourde f., courge f.

gourmand, n. gourmand m.

gourmet, n. gourmet m.

govern, vb. gouverner.

governess, n. gouvernante f.

government, n. gouvernement m.

governmental, adj. gouvernemental.

governor, n. gouverneur m.

governorship, n. fonctions de gouverneur f.pl., temps de gouvernement m.

gown, n. robe f.

grab, vb. saisir.

grace, n. grâce f.

graceful, adj. gracieux.

gracefully, adv. avec grâce.

graceless, adj. sans grâce, gauche.

gracious, adj. gracieux; (merciful) miséricordieux.

grackle, n. mainate m.

gradation, n. gradation f.

grade, 1. n. grade m.; (quality) qualité f. **2.** vb. classer.

grade crossing, n. passage (m.) à niveau.

gradual, adj. graduel, progressif.

gradually, adv. graduellement.

graduate, vb. graduer; (school) obtenir son diplôme; prendre ses grades.

graduation, n. remise (f.) des diplômes.

graft, n. corruption f.

grail, n. graal m.

grain, n. grain m.

gram, n. gramme m.

grammar, n. grammaire f.

grammarian, n. grammairien m.

grammar school, n. école primaire f.

grammatical, adj. grammatical.

gramophone, n. phonographe.

granary, n. grenier m.

grand, adj. grandiose; (in titles) grand; (fine, colloq.) épatant.

grandchild, n. petit-fils m.; petite-fille f.; petits-enfants m.pl.

granddaughter, n. petite-fille f.

grandee, n. grand m.

grandeur, n. grandeur f.

grandfather, n. grand-père m.

grandiloquent, adj. grandiloquent.

grandiose, adj. grandiose.

grand jury, n. jury d'accusation m.

grandly, adv. grandement, magnifiquement.

grandmother, n. grand'mère f.

grand opera, n. grand opéra m.

grandson, n. petit-fils m.

grandstand, n. grande tribune f.

granger, n. régisseur m.

granite, n. granit m.

granny, n. bonne-maman f.

grant, 1. n. concession f.; (money) subvention f. **2.** vb. accorder; (admit) admettre.

granular, adj. en grains, granulé.

granulate, vb. granuler, grener.

granulation, n. granulation f.

granule, n. granule m.

grape, n. raisin m.

grapefruit, n. pamplemousse f.

grapeshot, n. mitraille f.

grapevine, n. treille f.

graph, n. courbe f.

graphic, adj. graphique, pittoresque, explicite.

graphite, n. graphite m.

graphology, n. graphologie f.

grapple, 1. n. grappin m.; lutte f. **2.** vb. accrocher; en venir aux prises.

grasp, 1. n. (hold) prise f. **2.** vb. saisir.

grasping, adj. avide, cupide.

grass, n. herbe f.

grasshopper, n. sauterelle f.

grass-roots, adj. de la base, du people.

grassy, adj. herbeux, verdoyant.

grate, 1. n. grille f. **2.** vb. (cheese, etc.) râper; (make noise) grincer.

grateful, adj. reconnaissant.

gratify, vb. contenter, satisfaire.

grating, 1. n. grille f. **2.** adj. grinçant, discordant.

gratis, adv. gratis, gratuitement.

gratitude, n. gratitude f.

gratuitous, adj. gratuit.

gratuity, n. (tip) pourboire m.

grave, 1. n. tombe f. **2.** adj. grave.

gravel, n. gravier m.

gravely, adv. gravement, sérieusement.

gravestone, n. pierre sépulcrale f., tombe f.

graveyard, n. cimetière m.

gravitate, vb. graviter.

gravitation, n. gravitation f.

gravity, n. gravité f.

gravure, n. gravure f.

gravy, n. jus m.

gray, adj. gris.

grayish, adj. grisâtre.

gray matter, n. substance grise f., cendrée f.

graze, vb. paître.

grazing, n. pâturage m.

grease, 1. n. graisse f. **2.** vb. graisser.

great, adj. grand.

Great Dane, n. grand Danois m.

greatness, n. grandeur f.

Greece, n. Grèce f.

greediness, n. gourmandise f.

greedy, adj. gourmand.

Greek, 1. n. (person) Grec m., Grecque f.; (language) grec m. **2.** adj. grec m., grecque f.

green, adj. vert.

greenery, n. verdure f.

greenhouse, n. serre f.

greet, vb. saluer.

greeting, n. salutation f.; (reception) accueil m.

gregarious, adj. grégaire.

grenade, n. grenade f.

grenadine, n. grenadine f.

greyhound, n. lévrier m.

grid, n. gril m.

griddle, n. gril m.

gridiron, n. gril m.

grief, n. chagrin m.

grievance, n. grief m.

grieve, vb. affliger, tr.; chagriner, tr.

grievous, adj. douloureux.

grill, 1. n. gril m. **2.** vb. griller.

grillroom, n. grill-room m.

grim, adj. sinistre.

grimace, n. grimace f.

grime, n. saleté f.; noirceur f.

grimy, adj. sale, noirci, encrassé.

grin, n. large sourire m.

grind, vb. (crush) moudre; (sharpen) aiguiser.

grindstone, n. meule f.

gringo, n. Anglo-américain m.

grip, n. prise f.

gripe, vb. saisir, empoigner; grogner.

grisly, adj. hideux, horrible.

grist, n. blé à moudre m., mouture f.

gristle, n. cartilage m.

grit, n. grès m., sable m.; (fig.) cran m., courage m.

grizzled, adj. grison, grisonnant.

groan, 1. n. gémissement m. **2.** vb. gémir.

grocer, n. épicier m.

grocery, n. épicerie f.

grog, n. grog m.

groggy, adj. gris, titubant.

groin, n. aine f.

groom, 1. n. (horses) palefrenier m.; (bridegroom) nouveau marié m. **2.** vb. (horses) panser.

groove, n. rainure f.

grope, vb. tâtonner.

grosgrain, adj. de grosgrain.

gross, adj. (bulky) gros m., grosse f.; (coarse) grossier; (comm.) brut.

grossly, adv. grossièrement.

grossness, n. grossièreté f., énormité f.

grotesque, adj. and n. grotesque m.

grotto, n. grotte f.

grouch, 1. n. maussaderie f.; grogneur m. **2.** vb. grogner.

ground, n. (earth) terre f.; (territory) terrain m.; (reason) raison f.; (background) fond m.

ground hog, n. marmotte d'Amérique f.

groundless, adj. sans fondement.

ground swell, n. houle f., lame de fond f.

groundwork, n. fondement m., fond m., base f.

group, 1. n. groupe m. **2.** vb. grouper, tr.

groupie, n. groupie f.; membre (m.) d'un groupe de jeunes filles.

grouse, 1. n. tétras m. **2.** vb. grogner.

grove, n. bocage m., bosquet m.

grovel, vb. ramper, se vautrer.

grow, vb. croître; (persons) grandir; (become) devenir; (cultivate) cultiver.

growl, vb. grogner.

grown, adj. fait, grand.

grownup, *adj. and n.* grand *m.,* adulte *m.f.*

growth, *n.* croissance *f.;* (increase) accroissement *m.*

grub, 1. *n.* larve *f.,* ver blanc *m.;* (slang) nourriture *f.* 2. *vb.* défricher, fouiller.

grubby, *adj.* véreux, *(fig.)* sale.

grudge, *n.* rancune *f.*

gruel, *n.* gruau *m.*

gruesome, *adj.* lugubre, terrifiant.

gruff, *adj.* bourru.

grumble, *vb.* grommeler.

grumpy, *adj.* bourru, morose.

grunt, 1. *n.* grognement *m.* 2. *vb.* grogner.

guarantee, 1. *n.* garantie *f.* 2. *vb.* garantir.

guarantor, *n.* garant *m.*

guaranty, *n.* garantie *f.*

guard, 1. *n.* garde *f.* 2. *vb.* garder.

guarded, *adj.* prudent, circonspect, réservé.

guardhouse, *n.* corps de garde *m.,* poste *m.*

guardian, *n.* gardien *m.;* (law) tuteur *m.*

guardianship, *n.* tutelle *f.*

guardsman, *n.* garde *m.*

guava, *n.* goyave *f.*

gubernatorial, *adj.* du gouverneur, du gouvernement.

guerrilla, *n.* guérilla *f.*

guess, 1. *n.* conjecture *f.* 2. *vb.* deviner.

guesswork, *n.* conjecture *f.*

guest, *n.* invité *m.*

guffaw, 1. *n.* gros rire *m.* 2. *vb.* s'esclaffer.

guidance, *n.* direction *f.*

guide, 1. *n.* guide *m.* 2. *vb.* guider.

guidebook, *n.* guide *m.*

guided missile, *n.* missile *(m.)* téléguidé.

guidepost, *n.* poteau indicateur *m.*

guild, *n.* corporation *f.,* corps de métier *m.*

guile, *n.* astuce *f.,* artifice *m.*

guillotine, *n.* guillotine *f.*

guilt, *n.* culpabilité *f.*

guiltily, *adv.* criminellement.

guiltless, *adj.* innocent.

guilty, *adj.* coupable.

guimpe, *n.* guimpe *f.*

guinea fowl, *n.* pintade *f.*

guinea pig, *n.* cobaye *m.*

guise, *n.* guise *f.,* façon *f.*

guitar, *n.* guitare *f.*

gulch, *n.* ravin *m.*

gulf, *n.* (geog.) golfe *m.;* (fig.) gouffre *m.*

gull, *n.* mouette *f.*

gullet, *n.* gosier *m.*

gullible, *adj.* crédule, facile à duper.

gully, *n.* ravin *m.*

gulp, 1. *n.* goulée *f.,* gorgée *f.,* trait *m.* 2. *vb.* avaler, gober.

gum, *n.* gomme *f.;* (teeth) gencive *f.*

gumbo, *n.* gombo *m.*

gummy, *adj.* gommeux.

gumption, *n.* initiative *f.,* audace *f.*

gun, *n.* (cannon) canon *m.;* (rifle) fusil *m.*

gunboat, *n.* canonnière *f.*

gunman, *n.* partisan armé *m.,* voleur armé *m.,* bandit *m.*

gunner, *n.* artilleur *m.*

gunpowder, *n.* poudre (*f.*) à canon.

gunshot, *n.* portée (*f.*) de fusil.

gunwale, *n.* plat-bord *m.*

gurgle, *vb.* faire glouglou, gargouiller.

guru, *n.* gourou *m.*

gush, 1. *n.* jaillissement *m.* 2. *vb.* jaillir.

gusher, *n.* source jaillissante *f.,* personne exubérante *f.*

gusset, *n.* gousset *m.,* soufflet *m.*

gust, *n.* (wind) rafale *f.*

gustatory, *adj.* gustatif.

gusto, *n.* goût *m.,* délectation *f.,* verve *f.*

gusty, *adj.* venteux, orageux.

gut, 1. *n.* boyau *m.,* intestin *m.* 2. *vb.* éventrer, vider.

gutter, *n.* (roof) gouttière *f.;* (street) ruisseau *m.*

guttural, *adj.* guttural.

guy, 1. *n.* type *m.,* individu *m.* 2. *vb.* se moquer de.

guzzle, *vb.* ingurgiter, boire avidement.

gym, *n.* gymnase *m.*

gymnasium, *n.* gymnase *m.*

gymnast, *n.* gymnaste *m.*

gymnastic, *adj.* gymnastique.

gymnastics, *n.* gymnastique *f.*

gynecology, *n.* gynécologie *f.*

gypsum, *n.* gypse *m.*
gypsy, *n.* gitan *m.*

gyrate, *vb.* tournoyer.
gyroscope, *n.* gyroscope *m.*

H

habeas corpus, *n.* habeas corpus *m.*

haberdasher, *n.* chemisier *m.*; mercier *m.*

haberdashery, *n.* chemiserie *f.*, mercerie *f.*

habiliment, *n.* habillement *m.*, apprêt *m.*

habit, *n.* habitude *f.*

habitable, *adj.* habitable.

habitat, *n.* habitat *m.*

habitation, *n.* habitation *f.*

habitual, *adj.* habituel.

habituate, *vb.* habituer, accoutumer.

habitué, *n.* habitué *m.*

hack, 1. *n.* (tool) pioche *f.*; (horse) cheval *(m.)* de louage; (vehicle) voiture *(f.)* de louage. **2.** *vb.* **(h. up)** hacher; (notch) entailler.

hackneyed, *adj.* banal, rebattu.

hacksaw, *n.* scie *(f.)* à métaux.

haddock, *n.* aigle fin *m.*

haft, *n.* manche *m.*, poignée *f.*

hag, *n.* vieille sorcière *f.*

haggard, *adj.* hagard.

haggle, *vb.* marchander.

hagridden, *adj.* tourmenté par le cauchemar.

Hague (The), *n.* La Haye *f.*

hail, 1. *n.* grêle *f.* **2.** *vb.* (weather) grêler; (salute) saluer; (come from) venir de. **3.** *interj.* salut.

Hail Mary, *n.* Ave Maria *m.*

hailstone, *n.* grêlon *m.*

hailstorm, *n.* tempête *(f.)* de grêle.

hair, *n.* cheveux *m.pl.*; (single, on head) cheveu *m.*; (on body, animals) poil *m.*

haircut, *n.* coupe *(f.)* de cheveux.

hairdo, *n.* coiffure *f.*

hairdresser, *n.* coiffeur *m.*

hairline, *n.* délié *m.*

hairpin, *n.* épingle *(f.)* à cheveux.

hair-raising, *adj.* horripilant, horrifique.

hair's-breadth, *n.* l'épaisseur d'un cheveu *f.*

hairspray, *n.* laque *f.*

hairy, *adj.* velu, poilu.

halcyon, 1. *n.* alcyon *m.* **2.** *adj.* calme.

hale, *adj.* sain.

half, 1. *n.* moitié *f.* **2.** *adj.* demi. **3.** *adv.* à moitié.

half-and-half, *n.* moitié de l'un, moitié de l'autre *f.*

halfback, *n.* demi-arrière *m.*

half-baked, *adj.* à moitié cuit, inexpérimenté, incomplet.

half-breed, *n.* métis *m.*

half brother, *n.* frère de père *m.*, frère de mère *m.*

half dollar, *n.* demi-dollar *m.*

half-hearted, *adj.* sans enthousiasme.

half-mast, *adv.* à mi-mât.

halfpenny, *n.* petit sou *m.*

halfway, *adv.* à mi-chemin.

half-wit, *n.* niais *m.*, sot *m.*

halibut, *n.* flétan *m.*

hall, *n.* (large room) salle *f.*; (entrance) vestibule *m.*

hallmark, *n.* contrôle *m.*

hallow, *vb.* sanctifier.

Halloween, *n.* la veille *(f.)* de la Toussaint.

hallucination, *n.* hallucination *f.*

hallway, *n.* corridor *m.*, vestibule *m.*

halo, *n.* auréole *f.*

halt, 1. *n.* halte *f.* **2.** *vb.* arrêter, s'arrêter.

halter, *n.* licou *m.*, longe *f.*, corde *f.*

halve, *vb.* diviser en deux, partager en deux.

halyard, *n.* drisse *f.*

ham, *n.* jambon *m.*

hamburger, *n.* hamburger *m.*

hamlet, *n.* hameau *m.*

hammer, 1. *n.* marteau *m.* **2.** *vb.* marteler.

hammock, *n.* hamac *m.*

hamper, 1. *n.* pannier *m.* **2.** *vb.* embarrasser, gêner.

hamstring, *vb.* couper le jarret à, couper les moyens à.

hand, *n.* main *f.*

handbag, *n.* sac *(m.)* à main.

handball, n. balle f.
handbook, n. manuel m.
handcuff, 1. n. menotte f. 2. vb. mettre les menottes à.
handful, n. poignée f.
handicap, n. handicap m., désavantage m.
handicraft, n. artisanat m.
handiwork, n. main-d'œuvre f.
handkerchief, n. mouchoir m.
handle, 1. n. manche m. 2. vb. manier.
handlebar, n. guidon m.
handmade, adj. fait à la main, fabriqué à la main.
handmaid, n. servante f.
hand organ, n. orgue portatif m., orgue de Barbarie.
handout, n. aumône f.; compte rendu (m.) communiqué à la presse.
hand-pick, vb. trier à la main, éplucher à la main.
handsome, adj. beau m., belle f.
hand-to-hand, adj. corps à corps.
handwriting, n. écriture f.
handy, adj. (person) adroit; (thing) commode; (at hand) sous la main.
handyman, n. homme (m.) à tout faire, bricoleur m., factotum.
hang, vb. pendre.
hangar, n. hangar m.
hangdog, adj. avec une mine patibulaire, avec un air en dessous.
hanger-on, n. dépendant m., parasite m.
hang glider, n. glisseur (m.) duquel l'usager pend.
hanging, 1. n. suspension f., pendaison f. 2. adj. suspendu, pendant.
hangman, n. bourreau m.
hangnail, n. envie f.
hangout, n. repaire m., nid m.
hangover, n. gueule (f.) de bois.
hang-over, n. reste m., reliquat m.
hangup, n. difficulté psychologique f.
hank, n. écheveau m., torchette f.
hanker, vb. désirer vivement, convoiter.
haphazard, adv. au hasard.
happen, vb. (take place) arriver; (chance to be) se trouver.

happening, n. événement m.
happily, adv. heureusement.
happiness, n. bonheur m.
happy, adj. heureux.
happy-go-lucky, adj. sans souci, insouciant.
harakiri, n. hara-kiri m.
harangue, 1. n. harangue f. 2. vb. haranguer.
harass, vb. harceler, tracasser.
harbinger, n. avant-coureur m., précurseur m.
harbor, 1. n. (refuge) asile m.; (port) port m. 2. vb. héberger.
hard, 1. adj. dur; (difficult) difficile. 2. adv. fort.
hard-bitten, adj. tenace, dur à cuire.
hard-boiled, adj. dur, tenace, boucané.
hard coal, n. anthracite m.
hard disk, n. disque (m.) dur.
harden, vb. durcir.
hard-headed, adj. pratique, positif.
hard-hearted, adj. insensible, impitoyable, au cœur dur.
hardiness, n. robustesse f., vigueur f.
hardly, adv. (in a hard manner) durement; (scarcely) à peine; (h. ever) presque jamais.
hardness, n. dureté f.; (difficulty) difficulté f.
hardship, n. privation f.
hardtack, n. galette f., biscuit de mer m.
hardware, n. quincaillerie f., matériel m.
hardwood, n. bois dur m.
hardy, adj. robuste.
hare, n. lièvre m.
harebrained, adj. écervelé, étourdi.
harelip, n. bec-de-lièvre m.
harem, n. harem m.
hark, 1. vb. prêter l'oreille à. 2. interj. écoutez!
Harlequin, n. Arlequin m.
harlot, n. prostituée f., fille de joie f.
harm, 1. n. mal m. 2. vb. nuire à.
harmful, adj. nuisible.
harmless, adj. inoffensif.
harmonic, adj. harmonique.
harmonica, n. harmonica m.

harmonious, *adj.* harmonieux.

harmonize, *vb.* harmoniser.

harmony, *n.* harmonie *f.*

harness, 1. *n.* harnais *m.* **2.** *vb.* harnacher.

harp, *n.* harpe *f.*

harpoon, 1. *n.* harpon *m.* **2.** *vb.* harponner.

harpsichord, *n.* clavecin *m.*

harridan, *n.* vieille sorcière *f.*, vieille mégère *f.*

harrowing, *adj.* déchirant.

harry, *vb.* harceler.

harsh, *adj.* rude.

harshness, *n.* rudesse *f.*

harvest, 1. *n.* moisson *f.* **2.** *vb.* moissoner.

hash, 1. *n.* hachis *m.*, émincé *m.* **2.** *vb.* hacher (de la viande).

hashish, *n.* hachisch *m.*

hasn't, *vb.* n'a pas.

hassle, 1. *vb.* harceler. **2.** *n.* harcèlement *m.*

hassock, *n.* agenouilloir *m.*

haste, *n.* hâte *f.*

hasten, *vb.* hâter, *tr.*

hastily, *adv.* à la hâte.

hasty, *adj.* précipité.

hat, *n.* chapeau *m.*

hatch, *vb.* (hen) couver; (egg) éclore.

hatchback, *adj.* (auto) avec hayon arrière.

hatchery, *n.* établissement *(m.)* de pisciculture.

hatchet, *n.* hachette *f.*

hate, *vb.* haïr.

hateful, *adj.* odieux.

hatred, *n.* haine *f.*

haughtiness, *n.* arrogance *f.*, hauteur *f.*

haughty, *adj.* hautain.

haul, *vb.* traîner.

haunch, *n.* hanche *f.*, cuissot *m.*

haunt, *vb.* hanter.

have, *vb.* avoir; **(h. to,** necessity) devoir.

haven, *n.* havre *m.; (refuge)* asile *m.*

haven't, *vb.* n'ont pas.

havoc, *n.* ravage *m.*

hawk, 1. *n.* faucon *m.* **2.** *vb.* colporter.

hawker, *n.* colporteur *m.*, marchand ambulant *m.*

hawser, *n.* haussière *f.*, amarre *f.*

hawthorn, *n.* aubépine *f.*

hay, *n.* foin *m.*

hay fever, *n.* fièvre *(f.)* des foins.

hayfield, *n.* champs *(m.)* de foin.

hayloft, *n.* fenil *m.*, grenier *m.*

haystack, *n.* meule *(f.)* de foin.

hazard, 1. *n.* hasard *m.* **2.** *vb.* hasarder, risquer.

hazardous, *adj.* hasardeux.

haze, *n.* brume *(f.)* légère.

hazel, *n.* noisetier *m.;* couleur de noisette *f.*

hazy, *adj.* brumeux, nébuleux.

he, *pron.* il; (alone, stressed, with another subject) lui.

head, *n.* tête *f.*

headache, *n.* mal *(m.)* de tête.

headband, *n.* bandeau *m.*

headfirst, *adv.* la tête la première.

headgear, *n.* garniture *(f.)* de tête, coiffure *f.*

head-hunting, *n.* chasse *(f.)* aux têtes.

heading, *n.* rubrique *f.*

headlight, *n.* phare *m.*, projecteur *m.*

headline, *n.* titre *m.*

headlong, *adv.* la tête la première.

headman, *n.* chef *m.*

headmaster, *n.* directeur *m.*

head-on, *adj. and adv.* de front.

headquarters, *n.* (mil.) quartier *(m.)* général; *(comm.)* bureau *(m.)* principal.

headstone, *n.* pierre angulaire *f.*

headstrong, *adj.* volontaire, têtu, entêté.

headwaters, *n.* cours supérieur (d'une rivière) *m.*, eau d'amont *m.*

headway, *n.* progrès *m.*

headwork, *n.* travail de tête *m.*, travail intellectuel *m.*

heady, *adj.* impétueux, capiteux.

heal, *vb.* guérir.

health, *n.* santé *f.*

health foods, *n.* aliments *(m.pl.)* diététiques.

healthful, *adj.* salubre.

healthy, *adj.* sain.

heap, 1. *n.* tas *m.* **2.** *vb.* entasser.

hear, *vb.* entendre.

hearing, *n.* audition *f.;* ouïe *f.*

hearsay, *n.* ouï-dire *m.*

hearse, n. catafalque m., corbillard m.

heart, n. cœur m.

heartache, n. chagrin m.

heart attack, n. crise (f.) cardiaque.

heartbreak, n. déchirement de cœur m.

heartbroken, adj. avec le cœur brisé, navré.

heartburn, n. brûlures (f.pl.) d'estomac. aigreur f.

heartfelt, adj. sincère, qui va au cœur.

hearth, n. foyer m., âtre m.

heartless, adj. sans cœur, insensible, sans pitié.

heart-rending, adj. à fendre le cœur, navrant, déchirant.

heartsick, adj. écœuré.

heart-stricken, adj. frappé au cœur, navré.

heart-to-heart, adj. à cœur ouvert, intime.

hearty, adj. cordial.

heat, 1. n. chaleur f. 2. vb. chauffer.

heated, adj. chaud, chauffé, animé.

heath, n. bruyère f., lande f.

heathen, adj. and n. païen m., païenne f.

heather, n. bruyère f., brande f.

heatstroke, n. coup (m.) de chaleur.

heat wave, n. vague (f.) de chaleur, canicule f.

heave, vb. (lift) lever; (utter) pousser; (rise) se soulever, intr.

heaven, n. ciel m., pl. cieux.

heavenly, adj. céleste.

heavy, adj. lourd.

heavyweight, n. poids lourd m.

Hebrew, 1. n. (language) hébreu m. 2. adj. hébreu.

Hebrides, n. les Hébrides f.pl.

heckle, vb. poser des questions embarrassantes.

hectare, n. hectare m.

hectic, adj. (restless) agité.

hectograph, 1. n. hectographe m., autocopiste m. 2. vb. hectographier, autocopier.

hedge, n. haie f.

hedgehog, n. hérisson m.

hedgehop, vb. voler à ras de terre.

hedgerow, n. bordure de haies f.

hedonism, n. hédonisme m.

heed, 1. n. attention f. 2. vb. faire attention à.

heedless, adj. étourdi, imprudent, insouciant.

heel, n. talon m.

hefty, adj. fort, solide, costaud.

hegemony, n. hégémonie f.

heifer, n. génisse f.

height, n. hauteur f.

heighten, vb. rehausser, augmenter.

heinous, adj. odieux, atroce, abominable.

heir, n. héritier m.

heir apparent, n. héritier présomptif m.

heirloom, n. meuble m. (or bijou m.) de famille.

heir presumptive, n. héritier présomptif m.

helicopter, n. hélicoptère m.

heliocentric, adj. héliocentrique.

heliograph, n. héliographe m.

heliotrope, n. héliotrope m.

heliport, n. héliport m.

helium, n. hélium m.

hell, n. enfer m.

Hellenism, n. hellénisme m.

hellish, adj. infernal, diabolique.

hello, interj. (telephone) allô.

helm, n. barre (f.) du gouvernail.

helmet, n. casque m.

helmsman, n. homme de barre m., timonier m.

help, 1. n. aide f. 2. vb. aider; (at table) servir. 3. interj. au secours!

helper, n. aide m.f.

helpful, adj. (person) serviable; (thing) utile.

helpfulness, n. serviabilité f., utilité f.

helping, 1. n. portion f. 2. adj. secourable.

helpless, adj. (forlorn) délaissé; (powerless) impuissant.

helter-skelter, adv. pêle-mêle, en désordre.

hem, 1. n. ourlet m. 2. vb. ourler.

hematite, n. hématite f.

hemisphere, n. hémisphère m.

hemlock, n. ciguë f.

hemoglobin, n. hémoglobine f.

hemophilia, n. hémophilie f.

hemorrhage, n. hémorragie f.

hemorrhoid, n. hémorroïde f.
hemp, n. chanvre m.
hemstitch, 1. n. ourlet m. **2.** vb. ourler.
hen, n. poule f.
hence, adv. (time, place) d'ici; (therefore) de là.
henceforth, adv. désormais.
henchman, n. homme de confiance m., acolyte m., satellite m.
henequen, n. henequen m.
henna, 1. n. henné m. **2.** vb. teindre au henné.
henpeck, vb. mener par le bout du nez.
hepatic, adj. hépatique.
hepatica, n. hépatique f.
hepatitis, n. hépatite f.
her, 1. adj. son m., sa f., ses pl. **2.** pron. (direct) la; (indirect) lui; (alone, stressed, with prep.) elle.
herald, n. héraut m.
heraldic, adj. héraldique.
heraldry, n. l'héraldique f.
herb, n. herbe f.
herbaceous, adj. herbacé.
herbarium, n. herbier m.
herculean, adj. herculéen.
herd, n. troupeau m.
here, adv. ici; (**h. is**) voici.
hereabout, adv. par ici, près d'ici.
hereafter, adv. dorénavant.
hereby, adv. par ceci, par ce moyen, par là.
hereditary, adj. héréditaire.
heredity, n. hérédité f.
herein, adv. ici; (**h. enclosed**) ci-enclus.
heresy, n. hérésie f.
heretic, n. hérétique m.f.
heretical, adj. hérétique.
hereto, adv. ci-joint.
heretofore, adv. jusqu'ici.
herewith, adv. avec ceci, ci-joint.
heritage, n. héritage m., patrimoine m.
hermetic, adj. hermétique.
hermit, n. ermite m.
hermitage, n. ermitage m.
hernia, n. hernie f.
hero, n. héros m.
heroic, adj. héroïque.
heroically, adv. héroïquement.
heroin, n. héroïne f.
heroine, n. héroïne f.

heroism, n. héroïsme m.
heron, n. héron m.
herpes, n. herpès m.
herring, n. hareng m.
herringbone, n. arête (f.) de hareng.
hers, pron. le sien m., la sienne f.
herself, pron. elle-même; (reflexive) se.
hertz, n. hertz m.
hesitancy, n. hésitation f., incertitude f.
hesitant, adj. hésitant, irrésolu.
hesitate, vb. hésiter.
hesitation, n. hésitation f.
heterodox, adj. hétérodoxe.
heterodoxy, n. hétérodoxie f.
heterogeneous, adj. hétérogène.
heterosexual, adj. hétérosexuel.
hew, vb. couper, tailler.
hexagon, n. hexagone m.
heyday, n. apogée m., beaux jours m.pl.
hi, interj. salut!
hiatus, n. lacune f.
hibernate, vb. hiberner, hiverner.
hibernation, n. hibernation f.
hibiscus, n. hibiscus m.
hiccup, 1. n. hoquet m. **2.** vb. hoqueter.
hickory, n. noyer (blanc) d'Amérique m.
hide, 1. vb. cacher, tr. **2.** n. peau f.
hideous, adj. hideux.
hide-out, n. cachette f., lieu (m.) de retraite.
hierarchical, adj. hiérarchique.
hierarchy, n. hiérarchie f.
hieroglyphic, adj. hiéroglyphique.
hi-fi, 1. n. hi-fi f. **2.** adj. hi-fi.
high, adj. haut.
highbrow, n. intellectuel m.
high fidelity, n. haute fidélité f.
high-handed, adj. arbitraire, tyrannique.
high-hat, vb. traiter de haut en bas.
highland, n. haute terre f.
highlight, 1. n. clou m. **2.** vb. mettre en relief.
highly, adv. extrêmement.
high-minded, adj. à l'esprit élevé, généreux.
Highness, n. (title) Altesse f.
high school, n. lycée m.
high seas, n. haute mer f.

high-strung, *adj.* nerveux, impressionable.

high-tech, *n. and adj.* de pointe.

high tide, *n.* marée haute *f.*

highway, *n.* grande route *f.*

hijack, *vb.* détourner.

hijacker, *n.* pirate de l'air *m.*

hike, *n.* excursion (*f.*) à pied.

hilarious, *adj.* hilare.

hilariousness, *n.* hilarité *f.*

hilarity, *n.* hilarité *f.*

hill, *n.* colline *f.*

hilt, *n.* poignée *f.,* garde *f.*

him, *pron.* (direct) le; (indirect) lui; (alone, stressed, with prep.) lui.

himself, *pron.* lui-même; (reflexive) se.

hinder, *vb.* (impede) gêner; (prevent) empêcher.

hindmost, *adj.* dernier.

hindquarter, *n.* arrière-main *m.,* arrière-train *m.*

hindrance, *n.* empêchement *m.,* obstacle *m.,* entrave *f.*

hindsight, *n.* (with h.) avec du recul.

Hindu, **1.** *n.* Hindou *m.* **2.** *adj.* hindou.

hinge, *n.* gond *m.*

hint, **1.** *n.* allusion *f.* **2.** *vb.* insinuer.

hinterland, *n.* hinterland *m.,* arrière-pays *m.*

hip, *n.* hanche *f.*

hippie, *n.* hippie *m.f.*

hippodrome, *n.* hippodrome *f.*

hippopotamus, *n.* hippopotame *m.*

hire, *vb.* louer; (servant) engager.

hireling, *n.* mercenaire *m.,* stipendié *m.*

hirsute, *adj.* hirsute, velu.

his, **1.** *adj.* son *m.,* sa *f.,* ses *pl.* **2.** *pron.* le sien *m.,* la sienne *f.*

Hispanic, *adj.* hispanique.

hiss, *vb.* siffler.

historian, *n.* historien *m.*

historic, *adj.* historique.

historical, *adj.* historique.

history, *n.* histoire *f.*

histrionic, *adj.* histrionique, théâtral.

histrionics, *n.* parade d'émotions *f.,* démonstration peu sincère *f.*

hit, **1.** *n.* coup *m.;* (success) succès *m.* **2.** *vb.* frapper.

hitch, **1.** *n.* (obstacle) anicroche *f.* **2.** *vb.* (fasten) accrocher, *tr.*

hitchhike, *vb.* faire de l'auto-stop.

hither, **1.** *adv.* ici. **2.** *adj.* le plus rapproché.

hitherto, *adj.* jusqu'ici.

hive, *n.* ruche *f.*

hives, *n.* éruption *f.,* varicelle pustuleuse *f.,* urticaire *f.*

hoard, **1.** *n.* amas *m.* **2.** *vb.* amasser; (money) thésauriser.

hoarse, *adj.* enroué.

hoax, *n.* mystification *f.*

hobble, *vb.* boitiller, clopiner, entraver.

hobby, *n.* marotte *f.*

hobbyhorse, *n.* dada *m.,* cheval de bois *m.*

hobgoblin, *n.* lutin *m.,* esprit follet *m.*

hobnail, **1.** *n.* caboche *f.,* clou (*n.*) à ferrer. **2.** *vb.* ferrer.

hobnob, *vb.* boire avec, fréquenter.

hobo, *n.* vagabond *m.,* clochard *m.,* ouvrier ambulant *m.*

hock, **1.** *n.* jarret *m.* **2.** *vb.* mettre au clou.

hockey, *n.* hockey *m.*

hocuspocus, *n.* passe-passe *m.*

hod, *n.* auge *f.*

hodgepodge, *n.* mélange confus *m.*

hoe, **1.** *n.* houe *f.* **2.** *vb.* houer.

hog, *n.* porc *m.*

hogshead, *n.* tonneau *m.,* barrique *f.*

hog-tie, *vb.* lier les quatre pattes.

hoist, **1.** *n.* treuil *m.,* grue *f.* **2.** *vb.* hisser.

hold, **1.** *n.* prise *f.;* (ship) cale *f.* **2.** *vb.* tenir; (contain) contenir; (h. back) retenir; (h. up) arrêter, détenir, entraver.

holdup, *n.* arrêt *m.,* suspension *f.;* coup (*m.*) à main armée.

hole, *n.* trou *m.*

holiday, *n.* jour (*m.*) de fête; fête *f.;* (h.s) vacances *f.pl.*

holiness, *n.* sainteté *f.*

holistic, *adj.* holistique.

Holland, *n.* les Pays-Bas *m.pl.,* Hollande *f.*

hollow, *adj. and n.* creux *m.*

holly, *n.* houx *m.*

hollyhock, n. passe-rose f., rose-trémière f.

holocaust, n. holocauste m.

hologram, n. hologramme m.

holography, n. holographie f.

holster, n. étui m.

holy, adj. saint.

Holy See, n. Saint-Siège m.

Holy Spirit, n. Saint-Esprit m.

Holy Week, n. semaine sainte f.

homage, n. hommage m.

home, n. maison f.; (hearth) foyer (m.) domestique; **(at h.)** à la maison, chez soi.

homeland, n. patrie f.

homeless, 1. adj. sans asile, sans abri. **2.** n. sans abri m.

homelike, adj. qui resemble au foyer domestique.

homely, adj. laid.

homemade, adj. fait à la maison.

home rule, n. autonomie f.

homesick, adj. **(be h.)** avoir le mal du pays.

homespun, adj. (étoffe) de fabrication domestique, fait à la maison, simple.

homestead, n. ferme f., bien de famille m.

homeward, adj. de retour.

homework, n. travail fait à la maison m.; devoirs m.pl.

homicide, n. homicide m.

homily, n. homélie f.

homing pigeon, n. pigeon messager m.

hominy, n. bouillie (f.) de farine de maïs, semoule (f.) de maïs.

homogeneous, adj. homogène.

homonym, n. homonyme m.

homosexual, n. and adj. homosexuel m., homosexuelle f.

Honduras, n. Honduras m.

hone, vb. aiguiser, affiler.

honest, adj. honnête.

honestly, adv. honnêtement, de bonne foi.

honesty, n. honnêteté f.

honey, n. miel m.

honeybee, n. abeille domestique f.

honeycomb, 1. n. rayon de miel m. **2.** vb. cribler, affouiller.

honeydew melon, n. melon m.

honeymoon, n. lune (f.) de miel.

honeysuckle, n. chèvre-feuille m.

honor, 1. n. honneur m. **2.** vb. honorer.

honorable, adj. honorable.

honorary, adj. honoraire.

hood, n. capuchon m.; (vehicle) capote f.

hoodlum, n. voyou m.

hoodwink, vb. tromper, bander les yeux à.

hoof, n. sabot m.

hook, 1. n. croc m.; (fishing) hameçon m. **2.** vb. accrocher.

hooked, adj. crochu, recourbé; **(be h. on)** (drugs) se droguer à; (hobbies, etc.) être fana de.

hooked rug, n. tapis (m.) à points noués simples.

hooker, n. (colloquial) prostituée f.

hookworm, n. ankylostome m.

hoop, n. cercle m.

hoop skirt, n. jupe (f.) à paniers, vertugadin m.

hoot, 1. n. ululation f., hululement m., huée f. **2.** vb. hululer, huer.

hop, 1. n. (plant) houblon m. **2.** vb. sautiller.

hope, 1. n. espérance f., espoir m. **2.** vb. espérer.

hopeful, adj. plein d'espoir.

hopeless, adj. désespéré.

hopelessness, n. désespoir m., état désespéré m.

hopscotch, n. marelle f.

horde, n. horde f.

horizon, n. horizon m.

horizontal, adj. horizontal.

hormone, n. hormone f.

horn, n. corne f.; (music) cor m.; (auto) klaxon m.

hornet, n. frelon m., guêpe-frelon f.

horny, adj. corné, calleux.

horoscope, n. horoscope m.

horrendous, adj. horrible, horripilant.

horrible, adj. horrible.

horrid, adj. affreux.

horrify, vb. horrifier.

horror, n. horreur f.

horror film, n. film (m.) d'horreur.

horse, n. cheval m.

horseback, *n.* (**on h.**) à cheval.
horsefly, *n.* taon *m.*
horsehair, *n.* crin *m.*
horseman, *n.* cavalier *m.*
horsemanship, *n.* équitation *f.,* manège *m.*
horseplay, *n.* jeu (*m.*) de mains, badinerie grossière *f.*
horsepower, *n.* puissance (*f.*) en chevaux.
horse-racing, *n.* courses (*f.pl.*) de chevaux.
horseradish, *n.* raifort *m.*
horseshoe, *n.* fer à cheval *m.*
horsewhip, 1. *n.* cravache *f.* **2.** *vb.* cravacher, sangler.
hortatory, *adj.* exhortatif.
horticulture, *n.* horticulture *f.*
hose, *n.* (pipe) tuyau *m.*; (stockings) bas *m.pl.*
hosiery, *n.* bonneterie *f.*
hospice, *n.* hospice *m.*
hospitable, *adj.* hospitalier.
hospital, *n.* hôpital *m.*
hospitality, *n.* hospitalité *f.*
hospitalization, *n.* hospitalisation *f.*
hospitalize, *vb.* hospitaliser.
host, *n.* hôte *m.*; (show) animateur *m.*; (religion) hostie *f.*
hostage, *n.* otage *m.*
hostel, *n.* hôtellerie *f.,* auberge *f.*
hostelry, *n.* hôtellerie *f.,* auberge *f.*
hostess, *n.* hôtesse *f.*
hostile, *adj.* hostile, agressif, contre.
hostility, *n.* hostilité *f.*
hot, *adj.* chaud.
hotbed, *n.* couche *f.,* foyer ardent *m.*
hot dog, *n.* saucisse chaude *f.*
hotel, *n.* hôtel *m.*
hot-headed, *adj.* impétueux, exalté, emporté.
hothouse, *n.* serre *f.*
hound, 1. *n.* chien (*m.*) de chasse. **2.** *vb.* poursuivre, pourchasser.
hour, *n.* heure *f.*
hourglass, *n.* sablier *m.*
hourly, *adv.* à chaque heure, à l'heure.
house, 1. *n.* maison *f.*; (legislature) chambre *f.* **2.** *vb.* loger; abriter.
housecoat, *n.* peignoir *m.*
housefly, *n.* mouche domestique *f.*

household, *n.* (house, family) ménage, *m.,* (family) famille *f.*; (servants) domestiques *m.pl.*
housekeeper, *n.* gouvernante *f.*
housekeeping, *n.* ménage *m.,* économie domestique *f.*
housemaid, *n.* fille (*f.*) de service, bonne *f.,* femme de chambre *f.*
housewarming (party), *n.* pendaison (*f.*) de la crémaillère.
housewife, *n.* ménagère *f.,* femme (*f.*) au foyer.
housework, *n.* ménage *m.*
housing, *n.* logement *m.*
hovel, *n.* taudis *m.,* bicoque *f.*
hover, *vb.* planer.
hovercraft, *n.* aéroglisseur *m.*
how, *adv.* comment; (**h. are you**) comment allez-vous?; (**h. much**) combien (de); (in exclamation) comme.
however, *adv.* (in whatever way) de quelque manière que; (with adj.) si . . . que; (nevertheless) cependant.
howitzer, *n.* obusier *m.*
howl, *vb.* hurler.
hub, *n.* moyeu *m.,* centre *m.*
hubbub, *n.* vacarme *m.,* tintamarre *m.*
huckleberry, *n.* airelle *f.*
huddle, 1. *n.* tas confus *m.,* fouillis *m.* **2.** *vb.* entasser.
hue, *n.* couleur *f.*
huff, 1. *n.* emportement *m.,* accès de colère *m.* **2.** *vb.* gonfler, enfler.
hug, 1. *n.* étreinte *f.* **2.** *vb.* serrer dans ses bras.
huge, *adj.* énorme.
hulk, *n.* carcasse *f.,* ponton *m.*
hull, *n.* coque *f.,* corps *m.*
hullabaloo, *n.* vacarme *m.*
hum, *vb.* (insect) bourdonner; (sing) fredonner.
human, humane, *adj.* humain.
human being, *n.* être (*m.*) humain.
humanism, *n.* humanisme *m.*
humanitarian, *adj.* humanitaire.
humanities, *n.* humanités *f.pl.*
humanity, *n.* humanité *f.*
humanly, *adv.* humainement.
humble, *adj.* humble.
humbug, *n.* blague *f.,* tromperie *f.,* fumisterie *f.*

humdrum, *adj.* monotone, assommant.

humid, *adj.* humide.

humidify, *vb.* humidifier.

humidor, *n.* boîte à cigares *f.*

humiliate, *adj.* humilier.

humiliation, *n.* humiliation *f.*

humility, *n.* humilité *f.*

humor, 1. *n.* (wit) humour *m.*; (medical, mood) humeur *f.* **2.** *vb.* se prêter aux caprices de.

humorous, *adj.* (witty) humoristique; (funny) drôle.

hump, *n.* bosse *f.*

humpback, *n.* bossu *m.*

humus, *n.* humus *m.,* terreau *m.*

hunch, 1. *n.* bosse *f.*; pressentiment *m.* **2.** *vb.* arrondir, voûter.

hunchback, *n.* bossu *m.*

hundred, *adj. and n.* cent *m.*

hundredth, *n. and adj.* centième *m.f.*

Hungarian, 1. *n.* (person) Hongrois *m.*; (language) hongrois *m.* **2.** *adj.* hongrois.

Hungary, *n.* Hongrie *f.*

hunger, *n.* faim *f.*

hunger strike, *n.* grève *(f.)* de la faim.

hungry, *adj.* affamé; **(be h.)** avoir faim.

hunk, *n.* gros morceau *m.*

hunt, *vb.* chasser.

hunter, *n.* chasseur *m.*

hunting, *n.* chasse *f.*

huntress, *n.* chasseuse *f.,* chasseresse *f.*

hurdle, *n.* claie *f.*

hurl, *vb.* lancer.

hurrah, hurray, *interj.* houra!

hurricane, *n.* ouragan *m.*

hurry, 1. *n.* hâte *f.*; **(in a h.)** à la hâte. **2.** *vb.* presser, *tr.*; se presser, *intr.*

hurt, *vb.* faire mal (à).

hurtful, *adj.* nuisible, pernicieux, préjudiciable.

hurtle, *vb.* se choquer, se heurter.

husband, *n.* mari *m.*

husbandry, *n.* agriculture *f.,* économie *f.*

hush, 1. *interj.* chut! paix! **2.** *vb.* taire, imposer silence à.

husk, 1. *n.* cosse *f.,* gousse *f.* **2.** *vb.* écosser, éplucher.

husky, 1. *adj.* (body) cossu; (voice) rauque, enroué. **2.** *n.* chien *(m.)* de traineau.

hustle, *vb.* bousculer, se presser.

hut, *n.* cabane *f.*

hutch, *n.* huche *f.,* clapier *m.*

hyacinth, *n.* jacinthe *f.*

hybrid, *n.* hybride *m.*

hydrangea, *n.* hortensia *m.*

hydrant, *n.* prise d'eau *f.,* bouche d'incendie *f.*

hydraulic, *adj.* hydraulique.

hydrochloric acid, *n.* acide *(m.)* chlorhydrique.

hydroelectric, *adj.* hydroélectrique.

hydrofoil, *n.* hydroptère *m.*

hydrogen, *n.* hydrogène *m.*

hydrophobia, *n.* hydrophobie *f.*

hydroplane, *n.* hydroplane *m.*

hydrotherapy, *n.* hydrothérapie *f.*

hyena, *n.* hyène *f.*

hygiene, *n.* hygiène *f.*

hygienic, *adj.* hygiénique.

hymn, *n.* (song, anthem) hymne *m.*; (church) hymne *f.*

hymnal, *n.* hymnaire *m.,* recueil d'hymnes *m.*

hype, 1. *n.* tapage *(m.)* publicitaire. **2.** *vb.* faire du tapage autour de.

hyperacidity, *n.* hyperacidité *f.*

hyperbole, *n.* hyperbole *f.*

hypercritical, *adj.* hypercritique.

hypermarket, *n.* hypermarché *m.*

hypersensitive, *adj.* hypersensible.

hypertension, *n.* hypertension *f.*

hyphen, *n.* trait *(m.)* d'union.

hyphenate, *vb.* mettre un trait d'union à.

hypnosis, *n.* hypnose *f.*

hypnotic, *adj.* hypnotique.

hypnotism, *n.* hypnotisme *m.*

hypnotize, *vb.* hypnotiser.

hypochondria, *n.* hypocondrie *f.*

hypochondriac, *n. and adj.* hypocondriaque *m.*

hypocrisy, *n.* hypocrisie *f.*

hypocrite, *n.* hypocrite *m.f.*

hypocritical, *adj.* hypocrite.

hypodermic, *adj.* hypodermique.

hypotenuse, *n.* hypoténuse *f.*

hypothermia, *n.* hypothermie *f.*

hypothesis, *n.* hypothèse *f.*

hypothetical, *adj.* hypothétique.

hysterectomy, n. hystérectomie f.
hysteria, n. hystérie f.

hysterical, adj. hystérique.
hysterics, n.pl. crise (f.) de nerfs.

I

I, pron. je; (alone, stressed, with another subject) moi.
iambic, adj. iambique.
Iberia, n. Ibérie f.
ice, n. glace f.
iceberg, n. iceberg m., gros bloc de glace m.
ice-box, n. glacière f.
ice cream, n. glace f.
ice cube, n. glaçon m.
Iceland, n. Islande f.
ice skate, 1. n. patin à glace m. **2.** vb. patiner.
ichthyology, n. ichtyologie f.
icicle, n. glaçon m.
icing, n. glacé m.
icon, n. icône f.
icy, adj. glacial.
idea, n. idée f.
ideal, adj. and n. idéal m.
idealism, n. idéalisme m.
idealist, n. idéaliste m.f.
idealistic, adj. idéaliste.
idealize, vb. idéaliser.
ideally, adv. idéalement, en idée.
identical (with), adj. identique (à).
identifiable, adj. identifiable.
identification, n. identification f.
identify, vb. identifier.
identity, n. identité f.
ideology, n. idéologie f.
idiocy, n. idiotie f., idiotisme m.
idiom, n. (language) idiome m.; (peculiar expression) idiotisme m.
idiot, adj. and n. idiot m.
idiotic, adj. idiot.
idle, adj. (unoccupied) désœuvré; (lazy) paresseux; (futile) vain.
idleness, n. oisiveté f.
idol, n. idole f.
idolatry, n. idolâtrie f.
idolize, vb. idolâtrer.
idyl, n. idylle f.
idyllic, adj. idyllique.
if, conj. si.
ignite, vb. allumer, mettre en feu.
ignition, n. ignition f., allumage m.
ignoble, adj. ignoble; (low birth) plébéien.

ignominious, adj. ignominieux.
ignoramus, n. ignorant m., ignare m.
ignorance, n. ignorance f.
ignorant, adj. ignorant; (be i. of) ignorer.
ignore, vb. feindre d'ignorer.
ill, 1. n. mal. **2.** adj. (sick) malade; (bad) mauvais. **3.** adv. mal.
illegal, adj. illégal.
illegible, adj. illisible.
illegibly, adv. illisiblement.
illegitimacy, n. illégitimité f.
illegitimate, adj. illégitime.
illicit, adj. illicite.
illiteracy, n. analphabétisme m.
illiterate, adj. illettré, analphabète.
illness, n. maladie f.
illogical, adj. illogique.
illuminate, vb. illuminer.
illumination, n. illumination f., enluminure f.
illusion, n. illusion f.
illusive, adj. illusoire.
illustrate, vb. illustrer.
illustration, n. illustration f.; (example) exemple m.
illustrative, adj. explicatif, qui éclaircit.
illustrious, adj. illustre.
ill will, adj. mauvais vouloir m., malveillance f.
image, n. image f.
imagery, n. images f.pl., langage figuré m.
imaginable, adj. imaginable.
imaginary, adj. imaginaire.
imagination, n. imagination f.
imaginative, adj. imaginatif.
imagine, vb. imaginer, tr.
imam, n. imam m.
imbalance, n. déséquilibre m.
imbecile, n. imbécile m.
imbue, vb. imprégner.
imitate, vb. imiter.
imitation, n. imitation f.
imitative, adj. imitatif.
immaculate, adj. immaculé, sans tache.

immanent, *adj.* immanent.

immaterial, *adj.* immatériel, incorporel, sans conséquence.

immature, *adj.* pas mûr, prématuré.

immediate, *adj.* immédiat.

immediately, *adv.* immédiatement, tout de suite.

immense, *adj.* immense.

immerse, *vb.* immerger, plonger.

immigrant, *n.* immigrant *m.,* immigré *m.*

immigrate, *vb.* immigrer.

imminent, *adj.* imminent.

immobile, *adj.* fixe, immobile.

immobilize, *vb.* immobiliser.

immoderate, *adj.* immodéré, intempéré, outré.

immodest, *adj.* immodeste, impudique, présomptueux.

immoral, *adj.* immoral.

immorality, *n.* immoralité *f.*

immorally, *adv.* immoralement.

immortal, *adj. and n.* immortel *m.*

immortality, *n.* immortalité *f.*

immortalize, *vb.* immortaliser.

immovable, *adj.* fixe, immuable, inébranlable.

immune, *adj.* immunisé.

immunity, *n.* exemption *f.,* immunité *f.*

immunize, *vb.* immuniser.

immutable, *adj.* immuable, inaltérable.

impact, *n.* choc *m.,* impact *m.*

impair, *vb.* affaiblir, altérer, compromettre.

impale, *vb.* empaler.

impart, *vb.* donner, communiquer, transmettre.

impartial, *adj.* impartial.

impasse, *n.* impasse *f.*

impassioned, *adj.* passionné.

impassive, *adj.* impassible.

impatience, *n.* impatience *f.*

impatient, *adj.* impatient.

impeach, *vb.* attaquer, accuser, récuser.

impede, *vb.* entraver, empêcher.

impediment, *n.* entrave *f.,* obstacle *m.,* empêchement *m.*

impel, *vb.* pousser, forcer.

impending, *adj.* imminent.

impenetrable, *adj.* impénétrable.

impenitent, *adj.* impénitent.

imperative, 1. *n.* (*gramm.*) impératif *m.* **2.** *adj.* (*gramm.*) impératif; urgent, impérieux.

imperceptible, *adj.* imperceptible.

imperfect, *adj. and n.* imparfait *m.*

imperfection, *n.* imperfection *f.*

imperial, *adj.* impérial.

imperialism, *n.* impérialisme *m.*

imperil, *vb.* mettre en péril, exposer au danger.

imperious, *adj.* impérieux, arrogant.

impersonal, *adj.* impersonnel.

impersonate, *vb.* personnifier, représenter.

impersonation, *n.* personnification *f.,* incarnation *f.*

impersonator, *n.* personnificateur *m.*

impertinence, *n.* impertinence *f.*

impervious, *adj.* impénétrable, imperméable.

impetuous, *adj.* impétueux.

impetus, *n.* élan *m.,* vitesse acquise *f.*

impinge, *vb.* se heurter à, empiéter sur.

implacable, *adj.* implacable.

implant, *vb.* inculquer, implanter.

implement, *n.* outil *m.*

implicate, *vb.* impliquer, entremêler.

implication, *n.* implication *f.*

implicit, *adj.* implicite.

implied, *adj.* implicite, tacite.

implore, *vb.* implorer.

imply, *vb.* impliquer.

impolite, *adj.* impoli.

imponderable, *adj.* impondérable.

import, 1. *n.* article (*m.*) d'importation, importation *f.* **2.** *vb.* importer.

importance, *n.* importance *f.*

important, *adj.* important.

importation, *n.* importation *f.*

importune, *vb.* importuner.

impose (on), *vb.* imposer (à).

imposition, *n.* imposition *f.*

impossibility, *n.* impossibilité *f.*

impossible, *adj.* impossible.

impotence, *n.* impuissance *f.*

impotent, *adj.* impuissant.

impound, *vb.* confisquer.

impoverish, *vb.* appauvrir.

impractical, *adj.* pas pratique.

impregnable, *adj.* imprenable, inexpugnable.

impregnate, *vb.* imprégner, féconder.

impresario, *n.* imprésario *m.*

impress, *vb.* (imprint) imprimer; (affect) faire une impression à.

impression, *n.* impression *f.*

impressive, *adj.* impressionnant.

imprison, *vb.* emprisonner.

imprisonment, *n.* emprisonnement *m.*

improbable, *adj.* improbable.

impromptu, *adv., adj. and n.* impromptu *m.*

improper, *adj.* (inaccurate) impropre; (unbecoming) malséant.

improve, *vb.* améliorer, *tr.*

improvement, *n.* amélioration *f.*

improvise, *vb.* improviser.

impudent, *adj.* insolent, effronté, impertinent.

impugn, *vb.* attaquer, contester, impugner.

impulse, *n.* impulsion *f.*

impulsion, *n.* impulsion *f.*

impulsive, *adj.* impulsif.

impunity, *n.* impunité *f.*

impure, *adj.* impur.

impurity, *n.* impureté *f.*

impute, *vb.* imputer.

in, *prep.* en; (with art. or adj.) dans; (town) à.

inability, *n.* incapacité *f.*

inaccurate, *adj.* inexact.

inadequate, *adj.* insuffisant.

inadvertent, *adj.* inattentif, négligent, involontaire.

inalienable, *adj.* inaliénable.

inane, *adj.* inepte, niais, bête.

inappropriate, *adj.* mal à propos.

inaugural, *adj.* inaugural.

inaugurate, *vb.* inaugurer.

inauguration, *n.* inauguration *f.*

inborn, *adj.* inné.

inbred, *adj.* inné.

Inca, *n.* Inca *m.*

incandescence, *n.* incandescence *f.*

incandescent, *adj.* incandescent.

incantation, *n.* incantation *f.*, conjuration *f.*

incapable, *adj.* incapable.

incapacitate, *vb.* rendre incapable, priver de capacité légale.

incarcerate, *vb.* incarcérer, emprisonner.

incarnate, 1. *vb.* incarner. **2.** *adj.* incarné, fait chair.

incarnation, *n.* incarnation *f.*

incendiary, 1. *n.* incendiaire *m.* **2.** *adj.* incendiaire, séditieux.

incense, *n.* encens *m.*

incentive, *n.* stimulant *m.*, aiguillon *m.*

inception, *n.* commencement *m.*, début *m.*

incessant, *adj.* incessant, continuel.

incest, *n.* inceste *m.*

inch, *n.* pouce *m.*

incidence, *n.* incidence *f.*

incident, *n.* incident *m.*

incidental, *adj.* fortuit.

incidentally, *adv.* incidemment, en passant.

incinerator, *n.* incinérateur *m.*

incipient, *adj.* naissant, qui commence.

incision, *n.* incision *f.*, entaille *f.*

incisive, *adj.* incisif, tranchant.

incisor, *n.* incisive *f.*

incite, *vb.* inciter, instiguer.

inclination, *n.* inclinaison *f.*, penchant *m.*

incline, *vb.* incliner.

inclose, *see* **enclose.**

include, *vb.* comprendre.

inclusive, *adj.* inclusif.

incognito, *adj. and adv.* incognito.

income, *n.* revenu *m.*

incomparable, *adj.* incomparable.

incompetent, *adj.* incompétent.

inconsiderate, *adj.* peu prévenant.

inconvenience, 1. *n.* inconvénient *m.* **2.** *vb.* incommoder.

inconvenient, *adj.* incommode.

incorporate, *vb.* incorporer.

incorrigible, *adj.* incorrigible.

increase, 1. *n.* augmentation *f.* **2.** *vb.* augmenter.

incredible, *adj.* incroyable.

incredulity, *n.* incrédulité *f.*

incredulous, *adj.* incrédule.

increment, *n.* augmentation *f.*, accroissement *m.*

incriminate, *vb.* incriminer.

incrimination, *n.* incrimination *f.*

incrust, *vb.* incruster.

incubator, *n.* incubateur *m.*

inculcate, vb. inculquer.
incumbency, n. période (f.) d'exercice, charge f.
incumbent, 1. n. titulaire m., bénéficiaire m. **2.** adj. couché, posé, appuyé.
incur, vb. encourir.
incurable, adj. incurable.
indebted, adj. endetté.
indecent, adj. indécent.
indecisive, adj. indécis.
indeed, adv. en effet.
indefatigable, adj. infatigable, inlassable.
indefinite, adj. indéfini.
indefinitely, adv. indéfiniment.
indelible, adj. indélébile, ineffaçable.
indemnify, vb. garantir, indemniser, dédommager.
indemnity, n. garantie f., indemnité f., dédommagement m.
indent, vb. denteler, découper, entailler.
indentation, n. découpage m., renfoncement m., entendement m.
independence, n. indépendance f.
independent, adj. indépendant.
in-depth, adj. profond.
index, n. index m.
India, n. Inde f.
Indian, 1. n. Indien m. **2.** adj. indien.
indicate, vb. indiquer.
indication, n. indication f.
indicative, adj. and n. indicatif m.
indicator, n. indicateur m.
indict, vb. accuser, inculper.
indictment, n. accusation f., inculpation f., réquisitoire m.
indifference, n. indifférence f.
indifferent, adj. indifférent.
indigenous, adj. indigène.
indigent, adj. indigent, pauvre.
indigestion, n. dyspepsie f., indigestion f.
indignant, adj. indigné.
indignation, n. indignation f.
indignity, n. indignité f., affront m.
indirect, adj. indirect.
indiscreet, adj. indiscret.
indiscretion, n. imprudence f.
indiscriminate, adj. aveugle, qui ne fait pas de distinction.
indispensable, adj. indispensable.

indisposed, adj. (unwilling) peu enclin, peu disposé; (ill) indisposé, souffrant.
individual, 1. n. individu m. **2.** adj. individuel.
individuality, n. individualité f.
individually, adv. individuellement.
indivisible, adj. indivisible.
indoctrinate, vb. endoctriner, instruire.
Indonesia, n. Indonésie f.
indoor, adj. d'intérieur.
indoors, adv. à la maison.
indorse, vb. endosser, appuyer, sanctionner.
induce, vb. (persuade) persuader; (produce) produire.
induct, vb. installer, conduire.
induction, n. induction f.; installation f.
inductive, adj. inductif.
indulge, vb. contenter, favoriser.
indulgence, n. indulgence f.
indulgent, adj. indulgent.
industrial, adj. industriel.
industrialist, n. industriel m.
industrious, adj. travailleur.
industry, n. industrie f.; (diligence) assiduité f.
inebriated, adj. sou.
ineligible, adj. inéligible.
inept, adj. inepte, mal à propos.
inert, adj. inerte, apathique.
inertia, n. inertie f.
inevitable, adj. inévitable.
inexplicable, adj. inexplicable.
infallible, adj. infaillible.
infamous, adj. infâme.
infamy, n. infamie f.
infancy, n. (première) enfance f.
infant, n. enfant m.
infantile, adj. enfantin, infantile.
infantryman, n. soldat (m.) d'infanterie, fantassin m.
infatuated, adj. infatué, entiché.
infect, vb. infecter.
infection, n. infection f.
infectious, adj. infectieux, infect, contagieux.
infer, vb. déduire.
inference, n. inférence f.
inferior, adj. and n. inférieur m.

inferiority complex, n. complexe (m.) d'infériorité.

infernal, adj. infernal.

inferno, n. enfer m.

infest, vb. infester.

infidel, n. infidèle m., incroyant m.

infidelity, n. infidélité f.

infighting, n. querelles (f.pl.) internes.

infiltrate, vb. infiltrer.

infinite, adj. and n. infini m.

infinitesimal, adj. infinitésimal.

infinitive, n. infinitif m.

infinity, n. infinité f.

infirm, adj. infirme, faible, maladif.

infirmary, n. infirmerie f.

infirmity, n. infirmité f.

inflame, vb. enflammer, tr.

inflammable, adj. inflammable.

inflammation, n. inflammation f.

inflammatory, adj. incendiaire, inflammatoire.

inflate, vb. gonfler.

inflation, n. (currency) inflation f.

inflection, n. inflection f.

inflict, vb. (penalty) infliger.

infliction, n. infliction f., châtiment m.

influence, n. influence f.

influential, adj. influent.

influenza, n. grippe f., influenza f.

inform, vb. (tell) informer.

informal, adj. (without formality) sans cérémonie.

informant, n. informateur m.

information, n. renseignements m.pl.

informative, adj. instructif.

informer, n. indicateur m.

infringe, vb. enfreindre, violer.

infuriate, vb. rendre furieux.

ingenious, adj. ingénieux.

ingenuity, n. ingéniosité f.

ingrained, adj. enraciné.

ingredient, n. ingrédient m.

inhabit, vb. habiter.

inhabitant, n. habitant m.

inhale, vb. inhaler, aspirer, humer.

inherent, adj. inhérent.

inherit, vb. hériter.

inheritance, n. héritage m.

inhibit, vb. empêcher; (psychology) inhiber.

inhibition, n. inhibition f., défense expresse f., prohibition f.

inhuman, adj. inhumain.

inimical, adj. ennemi, hostile, défavorable.

inimitable, adj. inimitable.

iniquity, n. iniquité f.

initial, 1. n. initiale f. **2.** adj. initial. **3.** vb. parafer.

initialize, vb. initialiser.

initiate, vb. (begin) commencer; (admit) initier.

initiation, n. commencement m., début m., initiation f.

initiative, n. initiative f.

inject, vb. injecter.

injection, n. injection f.

injunction, n. injonction f., ordre m.

injure, vb. (harm) nuire à; (wound) blesser; (damage) abîmer.

injurious, adj. (harmful) nuisible; (offensive) injurieux.

injury, n. (person) préjudice m.; (body) blessure f.; (thing) dommage m.

injustice, n. injustice f.

ink, n. encre f.

inland, adj. and n. intérieur m.

inlet, n. entrée f., admission f., débouché m.

inmate, n. habitant m., hôte m., pensionnaire m.

inn, n. auberge f.

innate, adj. inné.

inner, adj. intérieur.

inning, n. tour (m.) de batte.

innocence, n. innocence f.

innocent, adj. innocent.

innocuous, adj. inoffensif.

innovation, n. innovation f.

innuendo, n. insinuation f., allusion malveillante f.

innumerable, adj. innombrable.

inoculate, vb. inoculer.

inoculation, n. inoculation f., vaccination préventive f.

inoffensive, adj. inoffensif.

input, n. entrée (f.) (de données).

inquest, n. enquête f.

inquire (about), vb. se renseigner (sur).

inquiry, n. (investigation) recherche f.; (question) demande f.; (official) enquête f.

inquisition, *n.* Inquisition *f.;* enquête *f.,* recherche *f.*

inquisitive, *adj.* curieux, questionneur, indiscret.

inroad, *n.* incursion *f.,* invasion *f.,* empiétement *m.*

insane, *adj.* fou *m.,* folle *f.*

insanity, *n.* folie *f.,* insanité *f.,* démence *f.*

inscribe, *vb.* inscrire, graver.

inscription, *n.* inscription *f.*

insect, *n.* insecte *m.*

insecticide, *n.* insecticide *m.*

insecure, *adj.* peu sûr.

insensitive, *adj.* insensible.

inseparable, *adj.* inséparable.

insert, *vb.* insérer.

insertion, *n.* insertion *f.*

inside, 1. *n.* dedans *m.* **2.** *adj.* intérieur. **3.** *prep.* à l'intérieur de. **4.** *adv.* (en) dedans.

insidious, *adj.* insidieux.

insight, *n.* perspicacité *f.,* pénétration *f.*

insignia, *n.* insignes *m.pl.*

insignificance, *n.* insignifiance *f.*

insignificant, *adj.* insignifiant.

insinuate, *vb.* insinuer.

insinuation, *n.* insinuation *f.*

insipid, *adj.* insipide, fade.

insist, *vb.* insister.

insistence, *n.* insistance *f.*

insistent, *adj.* qui insiste, importun.

insolence, *n.* insolence *f.*

insolent, *adj.* insolent.

insomnia, *n.* insomnie *f.*

inspect, *vb.* examiner, inspecter.

inspection, *n.* inspection *f.*

inspector, *n.* inspecteur *m.*

inspiration, *n.* inspiration *f.*

inspire, *vb.* inspirer.

install, *vb.* installer.

installation, *n.* installation *f.,* montage *m.*

installment, *n.* acompte *m.,* versement partiel *m.,* paiement à compte *m.*

instance, *n.* exemple *m.*

instant, *n.* instant *m.*

instantaneous, *adj.* instantané.

instantly, *adv.* à l'instant.

instead, *adv.* au lieu de cela.

instead of, *prep.* au lieu de.

instigate, *vb.* instiguer.

instill, *vb.* instiller, faire pénétrer, inculquer.

instinct, *n.* instinct *m.*

instinctive, *adj.* instinctif.

institute, *vb.* instituer.

institution, *n.* institution *f.*

instruct, *vb.* instruire.

instruction, *n.* instruction *f.*

instructive, *adj.* instructif.

instructor, *n.* *(mil.)* instructeur *m.;* (university) chargé *(m.)* de cours.

instrument, *n.* instrument *m.*

instrumental, *adj.* instrumental, contributif (à).

insufferable, *adj.* insupportable, intolérable.

insufficient, *adj.* insuffisant.

insular, *adj.* insulaire.

insulate, *vb.* isoler.

insulation, *n.* isolement *m.,* isolation *f.*

insulator, *n.* isolant *m.,* isolateur *m.*

insulin, *n.* insuline *f.*

insult, 1. *vb.* insulter. **2.** *n.* insulte *f.*

insuperable, *adj.* insurmontable.

insurance, *n.* assurance *f.*

insure, *vb.* assurer.

insurgent, *adj. and n.* insurgé *m.*

insurrection, *n.* insurrection *f.,* soulèvement *m.*

intact, *adj.* intact.

intake, *n.* admission(s) *f.pl.;* (technical) prise *f.*

intangible, *adj.* intangible, impalpable.

integral, *adj.* intégrant.

integrate, *vb.* intégrer, compléter, rendre entier.

integrity, *n.* intégrité *f.*

intellect, *n.* (mind) esprit *m.;* (faculty) intellect *m.*

intellectual, *adj. and n.* intellectuel *m.*

intelligence, *n.* intelligence *f.;* (information) renseignements *m.pl.*

intelligent, *adj.* intelligent.

intelligentsia, *n.* l'intelligence *f.*

intelligible, *adj.* intelligible.

intend, *vb.* avoir l'intention de; (destine for) destiner à.

intense, *adj.* intense.

intensify, *vb.* intensifier.

intensity, *n.* intensité *f.*

intensive, *adj.* intensif.

intent, *adj.* **(i. on)** (absorbed in) absorbé dans; (determined to) déterminé à.

intention, *n.* intention *f.*

intentional, *adj.* intentionnel, voulu, fait exprès.

inter, *vb.* enterrer.

interact, *vb.* communiquer, avoir une action réciproque.

intercede, *vb.* intervenir, intercéder.

intercept, *vb.* intercepter, capter.

interchange, *n.* échange *m.*

intercom, *n.* interphone *m.*

intercourse, *n.* commerce *m.*, relations *f.pl.*, rapports *m.pl.*

interdict, *vb.* interdire, prohiber.

interest, 1. *n.* intérêt *m.* **2.** *vb.* intéresser.

interesting, *adj.* intéressant.

interface, *n.* entreface *f.*

interfere, *vb.* (person) intervenir (dans); **(i. with)** (hinder) gêner.

interference, *n.* (person) intervention *f.*

interim, *adv.* entre temps, en attendant.

interior, *adj. and n.* intérieur *m.*

interject, *vb.* lancer, émettre.

interjection, *n.* interjection *f.*

interloper, *n.* intrus *m.*

interlude, *n.* intermède *m.*, interlude *m.*

intermarry, *vb.* se marier.

intermediary, *n.* intermédiaire *m.f.*

intermediate, *adj. and n.* intermédiaire *m.f.*

interment, *n.* enterrement *m.*

intermission, *n.* interruption *f.*, relâche *f.*; (theater) entr'acte *m.*

intermittent, *adj.* intermittent.

intern, 1. *n.* interne *m.* **2.** *vb.* interner.

internal, *adj.* interne.

Internal Revenue Service, *n.* fisc *m.*

international, *adj.* international.

internationalism, *n.* internationalisme *m.*

interne, *n.* interne *m.*

interplay, *n.* effect (*m.*) réciproque, interaction *f.*

interpolate, *vb.* interpoler.

interpose, *vb.* interposer, *tr.*

interpret, *vb.* interpréter.

interpretation, *n.* interprétation *f.*

interpreter, *n.* interprète *m.f.*

interrogate, *vb.* interroger, questionner.

interrogation, *n.* interrogation *f.*

interrogative, 1. *adj.* interrogateur. **2.** *n.* interrogatif *m.*

interrupt, *vb.* interrompre.

interruption, *n.* interruption *f.*

intersect, *vb.* entrecouper, intersecter, entrecroiser.

intersection, *n.* intersection *f.*

intersperse, *vb.* entremêler, parsemer, intercaler.

intertwine, *vb.* (s') entrelacer.

interval, *n.* intervalle *m.*

intervene, *vb.* intervenir.

intervention, *n.* intervention *f.*

interview, *n.* entrevue *f.*; (press) interview *m.f.*

intestine, *n.* intestin *m.*

intimacy, *n.* intimité *f.*

intimate, *adj.* intime.

intimidate, *vb.* intimider.

intimidation, *n.* intimidation *f.*

into, *prep.* en; (with art. or adj.) dans.

intonation, *n.* intonation *f.*

intone, *vb.* entonner, psalmodier.

intoxicate, *vb.* enivrer.

intoxication, *n.* intoxication *f.*, ivresse *f.*

intractable, *adj.* très difficile.

intransigent, *adj.* intransigeant.

intravenous, *adj.* intraveineux.

intrepid, *adj.* intrépide, brave, courageux.

intricacy, *n.* complexité *f.*, nature compliquée *f.*

intricate, *adj.* compliqué.

intrigue, *n.* intrigue *f.*

intrinsic, *adj.* intrinsèque.

introduce, *vb.* (bring in) introduire; (present) présenter.

introduction, *n.* introduction *f.*; (presenting) présentation *f.*

introductory, *adj.* introductoire, d'introduction.

introspection, *n.* introspection *f.*, recueillement *m.*

introvert, *n.* introverti *m.*

intrude on, *vb.* importuner.

intruder, *n.* intrus *m.*

intuition, *n.* intuition *f.*

intuitive, adj. intuitif.
inundate, vb. inonder.
invade, vb. envahir.
invader, n. envahisseur m., transgresseur m.
invalid, adj. and n. infirme m.f.
invaluable, adj. inestimable.
invariable, adj. invariable.
invasion, n. invasion f.
invective, n. invective f.
inveigle, vb. attirer, séduire, leurrer.
invent, vb. inventer.
invention, n. invention f.
inventive, adj. inventif, trouveur.
inventor, n. inventeur m.
inventory, n. inventaire m.
inverse, adj. inverse.
invertebrate, 1. n. invertébré m. **2.** adj. invertébré.
invest, vb. investir; (money) placer.
investigate, vb. faire des recherches (sur).
investigation, n. investigation f.
investment, n. placement m.
inveterate, adj. invétéré, enraciné.
invidious, adj. odieux, haïssable, ingrat.
invigorate, vb. fortifier, vivifier.
invincible, adj. invincible.
invisible, adj. invisible.
invitation, n. invitation f.
invite, vb. inviter.
invocation, n. invocation f.
invoice, n. facture f.
invoke, vb. invoquer.
involuntary, adj. involontaire.
involve, vb. (implicate) impliquer; (entail) entraîner.
invulnerable, adj. invulnérable.
inward, adj. intérieur.
iodine, n. iode m.
Iran, n. Iran m.
Iraq, n. Irak m., Iraq m.
irate, adj. en colère, courroucé, furieux.
Ireland, n. Irlande f.
iridium, n. iridium m.
iris, n. iris m.
Irish, adj. irlandais.
Irishman, n. Irlandais m.
irk, vb. ennuyer.
iron, n. fer m.

ironworks, n. fonderie de fonte f., usine métallurgique f.
irony, n. ironie f.
irrational, adj. irrationnel, déraisonnable, absurde.
irrefutable, adj. irréfutable, irrécusable.
irregular, adj. irrégulier.
irregularity, n. irrégularité f.
irrelevant, adj. non pertinent, hors de propos.
irresistible, adj. irrésistible.
irresponsible, adj. irresponsable.
irreverent, adj. irrévérent, irrévérencieux.
irrevocable, adj. irrévocable.
irrigate, vb. irriguer, arroser.
irrigation, n. irrigation f.
irritability, n. irritabilité f.
irritable, adj. irritable, irascible.
irritant, n. irritant m.
irritate, vb. irriter.
irritation, n. irritation f.
Islam, n. Islam m.
Islamic, adj. islamique.
island, n. île f.
isolate, vb. isoler.
isolation, n. isolement m.
isolationist, n. isolationniste m.
isosceles, adj. isoscèle.
Israel, n. Israël m.
Israeli 1. n. Israëlien m. **2.** adj. israëlien.
issuance, n. délivrance f.
issue, 1. n. (way out, end) issue f.; (result) résultat m.; (question) question f.; (publication) numéro m.; (money, bonds) émission f. **2.** vb. (come out) sortir; (publish) publier; (money) émettre.
isthmus, n. isthme m.
it, pron. (subject) il m.; elle f.; (object) le m., la f.; (of it) en; (in it, to it) y.
Italian, 1. n. (person) Italien m.; (language) italien m. **2.** adj. italien.
italics, n. italique m.
Italy, n. Italie f.
itch, 1. n. démangeaison f. **2.** vb. démanger.
item, n. (article) article m.; (detail) détail m.
itemize, vb. détailler.

itinerant, *adj.* ambulant.

itinerary, *n.* itinéraire *m.*

its, 1. *adj.* son *m.*, sa *f.*, ses *pl.* **2.** *pron.* le sien *m.*, la sienne *f.*

itself, *pron.* lui-même *m.*, elle-même *f.*; (reflexive) se.

ivory, *n.* ivoire *m.*

ivy, *n.* lierre *m.*

J

jab, 1. *n.* coup *m.*, coup sec *m.* **2.** *vb.* piquer, donner un coup sec.

jackal, *n.* chacal *m.*

jackass, *n.* âne *m.*; idiot *m.*

jacket, *n.* (man) veston *m.*; (woman) jaquette *f.*

jackknife, *n.* couteau *(m.)* de poche.

jack-of-all-trades, *n.* maître Jacques *m.*, factotum *m.*, homme *(m.)* à tous les métiers.

jade, *n.* (horse) rosse *f.*, haridelle *f.*; (woman) drôlesse *f.*, coureuse *f.*; (mineral) jade *m.*

jaded, *adj.* surmené, éreinté, blasé, fatigué.

jagged, *adj.* déchiqueté, entaillé, dentelé.

jaguar, *n.* jaguar *m.*

jail, *n.* prison *f.*

jailer, *n.* gardien *m.*, geôlier *m.*

jam, 1. *n.* foule *f.*, presse *f.*; (traffic) embouteillage *m.*; (food) confiture *f.* **2.** *vb.* serrer, presser.

Jamaica, *n.* Jamaïque *f.*

jamb, *n.* jambage *m.*, montant *m.*, chambranle *m.*

jangle, 1. *n.* cliquetis *m.* **2.** *vb.* cliqueter.

janitor, *n.* concierge *m.*

January, *n.* janvier *m.*

Japan, *n.* Japon *m.*

Japanese, 1. *n.* (person) Japonais *m.*; (language) japonais *m.* **2.** *adj.* japonais.

jar, 1. *n.* (container) pot *m.*; (sound) son *(m.)* discordant; (shock) secousse *f.* **2.** *vb.* secouer, heurter.

jargon, *n.* jargon *m.*

jasmine, *n.* jasmin *m.*

jaundice, *n.* jaunisse *f.*

jaunt, *n.* petite excursion *f.*, balade *f.*

javelin, *n.* javelot *m.*, javeline *f.*

jaw, *n.* mâchoire *f.*

jay, *n.* geai *m.*

jaywalk, *vb.* se promener d'une façon distraite ou imprudente.

jazz, *n.* jazz *m.*

jealous, *adj.* jaloux.

jealousy, *n.* jalousie *f.*

jeans, *n.* jeans *m.pl.*

jeer, 1. *n.* raillerie *f.*; moquerie *f.*, huée *f.* **2.** *vb.* se moquer de, huer.

jelly, *n.* gelée *f.*

jellyfish, *n.* méduse *f.*

jeopardize, *vb.* exposer au danger, mettre en danger, hasarder.

jeopardy, *n.* danger *m.*, péril *m.*

jerk, 1. *n.* saccade *f.*; (person) pauvre type *m.*

jerkin, *n.* justaucorps *m.*, pourpoint *m.*

jerky, *adj.* saccadé, coupé.

jersey, *n.* jersey *m.*, tricot *(m.)* de laine.

Jerusalem, *n.* Jérusalem *f.*

jest, 1. plaisanterie *f.*, raillerie *f.*, badinage *m.* **2.** *vb.* plaisanter, railler, badiner.

jester, *n.* railleur *m.*, farceur *m.*, bouffon *m.*

Jesuit, *n.* jésuite *m.*

Jesus, *n.* Jésus *m.*

jet, *n.* (mineral) jais *m.*; (water, gas) jet *m.*; **(j. plane)** avion *(m.)* à réaction.

jet lag, *n.* (réaction au) décalage *(m.)* horaire.

jetsam, *n.* épaves *f.pl.*

jettison, *vb.* se délester.

jetty, *n.* jetée *f.*, môle *m.*

Jew, *n.* Juif *m.*, Juive *f.*

jewel, *n.* bijou *m.*

jeweler, *n.* bijoutier *m.*, jouaillier *m.*

jewelry, *n.* bijouterie *f.*

Jewish, *adj.* juif *m.*, juive *f.*

jib, *n.* foc *m.*

jibe, vb. être en accord, s'accorder.

jiffy, n. instant m., clin d'œil m.

jig, 1. n. gigue f.; calibre m., gabarit m. **2.** vb. danser la gigue, sautiller.

jilt, vb. délaisser, plaquer, planter.

jingle, 1. n. tintement m., cliquetis m. **2.** vb. tinter, cliqueter.

jinx, n. porte-malheur m.

jittery, adj. très nerveux.

job, n. (work) travail m.; (employment) emploi m.

jobber, n. intermédiaire m., marchandeur m., sous-traitant m.

jockey, n. jockey m.

jocular, adj. facétieux, jovial, rieur.

jocund, adj. enjoué.

jodhpurs, n. pantalon (m.) d'équitation.

jog, 1. n. coup m., secousse f., cahot m. **2.** vb. pousser, secouer, cahoter; faire du jogging.

jogging, n. jogging m.

joggle, 1. n. petite secousse f. **2.** vb. secouer légèrement.

join, vb. (things) joindre; (group, etc.) se joindre à.

joiner, n. menuisier m.

joint, 1. n. joint m.; (anatomy) articulation f. **2.** adj. (in common) commun; (in partnership) co-.

jointly, adv. ensemble, conjointement.

joist, n. solive f., poutre f.

joke, 1. n. plaisanterie f. **2.** vb. plaisanter.

joker, n. farceur m., blagueur m.; joker m.

jolly, adj. joyeux.

jolt, 1. n. cahot m., choc m., secousse f. **2.** vb. cahoter, secouer, ballotter.

jonquil, n. jonquille f.

Jordan, n. Jordanie f.

jostle, vb. coudoyer tr.

jot, vb. **(j. down)** noter.

jounce, 1. n. cahot m., secousse f. **2.** vb. cahoter.

journal, n. journal m.

journalism, n. journalisme m.

journalist, n. journaliste m.f.

journey, 1. n. voyage m. **2.** vb. voyager.

journeyman, n. compagnon m.

jovial, adj. jovial, gai.

jowl, n. mâchoire f.

joy, n. joie f.

joyful, adj. joyeux.

joyous, adj. joyeux.

joystick, n. manette f.

jubilant, adj. réjoui, jubilant, exultant.

jubilee, n. jubilé m.

Judaism, n. judaïsme m.

judge, 1. n. juge m. **2.** vb. juger.

judgment, n. jugement m.

judicial, adj. judiciaire.

judiciary, adj. judiciaire.

judicious, adj. judicieux, sensé.

jug, n. cruche f.

juggle, vb. jongler.

jugular, adj. jugulaire.

juice, n. jus m.

juicy, adj. juteux.

July, n. juillet m.

jumble, 1. n. brouillamini m., fouillis m., fatras m. **2.** vb. brouiller, mêler confusément.

jump, 1. n. saut m. **2.** vb. sauter.

jumper cables, n. câbles (m.pl.) de démarrage.

jumpy, adj. nerveux.

junction, n. jonction f.; (rail) embranchement m.

juncture, n. jointure f., jonction f., conjoncture f.

June, n. juin m.

jungle, n. jungle f., brousse f.

junior, adj. and n. (age) cadet m.; (rank) subalterne m.

juniper, n. genévrier m., genièvre m.

junk, n. (waste) rebut m.

junket, n. jonchée f.; festin m.; partie de plaisir f.

jurisdiction, n. juridiction f.

jurisprudence, n. jurisprudence f.

jurist, n. juriste m., légiste m.

juror, m. juré m., membre du jury m.

jury, n. jury m.

just, 1. adj. juste. **2.** adv. (exactly) juste; (barely) à peine; **(have j.)** venir de.

justice, n. justice f.

justifiable, adj. justifiable, justifié.

justification, n. justification f.

justify, vb. justifier.

jut, vb. être en saillie.

jute, n. jute m.

juvenile, adj. juvénile.

K

kale, n. chou m.

kaleidoscope, n. kaléidoscope m.

kangaroo, n. kangourou m.

karakul, n. karakul m., caracul m.

karat, n. carat m.

karate, n. karaté m.

keel, n. quille f.

keen, adj. (edge) aiguisé; (pain, point) aigu; (look, mind) pénétrant; (**k. on**) enthousiaste de.

keep, vb. tenir; (reserve, protect, retain) garder; (remain) rester; (continue) continuer à.

keeper, n. gardien m.

keepsake, n. souvenir m.

keg, n. caque f., barillet m., tonnelet m.

kennel, n. chenil m.

Kenya, n. Kenya m.

kerchief, n. fichu m., mouchoir m.

kernel, n. (grain) grain m.; (nut) amande f.; (fig.) noyau m.

kerosene, n. pétrole m.

ketchup, n. sauce (f.) piquante à base de tomates.

kettle, n. bouilloire f.

kettledrum, n. timbale f.

key, n. clef, clé f.; (piano, typewriter) touche f.

keyboard, n. clavier m.

keyhole, n. entrée (f.) de clef.

khaki, n. kaki m.

kick, 1. n. coup (m.) de pied; (gun) recul m. **2.** vb. donner un coup de pied à.

kid, n. (animal, skin) chevreau m.; (child) gosse m.f.

kidnap, vb. enlever de vive force.

kidnapper, n. auteur (m.) de l'enlèvement, ravisseur m.

kidney, n. rein m.; (food) rognon m.

kidney bean, n. haricot nain m.

kill, vb. tuer.

killer, n. tueur m., meurtrier m.

killing, n. meurtre m.

kiln, n. four (céramique) m., séchoir m.

kilobyte, n. kilo-octet m.

kilocycle, n. kilocycle m.

kilogram, n. kilogramme m.

kilohertz, n. kilohertz m.

kilowatt, n. kilowatt m.

kilt, n. kilt m.

kimono, n. kimono m.

kin, n. (relation) parent m.

kind, 1. n. genre m. **2.** adj. aimable.

kindergarten, n. jardin (m.) d'enfants, école maternelle f.

kindle, vb. allumer, f.

kindling, n. allumage m., bois d'allumage m.

kindly, adv. avec bonté.

kindness, n. bonté f.

kindred, 1. n. parenté f., affinité f. **2.** adj. analogue.

kinetic, adj. cinétique f.

king, n. roi m.

kingdom, n. royaume m.

kink, 1. n. nœud m., tortillement m. **2.** vb. se nouer.

kinky, adj. excentrique.

kiosk, n. kiosque m.

kipper, n. kipper m., hareng (m.) légèrement salé et fumé.

kiss, 1. n. baiser m. **2.** vb. embrasser.

kitchen, n. cuisine f.

kite, n. cerf-volant m.

kitten, n. petit chat m.

kitty, n. (money) cagnotte f.

kleptomania, n. kleptomanie f.

kleptomaniac, n. kleptomane m.

knack, n. tour de main m., talent m., truc m.

knapsack, n. havresac m.

knead, vb. pétrir, malaxer.

knee, n. genou m.

kneecap, n. genouillère f.

kneel, vb. s'agenouiller.

knell, n. glas m.

knickers, n. pantalon m.; (underwear) culotte f.

knife, n. couteau m.

knight, n. chevalier m.

knit, vb. (with needles) tricoter.

knob, n. bouton m.

knock, 1. n. coup m. **2.** vb. frapper.

knot, n. nœud m.
knotty, adj. plein de nœuds.
know, vb. savoir; (be acquainted with) connaître.
knowledge, n. connaissance f.; (learning) savoir m.

knuckle, n. articulation (f.) du doigt, jointure (f.) du doigt.
Kodak, n. kodak m.
Koran, n. Coran m.
Korea, n. Corée f.
Kosher, adj. kascher.

L

lab, n. labo m.
label, n. étiquette f.
labor, 1. n. travail m.; (workers) ouvriers m.pl. **2.** vb. peiner.
laboratory, n. laboratoire m.
laborer, n. travailleur m.
laborious, adj. laborieux.
labor union, n. syndicat m.
laburnum, n. cytise m.
labyrinth, n. labyrinthe m.
lace, 1. n. dentelle f.; (string) lacet m.
lacerate, vb. lacérer, déchirer.
laceration, n. lacération f.
lack, 1. n. manque m. **2.** vb. manquer de.
lackadaisical, adj. affecté.
laconic, adj. laconique.
lacquer, n. vernis-laque m.
lactic, adj. lactique.
lactose, n. lactose f.
lacy, adj. de dentelle.
ladder, n. échelle f.
ladle, n. cuiller (f.) à pot.
lady, n. dame f.
ladybug, n. coccinelle f.
lag behind, vb. rester en arrière.
lagoon, n. lagune f.
laid-back, adj. décontracté.
lair, n. tanière f., repaire m.
laissez faire, n. laisser-faire m.
laity, n. les laïques m.pl.
lake, n. lac m.
lamb, n. agneau m.
lame, adj. boiteux.
lament, vb. se lamenter (sur); (mourn) pleurer.
lamentable, adj. lamentable, déplorable.
lamentation, n. lamentation f.
laminate, vb. laminer, écacher.
lamp, n. lampe f.
lampoon, 1. n. pasquinade f., satire f. **2.** vb. lancer des satires.
lance, n. lance f.

land, 1. n. terre f. **2.** vb. (boat) débarquer; (plane) atterrir.
landholder, n. propriétaire foncier m.
landing, n. débarquement m., mise à terre f.
landlord, n. propriétaire m.f.
landmark, n. borne f.
landscape, n. paysage m.
landslide, n. éboulement m.
landward, adv. vers la terre.
lane, n. (country) sentier m.; (town) ruelle f.; (highway) file f.
language, n. langue f.; (form of expression) langage m.
languid, adj. languissant.
languish, vb. languir.
languor, n. langueur f.
lanky, adj. grand et maigre.
lanolin, n. lanoline f.
lantern, n. lanterne f.
lap, n. (of body) genoux m.pl.; (of track) tour (m.) (de piste).
lapel, n. revers m.
lapin, n. lapin m.
lapse, 1. n. (of time) laps m.; (error) faute f. **2.** vb. passer.
laptop computer, n. portable m.
larceny, n. larcin m., vol m.
lard, n. saindoux m.
large, adj. grand.
largely, adv. en grande partie.
largo, n. largo m.
lariat, n. lasso m.
lark, n. alouette f.
larkspur, n. pied d'alouette m., delphinium m.
larva, n. larve f.
laryngitis, n. laryngite f.
larynx, n. larynx m.
lascivious, adj. lascif.
laser, n. laser m.
lash, 1. n. (whip) lanière f.; (blow)

coup (m.) de fouet. **2.** vb. fouetter.

lass, n. jeune fille f.

lassitude, n. lassitude f.

lasso, n. lasso m.

last, 1. adj. dernier; **(at l.)** enfin. **2.** vb. durer.

lasting, adj. durable.

latch, n. loquet m.

late, adj. and adv. (on in day, etc.) tard; (after due time) en retard; (dead) feu; (recent) dernier.

latecomer, n. retardataire m.

lately, adv. dernièrement.

latent, adj. latent, caché.

lateral, adj. latéral.

lath, n. latte f.

lathe, n. tour m.

lather, n. (soap) mousse f.; (horse) écume f.

Latin, 1. n. (person) Latin m.; (language) latin m. **2.** adj. latin.

Latin America, n. Amérique (f.) latine.

latitude, n. latitude f.

latrine, n. latrine f.

latter, adj. and pron. dernier.

lattice, n. treillis m.

laud, vb. louer.

laudable, adj. louable.

laudanum, n. laudanum m.

laudatory, adj. élogieux.

laugh, n. rire m.

laugh (at), vb. rire (de).

laughable, adj. risible.

laughter, n. rire m.

launch, 1. n. (boat) chaloupe f. **2.** vb. lancer, tr.

launder, vb. blanchir.

launderette, n. buanderie f., laverie (f.) (automatique).

laundry, n. (works) blanchisserie f.; (washing) lessive f.

laundryman, n. blanchisseur m.

laureate, adj. and n. lauréat m.f.

laurel, n. laurier m.

lava, n. lave f.

lavaliere, n. lavallière f.

lavatory, n. lavabo m.; cabinet (m.) de toilette.

lavender, n. lavande f.

lavish, 1. adj. (person) prodigue; (thing) somptueux. **2.** vb. prodiguer.

law, n. loi f.; (jurisprudence) droit m.

law court, n. tribunal m.

lawful, adj. légal.

lawless, adj. sans loi.

lawn, n. pelouse f.

lawsuit, n. procès m.

lawyer, n. (counselor) avocat m.; (attorney) avoué m.; (jurist) jurisconsulte m.

lax, adj. lâche, mou, relâché.

laxative, n. laxatif m.

laxity, n. relâchement m.

lay, 1. vb. poser; **(l. off)** licencier. **2.** adj. laïque.

layer, n. couche f.

layman, n. laïque m.

lazy, adj. paresseux.

lead, 1. n. plomb m.; (pencil) mine f. **2.** vb. mener, conduire.

leaden, adj. de plomb.

leader, n. chef m.

leading, adj. principal.

lead pencil, n. crayon (m.) à la mine de plomb.

leaf, n. feuille f.

leaflet, n. feuillet m.

leafy, adj. feuillu.

league, n. (compact) ligue f.; (measure) lieue f.

League of Nations, n. La Société (f.) des Nations.

leak, 1. n. (liquid) fuite f.; (boat) voie (f.) d'eau. **2.** vb. fuir; faire eau.

leakage, n. fuite d'eau f.

leaky, adj. qui coule, qui fait eau.

lean, 1. adj. maigre. **2.** vb. intr. **(l. against)** s'appuyer sur; (stoop) se pencher. **3.** vb., tr., appuyer.

leap, vb. sauter.

leap year, n. année bissextile f.

learn, vb. apprendre.

learned, adj. savant, docte.

learning, n. science f., instruction f., érudition f.

lease, n. bail m.

leash, n. laisse f., attache f.

least, 1. n. moins m. **2.** adj. (le) moindre. **3.** adv. (le) moins.

leather, n. cuir m.

leathery, adj. coriace.

leave, 1. n. permission f. **2.** vb. laisser; (go away from) quitter.

leaven, 1. n. levain m. **2.** vb. faire lever, modifier.

Lebanon, n. Liban m.

lecherous, adj. lascif, libertin.

lecture, n. conférence f.

lecturer, n. conférencier m.

ledge, n. bord m.; (of rocks) chaîne f.

ledger, n. grand livre m.

lee, n. côté m. f. sous le vent.

leech, n. sangsue f.

leek, n. poireau m.

leer, 1. n. œillade f., regard de côté m. **2.** vb. lorgner.

leeward, adj. and adv. sous le vent.

left, adj. and n. gauche f.; (on, to the l.) à gauche.

leftist, n. gaucher m.; (politics) gauchiste m.

left wing, n. l'aile gauche f.; (politics) la gauche.

leg, n. (man, horse) jambe f.; (most animals) patte f.

legacy, n. legs m.

legal, adj. légal.

legalize, vb. rendre légal.

legation, n. légation f.

legend, n. légende f.

legendary, adj. légendaire.

legible, adj. lisible.

legion, n. légion f.

legislate, vb. faire les lois.

legislation, n. législation f.

legislator, n. législateur m.

legislature, n. législature f.

legitimate, adj. légitime.

legume, n. légume m.

leisure, n. loisir m.

leisurely, adv. à loisir.

lemon, n. citron m.

lemonade, n. citron (m.) pressé.

lend, vb. prêter.

length, n. (dimension) longueur f.; (time) durée f.

lengthen, vb. allonger, tr.

lengthwise, adv. en long.

lengthy, adj. assez long.

lenient, adj. indulgent.

lens, n. lentille f.; (camera) objectif m.

Lent, n. carême m.

Lenten, adj. de carême.

lentil, n. lentille f.

lento, adv. lento.

leopard, n. léopard m.

leotard, n. maillot (m.) (de danseur, etc.).

leper, n. lépreux m.

leprosy, n. lèpre f.

lesbian, 1. adj. lesbien. **2.** n. lesbienne f.; tribade f.

lesion, n. lésion f.

less, 1. adj. (smaller) moindre; (not so much) moins de. **2.** adv. (l. than) moins (de).

lessen, vb. diminuer.

lesser, adj. moindre.

lesson, n. leçon f.

lest, conj. de peur que . . . (ne).

let, vb. laisser; (lease) louer.

letdown, n. déception f.

lethal, adj. mortel.

lethargic, adj. léthargique.

lethargy, n. léthargie f.

letter, n. lettre f.

letterhead, n. en-tête de lettre m.

lettuce, n. laitue f.

leukemia, n. leucémie f.

levee, n. lever m.

level, 1. adj. (flat) égal; (l. with) au niveau de. **2.** n. niveau m.

lever, n. levier m.

levity, n. légèreté f.

levy, 1. n. levée f. **2.** vb. lever.

lewd, adj. impudique.

lexicon, n. lexique m.

liability, n. responsabilité f.

liable, adj. (responsible for) responsable de; (subject to) sujet à.

liar, n. menteur m.

libation, n. libation f.

libel, n. diffamation f.

libelous, adj. diffamatoire.

liberal, adj. libéral; (generous) généreux.

liberalism, n. libéralisme m.

liberality, n. libéralité f.

liberate, vb. libérer.

liberation, n. libération f.

libertine, 1. n. libre-penseur m. **2.** adj. libertin.

liberty, n. liberté f.

libidinous, adj. libidineux.

libido, n. libido m.

librarian, n. bibliothécaire m.f.

library, n. bibliothèque f.

libretto, n. livret m.

Libya, n. Libye f.

license, n. permis m.; (tradesmen)

patente *f.*; (abuse of freedom) licence *f.*

licentious, *adj.* licencieux.

lick, *vb.* lécher.

licorice, *n.* réglisse *f.*

lid, *n.* couvercle *m.*

lie, 1. *n.* mensonge *m.* **2.** *vb.* (fib) mentir; (recline) être couché; (**l. down**) se coucher; (be situated) se trouver.

lien, *n.* privilège *m.*

lieutenant, *n.* lieutenant *m.*

life, *n.* vie *f.*

lifeboat, *n.* bateau *(m.)* de sauvetage.

life buoy, *n.* bouée *(f.)* de sauvetage.

lifeguard, *n.* maître-nageur *m.*

life insurance, *n.* assurance-vie *f.*

lifeless, *adj.* sans vie.

life preserver, *n.* appareil *(m.)* de sauvetage.

life sentence, *n.* condamnation *(f.)* à perpétuité.

life style, *n.* manière de vivre *f.*

life-support system, *n.* respirateur *(m.)* artificiel.

lifetime, *n.* vie *f.*, vivant *m.*

lift, *n.* lever.

ligament, *n.* ligament *m.*

ligature, *n.* ligature *f.*

light, 1. *n.* lumière *f.* **2.** *adj.* (not heavy) léger; (not dark) clair. **3.** *vb.* allumer, *tr.*

lighten, *vb.* (relieve) alléger, *tr.*; (brighten) éclairer, *tr.*

lighter, *n.* (cigarette) briquet *m.*

lighthouse, *n.* phare *m.*

lighting, *n.* éclairage *m.*

lightly, *adv.* légèrement.

lightness, *n.* légèreté *f.*

lightning, *n.* (flash of) éclair *m.*

lightweight, 1. *adj.* léger. **2.** *n.* (boxing) poids *(m.)* léger.

lignite, *n.* lignite *m.*

likable, *adj.* agréable.

like, 1. *adj.* pareil. **2.** *vb.* aimer; plaire à. **3.** *prep.* comme.

likelihood, *n.* probabilité *f.*

likely, *adj.* probable.

liken, *vb.* comparer.

likeness, *n.* ressemblance *f.*

likewise, *adv.* de même.

lilac, *n.* lilas *m.*

lilt, 1. *n.* forte cadence *f.* **2.** *vb.* chanter gaiement.

lily, *n.* lis *m.*; (**l. of the valley**) muguet *m.*

limb, *n.* membre *m.*; (tree) grosse branche *f.*

limber, 1. *adj.* souple, flexible. **2.** *vb.* assouplir.

limbo, *n.* limbes *m.pl.*

lime, *n.* (mineral) chaux *f.*; (tree) tilleul *m.*; (fruit) lime *f.*, citron *(m.)* vert.

limelight, *n.* lumière oxhydrique *f.*

limestone, *n.* pierre à chaux *f.*, calcaire *m.*

limewater, *n.* eau de chaux *f.*

limit, 1. *n.* limite *f.* **2.** *vb.* limiter.

limitation, *n.* limitation *f.*

limitless, *adj.* sans limite, sans bornes.

limousine, *n.* limousine *f.*

limp, 1. *adj.* flasque. **2.** *vb.* boiter.

limpid, *adj.* limpide.

linden, *n.* tilleul *m.*

line, *n.* ligne *f.*

lineage, *n.* lignée *f.*, race *f.*

lineal, *adj.* linéaire.

linen, *n.* (cloth) toile *f.*; (sheets, etc.) linge *m.*

linger, *vb.* s'attarder.

lingerie, *n.* lingerie *f.*

linguist, *n.* linguiste *m.f.*

linguistic, *adj.* linguistique.

linguistics, *n.* linguistique *f.*

liniment, *n.* liniment *m.*

lining, *n.* (clothes) doublure *f.*

link, 1. *n.* (chain) chaînon *m.*; (fig.) lien *m.* **2.** *vb.* (re)lier.

linoleum, *n.* linoléum *m.*

linseed, *n.* graine *(f.)* de lin.

lint, *n.* charpie *f.*

lion, *n.* lion *m.*

lip, *n.* lèvre *f.*

lipstick, *n.* rouge *(m.)* à lèvres.

liquefy, *vb.* liquéfier.

liqueur, *n.* liqueur *f.*

liquid, *n.* and *adj.* liquide *m.*

liquidate, *vb.* liquider.

liquidation, *n.* liquidation *f.*, acquittement *m.*

liquor, *n.* boisson *(f.)* alcoolique.

lisp, *vb.* zézayer.

list, 1. *n.* liste *f.* **2.** *vb.* enregistrer.

listen (to), *vb.* écouter.

listless, *adj.* inattentif.

litany, n. litanie f.
literacy, n. degré (m.) d'aptitude à lire et à écrire.
literal, adj. littéral.
literary, adj. littéraire.
literate, adj. lettré.
literature, n. littérature f.
lithe, adj. flexible, pliant.
lithograph, vb. lithographier.
lithography, n. lithographie f.
litigant, n. plaideur f.
litigation, n. litige m.
litmus, n. tournesol m.
litter, n. (vehicle, animals' bedding) litière f.; (disorder) fouillis m.; (animals' young) portée f.
little, 1. adj. and adv. peu. **2.** adj. (small) petit; (not much) peu (de).
liturgical, adj. liturgique.
liturgy, n. liturgie f.
live, vb. vivre.
livelihood, n. vie f., subsistance f., gagne-pain m.
lively, adj. vif m., vive f.
liven, vb. animer, activer.
liver, n. foie m.
livery, n. livrée f.
livestock, n. bétail m.
livid, adj. livide, blême.
lizard, n. lézard m.
llama, n. lama m.
lo, interj. voilà.
load, 1. n. (cargo) charge f.; (burden) fardeau m. **2.** vb. charger.
loaf, 1. n. pain m. **2.** vb. flâner.
loafer, n. fainéant m.
loam, n. terre grasse f.
loan, 1. n. (thing) prêt m.; (borrowing) emprunt m. **2.** vb. prêter.
loath, adj. fâché, peiné.
loathe, vb. détester.
loathing, n. dégoût m.
loathsome, adj. dégoûtant m.
lobby, 1. n. (hall) vestibule m.; (politics) groupe (m.) de pression. **2.** vb. faire pression sur.
lobe, n. lobe m.
lobster, n. homard m.
local, adj. local.
locale, n. localité f.; scène f.
locality, n. localité f.
localize, vb. localiser.
locate, vb. localiser.
location, n. placement m.

lock, 1. n. (door) serrure f.; (hair) mèche f. **2.** vb. fermer à clef.
locker, n. armoire f.; (baggage) consigne automatique f.
locket, n. médaillon m.
lockjaw, n. tétanos m.
locksmith, n. serrurier m.
locomotion, n. locomotion f.
locomotive, n. locomotive f.
locust, n. sauterelle f.
locution, n. locution f.
lode, n. filon m.
lodge, vb. loger.
lodger, n. locataire m.
lodging, n. logement m.
loft, n. grenier m.
lofty, adj. élevé; (proud) hautain.
log, n. (wood) bûche f.; (boat) loch m.
logarithm, n. logarithme m.
loge, n. loge f.
logic, n. logique f.
logical, adj. logique.
logo, n. emblème m.
loins, n. reins m.pl.
loiter, vb. flâner.
lollipop, n. sucre d'orge m., sucette f.
London, n. Londres m.
lone, lonely, lonesome, adj. solitaire.
loneliness, n. solitude f.
long, 1. adj. long m., longue f. **2.** adv. longtemps.
longevity, n. longévité f.
long for, vb. désirer ardemment.
longing, n. désir ardent m.
longitude, n. longitude f.
longitudinal, adj. longitudinal.
look, 1. n. regard m.; aspect m. **2.** vb. (l. at) regarder; (l. for) chercher; (l. after) soigner; (seem) paraître.
looking glass, n. miroir m.
loom, 1. n. métier m. **2.** vb. se dessiner.
loop, n. boucle f.
loophole, n. meurtrière f., échappatoire f.
loose, adj. (not tight) lâche; (detached) détaché; (morals) relâché.
loosen, vb. desserrer.
loot, 1. n. butin m. **2.** vb. piller.
lop, vb. élaguer, ébrancher.
loquacious, adj. loquace.
lord, n. seigneur m.; (title) lord m.

lordship, n. seigneurie f.
lorgnette, n. lorgnette f.
lose, vb. perdre.
loss, n. perte f.
lot, n. (fortune) sort m.; (land) terrain m.; (much) beaucoup.
lotion, n. lotion f.
lottery, n. loterie f.
lotus, n. lotus m., lotos m.
loud, 1. adj. fort; (noisy) bruyant.
2. adv. haut.
loudspeaker, n. haut-parleur m.
lounge, 1. n. sofa m.; hall m. **2.** vb. flâner.
louse, n. pou m.
lout, n. rustre m.
louver, n. auvent m.
lovable, adj. aimable.
love, 1. n. amour m. **2.** vb. aimer.
love affair, n. liaison (f.) amoureuse.
lovely, adj. beau m., belle f.
lover, n. amoureux m.
low, adj. bas m., basse f.
lowboy, n. commode basse f.
lowbrow, adj. peu intellectuel.
lower, vb. baisser.
lowly, adj. humble.
loyal, adj. loyal.
loyalist, n. loyaliste m.f.
loyalty, n. loyauté f.
lozenge, n. pastille f.
lubricant, n. lubrifiant m.
lubricate, vb. lubrifier.
lucid, adj. lucide.
luck, n. chance f.
lucky, adj. (person) heureux.
lucrative, adj. lucratif.
ludicrous, adj. risible.
lug, vb. traîner, tirer.
luggage, n. bagages m.pl.
lukewarm, adj. tiède.

lull, n. moment (m.) de calme.
lullaby, n. berceuse f.
lumbago, n. lumbago m.
lumber, n. bois (m.) de charpente.
luminous, adj. lumineux.
lump, 1. n. (gros) morceau m. **2.** vb. (l. together) mettre en tas.
lumpy, adj. grumeleux.
lunacy, n. folie f.
lunar, adj. lunaire.
lunatic, n. aliéné m.
lunch, 1. n. déjeuner m. **2.** vb. déjeuner.
luncheon, n. déjeuner m.
lung, n. poumon m.
lunge, 1. n. botte f. **2.** vb. se fendre.
lurch, 1. n. embardée f. **2.** vb. faire une embardée.
lure, vb. (animal) leurrer; (attract) attirer.
lurid, adj. blafard, sombre.
lurk, vb. se cacher, rôder.
luscious, adj. délicieux.
lush, adj. luxuriant.
lust, n. luxure f.
luster, n. lustre m.
lustful, adj. lascif, sensuel.
lustrous, adj. brillant, lustré.
lusty, adj. vigoureux.
lute, n. luth m.
Lutheran, n. Luthérien m.
Luxemburg, n. Luxembourg m.
luxuriant, adj. exubérant.
luxurious, adj. (thing) luxueux.
luxury, n. luxe m.
lying, n. mensonge m.
lymph, n. lymphe f.
lynch, vb. lyncher.
lyre, n. lyre f.
lyric, adj. lyrique.
lyricism, n. lyrisme f.
lyrics, n. (of song) paroles f.pl.

M

macaroni, n. macaroni m.
machine, n. machine f.
machine gun, n. mitrailleuse f.
machinery, n. machines f.pl; (fig.) mécanisme m.
machinist, n. machiniste m.
machismo, n. phallocratie f.
macho, 1. adj. phallocrate, macho.
2. n. homme phallocrate m.

mackerel, n. maquereau m.
mackinaw, n. mackinaw m.
macrobiotic, adj. macrobiotique.
mad, adj. fou m., folle f.
madness, n. folie f.
Madagascar, n. Madagascar m.
madam, n. madame f.
madcap, n. and adj. écervelé.
madden, vb. exaspérer.

made, *adj.* fait, fabriqué.

mafia, *n.* mafia *f.*

magazine, *n.* revue *f.*

maggot, *n.* ver *m.*

magic, 1. *n.* magie *f.* **2.** *adj.* magique.

magician, *n.* magicien *m.*

magistrate, *n.* magistrat *m.*

magnanimous, *adj.* magnanime.

magnate, *n.* magnat *m.*

magnesium, *n.* magnésium *m.*

magnet, *n.* aimant *m.*

magnetic, *adj.* magnétique.

magnificence, *n.* magnificence *f.*

magnificent, *adj.* magnifique.

magnify, *vb.* grossir.

magnitude, *n.* grandeur *f.*

mahogany, *n.* acajou *m.*

maid, *n.* (servant) bonne *f.*; (old m.) vieille fille *f.*

maiden, *adj.* de jeune fille.

mail, 1. *n.* courrier *m.* **2.** *vb.* envoyer par la poste.

mailbox, *n.* boîte *(f.)* aux lettres.

mail carrier, mailman, *n.* facteur *m.*

maim, *vb.* estropier, mutiler.

main, *adj.* principal.

mainframe, *n.* unité centrale (d'un informateur) *f.*

mainland, *n.* terre *(f.)* ferme.

mainly, *adv.* surtout.

mainspring, *n.* grand ressort *m.*; mobile essentiel *m.*

maintain, *vb.* maintenir; (support) soutenir.

maintenance, *n.* entretien *m.*

maize, *n.* maïs *m.*

majestic, *adj.* majestueux.

majesty, *n.* majesté *f.*

major, 1. *n. (mil.)* commandant *m.*; (school) sujet *(m.)* principal. **2.** *adj.* majeur.

majority, *n.* majorité *f.*

major scale, mode, or key, *n.* ton majeur *m.*, mode majeur *m.*

make, 1. *n.* fabrication *f.* **2.** *vb.* faire.

make-believe, 1. *n.* trompe l'œil *m.* **2.** *vb.* feindre.

maker, *n.* fabricant *m.*

makeshift, 1. *n.* expédient *m.* **2.** *adj.* provisoire.

make-up, *n.* (face) maquillage *m.*

maladjusted, *adj.* mal adapté, mal ajusté.

maladjustment, *n.* mauvaise adaptation *f.*

malady, *n.* maladie *f.*

malaria, *n.* malaria *f.*

male, *adj. and n.* mâle *m.*

malevolent, *adj.* malveillant.

malice, *n.* méchanceté *f.*

malicious, *adj.* méchant.

malign, *vb.* calomnier.

malignant, *adj.* malin *m.*, maligne *f.*

mall, *n.* centre *(m.)* commercial.

malleable, *adj.* malléable.

malnutrition, *n.* mauvaise hygiène *(f.)* alimentaire.

malpractice, *n.* faute *(f.)* professionnelle.

malt, *n.* malt *m.*

Malta, *n.* Malte *f.*

mammal, *n.* mammifère *m.*

man, *n.* homme *m.*

manage, 1. *vb. tr.* (administer) gérer; (conduct) diriger; (person, animal) dompter. **2.** *vb. intr.* se tirer d'affaire; **(m. to)** réussir à.

management, *n.* direction *f.*, gestion *f.*

manager, *n.* directeur *m.*; (household) ménager *m.*; gérant *m.*

mandate, *n.* (politics) mandat *m.*

mandatory, *adj.* obligatoire.

mandolin, *n.* mandoline *f.*

mane, *n.* crinière *f.*

maneuver, *n.* manœuvre *f.*

manganese, *n.* manganèse *m.*

manger, *n.* mangeoire *f.*

mangle, *vb.* mutiler.

manhood, *n.* virilité *f.*

mania, *n.* (craze) manie *f.*; (madness) folie *f.*

maniac, *n. and adj.* fou *m.*, folle *f.*

manic-depressive, *n. and adj.* maniaco-dépressif *m.*

manicure, *n.* (person) manucure *m.f.*; (care of hands) soin *(m.)* des mains.

manifest, 1. *adj.* manifeste. **2.** *vb.* manifester.

manifesto, *n.* manifeste *m.*

manifold, *adj.* (varied) divers; (numerous) nombreux.

manipulate, *vb.* manipuler.

mankind, *n.* genre *(m.)* humain.

manly, *adj.* viril.

man-made, *adj.* artificiel.

manner, *n.* manière *f.*; (customs) mœurs *f.pl.*

mannerism, *n.* maniérisme *m.*; affectation *f.*

manor, *n.* manoir *m.*

manpower, *n.* main-d'œuvre *f.*

mansion, *n.* (country) château *m.*; (town) hôtel *m.*

manslaughter, *n.* homicide involontaire *m.*

mantel, *n.* (framework) manteau *m.*; (shelf) tablette *f.*

mantle, *n.* manteau *m.*

manual, *adj. and n.* manuel *m.*

manufacture, 1. *n.* manufacture *f.*; (product) produit *(m.)* manufacturé. **2.** *vb.* fabriquer.

manufacturer, *n.* fabricant *m.*

manure, *n.* fumier *m.*

manuscript, *adj. and n.* manuscrit *m.*

many, 1. *adj.* beaucoup de, un grand nombre de; (too m.) trop de; (so m.) tant de; (how m.) combien de. **2.** *pron.* beaucoup.

map, *n.* carte *(f.)* géographique.

maple, *n.* érable *m.*

mar, *vb.* gâter.

marble, *n.* marbre *m.*

march, 1. *n.* marche *f.* **2.** *vb.* marcher.

March, *n.* mars *m.*

mare, *n.* jument *f.*

margarine, *n.* margarine *f.*

margin, *n.* marge *f.*

marijuana, *n.* marijuana *f.*; marie-jeanne *f.*

marinate, *vb.* faire mariner.

marine, 1. *n.* (ships) marine *f.*; (soldier) fusilier *(m.)* marin. **2.** *adj.* marin; (insurance) maritime.

mariner, *n.* marin *m.*

marionette, *n.* marionnette *f.*

marital, *adj.* conjugal.

maritime, *adj.* maritime.

marjoram, *n.* marjolaine *f.*

mark, 1. *n.* marque *f.*; (target) but *m.*; (school) point *m.* **2.** *vb.* marquer.

market, 1. *n.* marché *m.* **2.** *vb.* commercialiser.

marketing, *n.* marketing *m.*

market place, *n.* place *(f.)* du marché.

market research, *n.* étude *(f.)* de marché.

marmalade, *n.* confiture *f.*

maroon, 1. *adj. and n.* rouge *(m.)* foncé. **2.** *vb.* abandonner (dans une île déserte).

marquee, *n.* (tente) marquise *f.*

marquis, *n.* marquis *m.*

marriage, *n.* mariage *m.*

married, *adj.* marié.

marrow, *n.* moelle *f.*

marry, *vb.* épouser; se marier (avec).

marsh, *n.* marais *m.*

marshal, *n.* maréchal *m.*

marshmallow, *n.* guimauve (plant) *f.*

martial, *adj.* martial.

martinet, *n.* officier *(m.)* strict sur la discipline.

martyr, *n.* martyr *m.*

martyrdom, *n.* martyre *m.*

marvel, 1. *n.* merveille *f.* **2.** *vb.* (m. at) s'étonner de.

marvelous, *adj.* merveilleux.

Marxist, *n. and adj.* marxiste *m.f.*

mascara, *n.* mascara *m.*

mascot, *n.* mascotte *f.*

masculine, *adj.* masculin.

mash, *n.* (food) purée *f.*

mask, 1. *n.* masque *m.* **2.** *vb.* masquer.

masochist, *n.* masochiste *m.f.*

mason, *n.* maçon *m.*

masquerade, *n.* mascarade *f.*, bal masqué *m.*

mass, *n.* masse *f.*

Mass, *n.* messe *f.*

massacre, 1. *n.* massacre *m.* **2.** *vb.* massacrer.

massage, *n.* massage *m.*

masseur, *n.* masseur *m.*

massive, *adj.* massif.

mass media, *n.* mass-media *m.pl.*

mass meeting, *n.* réunion *f.*

mass production, *n.* fabrication *(f.)* en série.

mast, *n.* mât *m.*

master, 1. *n.* maître *m.* **2.** *vb.* maîtriser.

masterpiece, *n.* chef-d'œuvre *m.*

mastery, *n.* maîtrise *f.*

masticate, *vb.* mâcher.

mat, n. (door) paillasson m.

match, 1. n. (for fire) allumette f.; (equal) égal m.; (marriage) mariage m.; (person to marry) parti m.; (sport) partie f. **2.** vb. assortir, tr.

match box, n. boîte (f.) d'allumettes.

mate, 1. n. (fellow-worker) camarade m.f.; (of pair) compagnon m.; compagne f.; (boat) officier m. **2.** vb. s'accoupler.

material, 1. n. matière f.; (cloth) étoffe f. **2.** adj. matériel.

materialism, n. matérialisme m.

materialize, vb. matérialiser, tr.; se réaliser, intr.

maternal, adj. maternel.

maternity, n. maternité f.

math, n. maths f.pl.

mathematical, adj. mathématique.

mathematics, n. mathématiques f.pl.

matinee, n. matinée f.

mating, n. accouplement m.

mating season, n. saison (f.) des amours.

matriarch, n. femme (f.) qui porte les chausses.

matrimony, n. mariage m.

matrix, n. matrice f.

matron, n. (institution) intendante f.

matter, 1. n. (substance) matière f.; (subject) sujet m.; (question, business) affaire f.; (what is the m.?) qu'est-ce qu'il y a? **2.** vb. importer.

mattress, n. matelas m.

mature, 1. adj. mûr. **2.** vb. mûrir.

maturity, n. maturité f.; (comm.) échéance f.

maudlin, adj. larmoyant.

mausoleum, n. mausolée m.

maxim, n. maxime f.

maximum, n. maximum m.

may, vb. pouvoir.

May, n. mai m.

maybe, adv. peut-être.

mayhem, n. mutilation f.

mayonnaise, n. mayonnaise f.

mayor, n. maire m.

maze, n. labyrinthe m.

me, pron. (unstressed direct and in-

direct) me; (alone, stressed, with prep.) moi.

meadow, n. (small) pré m.; (large) prairie f.

meager, adj. maigre.

meal, 1. n. (repast) repas m.; (grain) farine f.

mean, 1. n. (math.) moyenne f.; (m.s, financial) moyens m.pl.; (m.s, way to do) moyen m. **2.** adj. humble; (stingy) avare; (contemptible) méprisable. **3.** vb. (signify) vouloir dire; (purpose) se proposer (de); (destine) destiner (à).

meaning, n. sens m.

meaningful, adj. significatif.

meanness, n. méchanceté f.

meantime, meanwhile, adv. sur ces entrefaites.

measles, n. rougeole f.

measure, 1. n. mesure f. **2.** vb. mesurer.

measurement, n. mesurage m.

meat, n. viande f.

mechanic, n. mécanicien m.; (auto) garagiste m.

mechanical, 1. adj. mécanique. **2.** (fig.) machinal.

mechanism, n. mécanisme m.

mechanize, vb. mécaniser.

medal, n. médaille f.

meddle, vb. se mêler (de).

media, n. media m.pl.

median, n. médian.

mediate, vb. agir en médiateur.

medical, adj. médical.

medicate, vb. médicamenter.

medication, n. médicament m.

medicine, n. médecine f.

medieval, adj. médiéval.

mediocre, adj. médiocre.

mediocrity, n. médiocrité f.

meditate, vb. méditer.

meditation, n. méditation f.

Mediterranean, 1. adj. méditerranéen. **2.** n. **(M. Sea)** Méditerranée f.

medium, 1. n. milieu m.; (agent) intermédiaire m.; (psychic person) médium m. **2.** adj. moyen.

medley, n. mélange m.

meek, adj. doux m.; douce f.

meekness, n. douceur f.

meet, vb. rencontrer, tr.; (become

acquainted with) faire la connaissance de; (expenses) faire face à.

meeting, n. réunion f.

megabyte, n. méga-octet m.

megahertz, n. mégahertz m.

megaphone, n. mégaphone m.

melancholic, adj. mélancolique.

melancholy, n. mélancolie f.

mellow, adj. moelleux.

melodious, adj. mélodieux.

melodrama, n. mélodrame m.

melody, n. mélodie f.

melon, n. melon m.

melt, vb. fondre.

meltdown, n. fusion f.

member, n. membre m.

membership, n. adhésion f.

membrane, n. membrane f.

memento, n. mémento m.

memo, n. note f.

memoir, n. mémoire m.

memorable, adj. mémorable.

memorandum, n. mémorandum m.

memorial, 1. n. souvenir m., monument m. 2. adj. commémoratif.

memorize, vb. apprendre par cœur.

memory, n. mémoire f.

menace, 1. n. menace f. 2. vb. menacer.

menagerie, n. ménagerie f.

mend, vb. (clothes) raccommoder; (correct) corriger.

mendacious, adj. menteur.

mendicant, n. and adj. mendiant m.

menial, adj. servile.

meningitis, n. méningite f.

menstruation, n. menstruation f.

menswear, n. habillements masculins m.pl.

mental, adj. mental.

mentality, n. mentalité f.

menthol, n. menthol m.

mention, 1. n. mention f. 2. vb. mentionner; (don't m. it) il n'y a pas de quoi.

menu, n. menu m.

mercantile, adj. mercantile.

mercenary, adj. and n. mercenaire m.

merchandise, n. marchandise(s) f. (pl.).

merchant, 1. n. négociant m. 2. adj. marchand.

merchant marine, n. marine marchande f.

merciful, adj. miséricordieux.

merciless, adj. impitoyable.

mercury, n. mercure m.

mercy, n. miséricorde f.; (at the m. of) à la merci de.

mere, adj. simple.

merely, adv. simplement.

merge, vb. fusionner.

merger, n. fusion f.

merit, 1. n. mérite m. 2. vb. mériter.

meritorious, adj. (person) méritant; (deed) méritoire.

mermaid, n. sirène f.

merriment, n. gaieté f.

merry, adj. gai.

merry-go-round, n. carrousel m.

mesh, n. maille f.

mesmerize, vb. magnétiser.

mess, 1. n. (muddle) fouillis m.; gâchis m.; (mil.) popote f. 2. vb. gâcher.

message, n. message m.

messenger, n. messager m., coursier m.

messy, adj. (dirty) malpropre.

metabolism, n. métabolisme m.

metal, n. métal m.

metallic, adj. métallique.

metamorphosis, n. métamorphose f.

metaphor, n. métaphore f.

metaphysics, n. métaphysique f.

meteor, n. météore m.

meteorology, n. météorologie f.

meter, 1. n. (measure) mètre m.; (device) compteur m.

method, n. méthode f.

meticulous, adj. méticuleux.

metric, n. métrique.

metropolis, n. métropole f.

metropolitan, adj. métropolitain.

mettle, n. ardeur f.

Mexican, 1. n. Mexicain m. 2. adj. mexicain.

Mexico, n. Mexique m.

mezzanine, n. mezzanine f.

microbe, n. microbe m.

microchip, n. microplaquette f., puce f.

microcomputer, n. micro-ordinateur m.

microcosm, n. microcosme m.
microfiche, n. microfiche f.
microfilm, n. microfilm m.
microform, n. microforme f.
microphone, n. microphone m.
microscope, n. microscope m.
microscopic, adj. microscopique.
microwave, n. micro-onde f.; (m. oven) four (m.) à micro-ondes.
mid, adj. mi-.
middle, 1. n. milieu m. **2.** adj. du milieu.
middle-aged, adj. d'un certain âge.
Middle Ages, n. moyen âge m.
middle class, n. classe moyenne f., bourgeoisie f.
Middle East, n. Moyen Orient m.
midget, n. nain m.
midnight, n. minuit m.
midriff, n. diaphragme m.
midwife, n. sage-femme f.
mien, n. mine f., air m.
might, n. puissance f.
mighty, adj. puissant.
migraine, n. migraine f.
migrate, vb. émigrer.
migration, n. migration f.
mike, n. (colloquial) micro m.
mild, adj. doux m., douce f.
mildew, n. rouille f.
mile, n. mille m.
mileage, n. kilométrage m.
milestone, n. borne routière f.
militarism, n. militarisme m.
military, adj. militaire.
militia, n. milice f.
milk, n. lait m.
milkman, n. laitier m.
milky, adj. laiteux.
mill, 1. n. (grinding) moulin m.; (spinning) filature f.; (factory) usine f. **2.** vb. (grind) moudre; (crowd) fourmiller.
millennium, n. millénaire m.
miller, n. meunier m.
millimeter, n. millimètre m.
milliner, n. modiste f.
millinery, n. modes f.pl.
million, n. million m.
millionaire, adj. and n. millionnaire m.f.
mimic, 1. n. mime m. **2.** adj. mimique. **3.** vb. imiter.
mince, vb. (chop) hacher.
mind, 1. n. esprit m.; (opinion) avis

m.; (desire) envie f. **2.** vb. (heed) faire attention à; (listen to) écouter; (apply oneself to) s'occuper de; (take care) prendre garde; (look after) garder; (never m.) n'importe.
mindful, adj. attentif.
mine, 1. n. mine f. **2.** pron. le mien m., la mienne f., les miens m.pl., les miennes f.pl.
mine field, n. champ (m.) de mines.
miner, n. mineur m.
mineral, adj. and n. minéral m.
mine sweeper, n. dragueur (m.) de mines.
mingle, vb. mêler, tr.
miniature, n. miniature f.
miniaturize, vb. miniaturiser.
minimize, vb. réduire au minimum.
minimum, n. minimum m.
minimum wage, n. salaire minimum m.
mining, n. exploitation minière f., pose de mines f.
minister, n. ministre m.
ministry, n. ministère m.
mink, n. vison m.
minnow, n. vairon m.
minor, adj. and n. mineur m.
minority, n. minorité f.
minstrel, n. ménestrel m.
mint, n. (plant) menthe f.; (place) Hôtel (m.) de la Monnaie.
minus, prep. moins.
minute, 1. n. minute f.; (of meeting) procès-verbal m. **2.** adj. (very small) minuscule; (detailed) minutieux.
miracle, n. miracle m.
miraculous, adj. miraculeux.
mirage, n. mirage m.
mire, n. boue f., bourbier m.
mirror, n. miroir m.
mirth, n. gaieté f.
misadventure, n. mésaventure f., contretemps m.
misappropriate, vb. détourner, dépréder.
misbehave, vb. se conduire mal.
miscellaneous, adj. divers.
mischief, n. (harm) mal m.; (mischievousness) malice f.

mischievous, *adj.* espiègle; (wicked) méchant.

misconstrue, *vb.* mal interpréter, tourner en mal.

misdemeanor, *n.* délit *m.*

miser, *n.* avare *m.f.*

miserable, *adj.* (unhappy) malheureux; (wretched) misérable.

miserly, *adj.* avare.

misery, *n.* (affliction) souffrance(s) *f.(pl.);* (poverty) misère *f.*

misfit, *n.* vêtement manqué *m.;* inadapté *n.,* inapte *m.f.*

misfortune, *n.* malheur *m.*

misgiving, *n.* doute *m.*

mishap, *n.* mésaventure *f.*

mislead, *vb.* tromper, égarer.

misplace, *vb.* mal placer.

misprint, *n.* faute *(f.)* d'impression.

mispronounce, *vb.* mal prononcer, estropier.

miss, *vb.* manquer; **(I m. you)** vous me manquez.

miss, *n.* mademoiselle *f.*

missile, *n.* projectile *m.*

missing, *adj.* (thing) qui manque; (person) disparu.

mission, *n.* mission *f.*

missionary, *adj. and n.* missionnaire *m.f.*

misspell, *vb.* mal orthographier.

mist, *n.* brume *f.*

mistake, 1. *n.* erreur *f.* **2.** *vb.* (misunderstand) comprendre mal; (make a mistake) se tromper (de).

mister, *n.* monsieur *m.*

mistletoe, *n.* gui *m.*

mistreat, *vb.* maltraiter.

mistress, *n.* maîtresse *f.*

mistrust, 1. *n.* méfiance *f.* **2.** *vb.* se méfier de.

misty, *adj.* brumeux.

misunderstand, *vb.* mal comprendre.

misuse, *vb.* (misapply) faire mauvais usage (de); (maltreat) maltraiter.

mite, *n.* denier *m.,* obole *f.*

mitigate, *vb.* atténuer.

mitten, *n.* moufle *f.*

mix, *vb.* mêler, *tr.*

mixture, *n.* mélange *m.*

mix-up, *n.* embrouillement *m.*

moan, 1. *n.* gémissement *m.* **2.** *vb.* gémir.

moat, *n.* fossé *m.*

mob, 1. *n.* foule *f.;* (pejorative) populace *f.* **2.** *vb.* assaillir.

mobile, *adj.* mobile.

mobile phone, *n.* téléphone *(m.)* portatif.

mobilization, *n.* mobilisation *f.*

mobilize, *vb.* mobiliser.

mock, *vb.* **(m. at)** se moquer de; (imitate) singer.

mockery, *n.* moquerie *f.*

mod, *adj.* à la mode.

mode, *n.* mode *m.*

model, *n.* modèle *m.*

modem, *n.* modem *m.*

moderate, 1. *adj.* modéré. **2.** *vb.* modérer.

moderation, *n.* modération *f.*

modern, *adj.* moderne.

modernize, *vb.* moderniser.

modest, *adj.* modeste.

modesty, *n.* modestie *f.*

modify, *vb.* modifier.

modish, *adj.* à la mode.

modulate, *vb.* moduler.

module, *n.* module *m.*

moist, *adj.* moite.

moisten, *vb.* humecter.

moisture, *n.* humidité *f.*

molar, *n. and adj.* molaire *f.*

molasses, *n.* mélasse *f.*

mold, 1. *n.* (casting) moule *m.;* (mildew) moisissure *f.* **2.** *vb.* (shape) mouler; (get moldy) moisir.

moldy, *adj.* moisi.

mole, *n.* (animal) taupe *f.;* (spot) grain *(m.)* de beauté.

molecule, *n.* molécule *f.*

molest, *vb.* molester.

mollify, *vb.* adoucir, apaiser.

molten, *adj.* fondu, coulé.

moment, *n.* moment *m.*

momentary, *adj.* momentané.

momentous, *adj.* important.

mommy, *n.* maman *f.*

Monaco, *n.* Monaco *f.*

monarch, *n.* monarque *m.*

monarchy, *n.* monarchie *f.*

monastery, *n.* monastère *m.*

Monday, *n.* lundi *m.*

monetary, *adj.* monétaire.

money, n. argent m.; (comm.) monnaie f.
money order, n. mandat m.
mongrel, n. métis m.
monitor, n. moniteur m.
monk, n. moine m.
monkey, n. singe m.
monologue, n. monologue m.
monoplane, n. monoplan m.
monopolize, vb. monopoliser.
monopoly, n. monopole m.
monosyllable, n. monosyllabe m.
monotone, n. monotone m.
monotonous, adj. monotone.
monotony, n. monotonie f.
monsoon, n. mousson f.
monster, n. monstre m.
monstrosity, n. monstruosité f.
monstrous, adj. monstrueux.
month, n. mois m.
monthly, adj. mensuel.
monument, n. monument m.
monumental, adj. monumental.
mood, n. humeur f.; (gramm.) mode m.
moody, adj. de mauvaise humeur.
moon, n. lune f.
moonlight, 1. n. clair (m.) de lune. **2.** vb. travailler au noir.
moor, n. lande f.
mooring, n. amarrage m.
moot, adj. discutable.
mop, n. balai (m.) à laver.
mope, vb. bouder.
moped, n. cyclomoteur m.
moral, 1. n. morale f.; (m.s) moralité f. **2.** adj. moral.
morale, n. moral m.
moralist, n. moraliste m.f.
morality, n. moralité f.; (ethics) morale f.
morally, adv. moralement.
morbid, adj. morbide.
more, 1. pron. en . . . davantage. **2.** adj. and adv. plus; (m. than) plus de; (no m.) ne . . . plus.
moreover, adv. de plus.
mores, n. mœurs f.pl.
morgue, n. morgue f.
morning, n. matin m.; (length of m.) matinée f.; (good m.) bonjour.
Morocco, n. Maroc m.
moron, n. idiot m.
morose, adj. morose.
morphine, n. morphine f.

Morse code, n. l'alphabet Morse m.
morsel, n. morceau m.
mortal, adj. and n. mortel m.
mortality, n. mortalité f.
mortar, n. mortier m.
mortgage, 1. n. hypothèque f. **2.** vb. hypothéquer.
mortician, n. entrepreneur (m.) de pompes funèbres.
mortify, vb. mortifier.
mortuary, adj. mortuaire.
mosaic, 1. n. mosaïque f. **2.** adj. en mosaïque.
Moscow, n. Moscou m.
Moslem, adj. and n. musulman m.
mosque, n. mosquée f.
mosquito, n. moustique m.
moss, n. mousse f.
most, 1. n. le plus. **2.** adj. le plus (de); la plupart (de). **3.** adv. (with adj. and vb.) le plus; (intensive) très.
mostly, adv. pour la plupart; (time) la plupart du temps.
moth, n. papillon (m.) de nuit; (clothes) mite f.
mother, n. mère f.
mother-in-law, n. belle-mère f.
mother-of-pearl, n. nacre f.
mother tongue, n. langue (f.) maternelle.
motif, n. motif m.
motion, n. mouvement m.; (gesture) signe m.; (proposal) motion f.
motionless, adj. immobile.
motion-picture, n. film m.
motivate, vb. motiver.
motive, n. motif m.
motley, 1. adj. bigarré. **2.** n. livrée de bouffon m.
motor, n. moteur m.
motorboat, n. canot (m.) automobile.
motorcycle, n. motocyclette f.
motorist, n. automobiliste m.
motto, n. devise f.
mound, n. tertre m.
mount, 1. n. (hill) mont m.; (horse, structure) monture f. **2.** vb. monter.
mountain, n. montagne f.
mountain bike, n. vélo (m.) tout terrain, VTT m.

mountaineer, n. montagnard m., alpiniste m.

mountainous, adj. montagneux.

mountebank, n. saltimbanque m., charlatan m.

mourn, vb. pleurer.

mournful, adj. triste.

mourning, n. deuil m.

mouse, n. souris f.

mouth, n. bouche f.

mouthful, n. bouchée f.

mouthpiece, n. embouchure f., embout m.

movable, adj. mobile.

move, vb. mouvoir, tr.; remuer; (stir) bouger; (affect with emotion) émouvoir; (change residence) déménager; (propose) proposer.

movement, n. mouvement m.

movie, n. film m.

movie camera, n. caméra f.

moving, 1. n. déménagement m. **2.** adj. touchant.

mow, vb. faucher; (lawn) tondre.

Mr., n. M. m. (abbr. for Monsieur).

Mrs., n. Mme. f. (abbr. for Madame).

much, adj., pron. and adv. beaucoup (de); (**too m.**) trop (de); (**so m.**) tant (de); (**how m.**) combien (de).

mucilage, n. mucilage m.

muck, n. fumier m.

mucous, adj. muqueux.

mud, n. boue f.

muddy, adj. boueux.

muff, n. manchon m.

muffin, n. petit pain m.

muffle, vb. emmitoufler.

mug, 1. n. gobelet m., pot m., chope f. **2.** vb. attaquer.

muggy, adj. lourd, moite.

mulatto, n. mulâtre m.

mule, n. mulet m.

mullah, n. mollah m.

multicolored, adj. multicolore.

multifarious, adj. divers.

multinational, adj. multinational.

multiple, adj. multiple.

multiplication, n. multiplication f.

multiplicity, n. multiplicité f.

multiply, vb. multiplier, tr.

multitude, n. multitude f.

mumble, vb. marmonner.

mummy, n. (embalmed) momie f.; maman f.

mumps, n. oreillons m.pl.

munch, vb. mâcher.

mundane, adj. banal.

municipal, adj. municipal.

munificent, adj. munificent.

munition, n. munition(s) f. (pl.).

mural, n. (painting) peinture (f.) murale.

murder, n. meurtre m.

murderer, n. meurtrier m.

murmur, 1. n. murmure m. **2.** vb. murmurer.

muscle, n. muscle m.

muscular, adj. musculaire; (strong) musclé.

muse, 1. n. muse f. **2.** vb. méditer.

museum, n. musée m.

mushroom, n. champignon m.

music, n. musique f.

musical, adj. musical; (person) musicien.

musical comedy, n. comédie musicale f.

musician, n. musicien m.

Muslim, adj. and n. musulman m.

muslin, n. mousseline f.

mussel, n. moule f.

must, vb. devoir; falloir (used impersonally, il faut que).

mustache, n. moustache f.

mustard, n. moutarde f.

muster, vb. rassembler, tr.

musty, adj. moisi, suranné.

mutation, n. mutation f.

mute, adj. muet.

mutilate, vb. mutiler.

mutiny, n. mutinerie f.

mutter, vb. grommeler.

mutton, n. mouton m.

mutual, adj. mutuel.

muzzle, n. muselière f.

my, adj. mon m., ma f., mes pl.

myopia, n. myopie f.

myriad, n. myriade f.

myself, pron. moi-même; (reflexive) me.

mysterious, adj. mystérieux.

mystery, n. mystère m.

mystic, adj. mystique.

mystify, vb. mystifier.
myth, n. mythe m.

mythical, adj. mythique.
mythology, n. mythologie f.

N

nab, vb. attraper, saisir.
nag, vb. gronder.
nail, 1. n. (person, animal) ongle m.; (metal) clou m.; **(n. polish)** vernis (m.) à ongles. **2.** vb. clouer.
naïve, adj. naïf m., naïve f.
naked, adj. nu.
name, 1. n. nom m. **2.** vb. nommer.
namely, adv. à savoir.
namesake, n. homonyme m.
nanny, n. nounou f.
nap, n. petit somme m.
nape, n. nuque f.
napkin, n. serviette f.
narcissus, n. narcisse f.
narcotic, adj. and n. narcotique m.
narrate, vb. raconter.
narrative, n. récit m.
narrow, adj. étroit.
narrow-minded, adj. à l'esprit étroit.
nasal, adj. nasal.
nasty, adj. méchant.
natal, adj. natal.
nation, n. nation f.
national, adj. national.
nationalism, n. nationalisme m.
nationality, n. nationalité f.
nationalization, n. nationalisation f.
nationalize, vb. nationaliser.
nationwide, 1. adj. à l'échelle du pays entier. **2.** adv. à travers tout le pays.
native, 1. n. autochtone m.f., (non-European) indigène m.f. **2.** adj. natif (place) natal; (language) maternel.
nativity, n. naissance f.
NATO, n. OTAN f.
natural, adj. naturel.
naturalist, n. naturaliste m.f.
naturalize, vb. naturaliser.
naturalness, n. naturel m.
nature, n. nature f.
naughty, adj. méchant.
nausea, n. nausée f.
nauseous, adj. nauséeux.
nautical, adj. marin.

naval, adj. naval.
nave, n. nef f.
navigable, adj. navigable.
navigate, vb. naviguer.
navigation, n. navigation f.
navigator, n. navigateur m.
navy, n. marine f.
navy yard, n. arsenal maritime m.
Nazi, n. Nazi m.
near, 1. adj. proche. **2.** adv. près. **3.** prep. près de.
nearly, adv. de près; (almost) presque.
near-sighted, adj. myope.
neat, adj. soigné, net.
neatness, n. propreté f.
nebula, n. nébuleuse f.
nebulous, adj. nébuleux.
necessary, adj. nécessaire.
necessity, n. nécessité f.
neck, 1. n. cou m. **2.** vb. se peloter.
necklace, n. collier m.
necktie, n. cravate f.
nectar, n. nectar m.
need, 1. n. besoin m. **2.** vb. avoir besoin de.
needful, adj. nécessaire.
needle, n. aiguille f.
needle point, n. pointe d'aiguille f.
needless, adj. inutile.
needy, adj. nécessiteux.
nefarious, adj. infâme.
negative, adj. négatif.
neglect, 1. n. négligence f. **2.** vb. négliger (de).
negligee, n. négligée f.
negligent, adj. négligent.
negligible, adj. négligeable.
negotiate, vb. négocier.
negotiation, n. négociation f.
Negro, adj. and n. nègre m.
neighbor, n. voisin m.; (fellow man) prochain m.
neighborhood, n. voisinage m.
neighborly, adj. amical.
neither, 1. adj. and pron. ni l'un ni l'autre. **2.** adv. non plus. **3.** conj. **(n. . . . nor)** ni . . . ni.
neon, n. néon m.

neophyte, n. néophyte m.
nephew, n. neveu m.
nepotism, n. népotisme m.
nerve, n. nerf m.
nerve-racking, adj. angoissant.
nervous, adj. nerveux.
nervous system, n. système nerveux m.
nest, n. nid m.
nestle, vb. se nicher.
net, 1. n. filet m. **2.** adj. net m., nette f.
Netherlands, the, n. les Pays-Bas m.pl., Hollande f.
network, n. réseau m.
neuralgia, n. névralgie f.
neurology, n. neurologie f.
neurotic, adj. and n. névrosé m.
neutral, adj. and n. neutre m.
neutron, n. neutron m.
neutron bomb, n. bombe (f.) à neutrons.
never, adv. jamais.
nevertheless, adv. néanmoins.
new, adj. nouveau m., nouvelle f.; (not used) neuf m., neuve f.
newborn, adj. nouveau né.
newlyweds, n. jeunes mariés m.pl.
news, n. (piece of news) nouvelle f.
newsboy, n. vendeur (m.) de journaux.
newscast, n. journal parlé m., informations f.pl.
newscaster, n. présentateur m.
newspaper, n. journal m.
newsreel, n. film (m.) d'actualité.
newsstand, n. kiosque (m.) à journaux.
New Testament, n. le Nouveau Testament m.
new year, n. nouvel an m.
New Zealand, n. Nouvelle-Zélande f.
next, 1. adj. prochain. **2.** adv. ensuite. **3.** prep. auprès de.
nibble, vb. grignoter.
nice, adj. (person) gentil; (thing) joli.
niche, n. niche f., (fig.) place f., situation f.
nick, n. entaille f.
nickel, n. nickel m.
nickname, n. surnom m.
nicotine, n. nicotine f.
niece, n. nièce f.

Nigeria, n. Nigéria m.f.
niggardly, adj. chiche.
night, n. nuit f.; (evening) soir m.
nightclub, n. boîte (f.) de nuit, établissement (m.) de nuit.
nightgown, n. chemise (f.) de nuit.
nightingale, n. rossignol m.
nightly, adv. tous les soirs; toutes les nuits.
nightmare, n. cauchemar m.
night-school, n. cours (m.) du soir.
nimble, adj. agile.
nine, adj. and n. neuf m.
nineteen, adj. and n. dix-neuf m.
ninety, adj. and n. quatre-vingt-dix m.
ninth, adj. and n. neuvième m.f.
nip, 1. n. pincement m., pinçade f. **2.** vb. pincer.
nipple, n. mamelon m.
nitrogen, n. nitrogène m.
no, 1. adj. pas de. **2.** interj., adv. non.
nobility, n. noblesse f.
noble, adj. noble.
nobleman, n. gentilhomme m.
nobly, adv. noblement.
nobody, pron. personne.
nocturnal, adj. nocturne.
nod, 1. n. signe (m.) de la tête. **2.** vb. incliner la tête.
node, n. nœud m.
no-frills, adj. simple.
noise, n. bruit m.
noiseless, adj. silencieux.
noisome, adj. puant, fétide.
noisy, adj. bruyant.
nomad, n. nomade m.f.
nominal, adj. nominal.
nominate, vb. (appoint) nommer; (propose) désigner.
nomination, n. (appointment) nomination f.; (proposal) désignation f.
nominee, n. personne nommée f., candidat choisi m.
nonaligned, adj. (in politics) non-aligné.
nonchalant, adj. nonchalant.
noncombatant, adj. and n. non-combattant m.
noncommissioned, adj. sans brevet.

noncommittal, *adj.* qui n'engage à rien.

nondescript, *adj.* indéfinissable.

none, *pron.* aucun.

nonentity, *n.* nullité *f.*

nonplussed, *adj.* perplexe.

non-proliferation, *n.* non-prolifération *f.*

nonresident, *n. and adj.* non-résident *m.*

nonsense, *n.* absurdité *f.*

non-smoker, *n.* non-fumeur *m.*

nonstop, *adj.* sans arrêt.

noodles, *n.* nouilles *f.pl.*

nook, *n.* coin *m.,* recoin *m.*

noon, *n.* midi *m.*

noose, *n.* nœud coulant *m.*

nor, *conj.* ni; (and not) et ne ... pas.

norm, *n.* norme *f.*

normal, *adj.* normal.

normally, *adv.* normalement.

Normandy, *n.* Normandie *f.*

north, *n.* nord *m.*

North America, *n.* Amérique *(f.)* du Nord.

northeast, *n.* nord-est *m.*

northern, *adj.* du nord.

North Pole, *n.* pôle nord *m.*

northwest, *n.* nord-ouest *m.*

Norway, *n.* Norvège *f.*

Norwegian, 1. *n.* (person) Norvégien *m.;* (language) norvégien *m.* **2.** *adj.* norvégien.

nose, *n.* nez *m.*

nosebleed, *n.* saignement *(m.)* du nez.

nose dive, *n.* vol piqué *m.*

nostalgia, *n.* nostalgie *f.*

nostril, *n.* narine *f.;* (animals) naseau *m.*

nostrum, *n.* panacée *f.,* remède *(m.)* de charlatan.

nosy, *adj.* curieux.

not, *adv.* (ne) pas.

notable, *adj. and n.* notable *m.*

notary, *n.* notaire *m.*

notation, *n.* notation *f.*

note, **1.** *n.* note *f.;* (letter, finance) billet *m.;* (distinction) marque *f.* **2.** *vb.* noter.

notebook, *n.* (small) carnet *m.;* (large) cahier *m.*

noted, *adj.* célèbre.

notepaper, *n.* papier *(m.)* à notes.

noteworthy, *adj.* remarquable, mémorable.

nothing, *pron.* rien.

notice, 1. *n.* (announcement) avis *m.;* (attention) attention *f.;* (forewarning) préavis *m.* **2.** *vb.* remarquer.

noticeable, *adj.* remarquable; apparent.

notification, *n.* notification *f.*

notify, *vb.* avertir.

notion, *n.* idée *f.*

notoriety, *n.* notoriété *f.*

notorious, *adj.* notoire.

notwithstanding, 1. *adv.* tout de même. **2.** *prep.* malgré.

noun, *n.* substantif *m.*

nourish, *vb.* nourrir.

nourishment, *n.* nourriture *f.*

novel, 1. *n.* roman *m.* **2.** *adj.* nouveau, original.

novelist, *n.* romancier *m.*

novelty, *n.* nouveauté *f.*

November, *n.* novembre *m.*

novice, *n.* novice *m.f.*

now, *adv.* maintenant; **(n. and then)** de temps en temps.

nowadays, *adv.* de nos jours.

nowhere, *adv.* nulle part.

nozzle, *n.* ajutage *m.,* jet *m.*

nuance, *n.* nuance *f.*

nuclear, *adj.* nucléaire.

nuclear physics, *n.* physique nucléaire *f.*

nuclear warhead, *n.* cône *(m.)* de charge nucléaire.

nuclear waste, *n.* déchets nucléaires *m.pl.*

nucleus, *n.* noyau *m.*

nude, *adj. and n.* nu *m.*

nugget, *n.* pépite *f.*

nuisance, *n.* (thing) ennui *m.;* (person) peste *f.*

nuke, 1. *n.* arme nucléaire *f.* **2.** *vb.* détruire avec des armes nucléaires.

nullify, *vb.* annuler, nullifier.

numb, 1. *adj.* engourdi. **2.** *vb.* engourdir.

number, 1. *n.* nombre *m.;* (in a series, street, etc.) numéro *m.* **2.** *vb.* compter, numéroter.

numeral, *n.* chiffre *m.*

numerical, *adj.* numérique.

numerous, *adj.* nombreux.

nun, *n.* religieuse *f.*, nonne *f.*
nuncio, *n.* nonce *m.*
nuptial, *adj.* nuptial.
nurse, 1. *n.* (hospital) infirmière *f.*; (wet-n.) nourrice *f.* **2.** *vb.* soigner; (suckle) allaiter.
nursery, *n.* (children) chambre *(f.)* des enfants; (plants) pépinière *f.*
nurture, 1. *n.* nourriture *f.* **2.** *vb.* nourrir, entretenir.

nut, 1. *n.* noix *f.;* (metal) écrou *m.* **2.** *adj.* **(n.s)** (colloquial) dingue.
nutcracker, *n.* casse-noix *m.*
nutmeg, *n.* muscade *f.*
nutrition, *n.* nutrition *f.*
nutritious, *adj.* nutritif.
nutshell, *n.* coquille *(f.)* de noix; (in a n.) en deux mots.
nylon, *n.* nylon *m.*
nymph, *n.* nymphe *f.*

O

oak, *n.* chêne *m.*
oar, *n.* rame *f.*
oasis, *n.* oasis *f.*
oath, *n.* serment *m.;* (curse) juron *m.*
oatmeal, *n.* farine *(f.)* d'avoine.
oats, *n.* avoine *f.*
obdurate, *adj.* obstiné, têtu.
obedience, *n.* obéissance *f.*
obedient, *adj.* obéissant.
obeisance, *n.* salut *m.*
obelisk, *n.* obélisque *m.*
obese, *adj.* obèse.
obey, *vb.* obéir à.
obituary, *n.* nécrologe *m.*
object, 1. *n.* objet *m.* **2.** *vb.* objecter.
objection, *n.* objection *f.*
objectionable, *adj.* répréhensible.
objective, *adj. and n.* objectif *m.*
obligation, *n.* obligation *f.*
obligatory, *adj.* obligatoire.
oblige, *vb.* obliger.
oblivion, *n.* oubli *m.*
obnoxious, *adj.* odieux.
oboe, *n.* hautbois *m.*
obscene, *adj.* obscène.
obscure, *adj.* obscur.
obsequious, *adj.* obséquieux.
observance, *n.* observance *f.*
observation, *n.* observation *f.*
observe, *vb.* observer.
observer, *n.* observateur *m.*
obsess, *vb.* obséder.
obsession, *n.* obsession *f.*
obsolescence, *n.* vieillissement *m.*
obsolete, *adj.* désuet.
obstacle, *n.* obstacle *m.*
obstetrician, *n.* médecin-accoucheur *m.*
obstinate, *adj.* obstiné.

obstreperous, *adj.* tapageur.
obstruct, *vb.* obstruer.
obstruction, *n.* obstruction *f.*
obtain, *vb.* obtenir.
obtrude, *vb.* mettre en avant.
obtuse, *adj.* obtus.
obviate, *vb.* prévenir, éviter.
obvious, *adj.* évident.
occasion, *n.* occasion *f.*
occasional, *adj.* (not regular) de temps en temps.
occult, *adj.* occulte.
occupant, *n.* occupant *m.*
occupation, *n.* occupation *f.;* (vocation) métier *m.*
occupy, *vb.* occuper.
occur, *vb.* (happen) avoir lieu; (come to the mind) se présenter à l'esprit.
occurrence, *n.* occurrence *f.*
ocean, *n.* océan *m.*
o'clock, *see* clock.
octagon, *n.* octogone *m.*
octave, *n.* octave *f.*
October, *n.* octobre *m.*
octopus, *n.* poulpe *m.*
ocular, *adj.* oculaire.
oculist, *n.* oculiste *m.f.*
odd, *adj.* (not even) impair; (unmatched) dépareillé; (strange) bizarre.
oddity, *n.* singularité *f.*
odds, *n.* inégalité *f.*, (betting) cote *f.*
odious, *adj.* odieux.
odor, *n.* odeur *f.*
of, *prep.* de.
off, 1. *adv.* (away) à . . . distance; (cancelled) rompu. **2.** *prep.* de.

offend, vb. offenser; **(o. against the law)** enfreindre la loi.

offender, n. offenseur m.; (law) délinquant m.

offense, n. offense f.; (transgression) délit m.

offensive, 1. n. offensive f. **2.** adj. (mil., etc.) offensif (word, etc.) offensant.

offer, 1. n. offre f. **2.** vb. offrir.

offering, n. offre f., offrande f.

offhand, 1. adj. spontané. **2.** adv. sans préparation.

office, n. (service) office m.; (function) fonctions f.pl.; (room) bureau m.

officer, n. (mil.) officier m.; (public) fonctionnaire m.

official, adj. officiel.

officiate, vb. officier.

officious, adj. officieux.

off-line, adj. and adv. (computer) (en mode) autonome.

off-peak, adj. aux heures creuses.

offshore, 1. adv. vers le large. **2.** adj. du côté de la terre.

offspring, n. descendant m.

often, adv. souvent.

oil, n. huile f.

oilcloth, n. toile cirée f.

oily, adj. huileux.

ointment, n. onguent m.

okay, interj. très bien, d'accord.

old, adj. vieux (vieil) m., vieille f.; **(how o. are you?)** quel âge avez-vous?

old-fashioned, adj. démodé.

Old Testament, n. l'Ancien Testament m.

olfactory, adj. olfactif.

oligarchy, n. oligarchie f.

olive, n. (tree) olivier m.; (fruit) olive f.

ombudsman, n. (in France) médiateur m.; (in Quebec) protecteur (m.) du citoyen.

omelet, n. omelette f.

omen, n. présage m.

ominous, adj. de mauvais augure.

omission, n. omission f.

omit, vb. omettre.

omnibus, n. omnibus m.

omnipotent, adj. omnipotent, tout-puissant.

on, prep. sur.

once, adv. une fois; (formerly) autrefois; **(at o., without delay)** tout de suite; **(at o., at the same time)** à la fois.

one, 1. adj. un; (only) seul. **2.** n. un m. **3.** pron. un; (indefinite subject) on, (indefinite object) vous; **(the o.)** celui; (this o.) celui-ci; (that o.) celui-là; **(which o.)** lequel.

oneself, pron. soi-même; (reflexive) se.

one-sided, adj. unilatéral.

one-way, adj. (street, traffic) à sens unique; non connecté.

onion, n. oignon m.

onionskin, n. pelure (f.) d'oignon, (paper) papier pelure m.

on-line, adj. and adv. en ligne; connecté.

only, 1. adj. seul. **2.** adv. seulement.

onslaught, n. assaut m.

onward, adj. and adv. en avant.

opal, n. opale f.

opaque, adj. opaque.

OPEC, n. OPEP f.

open, 1. adj. ouvert; **(o.-minded)** à l'esprit ouvert. **2.** vb. ouvrir.

opening, n. ouverture f.

opera, n. opéra m.

opera glasses, n. jumelles f.pl.

operate, vb. opérer; (put into operation) actionner.

operatic, adj. d'opéra.

operation, n. opération f.; (functioning) fonctionnement m.

operator, n. opérateur m.; (switchboard) standardiste m.f.

operetta, n. opérette f.

opinion, n. opinion f.

opponent, n. adversaire m.f.

opportunism, n. opportunisme m.

opportunity, n. occasion f.

oppose, vb. (put in opposition) opposer; (resist) s'opposer à.

opposite, 1. adj. opposé. **2.** adv. vis-à-vis. **3.** prep. en face de.

opposition, n. opposition f.

oppress, vb. opprimer.

oppression, n. oppression f.

oppressive, adj. oppressif; (heat, etc.) accablant.

opt, vb. **(o. for)** opter pour; **(o. out of)** refuser de participer à.

optic, adj. optique.

optician, n. opticien m.

optimism, *n.* optimisme *m.*
optimistic, *adj.* optimiste.
option, *n.* option *f.*
optional, *adj.* facultatif.
optometry, *n.* optométrie *f.*
opulent, *adj.* opulent, riche.
or, *conj.* ou; (with negative) ni.
oracle, *n.* oracle *m.*
oral, *adj.* oral.
orange, *n.* orange *f.*
orangeade, *n.* orangeade *f.*
oration, *n.* discours *m.*
orator, *n.* orateur *m.*
oratory, *n.* art (*m.*) oratoire.
orbit, *n.* orbite *f.*
orchard, *n.* verger *m.*
orchestra, *n.* orchestre *m.*
orchid, *n.* orchidée *f.*
ordain, *vb.* ordonner.
ordeal, *n.* épreuve *f.*
order, 1. *n.* ordre *m.;* (comm.) commande *f.* **2.** *vb.* ordonner; (comm.) commander.
orderly, *adj.* ordonné.
ordinance, *n.* ordonnance *f.*
ordinary, *adj. and n.* ordinaire *m.*
ordination, *n.* ordination *f.*
ore, *n.* minerai *m.*
organ, *n.* (music) orgue *m.;* (body) organe *m.*
organdy, *n.* organdi *m.*
organic, *adj.* organique.
organism, *n.* organisme *m.*
organist, *n.* organiste *m.f.*
organization, *n.* organisation *f.;* (group) organisme *m.*
organize, *vb.* organiser.
orgasm, *n.* orgasme *m.*
orgy, *n.* orgie *f.*
orient, *vb.* orienter.
Orient, *n.* Orient *m.*
Oriental, 1. *n.* Oriental *m.* **2.** *adj.* oriental.
orientation, *n.* orientation *f.*
orifice, *n.* orifice *m.*
origin, *n.* origine *f.*
original, *adj.* (new, unique) original; (from the origin) originel.
originality, *n.* originalité *f.*
originate from, *vb.* provenir de.
ornament, *n.* ornement *m.*
ornamental, *adj.* ornemental.
ornate, *adj.* orné.
ornithology, *n.* ornithologie *f.*
orphan, *n.* orphelin *m.*

orphanage, *n.* orphelinat *m.*
orthodox, *adj.* orthodoxe.
orthopedics, *n.* orthopédie *f.*
osmosis, *n.* osmose *f.*
ostensible, *adj.* prétendu.
ostentation, *n.* ostentation *f.*
ostentatious, *adj.* plein d'ostentation, ostentatoire.
osteopath, *n.* ostéopathe *m.f.*
ostracize, *vb.* ostraciser.
ostrich, *n.* autruche *f.*
other, *adj. and pron.* autre.
otherwise, *adv.* autrement.
ought, *vb.* devoir.
ounce, *n.* once *f.*
our, *adj.* notre *sg.,* nos *pl.*
ours, *pron.* le nôtre.
ourself, *pron.* nous-même; (reflexive) nous.
oust, *vb.* évincer.
ouster, *n.* éviction *f.*
out, *adv.* dehors.
outbreak, *n.* (beginning) commencement *m.;* (insurrection) révolte *f.,* éruption *f.*
outburst, *n.* éruption *f.*
outcast, *n.* paria *m.*
outcome, *n.* résultat *m.*
outdated, *adj.* suranné.
outdoors, *adv.* dehors.
outer, *adj.* extérieur.
outfit, *n.* équipement *m.;* (clothes) tenue *f.*
outgrow, *vb.* devenir trop grand pour.
outgrowth, *n.* conséquence *f.*
outing, *n.* promenade *f.*
outlandish, *adj.* bizarre.
outlaw, 1. *vb.* proscrire. **2.** *n.* hors-la-loi *m.*
outlet, *n.* issue *f.;* prise (*f.*) de courant.
outline, 1. *n.* contour *m.;* (general idea) aperçu *m.* **2.** *vb.* (drawing) tracer; (plan) exposer à grands traits.
out of, *prep.* hors de; (because of) par; (without) sans.
out-of-date, *adj.* suranné.
output, *n.* rendement *m.*
outrage, *n.* outrage *m.*
outrageous, *adj.* outrageant.
outrank, *vb.* occuper un rang supérieur.
outright, *adv.* complètement.

outrun, vb. dépasser.

outset, n. début m.

outside, 1. adv. dehors. **2.** prep. en dehors de.

outsider, n. étranger m.

outskirts, n. limites f.pl.

outstanding, adj. exceptionnel; non réglé.

outward, adj. extérieur.

oval, adj. and n. ovale m.

ovary, n. ovaire m.

ovation, n. ovation f.

oven, n. four m.

over, 1. prep. (on) sur; (above) au-dessus de; (beyond) au delà de; (more than) plus de. **2.** adv. **(all o.)** partout; (more) davantage; (finished) fini; (with adj.) trop.

overbearing, adj. arrogant.

overcast, adj. (weather) couvert.

overcoat, n. pardessus m.

overcome, vb. vaincre; **(be o. by)** succomber à.

overdose, n. dose (f.) excessive, overdose f.

overdue, adj. arriéré, échu.

overflow, vb. déborder.

overhaul, vb. examiner en détail, remettre au point.

overhead, 1. adj. (comm.) général. **2.** adv. en haut.

overkill, n. exagération rhétorique f.

overlook, vb. (look onto) avoir vue sur; (neglect) négliger.

overnight, adv. pendant la nuit.

overpower, vb. (subdue) subjuguer; (crush) accabler.

overrule, vb. décider contre.

overrun, vb. envahir.

overseas, adv. outre-mer, à l'étranger.

oversee, vb. surveiller.

oversight, n. inadvertance f.

overstuffed, adj. rembourré.

overt, adj. manifeste.

overtake, vb. rattraper; (accident, etc.) arriver à.

overthrow, vb. renverser.

overtime, n. heures (f.pl.) supplémentaires.

overture, n. ouverture f.

overturn, vb. renverser, tr.

overview, n. vue d'ensemble f.

overweight, n. excédent m.

overwhelm, vb. accabler (de).

overwork, vb. surmener, tr.

owe, vb. devoir.

owing, 1. prep. à cause de, en raison de. **2.** adj. dû.

owl, n. hibou m.

own, 1. adj. propre. **2.** vb. posséder; (admit) avouer; (acknowledge) reconnaître.

owner, n. propriétaire m.-f.

ox, n. bœuf m.

oxygen, n. oxygène m.

oxygen mask, n. masque (m.) d'oxygène.

oyster, n. huître f.

ozone, n. ozone m.; **(o. hole)** trou (m.) d'ozone. **(o. layer)** couche (f.) d'ozone.

P

pace, 1. n. (step) pas m.; (gait) allure f. **2.** vb. arpenter.

pacemaker, n. stimulateur (m.) cardiaque.

pacific, adj. pacifique.

Pacific Ocean, n. océan Pacifique m.

pacifism, n. pacifisme m.

pacify, vb. pacifier.

pack, 1. n. paquet m.; (animals) meute f.; (persons) bande f. **2.** vb. emballer; (crowd) entasser.

package, n. paquet m.

packet, n. paquet m.

packing, n. emballage m.

pact, n. pacte m., contrat m.

pad, 1. n. (stuffing) bourrelet m.; (cotton, ink) tampon m.; (paper) bloc m. **2.** vb. (clothes) ouater; (stuff) bourrer.

padding, n. remplissage m., rembourrage m.

paddle, n. pagaie f.

paddock, n. enclos m.

padlock, n. cadenas m.

pagan, adj. and n. païen m.

page, n. (book) page f.; (attendant) page m.
pageant, n. spectacle m.
pager, n. récepteur (m.) d'appels.
pagoda, n. pagode f.
pail, n. seau m.
pain, 1. n. douleur f.; (trouble) peine f. **2.** vb. (hurt) faire mal (à); (distress) faire de la peine (à).
painful, adj. douloureux.
painstaking, adj. soigneux.
paint, 1. n. peinture f. **2.** vb. peindre.
painter, n. peintre m.
painting, n. peinture f.
pair, n. paire f.
pajamas, n. pyjama m.
Pakistan, n. Pakistan m.
pal, n. copain m.
palace, n. palais m.
palatable, adj. d'un goût agréable, agréable au palais.
palate, n. palais m.
palatial, adj. qui ressemble à un palais, magnifique.
pale, adj. pâle.
paleness, n. pâleur f.
Palestine, n. Palestine f.
palette, n. palette f.
pall, 1. n. drap funéraire m. **2.** vb. s'affadir.
pallbearer, n. porteur (d'un cordon du poêle) m.
pallid, adj. pâle, blême.
palm, n. (tree) palmier m.; (branch) palme f.; (hand) paume f.
palpable, adj. manifeste.
palpitate, vb. palpiter.
paltry, adj. mesquin.
pamper, vb. choyer.
pamphlet, n. brochure f.
pan, n. (cooking) casserole f.
panacea, n. panacée f.
Pan-American, adj. panaméricain.
pancake, n. crêpe f.
pancreas, n. pancréas m.
pandemonium, n. tumulte m., chaos m.
pander to, vb. flatter bassement.
pane, n. (window) vitre f.
panel, n. panneau m.
pang, n. angoisse f.
panic, n. panique f.
panorama, n. panorama m.

pant, vb. haleter.
pantomime, n. pantomime m.
pantry, n. office f.
pants, n. pantalon m.
panty hose, n. collant m.
papal, adj. papal.
paper, n. papier m.
paperback, n. livre (m.) de poche.
par, n. pair m., égalité f.
parable, n. parabole f.
parachute, n. parachute m.
parade, n. parade f.
paradise, n. paradis m.
paradox, n. paradoxe m.
paraffin, n. paraffine f.
paragon, n. modèle m.
paragraph, n. alinéa m., paragraphe m.
parakeet, n. perruche f.
parallel, 1. n. (line) parallèle f.; (geography, comparison) parallèle m. **2.** adj. parallèle.
paralyze, vb. paralyser.
paramedic, n. assistant médical m.
parameter, n. paramètre m.
paramount, adj. souverain.
paranoia, n. paranoïa f.
paranoid, adj. paranoïaque.
paraphrase, vb. paraphraser.
parasite, n. parasite m.
parcel, n. paquet m.; **(p. post)** colis postal m.
parch, vb. dessécher, tr.
parchment, n. parchemin m.
pardon, 1. n. pardon m. **2.** vb. pardonner.
pare, vb. (fruit) peler.
parent, n. père m.; mère f.; **(parents)** parents m.pl.
parentage, n. naissance f.
parenthesis, n. parenthèse f.
parish, n. paroisse f.
Parisian, 1. n. Parisien m. **2.** adj. parisien.
parity, n. parité f., égalité f.
park, 1. n. parc m. **2.** vb. stationner.
parking lot, n. parking m.
parking meter, n. parcmètre m.
parley, n. conférence f., pourparler m.
parliament, n. parlement m.
parliamentary, adj. parlementaire.
parlor, n. petit salon m.
parochial, adj. paroissial; (limited in outlook) de clocher.

parody, n. parodie f.

parole, 1. n. parole f. **2.** vb. libérer conditionnellement.

paroxysm, n. paroxysme m.

parrot, n. perroquet m.

parsley, n. persil m.

parsimonious, adj. parcimonieux.

parson, n. pasteur m.

part, 1. n. (of a whole) partie f.; (share) part f. **2.** vb. (divide) diviser; (share) partager; (of people) se séparer.

partake of, vb. participer à.

partial, adj. partiel; (favoring) partial.

participant, adj. and n. participant m.

participate, vb. participer.

participation, n. participation f.

participle, n. participe m.

particle, n. particule f.

particular, 1. n. détail m. **2.** adj. particulier; (person) exigeant.

parting, n. séparation f.; (hair) raie f.

partisan, n. partisan m.

partition, n. partage m.; (wall) cloison f.

partly, adv. en partie.

partner, n. associé m.

part of speech, n. partie (f.) du discours.

partridge, n. perdrix f.

part-time, adj. and adv. à temps partiel.

party, n. (faction) parti m.; (social) réception f.; (group of people) groupe m.; (law) partie f.

pass, 1. n. (mountain) col m.; (permission) laissez-passer m. **2.** vb. passer.

passable, adj. traversable, passable, assez bon.

passage, n. passage m.

passenger, n. (land) voyageur m.; (sea, air) passager m.

passer-by, n. passant m.

passion, n. passion f.

passionate, adj. passionné.

passive, adj. and n. passif m.

Passover, n. Pâque f.

passport, n. passeport m.

password, n. mot (m.) de passe.

past, 1. adj. and n. passé m. **2.** prep. (beyond) au delà de; (more than)

plus de; **(half p. four)** quatre heures et demie.

paste, 1. n. pâte f.; (glue) colle f. **2.** vb. coller.

pasteurize, vb. pasteuriser.

pastime, n. passe-temps m.

pastor, n. pasteur m.

pastry, n. pâtisserie f.

pasture, n. pâturage m.

pasty, adj. empâté, pâteux.

pat, vb. taper.

patch, 1. n. pièce f. **2.** vb. rapiécer.

patchwork, n. patchwork m.

patent, n. brevet (m.) d'invention.

patent leather, n. cuir (m.) verni.

paternal, adj. paternel.

paternity, n. paternité f.

path, n. sentier m.

pathetic, adj. pathétique.

pathology, n. pathologie f.

pathos, n. pathétique m.

patience, n. patience f.

patient, 1. n. malade m.f. **2.** adj. patient.

patio, n. patio m.

patriarch, n. patriarche m.

patriot, n. patriote m.f.

patriotic, adj. patriotique.

patriotism, n. patriotisme m.

patrol, n. patrouille f.

patrolman, n. agent (de police) m., patrouilleur m.

patron, n. protecteur m.; (comm.) client m.

patronize, vb. subventionner; traiter avec condescendance.

pattern, n. modèle m.; (design) dessin m.; schéma m.

pauper, n. indigent m., pauvre m., mendiant m.

pause, n. pause f.

pave, vb. paver.

pavement, n. pavé m.; (sidewalk) trottoir m.

pavestone, n. pavé m.

pavilion, n. pavillon f.

paw, n. patte f.

pawn, 1. n. pion m. **2.** vb. mettre en gage, engager.

pay, 1. n. salaire m. **2.** vb. payer.

payment, n. paiement m.

pay phone, n. cabine (f.) téléphonique.

pea, n. pois m.

peace, n. paix f.

peaceable, peaceful, *adj.* paisible.

peach, *n.* pêche *f.*

peacock, *n.* paon *m.*

peak, *n.* sommet *m.*

peal, 1. *n.* retentissement *m.* **2.** *vb.* sonner, retentir.

peanut, *n.* arachide *f.*

pear, *n.* poire *f.*

pearl, *n.* perle *f.*

peasant, *n.* paysan *m.*

pebble, *n.* caillou *m.*

peck, *vb.* becqueter.

peculiar, *adj.* particulier; (unusual) singulier.

pecuniary, *adj.* pécuniaire.

pedagogue, *n.* pédagogue *m.*

pedagogy, *n.* pédagogie *f.*

pedal, *n.* pédale *f.*

pedant, *n.* pédant *m.*

peddle, *vb.* colporter.

peddler, *n.* colporteur *m.,* camelot *m.*

pedestal, *n.* piédestal *m.*

pedestrian, *n.* piéton *m.*

pediatrician, *n.* pédiatre *m.*

pedigree, *n.* généalogie *f.*

pee, *vb.* (colloquial) faire pipi.

peek, 1. *n.* coup d'œil furtif *m.* **2.** *vb.* regarder à la dérobée.

peel, 1. *n.* pelure *f.* **2.** *vb.* peler.

peep, *vb.* regarder furtivement.

peer, 1. *n.* pair *m.* **2.** *vb.* scruter.

peevish, *adj.* irritable.

peg, *n.* cheville *f.*

pejorative, *adj.* péjoratif.

pelican, *n.* pélican *m.*

pelt, 1. *n.* peau *f.,* fourrure *f.* **2.** *vb.* lancer, jeter.

pelvis, *n.* bassin *m.*

pen, *n.* plume *f.;* (ballpoint) stylo *(m.)* à bille.

penalty, *n.* peine *f.*

penance, *n.* pénitence *f.*

penchant, *n.* penchant *m.*

pencil, *n.* crayon *m.*

pendant, *n.* pendentif *m.*

pending, *prep.* pendant.

penetrate, *vb.* pénétrer.

penetration, *n.* pénétration *f.*

penicillin, *n.* pénicilline *f.*

peninsula, *n.* péninsule *f.*

penis, *n.* pénis *m.*

penitent, 1. *adj.* pénitent, contrit. **2.** *n.* pénitent *m.*

penknife, *n.* canif *m.*

penniless, *adj.* sans le sou.

penny, *n.* sou *m.*

pension, *n.* pension *f.*

pensive, *adj.* pensif.

Pentecost, *n.* Pentecôte *f.*

pent-up, *adj.* refoulé.

penury, *n.* pénurie *f.*

people, 1. *n.* gens *m.f.pl.;* (of a country) peuple *m.* **2.** *vb.* peupler.

pep, *n.* énergie *f.*

pepper, *n.* poivre *m.*

per, *prep.* par; **(p. hour)** par heure; **(p. year)** par an.

perambulator, *n.* voiture *(f.)* d'enfant.

perceive, *vb.* apercevoir, *tr.*

percent, pour cent.

percentage, *n.* pourcentage *m.*

perceptible, *adj.* perceptible.

perception, *n.* perception *f.*

perch, 1. *n.* (for birds) perchoir *m.;* (fish) perche *f.* **2.** *vb.* se percher.

perdition, *n.* perte *f.*

peremptory, *adj.* péremptoire.

perennial, *adj.* perpétuel; (plant) vivace.

perfect, *adj.* parfait.

perfection, *n.* perfection *f.*

perforation, *n.* perforation *f.*

perform, *vb.* accomplir, (theater) jouer.

performance, *n.* (task) accomplissement *m.;* (theater) représentation *f.*

perfume, *n.* parfum *m.*

perfunctory, *adj.* fait pour la forme, superficiel.

perhaps, *adv.* peut-être.

peril, *n.* péril *m.*

perilous, *adj.* périlleux.

perimeter, *n.* périmètre *m.*

period, *n.* période *f.;* (full stop) point *m.*

periodic, *adj.* périodique.

periodical, *n.* périodique *m.*

peripheral, *adj.* périphérique.

periphery, *n.* périphérie *f.*

perish, *vb.* périr.

perishable, *adj.* périssable.

perjury, *n.* parjure *m.*

permanent, *adj.* permanent.

permeate, *vb.* filtrer.

permissible, *adj.* admissible.

permission, *n.* permission *f.*

permit, 1. n. permis m. **2.** vb. permettre.

pernicious, adj. pernicieux.

peroxide, n. eau (f.) oxygénée.

perpendicular, adj. perpendiculaire, vertical.

perpetrate, vb. perpétrer.

perpetual, adj. perpétuel.

perplex, vb. mettre dans la perplexité.

perplexity, n. perplexité f., embarras m.

persecute, vb. persécuter.

persecution, n. persécution f.

perseverance, n. persévérance f.

persevere, vb. persévérer.

Persian, adj. persan; **(P. Gulf)** golfe (m.) persique.

persist, vb. persister.

persistent, adj. persistant.

person, n. personne f.

personage, n. personnage m.

personal, adj. personnel.

personal computer, n. ordinateur (m.) personnel.

personality, n. personnalité f.

personally, adv. personnellement.

personnel, n. personnel m.

perspective, n. perspective f.

perspiration, n. transpiration f.

perspire, vb. transpirer.

persuade, vb. persuader.

persuasive, adj. persuasif.

pertain, vb. appartenir.

pertinent, adj. pertinent.

perturb, vb. troubler.

Peru, n. Pérou m.

peruse, vb. lire attentivement.

pervade, vb. pénétrer.

perverse, adj. entêté (dans l'erreur).

perversion, n. perversion f.

pessimism, n. pessimisme m.

pester, vb. importuner.

pestilence, n. pestilence f.

pet, n. (animal) animal (m.) familier.

petal, n. pétale m.

petition, n. pétition f.

petrified, adj. mort de peur.

petroleum, n. pétrole m.

petticoat, n. jupon m.

petty, adj. insignifiant.

petulant, adj. boudeur.

pew, n. banc (m.) (d'église).

phantom, n. fantôme m.

pharmacist, n. pharmacien m.

pharmacy, n. pharmacie f.

phase, n. phase f.

phenomenal, adj. phénoménal.

phenomenon, n. phénomène m.

philanthropy, n. philanthropie f.

Philippines, n. Philippines f.pl.

philosopher, n. philosophe m.

philosophical, adj. philosophique.

philosophy, n. philosophie f.

phobia, n. phobie f.

phone, 1. n. téléphone m. **2.** vb. téléphoner.

phone booth, n. cabine (f.) téléphonique.

phonetics, n. phonétique f.

phonograph, n. phonographe m.

photocopier, n. photocopieur m.

photocopy, 1. n. photocopie f. **2.** vb. photocopier.

photograph, photography, n. photographie f.

photographer, n. photographe m.

phrase, n. expression f.; (gramm.) bout (m.) de phrase.

physical, adj. physique.

physical therapy, n. kinésithérapie f.

physician, n. médecin m.

physics, n. physique f.

physiology, n. physiologie f.

pianist, n. pianiste m.f.

piano, n. piano m.

pick, 1. vb. (choose) choisir; (gather) cueillir. **2.** n. pioche f.

pickles, n. conserves (f.pl.) au vinaigre.

picnic, n. pique-nique m.

picture, n. tableau m.; (motion picture) film m.

picturesque, adj. pittoresque.

pie, n. tarte f.

piece, n. morceau m.

pier, n. jetée f.; quai m.

pierce, vb. percer.

piety, n. piété f.

pig, n. cochon m.

pigeon, n. pigeon m.

pigeonhole, n. (for papers, etc.) case f.

pigment, n. pigment m.

pigtail, n. natte f.

pile, 1. n. (construction) pieu m.; (heap) tas m. **2.** vb. entasser.

pilgrim, n. pèlerin m.

pilgrimage, n. pèlerinage m.

pill, n. pilule f.

pillage, 1. n. pillage m. **2.** vb. piller.

pillar, n. pilier m.

pillow, n. oreiller m.

pillowcase, n. taie (f.) d'oreiller.

pilot, n. pilote m.

pimp, n. maquereau m., souteneur m.

pimple, n. bouton m.

pin, 1. n. épingle f. **2.** vb. épingler.

pinball, n. flipper m.

pinch, vb. pincer.

pine, 1. n. pin m. **2.** vb. languir.

pineapple, n. ananas m.

pink, adj. and n. rose m.

pinnacle, n. pinacle m.

pint, n. pinte f.

pioneer, n. pionnier m.

pious, adj. pieux.

pipe, n. tuyau m.; (smoking) pipe f.

pipeline, n. pipeline m.

piper, n. (bagpipe) joueur (m.) de cornemuse.

piquant, adj. piquant.

pirate, n. pirate m.

pistol, n. pistolet m.

piston, n. piston m.

pit, n. fosse f.

pitch, 1. n. (substance) poix f.; (throw) jet m.; (height) hauteur f.; (music) ton m. **2.** vb. (throw) lancer.

pitcher, n. (vessel) cruche f.; (baseball) lanceur m.

pitfall, n. trappe f.

pitiful, adj. pitoyable.

pitiless, adj. impitoyable.

pity, 1. n. pitié f.; (what a p.!) quel dommage! **2.** vb. plaindre.

pivot, n. pivot m., axe m.

pizza, n. pizza f.

placate, vb. calmer.

place, 1. n. endroit m.; (locality) lieu m.; (position occupied) place f. **2.** vb. mettre.

placid, adj. placide.

plagiarize, vb. plagier.

plague, n. (disease) peste f.; (fig.) fléau m.

plaid, n. (blanket) plaid m.; (textile) tartan m.

plain, 1. n. plaine f. **2.** adj. (clear) clair; (simple) simple; (of person) quelconque.

plaintiff, n. demandeur m., plaignant m.

plan, 1. n. plan m. **2.** vb. prévoir, projeter.

plane, n. (surface) plan m.; (tool) rabot m.; (tree) platane m.; (airplane) avion m.

planet, n. planète f.

plank, n. planche f.

planning, n. planification f.; (family p.) planning (m.) familial.

plant, 1. n. plante f. **2.** vb. planter.

plantation, n. plantation f.

planter, n. planteur m.

plasma, n. plasma m.

plaster, n. plâtre m.

plastic, adj. plastique.

plate, n. plaque f.; (for eating) assiette f.

plateau, n. plateau m.

platform, n. plate-forme f.; (railroad) quai m.

platinum, n. platine f.

platonic, adj. platonique.

platoon, n. (military) section f.

platter, n. plat m.

plausible, adj. plausible.

play, 1. n. jeu m.; (drama) pièce (f.) de théâtre. **2.** vb. jouer; (game) jouer à; (instrument) jouer de.

player, n. jouer m.; (theater) acteur m.

playful, adj. enjoué.

playground, n. (children) terrain (m.) de jeu.

playmate, n. camarade (m.f.) de jeu.

playwright, n. dramaturge m.

plea, n. défense f.; (excuse) excuse f.

plead, vb. plaider; (allege) alléguer.

pleasant, adj. agréable.

please, vb. plaire à; (satisfy) contenter; (if you p.) s'il vous plaît.

pleasure, n. plaisir m.

pleat, n. pli m.

pledge, n. gage m.; (promise) engagement m.

plentiful, adj. abondant.

plenty, n. abondance f.

pliable, adj. pliable.

pliers, n. pinces f.pl.

plight, n. état m.

plot, 1. n. (literature) intrigue f.; (conspiracy) complot m. **2.** vb. comploter.

plow, 1. n. charrue f. **2.** vb. labourer.

pluck, n. courage m.

plug, n. tampon m.; (electric) prise (f.) de courant.

plum, n. prune f.

plumber, n. plombier m.

plume, n. panache m.

plump, adj. grassouillet.

plunder, vb. piller.

plunge, 1. n. plongeon m. **2.** vb. plonger.

pluperfect, n. plus-que-parfait m.

plural, adj. and n. pluriel m.

plus, n. plus m.

pneumonia, n. pneumonie f.

poach, vb. (of eggs) pocher.

poacher, n. braconnier m.

pocket, n. poche f.

pocketbook, n. sac (m.) à main.

podiatrist, n. podologue m.f.

poem, n. poésie f.; (long) poème f.

poet, n. poète m.

poetic, adj. poétique.

poetry, n. poésie f.

poignant, adj. poignant.

point, 1. n. point m.; (sharp end) pointe f. **2.** vb. (gun, etc.) pointer; (indicate) désigner.

pointed, adj. pointu; (ironical) mordant.

poise, n. équilibre m.

poison, 1. n. poison m. **2.** vb. empoisonner.

poisonous, adj. empoisonné; (plant) vénéneux; (animal) venimeux.

Poland, n. Pologne f.

polar, adj. polaire.

polar bear, n. ours (m.) blanc.

Pole, n. Polonais m.

pole, n. (geography) pôle m.; (wood) perche f.

polemic, n. polémique f.

police, n. police f.

policeman, n. agent (m.) de police.

policy, n. politique f.; (insurance) police f.

polio, n. polio f.

Polish, adj. and n. polonais m.

polish, vb. polir; (shoes) cirer.

polite, adj. poli.

politic, political, adj. politique.

politician, n. politicien m.

politics, n. politique f.

poll, n. (voting) scrutin m.; (opinion) sondage m.

pollen, n. pollen m.

pollute, vb. polluer.

polygamy, n. polygamie f.

pomegranate, n. grenade f.

pomp, n. pompe f.

pompous, adj. pompeux.

pond, n. étang m.

ponder, vb. réfléchir.

ponderous, adj. pesant.

pony, n. poney m.

poodle, n. caniche m.

pool, n. mare f.; (swimming) piscine f.

poor, adj. pauvre.

pop, n. petit bruit (m.) sec.

pope, n. pape m.

popular, adj. populaire.

popularity, n. popularité f.

population, n. population f.

porcelain, n. porcelaine f.

porch, n. véranda f.

porcupine, n. porc-épic m.

pore, 1. n. pore m. **2.** vb. (p. over) s'absorber dans.

pork, n. porc m.

pornography, n. pornographie f.

porous, adj. poreux.

porpoise, n. marsouin m.

port, n. (harbor) port m.; (naut.) bâbord m.; (wine) porto m.

portable, adj. portatif.

portal, n. portail m.

portfolio, n. portefeuille m.

portion, n. portion f.

portrait, n. portrait m.

portray, vb. (paint) peindre; (describe) dépeindre.

Portugal, n. Portugal m.

Portuguese, 1. n. (person) Portugais m.; (language) portugais m. **2.** adj. portugais.

pose, 1. n. pose f. **2.** vb. poser.

position, n. position f.

positive, 1. n. positif m. **2.** adj. positif.

possess, vb. posséder.

possession, n. possession f.

possibility, n. possibilité f.

possible, adj. possible.

possibly, adv. il est possible que . . .; (perhaps) peut-être.

post, 1. n. (mail) poste f.; (wood) poteau m.; (place) poste m. **2.** vb. (mail) mettre à la poste; (placard) afficher.

postage, n. affranchissement m.

postal, adj. postal.

post card, n. carte (f.) postale.

poster, n. affiche f.

posterior, adj. postérieur.

posterity, n. postérité f.

post office, n. bureau (m.) de poste.

postman, n. facteur m.

postmark, n. cachet (m.) de la poste.

postpone, vb. remettre.

postscript, n. post-scriptum m.

posture, n. posture f.

postwar, adj. d'après-guerre.

pot, n. pot m.; (saucepan) marmite f.; (marijuana) herbe f., kif m.

potato, n. pomme (f.) de terre; **(French-fried p.s)** frites f.pl.

potent, adj. puissant.

potential, adj. and n. potentiel m.

pottery, n. poterie f.

pouch, n. sac m.

poultry, n. volaille f.

pound, n. livre f.

pour, vb. verser; (rain) tomber à verse.

pout, vb. bouder.

poverty, n. pauvreté f.

powder, n. poudre f.

power, n. pouvoir m.; (nation, mathematics) puissance f.

powerful, adj. puissant.

powerless, adj. impuissant.

practical, adj. pratique.

practically, adv. pratiquement.

practice, 1. n. (exercise) exercice m.; (habit) habitude f.; (not theory) pratique f. **2.** vb. pratiquer; (piano, etc.) s'exercer (à).

practiced, adj. expérimenté.

pragmatic, adj. pragmatique.

prairie, n. savane f.

praise, 1. n. éloge m. **2.** vb. louer.

prank, n. fredaine f.

pray, vb. prier.

prayer, n. prière f.

preach, vb. prêcher.

preacher, n. prédicateur m.

precarious, adj. précaire.

precaution, n. précaution f.

precede, vb. précéder.

precedent, n. précédent m.

precept, n. précepte m.

precinct, n. circonscription f.

precious, adj. précieux.

precipice, n. précipice m.

precipitate, vb. précipiter.

precise, adj. précis.

precision, n. précision f.

preclude, vb. empêcher.

precocious, adj. précoce.

precondition, n. condition (f.) requise.

predecessor, n. prédécesseur m.

predestination, n. prédestination f.

predicament, n. situation (f.) difficile.

predict, vb. prédire.

predispose, vb. prédisposer.

predominant, adj. prédominant.

preempt, vb. (acquire) acquérir d'avance; (forestall) prévenir.

prefabricate, vb. préfabriquer.

preface, n. préface f.

prefer, vb. préférer.

preferable, adj. préférable.

preference, n. préférence f.

prefix, n. préfixe m.

pregnant, adj. enceinte.

prejudice, n. préjugé m.

preliminary, adj. préliminaire.

prelude, n. prélude m.

premarital, adj. avant le mariage.

premature, adj. prématuré.

premeditate, vb. préméditer.

premier, n. premier ministre m.

première, n. première f.

premise, n. (place) lieux m.pl.; (logic) prémisse f.

premium, n. prix m.

preoccupation, n. préoccupation f.

preparation, n. préparation f.; préparatifs m.pl.

preparatory, adj. préparatoire.

prepare, vb. préparer, tr.

preponderant, adj. prépondérant.

preposition, n. préposition f.

preposterous, adj. absurde.

prerequisite, n. nécessité (f.) préalable.

prerogative, n. prérogative f.
prescribe, vb. prescrire.
prescription, n. prescription f.; (medical) ordonnance f.
presence, n. présence f.
present, 1. adj. présent. **2.** n. présent m.; (gift) cadeau m. **3.** vb. présenter.
presentable, adj. présentable.
presentation, n. présentation f.
presently, adv. tout à l'heure.
preservative, n. préservateur m., conservateur m.
preserve, 1. n. (jam) confiture f. **2.** vb. (protect) préserver; (keep) conserver.
preside, vb. présider.
president, n. président m.
press, 1. n. presse f. **2.** vb. presser; (iron) repasser.
press conference, n. conférence (f.) de presse.
pressure, n. pression f.
prestige, n. prestige m.
presume, vb. présumer.
presumptuous, adj. présomptueux.
pretend, vb. (claim, aspire) prétendre; (feign) simuler.
pretense, n. faux semblant m.
pretentious, adj. prétentieux.
pretext, n. prétexte m.
pretty, adj. joli.
prevail, vb. prévaloir; **(p. upon)** décider.
prevalent, adj. répandu.
prevent, vb. (impede) empêcher; (forestall) prévenir.
prevention, n. empêchement m.
preventive, adj. préventif.
preview, n. avant-première f.
previous, adj. antérieur.
prewar, adj. d'avant-guerre.
prey, n. proie f.
price, n. prix m.
priceless, adj. inestimable.
prick, 1. n. piqûre f. **2.** vb. piquer.
pride, n. orgueil m.
priest, n. prêtre m.
prim, adj. guindé.
primarily, adv. principalement.
primary, adj. premier; (school, geology) primaire.
prime, 1. n. comble m. **2.** adj. pre-

mier, de première qualité. **3.** vb. amorcer.
primitive, adj. primitif.
prince, n. prince m.
princess, n. princesse f.
principal, adj. principal.
principle, n. principe m.
print, 1. n. (mark) empreinte f.; (book) impression f.; (photo) épreuve f. **2.** vb. imprimer.
printout, n. feuille (f.) imprimée produite par un ordinateur.
prior, 1. adj. antérieur. **2.** adv. **(p. to doing)** avant de faire.
priority, n. priorité f.
prism, n. prisme m.
prison, n. prison f.
prisoner, n. prisonnier m.
privacy, n. intimité f., solitude f., vie (f.) privée.
private, adj. particulier; (not public) privé.
privation, n. privation f.
privilege, n. privilège m.
prize, n. prix m.
probability, n. probabilité f.
probable, adj. probable.
probation, n. **(on p.)** en liberté (f.) surveillée.
probe, vb. sonder.
problem, n. problème m.
procedure, n. procédé m.
proceed, vb. procéder; (advance) avancer.
process, n. (method) procédé m., processus m.; (progress) développement m.
procession, n. cortège m.; (religious) procession f.
proclaim, vb. proclamer.
proclamation, n. proclamation f.
procrastinate, vb. différer.
procure, vb. procurer.
prodigal, adj. and n. prodigue m.
prodigy, n. prodige m.
produce, vb. produire.
product, n. produit m.
production, n. production f.
production line, n. chaîne (f.) (de fabrication).
productive, adj. productif.
profane, adj. profane.
profess, vb. professer.
profession, n. profession f.
professional, adj. professionnel.

professor, n. professeur m.

proficient, adj. capable.

profile, n. profil m.

profit, 1. n. profit m. **2.** vb. profiter.

profitable, adj. profitable.

profound, adj. profond.

profuse, adj. (of thing) profus; (of person) prodigue.

program, 1. n. programme m. **2.** vb. programmer.

programming, n. programmation f.

progress, n. progrès m.; (motion forward) marche f.

progressive, adj. progressif.

prohibit, vb. défendre.

prohibition, n. défense f.

prohibitive, adj. prohibitif.

project, 1. n. projet m. **2.** vb. projeter; (jut out) faire saillie.

projection, n. projection f.; (jutting out) saillie f.

projector, n. projecteur m.

proletariat, n. prolétariat m.

proliferation, n. prolifération f.

prologue, n. prologue m.

prolong, vb. prolonger.

prominent, adj. saillant.

promiscuous, adj. (indiscriminate) sans distinction.

promise, 1. n. promesse f. **2.** vb. promettre.

promote, vb. (raise) promouvoir; (encourage) encourager.

promotion, n. promotion f.

prompt, 1. adj. prompt. **2.** n. (computer) message (m.) (de guidage). **3.** vb. provoquer, (theater) souffler.

pronoun, n. pronom m.

pronounce, vb. prononcer.

pronunciation, n. prononciation f.

proof, n. (evidence) preuve f.; (test) épreuve f.

prop, n. appui m.

propaganda, n. propagande f.

propagate, vb. propager, tr.

propel, vb. propulser.

propeller, n. hélice f.

proper, adj. propre; (respectable, fitting) convenable.

property, n. propriété f.

prophecy, n. prophétie f.

prophesy, vb. prophétiser.

prophet, n. prophète m.

prophetic, adj. prophétique.

proportion, n. proportion f.

proportionate, adj. proportionné.

proposal, n. proposition f.; demande (f.) en mariage.

propose, vb. proposer, tr.

proposition, n. (proposal, grammar) proposition f.; (undertaking) affaire f.

proprietor, n. propriétaire m.f.

prosaic, adj. prosaïque.

proscribe, vb. proscrire.

prose, n. prose f.

prosecute, vb. poursuivre.

prosecution, n. poursuites (f.pl.) judiciaires.

prosecuting attorney, n. procureur m.

prospect, n. perspective f.

prospective, adj. en perspective.

prosper, vb. prospérer.

prosperity, n. prospérité f.

prosperous, adj. prospère.

prostate, n. prostate f.

prostitute, 1. n. prostituée f. **2.** vb. prostituer.

prostrate, adj. prosterné.

protagonist, n. protagoniste m.

protect, vb. protéger.

protection, n. protection f.

protective, adj. protecteur.

protector, n. protecteur m.

protégé, n. protégé m.

protein, n. protéine f.

protest, 1. n. protestation f.; (comm.) protêt m. **2.** vb. protester.

Protestant, 1. n. Protestant m. **2.** adj. protestant.

protocol, n. protocole m.

protrude, vb. saillir.

proud, adj. fier.

prove, vb. prouver; (test) éprouver.

proverb, n. proverbe m.

provide (with) vb. pourvoir (de), tr.

providence, n. (foresight) prévoyance f.; (divine) providence f.

province, n. province f.

provincial, adj. and n. provincial m.

provision, n. (stock) provision f.

provocation, n. provocation f.

provoke, vb. provoquer; (irritate) irriter.

prowess, n. prouesse f.
prowl, vb. rôder.
proximity, n. proximité f.
prude, n. prude f.
prudence, n. prudence f.
prudent, adj. prudent.
prune, n. pruneau m.
Prussia, n. Prusse f.
Prussian, 1. n. Prussien m. **2.** adj. prussien.
pry, vb. fureter.
psalm, n. psaume m.
psychedelic, adj. psychédélique.
psychiatry, n. psychiatrie f.
psychoanalysis, n. psychanalyse f.
psychological, adj. psychologique.
psychology, n. psychologie f.
psychothérapie, n. psychothérapie f.
ptomaine, n. ptomaïne f.
public, 1. n. public m. **2.** adj. public m., publique f.
publication, n. publication f.
publicity, n. publicité f.
public transport, n. transports (m.pl.) en commun.
publish, vb. publier.
publisher, n. éditeur m.
pudding, n. pouding m.
puddle, n. flaque f.
puff, n. (smoke etc.) bouffée f.
pugnacious, adj. batailleur, combattif.
pull, vb. tirer.
pulley, n. poulie f.
pulp, n. pulpe f.
pulpit, n. chaire f.
pulsar, n. pulsar m.
pulsate, vb. battre.
pulse, n. pouls m.
pump, 1. n. pompe f. **2.** vb. pomper.

pumpkin, n. potiron m.; citrouille f.
pun, n. calembour m.
punch, 1. n. (tool) poinçon m.; (blow) coup (m.) de poing; (beverage) punch m. **2.** vb. (pierce) percer; (pummel) gourmer.
punctual, adj. ponctuel.
punctuate, vb. ponctuer.
puncture, n. piqûre f.
punish, vb. punir.
punishment, n. punition f.
pupil, n. (school) élève m.f.; (eye) pupille f.
puppet, n. marionnette f.
puppy, n. petit chien m.
purchase, 1. n. achat m. **2.** vb. acheter.
pure, adj. pur.
puree, n. purée f.
purge, vb. purger.
purify, vb. purifier.
puritan, n. puritain m.
purity, n. pureté f.
purple, adj. violet.
purpose, n. but m.; (to the p.) à propos.
purposely, adv. exprès.
purse, n. bourse f.
pursue, vb. poursuivre.
pursuit, n. poursuite f.; (occupation) occupation f.; (p. plane) avion (m.) de chasse.
push, 1. n. poussée f. **2.** vb. pousser.
pussy(cat), n. minet m.
put, vb. mettre.
puzzle, 1. n. problème m. **2.** vb. embarrasser.
pyramid, n. pyramide f.
Pyrenees, n. Pyrénées f.pl.
python, n. python m.

Q

quadrangle, n. cour f.
quadraphonic, adj. quadriphonique.
quail, n. caille f.
quaint, adj. (strange) étrange.
quake, vb. trembler.
qualification, n. (reservation) réserve f.; (aptitude) compétence f.; (description) qualification f.
qualify, vb. qualifier; (modify) modifier.
quality, n. qualité f.
qualm, n. scrupule m.
quandary, n. dilemme m.
quantity, n. quantité f.

quarantine, *n.* quarantaine *f.*

quarrel, 1. *n.* querelle *f.* **2.** *vb.* se quereller.

quarry, *n.* carrière *f.*

quart, *n.* (approximately) litre *m.*

quarter, *n.* quart *m.;* (district, moon, beef) quartier *m.*

quarterly, *adj.* trimestriel.

quartet, *n.* quatuor *m.*

quartz, *n.* quartz *m.*

quasar, *n.* quasar *m.*

quaver, *vb.* chevroter.

queen, *n.* reine *f.*

queer, *adj.* bizarre.

quell, *vb.* réprimer.

quench, *vb.* éteindre.

querulous, *adj.* récriminateur.

query, *n.* question *f.*

quest, *n.* recherche *f.*

question, 1. *n.* question *f.* **2.** *vb.* interroger; (raise questions) mettre en doute.

questionable, *adj.* douteux.

question mark, *n.* point *(m.)* d'interrogation.

questionnaire, *n.* questionnaire *m.*

quibble, *vb.* ergoter.

quick, 1. *adj.* rapide; (lively) vif. **2.** *adv.* vite.

quicken, *vb.* accélérer.

quiet, 1. *n.* tranquillité *f.* **2.** *adj.* tranquille.

quilt, *n.* courtepointe *f.*

quinine, *n.* quinine *f.*

quip, *n.* mot *(m.)* piquant.

quit, *vb.* quitter.

quite, *adv.* tout à fait.

quiver, *vb.* trembloter.

quiz, 1. *n.* petit examen *m.* **2.** *vb.* examiner.

quorum, *n.* quorum *m.*

quota, *n.* (share) quote-part *f.;* (immigration, etc.) contingent *m.*

quotation, *n.* citation *f.; (comm.)* cote *f.*

quote, *vb.* citer.

quotient, *n.* quotient *m.*

R

rabbi, *n.* rabbin *m.*

rabbit, *n.* lapin *m.*

rabble, *n.* tourbe *f.*

rabid, *adj.* enragé.

rabies, *n.* rage *f.*

race, 1. *n.* (people) race *f.;* (contest) course *f.* **2.** *vb.* lutter à la course (avec).

race-track, *n.* piste *f.*

racial, *adj.* racial.

racism, *n.* racisme *m.*

rack, *n.* râtelier *m.;* (torture) chevalet *(m.)* de torture.

racket, *n.* (tennis) raquette *f.;* (noise) tintamarre *m.*

radar, *n.* radar *m.*

radiance, *n.* éclat *m.*

radiant, *adj.* radieux.

radiate, *vb.* irradier.

radiation, *n.* rayonnement *m.*

radiator, *n.* radiateur *m.*

radical, *adj. and n.* radical *m.*

radio, *n.* télégraphie *(f.)* sans fil (commonly T.S.F.), radio *f.*

radioactive, *adj.* radio-actif.

radish, *n.* radis *m.*

radium, *n.* radium *m.*

radius, *n.* rayon *m.*

raft, *n.* radeau *m.*

rafter, *n.* chevron *m.*

rag, *n.* chiffon *m.*

rage, *n.* rage *f.*

ragged, *adj.* en haillons.

ragweed, *n.* ambroisie *f.*

raid, 1. *n.* (police) descente *f.; (mil.)* raid *m.* **2.** *vb.* faire un raid sur.

rail, *n.* (bar) barre *f.;* (railroad) rail *m.*

railroad, *n.* chemin *(m.)* de fer.

railway station, *n.* gare *f.*

rain, 1. *n.* pluie *f.* **2.** *vb.* pleuvoir.

rainbow, *n.* arc-en-ciel *m.*

raincoat, *n.* imperméable *m.*

rainfall, *n.* chute *(f.)* de pluie.

rain forest, *n.* forêt *(f.)* tropicale humide.

rainy, *adj.* pluvieux.

raise, *vb.* (bring up, erect, promote) élever; (lift) lever; (plants) cultiver.

raisin, *n.* raisin *(m.)* sec.

rake, 1. *n.* râteau *m.* **2.** *vb.* râteler.

rally, *n.* (mil.) ralliement *m.;* (meeting) rassemblement *m.*

ram, *n.* bélier *m.*

ramble, *vb.* rôder; (speech) divaguer.

ramp, *n.* rampe *f.*

rampart, *n.* rempart *m.*

rancid, *adj.* rance.

random, *n.* hasard *m.*

range, 1. *n.* (scope) étendue *f.;* (mountains) chaîne *f.;* (distance) portée *f.;* (stove) fourneau *m.* **2.** *vb.* s'étendre.

rank, 1. *n.* rang *m.* **2.** *vb.* ranger, tr.

ransack, *vb.* (search) fouiller; (pillage) saccager.

ransom, *n.* rançon *f.*

rant, *vb.* fulminer.

rap, 1. *n.* coup *m.;* **(r. music)** rap *m.* or *f.* **2.** *vb.* frapper.

rape, *n.* viol *m.*

rapid, *adj.* and *n.* rapide *m.*

rapture, *n.* ravissement *m.*

rare, *adj.* rare; (meat) saignant.

rascal, *n.* coquin *m.*

rash, 1. *n.* éruption *f.* **2.** *adj.* téméraire.

raspberry, *n.* framboise *f.*

rat, *n.* rat *m.*

rate, 1. *n.* taux *m.;* (speed) vitesse *f.;* **(at any r.)** en tout cas; **(first-r.)** de premier ordre. **2.** *vb.* estimer.

rather, *adv.* plutôt.

ratify, *vb.* ratifier.

rating, *n.* classement *m.;* **(TV r.s)** Audimat *m.*

ration, *n.* ration *f.*

rational, *adj.* raisonnable; (mathematics, philosophy) rationnel.

rat race, *n.* foire *(f.)* empoigne.

rattle, *n.* (toy) hochet *m.;* (noise) fracas *m.*

raucous, *adj.* rauque.

rave, *vb.* délirer; **(r. about)** s'extasier sur.

raven, *n.* corbeau *m.*

ravenous, *adj.* vorace.

raw, *adj.* cru.

ray, *n.* rayon *m.*

rayon, *n.* rayonne *f.*

razor, *n.* rasoir *m.*

reach, 1. *n.* portée *f.* **2.** *vb.* atteindre; (extend) étendre, *tr.;* (arrive) arriver à.

react, *vb.* réagir.

reaction, *n.* réaction *f.*

reactionary, *adj.* réactionnaire.

read, *vb.* lire.

reader, *n.* (person) lecteur *m.;* (book) livre *(m.)* de lecture.

readily, *adv.* promptement.

ready, *adj.* prêt.

real, *adj.* réel.

realist, *n.* réaliste *m.f.*

reality, *n.* réalité *f.*

realization, *n.* réalisation *f.*

realize, *vb.* (notice) s'apercevoir de; (make real) réaliser, *tr.*

really, *adv.* vraiment.

realm, *n.* royaume *m.*

Realtor, *n.* agent *(m.)* immobilier.

reap, *vb.* moissonner.

rear, 1. *n.* (hind part) queue *f.;* (mil.) arrière-garde *f.* **2.** *adj.* situé à l'arrière. **3.** *vb.* élever.

rear-view mirror, *n.* rétroviseur *m.*

reason, 1. *n.* raison *f.* **2.** *vb.* raisonner.

reasonable, *adj.* raisonnable.

reassure, *vb.* rassurer.

rebate, *n.* rabais *m.*

rebel, 1. *adj.* and *n.* rebelle *m.f.* **2.** *vb.* se rebeller.

rebellion, *n.* rébellion *f.*

rebellious, *adj.* rebelle.

rebirth, *n.* renaissance *f.*

rebound, *n.* rebond *f.*

rebuff, *vb.* repousser.

rebuke, 1. *n.* réprimande *f.* **2.** *vb.* réprimander.

rebuttal, *n.* réfutation *f.*

recall, *vb.* (call back) rappeler; (remember) se rappeler.

recap, *vb.* récapituler.

recede, *vb.* s'éloigner.

receipt, *n.* (for payment) quittance *f.*

receive, *vb.* recevoir.

receiver, *n.* (phone) récepteur *m.*

recent, *adj.* récent.

receptacle, *n.* réceptacle *m.;* récipient *m.*

reception, *n.* réception *f.;* (welcoming) accueil *m.*

receptive, *adj.* réceptif.

recess, n. recoin m.; (parliament) vacances f.pl.; (school) récréation f.

recession, n. récession f.

recipe, n. recette f.

reciprocal, adj. réciproque.

reciprocate, vb. payer de retour.

recite, vb. réciter.

reckless, adj. téméraire.

reckon, vb. compter.

reclaim, v. (person) corriger; (land) défricher.

recline, vb. reposer, tr.

recognition, n. reconnaissance f.

recognize, vb. reconnaître.

recoil, vb. reculer.

recollect, vb. se rappeler.

recommend, vb. recommander.

recommendation, n. recommandation f.

recompense, n. récompense f.

reconcile, vb. réconcilier.

record, 1. n. (register) registre m.; (mention) mention f.; (known facts of person) antécédents m.pl.; (sports) record m.; (phonograph) disque m. 2. vb. enregistrer.

record player, n. tourne-disques m.

recount, vb. raconter.

recoup, vb. récupérer.

recover, vb. recouvrer m.; (from illness) se rétablir.

recovery, n. recouvrement m.; (health) rétablissement m.

recreation, n. récréation f.

recruit, 1. n. recrue f. 2. vb. recruter.

rectangle, n. rectangle m.

rectify, vb. rectifier.

recuperate, vb. se rétablir, intr.

recur, vb. revenir.

recycle, vb. recycler.

recycling, n. recyclage m.

red, adj. and n. rouge m.

red tape, n. paperasse f.

redeem, vb. racheter.

redemption, n. rachat m.; (theology) rédemption f.

redo, vb. refaire.

redress, 1. n. justice f.; réparation f. 2. vb. redresser, réparer; faire justice à.

reduce, vb. réduire.

reduction, n. réduction f.; (on price) remise f.

redundant, adj. superflu.

reed, n. roseau m.; (music) anche f.

reef, n. récif m.

reel, n. bobine f.

refer, vb. référer.

referee, n. arbitre m.

reference, n. référence f.

referendum, n. référendum m.

refill, vb. remplir (à nouveau).

refine, vb. raffiner.

refinement, n. raffinement m.

reflect, vb. réfléchir.

reflection, n. réflexion f.

reflex, adj. and n. réflexe m.

reform, 1. n. réforme f. 2. vb. réformer, tr.

reformation, n. réforme f.

refractory, adj. réfractaire.

refrain from, vb. se retenir de.

refresh, vb. rafraîchir.

refreshment, n. rafraîchissement m.

refrigerator, n. frigidaire m.

refuge, n. refuge m.

refugee, n. réfugié m.

refund, 1. n. remboursement m. 2. vb. rembourser.

refurbish, vb. remettre à neuf.

refusal, n. refus m.

refuse, 1. n. rebut m. 2. vb. refuser.

refute, vb. réfuter.

regain, vb. regagner.

regal, adj. royal.

regard, 1. n. égard m.; (r.s, compliments) amitiés f.pl. 2. vb. regarder.

regardless of, adj. sans tenir compte de.

regent, adj. and n. régent m.

regime, n. régime m.

regiment, n. régiment m.

region, n. région f.

register, 1. n. registre m. 2. vb. enregistrer; (letter) recommander.

registration, n. enregistrement m.

regret, 1. n. regret m. 2. vb. regretter.

regroup, vb. (se) regrouper.

regular, adj. régulier.

regularity, n. régularité f.

regulate, vb. régler.

regulation, n. règlement m.

regulator, n. régulateur m.

rehabilitate, *vb.* réhabiliter.
rehearse, *vb.* répéter.
reign, 1. *n.* règne *m.* **2.** *vb.* régner.
reimburse, *vb.* rembourser.
rein, *n.* rêne *f.*
reindeer, *n.* renne *m.*
reinforce, *vb.* renforcer.
reinforcement, *n.* renfort *m.*
reinstate, *vb.* rétablir, réintégrer.
reject, *vb.* rejeter.
rejoice, *vb.* réjouir, *tr.*
rejoin, *vb.* (join again) rejoindre; (reply) répliquer.
relapse, 1. *n.* rechute *f.* **2.** *vb.* rechuter.
relate, *vb.* raconter; (have reference to) se rapporter (à); (r. to) entrer en rapport avec.
relation, *n.* relation *f.;* (relative) parent *m.*
relationship, *n.* rapport *m.,* relations *f.pl.*
relative, 1. *n.* parent *m.* **2.** *adj.* relatif.
relax, *vb.* relâcher.
relay, 1. *n.* relais *m.* **2.** *vb.* relayer.
release, 1. *n.* délivrance *f.* **2.** *vb.* libérer.
relent, *vb.* se laisser attendrir.
relevant, *adj.* pertinent.
reliability, *n.* sûreté *f.*
reliable, *adj.* digne de confiance.
reliant, *adj.* confiant.
relic, *n.* relique *f.*
relief, *n.* (ease) soulagement *m.;* (help) secours *m.;* (projection) relief *m.*
relieve, *vb.* (ease) soulager; (help) secourir.
religion, *n.* religion *f.*
religious, *adj.* religieux.
relinquish, *vb.* abandonner.
relish, 1. *n.* goût *m.* **2.** *vb.* goûter.
relocate, *vb.* s'installer ailleurs.
reluctant, *adj.* peu disposé (à).
rely upon, *vb.* compter sur.
remain, *vb.* rester.
remainder, *n.* reste *m.*
remark, 1. *n.* remarque *f.* **2.** *vb.* remarquer.
remarkable, *adj.* remarquable.
remedy, 1. *n.* remède *m.* **2.** *vb.* remédier à.
remember, *vb.* se souvenir de.
remembrance, *n.* souvenir *m.*

remind of, *vb.* rappeler à (person recalling).
reminisce, *vb.* raconter ses souvenirs.
remiss, *adj.* negligent.
remission, *n.* rémission *f.*
remit, *vb.* remettre.
remnant, *n.* reste *m.,* vestige *m.,* (of cloth) coupon *m.*
remorse, *n.* remords *m.*
remote, *adj.* éloigné; (vague) vague.
removable, *adj.* transportable.
removal, *n.* enlèvement *m.*
remove, *vb.* enlever.
rend, *vb.* déchirer.
render, *vb.* rendre.
rendezvous, *n.* rendez-vous *f.*
renew, *vb.* renouveler.
renewal, *n.* renouvellement *m.*
renounce, *vb.* (give up) renoncer à; (repudiate) répudier.
renovate, *vb.* renouveler.
renown, *n.* renommée *f.*
rent, 1. *n.* loyer *m.* **2.** *vb.* louer.
repair, 1. *n.* réparation *f.* **2.** *vb.* réparer.
repay, *vb.* (give back) rendre; (refund) rembourser.
repeat, *vb.* répéter.
repel, *vb.* repousser.
repent, *vb.* se repentir (de).
repentance, *n.* repentir *m.*
repertoire, repertory, *n.* répertoire *m.*
repetition, *n.* répétition *f.*
replace, *vb.* (place again) replacer; (take place of) remplacer.
replay, *n.* répétition *f.*
replenish, *vb.* réapprovisionner.
reply, 1. *n.* réponse *f.* **2.** *vb.* répondre.
report, 1. *n.* rapport *m.;* (rumor) bruit *m.* **2.** *vb.* rapporter; (inform against) dénoncer.
report card, *n.* bulletin *(m.)* scolaire.
repose, *n.* repos *m.*
represent, *vb.* représenter.
representation, *n.* représentation *f.*
representative, 1. *n.* représentant *m.;* (politics) député *m.* **2.** *adj.* représentatif.
repress, *vb.* réprimer.

reprimand, n. réprimande f.

reprisals, n. représailles f.pl.

reproach, 1. n. reproche m. **2.** vb. faire des reproches à.

reproduce, vb. reproduire, tr.

reproduction, n. reproduction f.

reproof, n. réprimande f.

reprove, vb. réprimander.

reptile, n. reptile m.

republic, n. république f.

republican, adj. and n. républicain m.

repudiate, vb. répudier.

repugnant, adj. répugnant.

repulse, vb. repousser.

repulsive, adj. répulsif.

reputation, n. réputation f.

repute, 1. n. renom m. **2.** vb. réputer.

request, 1. n. requête f. **2.** vb. demander.

require, vb. exiger.

requirement, n. exigence f.

requisite, adj. nécessaire.

requisition, n. réquisition f.

rescind, vb. annuler.

rescue, 1. n. délivrance f. **2.** vb. délivrer.

research, n. recherche f.

resemble, vb. ressembler à.

resent, vb. être froissé de.

reservation, n. réserve f.

reserve, 1. n. réserve f. **2.** vb. réserver.

reservoir, n. réservoir m.

reside, vb. résider.

residence, n. résidence f.

resident, 1. n. habitant m. **2.** adj. résidant.

resign, vb. résigner; (from post se démettre (de), démissionner.

resignation, n. résignation f.; (from post) démission f.

resist, vb. résister (à).

resistance, n. résistance f.

resolute, adj. résolu.

resolution, n. résolution f.

resolve, vb. résoudre.

resonant, adj. résonnant.

resort, 1. n. (resource) ressource f.; (recourse) recours m.; (place) lieu (m.) de séjour. **2.** vb. avoir recours.

resound, vb. résonner.

resource, n. ressource f.

respect, 1. n. respect m.; (reference) rapport m. **2.** vb. respecter.

respectable, adj. respectable.

respectful, adj. respectueux.

respective, adj. respectif.

respiration, n. respiration f.

respite, n. répit m.

respond, vb. répondre.

response, n. réponse f.

responsibility, n. responsabilité f.

responsible, adj. responsable.

rest, 1. n. (repose) repos m.; (remainder) reste m.; (the r., the others) les autres m.f.pl. **2.** vb. se reposer.

restaurant, n. restaurant m.

restful, adj. qui repose.

restive, adj. agité.

restless, adj. (anxious) inquiet.

restoration, n. restauration f.

restore, vb. remettre; (repair) restaurer.

restrain, vb. contenir.

restraint, n. contrainte f.

restrict, vb. restreindre.

result, 1. n. résultat m. **2.** vb. résulter.

resume, vb. reprendre.

résumé, n. résumé m.

resurrect, vb. ressusciter.

retail, n. détail m.

retain, vb. retenir.

retaliate, vb. user de représailles.

retard, vb. retarder.

retarded, adj. arriéré.

reticent, adj. réservé.

retina, n. rétine f.

retire, vb. se retirer.

retort, n. riposte f.

retract, vb. (se) rétracter.

retreat, 1. n. retraite f. **2.** vb. se retirer.

retribution, n. châtiment m.

retrieve, vb. recouvrer.

retrospect, n. renvoi m., (in r.) coup d'œil (m.) rétrospectif.

return, 1. n. retour m.; (returns, comm.) recettes f.pl. **2.** vb. (give back) rendre; (go back) retourner; (come back) revenir.

reunion, n. réunion f.

reunite, vb. réunir.

reveal, vb. révéler.

revel, vb. s'ébattre.

revelation, n. révélation f.

revelry, n. bacchanale f.

revenge, 1. n. vengeance f. **2.** vb. (r. oneself) se venger.

revenue, n. revenu m.

reverberate, vb. réverbérer, réfléchir, répercuter.

revere, vb. révérer.

reverence, n. révérence f.

reverend, adj. révérend.

reverent, adj. respectueux.

reverie, n. rêverie f.

reverse, 1. n. (opposite) contraire m.; (defeat, medal) revers m.; (gear) marche (f.) arrière. **2.** vb. renverser.

revert, vb. revenir.

review, n. revue f.

revise, vb. réviser.

revision, n. révision f.

revival, n. renaissance f.; (religious) réveil m., renouveau m.

revive, vb. revivre, intr.; faire revivre, tr.

revoke, vb. révoquer.

revolt, 1. n. révolte f. **2.** vb. se révolter.

revolution, n. révolution f.

revolutionary, adj. révolutionnaire.

revolve, vb. tourner, intr.

revolver, n. revolver m.

reward, 1. n. récompense f. **2.** vb. récompenser.

rewind, vb. rembobiner.

rheumatism, n. rhumatisme m.

Rhine, n. Rhin m.

Rhone, n. Rhône m.

rhinoceros, n. rhinocéros m.

rhubarb, n. rhubarbe f.

rhyme, 1. n. rime f. **2.** vb. rimer.

rhythm, n. rythme m.

rhythmical, adj. rythmique.

rib, n. côte f.

ribbon, n. ruban m.

rice, n. riz m.

rich, adj. riche.

rid, vb. débarrasser.

riddle, n. énigme f.

ride, 1. n. promenade f. **2.** vb. (horse) aller à cheval; (vehicle) aller en voiture.

rider, n. (on horse) cavalier m.

ridge, n. crête f.

ridicule, 1. n. ridicule m. **2.** vb. se moquer de.

ridiculous, adj. ridicule.

rifle, n. fusil m.

rift, n. désaccord m.

rig, 1. n. (vessel) gréement m.; (outfit) tenue f. **2.** vb. gréer.

right, 1. n. droit m.; (not left) droite f. **2.** adj. (straight, not left) droit; (correct, proper) juste; (be r., of person) avoir raison; (all r.) c'est bien. **3.** adv. (straight) droit; (not left) à droite; (justly) bien.

righteous, adj. vertueux.

righteousness, n. justice f.

right of way, n. droit de passage m.; (automobiles) priorité (f.) de passage.

right wing, n. la droite f.

rigid, adj. rigide.

rigor, n. rigueur f.

rigorous, adj. rigoureux.

rim, n. bord m.; (wheel) jante f.

ring, 1. n. anneau m.; (ornament) bague f.; (circle) cercle m.; (arena) arène f.; (sound) son m.; (phone) coup (m.) de téléphone. **2.** vb. sonner.

rinse, vb. rincer.

riot, n. émeute f.

rip, 1. n. fente f. **2.** vb. fendre, tr.

ripe, adj. mûr.

ripen, vb. mûrir.

ripoff, 1. n. vol m. **2.** vb. voler.

ripple, 1. n. (on water) ride f. **2.** vb. rider, tr.

rise, 1. n. (ground) montée f.; (increase) augmentation f.; (rank) avancement m. **2.** vb. se lever.

risk, 1. n. risque m. **2.** vb. risquer.

rite, n. rite m.

ritual, adj. rituel.

rival, 1. adj. and n. rival m. **2.** vb. rivaliser avec.

rivalry, n. rivalité f.

river, n. fleuve m.

river bank, n. rive f., berge f.

rivet, n. rivet m.

Riviera, n. Côte (f.) d'Azur.

road, n. route f.

roam, vb. errer (par).

roar, vb. (person) hurler; (lion) rugir; (bull, sea) mugir; (thunder, cannon) gronder; (laughter) éclater de.

roast, 1. n. rôti m. **2.** vb. rôtir.

rob, vb. voler.

robber, n. voleur m.

robbery, n. vol m.

robe, n. robe f.

robin, n. rouge-gorge m.

robot, n. automate m., robot m.

robust, adj. robuste.

rock, 1. n. rocher m. **2.** vb. balancer; (child) bercer. **3.** adj. (music) rock.

rocket, n. fusée f.

rocking chair, n. fauteuil (m.) à bascule.

rocky, adj. rocheux.

rod, n. verge f.

rodent, adj. and n. rongeur m.

roe, n. (animal) chevreuil m.; (of fish) œufs (m.pl.) de poisson.

rogue, n. coquin m.

roguish, adj. coquin.

role, n. rôle m.

roll, 1. n. rouleau m.; (bread) petit pain m.; (list) liste f.; **(r.-call)** appel m.; (boat) roulis m. **2.** vb. rouler.

roller, n. rouleau m.

roller skate, n. patin (m.) à roulette.

Roman, 1. n. Romain m. **2.** adj. romain.

romance, n. roman (m.) de chevalerie.

Romania, n. Roumanie f.

Romanian, 1. n. (person) Roumain m.; (language) roumain m. **2.** adj. roumain.

romantic, adj. romanesque; (poetry, music) romantique.

romp, 1. n. tapage m. **2.** vb. batifoler.

roof, n. toit m.

room, n. (space) place f.; (private use) chambre f.; (public use) salle f.

roommate, n. camarade (m.f.) de chambre.

rooster, n. coq m.

root, 1. n. racine f.; (source) source f. **2.** vb. enraciner, tr.

rope, n. corde f.

rosary, n. rosaire m.

rose, n. rose f.

rosemary, n. romarin m.

rosin, n. colophane f.

rosy, adj. de rose.

rot, 1. n. pourriture f. **2.** vb. pourrir.

rotary, adj. rotatoire.

rotate, vb. tourner.

rotation, n. rotation f.

rotten, adj. pourri.

rouge, n. rouge m.

rough, adj. rude; (sea weather) gros m., grosse f.

round, 1. n. rond m. **2.** n. rond m.; (circuit) tournée f.

round trip, n. voyage (m.) aller et retour.

rouse, vb. (wake) réveiller; (stir up) secouer.

rout, n. (mil.) déroute f.

route, n. route f.

routine, n. routine f.

rove, vb. errer (par).

rover, n. rôdeur m.

row, 1. n. rang m.; dispute f. **2.** vb. ramer.

rowboat, n. barque f.

rowdy, adj. tapageur.

rowing, n. aviron m.

royal, adj. royal.

royalty, n. royauté f.; (of author) droits (m.pl.) d'auteur.

rub, vb. frotter.

rubber, n. caoutchouc m.

rubbish, n. rebuts m.pl.; (nonsense) bêtises f.pl.

ruby, n. rubis m.

rudder, n. gouvernail m.

ruddy, adj. rouge.

rude, adj. (rough) rude; (impolite) impoli.

rudiment, n. rudiment m.

rue, vb. regretter.

ruffian, n. bandit m.

ruffle, n. (frill) fraise f.

rug, n. tapis m.

rugged, adj. (rough) rude; (uneven) raboteux.

ruin, 1. n. ruine f. **2.** vb. ruiner.

ruinous, adj. ruineux.

rule, 1. n. règle f.; (authority) autorité f. **2.** vb. gouverner; (decide) décider.

ruler, n. souverain m.; (for lines) règle f.

rum, n. rhum m.

rumba, n. rumba f.

rumble, vb. gronder.
rumor, n. rumeur f.
run, vb. intr. courir; (of engine) marcher; (of colors) déteindre; (of liquids) couler; (r. away) s'enfuir.
run-down, adj. épuisé.
rung, n. échelon m.
runner, n. (person) coureur m.; (table) chemin (m.) de table.
running, n. course f., gestion f., direction f.
rupture, n. rupture f.
rural, adj. rural.
rush, 1. n. (haste) hâte f.; (onrush) ruée f.; (air, water) coup m.; (plant) jonc m. **2.** vb. se précipiter, intr.
Russia, n. Russie f.
Russian, 1. n. (person) Russe m.f.; (language) russe m. **2.** adj. russe.
rust, 1. n. rouille f. **2.** vb. rouiller, tr.
rustic, adj. rustique.
rustle, n. (leaves) bruissement m.; (skirt) frou-frou m.
rusty, adj. rouillé.
rut, n. ornière f.
ruthless, adj. impitoyable.
rye, n. seigle m.; (whiskey) whisky m.

S

Sabbath, n. sabbat m.
saber, n. sabre m.
sable, n. zibeline f.
sabotage, 1. n. sabotage m. **2.** vb. saboter.
saboteur, n. saboteur m.
saccharin, n. saccharine f.
sachet, n. sachet m.
sack, 1. n. sac m. **2.** vb. saccager.
sacrament, n. sacrement m.
sacred, adj. sacré.
sacrifice, 1. n. sacrifice m. **2.** vb. sacrifier.
sacrilege, n. sacrilège m.
sad, adj. triste.
sadden, vb. attrister, tr.
saddle, n. selle f.
sadism, n. sadisme m.
sadistic, adj. sadique.
sadness, n. tristesse f.
safe, 1. n. coffre-fort m. **2.** adj. sûr; (s. and sound) sain et sauf; (s. from) à l'abri de.
safeguard, vb. sauvegarder.
safe sex, n. rapports (m.pl.) sexuels sans risques.
safety, n. sûreté f., sécurité f.
safety pin, n. épingle (f.) anglaise.
sag, vb. s'affaisser.
sage, n. (person) sage m.; (plant) sauge f.
sail, 1. n. voile f. **2.** vb. naviguer; (depart) partir.
sailboat, n. canot (m.) à voiles.
sailor, n. marin m.
saint, adj. and n. saint m.
sake, n. (for the s. of) pour l'amour de.
salad, n. salade f.
salami, n. salami m.
salary, n. appointements m.pl.
sale, n. vente f.
salesman, n. vendeur m.
sales tax, n. impôt (m.) sur les ventes.
saliva, n. salive f.
salmon, n. saumon m.
salt, 1. n. sel m. **2.** vb. saler.
salute, 1. n. salut m. **2.** vb. saluer.
salvage, n. sauvetage m.
salvation, n. salut m.
salve, n. onguent m.
same, 1. adj. and pron. même. **2.** adv. de même.
sample, n. échantillon m.
sanatorium, n. sanatorium m.
sanctify, vb. sanctifier.
sanction, n. sanction f.
sanctity, n. sainteté f.
sanctuary, n. sanctuaire m.
sand, n. sable m.
sandal, n. sandale f.
sandwich, n. sandwich m.
sandy, adj. sablonneux.
sane, adj. sain d'esprit.
sanitary, adj. sanitaire.
sanitary napkin, n. serviette (f.) hygiénique.
sanitation, n. hygiène f.
sanity, n. santé (f.) d'esprit.
Santa Claus, n. Père Noël m.
sap, n. sève f.

sapphire, n. saphir m.

sarcasm, n. sarcasme m.

sardine, n. sardine f.

Sardinia, n. Sardaigne f.

sash, n. ceinture f.

satellite, n. satellite m.

satellite dish, n. antenne (f.) parabolique.

satellite television, n. télévision (f.) par cable.

satin, n. satin m.

satire, n. satire f.

satisfaction, n. satisfaction f.

satisfactory, adj. satisfaisant.

satisfy, vb. satisfaire.

saturate, vb. saturer.

Saturday, n. samedi m.

sauce, n. sauce f.

saucer, n. soucoupe f.

saucy, adj. impertinent.

Saudi Arabia, n. Arabie (f.) Saoudite.

sausage, n. saucisse f.

savage, adj. and n. sauvage m.f.

save, vb. sauver; (put aside) mettre de côté; (economize) épargner.

saving, n. épargne f.

savings bank, n. caisse (f.) d'épargne.

savior, n. sauveur m.

savor, n. saveur f.

savory, adj. savoureux.

saw, 1. n. scie f. **2.** vb. scier.

say, vb. dire.

scab, n. croûte f., gale f.

scaffold, n. échafaud m.

scald, vb. échauder.

scale, 1. n. (fish) écaille f.; (balance) balance f.; (series, graded system, map) échelle f.; (music) gamme f. **2.** vb. escalader.

scallop, n. coquille (f.) Saint-Jacques; (sewing) feston m.

scalp, 1. n. cuir (m.) chevelu m. **2.** vb. scalper.

scan, 1. vb. (examine) scruter; (verse) scander. **2.** n. échographie f.

scandal, n. scandale m.

scandalous, adj. scandaleux.

Scandinavia, n. Scandinavie f.

Scandinavian, 1. n. Scandinave m.f. **2.** adj. scandinave.

scant(y), adj. limité, faible.

scar, n. cicatrice f.

scarce, adj. rare.

scare, vb. effrayer.

scarf, n. écharpe f.

scarlet, adj. and n. écarlate f.; **(s. fever)** scarlatine f.

scary, adj. effrayant.

scathing, adj. cinglant.

scatter, vb. éparpiller.

scavenger, n. boueur m.

scenario, n. scénario m.

scene, n. scène f.

scenery, n. (theater) décors m.pl.; (landscape) paysage m.

scent, 1. n. parfum m., odeur f. **2.** vb. flairer, sentir.

schedule, n. horaire m.

scheme, n. plan m.

schizophrenic, adj. and n. schizophrène m.f.

scholar, n. savant m.

scholarship, n. (school) bourse f.

school, n. école f.

sciatica, n. sciatique f.

science, n. science f.

science fiction, n. science-fiction f.

scientist, n. scientifique m.f.

scissors, n. ciseaux m.pl.

scoff at, vb. se moquer de.

scold, vb. gronder.

scoop out, vb. évider.

scope, n. (extent) portée f.; (outlet) carrière f.

scorch, vb. roussir.

score, n. (games) points m.pl.; (twenty) vingtaine f.; (music) partition f.

scorn, 1. n. mépris m. **2.** vb. mépriser.

scornful, adj. dédaigneux.

Scotch, Scottish, adj. écossais.

Scotchman, Scotsman, n. Écossais m.

Scotch tape, n. ruban adhésif m.

Scotland, n. Écosse f.

scour, vb. nettoyer.

scourge, n. fléau m.

scout, n. éclaireur m.; **(boy s.)** boy-scout m.

scowl, vb. se renfrogner.

scramble, vb. avancer péniblement.

scrap, 1. n. petit morceau m. **2.** vb. mettre au rebut.

scrape, scratch, 1. n. égratinure f. **2.** vb. gratter.

scream, 1. n. cri m. **2.** vb. crier.
screen, n. écran m.; **(folding s.)** paravent m.
screen play, n. scénario m.
screw, 1. n. vis f. **2.** vb. visser, tr.
screwdriver, n. tournevis m.
scribble, vb. griffonner.
script, n. écriture f., scénario m.
scroll, n. rouleau m.
scrub, vb. frotter.
scruple, n. scrupule m.
scrupulous, adj. scrupuleux.
scrutinize, vb. scruter.
scuba-diving, n. plongée (f.) sous-marine.
sculptor, n. sculpteur m.
sculpture, n. sculpture f.
scythe, n. faux f.
sea, n. mer f.
seabed, n. lit (m.) de la mer.
seacoast, n. littoral m.
seagull, n. mouette f.
seal, 1. n. (animal) phoque m.; (stamp) sceau m. **2.** vb. sceller.
seam, n. couture f.
seaport, n. port (m.) de mer.
search, 1. n. recherche f. **2.** vb. chercher.
seasickness, n. mal (m.) de mer.
season, 1. n. saison f. **2.** vb. assaisonner.
seat, 1. n. siège m. **2.** vb. asseoir.
seat-belt, n. ceinture (f.) de sécurité.
seclude, vb. isoler.
second, 1. n. seconde f. **2.** adj. second, deuxième.
secondary, adj. secondaire.
secret, adj. and n. secret m.
secretary, n. secrétaire m.f.
sect, n. secte f.
section, n. section f.
sectional, adj. régional.
secular, adj. (church) séculier; (education) laïque; (time) séculaire.
secure, 1. adj. sûr. **2.** vb. **(make s.)** mettre en sûreté; (make fast) fixer; (obtain) obtenir.
security, n. sûreté f.; (comm., law) caution f.; (finance, pl.) valeurs f.pl.
sedative, adj. and n. sédatif m.
sediment, n. sédiment m.
seduce, vb. séduire.
see, vb. voir.

seed, n. semence f.; (vegetables, etc.) graine f.
seek, vb. chercher.
seem, vb. sembler.
seep, vb. suinter.
segment, n. segment m.
segregate, vb. séparer.
seize, vb. saisir.
seizure, n. crise f., attaque f.
seldom, adv. rarement.
select, vb. choisir.
selection, n. sélection f.
self, n. moi m., personne f.
self-centered, adj. égocentrique.
selfish, adj. égoïste.
selfishness, n. égoïsme m.
self-righteous, adj. suffisant.
self-service, adj. and n. libre-service m.
sell, vb. vendre, tr.
semantics, n. sémantique f.
semester, n. semestre m.
semicircle, n. demi-cercle m.
semicolon, n. point-virgule m.
seminary, n. séminaire m.
Semite, n. Sémite m.f.
senate, n. sénat m.
senator, n. sénateur m.
send, vb. envoyer; **(s. back)** renvoyer.
senile, adj. sénile.
senior, adj. and n. (age) aîné m.; (rank) supérieur m.
senior citizen, n. personne (f.) du troisième âge.
seniority, n. ancienneté f.
sensation, n. sensation f.
sensational, adj. sensationnel.
sense, n. sens m.
sensible, adj. (wise) sensé; (appreciable) sensible.
sensitive, adj. sensible.
sensual, adj. sensuel.
sensuous, adj. sensuel.
sentence, n. (gramm.) phrase f.; (law) sentence f.
sentiment, n. sentiment m.
sentimental, adj. sentimental.
separate, 1. adj. séparé. **2.** vb. séparer, tr.
separation, n. séparation f.
September, n. septembre m.
sequence, n. suite f.
serene, adj. serein.
serenade, n. sérénade f.

serene, *adj.* serein.
sergeant, *n.* sergent *m.*
serial, *n.* roman-feuilleton *m.*
series, *n.* série *f.*
serious, *adj.* sérieux.
sermon, *n.* sermon *m.*
serpent, *n.* serpent *m.*
serum, *n.* sérum *m.*
servant, *n.* (domestic) domestique *m./f.;* (public) employé *m.*
serve, *vb.* servir.
service, *n.* service *m.;* (church) office *m.*
service station, *n.* station-service *f.*
servitude, *n.* servitude *f.*
session, *n.* session *f.*
set, 1. *n.* ensemble *m.* **2.** *adj.* fixe; (decided) résolu. **3.** *vb. tr.* (put) mettre; (regulate) régler; (jewels) monter; (fix) fixer. **4.** *vb. intr.* (sun, etc.) se coucher; **(s. about)** se mettre à.
settle, *vb.* (establish) établir, *tr.;* (fix) fixer; (decide) décider; (arrange) arranger; (pay) payer; **(s. down to,** *intr.*) se mettre à.
settlement, *n.* (colony) colonie *f.;* (accounts) règlement *m.*
settler, *n.* colon *m.*
seven, *adj. and n.* sept *m.*
seventeen, *adj. and n.* dix-sept *m.*
seventh, *adj. and n.* septième *m.f.*
seventy, *adj. and n.* soixante-dix *m.*
sever, *vb.* séparer, couper.
several, *adj. and pron.* plusieurs.
severe, *adj.* sévère.
severity, *n.* sévérité *f.*
sew, *vb.* coudre.
sewer, *n.* égout *m.*
sex, *n.* sexe *m.*
sexism, *n.* sexisme *m.*
sexist, *adj.* sexiste.
sexual, *adj.* sexuel.
shabby, *adj.* (clothes) usé; (person) mesquin.
shack, *n.* cabane *f.*
shade, 1. *n.* ombre *f.;* (colors) nuance *f.;* (window) store *m.* **2.** *vb.* ombrager.
shadow, *n.* ombre *f.*
shady, *adj.* ombragé; (not honest) louche.
shaft, *n.* (mine) puits *m.*
shaggy, *adj.* poilu, hirsute.

shake, *vb. tr.* secouer; trembler; **(s. hands)** serrer la main à.
shallow, *adj.* peu profond.
shame, *n.* honte *f.*
shameful, *adj.* honteux.
shampoo, *n.* shampooing *m.*
shape, 1. *n.* forme *f.* **2.** *vb.* former.
share, 1. *n. part f.;* (finance) action *f.* **2.** *vb.* partager.
shareholder, *n.* actionnaire *m.*
shark, *n.* requin *m.*
sharp, *adj.* (cutting) tranchant; (clever) fin; (piercing) perçant; (music) dièse.
sharpen, *vb.* aiguiser.
shatter, *vb.* briser.
shave, *vb.* raser, *tr.*
shaving brush, *n.* blaireau *m.*
shaving cream, *n.* crème *(f.)* à raser.
shawl, *n.* châle *m.*
she, *pron.* elle.
sheaf, *n.* (grain) gerbe *f.*
shear, *vb.* tondre.
shears, *n.* cisailles *f.pl.*
sheath, *n.* étui *m.*
shed, 1. *n.* hangar *m.* **2.** *vb.* verser.
sheen, *n.* lustre *m.*
sheep, *n.* mouton *m.*
sheet, *n.* (bed) drap *m.;* (paper, metal) feuille *f.*
shelf, *n.* rayon *m.*
shell, *n.* coquille *f.;* (of building) carcasse *f.;* (explosive) obus *m.*
shellac, *n.* laque *f.*
shellfish, *n.* coquillages *m.pl.*
shelter, 1. *n.* abri *m.* **2.** *vb.* abriter.
shepherd, *n.* berger *m.*
sherbet, *n.* sorbet *m.*
sherry, *n.* xérès *m.*
shield, *n.* bouclier *m.*
shift, 1. *n.* (change) changement *m.;* (workers) équipe *f.;* (expedient) expédient *m.;* (shirt) chemise *f.* **2.** *vb.* changer; **(s. gears)** changer de vitesse.
shin, *n.* tibia *m.*
shine, *vb.* briller, *intr.;* (shoes) cirer.
shiny, *adj.* luisant.
ship, *n.* navire *m.;* vaisseau *m.*
shipment, *n.* envoi *m.*
shirk, *vb.* esquiver.
shirt, *n.* chemise *f.*

shiver, 1. n. frisson m. 2. vb. frissonner.

shock, 1. n. choc m. 2. vb. choquer.

shock absorber, n. amortisseur m.

shoe, n. soulier m., chaussure f.

shoelace, n. lacet m.

shoemaker, n. cordonnier m.

shoot, vb. tirer; (person) fusiller; (hit) atteindre; (rush) se précipiter.

shop, 1. n. boutique f.; (factory) atelier m. 2. vb. faire des emplettes.

shopping, n. achats m.pl.

shop window, n. vitrine f.

shore, n. rivage m.

short, adj. court.

shortage, n. manque m., insuffisance f.

short-circuit, n. court-circuit m.

shorten, vb. raccourcir.

shorthand, n. sténographie f.

short story, n. nouvelle f.

shot, n. coup m.

should, vb. devoir (in conditional).

shoulder, n. épaule f.

shoulder blade, n. omoplate f.

shout, 1. n. cri m. 2. vb. crier.

shove, vb. pousser.

shovel, n. pelle f.

show, 1. n. (exhibition) exposition f.; (spectacle, performance) spectacle m.; (semblance) semblant m.; (display) parade f. 2. vb. montrer, tr.

shower, n. (rain) averse f.; (washing) douche f.

shrapnel, n. éclats (m.pl.) d'obus.

shrewd, adj. sagace.

shriek, 1. n. cri (m.) perçant. 2. vb. hurler.

shrill, adj. aigu.

shrimp, n. crevette f.

shrine, n. châsse f.

shrink, vb. rétrécir, tr.

shroud, n. linceul m.

shrub, n. arbrisseau m.

shudder, 1. n. frisson m. 2. vb. frissonner.

shun, vb. fuir.

shut, vb. fermer.

shuttle, 1. n. navette f. 2. vb. faire la navette.

shutter, n. volet m.

shy, adj. timide.

sick, adj. malade.

sickness, n. maladie f.

side, n. côté m.

sidewalk, n. trottoir m.

siege, n. siège m.

sieve, n. tamis m.

sift, vb. cribler.

sigh, 1. n. soupir m. 2. vb. soupirer.

sight, n. vue f.; (spectacle) spectacle m.

sightseeing, n. tourisme m.

sign, 1. n. signe m.; (placard) enseigne f. 2. vb. signer.

signal, n. signal m.

signature, n. signature f.

significance, n. (meaning) signification f.; (importance) importance f.

significant, adj. significatif.

signify, vb. signifier.

sign language, n. langage (m.) des sourds-muets.

silence, n. silence m.

silent, adj. silencieux.

silicon, n. silicium m.; (s. chip) microplaquette f.

silk, n. soie f.

silken, adj. de soie.

silly, adj. sot m., sotte f.

silver, 1. n. argent m. 2. adj. d'argent.

silverware, n. argenterie f.

similar, adj. semblable.

simple, adj. simple.

simplicity, n. simplicité f.

simplify, vb. simplifier.

simply, adv. simplement.

simultaneous, adj. simultané.

sin, 1. n. péché m. 2. vb. pécher.

since, 1. adv., prep. depuis. 2. conj. (time) depuis que; (cause) puisque.

sincere, adj. sincère.

sincerity, n. sincérité f.

sinful, adj. (person) pécheur m., pécheresse f.; (act) coupable.

sing, vb. chanter.

singer, n. chanteur m.

single, adj. (only one) seul; (particular) particulier; (not married) célibataire.

singular, adj. and n. singulier m.

sinister, adj. sinistre.

sink, 1. n. (kitchen) évier m., (bathroom) lavabo m. 2. vb. enfoncer, *tr.;* (vessel) couler à fond; (diminish, weaken) baisser.

sinner, *n.* pécheur *m.,* pécheresse *f.*

sinus, *n.* sinus *m.*

sip, *vb.* siroter.

sirloin, *n.* aloyau *m.*

sister, *n.* sœur *f.*

sister-in-law, *n.* belle-sœur *f.*

sit, *vb.* **(s. down)** s'asseoir; (be seated) être assis.

sitcom, *n.* comédie *(f.)* de situation

site, *n.* emplacement *m.*

sit-in, *n.* occupation *(f.)* (de locaux).

situate, *vb.* situer.

situation, *n.* situation *f.*

six, *adj. and n.* six *m.*

sixteen, *adj. and n.* seize *m.*

sixteenth, *adj. and n.* seizième *m.f.*

sixth, *adj. and n.* sixième *m.f.*

sixty, *adj. and n.* soixante *m.*

size, *n.* grandeur *f.;* (person) taille *f.;* (shoes, gloves) pointure *f.;* (book, packaged merchandise) format *m.*

skate, 1. *n.* patin *m.* 2. *vb.* patiner.

skateboard, *n.* planche *(f.)* à roulettes.

skeleton, *n.* squelette *m.*

skeptic, *n.* sceptique *m.f.*

skeptical, *adj.* sceptique.

sketch, 1. *n.* croquis *m.* 2. *vb.* esquisser.

ski, 1. *n.* ski *m.* 2. *vb.* faire du ski.

skill, *n.* adresse *f.*

skillful, *adj.* adroit.

skim, *vb.* (milk) écrémer; (book) feuilleter; (surface) effleurer.

skin, 1. *n.* peau *f.* 2. *vb.* écorcher.

skinny, *adj.* maigre.

skip, *vb.* sauter.

skirt, *n.* jupe *f.*

skull, *n.* crâne *m.*

sky, *n.* ciel *m.*

skyscraper, *n.* gratte-ciel *m.*

slab, *n.* dalle *f.*

slack, *adj.* lâche.

slacken, *vb.* (slow up) ralentir; (loosen) relâcher.

slacks, *n.* pantalon *m.*

slander, 1. *n.* calomnie *f.* 2. *vb.* calomnier.

slang, *n.* argot *m.*

slant, 1. *n.* (slope) pente *f.;* (bias) biais *m.* 2. *vb.* incliner.

slap, 1. *n.* claque *f.* 2. *vb.* gifler.

slash, *n.* taillade *f.*

slate, *n.* ardoise *f.*

slaughter, 1. *n.* (people) massacre *m.;* (animals) abattage *m.* 2. *vb.* massacrer; abattre.

slaughterhouse, *n.* abattoir *m.*

slave, *n.* esclave *m.f.*

slavery, *n.* esclavage *m.*

slay, *vb.* tuer.

sled, *n.* traîneau *m.*

sleep, 1. *n.* sommeil *m.;* **(go to s.)** s'endormir. 2. *vb.* dormir.

sleeping bag, *n.* sac de couchage *m.*

sleeping pill, *n.* somnifère *m.*

sleepy, *adj.* somnolent; **(be s.)** avoir sommeil.

sleet, 1. *n.* grésil *m.* 2. *vb.* grésiller.

sleeve, *n.* manche *f.*

sleigh, *n.* traîneau *m.*

slice, *n.* tranche *f.*

slide, 1. *n.* (sliding) glissade *f.;* (microscope) lamelle *f.;* (lantern) plaque *(f.)* de projection. 2. *vb.* glisser.

slight, *adj.* léger; mince.

slim, *adj.* mince.

sling, 1. *n.* fronde *f.;* (medical) écharpe *f.* 2. *vb.* (throw) lancer; (hang) suspendre.

slip, 1. *n.* (sliding) glissade *f.;* (tongue, pen) lapsus *m.;* (mistake) faux pas *m.;* (paper) fiche *f.;* (garment) sous-jupe *f.* 2. *vb.* glisser; (err) faire une faute.

slipper, *n.* pantoufle *f.*

slippery, *adj.* glissant.

slit, 1. *n.* fente *f.* 2. *vb.* fendre.

slogan, *n.* mot *(m.)* d'ordre; (politics) cri *(m.)* de guerre.

slope, 1. *n.* pente *f.* 2. *vb.* incliner.

sloppy, *adj.* mal soigné.

slot, *n.* fente *f.*

slow, *adj.* lent; (clock) en retard.

slowness, *n.* lenteur *f.*

sluggish, *adj.* paresseux.

slum, *n.* quartier *(m.)* pauvre.

slumber, *vb.* sommeiller.

sly, *adj.* (crafty) rusé; (secretive) sournois.

smack, 1. n. (a bit) soupçon m.; (noise) claquement m. **2.** vb. gifler.

small, adj. petit.

smallpox, n. petite vérole f.

smart, 1. adj. (clever) habile; (stylish) élégant. **2.** vb. cuire.

smash, 1. vb. briser, tr. **2.** n. coup m.; (fig.) collision f.

smear, 1. n. tache f. **2.** vb. salir.

smell, 1. n. odeur f. **2.** vb. sentir.

smelt, 1. n. éperlan m. **2.** vb. fondre.

smile, n., vb. sourire m.

smite, vb. frapper.

smog, n. brouillard (m.) mélangé de fumée.

smoke, 1. n. fumée f. **2.** vb. fumer.

smolder, vb. couver.

smooth, 1. adj. lisse. **2.** vb. lisser.

smother, vb. étouffer.

smug, adj. suffisant.

smuggle, vb. faire passer en contrebande.

snack, n. casse-croute m.

snag, n. obstacle (m.) caché.

snail, n. escargot m.

snake, n. serpent m.

snap, 1. n. (bite) coup (m.) de dents; (sound) coup (m.) sec. **2.** vb.tr. (with teeth) happer; (sound) faire claquer.

snapshot, n. instantané m.

snare, n. piège m.

snarl, vb. grogner.

snatch, vb. saisir.

sneak, vb. se glisser furtivement.

sneakers, n. tennis m.pl., basket m.pl.

sneer, vb. ricaner.

sneeze, 1. n. éternuement m. **2.** vb. éternuer.

sniff, vb. renifler.

snob, n. snob m.

snore, vb. ronfler.

snorkel, n. tuba m.

snow, 1. n. neige f. **2.** vb. neiger.

snug, adj. confortable.

snuggle, vb. se pelotonner.

so, adv. si; tellement; (thus) ainsi; **(s. that)** de sorte que.

soak, vb. tremper.

soap, n. savon m.

soar, vb. prendre son essor.

sob, 1. n. sanglot m. **2.** vb. sangloter.

sober, adj. (sedate) sérieux; (not drunk) qui n'est pas ivre.

soccer, n. football m.

sociable, adj. sociable.

social, adj. social.

socialism, n. socialisme m.

socialist, adj. and n. socialiste m.f.

social worker, n. assistant (m.f.) social.

society, n. société f.

sociology, n. sociologie f.

sock, n. chaussette f.

socket, n. douille f.

sod, n. motte f.

soda, n. soude f.; **(s. water)** eau (f.) de Seltz.

sofa, n. canapé m.

soft, adj. doux m., douce f.; (yielding) mou m., molle f.

soften, vb. amollir, tr.

software, n. logiciel m.

soil, 1. n. terroir m. **2.** vb. souiller.

sojourn, 1. n. séjour m. **2.** vb. séjourner.

solace, n. consolation f.

solar, adj. solaire.

soldier, n. soldat m.

sole, n. (shoe) semelle f.; (fish) sole f.

solemn, adj. solennel.

solemnity, n. solennité f.

solicit, vb. solliciter.

solicitous, adj. empressé.

solid, adj. and n. solide m.

solidity, n. solidité f.

solidarity, n. solidarité f.

solitary, adj. solitaire.

solitude, n. solitude f.

solo, n. solo m.

solution, n. solution f.

solve, vb. résoudre.

solvent, adj. (comm.) solvable.

somber, adj. sombre.

some, 1. adj. quelque; (partitive) de. **2.** pron. certains; (with verb) en.

somebody, someone, pron. quelqu'un.

something, pron. quelque chose m.

sometime, adv. (past) autrefois; (future) quelque jour.

sometimes, adv. quelquefois.

somewhat, adv. quelque peu.

somewhere, adv. quelque part.

son, n. fils m.

song, n. chanson f.; chant m.

son-in-law, n. gendre m.

soon, adv. bientôt, tôt.

soot, n. suie f.

soothe, vb. calmer.

sophisticated, adj. blasé.

soprano, n. soprano m.

sordid, adj. sordide.

sore, adj. (aching) douloureux; (have a s. throat, etc.) avoir mal à. . . .

sorrow, n. tristesse f., douleur f., chagrin m.

sorrowful, adj. (person) affligé.

sorry, 1. adj. désolé, triste; (be s.) regretter. 2. interj. pardon!

sort, 1. n. sorte f. 2. vb. trier.

soul, n. âme f.

sound, 1. n. son m. 2. adj. (healthy) sain, solide. 3. vb. sonner.

soundproof, adj. insonorisé.

soup, n. potage m., soupe, f.

sour, adj. aigre.

source, n. source f.

south, n. sud m.

South America, n. Amérique (f.) du Sud.

southeast, n. sud-est m.

southern, adj. du sud.

South Pole, n. pôle sud m.

southwest, n. sud-ouest m.

souvenir, n. souvenir m.

Soviet, adj. soviétique; (S. Union) Union (f.) soviétique.

sow, vb. semer.

spa, n. station (f.) thermale.

space, n. espace m.

space shuttle, n. navette spatiale f.

spacious, adj. spacieux.

spade, n. bêche f.; (cards) pique m.

Spain, n. Espagne f.

span, n. (hand) empan m.; (bridge) travée f.

Spaniard, n. Espagnol m.

Spanish, adj. and n. espagnol m.

spank, vb. fesser.

spanking, n. fessée f.

spare, 1. adj. (in reserve) de réserve. 2. vb. épargner.

spark, n. étincelle f.

sparkle, vb. étinceler.

sparrow, n. moineau m.

spasm, n. spasme m.

speak, vb. parler.

speaker, n. (public) orateur m.

spec, (on s.) à tout hasard.

special, adj. spécial.

specialist, n. spécialiste m.f.

specially, adv. spécialement.

specialty, n. spécialité f.

species, n. espèce f.

specific, adj. spécifique.

specify, vb. spécifier.

specimen, n. spécimen m.

spectacle, n. spectacle m.

spectacular, adj. spectaculaire.

spectator, n. spectateur m.

speculate, vb. spéculer.

speculation, n. spéculation f.

speech, n. (address) discours m.; (utterance) parole f.

speed, n. vitesse f.

speedometer, n. compteur (m.) (de vitesse).

speedy, adj. rapide.

spell, 1. n. (incantation) charme m.; (period) période f. 2. vb. épeler.

spelling, n. orthographe f.

spend, vb. (money) dépenser; (time) passer.

sphere, n. sphère f.

spice, n. épice f.

spider, n. araignée f.

spike, n. pointe f.

spill, vb. répandre, tr.

spin, vb. (thread) filer; (twirl) tourner.

spinach, n. épinards m.pl.

spine, n. épine f.; (backbone) épine (f.) dorsale.

spiral, 1. n. spirale f. 2. adj. spiral.

spirit, n. esprit m.

spiritual, adj. spirituel.

spiritualism, n. spiritisme m.; spiritualisme m.

spit, 1. n. (saliva) crachat m.; (for roast) broche f. 2. vb. cracher.

spite, n. dépit m.; (in s. of) malgré.

spiteful, adj. méchant.

splash, vb. éclabousser.

splendid, adj. splendide.

splendor, n. splendeur f.

splinter, n. éclat m.

split, vb. fendre.

spoil, 1. n. butin m. 2. vb. gâter.

sponge, n. éponge f.

sponsor, n. (law) garant m.

spontaneity, n. spontanéité f.

spontaneous, adj. spontané.

spool, n. bobine f.
spoon, n. cuiller f.
spoonful, n. cuillerée f.
sporadic, adj. sporadique.
sport, n. sport m.; (fun) jeu m.
spot, 1. n. (stain) tache f.; (place) endroit m. **2.** vb. tacher; (recognize) reconnaître.
spotless, adj. immaculé.
spouse, n. époux m., épouse f.
spout, 1. n. (teapot, etc.) bec m. **2.** vb. jaillir.
sprain, n. entorse f.
sprawl, vb. s'étaler.
spray, n. (sea) embrun m.
spread, 1. n. étendue f. **2.** vb. étendre, tr.
spreadsheet, n. tableur m.
spree, n. (go on a s.) faire la noce.
sprightly, adj. éveillé.
spring, 1. n. (season) printemps m.; (source) source f.; (leap) saut m.; (device) ressort m. **2.** vb. (leap) sauter; (water) jaillir.
sprinkle, vb. asperger.
spry, adj. alerte.
spur, 1. n. éperon m. **2.** vb. éperonner.
spurious, adj. faux m., fausse f.
spurn, vb. repousser.
spurt, 1. n. jet m. **2.** vb. jaillir.
spy, 1. n. espion m. **2.** espionner, apercevoir.
squad, n. escouade f.
squadron, n. escadron m.
squalid, adj. misérable.
squall, n. rafale f.
squander, vb. gaspiller.
square, 1. n. (geom.) carré m.; (in town) place f. **2.** adj. carré.
squash, n. (vegetable) courge f.; (game) squash m. **2.** vb. écraser.
squat, vb. s'accroupir.
squeak, 1. vb. crier, grincer. **2.** n. grincement m.
squeeze, vb. serrer; (lemon) presser.
squid, n. calamar m.
squirrel, n. écureuil m.
squirt, n. seringuer.
stab, vb. poignarder.
stability, n. stabilité f.
stabilize, vb. stabiliser.
stable, 1. n. écurie f. **2.** adj. stable.

stack, n. (hay) meule f.; (pile) pile f.; (chimney) souche f.
staff, n. (stick) bâton m.; (mil.) état-major m.; (personnel) personnel m.
stage, n. (theater) scène f.; (in development) période f.; (stopping-place) étape f.
stagflation, n. stagflation f.
stagger, vb. (totter) chanceler.
stagnant, adj. stagnant.
stain, 1. n. tache f. **2.** vb. (spot) tacher; (color) teinter.
staircase, stairway, n. escalier m.
stairs, n. escalier m.
stake, 1. n. (post) pieu m.; (at s.) en jeu. **2.** vb. (gaming) mettre au jeu.
stale, adj. (bread) rassis; (food) pas frais.
stalk, 1. n. tige f. **2.** vb. traquer.
stall, 1. n. (stable, church) stalle f. **2.** vb. temporiser.
stamina, n. vigueur f.
stammer, vb. bégayer.
stamp, 1. n. timbre(-poste) m. **2.** vb. (letter) timbrer; (with foot) frapper du pied.
stampede, n. sauve-qui-peut n.; débandade f.
stand, 1. n. (position) position f.; (resistance) résistance f.; (stall) étalage m.; (vehicles) station f. **2.** vb. tr. (put) poser; (endure) supporter. **3.** vb. intr. (upright) se tenir debout; (be situated, be located) se trouver; (stop) s'arrêter.
standard, n. (flag) étendard m.; (measure, etc.) étalon m.; (living, etc.) niveau m.
stanza, n. strophe f.
staple, 1. n. agrafe f. **2.** vb. agrafer.
stapler, n. agrafeuse f.
star, n. étoile f.; (movie) vedette f.
starch, n. amidon m.
stare, vb. regarder fixement.
stark, adj. pur, austère.
start, 1. n. (beginning) commencement m.; (surprise, etc.) tressaillement m. **2.** vb. commencer, tressaillir.
startle, vb. effrayer.
starvation, n. faim f.
starve, vb. intr. mourir de faim.
state, 1. n. état m. **2.** vb. déclarer.

statement, *n.* déclaration *f.*
statesman, *n.* homme (*m.*) d'état.
static, *adj.* statique.
station, *n.* (railroad) gare *f.*; (bus, subway) station *f.*
stationary, *adj.* stationnaire.
stationery, *n.* papeterie *f.*
statistics, *n.* statistique *f.*
statue, *n.* statue *f.*
stature, *n.* stature *f.*
statute, *n.* statut *m.*
stay, *vb.* rester.
steady, *adj.* ferme; (constant) soutenu.
steak, *n.* bifteck *m.*
steal, *vb.* voler.
steam, *n.* vapeur *f.*
steamboat, *n.* bateau (*m.*) à vapeur.
steamship, *n.* vapeur *m.*
steel, *n.* acier *m.*
steep, *adj.* raide.
steeple, *n.* clocher *m.*
steer, 1. *n.* jeune bœuf *m.* 2. *vb.* gouverner.
stem, *n.* (plant) tige *f.*
stenographer, *n.* sténographe *m.f.*
stenography, *n.* sténographie *f.*
step, 1. *n.* pas *m.*; (of staircase) marche *f.* 2. *vb.* faire un pas.
stereo, *n.* stéréo *f.*; chaîne (*f.*) stéréo.
stepbrother, *n.* demi-frère *m.*
stepdaughter, *n.* belle-fille *f.*
stepfather, *n.* beau-père *m.*
stepmother, *n.* belle-mère *f.*
stepsister, *n.* belle-sœur *f.*
stereophonic, *adj.* stéréophonique.
stereotype, *n.* stéréotype *m.*
sterile, *adj.* stérile.
stern, *adj.* sévère.
stethoscope, *n.* stéthoscope *m.*
stew, *n.* ragoût *m.*
steward, *n.* (airline) steward *m.*
stewardess, *n.* (airline) hôtesse (*f.*) de l'air.
stick, 1. *n.* bâton *m.* 2. *vb.* (paste) coller, *tr.*; (remain) rester.
sticker, *n.* autocollant *m.*
sticky, *adj.* gluant.
stiff, *adj.* raide.
stiffness, *n.* raideur *f.*
stifle, *vb.* étouffer.

still, 1. *adj.* tranquille. 2. *adv.* encore. 3. *conj.* cependant.
stillness, *n.* tranquillité *f.*
stimulant, *n.* stimulant *m.*
stimulate, *vb.* stimuler.
stimulus, *n.* stimulant *m.*
sting, 1. *n.* piqûre *f.* 2. *vb.* (prick) piquer; (smart) cuire.
stingy, *adj.* mesquin.
stink, 1. *vb.* puer. 2. *n.* puanteur *f.*
stir, 1. *vb.* remuer; (person, *intr.*) bouger. 2. *n.* mouvement *m.*
stitch, 1. *n.* (sewing) point *m.*; (knitting) maille *f.* 2. *vb.* coudre.
stock, 1. *n.* (goods on hand) marchandises *f.pl.*; (finance) valeurs *f.pl.*, action *f.*
stockbroker, *n.* agent de change *m.*
stock exchange, *n.* Bourse *f.*
stocking, *n.* bas *m.*
stole, *n.* étole *f.*
stomach, *n.* estomac *m.*; (**s. ache**) mal (*m.*) à l'estomac.
stone, *n.* pierre *f.*
stool, *n.* escabeau *m.*
stoop, *vb.* se pencher.
stop, 1. *n.* arrêt *m.* 2. *vb.* arrêter, *tr.*; (prevent) empêcher (de); (cease) cesser.
storage, *n.* emmagasinage *m.*
store, 1. *n.* (shop) magasin *m.*; (supply) provision *f.* 2. *vb.* emmagasiner.
storm, 1. *n.* orage *m.* 2. *vb.* prendre d'assaut.
stormy, *adj.* orageux.
story, *n.* histoire *f.*; (floor) étage *m.*
stout, *adj.* gros *m.*, grosse *f.*
stove, *n.* fourneau *m.*
straight, *adj.* and *adv.* droit.
straighten, *vb.* redresser.
strain, 1. *n.* effort *m.* 2. *vb.* (stretch) tendre; (filter) passer.
strait, *n.* (geography) détroit *m.*
strand, *n.* (beach) plage *f.*; (hair) mèche *f.*; (thread) fil *m.*
strange, *adj.* étrange; (foreign) étranger.
stranger, *n.* étranger *m.*
strangle, *vb.* étrangler.
strap, *n.* courroie *f.*
strategic, *adj.* stratégique.
strategy, *n.* stratégie *f.*
straw, *n.* paille *f.*

strawberry, n. fraise f.

stray, adj. égaré.

streak, 1. n. raie f. 2. vb. rayer.

stream, n. courant m.; (small river) ruisseau m.

streamline, vb. caréner, simplifier, moderniser.

street, n. rue f.

strength, n. force f.

strengthen, vb. fortifier.

strenuous, adj. énergique.

streptococcus, n. streptocoque m.

stress, 1. n. force f.; tension f.; (gramm.) accent m. 2. vb. accentuer.

stretch, vb. étendre, tr.

stretcher, n. brancard m.

strict, adj. strict.

stride, n. enjambée f.

strife, n. lutte f.

strike, 1. n. grève f. 2. vb. frapper; (match, tr.) allumer; (clock) sonner; (workers) se mettre en grève.

string, n. ficelle f.; (music) corde f.

string bean, n. haricot vert m.

strip, 1. n. bande f. 2. vb. dépouiller.

stripe, n. bande f.; (mil.) galon m.

strive, vb. s'efforcer (de).

stroke, 1. n. coup m., caresse f. 2. vb. caresser.

stroll, n. tour m.

stroller, n. poussette f.

strong, adj. fort.

structure, n. structure f.

struggle, 1. n. lutte f. 2. vb. lutter.

stub, n. souche f.

stubborn, adj. opiniâtre, obstiné, têtu.

student, n. étudiant m.

studio, n. atelier m.

studious, adj. studieux.

study, 1. n. étude f.; (room) cabinet (m.) de travail. 2. vb. étudier.

stuff, 1. n. (materials) matériaux m.pl.; (textile) étoffe f. 2. vb. bourrer; (cooking) farcir.

stuffing, n. bourre f.; (cooking) farce f.

stumble, vb. trébucher.

stump, n. (tree) souche f.

stun, vb. étourdir.

stunt, n. tour (m.) de force.

stupid, adj. stupide.

stupidity, n. stupidité f.

sturdy, adj. vigoureux.

stutter, vb. bégayer.

style, n. style m.

stylish, adj. élégant.

subconscious, adj. subconscient.

subdue, vb. subjuguer.

subject, 1. n. sujet m. 2. adj. (people, country) assujetti; (liable) sujet. 3. vb. assujettir.

sublet, vb. sous-louer.

sublimate, vb. sublimer.

sublime, adj. sublime.

submarine, adj. n. sous-marin m.

submerge, vb. submerger.

submission, n. soumission f.

submit, vb. soumettre, tr.

subnormal, adj. sous-normal.

subordinate, adj. and n. subordonné m.

subpoena, n. citation f.

subscribe, vb. (consent, support) souscrire; (to paper, etc.) s'abonner.

subscription, n. souscription f.; (to paper, etc.) abonnement m.

subsequent, adj. subséquent, ultérieur.

subsidy, n. subvention f.

substance, n. substance f.

substantial, adj. substantiel; (well-to-do) aisé.

substitute, 1. n. remplaçant m., remplacement m. 2. vb. substituer.

substitution, n. substitution f.

subterfuge, n. subterfuge m., faux-fuyant m.

subterranean, adj. souterrain.

subtitle, n. sous-titre m.

subtle, adj. subtil.

subtract, vb. soustraire.

suburb, n. faubourg m., banlieue f.

subversive, adj. subversif.

subway, n. métro(politain) m.

succeed, vb. (come after) succéder à; (be successful) réussir (à).

success, n. succès m.

successful, adj. heureux.

succession, n. succession f.

successive, adj. successif.

successor, n. successeur m.

succumb, vb. succomber.

such, adj. tel; (intensive, s. a + adj.) un . . . aussi + adj.

suck, vb. sucer.

suction, n. succion f.

sudden, *adj.* soudain.

sue, *vb.* poursuivre.

suffer, *vb.* souffrir.

suffice, *vb.* suffire.

sufficient, *adj.* suffisant.

suffocate, *vb.* suffoquer.

sugar, *n.* sucre *m.*

suggest, *vb.* suggérer.

suggestion, *n.* suggestion *f.*

suicide, 1. *n.* suicide *m.* **2.** *vb.* (commit s.) se suicider, *intr.*

suit, 1. *n.* (law) procès *m.;* (clothes) (man's) complet *m.,* (woman's) tailleur *m.;* (cards) couleur *f.* **2.** *vb.* convenir (à).

suitable, *adj.* convenable.

suitcase, *n.* valise *f.*

sulk, *vb.* bouder.

sulphur, *n.* soufre *m.*

sum, *n.* somme *f.*

summary, 1. *n.* résumé *m.,* abrégé *m.* **2.** *adj.* sommaire, immédiat.

summer, *n.* été *m.*

summit, *n.* sommet *m.*

summon, *vb.* (convoke) convoquer; (bid to come) appeler.

sun, *n.* soleil *m.*

sunburn, *n.* hâle *m.,* coup *(m.)* de soleil.

Sunday, *n.* dimanche *m.*

sunglasses, *n.* lunettes *(f.pl.)* de soleil.

sunny, *adj.* ensoleillé.

sunshine, *n.* soleil *m.*

suntan, *n.* bronzage *m.*

superb, *adj.* superbe.

superficial, *adj.* superficiel.

superfluous, *adj.* superflu.

superimpose, *vb.* superposer.

superintendent, *n.* surveillant *m.*

superior, *adj. and n.* supérieur *m.*

superiority, *n.* supériorité *f.*

superlative, *n.* superlatif *m.*

supermarket, *n.* supermarché *m.*

supernatural, *adj. and n.* surnaturel *m.*

superpower, *n.* superpuissance *f.*

supersede, *vb.* remplacer.

superstar, *n.* superstar *f.*

superstition, *n.* superstition *f.*

superstitious, *adj.* superstitieux.

superstore, *n.* hypermarché *m.*

supervise, *vb.* surveiller.

supper, *n.* souper *m.*

supplement, *n.* supplément *m.*

supply, 1. *n.* approvisionnement *m.;* provision *f.* **2.** *vb.* fournir (de).

support, 1. *n.* appui *m.,* soutien *m.* **2.** *vb.* soutenir; (bear) supporter; (back up) appuyer.

suppose, *vb.* supposer.

suppress, *vb.* supprimer.

suppression, *n.* suppression *f.*

supreme, *adj.* suprême.

surcharge, *n.* prix *(m.)* supplémentaire; (tax) surtaxe *f.*

sure, *adj.* sûr.

surf, *n.* ressac *m.*

surface, *n.* surface *f.*

surfboard, *n.* planche *(f.)* de surf.

surfing, *n.* surf *m.*

surge, *n.* houle *f.*

surgeon, *n.* chirurgien *m.*

surgery, *n.* chirurgie *f.*

surpass, *vb.* surpasser.

surplus, *n.* surplus *m.*

surprise, 1. *n.* surprise *f.* **2.** *vb.* surprendre.

surrender, *vb.* rendre, *tr.*

surround, *vb.* entourer.

survey, 1. *vb.* contempler; (investigate) examiner. **2.** *n.* enquête *f.*

survival, *n.* survivance *f.,* survie *f.*

survive, *vb.* survivre.

susceptible, *adj.* susceptible (de).

suspect, 1. *vb.* soupçonner. **2.** *adj. and n.* suspect *m.*

suspend, *vb.* suspendre.

suspense, *n.* incertitude *f.;* (in s.) en suspens; (film, book) suspense *m.*

suspension, *n.* suspension *f.*

suspicion, *n.* soupçon *m.*

suspicious, *adj.* soupçonneux; (questionable) suspect.

sustain, *vb.* soutenir.

swallow, 1. *n.* (bird) hirondelle *f.* **2.** *vb.* avaler.

swamp, *n.* marais *m.*

swan, *n.* cygne *m.*

swap, *vb.* échanger.

swarm, *n.* essaim *m.*

sway, 1. *n.* (rule) domination *f.;* (motion) oscillation *f.* **2.** *vb.* (rule) gouverner; (motion) se balancer.

swear, *vb.* jurer.

sweat, 1. *n.* sueur *f.* **2.** *vb.* suer.

sweater, *n.* pull-over *m.*

Swede, *n.* Suédois *m.*

Sweden, *n.* Suède *f.*

Swedish, *adj. and n.* suédois *m.*

sweep, 1. *n.* (bend) courbe *f.;* (movement) mouvement *(m.)* circulaire. **2.** *vb.* balayer.

sweepstakes, *n.* poule *f.*

sweet, *adj.* doux *m.,* douce *f.;* sucré.

sweetheart, *n.* chéri *m.,* chérie *f.*

sweetness, *n.* douceur *f.*

swell, *vb.* gonfler, *tr.;* enfler, *tr.*

swift, *adj.* rapide.

swim, *vb.* nager.

swimsuit, *n.* maillot de bain *m.*

swindle, *vb.* escroquer.

swine, *n.* cochon *m.*

swing, *vb.* balancer, *tr.*

Swiss, 1. *n.* Suisse *m.* **2.** *adj.* suisse, helvétique.

switch, *n.* (elect.) interrupteur *m.*

switchboard, *n.* standard *m.*

Switzerland, *n.* Suisse *f.*

sword, *n.* épée *f.*

syllable, *n.* syllabe *f.*

symbol, *n.* symbole *m.*

symbolic, *adj.* symbolique.

symmetry, *n.* symétrie *f.*

sympathetic, *adj.* compatissant.

sympathy, *n.* compassion *f.*

symphony, *n.* symphonie *f.*

symptom, *n.* symptôme *m.*

synagogue, *n.* synagogue *f.*

synchronize, *vb.* synchroniser, *tr.*

syndicate, *n.* syndicat *m.*

syndrome, *n.* syndrome *m.*

synonym, *n.* synonyme *m.*

synthetic, *adj.* synthétique.

syphilis, *n.* syphilis *f.*

Syria, *n.* Syrie *f.*

syringe, *n.* seringue *f.*

syrup, *n.* sirop *m.*

system, *n.* système *m.*

systems analyst, *n.* analyste-programmeur *m.*

systematic, *adj.* systématique.

T

tabernacle, *n.* tabernacle *m.*

table, *n.* table *f.*

tablecloth, *n.* nappe *f.*

tablespoon, *n.* cuiller *(f.)* à soupe.

tablet, *n.* tablette *f.*

tabloid, *n.* (t. press) la presse *(f.)* populaire.

tack, 1. *n.* (nail) broquette *f.* **2.** *vb.* clouer.

tackle, 1. *n.* matériel *m.* **2.** *vb.* s'attaquer à.

tact, *n.* tact *m.*

tag, *n.* étiquette *f.*

tail, *n.* queue *f.*

tailor, *n.* tailleur *m.*

take, *vb.* prendre; (lead) conduire; (carry) porter; **(t. off)** (plane) décoller.

tale, *n.* conte *m.*

talent, *n.* talent *m.*

talk, 1. *n.* conversation *f.* **2.** *vb.* parler.

talkative, *adj.* bavard.

tall, *adj.* grand.

tame, *adj.* (animal) apprivoisé.

tamper, *vb.* toucher à.

tampon, *n.* tampon hygiénique *m.*

tan, 1. *n.* (leather) tan *m.;* (skin) hâle *m.;* (color) tanné *m.* **2.** *vb.* tanner.

tangible, *adj.* tangible.

tangle, *n.* embrouillement *m.*

tank, *n.* réservoir *m.;* (mil.) char *(m.)* d'assaut.

tap, 1. *n.* (water) robinet *m.;* (knock) petit coup *m.* **2.** *vb.* frapper légèrement.

tape, *n.* ruban *m.*

tape recorder, *n.* magnétophone *m.*

tapestry, *n.* tapisserie *f.*

tar, *n.* goudron *m.*

target, *n.* cible *f.*

tariff, *n.* tarif *m.*

tarnish, *vb.* ternir, *tr.*

tarragon, *n.* estragon *m.*

tart, 1. *n.* tarte *f.* **2.** *adj.* âpre.

task, *n.* tâche *f.*

taste, 1. *n.* goût *m.* **2.** *vb.* goûter.

tasty, *adj.* savoureux.

taut, *adj.* raide.

tavern, *n.* taverne *f.*

tax, 1. *n.* impôt *m.* **2.** *vb.* imposer.

taxi, *n.* taxi *m.*

taxi driver, *n.* chauffeur *(m.)* de taxi.

taxpayer, *n.* contribuable *m.*

tea, *n.* thé *m.*

teach, *vb.* enseigner; (to do) apprendre à.

teacher, *n.* instituteur *m.;* (school) professeur *m.*

team, *n.* (animals) attelage *m.;* (people) équipe *f.*

teapot, *n.* théière *f.*

tear, 1. *n.* larme *f.;* (rip) déchirure *f.* **2.** *vb.* déchirer.

tease, *vb.* taquiner.

teaspoon, *n.* cuiller (*f.*) à thé.

technical, *adj.* technique.

technician, *n.* technicien *m.*

technique, *n.* technique *f.*

technological, *adj.* technologique.

tedious, *adj.* ennuyeux.

teenager, *n.* adolescent *m.*

telegram, *n.* télégramme *m.*

telegraph, *n.* télégraphe *m.*

telephone, 1. *n.* téléphone *m.* **2.** *vb.* téléphoner.

telephone booth, *n.* cabine (*f.*) téléphonique.

telephone directory, *n.* annuaire *m.* (du téléphone).

telescope, *n.* télescope *m.*

televise, *vb.* téléviser.

television, *n.* télévision *f.*

tell, *vb.* dire; (story, etc.) raconter.

teller, *n.* (bank) caissier *m.,* guichetier *m.*

temper, *n.* (humor) humeur *f.;* (lose one's t.) s'emporter; (anger) colère *f.;* (metals) trempe *f.*

temperament, *n.* tempérament *m.*

temperamental, *adj.* instable.

temperance, *n.* tempérance *f.*

temperate, *adj.* (habit) sobre; (climate) tempéré.

temperature, *n.* température *f.*

tempest, *n.* tempête *f.*

template, *n.* patron *m.*

temple, *n.* temple *m.;* (forehead) tempe *f.*

temporary, *adj.* temporaire, provisoire.

tempt, *vb.* tenter.

temptation, *n.* tentation *f.*

ten, *adj. and n.* dix *m.*

tenant, *n.* locataire *m.f.*

tend, *vb.* tendre, *intr.;* (care for) soigner.

tendency, *n.* tendance *f.*

tender, *adj.* tendre.

tenderness, *n.* tendresse *f.*

tendon, *n.* tendon *m.*

tenement, *n.* taudis *m.*

tennis, *n.* tennis *m.*

tenor, *n.* (music) ténor *m.*

tense, *adj.* tendu.

tension, *n.* tension *f.*

tent, *n.* tente *f.*

tentative, *adj.* tentatif, expérimental.

tenth, *adj. and n.* dixième *m.f.*

term, *n.* terme *m.;* (school) trimestre *m.;* (conditions) conditions *f.pl.;* (political) mandat *m.*

terminal, 1. *n.* (electricity) borne *f.;* (computer) terminal *m.;* (airport) aérogare *f.* **2.** *adj.* incurable, terminal.

terrace, *n.* terrasse *f.*

terrible, *adj.* terrible.

terrific, *adj.* fantastique.

terrify, *vb.* terrifier.

territory, *n.* territoire *m.*

terror, *n.* terreur *f.*

test, 1. *n.* épreuve *f.* **2.** *vb.* mettre à l'épreuve.

testament, *n.* testament *m.*

testify, *vb.* témoigner (de); (declare) affirmer.

testimony, *n.* témoignage *m.*

text, *n.* texte *m.*

textile, *adj.* textile.

texture, *n.* texture *f.*

Thai, 1. *n.* Thaïlandais *m.* **2.** *adj.* thaïlandais.

than, *conj.* que; (with numerals) de.

thank, *vb.* remercier; (t. you) merci.

thankful, *adj.* reconnaissant.

that *sg., those pl.,* **1.** *adj.* ce, cet *m.,* cette *f.,* ces *pl.;* (opposed to *this*) ce . . . -là, *etc.* **2.** *demonstrative pron.* celui-là, celle-là *f.,* ceux-là *m.pl.,* celles-là *f.pl.;* (object not named) cela, *abbr.* ça; (what is t.?) qu'est-ce que c'est que ça? **3.** *relative pron.* qui (subject); que (object). **4.** *conj.* que; (purpose) pour que.

the, *art.* le *m.,* la *f.,* les *pl.*

theater, *n.* théâtre *m.*

theft, *n.* vol *m.*

their, *adj.* leur *sg.,* leurs *pl.*

theirs, *pron.* le leur *m.,* la leur *f.,* leurs *pl.*

them, *pron.* eux *m.*; elles *f.*; (unstressed, with verb) les (direct), leur (indirect).

theme, *n.* thème *m.*

themselves, *pron.* eux-mêmes *m.*; elles-mêmes *f.*; (reflexive) se.

then, *adv.* alors; (after that) ensuite.

thence, *adv.* (place) de là; (reason) pour cette raison.

theology, *n.* théologie *f.*

theoretical, *adj.* théorique.

theory, *n.* théorie *f.*

therapy, *n.* thérapie *f.*

there, *adv.* là; (with verb) y.

therefore, *adv.* donc.

thermometer, *n.* thermomètre *m.*

thermonuclear, *adj.* thermonucléaire.

thermostat, *n.* thermostat *m.*

these, *see* **this.**

they, *pron.* ils *m.*, elles *f.*

thick, *adj.* épais.

thicken, *vb.* épaissir, *tr.*

thickness, *n.* épaisseur *f.*

thief, *n.* voleur *m.*

thigh, *n.* cuisse *f.*

thimble, *n.* dé *m.*

thin, *adj.* mince.

thing, *n.* chose *f.*

think (of), *vb.* penser (à).

thinker, *n.* penseur *m.*

third, 1. *n.* tiers *m.* **2.** *adj.* troisième.

Third World, *n.* Tiers Monde *m.*

thirst, *n.* soif *f.*

thirsty, *adj.* (be t.) avoir soif.

thirteen, *adj. and n.* treize *m.*

thirty, *adj. and n.* trente *m.*

this, *sg.* **these** *pl.,* **1.** *adj.* ce, cet *m.*, cette *f.*, ces *pl.*; (opposed to *that*) ce . . . -ci, *etc.* **2.** *demonstrative pron.* celui-ci *m.*, celle-ci *f.*, ceux-ci *m.pl.*, celles-ci *f.pl.*; (object not named) ceci.

thorough, *adj.* complet.

those, *see* **that.**

though, *conj.* quoique.

thought, *n.* pensée *f.*

thoughtful, *adj.* pensif.

thoughtless, *adj.* étourdi.

thousand, *adj. and n.* mille *m.*

thread, *n.* fil *m.*

threat, *n.* menace *f.*

threaten, *vb.* menacer.

three, *adj. and n.* trois *m.*

thrift, *n.* économie *f.*

thrill, 1. *n.* tressaillement *m.* **2.** *vb.* tressaillir, *intr.*; faire frémir, *tr.*

thriller, *n.* livre *(m.)*/film *(m.)* à suspense.

thrive, *vb.* prospérer.

throat, *n.* gorge *f.*

throne, *n.* trône *m.*

through, *prep. and adv.* à travers; (be t.) avoir fini.

throughout, *adv.* partout.

throw, *vb.* jeter.

thrust, *vb.* pousser.

thumb, *n.* pouce *m.*

thumbtack, *n.* punaise *f.*

thunder, 1. *n.* tonnerre *m.* **2.** *vb.* tonner.

Thursday, *n.* jeudi *m.*

thus, *adv.* ainsi.

thwart, *vb.* contrarier.

thyme, *n.* thym *m.*

thyroid, *n.* thyroïde *f.*

ticket, *n.* billet *m.*

tickle, *vb.* chatouiller.

ticklish, *adj.* chatouilleux.

tide, *n.* marée *f.*

tidy, *adj.* ordonné, en ordre.

tie, 1. *n.* lien *m.*; (neck-t.) cravate *f.* **2.** *vb.* attacher; (bind) lier; (knot) nouer.

tier, *n.* gradin *m.*

tiger, *n.* tigre *m.*

tight, *adj.* serré; (drunk) gris.

tighten, *vb.* serrer.

tile, *n.* (roof) tuile *f.*

till, 1. *prep.* jusqu'a. **2.** *conj.* jusqu'à ce que.

tilt, *vb.* pencher.

timber, *n.* (building) bois *(m.)* de construction.

time, 1. *n.* temps *m.*; (occasion) fois *f.*; (clock) heure *f.*; (what t. is it?) quelle heure est-il?; (have a good t.) s'amuser bien. **2.** *vb.* (race) chronométrer; (program) minuter.

timeless, *adj.* éternel.

timetable, *n.* horaire *m.*

timid, *adj.* timide.

timidity, *n.* timidité *f.*

tin, *n.* étain *m.*

tin foil, *n.* papier *(m.)* d'aluminium.

tint, *n.* teinte *f.*

tiny, *adj.* tout petit.

tip, 1. *n.* (money) pourboire *m.;* (end) bout *m.* **2.** *vb.* (money) donner un pourboire à; (**t. over**) renverser.

tire, 1. *n.* (car, etc.) pneu *m.* **2.** *vb.* fatiguer.

tired, *adj.* fatigué.

tissue, *n.* tissu *m.;* mouchoir *m.*

title, *n.* titre *m.*

to, *prep.* à; (**in order t.**) pour.

toast, *n.* pain *(m.)* grillé.

tobacco, *n.* tabac *m.*

today, *adv.* aujourd'hui.

toe, *n.* orteil *m.*

together, *adv.* ensemble.

toil, *vb.* travailler dur.

toilet, *n.* toilettes *f.pl.;* (**t. paper**) papier *(m.)* hygiénique.

token, *n.* témoignage *m.;* (coin) jeton *m.*

tolerance, *n.* tolérance *f.*

tolerant, *adj.* tolérant.

tolerate, *vb.* tolérer.

toll, *n.* péage *m.*

tomato, *n.* tomate *f.*

tomb, *n.* tombeau *m.*

tomorrow, *adv.* demain.

ton, *n.* tonne *f.*

tone, *n.* ton *m.*

tongue, *n.* langue *f.*

tonic, *adj. and n.* tonique *m.*

tonight, *adv.* cette nuit; (evening) ce soir.

tonsil, *n.* amygdale *f.*

tonsillitis, *n.* amygdalite *f.*

too, *adv.* trop; (also) aussi.

tool, *n.* outil *m.*

tooth, *n.* dent *f.*

toothache, *n.* mal *(m.)* de dents.

toothbrush, *n.* brosse *(f.)* à dents.

toothpaste, *n.* dentifrice *m.*

top, *n.* (mountain, etc.) sommet *m.;* (table) dessus *m.*

topcoat, *n.* pardessus *m.*

topic, *n.* sujet *m.*

torch, *n.* torche *f.*

torment, 1. *n.* tourment *m.* **2.** *vb.* tourmenter.

tornado, *n.* tornade *f.*

torrent, *n.* torrent *m.*

torture, 1. *n.* torture *f.* **2.** *vb.* torturer.

toss, *vb.* (throw) jeter; s'agiter.

total, *adj.* n. total *m.*

totalitarian, *adj.* totalitaire.

touch, 1. *n.* (touching) attouchement *m.;* (sense) toucher *m.;* (small amount) pointe *f.;* (contact) contact *m.* **2.** *vb.* toucher.

touching, *adj.* touchant.

tough, *adj.* dur.

tour, 1. *n.* tour *m.* **2.** *vb.* visiter.

tourist, *n.* touriste *m.f.*

tournament, *n.* tournoi *m.*

tow, *vb.* remorquer.

toward, *prep.* (place, time) vers; (feelings, etc.) envers.

towel, *n.* serviette *f.*

tower, *n.* tour *f.*

town, *n.* ville *f.*

toy, *n.* jouet *m.*

trace, *n.* trace *f.*

track, *n.* piste *f.;* (railroad) voie *f.*

tract, *n.* (space) étendue *f.*

tractor, *n.* tracteur *m.*

trade, 1. *n.* commerce *m.;* (job) métier *m.* **2.** *vb.* commercer, échanger.

trader, *n.* commerçant *m.*

trade union, *n.* syndicat *m.*

tradition, *n.* tradition *f.*

traditional, *adj.* traditionnel.

traffic, *n.* circulation *f.*

tragedy, *n.* tragédie *f.*

tragic, *adj.* tragique.

trail, *n.* trace *f.*

train, 1. *n.* train *m.;* (dress) traîne *f.;* (retinue) suite *f.* **2.** *vb.* (sports) entraîner, *tr.;* (mil.) exercer, *tr.*

trait, *n.* trait *m.*

traitor, *n.* traître *m.*

tramp, *n.* (steps) bruit *(m.)* de pas; (person) chemineau *m.*

tranquil, *adj.* tranquille.

tranquillity, *n.* tranquillité *f.*

transaction, *n.* opération *f.*

transcript, *n.* transcription *f.*

transfer, 1. *n.* transport *m.;* (ticket) billet *(m.)* de correspondance. **2.** *vb.* transférer, *tr.*

transform, *vb.* transformer.

transfusion, *n.* transfusion *f.*

transistor, *n.* transistor *m.*

transition, *n.* transition *f.*

translate, *vb.* traduire.

translation, *n.* traduction *f.*

transmit, *vb.* transmettre.

transparent, *adj.* transparent.

transplant, 1. *vb.* transplanter. 2. *n.* transplantation *f.*

transport, transportation, 1. *n.* transport *m.* 2. *vb.* transporter.

transsexual, *adj.* transsexuel.

transvestite, *n.* travesti.

trap, 1. *n.* piège *m.* 2. *vb.* prendre au piège.

trash, *n.* (rubbish) rebut *m.*

trauma, *n.* traumatisme *m.*

travel, 1. *n.* voyage *m.* 2. *vb.* voyager.

traveler, *n.* voyageur *m.*

traveler's check, *n.* chèque *(m.)* de voyage.

tray, *n.* plateau *m.*

treacherous, *adj.* traître.

tread, *vb.* marcher.

treason, *n.* trahison *f.*

treasure, 1. *n.* trésor *m.* 2. *vb.* tenir beaucoup à.

treasurer, *n.* trésorier *m.*

treasury, *n.* trésor *m.*

treat, *vb.* traiter.

treatment, *n.* traitement *m.*

treaty, *n.* traité *m.*

tree, *n.* arbre *m.*

trek, *n.* voyage *(m.)* difficile.

tremble, *vb.* trembler.

tremendous, *adj.* terrible.

trench, *n.* tranchée *f.*

trend, *n.* tendance *f.*, mode *f.*

trespass, *vb.* empiéter.

triage, *n.* présélection *f.*

trial, *n.* (law) procès *m.*; (test) épreuve *f.*

triangle, *n.* triangle *m.*

tribe, *n.* tribu *f.*

tribulation, *n.* tribulation *f.*

tributary, 1. *n.* (river) affluent *m.* 2. *adj.* tributaire.

tribute, *n.* tribut *m.*

trick, 1. *n.* ruse *f.* 2. *vb.* duper.

trickle, *vb.* dégouliner.

tricky, *adj.* astucieux.

trifle, *n.* bagatelle *f.*

trigger, 1. *n.* détente *f.* 2. *vb.* déclencher.

trim, 1. *adj.* soigné, svelte. 2. *vb.* (put in order) arranger; (adorn) garnir; (cut) tailler.

Trinity, *n.* Trinité *f.*

trinket, *n.* breloque *f.*

trip, 1. *n.* voyage *m.* 2. *vb.* trébucher.

triple, *adj. and n.* triple *m.*

trite, *adj.* rebattu.

triumph, *n.* triomphe *m.*

triumphant, *adj.* triomphant.

trivial, *adj.* trivial.

trolley-car, *n.* tramway *m.*

troop, *n.* troupe *f.*

trophy, *n.* trophée *m.*

tropic, *n.* tropique *m.*

trot, 1. *n.* trot *m.* 2. *vb. intr.* trotter.

trouble, 1. *n.* (misfortune) malheur *m.*; (difficulty) difficulté *f.*; (inconvenience, med.) dérangement *m.* 2. *vb.* (worry) inquiéter, *tr.*; (inconvenience) déranger; (afflict) affliger.

troublesome, *adj.* gênant.

trough, *n.* auge *f.*

trousers, *n.* pantalon *m.*

trousseau, *n.* trousseau *m.*

trout, *n.* truite *f.*

truce, *n.* trêve *f.*

truck, *n.* camion *m.*

true, *adj.* vrai.

truly, *adv.* vraiment.

trumpet, *n.* trompette *f.*

trunk, *n.* (clothes) malle *f.*; (body, tree) tronc *m.*

trust, 1. *n.* confiance *f.* 2. *vb.* se confier à; (entrust) confier.

trustworthy, *adj.* digne de confiance.

truth, *n.* vérité *f.*

truthful, *adj.* sincère.

try, *vb.* essayer; (law) mettre en jugement.

tryst, *n.* rendez-vous *m.*

T-shirt, *n.* maillot *m.*, tee-shirt *m.*

tub, *n.* baignoire *f.*

tube, *n.* tube *m.*

tuberculosis, *n.* tuberculose *f.*

tuck, 1. *n.* (fold) pli *m.* 2. *vb.* ranger, rentrer.

Tuesday, *n.* mardi *m.*

tug, 1. *n.* (boat) remorqueur *m.* 2. *vb.* (pull) tirer; (boat) remorquer.

tuition, *n.* (frais de l')enseignement *m.*

tulip, *n.* tulipe *f.*

tumble, *vb.* (fall) tomber.

tummy, *n.* ventre *m.*

tumor, *n.* tumeur *f.*

tumult, *n.* tumulte *m.*

tuna, *n.* thon *m.*

tune, 1. n. air m.; (concord, harmony) accord m. 2. vb. accorder.
Tunisia, n. Tunisie f.
tunnel, n. tunnel m.
turban, n. turban m.
turf, n. gazon m.
Turk, n. Turc m., Turque f.
turkey, n. dindon m.
Turkey, n. Turquie f.
Turkish, 1. n. (language) turc m. 2. adj. turc m., turque f.
turmoil, n. tumulte m.
turn, 1. n. tour m.; (road) détour m. 2. vb. tourner, virer.
turning point, n. tournant m.
turnip, n. navet m.
turnover, n. (money) chiffre (m.) d'affaires.
turnpike, n. autoroute (f.) à péage.
turret, n. tourelle f.
turtle, n. tortue f.
tutor, 1. n. précepteur m. 2. vb. donner des leçons particulières à.
TV, n. télé f.
twelfth, adj. and n. douzième m.f.

twelve, adj. and n. douze m.
twentieth, adj. and n. vingtième m.f.
twenty, adj. and n. vingt m.
twice, adv. deux fois.
twig, n. brindille f.
twilight, n. crépuscule m.
twin, adj. and n. jumeau m., jumelle f.
twine, n. ficelle f.
twinkle, vb. scintiller.
twirl, vb. (faire) tournoyer.
twist, vb. tordre.
two, adj. and n. deux m.
tycoon, n. magnat m.
type, 1. n. type m.; (printing) caractère m. 2. vb. taper à la machine.
typewriter, n. machine (f.) à écrire.
typhoid fever, n. fièvre (f.) typhoïde.
typical, adj. typique.
typist, n. dactylo(graphe) m.f.
tyranny, n. tyrannie f.
tyrant, n. tyran m.

U

ubiquitous, adj. omniprésent.
udder, n. mamelle f.
Uganda, n. Ouganda m.
ugliness, n. laideur f.
ugly, adj. laid.
ulcer, n. ulcère m.
ulterior, adj. ultérieur.
ultimate, adj. dernier.
ultrasound, n. ultrason m.
umbrella, n. parapluie m.
umpire, n. arbitre m.f.
unable, adj. incapable; (u. to) dans l'impossibilité de.
unanimous, adj. unanime.
uncalled for, adj. déplacé.
uncanny, adj. bizarre.
uncertain, adj. incertain.
uncle, n. oncle m.
unconscious, 1. n. inconscient m. 2. adj. (aware) inconscient; (faint) sans connaissance; (u. of) sans conscience de.
uncouth, adj. grossier.
uncover, vb. découvrir.

under, 1. prep. sous. 2. adv. au-dessous.
underdeveloped, adj. sous-développé.
underestimate, vb. sous-estimer.
undergo, vb. subir.
underground, adj. souterrain, clandestin.
underline, vb. souligner.
underneath, adv. en-dessous.
underpants, n.pl. caleçon m., slip m.
underprivileged, adj. défavorisé.
undershirt, n. gilet (m.) de dessous.
understand, vb. comprendre.
understatement, n. litote f.
undertake, vb. entreprendre.
undertaker, n. entrepreneur (m.) de pompes funèbres.
underwear, n., sous-vêtements m.pl.
underworld, n. (crime) milieu m., pègre f.
undo, vb. défaire.

undress, *vb.* déshabiller, *tr.*

uneasy, *adj.* gêné.

uneven, *adj.* inégal.

unexpected, *adj.* inattendu.

unfair, *adj.* injuste.

unfit, *adj.* peu propre (à).

unfold, *vb.* déplier.

unforgettable, *adj.* inoubliable.

unfortunate, *adj.* malheureux.

unhappy, *adj.* malheureux.

uniform, *adj. and n.* uniforme *f.*

unify, *vb.* unifier.

union, *n.* union *f.*

unique, *adj.* unique.

unisex, *adj.* unisexuel.

unison, *n.* (in u.) à l'unisson.

unit, *n.* unité *f.*

unite, *vb.* unir, *tr.*

United Kingdom, *n.* Royaume (*m.*) Uni.

United Nations, *n.* Nations (*f.pl.*) Unies.

United States, *n.* États-Unis *m.pl.*

unity, *n.* unité *f.*

universal, *adj.* universel.

universe, *n.* univers *m.*

university, *n.* université *f.*

unless, *conj.* à moins que . . . ne.

unlike, *adj.* dissemblable.

unload, *vb.* décharger.

unlock, *vb.* ouvrir.

untie, *vb.* dénouer.

until, *conj.* jusqu'à ce que.

unusual, *adj.* insolite.

up, *prep.* vers le haut de.

upbringing, *n.* éducation *f.*

update, *vb.* mettre à jour.

uphold, *vb.* soutenir.

upholster, *vb.* tapisser.

upon, *prep.* sur.

upper, *adj.* supérieur.

upright, *adj.* droit.

uprising, *n.* soulèvement *m.*

uproar, *n.* vacarme *m.*

upset, *vb.* renverser.

upstairs, *adv.* en haut.

uptight, *adj.* tendu, crispé.

upward, 1. *adj.* dirigé en haut. **2.** *adv.* en montant.

uranium, *n.* uranium *m.*

urban, *adj.* urbain.

urge, *vb.* (beg) prier.

urgency, *n.* urgence *f.*

urgent, *adj.* urgent.

us, *pron.* nous.

use, 1. *n.* usage *m.* **2.** *vb.* employer, se servir de.

useful, *adj.* utile.

useless, *adj.* inutile.

usher, *n.* huissier *m.*

usual, *adj.* usuel.

utensil, *n.* ustensile *m.*

uterus, *n.* utérus *m.*

utilize, *vb.* utiliser, se servir de.

utmost, 1. *n.* le plus; (all one can) tout son possible. **2.** *adj.* (greatest) le plus grand.

utter, 1. *adj.* absolu. **2.** *vb.* prononcer; (cry) pousser.

utterance, *n.* émission *f.*

V

vacancy, *n.* vide *m.*, vacance *f.*

vacant, *adj.* vide.

vacate, *vb.* quitter, évacuer.

vacation, *n.* vacances *f.pl.*

vaccinate, *vb.* vacciner.

vaccine, *n.* vaccin *m.*

vacuum, *n.* vide *m.*; (v. cleaner) aspirateur *m.*

vagina, *n.* vagin *m.*

vagrant, *adj.* vagabond.

vague, *adj.* vague.

vain, *adj.* vain.

valiant, *adj.* vaillant.

valid, *adj.* valide.

valise, *n.* valise *f.*

valley, *n.* vallée *f.*

valor, *n.* valeur *f.*

valuable, *adj.* de valeur.

value, 1. *n.* valeur *f.* **2.** *vb.* évaluer.

value-added tax, *n.* taxe à la valeur ajoutée *f.*

valve, *n.* soupape *f.*

van, *n.* camionnette *f.*

vandal, *n.* vandale *m.f.*

vanguard, *n.* avant-garde *f.*

vanilla, *n.* vanille *f.*

vanish, *vb.* s'évanouir.

vanity, *n.* vanité *f.*

vanquish, *vb.* vaincre.

vapor, *n.* vapeur *f.*

variable, *adj.* variable.
variation, *n.* variation *f.*
varied, *adj.* varié.
variety, *n.* variété *f.*
various, *adj.* divers.
varnish, *n.* vernis *m.*
vary, *vb.* varier.
vase, *n.* vase *m.*
vasectomy, *n.* vasectomie *f.*
vassal, *n.* vassal *m.*
vast, *adj.* vaste.
vat, *n.* cuve *f.*
vault, *n.* voûte *f.*
veal, *n.* veau *m.*
vegetable, *n.* légume *m.*
vegetarian, *n.* végétarien *m.*
vehement, *adj.* véhément.
vehicle, *n.* véhicule *m.*
veil, *n.* voile *m.*
vein, *n.* veine *f.*
velocity, *n.* vitesse *f.*
velvet, *n.* velours *m.*
vending machine, *n.* distributeur
  (m.) automatique
venereal, *adj.* vénérien.
vengeance, *n.* vengeance *f.*
vent, *n.* ouverture *f.*
ventilate, *vb.* ventiler.
venture, 1. *n.* aventure *f.* **2.** *vb.* hasarder, *tr.*
verb, *n.* verbe *m.*
verbose, *adj.* verbeux.
verdict, *n.* verdict *m.*
verge, *n.* bord *m.*
verify, *vb.* vérifier.
vermouth, *n.* vermouth *m.*
versatile, *adj.* versatile.
verse, *n.* vers *m.pl.;* (line of poetry)
  vers *m.*
version, *n.* version *f.*
vertical, *adj.* vertical.
vertigo vertige *m.*
very, *adv.* très.
vessel, *n.* vaisseau *m.*
vest, *n.* gilet *m.*
veteran, *n.* vétéran *m.*
veterinarian, *n.* vétérinaire *m.f.*
veto, *n.* véto *m.*
vex, *vb.* vexer.
viaduct, *n.* viaduc *m.*
vibrate, *vb.* vibrer.
vibration, *n.* vibration *f.*
vice, *n.* vice *m.*
vicinity, *n.* voisinage *m.*

vicious, *adj.* méchant.
victim, *n.* victime *f.*
victor, *n.* vainqueur *m.*
victorious, *adj.* victorieux.
victory, *n.* victoire *f.*
videocassette recorder, *n.* magnétoscope *m.*
videodisc, *n.* vidéodisque *m.*
videotape, *n.* bande vidéo *f.*
Vietnam, *n.* Viêt-nam *m.*
view, *n.* vue *f.*
vigil, *n.* veille *f.*
vigilant, *adj.* vigilant.
vigor, *n.* vigueur *f.*
vile, *adj.* vil, abominable.
village, *n.* village *m.*
villain, *n.* scélérat *m.*
vindicate, *vb.* défendre.
vindictive, *adj.* vindicatif.
vine, *n.* vigne *f.*
vinegar, *n.* vinaigre *m.*
vineyard, *n.* vigne *f.,* vignoble *m.*
vintage, *n.* (grapes gathered) vendange *f.;* (year of wine) année *f.,*
  millésime, *m.*
viola, *n.* alto *m.*
violate, *vb.* violer.
violation, *n.* violation *f.*
violence, *n.* violence *f.*
violent, *adj.* violent.
violet, 1. *n.* violette *f.* **2.** *adj.* violet.
violin, *n.* violon *m.*
virgin, *n.* vierge *f.*
virile, *adj.* viril.
virtual, *adj.* vrai.
virtual reality, *n.* réalité *(f.)* vir-
  tuelle.
virtue, *n.* vertu *f.*
virtuous, *adj.* vertueux.
virus, *n.* virus *m.*
visa, *n.* visa *m.*
visible, *adj.* visible.
vision, *n.* vision *f.*
visit, 1. *n.* visite *f.* **2.** *vb.* visiter.
visitor, *n.* visiteur *m.*
visual, *adj.* visuel.
vital, *adj.* vital.
vitality, *n.* vitalité *f.*
vitamin, *n.* vitamine *f.*
vivacious, *adj.* vif *m.,* vive *f.*
vivid, *adj.* vif *m.,* vive *f.*
vocabulary, *n.* vocabulaire *m.*
vocal, *adj.* vocal.
vocation, *n.* vocation *f.*

vodka, *n.* vodka *f.*

vogue, *n.* vogue *f.*

voice, *n.* voix *f.*

void, *adj.* (law) nul.

volcano, *n.* volcan *m.*

volley, *n.* (gun fire) salve *f.* **volleyball,** *n.* volley(-ball) *m.*

volt, *n.* volt *m.*

voltage, *n.* tension *f.*, voltage *m.*

volume, *n.* volume *m.*

voluntary, *adj.* volontaire.

volunteer, 1. *n.* volontaire *m.* **2.** *vb.* s'engager.

vomit, *vb.* vomir.

vote, 1. *n.* vote *m.* **2.** *vb.* voter.

voter, *n.* votant *m.*

vouch for, *vb.* répondre de.

vow, *n.* vœu *m.*

vowel, *n.* voyelle *f.*

voyage, *n.* voyage *m.*

vulgar, *adj.* vulgaire.

vulnerable, *adj.* vulnérable.

vulture, *n.* vautour *m.*

W

wade, *vb.* traverser à gué.

wafer, *n.* gaufrette *f.*

waffle, *n.* gaufre (américaine) *f.*

wag, *vb.* agiter.

wage, *vb.* (war) faire la guerre.

wages, *n.* salaire *m.*

wagon, *n.* chariot *m.*

wail, *vb.* gémir.

waist, *n.* taille *f.*

wait (for), *vb.* attendre.

waiter, *n.* garçon *m.*, serveur *m.*

waitress, *n.* serveuse *f.*

wake (up), *vb.* réveiller, *tr.*; s'éveiller, *intr.*

Wales, *n.* pays *(m.)* de Galles.

walk, 1. *n.* promenade *f.* **2.** *vb.* marcher; **(take a w.)** se promener.

Walkman, *n.* baladeur *m.*, walkman *m.*

wall, *n.* mur *m.*

wallcovering, *n.* tenture *f.*

wallet, *n.* portefeuille *m.*

wallpaper, *n.* papier peint *m.*; papier à tapisser *m.*

walnut, *n.* noix *f.*

walrus, *n.* morse *m.*

waltz, *n.* valse *f.*

wander, *vb.* errer.

want, 1. *n.* besoin *m.* **2.** *vb.* vouloir.

war, *n.* guerre *f.*

ward, *n.* (hospital) salle *f.*; (charge) pupille *m.f.*

ware, *n.* marchandise *f.pl.*

warehouse, *n.* entrepôt *m.*

warhead, *n.* ogive *f.*

warlike, *adj.* guerrier.

warm, 1. *adj.* chaud; **(be w.)** avoir chaud. **2.** *vb.* chauffer.

warmth, *n.* chaleur *f.*

warn, *vb.* avertir.

warning, *n.* avertissement *m.*

warp, *vb.* détourner.

warrant, 1. *n.* mandat *m.* **2.** *vb.* garantir.

warranty, *n.* garantie *f.*

warrior, *n.* guerrier *m.*

warship, *n.* navire *(m.)* de guerre.

wash, *vb.* laver, *tr.*

washing machine, *n.* laveuse mécanique *f.*

washroom, *n.* salle *(f.)* de bain.

wasp, *n.* guêpe *f.*

waste, 1. *n.* (money) gaspillage *m.*; (time) perte *f.*; (rubbish) déchets *m.pl.* **2.** *vb.* gaspiller, perdre.

wastepaper basket, *n.* corbeille *(f.)* à papier.

watch, 1. *n.* (timepiece) montre *f.*; (guard) garde *f.* **2.** *vb.* veiller.

watchful, *adj.* vigilant.

watchmaker, *n.* horloger *m.*

watchman, *n.* gardien *m.*

water, *n.* eau *f.*

waterbed, *n.* aqualit *m.*

water color, *n.* aquarelle *f.*

watercress, *n.* cresson *m.*

waterfall, *n.* chute *(f.)* d'eau.

waterproof, *adj.* imperméable.

wave, 1. *n.* (sea) vague *f.*; (sound) onde *f.*; **(permanent w.)** ondulation *(f.)* permanente. **2.** *vb.* agiter; (hair) onduler; saluer.

waver, *vb.* vaciller.

wax, *n.* cire *f.*

way, *n.* (road) chemin *m.*; (distance) distance *f.*; (direction) côté *m.*; (manner) manière *f.*

we, *pron.* nous.

weak, *adj.* faible.

weaken, *vb.* affaiblir.

weakness, *n.* faiblesse *f.*

wealth, *n.* richesse *f.*

wealthy, *adj.* riche.

weapon, *n.* arme *f.*

wear, *vb.* porter; **(w. down)** user; **(w. out)** épuiser.

weary, *adj.* las.

weasel, *n.* belette *f.*

weather, *n.* temps *m.*

weave, *vb.* tisser.

weaver, *n.* tisserand *m.*

web, *n.* (fabric) tissu *m.*; (spider) toile *f.*

wedding, *n.* noces *f.pl.*

wedge, *n.* coin *m.*

Wednesday, *n.* mercredi *m.*

weed, *n.* mauvaise herbe *f.*

week, *n.* semaine *f.*

weekday, *n.* jour *(m.)* de semaine.

weekend, *n.* week-end *m.*, fin de semaine *f.*

weekly, *adj.* hebdomadaire.

weep, *vb.* pleurer.

weigh, *vb.* peser.

weight, *n.* poids *m.*

weird, *adj.* mystérieux.

welcome, *adj.* bienvenu.

welfare, *n.* bien-être *m.*

welfare work, *n.* travail *(m.)* social.

well, 1. *n.* (water) puits *m.* **2.** *adj.* bien.

well-known, *adj.* bien connu.

well-meaning, *adj.* bien intentionné.

well-off, *adj.* aisé.

Welsh, *adj.* gallois.

west, *n.* ouest *m.*

western, *adj.* de l'ouest.

westward, *adv.* vers l'ouest.

wet, 1. *adj.* mouillé; (weather) pluvieux. **2.** *vb.* mouiller.

whale, *n.* baleine *f.*

wharf, *n.* quai *m.*

what, 1. *adj.* quel. **2.** *pron.* (relative, that which) ce qui (subject), ce que (object); *interr.* qu'est-ce qui; quoi. **3.** *interj.* quoi!

whatever, 1. *adj.* quelque . . . qui (subject), . . . que (object). **2.** *pron.*

quoi qui (subject), . . . que (object).

wheat, *n.* blé *m.*

wheel, *n.* roue *f.*

wheel chair, *n.* fauteuil *(m.)* roulant.

when, *conj.* quand.

whenever, *conj.* toutes les fois que.

where, *conj.* où.

wherever, *conj.* partout où.

whether, *conj.* soit que; (if) si.

which, 1. *adj.* quel. **2.** *pron.* (relative) qui; lequel; *interr.* lequel.

whichever, *pron.* n'importe lequel.

while, *conj.* pendant que; (whereas) tandis que.

whim, *n.* caprice *m.*, lubie *f.*

whip, *n.* fouet *m.*

whirl, *vb.* faire tourner, *tr.*; tourner sur soi, *intr.*

whirlpool, *n.* tourbillon *m.*

whirlwind, *n.* tornade *f.*

whisker, *n.* (man) favori *m.*; (animals) moustache *f.*

whiskey, *n.* whiskey *m.*

whisper, *vb.* chuchoter.

whistle, 1. *n.* sifflet *m.* **2.** *vb.* siffler.

white, *adj.* blanc *m.*, blanche *f.*

who, *pron.* qui.

whoever, *pron.* qui que.

whole, *adj.* entier.

wholesale, *adj. and adv.* en gros.

wholesome, *adj.* sain.

wholly, *adv.* entièrement.

whom, *pron.* (relative) que; lequel; *interr.* qui.

whooping cough, *n.* coqueluche *f.*

whose, *pron.* (relative) dont; *interr.* de qui.

why, *adv.* pourquoi.

wicked, *adj.* méchant.

wickedness, *n.* méchanceté *f.*

wide, *adj.* large.

widen, *vb.* élargir, *tr.*

widespread, *adj.* répandu.

widow, *n.* veuve *f.*

widower, *n.* veuf *m.*

width, *n.* largeur *f.*

wield, *vb.* manier.

wife, *n.* femme *f.*

wig, *n.* perruque *f.*

wild, *adj.* sauvage.

wilderness, *n.* désert *m.*

wildlife, n. faune f.
will, 1. n. volonté f.; **(last w.)** testament m. **2.** vb. vouloir; (bequeath) léguer.
willful, adj. obstiné.
willing, adj. bien disposé.
willpower, n. volonté f.
wilt, vb. flétrir.
win, vb. gagner.
wind, n. vent m.
window, n. fenêtre f.
windshield, n. pare-brise m.
windsurfing, n. planche (f.) à voile.
windy, adj. venteux.
wine, n. vin m.
wing, n. aile f.
wink, 1. n. clin (m.) d'œil. **2.** vb. clignoter.
winner, n. gagnant m.
winter, n. hiver m.
wipe, vb. essuyer.
wire, n. fil (m.) de fer.
wireless, n. télégraphie (f.) sans fil (abbr. T.S.F.).
wisdom, n. sagesse f.
wise, adj. sage.
wish, 1. n. désir, souhait m. **2.** vb. désirer, souhaiter.
wit, n. esprit m.
witch, n. sorcière f.
with, prep. avec.
withdraw, vb. retirer, tr.
wither, vb. flétrir.
withhold, vb. refuser.
within, adv. dedans.
without, prep. sans.
witness, n. témoin m.
witty, adj. spirituel.
wizard, n. sorcier m.
woe, n. malheur m.
wolf, n. loup m.
woman, n. femme f.
womb, n. matrice f.
wonder, vb. (ask oneself) se demander; (be surprised) être étonné.
wonderful, adj. merveilleux.
woo, vb. faire la cour à.
wood, n. bois m.
wooden, adj. de bois.
wool, n. laine f.
woolen, adj. de laine.

word, n. mot m.
word processing, n. traitement (m.) de texte.
word processor, n. machine (f.) de traitement de texte.
work, 1. n. travail m. **2.** vb. travailler.
workaholic, n. bourreau (m.) de travail.
worker, n. travailleur m.
working class, n. classe (f.) ouvrière.
workman, n. ouvrier m.
world, n. monde m.
worldly, adj. mondain.
worldwide, adj. mondial.
worm, n. ver m.
worn, adj. usé.
worry, 1. n. souci m. **2.** vb. tracasser, préoccuper, tr.
worse, 1. adj. pire. **2.** adv. pis.
worship, 1. n. culte m. **2.** vb. adorer.
worst, 1. adj. (le) pire. **2.** adv. (le) pis.
worth, n. valeur f.; **(be w. while to)** valoir la peine de.
worthless, adj. indigne; (without value) sans valeur.
worthy, adj. digne.
would, vb. vouloir.
wound, 1. n. blessure f. **2.** vb. blesser.
wrap, vb. envelopper, emballer.
wrapping, n. couverture f., emballage m.
wrath, n. courroux m.
wreath, n. couronne f.
wreck, n. (ship) naufrage m.; (remains) débris m.pl.
wrench, vb. tordre.
wrestle, vb. lutter.
wretched, adj. misérable.
wring, vb. tordre.
wrinkle, 1. n. ride f. **2.** vb. rider tr.
wrist, n. poignet m.
wristwatch, n. montre-bracelet f.
write, vb. écrire.
writer, n. écrivain m.
writhe, vb. se tordre.
writing, n. écriture f.
wrong, 1. n. tort m. **2.** adj. faux m., fausse f.; **(be w.)** avoir tort.

xerox, *vb.* photocopier.
x-rays, *n.* rayons X *m.pl.*
xylophone, *n.* xylophone *m.*
yacht, *n.* yacht *m.*
yam, *n.* igname *f.*
yard, *n.* (house, etc.) cour *f.;* (lumber, etc.) chantier *m.;* (measure) yard *m.*
yarn, *n.* fil *m.*
yawn, **1.** *n.* bâillement *m.* **2.** *vb.* bâiller.
year, *n.* an *m.;* (duration) année *f.*
yearly, *adj.* annuel.
yearn for, *vb.* soupirer après.
yeast, *n.* levure *f.*
yell, *vb.* hurler.
yellow, *adj. and n.* jaune *m.*
yes, *adv.* oui; (after negative question) si.
yesterday, *adv.* hier.
yet, **1.** *adv.* encore. **2.** *conj.* néanmoins.
Yiddish, *n.* yiddish *m.*
yield, *vb.* (resign, submit) céder; (produce) produire.
yoga, *n.* yoga *m.*
yogurt, *n.* yaourt *m.*
yoke, *n.* joug *m.*
yolk, *n.* jaune *m.*
you, *pron.* vous; (familiar, *sg.)* tu (subject), toi (object), te (object, unstressed, with verb).

young, *adj.* jeune.
your, *adj.* votre *sg.,* vos *pl.;* (familiar form) ton *m.sg.,* ta *f.sg.,* tes *pl.*
yours, *pron.* le vôtre *f.,* les vôtres *pl.,* (familiar form) le tien *m.,* la tienne *f.,* les tiens *m.pl.,* les tiennes *f.pl.*
yourself, *pron.* vous-même; (familiar form) toi-même; (reflexive) vous, te.
youth, *n.* jeunesse *f.*
youthful, *adj.* (young) jeune; (of youth) de jeunesse.
Yugoslavia, *n.* Yougoslavie *f.*
yuppie, *n.* yuppie *m.*
zap, *vb.* (kill) descendre; (computer) effacer; (TV) zapper.
zeal, *n.* zèle *m.*
zealous, *adj.* zélé.
zebra, *n.* zèbre *m.*
zenith, *n.* zénith *m.*
zero, *n.* zéro *m.*
zest, *n.* entrain *m.;* (taste) saveur *f.*
zip code, *n.* code postal *m.*
zipper, *n.* fermeture *f.* éclair.
zone, *n.* zone *f.*
zoo, *n.* jardin *(m.)* zoologique.
zoology, *n.* zoologie *f.*
zoom, **1.** *vb.* passer en trombe. **2.** *n.* zoom *m.*
zucchini, *n.* courgette *f.*

Numerals

Cardinal

1 un, une	21 vingt et un	75 soixante-quinze
2 deux	22 vingt-deux	76 soixante-seize
3 trois	23 vingt-trois	77 soixante-dix-sept
4 quatre	24 vingt-quatre	78 soixante-dix-huit
5 cinq	25 vingt-cinq	79 soixante-dix-neuf
6 six	26 vingt-six	80 quatre-vingts
7 sept	27 vingt-sept	81 quatre-vingt-un
8 huit	28 vingt-huit	82 quatre-vingt-deux
9 neuf	29 vingt-neuf	90 quatre-vingt-dix
10 dix	30 trente	91 quatre-vingt-onze
11 onze	31 trente et un	92 quatre-vingt-douze
12 douze	32 trente-deux	100 cent
13 treize	40 quarante	101 cent un
14 quatorze	50 cinquante	102 cent deux
15 quinze	60 soixante	200 deux cents
16 seize	70 soixante-dix	300 trois cents
17 dix-sept	71 soixante et onze	301 trois cent un
18 dix-huit	72 soixante-douze	1,000 mille
19 dix-neuf	73 soixante-treize	5,000 cinq mille
20 vingt	74 soixante-quatorze	1,000,000 un million

Ordinal

1st premier, première	19th dix-neuvième
2nd deuxième, second	20th vingtième
3rd troisième	21st vingt-et-unième
4th quatrième	22nd vingt-deuxième
5th cinquième	30th trentième
6th sixième	40th quarantième
7th septième	50th cinquantième
8th huitième	60th soixantième
9th neuvième	70th soixante-dixième
10th dixième	80th quatre-vingtième
11th onzième	90th quatre-vingt-dixième
12th douzième	100th centième
13th treizième	101st cent-unième
14th quatorzième	102nd cent-deuxième
15th quinzième	103rd cent-troisième
16th seizième	300th trois-centième
17th dix-septième	1,000th millième
18th dix-huitième	1,000,000th millionième

Days of the Week

Sunday	dimanche
Monday	lundi
Tuesday	mardi
Wednesday	mercredi
Thursday	jeudi
Friday	vendredi
Saturday	samedi

Months

January	janvier
February	février
March	mars
April	avril
May	mai
June	juin
July	juillet
August	août
September	septembre
October	octobre
November	novembre
December	décembre

Weights and Measures

The French use the *Metric System* of weights and measures, a decimal system in which multiples are shown by the prefixes **déci-** (one-tenth); **centi-** (one hundredth); **milli-** (one thousandth); **hecto-** (hundred); and **kilo-** (thousand).

1 centimètre	=	.3937 inch
1 mètre	=	39.37 inches
1 kilomètre	=	.621 mile
1 centigramme	=	.1543 grain
1 gramme	=	15.432 grains
100 grammes	=	3.527 ounces
1 kilogramme	=	2.2046 pounds
1 tonne	=	2.204 pounds
1 centilitre	=	.338 ounce
1 litre	=	1.0567 quart (liquid);
		.908 quart (dry)
1 kilolitre	=	264.18 gallons

Useful Words and Phrases

Good day.	Bonjour.
Good afternoon.	Bonjour.
Good evening.	Bonsoir.
Good night.	Bonne nuit.
Good-bye.	Au revoir.
How are you?	Comment allez-vous?
Fine, thank you.	Très bien, merci.
Glad to meet you.	Enchanté de faire votre connaissance.
Thank you very much.	Merci beaucoup.
You're welcome.	Pas de quoi.
Please.	S'il vous plaît.
Good luck.	Bonne chance.
To your health.	A votre santé.
I am lost.	Je me suis égaré(e).
Please help me.	Aidez-moi, s'il vous plaît.
Do you understand?	Comprenez-vous?
I don't understand.	Je ne comprends pas.
Speak slowly, please.	Parlez lentement, s'il vous plaît.
Please repeat.	Répétez, s'il vous plaît.
I don't speak French.	Je ne parle pas français.
Do you speak English?	Parlez-vous anglais?
Does anyone here speak English?	Y a-t-il quelqu'un qui parle anglais?
How do you say . . . in French?	Comment dit-on . . . en français?
What do you call this?	Comment appelle-t-on ceci?
What is your name?	Comment vous appelez-vous?
My name is . . .	Je m'appelle . . .
I am an American.	Je suis américain.
May I introduce . . .	Permettez-moi de vous présenter . . .
How is the weather?	Quel temps fait-il?
What time is it?	Quelle heure est-il?
What is it?	Qu'est-ce que c'est?
I would like . . .	Je voudrais . . .
Please give me . . .	S'il vous plaît, donnez-moi . . .
Please bring me . . .	S'il vous plaît, apportez-moi . . .
How much does this cost?	Combien est ceci?
It is too expensive.	C'est trop cher.

May I see something cheaper?	Pourrais-je voir quelque chose à meilleur marché?
May I see something better?	Pourrais-je voir quelque chose de meilleur?
It is not exactly what I want.	Ce n'est pas exactement ce que je cherche.
I want to buy . . .	Je voudrais acheter . . .
Do you accept traveler's checks?	Acceptez-vous les chèques de voyage?
I want to eat.	Je voudrais manger.
Can you recommend a restaurant?	Pouvez-vous recommander un restaurant?
I am hungry.	J'ai faim.
I am thirsty.	J'ai soif.
May I see the menu?	Pourrais-je voir le menu?
Check, please.	L'addition, s'il vous plaît.
Is service included in the bill?	Le service est-il compris?
Where can I get a taxi?	Où pourrais-je trouver un taxi?
What is the fare to . . .	Quel est le tarif jusqu'à . . . ?
Please take me to this address.	Veuillez me conduire à cette adresse.
I have a reservation.	J'ai une réservation.
Where is the nearest drugstore?	Où est la pharmacie la plus proche?
Is there a hotel here?	Y a-t-il un hôtel ici?
Where is . . . ?	Où est . . . ?
Where is the men's (women's) room?	Où est la toilette pour messieurs (dames)?
What is the way to . . . ?	Quelle est la route de . . . ?
Take me to . . .	Conduisez-moi à . . .
I need . . .	J'ai besoin de . . .
I am ill.	Je suis malade.
Please call a doctor.	Appelez un docteur, s'il vous plaît.
Is there any mail for me?	Y a-t-il du courrier pour moi?
Please call the police.	Appelez la police, s'il vous plaît.
I want to send a telegram.	Je voudrais envoyer un télégramme.
Where can I change money?	Où puis-je changer de l'argent?
Where is the nearest bank?	Où est la banque la plus proche?
Will you accept checks?	Acceptez-vous des chèques?
What is the postage?	Quel est l'affranchissement?
Where can I mail this letter?	Où est-ce que je peux mettre cette lettre à la poste?

Please help me with my baggage	S'il vous plaît, aidez-moi avec mes bagages.		
Right away.	Tout de suite.		
Help!	Au secours!		
Who is it?	Qui est-ce que c'est?		
Come in.	Entrez.		
Stop.	Arrêtez.		
Hurry.	Dépêchez-vous.		
Go on.	Continuez.		
Right.	A droite.		
Left.	A gauche.		
Straight ahead.	Tout droit.		
Hello! *(on telephone)*	Allô!		
As soon as possible.	Aussitôt que possible.		
Pardon me.	Pardon *or* Pardonnez-moi *or* Je m'excuse.		
Look out!	Attention! *or* Faites attention!		
Just a minute!	Un instant!		

Signs

Caution	Attention	**Go Slow**	Ralentir
Danger	Danger	**No smoking**	Défense de fumer
Exit	Sortie	**No admittance**	Défense d'entrer
Entrance	Entrée	**Women**	Dames
Stop	Halte, Arrêtez	**Men**	Hommes
Closed	Fermé	**Lavatory**	Lavabos, toilettes
Open	Ouvert		

FOOD AND MENU TERMS

LES ENTRÉES *f.pl.*   APPETIZERS

artichaut *m.*	artichoke
assiette *f.* de charcuterie	cold cuts
assiette *f.* de crudités	raw vegetables
céleri *m.* rémoulade *f.*	shredded celery root in mayonnaise sauce
champignons *m.pl.* à la grecque	mushrooms in oil, lemon juice and herbs
coeur *m.* de palmier	hearts of palm
coquilles *f.pl.* St. Jacques	bay scallops in cream sauce
escargots *m.pl.*	snails (usually in garlic butter)
moules *f.pl.* (rémoulade)	mussels (in mayonnaise)
pâté *m.* de foie	liver pâté
pâté de campagne	pork pâté
pâté impérial	spring roll
salade *f.* verte	green salad
salade niçoise	salad usually including tuna, tomatoes, green beans, anchovies and olives
sardines *f.pl.* à l'huile	sardines in oil
saucisse *f.*	small fresh sausage
saucisson *m.*	large sausage, like salami
saucisson à l'ail	garlic sausage
saumon *m.* fumé	smoked salmon
terrine *f.*	cold pâté baked in earthenware casserole
thon *m.* mayonnaise	tuna salad with mayonnaise

POTAGES *m.pl.* AND SOUPES *f.pl.*   SOUPS

bisque *f.*	shellfish soup
bouillabaisse *f.*	Provençal fish soup
bouillon *m.*	clear broth
consommé *m.* (de volaille)	clear (chicken) soup
petite marmite *f.*	meat and vegetable broth cooked in earthenware casserole
pistou *m.*	rich vegetable, bean and pasta soup flavored with basil, garlic and olive oil
potage *m.* aux légumes	vegetable soup
potage crème Saint-Germain	cream of pea soup
soupe *f.* à l'oignon	onion soup
vichyssoise *f.*	cold, creamy leek and potato soup

LES PLATS *m.pl*	MAIN COURSES
Viandes *f.pl.*	**Meats**
agneau *m.*	lamb
carré *m.* d'agneau	rack of lamb
côte *f.* d'agneau	lamb chop
gigot *m.* d'agneau	leg of lamb
bifteck *m.*	steak
blanquette *f.*	traditional stew of veal, chicken, lamb or seafood in cream sauce
boeuf *m.* bourguignon	stew of beef chunks and vegetables in Burgundy wine sauce
boudin *m.*	meat sausage
boudin blanc	white sausage of veal, chicken or pork
boudin noir	pork blood sausage
brochette *f.*	cubes of meat or fish and vegetables cooked on skewer
chateaubriand *m.*	thick beef fillet, traditionally served with sautéed potatoes and sauce
côtelette *f.*	thin chop or cutlet
entrecôte *m.* or *f.*	beef rib steak
escalope *f.*	thin slice of meat or fish
filet mignon *m.*	filet mignon
jambon *m.*	ham
jarret *m.* (de veau, de porc, de boeuf)	knuckles (veal, pork, beef)
lapin *m.*	rabbit
pavé *m.*	thick slice of boned beef or calf's liver
porc *m.*	pork
carré de porc	pork loin
steak *m.* frites	steak with French fries
steak *m.* tartare	raw chopped steak
tournedos *m.*	center part of beef fillet
tripes *f.pl.* à la mode de Caen	beef entrails, carrots, leeks, and onions, cooked in water, cider and Calvados
veau *m.*	veal
côte de veau	veal chop

Volailles *f.pl.*	**Poultry**
caille *f.*	quail
canard *m.*	duck
canard à la presse	roast duck with sauce of natural juices, red wine and cognac
canard sauvage	wild duck, usually mallard
caneton *m.*	young male duck
coq *m.* (au vin)	mature male chicken (cooked in wine sauce)
coq jaune	chicken cooked in the local wine with butter, cream and tarragon
coq *m.* de bruyère	wood grouse
coquelet *m.* (sauté)	sautéed baby rooster
foie *m.*	liver
fricassé *m.*	stewed or sautéed mixture of fish or meat
perdrix *f.*	partridge
poulet *m.* rôti	roast chicken
poulet à la Kiev	chicken Kiev
poulet impérial	Vietnamese chicken
poulet basquaise	chicken Basque-style with tomatoes and sweet peppers
poulet fermier	free-range chicken
Fruits *m.pl.* de Mer and Poissons *m.pl.*	**Fish**
bar *m.*	bass
colin *m.*	hake
coquillage *m.*	shellfish
crevettes *f.pl.*	shrimp
escargots *m.pl.*	snails
grenouilles *f.pl.*	frogs' legs
homard *m.*	lobster
huîtres *f.pl.*	oysters
langouste *f.*	crayfish
langoustines *f.pl.*	prawns
moules *f.pl.*	mussels
saumon *m.*	salmon
sôle *f.*	sole
thon *m.*	tuna
truite *f.*	trout
turbot *m.*	turbot
Légumes *m.pl.*	**Vegetables**
asperges *f.pl.*	asparagus
avocat *m.*	avocado
brocoli *m.*	broccoli